Deviant Behavior

sixth edition

Deviant Behavior

Alex Thio

Ohio University

Allyn and Bacon

Boston ■ London ■ Toronto ■ Sydney ■ Tokyo ■ Singapore

Editor-in-chief, Social Sciences: *Karen Hanson*
Editorial Assistant: *Karen Corday*
Editorial Production Administrator: *Susan Brown*
Editorial Production Service: *Matrix Productions Inc.*
Composition Buyer: *Linda Cox*
Manufacturing Buyer: *Julie McNeil*
Compositor: *Monotype Composition*
Cover Administrator: *Linda Knowles*

Copyright © 2001 by Allyn & Bacon
A Pearson Education Company
160 Gould St.
Needham Heights, Mass. 02494
www.abacon.com

Library of Congress Cataloging-in-Publication Data

Thio, Alex.
    Deviant behavior / Alex Thio.—6th ed.
        p. cm.
    Includes bibliographical references and index.
    ISBN 0-321-05031-2
    1. Deviant behavior. I. Title.

    HM811.T46 2000
    302.5'42—dc21   00-025102

Photo Credits: Bob Daemmrich/Stock Boston: pp. 89, 202; Najlah Feanny/Stock Boston: p. 326; Frank Fournier/Woodfin Camp & Associates: p. 16; Tony Freeman/PhotoEdit: p. 354; Charles Gatewood/Stock Boston: p. 34; Kevin Horan/Stock Boston: p. 298; Sylvia Johnson/Woodfin Camp & Associates: p. 3; Cyrus McCrimmon/Denver Rocky Mountain News/Corbis Sygma: p. 59; Michael Newman/PhotoEdit: p. 119; Mark Richards/PhotoEdit: p. 236; T. Ross/The Image Works: p. 267; Eric Roth/Index Stock Imagery: p. 170; Miro Vintoniv/Stock Boston: p. 139.

Printed in the United States of America

10   9   8   7   6   5   4   3   2   1   RRDV   04   03   02   01   00

BRIEF CONTENTS

CONTENTS

12   **Drinking and Alcoholism**   **298**

13   White-Collar and Governmental Deviance   326

PREFACE

Like its predecessors, this new edition of *Deviant Behavior* is designed to make teaching and learning interesting and rewarding. Deviant behavior is by itself an exciting subject, and I have tried to make it more exciting with a direct, clear style of writing. No matter how complex and dull the theories and data about deviance may appear in scholarly journals and books, they are here described simply and interestingly, yet accurately. I have often thrown in ironic, stimulating, or thought-provoking remarks to enliven the book as well. Students should thus be able to grasp the contents easily. I have greatly enjoyed working on this edition. I hope that students will have fun reading it while learning about deviance.

Successful Features

The current edition retains all the features that have made the book a great success. These features include comprehensive coverage, vibrant writing, real-life vignettes, student-oriented examples, and critical analyses of theories and data. But perhaps the most important feature is the blend of readability and scholarship.

I have also tried to cover as much of the literature of deviance as possible. A wide spectrum of theories and specific deviant behaviors are analyzed here. In addition to discussing all the standard subjects, I have presented such important, and modern material as feminism, postmodernism, and shaming; phenomenological and Marxist theories as well as such emergent or newly recognized deviances as cyberporn, cigarette smoking, terrorism, homophobia, and governmental deviance. I have also presented an abundance of research data, including a substantial amount that demolishes our common assumptions about deviant behavior.

Students will not only be exposed to the full range of theories and data about deviance, they will also be challenged to think about and evaluate their own biases and preconceptions. In the chapter on homosexuality and homophobia, for example, students will learn how some people become homosexual, how gay men and lesbians are just as normal as straights, and how the homophobic society unjustly treats this sexual minority.

Continuing Upgrade

A number of social issues have recently come front and center in our national consciousness. They include such deviances as school violence, teen smoking, sexual deviance in cyberspace, and democide (killing of people by their government, such as the recent slaughter of an ethnic minority in Bosnia). Whole new sections are devoted to analyses of these subjects, along with a new postmodernist theory of deviance.

I have updated and modified the text to take into account significant new studies by sociologists and other behavioral scientists, as well as suggestions and criticisms from the reviewers of this text. It has also been necessary to correct or delete some old ideas and facts.

Noteworthy updatings and revisions include the nature of youthful violence, the difference between mass murderers and serial killers, sociological criticism of the ethological theory of killing, child molestation, the causes of marital rape, the rising suicide rate among African-American youth, the link between social class and mental illness, prostitutes' fight against AIDS, gays in the military, the comparison of the origins of homosexuality and left-handedness, the sharp increase in youthful drug use, the ranking of nations in alcohol consumption, official violence, carjacking, and the Russian Mafia. A number of chapter-opening vignettes have been replaced by new ones, including those about physical violence, rape, suicide, and mental disorder. In the first and third chapters the term "humanist" has been changed to "social constructionist" or "constructionist," which is much more appropriate for referring to a major perspective or type of theories in today's deviance literature. Finally, the chapter on same-sex orientation has been reorganized to accommodate many professors' suggestions that I first discuss homosexuality and then homophobia.

Pedagogy

Each chapter opens with a meaningful photo and a real-life vignette, not only to stimulate student interest but also to portray an important theme of the chapter. The end of each chapter is laid out in a question-and-answer format to promote thinking as well as retention. The list of suggested readings is annotated to help students decide which publications will suit their need for more information.

Supplements

Professor Peter Morrill of Bronx Community College has prepared a comprehensive Instructor's Manual/Test Bank to accompany this text. The Instructor's Manual includes detailed chapter outlines, suggestions for lectures, demonstrations, and student activities; annotated lists of films and videos; and additional resources pertinent to each chapter. The Test Bank portion of the manual presents multiple-choice, true/false, fill-in-the-blank, and essay questions.

Acknowledgments

I would like to express my profound gratitude to the numerous professors who have adopted the past five editions of this book for their classes. My thanks also go to those sociologists who have contributed to the success of the earlier editions with their criticisms and suggestions:

Roy Austin, Pennsylvania State University
James T. Carey, University of Illinois, Chicago Circle
Estelle Disch, Boston State College
Charles E. Frazier, University of Florida
John R. Hepburn, Arizona State University
Arthur C. Hill, Minneapolis Community College
Richard C. Hollinger, University of Florida
Gary Jensen, Vanderbilt University
Michael Kimmel, SUNY-Stony Brook
Hong Liu, University of Pittsburgh
Charles H. McCaghy, Bowling Green State University
James Messerschmidt, University of Southern Maine
David Prok, Baldwin Wallace College
Marion Sherman-Goldman, University of Oregon
Deanna Shields, Fairmont State College
Larry Stokes, University of Tennessee, Chattanooga
Kenrick S. Thompson, Northern Michigan University
Timothy N. Veiders, Niagara County Community College
J. D. Wemhaner, Tulsa Junior College
Arthur L. Wood, University of Connecticut

For helping me make the current edition better and more relevant to the new millennium, I am indebted to the following reviewers:

Dodd Bogart/University of New Mexico
Jerry Van Hoy/Purdue University
Eleanor M. Miller/University of Wisconsin–Milwaukee
Michael Olson/Frostburg State University
Gunnar Valgeirsson/California State University, Fresno

I would like to thank Professor Peter Morrill for preparing the excellent Instructor's Manual and Test Bank. Finally, I am grateful for the support of the able staff at Allyn and Bacon.

Alex Thio

ABOUT THE AUTHOR

Alex Thio (pronounced *TEE-oh*) is professor of Sociology at Ohio University. Born of Chinese parentage in Penang, Malaysia, he grew up in a multicultural environment. He acquired fluency in Mandarin (modern standard Chinese), two Chinese dialects (Fukienese and Hakka), Malay, and Indonesian. He also picked up a smattering of English and Dutch. He further took French and German in high school and college.

Professor Thio attended primary school in Malaysia and high school in Indonesia. He then came to the United States and worked his way through Central Methodist College in Missouri, where he majored in social sciences and took many literature and writing courses. Later, he studied sociology as a graduate student at the State University of New York at Buffalo, and he completed his doctorate while working as a research and teaching assistant.

Professor Thio regularly teaches courses in deviance, introductory sociology, social problems, and criminology. In addition to teaching, he enjoys writing. Aside from this book, he is the author of the popular texts, *Sociology: A Brief Introduction*, 4th edition (2000), and *Sociology*, 5th edition (1998), and has written many articles. The author is very grateful for the feedback he often receives from faculty and students, which he believes improves greatly the quality of his books. If you have any comments, suggestions, or questions, please write him at the Department of Sociology, Ohio University, Athens, OH 45701 (Internet: thio@ohiou.edu). He takes as much pleasure in responding to you as in hearing from you.

He lives in Athens, Ohio. His hobbies include reading, moviegoing, and traveling.

PART ONE

General Definitions and Theories of Deviant Behavior

Before we can study deviant behavior, we have to define it. Various sociologists define it differently, however, and each is influenced by certain philosophical assumptions about the nature of deviant reality. These assumptions and the resulting definitions will be the subject of Chapter 1.

Once we have considered what deviant behavior is, the next task will be to explain what causes it and to understand what it means to different people. This will be the subject of Chapters 2 and 3.

1 What Is Deviant Behavior?

Throughout her life, Aleta Walker, an overweight 36-year-old woman, has been ridiculed and abused for her weight, especially during her childhood and adolescence. Every day, when she walked down the halls at school, boys would step back and yell, "Wide load!" It was worse at lunchtime. As she said, "Every day there was this production of watching me eat lunch." One day, schoolmates threw food at her. Spaghetti splashed on her head and face, and the long greasy strands dripped onto her clothes. "Everyone was laughing and pointing. They were making pig noises. I just sat there," she said (Kolata, 1992).

Is Walker deviant for being overweight? Some people would say yes, but others would say no. In fact, some would say that it is her tormentors—the so-called normal people—who are deviant because they are grossly insensitive, nasty, or cruel. There is, in fact, a great deal of disagreement among people as to what they consider deviant. In a classic study, J. L. Simmons (1965) asked a sample of the general public who they thought was deviant. They mentioned 252 different kinds of people as deviants, including prostitutes, alcoholics, drug users, murderers, the mentally ill, the physically challenged, communists, atheists, liars, Democrats, Republicans, reckless drivers, self-pitiers, the retired, divorcees, Christians, suburbanites, movie stars, perpetual bridge players, pacifists, psychiatrists, priests, liberals, conservatives, junior executives, smart-aleck students, and know-it-all professors. If you are surprised that some of these people are considered deviant, your surprise simply adds to the fact that there is a good deal of disagreement among the public as to the conception of deviant behavior.

A similar lack of consensus exists among sociologists. We could say that the study of deviant behavior is probably the most "deviant" of all the subjects in sociology. Sociologists disagree more over the definition of deviant behavior than they do on any other subject.

Conflicting Definitions

Some sociologists simply say that deviance is a violation of any social rule, while others argue that deviance involves more than rule violation—that it also has the quality of provoking disapproval, anger, or indignation. Some advocate a broader definition, arguing that a person can be a deviant *without* violating any rule or doing something that rubs others the wrong way, such as individuals with physical or mental disabilities. These people are considered deviant in this view because they are disvalued by society. By contrast, some sociologists contend that deviance does not have to be conceived as only negative but instead can also be positive, such as being a genius, reformer, creative artist, or glamorous celebrity. Other sociologists disagree, considering "positive deviance" to be an oxymoron, a contradiction in terms (Goode, 1991; Dodge, 1985; Harman, 1985; Sagarin, 1985, 1975; Nettler, 1984, 1974; Hirschi, 1973; Merton, 1971; Cohen, 1966; Parsons, 1951).

All these sociologists apparently assume that, whether it is positive or negative, disturbing behavior or disvalued condition, deviance is real in and of itself, that is, endowed with a certain quality that distinguishes it from nondeviance. The logic behind this assumption is that if it is not real in the first place, it cannot be considered positive, negative, disturbing, or disvalued (Nettler 1984, 1974; Hirschi, 1973; Akers, 1968). But other sociologists disagree, arguing that deviance does not have to be real in order for behaviors and conditions to be labeled deviant. People can be falsely accused of being criminal, erroneously diagnosed as mentally ill, unfairly stereotyped as dangerous because of their skin color, and so on. Conversely, committing a deviant act does not necessarily make the person a deviant, especially when the act is kept secret, unlabeled by others as deviant. It is, therefore, the label "deviant"—not the act itself—that makes the individual deviant (Becker, 1963; Erikson, 1962).

Some sociologists go beyond the notion of labeling to define deviance by stressing the importance of power. They observe that relatively powerful people are capable of avoiding the fate suffered by the powerless—being falsely, erroneously, or unjustly labeled deviant. The key reason is that the powerful, either by themselves or through influencing public opinion or both, hold more power for labeling others' behavior as deviant. Understandably, sociologists who hold this view define deviance as any act considered by the powerful at a given time and place to be a violation of some social rule (Ermann and Lundman, 1996; Simon, 1996; Thio, 1973).

From this welter of conflicting definitions we can discern the influence of two opposing perspectives: positivism and social constructionism. The positivist perspective is associated with the sciences, such as physics, chemistry, or biology. The constructionist perspective is fundamental in the humanities, such as art, language, or philosophy. Each perspective influences how scientists and scholars see, study, and make sense of their subject. The two perspectives have long been transported into sociology, so that some sociologists are more influenced by the positivist perspective while others are more influenced by the constructionist one.

In the sociology of deviance the positivist generally defines deviance as intrinsically real, while the constructionist more often defines deviance as a social construction—an idea imputed by society to some behavior. Each perspective suggests other ideas about deviance, so that it has been referred to in various terms. Thus the positivist perspective has also been called objectivist, absolutist, determinist, structuralist, factist, and essentialist (Goode, 1997; Wittig, 1990; Henslin, 1988; Troyer and Markle, 1982). The constructionist perspective has also been referred to by the terms humanist, subjectivist, relativist, voluntarist, individualist, definitionist, critical, and postmodernist (Lyman, 1995; Goode, 1994; Seidman, 1994; Henslin, 1988; Troyer and Markle 1982). Each perspective suggests how to *define* deviance, but reveals through the definitions what *subject* to study, what *method* to use for the study, and what kind of *theory* to use to make sense of the subject.

The Positivist Perspective

The positivist perspective consists of three assumptions about what deviance is. These assumptions are known to positivists as absolutism, objectivism, and determinism.

Absolutism: Deviance as Absolutely Real

The positivist perspective holds deviance to be absolutely or intrinsically real, in that *it possesses some qualities that distinguish it from conventionality.* Similarly, deviant persons are assumed to have certain characteristics that make them different from conventional others. Thus, sociologists who are influenced by such a perspective tend to view deviant behavior as an attribute that inheres in the individual.

This view was first strongly held by the early criminologists who were the progenitors of today's sociology of deviance. Around the turn of this century, criminologists believed that criminals possessed certain biological traits that were absent in noncriminals. The biological traits were believed to include defective genes, bumps on the head, a long lower jaw, a scanty beard, and a tough body build. Since all these traits are inherited, criminals were believed to be born as such. Thus, if they were born criminals, they would always be criminals. As the saying goes, "If you've had it, you've had it." So, no matter where they might go—they could go anywhere in the world—they would still be criminals.

Then criminologists shifted their attention from biological to psychological traits. Criminals were thought to have certain mental characteristics that non-criminals did not. More specifically, criminals were thought to be feebleminded, psychotic, neurotic, psychopathic, or otherwise mentally disturbed. Like biological traits, these mental characteristics were believed to reside within individual criminals. And like biological traits, mental characteristics were believed to stay with the criminals, no matter what society or culture they might go to. Again, wherever they went, criminals would always remain criminals.

Today's positivist sociologists, however, have largely abandoned the use of biological and psychological traits to differentiate criminals from noncriminals. They recognize the important role of social factors in determining a person's status as a criminal. Such status does not remain the same across time and space; instead, it changes in different periods and with different societies. A polygamist may be a criminal in our society but a law-abiding citizen in Islamic countries. A person who sees things invisible to others may be a psychotic in our society but may become a spiritual leader among some South Pacific peoples. Nevertheless, positivist sociologists still regard deviance as absolutely or intrinsically real. Countering the relativist notion of deviance as basically a *label* imposed on an act, positivist Travis Hirschi (1973), for example, argues: "The person may not have committed a 'deviant' act, but he did (in many cases) do *something*. And it is just possible that what he did was a result of things that had happened to him in the past; it is also possible that the past in some inscrutable way remains with him and that if he were left alone he would *do it again*." Moreover, countering the relativist notion of mental illness as a label imputed to some people's behavior, Gwynn Nettler (1974) explicitly voices his absolutist stance: "Some people *are* more crazy than others; we can tell the difference; and calling lunacy a name does not *cause* it." These positivist sociologists seem to say that just as a rose by any other name would smell as sweet, so deviance by any other label is just as real.

Because they consider deviance real, positivist sociologists tend to focus their study on deviant behavior and deviant persons, rather than on nondeviants who label others deviants, such as lawmakers and law-enforcers, which constructionist sociologists are more likely to study, as will be explained later.

Objectivism: Deviance as an Observable Object

To positivist sociologists deviant behavior is an observable object in that a deviant person is like an object, a real something that can be studied objectively. Positivist sociologists therefore assume that they can be as objective in studying deviance as natural scientists can be in studying physical phenomena. The trick is to treat deviants as if they were objects, like those studied by natural scientists. Nonetheless, positivist sociologists cannot help being aware of the basic difference between their subject, human beings, and that of natural scientists, inanimate objects. As human beings themselves, positivist sociologists must have certain feelings about their subject. However, they try to control their personal biases by forcing themselves not to pass moral judgment on deviant behavior or share the deviant person's feelings. Instead, they try to concentrate on the subject matter as it outwardly appears. Further, these sociologists have tried to follow the scientific rule that all their ideas about deviant behavior should be subject to public test. This means that other sociologists should be able to analyze these ideas to see whether they are supported by facts.

Such a drive to achieve scientific objectivity has made today's positivist sociologists more objective than their predecessors. They have, therefore, produced works that can tell us much more about deviant behavior. No longer in vogue today are such value-loaded and subjective notions as maladjustment, moral failing, debauchery, demoralization, sickness, pathology, and abnormality. Replacing those outmoded notions are such value-free and objective concepts as innovation, retreatism, ritualism, rebellion, culture conflict, subcultural behavior, white-collar crime, norm violation, learned behavior, and reinforced behavior.

To demonstrate the objective reality of these concepts, positivist sociologists have used official reports and statistics, clinical reports, surveys of self-reported behavior, and surveys of victimization. Positivists recognize the unfortunate fact that the deviants who are selected by these methods do not accurately represent the entire population of deviants. The criminals and delinquents reported in the official statistics, for example, are a special group of deviants, because most crimes and delinquent acts are not discovered and therefore not included in the official statistics. Nevertheless, positivists believe that the quality of information obtained by these methods can be improved and refined. In the meantime, they consider the information, though inadequate, useful for revealing at least some aspect of the totality of deviant behavior. A major reason for using the information is to seek out the causes of deviant behavior. This brings us to the next, third assumption of the positivist perspective.

Determinism: Deviance as Determined Behavior

According to the positivist perspective deviance is determined or caused by forces beyond the individual's control. Natural scientists hold the same deterministic view about physical phenomena. When positivist sociologists follow natural scientists, they adopt the deterministic view and apply it to human behavior.

Overly enthusiastic about the prospect of turning their discipline into a science, early sociologists argued that, like animals, plants, and material objects that natural scientists study, humans do not have any free will. The reason is that acknowledgment of free will would contradict the scientific principle of determinism. If a murderer is thought to will or determine a murderous act, then it does not make sense to say that the murderous act is caused by forces (such as mental condition or family background) beyond the person's control. Therefore, in defending their scientific principle of determinism, early sociologists maintained their denial of free will.

However, today's positivist sociologists assume that humans do possess free will. Still, this assumption, they argue, does not undermine the scientific principle of determinism. No matter how much a person exercises free will by making choices and decisions, the choices and decisions do not just happen but are determined by some causes. If a woman chooses to kill her husband rather than continue to live with him, she certainly has free will or freedom of choice as long as no one forces her to do what she does. Yet some factor may *determine* or *cause* the woman's choice of one alternative over another, that is, determine the way she exercises her free will. One such causal factor may be a long history of abuse at the hands of her husband. Thus, according to today's positivist sociologists, there is no inconsistency between freedom and causality.

Although they allow for human freedom or choice, positivist sociologists do not use it to explain why people behave in a certain way. They will not, for example, explain why the woman kills by saying "because she chooses to kill." This is no explanation at all, since the idea of choice can also be used to explain why another woman does not kill her husband—by saying "because she chooses not to." According to positivists, killing and not killing, or more generally, deviant and conventional behavior, being contrary phenomena, cannot be explained by the same factor, such as choice. Further, the idea of choice simply cannot explain the difference between deviance and conventionality; it cannot explain why one person chooses to kill while the other chooses not to. Therefore, although positivists do believe in human choice, they will not attribute deviance to human choice. Instead, they explain deviance by using such concepts as wife abuse, broken homes, unhappy homes, lower-class background, economic deprivation, social disorganization, rapid social change, differential association, differential reinforcement, and lack of social control. Any one of these causes of deviance can be used to illustrate what positivists consider to be a real explanation of deviance because, for example, wife abuse is more likely to cause a woman to kill her husband than not. Positivist theories essentially point to factors like these as the causes of deviance.

In sum, the positivist perspective on deviant behavior consists of three assumptions. First, deviance is *absolutely real* in that it has certain qualities that distinguish it from conventionality. Second, deviance is an *observable object* in that a deviant person is like an object and thus can be studied objectively. Third, deviance is *determined* by forces beyond the individual's control.

The Constructionist Perspective

Since the 1960s the constructionist perspective has emerged to challenge the positivist perspective, which had earlier been predominant in the sociology of deviance. Let's examine the assumptions of the constructionist perspective that run counter to those of the positivist perspective.

Relativism: Deviance as a Label

The constructionist perspective holds the relativist view that deviant behavior by itself does not have any intrinsic characteristics unless it is thought to have these characteristics. The so-called intrinsically deviant characteristics do not come from the behavior itself; they come instead from some people's minds. To put it simply, an act appears deviant only because some people think it so. As Howard Becker (1963) says, "Deviant behavior is behavior that people so label." So, no deviant label, no deviant behavior. The existence of deviance depends on the label. Deviance, then, is a mental construct (an idea, thought, or image) expressed in the form of a label. Deviance, in other words, is socially constructed, defined as such by society.

Since, effectively, they consider deviance unreal, constructionists understandably stay away from studying it. They are more interested in the questions of whether and why a given act is defined by society as deviant. This leads to the study of people who label others as deviants—such as the police and other law-enforcing agents. If constructionists study so-called deviants, they do so by focusing on the nature of labeling and its consequences.

In studying law-enforcing agents, constructionists have found a huge lack of consensus on whether a certain person should be treated as a criminal. The police often disagree among themselves as to whether a suspect should be arrested, and judges often disagree among themselves as to whether those arrested should be convicted or acquitted. In addition, since laws vary from one state to another, the same type of behavior may be defined as criminal in one state but not so in another. Young adult males who father babies born to unwed teenage females, for example, can be prosecuted for statutory rape in California but not in most other states (Gleick, 1996). There is, then, a *relativity* principle in deviant behavior: Behavior gets defined as deviant relative to a given norm or standard of behavior, which is to say, to the way people react to it. If it is not related to the reaction of other people, a given behavior is in itself meaningless—it is impossible to say whether it is deviant or conforming. Constructionists strongly emphasize this relativistic view, according to which, deviance, like beauty, is in the eye of the beholder.

Subjectivism: Deviance as a Subjective Experience

To constructionists, the supposedly deviant behavior is a subjective, personal experience and the supposedly deviant person is a conscious, feeling, thinking, and reflective subject. Constructionists insist that there is a world of difference between humans (as active subjects) and nonhuman beings and things (as passive objects). Humans feel and reflect, and are thus distinguishable from animals, plants, things, and forces in nature, which cannot. Humans also have sacred worth and dignity, but things and forces do not. It is proper and useful for natural scientists to assume nature as an object and then study it, because this study can produce objective knowledge for controlling the natural world. It can also be useful for social scientists to assume and then study humans as objects because it may produce objective knowledge for controlling humans, but this violates the constructionist's humanist values and sensibilities.

As humanists, constructionists are opposed to the control of humans; instead, they advocate the protection and expansion of human worth, dignity, and freedom. One result of this humanist ideology is the observation that so-called objective knowledge about human behavior is inevitably superficial whenever it is used for controlling people. To control its black citizens, for example, the former white racist regime in South Africa needed only the superficial knowledge that they were identifiable and separable from whites. To achieve the humanist goal of protecting and expanding a certain people's human worth, dignity, and freedom, a deeper understanding is needed. This understanding requires appreciating and empathizing with each individual or group, experiencing what they experience, and seeing their lives and the world around them from their perspective. We must look at their experience from the inside as a participant rather than from the outside as a spectator. In a word, we must adopt the internal, subjective view rather than the external, objective one.

The same principle, according to constructionists, should hold for understanding deviants and their deviant behavior. Constructionists contrast this subjective approach with positivists' objective one. To constructionists, positivists treat deviance as if it were an immoral, unpleasant, or repulsive phenomenon that should be controlled, corrected, or eliminated. In consequence, positivists have used the objective approach by staying aloof from deviants, by studying the external aspects of their deviant behavior, and by relying upon a set of preconceived ideas for guiding their study. The result is a collection of *surface facts* about deviants, such as their poverty, lack of schooling, poor self-image, and low aspirations. All this may be used for controlling and eliminating deviance, but it does not tell us "what deviant people do in their daily round of activity and what they think about themselves, society, and their activities" (Becker, 1963).

In order to understand the life of a deviant, constructionists believe, we need to use the relatively subjective approach, which requires our appreciation for and empathy with the deviant. The aim of this subjective approach, according to David Matza (1969), "is to comprehend and to illuminate the subject's view and to interpret the world *as it appears to him.*" Thus constructionists tend to study deviants with such methods as ethnography, participant observation, or open-ended, in-depth interviews.

As a result of their subjective and empathetic approach, constructionists often present an image of deviants as basically the same as conventional people. The deaf, for example, are the same as the nondeaf in being able to communicate and live a normal life. They should therefore be respected rather than pitied. This implies that so-called deviant behavior, because it is like so-called conventional behavior, should not be controlled, cured, or eradicated by society.

Voluntarism: Deviance as a Voluntary Act

The constructionist perspective holds that supposedly deviant behavior is a voluntary act, an expression of human volition, will, or choice. Constructionists take this stand because they are disturbed by what they claim to be the dehumanizing implication of the positivist view of deviant behavior. The positivist view is said to imply that the human being is like "a robot, a senseless and purposeless machine reacting to every fortuitous change in the external and internal environment." But constructionists emphasize that human beings, because they possess free will and choice-making ability, determine their own behavior.

To support this voluntarist assumption, constructionists tend to analyze how social control agencies define some people as deviant and carry out the sanctions against them. Such analyses, as Edwin Lemert (1972) has observed, often accent "the arbitrariness of official action, stereotyped decision-making in bureaucratic contexts, bias in the administration of law, and the general preemptive nature of society's controls over deviants." All these convey the strong impression that control agents, being in positions of power, exercise their free will by actively, intentionally, and purposefully controlling the "deviants."

Constructionists also analyze people who have been labeled deviant. The "deviants" are not presented as if they were robots, passively and senselessly developing a poor self-image as conventional society expects of them. Rather, they are described as actively seeking positive meanings in their deviant activities. In constructionist Jack Katz's (1988) analysis, for example, murderers see themselves as morally superior to their victims. The killing is said to give the murderers the self-righteous feeling of defending their dignity and respectability because their victims have unjustly humiliated them by taunting or insulting them. Katz also portrays robbers as feeling themselves morally superior to their victims—regarding their victims as fools or "suckers" who deserve to be robbed. (More of this analysis will be presented in Chapter 3.) Such insight into the subjective, experiential world of deviance constitutes a noncausal, descriptive, or analytical theory.

In brief, the constructionist perspective consists of three assumptions. First, deviant behavior is not real in and of itself; it is, basically, a *label*. Second, supposedly deviant behavior is a *subjective* experience and therefore should be studied with subjectivity and empathy. And, third, putatively deviant behavior is a *voluntary, self-willed* act rather than one caused by forces in the internal and external environments.

An Integrated View

To know what deviant behavior is, then, we need both positivist and constructionist perspectives. (See Table 1.1 for a quick review of these two perspectives.) The combination of the two can give us a better picture than either one can by itself. The two perspectives may appear to be in sharp contradiction, but their differences are largely in emphasis. By giving consideration to one side, we do not

TABLE 1.1   A Summary of Two Perspectives

Positivist Perspective	Constructionist Perspective
Absolutism: Deviance is absolutely, intrinsically real; hence, deviance or deviants can be subject of study.	*Relativism:* Deviance is a label, defined as such at a given time and place; hence, labelers, labeling, and impact of labeling can be subject of study.
Objectivism: Deviance is an observable object; hence, objective research methods can be used.	*Subjectivism:* Deviance is a subjective experience; hence, subjective research methods can be used.
Determinism: Deviance is determined behavior, a product of causation; hence, causal, explanatory theory can be developed.	*Voluntarism:* Deviance is a voluntary act, an expression of free will; hence, noncausal, descriptive theory can be developed.

necessarily deny the reality of the other. Both positivist and constructionist sociologists, in emphasizing their own views, assume in a way their opponents to be correct. Each group merely thinks of the other's argument as less important than its own. Thus, while they accept constructionists' view of deviance as a label, positivists simply take it for granted, considering it less important than their own assumption of deviance as real behavior. On the other hand, while constructionists accept positivists' view of deviance as an act that has really occurred, they consider it more worthwhile to focus on society's definition of the act as deviant.

Now that we know the two opposing perspectives, we can bring them together. As Chinese people are fond of saying, "Things that oppose each other also complement each other" (Mao, 1967). Thus we may see deviant behavior as being both a real act and a label. One cannot exist without the other. If there is no real act, there is no deviant *behavior;* if there is no label, there is no *deviant* behavior. In order for us to use the label "deviant," the *behavior* must occur. Similarly, for us to understand that behavior, the *label* "deviant" must be used.

But in complementing each other the two conflicting perspectives are not necessarily equally applicable to all types of deviant behavior. On the contrary, one perspective seems more relevant than the other in studying the types of deviance that more easily fit its assumptions and the temperaments of the sociologists embracing that perspective.

Specifically, the positivist perspective is more relevant to the study of what society considers relatively *serious* types of deviant behavior, such as murder, rape, armed robbery, and the like. The study of these types of deviance responds well to the positivist perspective for three reasons. First, these forms of deviant behavior, which characteristically enter into the official statistics analyzed by positivists, can be defined as really deviant. Such deviant acts are intrinsically more harmful than conforming behavior, are likely to elicit wide consensus from the public as to their deviant characteristics, and therefore are easily distinguishable from conforming behavior. Second, people who commit serious crimes, such as murder and robbery, generally come from the lower classes, quite unlike the positivists who study them. These are crimes that positivists themselves—as researchers, scholars, or professors—generally would not commit or could not conceive themselves capable of committing. It is easy, therefore, for positivists to stay aloof from these criminals, analyzing their behavior objectively, without empathizing with them or romanticizing their behavior. Third, since positivists can easily separate themselves from the people who commit serious deviant acts, it is natural for them to study these deviants as if they were passive objects "out there" rather than active subjects "in here" (like positivists themselves). It is thus natural for positivists to investigate these "passive" individuals with an eye to seeking out the causes of their deviance rather than understanding the operation of their free will.

In the same way, the constructionist perspective is more pertinent to the *less serious* kinds of deviance, particularly those that do not gravely harm other people. This perspective, as a constructionist puts it, "finds itself at home in the world of hip, drug addicts, jazz musicians, cab drivers, prostitutes, night people, drifters, grifters, and skidders: the 'cool world'" (Gouldner, 1968). Again, three reasons explain the convenient fit between perspective and subject matter. First, there is a relative lack of consensus in society as to whether the less serious forms of deviant behavior are indeed deviant. Some members of society may label them deviant, while others may not. It is therefore logical for constructionists to emphasize that deviant behavior is basically a matter of labeling. Second, those so-called deviants are considered by society as less dangerous than the criminals typically studied by positivists. They also engage in the so-called deviant activities that constructionists themselves could enjoy, participate in, or at least feel themselves capable of engaging in—quite unlike the more dangerous acts committed by "common" criminals. Therefore, constructionists can more easily empathize with these supposed deviants and consider the latter's subjective experience useful for understanding deviance. Third, since they can empathize with these harmless deviants, it is natural for constructionists to consider them active subjects like themselves rather than passive objects. This may be why they emphasize the voluntary, self-willed nature of the putative deviants' experience.

At bottom, the types of deviant behavior—seen through the positivist and constructionist perspectives—differ in the *amount of public consensus* regarding their deviant nature. On the one side, a given deviant act is, from the positivist standpoint, "intrinsically real," largely because there is a relatively great public consensus that it is really deviant. On the other side, a given deviant act is, from the constructionist perspective, "not real in itself but basically a label," largely because there is a relative lack of public consensus supporting it as really deviant. We may integrate the two views by defining deviant behavior with public consensus in mind.

Deviant behavior, we may say, is *any behavior considered deviant by public consensus, which may range from the maximum to the minimum.* Defined this way, deviant behavior should not be regarded as a discrete entity that is clearly and absolutely distinguishable from conforming behavior. Instead, deviance should be viewed as an act located somewhere on a continuum from total conformity at one extreme to total deviance at the other. Given the pluralistic nature of U.S. society, with many different groups having conflicting views of whether a given act is deviant, most of the so-called deviant behaviors can be assumed to fall in the large gray areas between the two poles of the continuum. Hence deviant behavior actually means being more or less, rather than completely, deviant. It is a matter of degree rather than kind. Keeping this in the back of our minds, we may classify deviant behavior into two types, one more deviant than the other: higher- and lower-consensus deviance. *Higher-consensus deviance* is the type that has often been studied by positivist sociologists. *Lower-consensus deviance* is the type that has more frequently been studied by constructionist sociologists. Today, however, either positivists or constructionists are more interested than before in investigating both types of deviance.

Summary

1. How do sociologists define deviant behavior? In sociology there are many different definitions of deviant behavior. They can be divided into two major types, one influenced by the positivist perspective and the other by the constructionist perspective. The positivist perspective holds the absolutist view that deviant behavior is absolutely real, the objectivist view that deviance is an observable object, and the determinist view that deviance is determined behavior, a product of causation. The constructionist perspective consists of the relativist view that the so-called deviance is largely a label applied to an act at a given time and place, the subjectivist view that deviance is itself a subjective experience, and the voluntarist view that deviance is a voluntary, self-willed act.

2. Can we integrate those two perspectives? Yes. We can integrate them into a larger perspective that sees deviant behavior as an act located at some point on a continuum from maximal to minimal public consensus regarding the deviant nature of the act. With this integrated view, we can divide deviant behavior into two major types. One, *higher-consensus deviance,* is generally serious enough to earn a great amount of public consensus that it is really deviant. This type has often been the subject of research by positivist sociologists. The other, *lower-consensus deviance,* is generally less serious and thus receives a lesser degree of public consensus on its deviant reality. This type has more often attracted the interest of constructionist sociologists.

SUGGESTED READINGS

Bendle, Mervyn F. 1999. "The death of the sociology of deviance?" A critical analysis of the problems besetting the sociology of deviance and the emergence of a new paradigm for the field.

Conrad, Peter, and Joseph W. Schneider. 1992. *Deviance and Medicalization: From Badness to Sickness*. Philadelphia: Temple University Press. An analysis of the changing definitions of deviance, from religious to criminal to medical definitions.

Cullen, Francis T. 1984. *Rethinking Crime and Deviance Theory: The Emergence of a Structuring Tradition*. Totowa, N.J.: Rowman & Allanheld. Arguing the importance of the "structuring perspective" for understanding deviance, which shows how certain social and social-psychological conditions can determine the transformation of a general deviant tendency into a specific form of deviant behavior.

Dodge, David L. 1985. "The over-negativized conceptualization of deviance: A programmatic exploration." *Deviant Behavior*, 6, 17–37. Argues that sociologists would do well to start studying positive deviance.

Goode, Erich, and Nachman Ben-Yehuda. 1994. *Moral Panics: The Social Construction of Deviance*. Cambridge, Mass.: Blackwell. A constructionist analysis of how societies periodically overreact with excessive fear or outrage to such social events as witchcraft, drug abuse, and satanism.

Henslin, James M. 1988. "Structuralism and individualism in deviance theory." *Deviant Behavior*, 9, 211–223. Illustrating an example of the difference between the positivist and constructionist perspectives in the sociology of deviance.

Lyman, Stanford M. 1995. "Without morals or mores: Deviance in postmodernist social theory." *International Journal of Politics, Culture and Society*, 9, 197–235. A critical analysis of the constructionist view that the concept of deviance reflects an unjustifiable attempt to distinguish one group from another.

Pfohl, Stephen J. 1994. *Images of Deviance and Social Control: A Sociological History*. 2d ed. New York: McGraw-Hill. Presents nine perspectives of deviance, ranging from the earliest view of deviance as a demonic act to the latest conception of deviance as a way of "asserting lost power."

Scull, Andrew. 1984. "Competing perspectives on deviance." *Deviant Behavior*, 5, 275–289. A review of the theoretical debates in the sociology of deviance over the last two decades, with the warning that sociologists may get bogged down with metaphysical issues, unable to study real deviance in a real society.

Thio, Alex, and Thomas C. Calhoun (Eds.). 2001. *Readings in Deviant Behavior*. New York: HarperCollins. An anthology that includes articles on definitions, images, or notions of deviance.

Troyer, Ronald J., and Gerald E. Markle. 1982. "Creating deviance rules: A macroscopic model." *The Sociological Quarterly*, 23, 157–169. An attempt to integrate the positivist and constructionist perspectives (which the authors call "social factist and definitionist traditions") for studying how rules against deviance are made.

2 Positivist Theories: Explaining Deviance

One morning in 1996 in the tiny town of Dunblane, Scotland, a 43-year-old man strode into an elementary school with four loaded handguns. Two staff members tried to stop him, but he shot and wounded them both. Then he made his way to the gymnasium where teacher Gwen Mayor had just brought in her 29 first-graders for physical education class. The gunman opened fire from a corner of the room. The teacher was the first to die as she tried to shield the children. Then, the murderer moved around, methodically shooting at the screaming children, killing 16 and wounding 12. Only one child was unhurt; he had escaped by crawling into the alcove at the back of the gym. Finally, the killer pumped the last bullet into his own head (Pedersen, 1996).

Given such a shocking, monstrous act, positivist sociologists would ask what causes it. The answer could be found in the killer's past social experiences. The man had been "inadequately socialized" since birth, abandoned by his father when 18 months old and raised by his mother whom he had always thought to be his sister. Shunned by peers, he grew up to be a loner with a fascination for guns and an unhealthy interest in children. Boy Scout officials had dismissed him for "inappropriate behavior" as leader of a local troop. He was locally known as "Mr. Creepy." He was full of grievances against the town (Jackson, 1996). All these facts suggest the possible causes of the mass killing, and it is the focus on causes of deviance that characterizes all positivist theories of deviance.

There are many positivist causal theories of deviance. Here we will discuss only the most important ones, namely, strain theory, learning theory, and control theory.

Strain Theory

Strain theory was first developed by Robert Merton (1938). Later, Albert Cohen (1955) formulated his theory of juvenile delinquency, which appears to be an extension of Merton's ideas. Finally, two other sociologists, Richard Cloward and Lloyd Ohlin (1960), attempted to improve on Merton's theory. Today, sociologists often refer to these theories collectively as *strain* theory because they suggest in one way or another that the experience of societally induced strain forces people to engage in deviant activities (Agnew, 1995; Bernard, 1984; Mitchell, 1984). To Merton, the strain is the inability to realize a success goal; to Cohen, the strain is the failure to achieve high status; and to Cloward and Ohlin, the strain involves not having an illegitimate opportunity for success, a complexity to be explained further.

Merton: The Goal–Means Gap

[handwritten: o reactionary, o conflict theory]

Merton found something wrong with Freud's psychoanalytic theory of deviant behavior. The psychoanalytic theory says that criminal, pathological, or socially dangerous behavior represents the free expression of the libido, biological impulses, or animal desires the individual is born with. The defect of this theory, according to Merton, lies in its assumption that "the structure of society primarily restrains the free expression of man's fixed native impulses." That is, society *discourages* the individual from engaging in deviant activities. Merton called this assumption a "fallacious premise," because he believed just the opposite: society *encourages* the individual to engage in deviant activities. With such a premise, Merton developed his strain theory.

Many sociologists have long believed that Merton's theory was inspired by Émile Durkheim, who was the first to use the term *anomie* as a sociological concept. Thus they have called it *anomie theory*. But the implication of Durkheim's concept of anomie is contrary to the premise of Merton's theory. By *anomie* Durkheim referred to an absence of social norms, which implies the failure of a society to control its members' behavior through laws, customs, and other norms. Durkheim assumed that the lack of this normative control causes deviance. This is similar to Freud's assumption that deviance will break out if society fails to discourage it by restraining individuals' impulses. But Merton's theory assumes just the opposite: Deviance will occur if society encourages it by pressuring individuals to commit it. Precisely how does society do this?

In Merton's view U.S. society heavily emphasizes the cultural value of success. From kindergarten to college your teachers motivate you to achieve a high scholastic record and to have great ambition for your future. The books, magazines, and newspapers you read often carry success stories that encourage you to become successful yourself. The games, sports, and athletic events that you watch in the stadium or on television impress you with the supreme importance of winning. If you participate in an athletic event, the coach will prod you to win. If you simply want to enjoy the pleasure of playing the game, and sarcastically argue that "winning is not everything," the coach may argue back even more sarcastically: "Right, winning is not everything—winning is the *only* thing!" This cultural value of success is so pervasive in this society that people of *all* classes are expected to be ambitious, to entertain high aspirations; everyone is expected to have the desire to be a winner, to be somebody. Even poor people are told that their children have the chance of becoming president of the United States if they have as much ambition as the young, poverty-stricken Abraham Lincoln did. In this sense, the cultural *goal* of success is freely available to all people, regardless of their social-class backgrounds.

In contrast, the institutionalized, legitimate *means* of achieving the high success goal, such as getting a good job, are not freely available to all classes of people. The society is structured in such a way that people of the lower social classes, when compared with those of the higher, have less opportunity to realize their success aspirations. Lower-class people thus find themselves trapped in a very difficult situation. They have been encouraged by the society to hold high success aspirations but they are not given the opportunity to realize those aspirations. To get themselves out of that predicament, many lower-class people resort to *illegitimate* means of achieving their success aspirations, such as stealing, robbing, and other similar forms of deviant activities. So, lower-class people are more likely to engage in deviant activities.

We have just seen that the *cause* of those lower-class deviant activities is the societal condition marked by the inconsistency between society's *over*emphasis on the success goal and its *under*emphasis on the use of legitimate means for achieving that goal. Merton (1938) describes this goal–means disjunction in this way: "Contemporary American culture continues to be characterized by a heavy emphasis on wealth as a basic symbol of success, without a corresponding emphasis upon the legitimate avenues on which to march toward this goal." With this encouragement of high aspirations and denial of success opportunities, U.S. society, in effect, pressures us to commit deviance.

TABLE 2.1   A Typology of Responses to Goal–Means Gap

In U.S. society, according to Merton, there is too much emphasis on success but too little emphasis on the legitimate means for achieving success. Such inconsistency may cause deviant behavior, yet various people respond to it differently.

Response	Success Goal	Legitimate Means
1. Conformity	+	+
2. Innovation	+	−
3. Ritualism	−	+
4. Retreatism	−	−
5. Rebellion	−+	−+

Note: + indicates accepting; − signifies rejecting; and −+ means rejecting the old and introducing the new.
Source: Adapted from Robert K. Merton, *Social Theory and Social Structure.* New York: Free Press, 1968.

However, given this societal pressure toward deviance, not all of us would respond to it in the same way. Many lower-class people, as the previous discussion has implied, may respond to it by accepting the success goal while rejecting the use of legitimate means for realizing that goal. Merton refers to this deviant behavior as *innovation*. It is also the case that many other individuals of various social classes may respond differently to that same social condition. Therefore, along with innovation, Merton presents other types of adaptation (see Table 2.1).

1. *Conformity* is the most popular mode of adaptation. It involves accepting both the cultural goal of success and the use of legitimate means of working toward that goal. Presumably most of us choose this adaptation.

2. *Innovation* is largely found among lower-class people, who reject the use of legal means in favor of illegal ones in their attempts to achieve the high success goal that they have learned to accept. This form of deviant adaptation is the central subject of strain theory, and Merton discusses it much more than any other.

3. *Ritualism* is common among lower-middle-class people who lower their aspirations or abandon high success goals so that they can more easily realize their aspirations. But in their attempts to realize these modest aspirations, they almost compulsively—hence, ritualistically—abide by the institutional norm of toiling as conscientious, loyal workers. They tend to be proud of their hard, honest work while shrugging off their modest incomes.

4. *Retreatism* is a withdrawal from society into the shell of one's self. The retreatist does not care about success, nor does he or she care to work. Examples of such people are psychotics, outcasts, vagrants, vagabonds, tramps, alcoholics, and drug addicts.

5. *Rebellion* involves rejecting the prevailing social expectation that we work hard in the so-called rat race to reach the goal of great success. The rebel also attempts to overthrow the existing system and put in its place a new one with new goals and new means of reaching those goals. Thus, the rebel may abandon both the pursuit of fame and riches and the cutthroat competition needed to achieve this worldly goal. At the same time, the rebel may encourage people to seek goodwill toward others and to cooperate in attaining this heavenly goal.

Cohen: Status Frustration

The version of strain theory proposed by Cohen (1955) is fundamentally the same as Merton's. Like Merton, Cohen suggests that U.S. society encourages all classes of people to achieve status while at the same time making it difficult for lower-class people to really achieve it. As a consequence, lower-class people are compelled to achieve status in their own way—that is, to engage in deviant acts. Although the theme is the same as in Merton's theory, Cohen tells the story differently, replacing Merton's word *success* with *status*.

According to Cohen, lower-class boys, like their middle-class peers, want to have status. An important place to achieve status is the school, which they are forced to attend. But the school turns out to be a most unlikely place for lower-class boys, because it ensures their failure. How so? The school is run by middle-class teachers, promotes middle-class values and behavior, and judges the student's achievement by middle-class standards of behavior and performance. The school, then, is a middle-class status system. To achieve the status of a successful, competent, or good student in the middle-class setting, youngsters must possess middle-class values, virtues, and traits, such as verbal fluency, academic intelligence, the ability to delay gratification, courtesy, opposition to fistfights, and respect for property. In this status system, middle-class boys obviously have a good chance of becoming successful. Yet lower-class boys, who have not been socialized in the same way as middle-class boys, are thrown into a status system where they are expected to compete with middle-class boys. The result is not surprising: lower-class boys fail disastrously. Cohen (1955) describes their problem in this manner:

> In particular, different patterns of socialization are associated with the different social classes and middle-class socialization is far more effective in training children for such success than is lower-class socialization. For this and other reasons, lower-class children are more likely to experience failure and humiliation. In brief, they are caught up in a game in which others are typically the winners and they are the losers and the also-rans.

Being a loser or also-ran is obviously very frustrating. Driven by this frustration, which Cohen calls *status frustration,* lower-class boys go back to their own lower-class neighborhood and set up their own competitive system, which Cohen refers to as a *delinquent subculture*. In that subculture they can compete more fairly among themselves for high status in accordance with their own criteria of achievement. Their criteria of achievement are in direct opposition to the "respectable" middle-class or conventional criteria. They judge as wrong whatever values and behaviors are considered right by conventional standards, and they judge as right whatever values and behaviors are considered wrong by conventional standards. Given this, it is obvious that the lower-class boys' very attempt to achieve status among their peers is—according to conventional standards—delinquent. The so-called delinquent activities include stealing "for the hell of it," fighting, terrorizing "good" children, destroying property, and defying various conventional taboos.

In short, Cohen extends Merton's theory by adding the concept of status frustration. As you may remember, Merton suggests that the goal–means gap (discrepancy between success aspiration and opportunity) *by itself* pressures lower-class people into deviance: Goal–means gap → deviance. But Cohen's theory suggests that the goal–means gap can lead lower-class boys toward deviant activities only if the boys encounter *status frustration*. In other words, status frustration serves as the third, intervening variable that enables the goal–means gap to produce delinquent subculture: Goal–means gap → *status frustration* → deviance.

Nevertheless, Cohen's theory is basically the same as Merton's. Both assume that lower-class people are more likely than others to engage in deviant activities because society fails to help them fulfill the aspirations (for success or status) that it has induced in these people.

Cloward and Ohlin: Differential Illegitimate Opportunity

You may recall the way Merton formulates his theory: The lower classes tend to engage in deviance because they, like the upper classes, have been encouraged to hold high success goals but, unlike the upper classes, are denied the *legitimate* means or opportunity of achieving the success goals. Cloward and Ohlin (1960) accept this general idea. At the same time, however, they want to extend it by introducing the concept of differential *illegitimate* opportunity.

First, Cloward and Ohlin point out that Merton correctly directs our attention to the problem of differential legitimate opportunity—that the lower classes have less opportunity than other classes for achieving success in a legitimate, conforming manner. But Merton wrongly assumes that the lower classes, when confronted with the lack of opportunity, would automatically and successfully engage in deviant activities. In other words, Merton fails to recognize the fact that the lower classes, after being confronted with the problem of differential *legitimate* opportunity, are further confronted with the additional problem of differential *illegitimate* opportunity. The fact is that some members of the lower classes have less opportunity than others of the same classes for achieving success in an *illegitimate, deviant* manner. What Cloward and Ohlin want to emphasize is that while all lower-class people have the same lack of opportunity for engaging in legitimate and conforming activities, they do not have the same opportunity for participating in illegitimate and deviant activities. Thus, when some lower-class persons are pressured toward committing a deviant act such as theft or robbery, there is no guarantee that they will actually do it. Whether or not they will actually do it depends on the nature of their access to illegitimate opportunity in the lower-class neighborhood.

There are three types of illegitimate opportunity, each provided by a deviant subculture. The *criminal subculture* offers illegitimate opportunities for achieving success goals. If lower-class youngsters are integrated into this subculture, they are able to achieve their success goals by stealing, robbing, and fencing. This is the kind of deviant activity to which Merton assumes all lower-class youngsters will turn when they are denied conventional opportunities in the larger society. But, according to Cloward and Ohlin, many of these lower-class youths are not part of the criminal subculture and therefore do not enjoy criminal opportunities.

Yet some youths may find themselves in another neighborhood where the *conflict* subculture flourishes. In this subculture, a youngster has the opportunity to achieve "rep" or status within a violent delinquent gang. But that opportunity is available only to those youngsters who can meet such requirements as possessing great fighting skill and demonstrating enthusiasm for risking injury or death in gang warfare. Some lower-class adolescents fail to meet these requirements and are therefore denied the opportunity for achieving status within the conflict subculture.

There is, finally, a third, *retreatist* subculture, in which the only requirement for membership is the willingness to enjoy the use of drugs. Persons who are recruited into the retreatist subculture are likely to be those who have failed to achieve success in the criminal subculture or to attain status in the conflict subculture. Because of their failure to achieve success or status in *both* the delinquent underworld and the conventional upperworld, the retreatists have been called "double failures."

In brief, Cloward and Ohlin extend Merton's strain theory by introducing differential illegitimate opportunity as the third, intervening variable through which the goal–means gap leads to three different kinds of deviant activities: goal–means gap → *differential illegitimate opportunity* → different deviant activities. (Table 2.2 shows how this version of strain theory compares with the other two.) Nevertheless, Cloward and Ohlin basically agree with Merton that lower-class

TABLE 2.2 Three Versions of Strain Theory

Merton: Goal–means gap → deviance

Cohen: Goal–means gap → status frustration → deviance

Cloward and Ohlin: Goal–means gap → differential illegitimate opportunity → different deviant activities

Note: The sign "→" indicates "antecedes or causes," as in "A antecedes or causes B."

people are more inclined than others toward deviance because they are more likely to experience the discrepancy between success aspirations and the opportunity for realizing those aspirations.

Evaluating Strain Theory

Strain theory has at least two problems. First, there is no reliable evidence to support strain theory's claim that people of lower classes are more likely than those of other classes to engage in deviant activities. It is true that the official statistics on crime and delinquency, which strain theorists rely on, do support the theory. But the official statistics are largely unreliable and invalid. They are unreliable because law enforcers are much more likely to catch lower-class criminals and delinquents than higher-class ones. They are invalid because they do not reflect the total picture of deviance—they measure instead a very small portion of the totality of deviance, namely, the relatively serious types. If we modify the theory and say that lower-class people are more likely to commit what society considers *serious* types of deviance, then the theory does have adequate empirical support from both the official and unofficial reports on criminality and delinquency.

Second, there is no evidence to support the assumption of strain theory that lower-class people tend to hold the same level of success aspirations as do upper- and middle-class people. On the contrary, both theoretical analysis and empirical data show that lower-class people hold a significantly lower level of success aspirations (Thio, 1975). It is true, as strain theorists claim, that U.S. society *encourages* lower-class people to embrace high-success goals. But it is *not* necessarily true, as strain theorists assume, that lower-class people will end up embracing high-success goals. Merton and other strain theorists appear to have ignored the fact that while the manifest, intended function of U.S. success ideology is to get all social classes to entertain high aspirations, its latent, unintended, and real consequence turns out to be the higher social classes holding far higher aspirations than the lower classes.

Whatever its shortcomings, strain theory does have important redeeming value, aside from its being considered by many sociologists as highly interesting. Foremost to consider is that strain theory has contributed greatly to the sociological idea that the society, not the individual, causes deviant behavior. Before the theory was first published in 1938, many sociologists tended to seek the causes of deviance within the individual rather than without. The fact that, today, many sociologists take for granted the notion of deviance as caused by society is a testament to the contribution of strain theory.

Further, strain theory seems to have a valid premise: The discrepancy between aspirations and the opportunity to realize these aspirations produces pressures toward deviation. This premise appears valid as long as it is not used to make the unwarranted generalization that the lower classes are more pressured toward deviation in general than are other classes. Instead, we may use the premise to suggest that anybody, regardless of class, tends to engage in deviance if they experience a significant gap between aspiration and opportunity. Indeed, much research has shown that wherever the aspiration–opportunity gap strikes, it tends to generate deviation (Agnew, 1995; Menard, 1995; Bernard, 1984).

Social Learning Theory

According to social learning theory, the brainchild of Edwin Sutherland (1939), deviant behavior is learned through one's interaction with others. More specifically, Sutherland developed the theory of differential association to explain how the learning of deviance comes about. Later, other sociologists presented different theories about the same subject.

Sutherland: Differential Association

More than 50 years ago—at about the same time that Merton proposed strain theory—Sutherland (1939) introduced the theory of differential association. The heart of the theory is this: If an individual associates with people who hold deviant (or criminal) ideas more than with people who embrace conventional ideas, the individual is likely to become deviant.

We should note two things about the meaning of this statement. First, the people who hold deviant ideas do not have to be deviants—they can be anybody, even those who have not committed any deviance. What counts is the *idea* of committing deviance. Suppose a father tells his children that it's all right to steal when you are poor, he is giving them an idea of committing a deviant act. On the other hand, if the father tells his children that it's wrong to steal, he is giving them an antideviant idea. The emphasis here is on whether the father gives his children deviant or antideviant ideas, not whether the father himself is a deviant or nondeviant. Therefore, if people are given more ideas of committing deviant acts than ideas of performing conventional acts, they are likely to engage in deviance.

Second, the theory does *not* refer to only one type of association, that is, deviant association or exposure to deviant ideas. The theory does not suggest that, if individuals have a lot of contacts with deviant ideas, they will become deviant. Lawyers, for example, may have a lot of contacts with their criminal clients, but they will not necessarily become criminals themselves. The theory instead refers to both deviant and conventional contacts or, more precisely, to the *excess* of deviant over conventional contacts. This means that it is all right to have both kinds of contacts; only if we have a *greater* number of deviant contacts than conventional ones, are we likely to become deviant. This is suggested by the term *differential association*, which refers to the fact that deviants' *association* with deviant individuals and ideas *differs* from (or, more precisely, occurs more often than) their association with conventional ones. Defined in this way, differential association is theorized to be the cause of deviance: Differential association → deviant behavior.

Glaser: Differential Identification

According to Daniel Glaser (1956), Sutherland's theory actually conveys a rather "mechanistic image" of deviance. Such an image shows the individual as being mechanically pushed into deviant involvement by an association with deviants. It ignores the individual's role-taking and choice-making ability. Glaser, then, tries to correct this mechanistic image by suggesting that the experience of associating with deviants is harmless unless the individual *identifies* with them. As Glaser (1956) states:

> The theory of differential identification, in essence, is that a person pursues criminal behavior to the extent that he *identifies* with real or imaginary persons from whose perspective his criminal behavior seems acceptable. Such a theory focuses attention on the interaction in which choice of models occurs, including the individual's interaction with himself in rationalizing his conduct.

Glaser's theory may be taken to suggest that it is all right for us to associate with deviants in real life or in books and movies, as long as we do not take them so seriously that we identify with them, treating them as our heroes. If we do identify with them, we are likely to become deviants ourselves. In effect, Glaser suggests that deviance is likely to occur if differential identification intervenes between it and differential association: Differential association → *differential identification* → deviant behavior.

Burgess and Akers: Differential Reinforcement

According to Robert Burgess and Ronald Akers (1966a), Sutherland merely suggested, in very broad terms, that people with differential association must go through a learning process before they become deviant. Sutherland failed, they contend, to specify what that learning process entails. In trying to correct this failure, Burgess and Akers offer the idea of *differential reinforcement* as the substance of that learning process.

Burgess and Akers derive their idea from a well-known theory in psychology, which has been variously referred to as *social learning theory, behaviorist theory, operant behavior theory, operant conditioning theory,* and *reinforcement theory.* Generally, the theory says that we are motivated to continue behaving in a certain way if we have been rewarded for doing so, or to discontinue the behavior if we have been punished for it. You are, for example, likely to continue studying hard if you have been rewarded by good grades for studying hard in the past. When applied to deviant behavior, reinforcement theory says that people will continue to engage in deviant activities if they have been rewarded for doing so. Robbers, for example, will continue to rob if they have made much money from their robberies or if they have not been caught for their crimes.

One aspect of reinforcement theory that is most relevant to the Burgess-Akers reformulation of Sutherland's differential association theory is the Law of Differential Reinforcement. In technical language, the law states that "given a number of available operants, all of which produce the same reinforcer, that operant which produces the reinforcer in the greatest amount, frequency and probability will have the higher probability of occurrence" (Burgess and Akers,

TABLE 2.3   Three Versions of Social Learning Theory

Sutherland: Differential association → criminal behavior

Glaser: Differential association → differential identification → criminal behavior

Burgess and Akers: Differential association → differential reinforcement → criminal behavior

Note: The sign "→" indicates "antecedes or causes," as in "A antecedes or causes B."

1966b). This can be expressed in simple terms as follows: If you are given several options, such as studying hard, going to the movies, drinking in a tavern, and attending a wild party the night before an exam, you will most likely choose the option that has been most (or most greatly, frequently, and probably) satisfying to you in the past. When applied to deviant behavior, the law of differential reinforcement would explain that individuals will choose deviance over conventionality if they find deviance more (or more greatly, frequently, and probably) satisfying than conventionality.

By incorporating this law into Sutherland's differential association theory, Akers comes up with what he now calls *social learning theory*. He uses this expanded theory to explain deviant behavior this way: "Deviant behavior can be expected to the extent that [1] it has been differentially reinforced over alternative behavior and [2] is defined as desirable or justified when the individual is in a situation discriminative for the behavior" (Akers, 1998, 1985). This essentially means that people will likely commit a deviant act (1) if they find it more rewarding or satisfying than the other, conventional act, and (2) after they have been exposed to deviant ideas more than to antideviant ideas. Note that the first clause in Akers's statement of his theory represents his concept of differential reinforcement and the second clause basically expresses Sutherland's concept of "definitions favorable to violation of law." In short, Akers supplies what he and Burgess earlier seemed to consider as the missing link in Sutherland's theory: Differential association → *differential reinforcement* → deviant behavior. Table 2.3 summarizes how this version of differential theory differs from the other two discussed earlier.

Evaluating Social Learning Theory

First, it is difficult to determine precisely what "differential association" in Sutherland's theory is in real-life situations. As Sutherland and Cressey (1978) admit, people often cannot identify the persons from whom they have learned deviant and antideviant ideas. Although it is difficult to determine the exact, empirical meaning of differential association, many sociologists have claimed that their research data appear to support Sutherland's theory. But this need not be surprising. Actually, those sociologists have not found any empirical support for

Sutherland's theory, but only for their *own* interpretations of the theory. As James Short (1960), who has done considerable research to test the theory, observed: "Much support has been found for the principle of differential association *if* the liberties taken in the process of its operationalization [translation into empirical or testable terms] are granted."

Second, Glaser's differential identification theory appears to have received some support from empirical data. Victor Matthews (1968), for example, found that high school boys who identified with delinquent friends were likely to become delinquent themselves. But there is no conclusive evidence that identification with delinquent friends is the cause of delinquency or occurs before a person becomes delinquent. It is quite possible that youngsters may identify with delinquent friends only after—not before—having become delinquent themselves.

Third, the Burgess-Akers differential reinforcement theory cannot explain why a person *initially* commits a deviant act. The theory is useful, however, for explaining *repeated* deviance, namely, why some people *continue* to get involved in deviance after committing a deviant act for the first time. The reason, according to differential reinforcement theory, is that they have in the past been rewarded more than punished for their deviance, whereas others do not repeat a deviant act because they have been punished more than rewarded for the act. This formulation has indeed been borne out by many studies (see, for example, Krohn et al., 1985).

Control Theory

Control theory differs in at least two ways from the other major theories discussed above. First, both strain and learning theorists approach the problem of explaining deviant behavior head-on and ask: What causes deviance? Control theorists approach the problem in a roundabout way: What, they ask, causes conformity? They assume, in other words, that if they find out what causes conformity, they will know what causes deviance, for what causes deviance is simply the *absence* of what causes conformity. Second, both strain and learning theorists reject the Freudian idea that deviance can naturally, or by itself, burst forth from our inborn animal impulses. Instead, strain and learning theories maintain that deviance originates from certain social conditions, namely, the discrepancy between goals and means in society and the experience of learning from others. In contrast, control theorists seem to accept the Freudian idea because they assume that people are naturally inclined to commit deviant acts and will do so *unless* they are properly controlled.

In the eyes of control theorists, then, what causes conformity is social control over the individual, and therefore *the absence of social control causes deviance*. There are, however, many different theories about the specific nature of social control. We will focus on only three of the more important ones.

Hirschi: Social Bond and Self-Control

Travis Hirschi (1969) assumes that all of us are endowed like animals with the ability to commit deviant acts. But most of us do not take advantage of this ability, Hirschi suggests, because of our *strong bond* to society. In other words, our strong bond to society ensures our conformity. Conversely, if our social bond is weak, we will commit deviant acts.

According to Hirschi, there are four ways for individuals to bond themselves to society. The first is by *attachment* to conventional people and institutions. In the case of juveniles, they may show this attachment by loving and respecting their parents, making friends with conventional peers, liking school, and working hard to develop intellectual skills. A *commitment* to conformity is the second way. Individuals invest their time and energy in conventional types of action, such as getting an education, holding a job, developing an occupational skill, improving a professional status, building up a business, or acquiring a reputation for virtue. At the same time, people show a commitment to achievement through these activities. The third way is *involvement* in conventional activities. People simply keep themselves so busy doing conventional things that they do not have time for partaking in deviant activities or even thinking about deviant acts. A *belief* in the moral validity of social rules is the fourth way in which people bond themselves to society. Individuals have a strong moral belief that they should obey the rules of conventional society. A young person may show such moral belief through a respect for the police or through a positive attitude toward the law.

If these four elements of the individual's bond to conventional society are strong, the individual is likely to get stuck in conformity. If these elements are weak, the individual is likely to slide into deviance. In more recent publications, Hirschi argues that *weak self-control*, which he says results from poor socialization, is far more useful for explaining deviance. According to him, people with weak self-control are likely to commit deviant acts whether their social bond is strong or weak (Hirschi and Gottfredson, 1994; Gottfredson and Hirschi, 1990).

Braithwaite: Reintegrative Shaming

While Hirschi sees how society controls us through bonding, John Braithwaite (1989) looks at how society controls us through shaming. Shaming involves an expression of social disapproval designed to invoke remorse in the wrongdoer. There are two types of shaming: disintegrative and reintegrative. In *disintegrative shaming*, the wrongdoer is punished in such a way as to be stigmatized, rejected, or ostracized—in effect, banished from conventional society. It is the same as stigmatization. *Reintegrative shaming* is more positive; it involves making wrongdoers feel guilty while showing them understanding, forgiveness, or even respect. It is the kind of shaming that affectionate parents administer to their misbehaving child, or "hating the sin but loving the sinner." Thus, reintegrative shaming serves to reintegrate—or welcome back—the wrongdoer into conventional society.

According to Braithwaite, reintegrative shaming is more common in communitarian societies (marked by strong social relationships but weak individualism), such as Japan, whereas disintegrative shaming is more prevalent in less communitarian societies (characterized by weaker social relationships but stronger individualism), such as the United States. At the same time, reintegrative shaming usually discourages further deviance, while disintegrative shaming or stigmatization encourages it. This is taken to explain why crime rates are higher in the United States than in Japan.

Braithwaite concludes by arguing that the United States can significantly reduce its crime rates if it emphasizes reintegrative shaming rather than stigmatization in dealing with criminals, as Japanese society does. Since the early 1990s reintegrative shaming has appeared in the United States as "shaming penalties," which include drunk drivers being ordered by judges to display "DUI" bumper stickers, people convicted of public urination being ordered to sweep city streets, or men who solicit prostitutes being identified on newspapers, billboards, and radio shows. Dan Kahan (1997), a law professor at the University of Chicago, argues that the shaming is an effective deterrent to deviance.

The Deterrence Doctrine

While Braithwaite's theory deals largely with shaming as an *informal* social control (carried out by relatives, friends, neighbors, and the like), the deterrence doctrine focuses on *formal* social control (executed by judges and other law-enforcement agents). This version of control theory assumes that humans are basically rational, given to calculating the benefit and cost of committing a crime. If they find the cost greater than the benefit, they will refrain from committing the crime. The cost of crime, according to deterrence doctrine, is legal punishment, such as arrest, prosecution, imprisonment, or execution. Thus, the doctrine assumes that punishment (a form of social control) deters crime—and lack of punishment encourages it.

There are three ways in which punishment can be carried out, each being assumed to affect the likelihood of committing crime. First, punishment can be made more or less *severe*. According to deterrence doctrine, the more severe the punishment, the less likely the crime. Murder rates, for example, are expected to be lower in societies where convicted murderers are executed than in societies where the murderers are given a 20-year sentence. Second, punishment can be made more or less *certain*. Deterrence doctrine assumes that the more certain the commission of a crime will result in punishment, the less likely people will be to commit the crime. Shoplifting, for example, is expected to become less common if the chances of getting arrested for it go up from 50–50 to 100. Third, punishment can be made more or less *swift*. The more swiftly punishment is carried out, the less likely the crime is to occur. If it takes only several days for robbers to be arrested in a given city, the robbery rate in this city is likely to be lower than in another city where it takes longer to arrest robbers.

Whatever the mode of punishment, whether it be severe, certain, or swift, it is assumed to achieve two kinds of deterrence: general and specific. In *general deterrence* the punishment of a criminal deters the general public from committing crimes; in *specific deterrence* the punishment of a criminal deters the criminal from committing more crimes.

In sum, the three control theories suggest that some form of control prevents people from committing deviant acts, and the lack of controls prompts the commission of such acts. The theories differ largely in regard to what type of control can prevent deviance. Thus, they present various types of control, which include bond to society, reintegrative shaming, and legal punishment.

Evaluating Control Theory

First, many studies have supported Hirschi's social bond and self-control theory. Deviants such as juvenile delinquents, drug users, and drunk drivers have been found to have a weaker social bond or self-control than nondeviants (Krohn, 1995; Hirschi and Gottfredson, 1994; LaGrange and White, 1985; Minor, 1984; Wiatrowski, Griswold, and Roberts, 1981). But most of these studies, being cross-sectional rather than longitudinal, could not have controlled for (canceled out) the reciprocal effect of deviance on social bond or self-control. Often, it is the deviant experience that causes people to have a weaker social bond and self-control rather than the other way around. Therefore, the restraining effect of social bond or self-control on deviance may not be as strong as Hirschi and his colleagues believe (Kempf, 1993; Liska and Reed, 1985).

Second, Braithwaite is only partly convincing in his argument that the United States can reduce crime with reintegrative shaming—by treating criminals in the same lenient, compassionate way as Japan does. This treatment may work if applied to first-time offenders who have committed relatively minor crimes and still retain a sense of shame for their crimes. But it can hardly have the same positive impact on hardened criminals who have lost their sense of shame for their crimes. Moreover, since reintegrative shaming is part and parcel of a communitarian society, it seems to be the pervasiveness of such society's strong social relationships rather than reintegrative shaming that largely keeps the crime rate low.

Third, the deterrence doctrine has received only conflicting support from research. Various studies show, for example, that arresting wife-beaters deters further violence more than less severe forms of punishment such as ordering the offender to leave the victim for eight hours (Berk and Newton, 1985; Sherman and Berk, 1984). However, studies on released prisoners suggest just the opposite: The more severe their punishment (for example, the longer the sentence), the more likely it is that former inmates will commit crimes again (see, for example, Gibbs, 1975).

Just as the findings from those studies on *specific* deterrence are inconsistent, so are the data from studies that deal with *general* deterrence. A number of studies, for example, have found that the more severe the punishment for homicide, the lower the rate of homicide, and that the more certain the punishment for other major crimes (assault, rape, robbery, and auto theft), the lower the rates of these offenses (Bailey, Martin, and Gray, 1974; Tittle, 1969). But other studies found that certainty of punishment deters only economic crimes such as robbery and auto theft, not violent crimes such as homicide and assault (Paternoster and Iovanni, 1986; Piliavin, Gartner, Thornton, and Matsueda, 1986; see also Meier, Burkett, and Hickman, 1984; Geerken and Gove, 1977).

Finally, various control theories share a simplistic view of social control, regarding it as only a *preventer* of deviance. They fail to see control as a possible *cause* of deviance. The great ambition—along with excellent social and intellectual skills—that develops from social bond may prevent juvenile delinquency, as Hirschi's theory suggests, but the same ambition may cause corporate and political crimes. Similarly, contrary to Braithwaite's theory, reintegrative shaming may cause deviance, such as by encouraging judges to presume the accused as guilty, thereby violating the person's right to be presumed innocent. Also, contrary to the deterrence doctrine, the very process of law enforcement to deter crime may trigger lawbreaking acts. In taking action against a suspect, for example, a police officer may cause the suspect to commit such criminal acts as resisting arrest or assaulting an officer (Marx, 1981).

Table 2.4 presents the major points of all the theories discussed in this chapter.

Summary

1. How does strain theory explain the causation of deviant behavior? According to Merton's strain theory, lower-class people are more likely to get involved in deviant activities because the society has encouraged them to pursue a high-success goal without providing them with the means of achieving it. Cohen extends this theory by proposing that when their aspirations for status are frustrated in the middle-class milieu, lower-class youths are driven to achieve status among themselves by engaging in delinquency. Cloward and Ohlin extend Merton's theory by suggesting that whether potentially delinquent lower-class youth will actually become delinquent depends on whether they have access to illegitimate opportunity. **How good is strain theory?** There is no evidence for its assumption that, compared with middle and upper classes, the lower classes are more prone to deviance while holding the same level of success aspirations. Nevertheless, the theory has been valuable for replacing the psychological with the sociological explanation of deviance and for offering a valid premise concerning the aspiration–opportunity gap.

2. According to various versions of social learning theory, why do some people become deviant? Sutherland's differential association theory states that people will likely become deviant if they associate more with individuals who hold deviant ideas than with those who embrace antideviant ideas.

TABLE 2.4   Positivist Theories of Deviance

Strain Theory: Social strain causes deviance.

>   **Merton's goal–means gap:** Deviance is prevalent in society because the society encourages people to achieve success without providing equal opportunity for achieving it.

>   **Cohen's status frustration:** Deviance is prevalent among lower-class youths because they fail to achieve status in middle-class school environment.

>   **Cloward and Ohlin's differential illegitimate opportunity:** Lower-class youth are likely to engage in delinquent activities if they have access to illegitimate opportunity.

Social Learning Theory: Deviance is learned through social interaction.

>   **Sutherland's differential association:** People are likely to become deviant if they associate with people holding deviant ideas rather than with people holding antideviant ideas.

>   **Glaser's differential identification:** People are likely to become deviant if they identify themselves more with deviants than with nondeviants.

>   **Burgess and Akers' differential reinforcement:** Deviants are likely to continue engaging in deviant activities if they have been rewarded rather than punished for their past deviance.

Control Theory: Lack of social control causes deviance.

>   **Hirschi's social bond and self-control:** People are likely to become deviant if their bond to society and their self-control are weak.

>   **Braithwaite's reintegrative shaming:** People are likely to become deviant if they are not made to feel ashamed for their wrongdoing nor to feel they are an integral part of society.

>   **The deterrence doctrine:** People are likely to become deviant if they know their deviant acts are not punished with severity, certainty, or swiftness.

Glaser extends this theory by suggesting that the determining factor for turning the differential association into criminal action is differential identification, while Burgess and Akers designate differential reinforcement the determining factor. **Are Sutherland's theory and its extended versions any good?** Sutherland's theory has been criticized for lacking a precise, empirical meaning of "differential association," but many researchers claim to have found data supporting the theory. As for Glaser's theory, it has received some, though not conclusive, empirical support. The Burgess-Akers theory cannot explain initial acts of deviance but is useful for explaining repeated deviance.

   3. How does control theory explain deviance? According to the theory, what causes conformity is control, and therefore the lack of control causes deviance. Hirschi refers to this causal factor of conformity as *bond to society, or self-control.* Braithwaite calls it *reintegrative shaming,* and proponents of deterrence doctrine refer to it as *legal punishment.* **What are the strengths and weaknesses of various control theories?** Hirschi's theory has received a lot of support from research data, but the restraining effect of social bond on deviance may not be as strong as the theory suggests. Braithwaite's theory about reintegrative shaming being able to reduce crime in the United States may work for first-time offenders but not hardened criminals. The deterrence doctrine has received support from some studies but has been refuted by others.

SUGGESTED READINGS

Adler, Freda, and William S. Laufer (Eds.). 1995. *The Legacy of Anomie Theory.* New Brunswick, N.J.: Transaction. A series of essays that discuss the contribution of Merton's theory to the sociological research and understanding of deviance.

Agnew, Robert. 1992. "Foundation for a general strain theory of crime and delinquency." *Criminology, 30,* 47–87. A revision of Merton's strain theory that takes into account new studies on crime and delinquency.

Akers, Ronald L. 1998. *Social Learning and Social Structure: A General Theory of Crime and Deviance.* Boston: Northeastern University Press. A clear presentation of his social learning theory as well as research data supporting the theory.

Braithwaite, John. 1989. *Crime, Shame and Reintegration.* New York: Cambridge University Press. A theory about how society deters crime through the imposition of a social control called "reintegrative shaming."

Cullen, Francis T. 1988. "Were Cloward and Ohlin strain theorists? Delinquency and opportunity revisited." *Journal of Research in Crime and Delinquency, 25,* 214–241. Shows why Cloward and Ohlin are more opportunity theorists than strain theorists.

Hirschi, Travis, and Michael R. Gottfredson (Eds.). 1994. *The Generality of Deviance.* New Brunswick, N.J.: Transaction. A collection of articles about the editors' theory of self-control, which essentially shows how a lack of self-control can result from ineffective child rearing and then cause deviance.

Liska, Allen E., and Mark D. Reed. 1985. "Ties to conventional institutions and delinquency: Estimating reciprocal effects." *American Sociological Review, 50,* 547–560. Data in this study question the validity of many past studies that claimed to support control theory.

Marx, Gary T. 1981. "Ironies of social control: Authorities as contributors to deviance through escalation, nonenforcement, and covert facilitation." *Social Problems, 28,* 221–246. Discusses how authorities often help bring about deviance that they have set out to control.

Matsueda, Ross L. 1988. "The current state of differential association theory." *Crime & Delinquency, 34,* 277–306. Discusses the development of the theory as well as its strengths and weaknesses.

Mitchell, Richard G. 1984. "Alienation and deviance: Strain theory reconsidered." *Sociological Inquiry, 54,* 330–345. A theoretical attempt to extend Merton's strain theory by including the concept of alienation (the feeling that one's life is stifling, restrictive, and meaningless) as a cause of deviance.

Passas, Nikos, and Robert Agnew (Eds.). 1997. *The Future of Anomie Theory.* Boston: Northeastern University Press. A collection of articles analyzing , modifying, and expanding Merton's strain theory.

Tittle, Charles R. 1995. *Control Balance: Toward a General Theory of Deviance.* Boulder, Colo.: Westview. Presents a complicated theory of how the interaction among deviant motivation, opportunity, and constraint determines the probability of deviance.

3 Constructionist Theories: Understanding Deviance

In 1990 one male couple and two female couples applied for marriage licenses in Hawaii. The applications were turned down on the ground that only a man can marry a woman and vice versa. The couples went to court, charging the state with sexual discrimination. In 1993 the Hawaii Supreme Court ruled that prohibiting same-sex marriage would violate the Hawaii state constitution's guarantee of equal protection under the laws, unless the government could offer some compelling reason to ban such marriage. The case was sent back to Hawaii's First Circuit Court, and, in 1996, its judge ruled in favor of the couples. The key reason is that the judge, after listening to extensive testimony from sociologists and psychologists, found that the state had failed to prove what it believed to be the harmfulness of same-sex marriage on children or somebody else (Kunen, 1996).

This case boils down to whether same-sex marriage, or, by extension, homosexuality, is deviant or not. The Hawaii government apparently considers it deviant in the sense of being harmful. Positivist sociologists hold the same view, which is why they develop etiological theories that point out the causes of deviance. By contrast, the Hawaii Supreme Court, along with the gay and lesbian couples, regard same-sex marriage as similar to conventional marriage—harmless or nondeviant. Constructionist sociologists agree, which is why they are more interested in the meaning, rather than causation, of "deviance." They have thus developed theories mostly about how different groups impute conflicting meanings to "deviance" and how these meanings influence human behavior. In this chapter we will discuss the more important of such theories.

Labeling Theory

In the early 1960s, a group of sociologists developed what soon became widely known as labeling theory. It is actually a version of symbolic interactionism, a well-known sociological theory about social behavior in general (Becker, 1974, 1963; Erikson, 1962; Kitsuse, 1962).

A Version of Symbolic Interactionism

In defining what deviance is, labeling theorists call on two central ideas in symbolic interactionism. These two ideas are suggested by the very two words that make up the name of the theory. First, as suggested by the word *interaction*, deviance—like any other kind of human activity—is a collective action, involving more than one person's act. According to labeling theory, we should not focus on the deviant person alone as positivist sociologists do but rather on the *interaction* between the supposed deviant and other, conventional people. As Becker (1974) says:

> The positivist style [in positivist sociology] of studying deviance has focused on the deviant himself and has asked its questions mainly about him. Who is he? Is he likely to keep being that way? The new [labeling] approach sees it as always and everywhere a process of interaction between at least two kinds of people: those who commit (or are said to have committed) a deviant act and the rest of society, perhaps divided into several groups itself. The two groups are seen in complementary relationship. One cannot exist without the other.

Second, as suggested by the word *symbolic,* the interaction between the supposed deviant and the conformists is governed by the *meanings* that they impute to each other's actions and reactions. The meaning (variously referred to by symbolic interactionists as a symbol, significant gesture, interpretation, definition, or label) that people attach to an act is much more important than the act itself. The meaning, according to labeling theorists, comes through in how people respond to an act: A negative response means deviance; a positive response means NONDEVIANCE

nondeviance. As Kitsuse (1962) explains, "Forms of the behavior per se do not differentiate deviants from nondeviants; it is the responses of the conventional and conforming members of the society who identify and interpret behavior as deviant which sociologically transform persons into deviants."

In short, labeling theorists interpret deviance not as a static entity whose causes are to be sought out, but rather as *a dynamic process of symbolic interaction between both deviants and nondeviants.* Consequently, labeling theorists do not ask as positivists do: What causes deviant behavior? Instead, they ask at least two questions: (1) Who applies the *deviant* label to whom? and (2) What consequences does the application of this label have for the person labeled and for the people who apply the label? (These questions can be expressed in terms of symbolic interactionism: Who interprets whose behavior as deviant? And how does this interpretation affect the behavior of both parties involved in the matrix of interaction?)

Who Labels Whom?

According to labeling theorists, people who represent the forces of law and order as well as conventional morality typically apply the deviant label to those who have allegedly violated that law and morality. Examples of the *labelers* include the police, judges, prison guards, psychiatrists, mental hospital attendants, and other social control agents. On the other hand, examples of the *labeled* include criminals, juvenile delinquents, drug addicts, mental patients, and prostitutes.

Generally, the rich, white, or powerful and their representatives such as law-enforcing agents are more able to label others as deviant. As Becker (1974) says, "A major element in every aspect of the drama of deviance is the imposition of definitions—of situations, acts, and people—by *those powerful enough or legitimated to be able to do so.*" On the other side of the same coin, the poor, black, or powerless are more likely to be labeled deviant. Thus a poor or black person is more likely than a rich or white person to be arrested, prosecuted, or convicted as a criminal, even if both have committed similar crimes; to be declared insane or committed to a mental institution, even if both suffer from similar psychiatric conditions; and so on.

Consequences of Labeling

Labeling a person deviant may have some consequences for the person so labeled and also for the labeler.

Consequences for the Labeled.   According to labeling theorists, being labeled deviant produces *negative* consequences for the individual so labeled. One major consequence is that once people are labeled deviant, they tend to see themselves as deviant, which in turn leads them to continue the so-called deviant behavior. The issue here is not whether they have actually committed deviant acts; rather, whatever the nature of their acts, whenever they are defined as deviant by others, they also tend to define themselves as deviant, then continue to engage in the acts, and, finally, become confirmed deviants. This process of becoming deviant was long ago discussed by Frank Tannenbaum (1938). In his view, a child may engage in many forms of activities—such as breaking windows, annoying people, climbing over the roof, stealing apples, and playing hooky—and innocently consider all these enjoyable. But the parents, teachers, and police may, and often do, define these activities as a type of nuisance, delinquency, or evil. So they may "dramatize the evil" of these activities by admonishing, scolding, spanking, hauling into court, or jailing the child. Thus, dramatically labeled a delinquent, the child will likely become one, and, later, a criminal.

In discussing the process of becoming a criminal, Tannenbaum merely implied that there are two types of criminal acts. One is the *first* act, which the child considers innocent but which adults define as delinquent, and the second is the *final* behavior, which both child and adults define as delinquent. Later, Edwin Lemert (1951) made explicit the distinction between these two forms of behavior. He called the first *primary deviation,* and the second, *secondary deviation.*

Like Tannenbaum, Lemert sees the difference between primary and secondary deviance as more than temporal—more than the fact that one occurs earlier than the other, more than that primary deviance is committed essentially once while secondary deviance is continued or repeated deviance. Lemert sees primary deviance as a matter of value conflict, as a behavior that the society defines as deviant but that the performer of that behavior does not so define. This behavior becomes secondary deviance only when the person comes to agree with the society's definition of the behavior as deviant, seeing himself or herself as a deviant.

Labeling theorists are mostly interested in analyzing the process of becoming a secondary deviant—that is, in how a person goes from primary to secondary deviation. They refer to this analysis as a sequential, career, or identity-stabilizing model of deviance. Here is an example of the model described by Lemert (1951):

> The sequence of interaction leading to secondary deviation is roughly as follows: (1) primary deviation; (2) social penalties; (3) further primary deviation; (4) stronger penalties and rejections; (5) further deviation, perhaps with hostilities and resentment beginning to focus upon those doing the penalizing; (6) crisis reached in the tolerance quotient, expressed in formal action by the community stigmatizing of the deviant; (7) strengthening of the deviant conduct as a reaction to the stigmatizing and penalties; (8) ultimate acceptance of deviant social status and efforts at adjustment on the basis of the associated role.

So by the time the individual reaches the stage of accepting the social status of being a deviant, the individual becomes a secondary deviant. As such, the individual repeatedly engages in deviation as a way of life. Consider a man who has just been released from prison after serving a sentence for robbery. He is likely to be stigmatized as an "ex-con." As a stigmatized ex-con, he will find it difficult to get a good job. For that reason, he will be compelled to commit another robbery and thus launch his career as a robber.

In short, being labeled deviant often transforms primary deviance into secondary deviance; that is, once labeled a deviant, the individual tends to suffer the negative consequences of continuing to engage in deviant activities as a secondary, confirmed, or career deviant.

Consequences for the Labeler.   According to labeling theorists, labeling a person deviant tends to create *positive* consequences for the community that applies the label. One consequence is enhanced social order. As Erikson (1962) explains:

> As a trespasser against the group norms, he [the deviant] represents those factors which lie outside the group's boundaries: he informs us, as it were, what evil looks like, what shapes the devil can assume. And in doing so, he shows us the difference between the inside of the group and the outside. It may well be that without this ongoing drama at the outer edges of group space, the community would have no inner sense of identity and cohesion. . . . Thus deviance . . . may itself be, in controlled quantities, an important condition for preserving stability.

If some individuals are periodically singled out to be convicted and punished as criminals, conventional members of the community will know better the distinction between good and evil so that they will ally themselves with good and against evil. The deviant, in effect, does us a great service by teaching us what evil is like, presenting himself or herself as an object lesson for what we shall suffer if we do evil, and thus encouraging us to avoid punishment and do good. Therefore, when some individuals or groups are labeled deviant, there will follow some positive consequences for the community as the labeler, the most important consequence being the preservation and strengthening of social cohesion and social order.

Evaluating Labeling Theory

Labeling theory has enjoyed tremendous popularity among sociologists. They can easily see the significance of labeling in human interaction, and can find considerable data to support some basic ideas in labeling theory. Consider just a few findings:

- In an experimental study, higher-status subjects are more involved than lower-status ones in defining and rejecting others as deviants (Lauderdale et al., 1984).
- Higher-status members of a group are less likely than lower-status ones to incur sanctions for their own deviant behavior (Giordano, 1983).
- People known as "former mental patients" or given some other negative labels are more likely than others to have difficulty finding a job, a place to live, a group of friends, a marriage partner, or some other opportunity to achieve a goal (Link, 1982).

Despite a great deal of supportive data such as these, labeling theory has also drawn a lot of criticisms, of which only the most important are addressed here.

First, many sociologists have criticized labeling theory for not being able to answer the question of what causes deviance in the first place (Gove, 1980; Gibbs, 1966). This criticism misses the mark, though, because the theory is not meant to explain what causes primary deviance. The theory is intended to be nonetiological; it is not concerned with causal questions about primary deviance, except as they might relate to how labeling causes secondary deviance.

Second, research has failed to produce consistent support to labeling theorists' assumption that the deviant label leads the individual into further deviant involvement. Some studies show that labeling encourages further deviance, while many others do not. David Farrington and his fellow researchers, for example, found that juvenile delinquents who are publicly labeled (convicted in court for an offense) tend to commit more delinquent acts than their nonlabeled peers (Farrington, Osborn, and West, 1978; Farrington, 1977). But Charles Tittle (1980) found in his survey of 16 longitudinal studies that recidivism rates among released prisoners range from 24 to 68 percent with the average being 44 percent—not high enough, in Tittle's view, to support the labeling argument.

Finally, labeling theory cannot logically deal with hidden deviance and powerful deviants (Thio, 1973). By insisting that no behavior can be deviant unless labeled as such, labeling theory inevitably implies that hidden deviance, particularly the kind committed often in secrecy by powerful people, cannot be deviant because it is by definition unknown to others and therefore cannot be labeled by others as deviant. In addition, by stating that it is the more powerful people who typically impose the deviant label on the less powerful, labeling theorists in effect suggest that the powerful cannot be deviants because they can only be labelers.

Phenomenological Theory

Many sociologists have been influenced by labeling theory since the early 1960s. But toward the end of that decade, some sociologists took a step beyond labeling theory and developed another, new version of symbolic interactionism called *phenomenological theory.* (It has also been referred to as ethnomethodology, existential sociology, creative sociology, or sociology of everyday life.) As we have noted, labeling theory deals with societal reaction to deviance and the consequences of this reaction for the deviants and their labelers. But the theory does not get into the minds of these people. This is what phenomenological theory does. It delves into people's subjectivity (called a *phenomenon*), including their consciousness, perception, attitudes, feelings, and opinions about deviance. It assumes that all kinds of people, whether deviants or their labelers, are highly subjective in "constructing," defining, or interpreting deviance, although they may claim to be very objective (Handel, 1982; Morris, 1977).

Critique of Positivism

Phenomenologists first launch a philosophical attack on sociologists who adopt the positivist view of deviance. As we saw in Chapter 1, positivists take an objective and deterministic approach to deviance. They view a deviant person as an object whose behavior is determined or caused by various forces in the environment. Consequently, positivists ignore how the deviant person thinks and feels about his or her own deviant experience. By contrast, phenomenologists consider the deviant's subjective experience the heart of deviant reality. At the same time, they regard positivists' supposedly objective notion of deviant behavior as unreal, because it reflects their own preconception of the deviant as an object rather than the reality of the deviant as a thinking and feeling human.

In other words, positivists do not study a phenomenon as it really is but rather study *their own conception* of the phenomenon. They are, in effect, highly subjective—or certainly not as objective as they claim to be. Positivists have long assumed that the real phenomenon and the positivist conception of it are identical. But to phenomenologists, the real phenomenon is different from the positivist conception of it. The real phenomenon, in phenomenologists' view, is the immediate experience and consciousness of the person under study. Consider, for example, how the positivist view of a psychiatrist might differ from the subjective view of quiet, withdrawn Hopi Indians. To the psychiatrist, the Hopi are abnormal because their withdrawn behavior is defined by the psychiatric profession as a symptom of abnormality. The Hopi, to the contrary, see themselves as perfectly normal because their quiet demeanor is a virtue in Hopi culture.

Subjectivism as the Key to Deviant Reality

To phenomenologists, what deviance means is *fundamentally problematic:* People disagree over the meanings of deviance. Such disagreement frequently occurs among positivists when they try to observe and explain an individual's deviant behavior "objectively." In analyzing suicide, for example, constructionist sociologists find that doctors, coroners, and official statisticians—on whom positivist sociologists rely heavily for their definition of suicide—often disagree among themselves as to whether a given death is "suicide" (Pescosolido and Mendelsohn, 1986; Douglas, 1967). According to general agreement, a self-caused death should be interpreted as suicide if there is "intention to die." But since the *intention* to die is difficult to determine after the person is dead, disagreement is bound to exist over whether the deceased actually had this intention. Thus, those who believe there was intention to die would define the self-caused death as "suicide"; those who do not, would interpret it as "accidental death." All this implies that since the meanings of deviance are fundamentally problematic for positivists, their conception of deviance cannot possibly get at the essence of a deviant phenomenon.

The meanings that positivists ascribe to deviance are *abstract* in nature, that is, *independent* of concrete situations in which the deviant person is involved. By contrast, the meanings that the deviant person imputes to his or her own behavior are *situated* in nature, that is, tied to the concrete situations in which the subject is involved (Douglas, 1967). *Abstract meanings* are the positivist's so-called *objective*, scientific interpretation of the deviant subject's behavior, while *situated meanings* are the subject's *subjective* interpretation of the subject's own behavior. Alfred Schutz (1962), a founder of phenomenology, refers to the abstract, objective meanings as "constructs of the *second* degree," and the situated, subjective meanings as "constructs of the *first* degree." Phenomenologists insist that the positivists' supposedly objective idea about deviance is actually their *own* idea, far removed from, and at best a pale representation of, the deviant experience they study. Only the deviant person's subjective interpretation of the person's own experience is real. Thus, phenomenologists emphasize that to understand deviance, we should rely heavily on people's subjective interpretations of their own deviant experiences.

Still, phenomenologists' commitment to the subjective view is not total and absolute. They cannot always concur with the subject's own interpretation of his or her deviant experience. Taking the subject's interpretation at face value may distort the deviant reality, because the subject does not always know what he or she is talking about. So phenomenologists must "objectively" evaluate the subject's experience. Nevertheless, phenomenologists contend that their objective stance differs from that of the positivists. In order to observe and analyze an experience objectively, positivists try to make full use of their scientific preconceptions, propositions, methods, and knowledge. By contrast, phenomenologists attempt to expunge from their minds not only all these scientific notions but also their own personal ideas and beliefs so as to become totally receptive to the true meaning of the subject's experience. As one phenomenologist says, "The investigator goes into the situation to be studied with a totally open mind—open, in fact, in depth to all the stimuli that impinge upon his consciousness" (Bruyn, 1966). Phenomenologists have referred to this totally subject-oriented approach as *phenomenological bracketing, phenomenological reduction,* or *theoretic stance.* "The safeguarding of this subjective point of view," proclaimed Schutz (1964), "is the only but sufficient guarantee that the world of social reality will not be replaced by a fictional nonexisting world constructed by the scientific observer."

Uses of Phenomenology

Seeking to grasp the reality of deviance via their theoretic stance, phenomenologists have analyzed how their subjects feel and think about their deviance, themselves, and others. Let us examine just a few cases.

In his analysis of suicide, Douglas (1967) searched for the meanings that suicidal people attach to suicide, which lead them to kill themselves. These people, Douglas found, believe that although religious, legal, and other cultural values of our society condemn the act of suicide, most people do not hold a person morally responsible for self-killing. They are believed to blame instead the family, relatives, lover, employers, or society for having somehow caused the individual to commit suicide. Awareness of this moral meaning of suicide, which blames others for the act, removes whatever feelings of qualm and guilt might restrain suicide. Suicidal people find it easier to kill themselves, seeing their suicide as a way of making others feel guilty, of leaving this "wretched" world for a joyful union with God, or of attaining some other meaningful goal. In short, suicides see their self-destruction as a way of achieving some useful purpose rather than as conventional people see it—as a wasteful death.

Similarly, most people would regard hermaphrodites—individuals who have both male and female sex organs—as "freaks," but hermaphrodites see themselves as normal people. This fact shows up in Harold Garfinkel's (1967) study of Agnes, who had male genitals and female secondary sex characteristics. Agnes was 19, and had been born as a male and raised as a boy until high school. During adolescence Agnes developed large breasts, a slim waist, wide hips, and a soft skin. At 17 she had an attractive female figure. By then she dropped out of school, left home, moved to another city, and tried to begin a new life as a woman. A year later, she went to the UCLA Medical Center to request a sex-change operation. Before such surgery was approved, Agnes had to be thoroughly investigated to ensure that she really felt she was a woman. As a participant in this investigation, Garfinkel interviewed her extensively. He found that she saw herself as a normal woman, and did her best to convince others that she was. She told Garfinkel that she was merely a normal woman who happened to have a physical defect comparable to any other deformity, such as a harelip, clubfoot, or twisted spinal cord. Like any other normal person with a deformity, she felt that it was only natural for her to want to have hers—the penis—removed. Her self-concept as a normal woman further led her to claim that, as a sexual organ, her penis was "dead," that she had no sexual pleasure from it nor sexual attraction to women. She wanted to have it replaced by a surgically constructed vagina. Her self-concept as a normal woman also caused her to make sure that others would not suspect her of having a penis. Thus, on a beach she always wore a bathing suit with a skirt. In the apartment that she shared with a woman, she never undressed in her roommate's presence. On a date she always dodged necking and, in particular, petting below the waist.

Just as Agnes saw and presented herself as a normal person, Jack Katz (1988) more recently has found that criminals such as murderers and robbers also see themselves and their deviance in some positive way. Katz finds that murderers perceive themselves as morally superior to their victims. This is because, in most cases of homicide, the *victims* have humiliated their killers by teasing, daring, defying, taunting, or insulting them. The resulting rage leads to killing but at the same moment gives the killers the self-righteous feeling of defending their identity, dignity, or respectability.

Katz also finds that virtually all robbers feel themselves "morally superior" to their victims, regarding their victims as fools or suckers who deserve to be robbed. If robbers want to rob somebody on the street, they first ask the potential victim for the time, for directions, for a cigarette light, or for change. Each of these requests is intended to determine whether the person is a fool. The request for the time, for example, gives the robber the opportunity to know whether the prospective victim has an expensive watch. Complying with the request, then, is taken to establish the person as a fool and hence the right victim.

Katz further explores the experiential world of property criminals, violent-gang members, and "badasses." He finds that, in committing property crime such as vandalism, joyriding, and shoplifting, the criminals are enjoying a "sneaky thrill." This is how a shoplifter describes her experience: "Every time I would drop something into my bag, my heart would be pounding and I could feel this tremendous excitement, a sort of 'rush', go though me. . . . The experience was almost orgasmic for me. There was a build-up of tension as I contemplated the danger of a forbidden act, then a rush of excitement at the moment of committing the crime, and finally a delicious sense of release." Members of violent gangs enjoy their grandiose, elite stature on the street, which they seek to maintain by inflicting terror and violence on rival gangs. Badasses revel in being "real bad," namely, being tough, alien, and mean. Being tough means not being easily influenced by others or not being anxious about others' opinion of oneself. Being alien means being hostile to any form of conventionality, and being mean involves the readiness to hurt others in any way. As one badass says, "I'll jump you on the street, I'll 'come up side' your head. I'll fuck you up good" (Katz, 1988).

Evaluating Phenomenological Theory

Phenomenologists have offered a convincing argument about the inadequacy of positivism: Positivists cannot get at the essence of deviant reality. But the assumption of phenomenologists that they themselves can is less convincing. As we have observed, phenomenologists suggest that they can penetrate into the essence of human phenomena because they strive to keep a totally open mind, to suspend all beliefs and judgments about the phenomena in question, while positivists cannot do so because their preexisting concepts and knowledge distort their analysis. Can phenomenologists really keep a totally open mind so as to experience, observe, and depict the essence of reality? We could argue that they cannot either.

It is difficult to see how we can escape the human fate of having our observations influenced by our beliefs, judgments, ideas, and words. It is difficult to see how we can really empty our minds so that they can absorb the essence of a phenomenon. Some Zen Buddhists have methodically tried for a whole lifetime to empty their minds in the hope of achieving satori, the ultimate ability to see reality as it is. It is doubtful that they have ever succeeded (Watts, 1966). In his pilgrimage to Buddhist temples in Asia, the U.S. Trappist monk Thomas Merton (1973) found that a Tibetan Buddhist priest, despite his 30 years of meditation, still could not achieve "the ultimate emptiness." Neither could Merton himself. We may as well conclude that it is impossible for anybody to grasp the essence of reality. Positivists cannot do it. Neither can phenomenologists.

What phenomenologists actually do is only to create a version of human reality. The phenomenologist version may be unique, but it is not necessarily superior to the positivist or other versions. Since sociologists, whether they are phenomenologists, positivists, or others, differ in their value systems, ideological inclinations, observational methods, and sensitivity to human experience, they are bound to create different, competing, or conflicting versions of human reality. In this regard, however, we may point out the contribution of phenomenological theory. Its view of deviant behavior as comprehensible through the individual's subjective experience does differ, compete, or conflict with the positivist emphasis on the objective side of deviant reality, thereby enabling us to look at the subject with a broader perspective and understanding.

Nevertheless, the phenomenological version of deviant reality is not always convincing. In assuming that humans have free will, phenomenologists fail to recognize that powerless people cannot easily exercise their free will because it is often suppressed by their miserable life circumstances. As a result, phenomenologists have created a picture of powerless deviants as highly sophisticated, free-thinking, and choice-making philosophers. An example of this can be found in Matza's (1969) "rendition" of the supposedly true nature of deviance. Preoccupied with what he calls "the philosophical inner life" of his deviants, Matza has elevated them—including semiliterate juvenile delinquents—to the status of profound philosophers. All these philosopher-deviants are portrayed as being constantly engrossed in analyzing the intricate meanings of whatever happens to them. We may wonder how his deviants, being bogged down with such heavy philosophizing, could ever find time for, or be interested at all in, deviant *action* (Thio, 1974). Similarly, it is doubtful that most murderers, robbers, suicides, hermaphrodites, and other deviants have a positive view of themselves and their deviance. Some are bound to experience self-doubt, self-pity, or self-loathing from having been condemned, ridiculed, ostracized, or otherwise punished by society (Goode, 1990).

Conflict Theory

More than 60 years ago, a number of sociologists began to point out the pluralistic, heterogeneous, and conflictive nature of modern society (Fuller and Myers, 1941; Sellin, 1939; Waller, 1936). In a traditional or simple society, people share the same cultural values and therefore can have harmonious relationships with one another. Such value consensus and social harmony are absent in modern industrial societies, particularly in the United States. Instead, there is a great deal of social and cultural conflict. *Social conflict* has to do with the incompatible interests, needs, and desires of such diverse groups as business companies versus labor unions, conservative versus liberal political groups, whites versus blacks, and so on. *Cultural conflict* has to do with the discrepant norms and values that derive from definitions of right and wrong—that is, what is considered right in one subculture is considered wrong in another. For example, in the 1930s a Sicilian father in New Jersey, after killing his daughter's 16-year-old seducer, felt proud of having defended his family honor in a traditional way, but was very surprised when the police came to arrest him (Sellin, 1939). Either social or cultural conflict has been said to bring about criminal behavior, not only among immigrants but also among African Americans and other poor or oppressed groups. Therefore, conflict as well as its resulting criminality is an inherent, normal, and integral part of modern society. Those sociologists who held this view 50 years ago may be regarded as *conflict theorists.*

But those conflict theorists failed to develop systematically the notion of conflict as the source of criminal *definition* rather than behavior. They were still very much tied to the positivist concern with the causal explanation of criminal behavior. Only in the mid-1960s did a group of conflict theorists emerge to explore criminality systematically as a matter of definition. Since the mid-1970s, moreover, some of these new conflict theorists have begun to use the concepts of social inequality, Marxism, feminism, power, and linguistic domination to deal with the causation of deviance in a different way from the early conflict theorists. Let us see how these new conflict theorists view deviance.

Legal Reality Theory

According to William Chambliss (1969), there are two kinds of law. One is the *law on the books,* the ideal of law, and the other is the *law in action,* the reality of law. According to the law on the books, legal authorities *ought* to be fair and just by treating all citizens equally. However, the law in action shows that legal authorities are *actually* unfair and unjust, favoring the rich and powerful over the poor and weak (Chambliss and Seidman, 1971).

Many people may blame the discrepancy between the two types of law on the evil character of lawmaking and law-enforcing individuals, but Chambliss rejects such an individualistic interpretation. He shows how those individuals are heavily influenced by the historical and organizational background of the law, as follows.

Modern Anglo-American law stems from the legal system of early England. The English legal system was established in the eleventh century. Its central feature is that personal wrongs are considered transgressions against the state and that only the state has the right to punish the transgressors. This legal principle replaced the earlier nonlegal norm that personal wrongs, being a highly personal matter, should be settled through reconciliation by the private parties concerned. To carry out the new legal principle, the government used force and coercion as the means for handling wrongs and disputes; created two separate bodies, the lawmakers (legislature) and the law enforcers (judiciary); appointed judges to settle disputes between the state and individual citizens or between individual citizens themselves; and relied on peers (juries) to ultimately decide disputes.

Such was the general structure of the legal system in early England, and it still prevails in contemporary U.S. society. But the specific content of the laws as well as the specific manner of enforcing them has often changed to reflect the interests of the ruling classes. The vagrancy laws in fourteenth-century feudal England, for example, reflected the powerful landowners' need for cheap labor because the law required poor able-bodied men to work at low wages, made it unlawful for them to move from one place to another to avoid the low-paying jobs or to seek higher wages, and prohibited giving alms to able-bodied beggars. Then, in the sixteenth century, the vagrancy laws were changed to protect the interests of prosperous merchants who had to transport their goods from one town to another, as the new vagrancy laws were applied to the rogues, vagabonds, and highwaymen who often preyed on the traveling merchants. Today, in both England and the United States, the vagrancy laws are meant to control down-and-outers, the undesirable, the criminal, and nuisances, thereby reflecting the desire of the influential middle and upper classes to make their streets safe and peaceful. Historically, criminal law has, in effect if not in intent, served the interests of the rich and powerful rather than the interests of the poor and powerless. Under this historical influence, the legislators of today understandably tend to make laws that favor the rich and powerful.

Law enforcers such as police, prosecutors, and judges also tend to become the tools of power and privilege. This tendency is mostly the consequence of *organizational imperative.* It is in the nature of any organization to compel its members to perform tasks that will maximize reward and minimize trouble for the organization. The reward to be sought by the law-enforcing agency is public support; the trouble to be avoided is the withdrawal of such support, or worse. Thus, it is rewarding for the law-enforcing officials to arrest, prosecute, and convict powerless people such as skid-row drunks, vagrants, gamblers, prostitutes, rapists, thieves, and robbers. But it will likely cause trouble for the agency if the law enforcers make the same effort to process respectable middle- and upper-class citizens for their white-collar offenses. In view of such an organizational imperative, the law-enforcing officials are very likely to make the law serve the interests of the rich and powerful (Chambliss, 1969).

Social Reality Theory

While Chambliss attributes the unjust practice of law to historical changes and organizational imperative, Richard Quinney (1974) blames the unjust law itself directly on the capitalist system. "Criminal law," he says, "is used by the state and the ruling class to secure the survival of the capitalist system, and, as capitalist society is further threatened by its own contradictions, criminal law will be increasingly used in the attempt to maintain domestic order."

Such a critical view of capitalism is based on Quinney's (1975) conflict theory of criminality, which he calls "the social reality of crime." According to this theory, four factors jointly produce the capitalist society's high crime rates but also help to consolidate its established legal order as well as its dominant class. First, the dominant class *defines* as criminal those behaviors that threaten its interests. This means that criminal laws are largely made by powerful members of society. Second, the dominant class *applies* those laws to ensure the protection of its interests. This involves having the police, judges, and other members of the criminal justice system enforce the laws. Third, members of the subordinate class are compelled by their unfavorable life conditions to engage in those *actions* that have been defined as criminal. The poor, for example, are likely to commit a

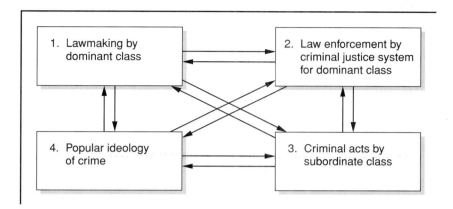

FIGURE 3.1 Quinney's Social Reality Theory. The interaction among these four factors helps produce and maintain a certain high level of crime in society.

crime because their poverty pressures them to do so. And, fourth, the dominant class uses these criminal acts as the basis for constructing and diffusing the *ideology* of crime. This is the belief that the subordinate class contains most of the society's dangerous criminal elements and therefore should most often be arrested, prosecuted, or imprisoned. These four factors are interrelated, supporting each other so as to produce and maintain a certain high level of crime in society. For example, such criminal acts as murder and robbery committed by the poor are likely to cause the dominant class to make and enforce the laws against the poor, which in turn would make life more difficult for the poor, thereby encouraging them to commit more crimes. Figure 3.1 summarizes Quinney's theory.

Quinney (1974) has also tried to turn his theory into a call for political action. As his theory implies, there is something terribly wrong with existing society. What is wrong is that members of the powerful class inevitably criminalize the actions of the powerless so as to exploit, oppress, and subjugate them, thereby preserving, consolidating, and perpetuating the status quo of social inequality. Thus, Quinney calls for the development of a revolutionary consciousness that should eventually lead to the creation of a democratic-socialist society that will end the oppression of the powerless by the powerful. More recently, a "new sociology of social control" has emerged that goes far beyond Quinney's notion about the capitalist state controlling, by itself, the powerless, deviant population. According to this new control theory, many institutions, organizations, professions, and agencies are increasingly involved in controlling troublesome, deviant people on behalf of the state (Garland, 1993; Davis and Stasz, 1990; Scull, 1988).

Marxist Theory

In describing how the powerful define and control the powerless as deviants, most conflict theorists such as those discussed above have virtually ignored the causes of deviance. More recently, however, a number of conflict theorists have turned their attention to the question of causality. They draw their ideas mostly from Marxism; hence, they are often referred to as *Marxist theorists* (Greenberg, 1981).

According to these theorists, the cause of deviance can be traced to the exploitative nature of capitalism. To increase profit, capitalists must find ways to enhance productivity at low labor costs, including introducing automation and other labor-saving devices, forcing workers to work faster and work overtime, relocating industries to cheap labor locations, such as some nonunionized places in the southern United States or in labor-rich developing countries, and importing workers from poor nations. No matter what method is used, it inevitably throws some of the existing labor force out of work. These unemployed laborers become what Marxists call *marginal surplus population,* relatively superfluous or useless to the economy. Their inability to maintain decent living conditions pressures them to commit crime.

Capitalism produces not only property crimes (such as robbery and theft) among the unemployed lower-class people; it also causes personal crimes (assault, rape, murder) and various other forms of deviance (alcoholism, suicide, and mental illness). As explained by Sheila Balkan, Ronald Berger, and Janet Schmidt (1980), economic "marginality leads to a lack of self-esteem and a sense of powerlessness and alienation, which create intense pressures on individuals. Many people turn to violence to vent their frustrations and strike out against symbols of authority, and others turn this frustration inward and experience severe emotional difficulties." This means that capitalism pressures people to commit crimes and become deviants by making them poor in the first place. Poverty, however, is not the only means by which capitalism generates deviance. According to Mark Colvin and John Pauly (1983), capitalist society can also produce crimes by exercising "coercive control" over the lower classes. Coercive control involves threatening to fire or actually firing poor workers in order to coerce them to work hard for their capitalist employers. It tends to create resentment. These workers are likely to feel alienated from society, showing an "alienative involvement" in it—a lack of attachment to it. Consequently, they are likely to engage in criminal activities.

However, the capitalistic pressure to commit crime and other forms of deviance is not confined to the lower classes, but reaches upward to affect the higher classes as well. By making possible the constant accumulation of profit, capitalism inevitably creates powerful empires of monopoly and oligopoly in the economy. These economic characteristics are an important cause of corporate crime. The reason is that "when only a few firms dominate a sector of the economy they can more easily collude to fix prices, divide up the market, and eliminate competitors" (Greenberg, 1981).

Feminist Theory

Virtually all theories about deviance are meant to apply to both sexes. The theories assume that what holds true for men also holds true for women. Feminist theorists, however, disagree. They argue that extant theories of deviance are actually about men only. Consequently, the theories may be valid for male behavior but not necessarily for female behavior. Consider, for example, Merton's anomie theory. First, this theory assumes that people are inclined to strive for material success. This may be true for men but not necessarily true for women. In fact, under the influence of patriarchal society, women have been socialized differently from men. Thus, women are traditionally less interested in achieving material success, which often requires one-upmanship, and more given to attaining emotional fulfillment through close, personal relations with others. Second, the theory assumes that if some women have a strong desire for economic success but no access to opportunities for achieving that goal, they would be as likely as men in the same situation to commit a crime. Today, given the greater availability of high positions for women in the economic world, the number of ambitious women in the "men's" world is on the rise. However, when these women are faced with the lack of opportunities for greater economic success, they are not as likely as men to engage in deviant activities. Finally, Merton's theory explicitly states that people in the United States are likely to commit a crime because their society overemphasizes the importance of entertaining high success goals while failing to provide the necessary opportunities for all its citizens to realize those goals. This may be relevant to men but less so to women. In fact, despite their greater lack of success opportunities, women still have lower crime rates than men (Heidensohn, 1995; Morris, 1987; Leonard, 1982).

The lack of relevancy to women in anomie and other conventional theories stems from a male-biased failure to take women into account. In redressing this problem, feminist theory understandably focuses on women. First, the theory deals with women as victims, mostly of rape and sexual harassment. These crimes against women are said to reflect the patriarchal society's attempt to put women in their place so as to perpetuate men's dominance (Heidensohn, 1995; Messerschmidt, 1986).

Feminist theory also zeroes in on women as offenders. It argues that although the rate of female crime has increased in recent years, the increase is not great enough to be significant. This is said to reflect the fact that gender equality is still far from being a social reality. Like employment opportunities, criminal opportunities are still much less available to women than men, hence women are still much less likely to engage in criminal activities. When women do commit a crime, they tend to commit the types of crime that reflect their continuing subordinate position in society. They are minor property crimes, such as shoplifting, passing bad checks, welfare fraud, and petty credit-card fraud. In fact, most of the recent increases in female crime involve these minor crimes. Largely, this reflects the increasing feminization of poverty—more women are falling below the poverty line today. Not surprisingly, most women criminals are unemployed, without a high school diploma, and single mothers with small children. They hardly fit the popular image of liberated women who benefit from whatever increase there has been in gender equality. There is no increase in female involvement in more profitable crimes, such as burglary, robbery, embezzlement, and business fraud, which are still primarily committed by men (Chesney-Lind, 1997; Steffensmeier, 1996; Weisheit, 1992; Daly and Chesney-Lind, 1988).

Power Theory

It seems obvious that power inequality affects the quality of people's lives: the rich and powerful live better than the poor and powerless. Similarly, power inequality affects the quality of *deviant* activities likely to be engaged in by people. Thus the powerful are more likely to engage in profitable deviant acts, such as corporate crime, while the powerless are more likely to commit less profitable deviant deeds, such as armed robbery. In other words, power—or the lack of it—determines to a large extent the *type* of deviance people are likely to carry out.

 Power can also be an important *cause* of deviance. More precisely, the likelihood of powerful people perpetrating profitable deviance is greater than the likelihood of powerless persons committing less profitable deviance. It is, for example, more likely for bank executives to rob customers quietly than for jobless persons to rob banks violently. Analysis of the deviance literature suggests three reasons why the powerful are more likely to commit profitable deviance than the powerless to commit less profitable deviance.

First, the powerful have a *stronger deviant motivation*. Much of this motivation stems from *relative deprivation*—from feeling unable to achieve relatively high aspirations. Compared with the powerless, whose aspirations are typically low, the powerful are more likely to raise their aspirations so high that they cannot be realized. The more people experience relative deprivation, the more likely they are to commit deviant acts (Cookson and Persell, 1985; Harry and Sengstock, 1978; Merton, 1957).

Second, the powerful enjoy *greater deviant opportunity*. Obviously, a rich banker enjoys more legitimate opportunities than a poor worker to make money. But suppose they both want to acquire *illegitimately* a large sum of money. The banker will have access to more and better opportunities that make it easy to defraud customers. The banker, further, has a good chance of getting away with it because the kind of skill needed to pull off the crime is similar to the skills required for holding the bank position in the first place. In contrast, the poor worker would find his or her illegitimate opportunity limited to crudely robbing the banker, an illegitimate opportunity being further limited by a high risk of arrest (Ermann and Lundman, 1996; Vaughan, 1983).

Third, the powerful are subjected to *weaker social control*. Generally, the powerful have more influence in the making and enforcement of laws. The laws against mostly higher-status criminals are therefore relatively lenient and seldom enforced, but the laws against largely lower-status criminals are harsher and more often enforced. For example, many lower-class murderers have been executed for killing one person, but not a single corporate criminal, for example, has ever faced the same fate for marketing some untested drug that "cleanly" kills many people. Given the lesser control imposed on them, the powerful are likely to feel freer to use some deviant means to amass their fortunes and power.

 In sum, due to social inequality, the powerful are likely to have a stronger deviant motivation, enjoy greater deviant opportunity, and encounter weaker social control, as compared with the powerless. As a consequence, the powerful are more likely to get involved in profitable deviancy than the powerless in less profitable deviancy.

Postmodernist Theory

Postmodernist theory is probably the newest attempt in sociology to shed light on the nature of deviance. It first emerged in the early twentieth century as a philosophical movement in France that *questioned* the basic values of *modernism* such as innovation, rationality, objectivity, and other similar values represented by modern science and technology. These modernist values were criticized for encouraging, among other things, objectification, depersonalization, alienation, and other social problems that make it difficult to people to form genuine or close relationships. The French philosophers, then, called for greater attention to postmodernist values including subjectivity, feeling, and intuition, so that a richer, more meaningful life can be attained.

This philosophical thought started to influence the arts and social sciences in the United States in the 1960s, and since the late 1980s it has become a well-known, though poorly understood, theoretical perspective in American sociology and, more specifically, criminology.

Postmodernist theory contains both old and new ideas in the sociology of deviance. First is the theory's attack on modern science's emphasis on the search for objective truth. To postmodernists, the so-called objectivity in modern science is actually subjective because it involves the scientists imposing their own "privileged" professional view on the subject under their investigation. The subjective view of the subject, whether the subject is a deviant, victim, or anybody who reacts in some way to the deviant act, is therefore suppressed, discounted, disregarded, or ignored. But, to postmodernists, the subject's own views are important for understanding deviance. By thus attacking positivism (the scientist's so-called objectivity) and advocating subjectivity, postmodernist theory is similar to phenomenological theory, which emerged in the late 1960s as we suggested earlier.

Another old idea in postmodernist theory is what its developers call "deconstructionism." This term is defined as "tearing a text [which means any phenomenon or event such as deviance] apart, revealing its contradictions and assumptions" (Rosenau, 1992). In other words, deconstruction is said to involve "the breaking up of something that has been built, as in 'demolition,' and exposing the way in which it is built" (Einstadter and Henry, 1995). This meaning of deconstructionism is basically the same as the meaning of what is popularly called "analysis," which involves, as Webster's dictionary says, studying something by separating a whole into its component parts. Further, because of its emphasis on the importance of subjectivity, the postmodernist's concept of deconstructionism is similar to the phenomenologist's idea of "phenomenological bracketing or reduction," which requires maximum sensitivity to the subject's experiences.

Postmodernist theory does have a new idea: linguistic domination. It is assumed that a linguistic conflict exists in any social interaction. There is, for

symbolic interactionism

example, a linguistic conflict between psychiatrists and mental patients. More specifically, the "privileged" language of the more powerful group (psychiatrists) dominates the everyday, ordinary language of the weaker group (patients). Consider the phrase "mentally ill." It means "diseased," "sick," or "in need of treatment" in the psychiatrist's language, but "touched by God," "possessed by the devil," "loony," and the like in the patient's everyday language. And it is the first set of meanings that is taken seriously, while the second set is suppressed or ignored (Arrigo and Bernard, 1997). Because language is assumed to influence the feeling and behavior of the individual, the linguistic domination shapes the deviant's life by defining and treating the person as a deviant. But our understanding of the nature of mental illness derives from the psychiatrist's language at the expense of the patient's language, which means that we cannot know how it feels to be mentally ill. To know more fully the nature of mental illness, postmodernists argue that we should also study the subject's suppressed language.

Evaluating Conflict Theory

In blaming the capitalist or inegalitarian society for the prevalence of deviant labeling and deviant activities, conflict theory seems to hold the *unconvincing* assumption that in the utopian, classless society, deviant labeling will stop and such nasty human acts as killing, robbing, raping, and otherwise hurting one another will disappear. It may be more realistic to assume as Durkheim did that deviance is inevitable, even in a society of saints, but that the type of deviance committed by saints can be expected to be mostly unserious or even trivial. More precisely, if full social equality were achieved, the serious forms of human nastiness would greatly decrease rather than completely disappear. This is because, with the abolition of poverty in a fully egalitarian society, there would not be any poor people left to produce, as they do now, a large volume of serious deviance and thus this volume would greatly shrink. But the formerly poor people would join the formerly rich to engage in less serious—or saintly—forms of deviant activities.

All the same, conflict theory greatly contributes to our understanding of how social inequality—such as in the form of capitalism and patriarchy—influences the making and enforcing of norms, rules, or laws, or the definition, production, and treatment of deviance in society (Heidensohn, 1995; Akers, 1985; Williams and Drake, 1980). Moreover, conflict theory is useful for explaining the motivations behind the formulation of laws, even, for example, why the powerful bother to pass laws against such nonpolitical acts as illicit sex, gambling, drinking, and loitering—the kind of deviance that does not seem to threaten their dominant position in society. The reason, according to conflict theory, is that those seemingly trivial deviances do threaten powerful people's vested interests by challenging the underlying values of capitalism, such as sobriety, individual responsibility, deferred gratification, industriousness, and the belief that the true pleasures in life can only be found in honest, productive labor. Laws against those

TABLE 3.1   Constructionist Theories of Deviance

Labeling Theory: Relatively powerful persons are more likely to label the less powerful as deviant than vice versa, and being labeled deviant by society leads people to see themselves as deviant and live up to this self-image by engaging in more deviancy.

Phenomenological Theory: Looking into people's subjective interpretation of their own experiences is key to understanding their deviant behavior.

Conflict Theory:

   Legal Reality: Law enforcement favors the rich and powerful over the poor and weak.

   Social Reality: The dominant class produces crime by making laws, enforcing laws, oppressing subordinate classes, and spreading crime ideology.

   Marxist: Deviance and crime stem from the exploitative nature of capitalism.

   Feminist: Conventional theories of deviance are largely inapplicable to women, and the status of women as victims and offenders reflects the continuing subordination of women in patriarchal society.

   Power: Because of strong deviant motivation, greater deviant opportunity, and weaker social control, the powerful are more likely to engage in profitable deviancy than are the powerless to engage in unprofitable deviancy.

   Postmodernist: "Privileged" language such as that of psychiatrists influences the lives of deviants.

"trivial" deviant acts serve to preserve these capitalist values, the capitalist system, and hence the dominant position of the powerful (Hepburn, 1977).

Table 3.1 shows the main points of all the theories discussed in this chapter.

Summary

1. What does labeling theory have to say about deviance? According to labeling theory, superordinate parties apply the deviant label to subordinate parties; being labeled deviant produces unfavorable consequences for the individual so labeled; and labeling some individuals as deviant generates favorable consequences for the community. The theory is generally convincing, and there are considerable data to support it. But it has been criticized for being unable to explain what causes deviance in the first place. It has also failed to receive consistent support from studies on the presumed negative consequences of labeling.

2. What is phenomenological theory all about? It claims that positivist sociologists cannot capture the essence of deviance, while phenomenological sociologists can cut into the heart of deviant experience with the scalpel of subjective interpretation, which they try to demonstrate with analyses of specific deviances. Phenomenologists are convincing in arguing that positivists cannot get into the essence of deviant reality. But their claim that they themselves can is excessive and unjustifiable. What they themselves can capture is only their own version of deviant reality, not the essence of that reality itself. In addition, phenomenologists tend to exaggerate the exercise of free will among powerless deviants, portraying them as sophisticated and positive thinkers.

3. How do various versions of conflict theory deal with deviance? According to legal reality, the enforcement of law is unjust, favoring the rich over the poor, the result of historical changes and organizational imperatives. Social reality theory attributes the capitalist society's high crime rates to the convergence of four forces: lawmaking by the elite, law enforcement for the elite, law violation by the masses, and popular beliefs about the poor as the criminal class. Marxist theory traces the source of lower-class deviance to the exploitative nature of capitalism and the origin of corporate crime to capitalism-generated monopoly. Feminist theorists criticize all other theories for being mostly relevant to men and therefore ignoring women, and ascribe the experience of women as offenders and victims to the patriarchal system of gender inequality. Power theory explains that the powerful are more likely to engage in profitable deviance than the powerless in less profitable deviance because the powerful experience stronger deviant motivation, greater deviant opportunity, and weaker social control. Postmodernist theory shows how "privileged" language (like that of powerful psychiatrists) influences the lives of deviants as well as our understanding of them.

4. What are the weaknesses and strengths of conflict theory? Conflict theory can be faulted for assuming that only capitalism or inequality can produce deviance but the utopian, classless society cannot. Nonetheless, conflict theory contributes greatly to our understanding of the making and enforcement of norms and laws, of the definition and production of deviance, and of the motivation behind the formulation of laws against seemingly trivial deviance.

SUGGESTED READINGS

Becker, Howard S. 1973. *Outsiders: Studies in the Sociology of Deviance,* enlarged edition. New York: Free Press. A classic collection of articles on the use of labeling theory in studying deviance.

Hagan, John. 1992. "The poverty of a classless criminology—The American Society of Criminology 1991 presidential address." *Criminology, 30,* 1–19. An effort to convince criminologists that it is important to use the class-related concept of power to understand the nature of crime.

Jensen, Gary F., and Kevin Thompson. 1990. "What's class got to do with it? A further examination of power-control theory." *American Journal of Sociology, 95,* 1009–1023. Reflects the continuing refusal of many sociologists to see the connection between class or power and deviance.

Katz, Jack. 1988. *Deductions of Crime: Moral and Sensual Attractions in Doing Evil.* New York: Basic Books. A phenomenological analysis of how various deviants, such as murderers and robbers, feel about their deviant acts.

Lauderdale, Pat, Jerry Parker, Phil Smith-Cunnien, and James Inverarity. 1984. "External threat and the definition of deviance." *Journal of Personality and Social Psychology, 46,* 1058–1068. An experimental study of whether an external threat to a group will result in the rejection of the group's deviant members.

Patterson, E. Britt. 1991. "Poverty, income inequality, and community crime rates." *Criminology, 29,* 755–776. Offers data showing that absolute poverty is significantly associated with higher rates of violent crime.

Regoli, Robert M., Eric D. Poole, and Finn Esbensen. 1985. "Labeling deviance: Another look." *Sociological Focus, 18,* 19–28. Calling for a revision of labeling theory that focuses on the process of labeling before the occurrence of a reaction to certain behavior.

Simpson, Sally S., and Christopher S. Koper. 1992. "Deterring corporate crime." *Criminology, 30,* 347–375. Analyzing the evidence concerning the deterrent impact of legal sanction on criminal corporate behavior.

Sorokin, Pitirim, and Walter Lunden. 1959. *Power and Morality: Who Shall Guard the Guardians?* Boston: Porter Sargent. A classic sociological statement on how power corrupts so that the ruling groups tend to become more criminal than the ruled.

Ward, David A., and Charles R. Tittle. 1993. "Deterrence or labeling: The effects of informal sanctions." *Deviant Behavior 14,* 43–64. Offers data showing how primary deviance leads to secondary deviance as suggested by labeling theory.

Winter, Michael F. 1996. "Social reaction, labeling, and social control: The contribution of Edwin M. Lemert." *History of the Human Sciences,* May, 53–77. Presents the main ideas of a major contributor to labeling theory

Specific Forms of Deviant Behavior

We have so far dealt with general analyses of deviant behavior. Chapter 1 has discussed how various sociologists define deviance in a general way. Chapters 2 and 3 have shown how various sociologists theorize about the causes and meanings of deviance, also in a general way.

These general analyses, however, assume that all forms of deviant behavior are in some respect similar to one another. This assumption inevitably ignores many unique aspects of each specific form of deviant behavior. Thus, in the following chapters, I will discuss the concrete characteristics of various deviances. Of course, we should not forget the general theories in the preceding chapters. I will apply them whenever they can directly shed light on the particular deviant act under investigation in order to give us a closer, sharper view and deeper understanding of each deviant behavior.

4 Physical Violence

Around 11:15 a.m. on an April day in 1999, Eric Harris and Dylan Klebold, students of Columbine High School in Littleton, Colorado, entered the school's cafeteria, where they opened fire with semiautomic rifles and threw pipe bombs. The gunmen killed two and caused some 500 other students to flee amid the flying bullets and exploding bombs. Then the killers went upstairs and entered the library. Laughing and taunting their victims, they shot ten more to death, many at point-blank range. Harris and Dylan asked at least two female students whether they believed in God, and immediately killed them when they answered "yes." Finally, after murdering 12 students and a teacher and wounding 23 students, the killers committed suicide in the library (Glick et al., 1999).

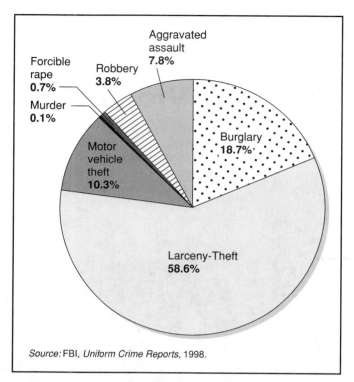

Source: FBI, *Uniform Crime Reports*, 1998.

FIGURE 4.1   Murder: Most Serious but Least Common. Of all the major offenses, murder makes up less than one-tenth of one percent.

In the last few years youthful killings in schools have surged. This is ironic because since 1994 the rate of homicides committed by young men has declined, while the rate of homicides by adults has fallen even more (Fox and Zawitz, 1999; Blumstein, 1995). In fact, homicide as a whole is a relatively rare form of crime. As Figure 4.1 suggests, we are far less likely to be murdered than to be a victim of any other major crime. We are even less likely to be murdered by others than to kill ourselves. Still, murder remains the most serious offense. Its cost to the victim is forever irreparable, and its cost to the victim's surviving loved ones is incalculably high.

Perhaps because it is the most horrendous act of physical violence, murder fascinates many of us. Thanks to a legion of novelists as well as television and movie producers, we often seek entertainment from a murder mystery, trying excitedly to figure out "who done it?" Yet our experiences with many manufactured murders may have led some of us to a distorted view of the real crime. We may fear strangers as our potential killers, while in reality most killings are done not by people unknown to us but by our acquaintances, friends, lovers, or relatives. We may also imagine that most murders are intriguing mysteries, while in real life they are no mysteries at all—the police can easily find out from the people at the murder scene who the culprit is. In this chapter we will examine in greater detail the real nature of homicide along with assault, school violence, and terrorism.

Who Is More Likely to Kill?

The most striking thing about killers is that they are mostly poor. Not surprisingly, blacks, being generally poorer than whites, are more likely than whites to commit homicide. Poor countries have higher rates of homicide than rich nations. Similarly, societies and individuals with violent pasts have relatively high rates of homicides. The South has more homicides than any other region in the United States. Here and abroad large cities have more killings than smaller cities. Men are far more likely than women to kill, and teenagers are more likely than adults to commit murder. Let us take a closer look at each of these facts.

Class and Race

Various studies have clearly indicated that homicides are concentrated heavily in the lower class. Over 90 percent of the murderers in the United States are semi-skilled workers, unskilled laborers, and welfare recipients. Poverty is definitely a factor in homicide. As such, poverty crosses racial lines: Poor whites have higher murder rates than better-off whites, and poor blacks have higher rates than richer blacks. There are several reasons for the strong link between poverty and murder. Compared with people of the higher classes, the poor are more likely to have financial, marital, and other stressful problems, which in turn tend to cause interpersonal conflict. The poor also tend more to resort to physical violence as a way of dealing with interpersonal conflict (Parker with Rebhun, 1995; Parker, 1989; Bailey, 1984).

Blacks generally have a much higher rate of homicide than whites. This fact makes it appear as if race plays an important role in homicide. Actually, though, being black has nothing to do with such violence. Instead, African Americans' higher rate of homicide simply reflects their higher rate of poverty, which, along with racial discrimination, generates greater frustration and alienation. In expressing their frustration, however, blacks tend more to kill their fellow blacks than to kill whites. In fact, most killings are *intra*racial, for whites also do away with whites more than blacks. *Inter*racial murders—in which blacks kill whites and vice versa—are rare because racial discrimination discourages interaction between blacks and whites (Shihadeh and Flynn, 1996; Greenberg and Schneider, 1994; Messner and Golden, 1992; Rose and McClain, 1990).

INTRA – within
INTER – between

Nation and Culture

The influence of poverty on homicide further shows up in comparisons between rich and poor nations. In general, less economically developed nations have been found to have high rates of homicide, while more developed countries have low rates. Among the industrialized nations, however, the United States has the highest rate. This is largely due to the greater amount of poverty in our society than in other industrialized countries such as Western Europe and Japan (Chesnais, 1992; Archer and Gartner, 1984; Quinney, 1965).

How does poverty explain the higher murder rates in most poor countries? The clue can be found in the high frequency of interaction among the poor themselves. The poor, who are more homicide-prone than the nonpoor, associate with each other more than with the nonpoor, thereby enhancing their opportunity of killing each other. This is particularly the case with developing countries, where the gap between rich and poor is greater than in developed countries. Research has suggested that social inequality is a great contributor to homicide because the poor often blame the rich—and others, rather than themselves—for their own plight (Szwarcwald et al., 1999; Lee and Bankston, 1999; Martinez, 1996; Shihadeh, 1994).

Among the poor developing countries, those in South America have unusually high homicide rates. Several sociologists have attributed these high rates to a "culture of violence." As Marshall Clinard and Daniel Abbot (1973) write, "The extremely high rate of homicide in Colombia represents a striking example of large-scale cultural violence, often called *Violencia Colombia*. There the use of violence has increased fantastically since 1948. Originally rural in nature, these violent activities permeate the cities, and despite army measures of control the homicide rate continues to be high." The culture of violence seems to have an element of machismo, the idea that men should be concerned about their manhood. In such a culture, men are encouraged to respond aggressively to an insult to their manhood. If they do not respond aggressively, they are made to feel like cowards. In any country, however, killers seem to have developed a similarly tough, macho attitude, because most have a violent past. A killer's violence usually began with minor assaults against others, gradually escalated to more and more serious assaults, and finally culminated in homicide (Peterson et al., 1980; Wolfgang, 1958).

Regions, Large Cities, and Rural Areas

Usually, the southern region has the highest murder rate, the western region has the next highest rate, and the northeastern and midwestern states have the lowest rate (FBI, 1996). There is nothing new about these regional differences; they have been around for a long time. What accounts for the southern leadership in homicide rates? Some sociologists have attributed it to the "subculture of violence" in the South, where violent behavior seems more acceptable than in other regions. For example, gun ownership and execution of murderers, which are assumed to reflect a violent subculture, are the most common in the South. Another reason could be the greater prevalence of rurality in the South. A study by Kenneth Wilkinson (1984) shows that the average murder rate in rural areas exceeds the rate in most cities. According to Wilkinson, the dispersion of people in rural areas (as contrasted with the congestion of people in most cities) reduces community integration, thereby forcing family members, friends, and acquain-

TABLE 4.1 How Urban and Rural Murder Rates Differ

Where People Live	Murder Rate in 1997 (per 100,000 population)
Large cities with population of	
250,000 or more	16.1
100,000 to 249,999	10.0
50,000 to 99,999	5.5
Rural areas	4.5
Small cities with population of	
25,000 to 49,999	4.0
10,000 to 24,999	3.2
Fewer than 10,000	3.1

Source: FBI, *Uniform Crime Reports,* 1998.

tances to spend too much time with each other. This enhances the opportunity for violent disruption in primary relationships (among relatives and acquaintances), and it is in such relationships that most homicides take place, a strange fact that we will discuss in another section.

The rurality-homicide connection, however, seems to run counter to the popular belief that there are more killings in *large* cities. Actually, it does not, because rurality is related to homicide only if we compare the homicide rates of rural areas with those of *most* cities, which are relatively *small,* having populations of fewer than 50,000 people. Rural areas do have higher homicide rates than these small cities. However, larger cities, with populations exceeding 50,000, have significantly higher murder rates than those for small cities and the rural areas (see Table 4.1).

Paradoxically, like rurality, large city size encourages homicides by reducing community integration. But unlike rurality, which reduces community integration through *population dispersion,* large city size diminishes community integration via *population heterogeneity.* However it comes about, the lack of community integration drives individuals—anonymous urbanites as much as isolated ruralites—into the same matrix of interactions among relatives and acquaintances that is likely to lead to homicides.

Gender and Age

Those homicidal interactions are far more likely to cause men than women to kill, because men are far more concerned about defending their manhood. Most of the killings involve a man doing away with another man. If a man and a woman are caught up in a homicidal interaction, he is more likely to be the offender and she the victim. Men who kill their wives or girlfriends do so mostly because they have persistently tried to *keep their victims in an abusive relationship.* Such killing, then, is the culmination of a long series of physically violent acts perpetrated by the men against their female victims. Moreover, men tend to kill in response to their wives' infidelity. Men would also kill their wives as part of a murder-suicide or a family massacre (Wilson and Daly, 1992).

In the fewer cases where women kill, they differ from their male counterparts in the choice of victims. Unlike male offenders, who are more likely to kill others of the *same* sex, female offenders are more likely to kill members of the *opposite* sex. In these opposite-sex killings, the female and male murderers usually commit the crime for different reasons. The women rarely kill in response to their husbands' infidelity even if their husbands are extremely adulterous. They usually send their husbands to the hereafter as a desperate attempt to *get out of an abusive relationship.* The women basically kill for self-preservation or in self-defense. Violence by women, then, is primarily defensive, in contrast to violence by men, which is distinctly offensive (Mann, 1996; Wilson and Daly, 1992; Goetting, 1987).

Males also kill at a younger age than females. When killing, people are more likely to target others of the same age group than older or younger victims. This is largely because people of about the same age spend more time interacting with one another than with others of a different age. In the few cases where older persons quarrel with younger ones, the older persons are more likely to end up dead, because the younger persons are more impulsive and hence quicker to shoot. While most homicides involve relatives and acquaintances, the younger killers are more likely than their older peers to target strangers and commit murder and robbery together (U.S. Census Bureau, 1999; Eigen, 1981; Mulvihill and Tumin with Curtis, 1969).

Today, the *overall* homicide rate in the United States is slightly lower than it was in the mid-1980s. But, as shown in Figure 4.2, since 1985 there has been a stunning upsurge in murders committed by *teenagers,* so that juvenile homicide is more than twice as common today as in the mid-1980s. Most of these killings take place in large cities' poor neighborhoods, where gang violence, drive-by shootings, and crack cocaine are relatively common. More important, many teenagers in poor inner cities carry guns, a new phenomenon since 1985. Contrary to popular belief, the primary reason for carrying guns is not seeking status among one's peers or trying to make an impression on others. Teenagers carry guns to protect themselves in their dangerous, high-crime neighborhoods (Fox, 1996; Blumstein, 1995; Wright, Sheley, and Smith, 1992). All the same, the increased possession of guns has contributed to the surge in teen murders. Other contributing factors include the larger number of dysfunctional families, the greater prevalence of drugs among the urban poor, the lower quality of public schools, and the increased glorification of violence on television, in the movies, and in video games. Since 1994, however, the teen murder rate has declined, largely as a result of the falloff in the crack market and increased confiscation of

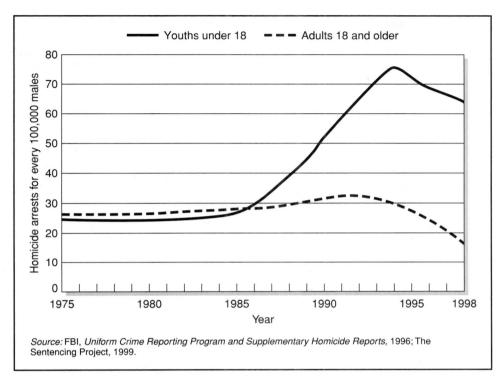

FIGURE 4.2   Youths Outpace Adults in Homicide

handguns from juveniles by police departments (Steinberg, 1999; Kleck and Hogan, 1999; Grossman, 1995; Butterfield, 1992).

Patterns of Killing

Various studies have found certain patterns in the majority of murder cases. However, these patterns mainly involve murders committed by lower-class people, not by middle- and upper-class persons. Traditionally, researchers have concentrated on lower-class homicides simply because they make up the overwhelming majority of murders. Thus, in this section, we will focus on the patterns of lower-class homicides, but will also note the characteristics of higher-class murders in cases where they differ.

Time of Killing   *July & August & December*

Most murders are committed in the heat of passion, and there does seem to be some, though relatively weak, connection between season of the year and murder. The number of homicides increases slightly during the hot late spring and summer, peaking in July and August, during which potential killers and victims, who are relatives, friends, and acquaintances rather than strangers, tend most to get together and drink cold beer in public places such as restaurants and taverns. Homicide decreases during the cool autumn and early spring, and drops even more during the winter months of January and February (U.S. Census Bureau, 1999; Wolfgang, 1958). But the number of homicides peaks again during the cold month of December, primarily due to its being a holiday season, which, like July and August, brings together the kinds of people who are more likely to get involved in homicide (Anderson, 1989).

Far stronger than the association between homicide and season is the link between homicide and days of the week as well as hours of the day. Homicide occurs most frequently during the weekend evenings, particularly on Saturday night. This may explain why the handgun most often used in homicide is popularly called a Saturday night special. These weekend killings are more likely to involve family members than the homicides occurring during the weekdays—the weekday homicides tend more to involve strangers. The reason is that people usually spend more time at home on weekends (Messner and Tardiff, 1985).

All this does not, however, hold true for the minority of cases involving middle-class and upper-class offenders. With these killers, researchers have failed to find any significant variation by the month of the year or day of the week. Why this class difference? Because murders in the middle and upper classes are more likely to be *calculative* or *premeditated,* while lower-class killings are more often carried out in a burst of rage, usually after some heavy drinking (Parker with Rebhun, 1995; Green and Wakefield, 1979).

What about the evening when the moon is full? Does the popularly believed lunar effect on homicide exist? Is it true, as "every policeman, bartender, and emergency-room attendant knows, that people tend to act crazy and become more violent when the moon is full"? One psychiatrist claimed to have found a higher incidence of homicides in Cleveland and Miami at the times of new and full moons. However, in analyzing the same data and other relevant studies, an astronomer found no correlation between lunar phases and homicide rates (*Sky and Telescope,* 1985).

Place of Killing

Men are about equally likely to commit murder in and outside the home, but women are far more likely to kill at home than outside it. In the past women most often did the killing in the kitchen, apparently because it is the place where women traditionally were accustomed to handling a knife—which can turn into a dangerous weapon when a quarrel flares up (Wolfgang, 1958). But nowadays, less likely to be confined to the kitchen as a result of greater gender equality, women tend more to kill in the living room (Mann, 1996). However, the bedroom is a more dangerous place for women than for men, as women are more frequently killed there by their husbands, boyfriends, or exes (Totman, 1978; Wolfgang, 1958). Perhaps men have been socially conditioned to use the bedroom as a place for demonstrating their "manliness" by sexually conquering women and end up using it as a place for physically subjugating them to death.

While women are more likely to kill at home, they are also more likely to be killed at home. A major reason is simply that they spend more time at home. Other types of people who spend more time at home are also more likely to have the same fate. These include the very young, the very old, minority groups, the married, and the unemployed (Messner and Tardiff, 1985).

Method of Killing

Killing a human may appear extraordinary when compared with, say, killing a rabbit. This consequently fires the imagination of many mystery writers, who help spread the popular notion that murderers often use mysterious, exotic, ingenious, or superclever methods to get rid of their victims. Yet research often shows that there is nothing special about the methods of killing. Most objects can be readily turned into murder weapons, as long as they are conveniently accessible when the murderous anger erupts. In our society firearms are easily available, and so they are most often used as murder weapons (Kristof, 1996b). Perhaps, seeing a gun while embroiled in a heated argument may incite a violent person to murderous action. As Shakespeare has it, "How oft the sight of means to do ill deeds, makes ill deeds done."

Of course, firearms in themselves cannot cause homicide, nor can their absence reduce the motivation to kill. It is true that "guns don't kill people, people do." Still, were guns less available, many heated arguments would have resulted in aggravated assaults rather than murders, thereby reducing the number of fatalities. An analysis of over 20,000 homicides and aggravated assaults in Chicago suggests that attacks with knives are five times *less* likely to result in death than attacks with guns (Wright, Rossi, and Daly, 1983). An enormous number of guns are in private hands: Half of all U.S. households own firearms of some kind, and a quarter of all families have handguns (Wright, 1995; Wright, Sheley, and Smith, 1992). It is, therefore, not surprising that many deaths in the United States result from gun homicides. Every year, our country has over 10,000 handgun homicides compared with less than 100 in other industrialized nations such as Canada, England, and Japan, where guns are much harder to get (Butterfield, 1996; Wright, 1995; Rodino, 1986).

The easy availability of guns in the United States appears to be a great equalizer for the poor. It gives power to the powerless. This may explain why lower-class people are more likely to use firearms than any other weapon when they kill. Shooting is also the most popular mode of murder among people of the higher classes. However, higher-class killers are much more likely than their lower-class peers to use more refined techniques of killing, such as poisoning, staging a hit-and-run car death, and hiring somebody else to do the killing (Green and Wakefield, 1979).

Varieties of Killing

Most killings are carried out against family members, friends, or acquaintances rather than strangers. Some killings happen as if the victim asks to be put to death. Some involve an attempt to win a seemingly trivial argument. Some serve as an adjunct to suicide. A few involve slaying more than one victim. Even fewer take place in schools and become widely known as school violence. Let us take a closer look at each form of killing.

Warm-Blooded Murder

Many people are apparently afraid of getting attacked and killed by strangers, particularly in big cities. Such fear came through clearly in the mid-1980s when Bernhard Goetz, the so-called Subway Vigilante, shot four young African Americans on a subway car in New York, though they allegedly had merely approached and asked him for money. It was also the same fear that drove many people to hail him as a hero. The fear that strangers will kill us unless we kill them first does not reflect reality. Compared with other major crimes, such as robbery, rape, and assault, homicide is the least likely to involve strangers. Of all the murders that occur every year, only a small percentage are committed by strangers. In fact, the majority of the murders involve relatives, friends, or acquaintances, as Figure 4.3 indicates. This situation is not unique to our society. It exists in many other countries as well (Clinard and Abbot, 1973).

It seems incredible that the people we know or even love are more likely to kill us than are total strangers. But, as three sociologists have explained, "This should really not be very surprising. Everyone is within easy striking distance of intimates for a large part of time. Although friends, lovers, spouses, and the like are a main source of pleasure in one's life, they are equally a main source of frustration and hurt. Few others can anger one so much" (Mulvihill and Tumin with Curtis, 1969). Ordinarily, killing requires a great deal of emotion. Therefore, it may be more difficult to kill a stranger about whom we don't have much feeling—unless we are professional killers, who typically dispatch their victims in a cold-blooded, unemotional manner (Levi, 1981). In sum, we are far less likely to become victims of cold-blooded murders carried out by strangers but more likely to die from warm-blooded, emotional murders at the hands of our relatives, friends, or acquaintances.

Doing the Victim a Favor

The general public often sympathizes with the murder victim but not with the offender at all. The public assumes that the murder victim is weak and meek, helplessly slain by the strong and aggressive offender. This assumption is not always correct. In at least one out of four homicides, the victim has first attacked the subsequent slayer, and such murder has been called *victim-precipitated homicide* (Wilbanks, 1984; Felson and Steadman, 1983; Luckenbill, 1977; Wolfgang, 1958). The following are typical cases of victim precipitation (Wolfgang, 1958):

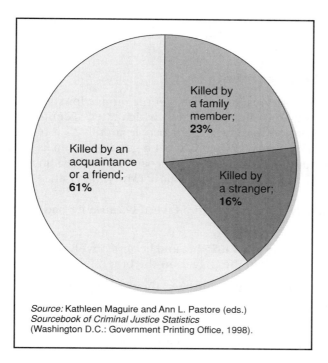

Killed by
a family
member;
23%

Killed by an
acquaintance
or a friend;
61%

Killed by
a stranger;
16%

Source: Kathleen Maguire and Ann L. Pastore (eds.)
Sourcebook of Criminal Justice Statistics
(Washington D.C.: Government Printing Office, 1998).

FIGURE 4.3   Most Victims Know Their Killers

■ A drunken husband, beating his wife in the kitchen, gave her a butcher knife and dared her to use it on him. She warned him that she would use it if he should strike her again. At the very instant he heard this warning, he slapped her in the face—and he was fatally stabbed.

■ A drunken man, with knife in hand, approached a person during a quarrel. When this person showed a gun, the drunk dared him to shoot. He did.

Because they provoke another person to kill them, Marvin Wolfgang (1967) assumes that these self-precipitated murder victims may have secretly wanted to kill *themselves.* This assumption may well be correct. But if they have suicide wishes, why do they not take it on themselves to end their own lives? Perhaps they have been influenced by what may be considered a culture of *showy masculinity,* characteristic of sexist society. This culture encourages males to show off their toughness and hide their tenderness, to act like a "man" and avoid acting like a "woman," or to engage in "manly" braggadocio and shun "feminine" quietism. Under the pressure of this culture, suicidally inclined men may *avoid* revealing their "sissy cowardice" or their plea for condescending sympathy from others in quietly ending their own lives. Instead, they are inclined to display masculine bravado and earn from others some "respect" as the worst person imaginable, by making an ostentatious assault on another person that is secretly designed for their own annihilation—the result being a victim-precipitated murder.

Winning a Trivial Argument

Murder is an extremely serious human act, yet the motive for committing it often appears downright trivial. Ordinary quarrels, which often seem to be over nothing, are the most common reason for poor people to kill. As a retired homicide detective in New York reports, "When you get a guy to 'fess up as to why he did it, you get very shoddy answers: 'He took my coat.' 'He stepped on my girlfriend's foot'" (Wilentz, 1985). Similar examples follow (Mulvihill et al., 1969):

■ A man was fatally shot in front of a tavern because he had refused to lend his assailant $1.

■ Two men were arguing over a $5 bet and became involved in a scuffle. Then one took out a gun and pulled the trigger on the other.

■ Two fellow workers were drinking beer; they argued over a $1 pool bet. One wound up in a morgue.

■ A man was drunk when he came home. He told his uncle to move over in bed. Seeing that his uncle would not, he stabbed him to death.

■ "Hey, you're lookin' at me."
"No, I ain't."
"Yes, you are. Why you lookin' at me?"
Minutes later one of them lay still in a puddle of blood.

Murder, then, is apparently a quick and effective way for the poor to win an argument—over trifles. Middle-class people usually use a much less drastic means, such as verbal or intellectual ability, to settle an argument. But the poor tend more to suffer from lack of such ability, and thus they are more often compelled to use their physical strength to end an argument with—and sometimes the life of—another person.

We may also note that arguments such as those illustrated above may appear trivial to us. Yet the same arguments are apparently taken by poor males as reasons for defending their dignity or honor as men. A dirty look, a little insult, a jostle would not usually get middle-class people into an argument, let alone impel them to spill another person's blood. The same triviality may be perceived differently by the poor. Why would the poor make such a mountain out of a molehill, and with such deadly consequences for themselves?

The explanation can be found in the economic and social oppression of the poor. The poor man's honor as a man—or, for that matter, as simply a human being—has been substantially diminished by the frustrating and humiliating forces in his life. Some of these forces are impersonal, such as the general condition of poverty, so that the poor man cannot fight back against them. Other humiliating forces can be found in people, such as the police, bureaucrats in a welfare or unemployment office, and employers—who usually treat him with far less respect than they do the more successful, higher-status persons. But since these people are more powerful, the poor man cannot fight back at them either.

As a consequence, he has extremely little honor left in him, and so, in order to live at least more honorably than an animal, he dearly hangs on to it. Although he cannot maintain this fragile honor in the larger society or in the presence of those more powerful than himself, he certainly can at his own home and in his neighborhood, among his equally honor-deprived family members, friends, and acquaintances. Because his honor as a man is already extremely fragile, the pressure of daily frustration and tension can easily crush it. Thus even a small insult from his relatives, friends, or acquaintances (who are, after all, his last strand of hope for keeping his honor) can mean, to him, the threat that all his honor will be taken away. With such a perception, he will very likely fight like mad to defend his honor, even to the extent of killing the person who has "dissed" him. In fact, as many researchers have found, most homicides result from what they call *character contest*, in which the offender and victim try to defend their honor after it has been threatened by the other (Athens, 1985; Felson and Steadman, 1983; Luckenbill, 1977).

An Adjunct to Suicide

We have speculated that the so-called victims of victim-precipitated homicide may have wanted to die and contributed greatly to their own deaths. There is yet a different group of offenders with the same suicidal tendency. They are homicide-suicide offenders, who first kill another person and then finish themselves off. The difference between these two types of offenders is obvious. While the "victim" of victim-precipitated homicide conceals the suicide wishes, the homicide-suicide offender reveals them.

Homicide-suicide is relatively rare, no more than 3 or 4 percent of all murders in the United States and approximately 10 percent in Canada. Virtually all homicide-suicides are male. They are usually severely depressed, violent, and jealous people, who impulsively kill their wives and often children as well (Gillespie, Hearn, and Silverman, 1998; Lecomte and Fornes, 1998; Cohen, Llorente, and Eisdorfer, 1998).

Two conflicting views can be found on the nature of homicide-suicide: one sociological, seeing homicide-suicide as a form of *normality;* the other psychiatric, viewing it as a symptom of *abnormality.* According to the sociological view, the murderer-suicide is a normal person because, after killing the loved one, he is able to feel remorse, just as we would expect normal people to feel after they had done such a horrible thing. By contrast, the psychiatrist sees the murderer-suicide as a psychotic, believing that, instead of feeling remorse, the offender anticipates a reunion with the victim in another world, and therefore kills himself in order to achieve that goal (Dorpat, 1967; Wolfgang, 1958).

Autocide:
suicide by car

These two conflicting views can be reconciled. It is true that some murderer-suicides are "normal." It is also true that other murderer-suicides are "psychotic." But these two types of murderer-suicides may have one thing in common—both are unaffected by the culture of showy masculinity discussed before. Instead of acting like "tough guys," as required by that culture, both behave like "weaklings." In effect, the normal one begs the mortally wronged victim (who is usually his wife or girlfriend) for pardon, and the psychotic one dreams for some happy reconciliation in another world. Both behave like—when seen from the standpoint of the "tough guy" culture—mushy characters in a tear-jerking love story.

Sociologist David Phillips (1981, 1980) has discovered homicide-suicides of a third kind. They resemble the so-called victims of victim-precipitated murder in that they conceal their suicidal wishes, but they carry out these wishes with more ingenuity. They "disguise their homicide-suicides as accidents to protect their survivors from insurance problems and from social stigma." One example of these disguised homicide-suicides is a pilot who deliberately crashes his airplane with passengers onboard, but who makes the crash appear convincingly like an accident. Phillips argues that many plane crashes actually involve the pilots committing murder-suicides. This argument is based on his finding that after a murder-suicide is publicized in the mass media there is an increase in both noncommercial and commercial plane crashes, a trend that persists for approximately nine days. Phillips assumed that the mass media, with their spate of murder-suicide stories, encourage those suicidal pilots to commit murder-suicides. He later reinforced this assumption by showing in another study the impact of mass media on homicides in general. That study indicated that between 1973 and 1978 homicides increased by more than 12 percent on the third day following highly publicized heavyweight championship prizefights (Phillips, 1983; see also Baron and Reiss, 1985; Phillips and Bollen, 1985; Altheide, 1981).

— difference —

Mass and Serial Murder

In 1997 Andrew Cunanan killed the famous fashion designer Gianni Versace in Miami Beach after having murdered four other men in other cities. In 1992 Jeffrey Dahmer of Milwaukee, Wisconsin, pleaded guilty to killing 15 young men, one after another. He reportedly had sex with some of the corpses, dismembered some of the bodies, and kept in his refrigerator a severed head as well as a heart that he planned to eat later. Earlier, in 1985, another serial killer struck terror in the Los Angeles area. Called the Night Stalker, he sneaked into the homes of 19 people at night and killed them as they slept. Just a year before, a mass murderer walked into a McDonald's restaurant in San Diego carrying a rifle, a shotgun, and a pistol with hundreds of rounds of ammunition. He opened fire on everybody, killing 21 people—mostly children—and wounding 19 others. These types of killing—mass and serial murders—attract considerable attention from the media and public. Just the same, they are extremely rare.

Mass murder involves killing a number of people at about the same time and place. It usually ends with the murderer dying at the scene of the carnage. The murderer's death results from either committing suicide or forcing the police to take lethal action. Despite the shocking nature of their crime, most mass murderers are not mentally ill. As sociologists Jack Levin and James Fox (1985) conclude after studying mass murderers, "The mass killer appears to be *extraordinarily ordinary*. He is indistinguishable from everyone else. Indeed, he may be the neighbor next door, a co-worker at the next desk, or a member of the family."

Some mass murderers are *disgruntled employees* who want to get even with their boss who has wronged them in some way, by firing them, for example. But in the process of killing their boss, they end up murdering their coworkers as well. Other mass murderers are *heads of family* who kill their wives and children after having long felt alone, alienated, helpless, and depressed, aggravated by heavy drinking. Some mass murderers are *"pseudocommandos,"* who turn their home into an arsenal and then lash out at what they consider to be an unjust or evil world. Finally, some mass murderers *work as a team under the direction of a charismatic leader* (Holmes and Holmes, 1992). Examples are those who participated in the 1969 mass killings ordered by Charles Manson in California, in the 1993 bombing of the World Trade Center in New York City, or in the more recent killing of Muslims in Bosnia and of ethnic Albanians in Kosovo, as well as many other terrorist acts against innocent citizens in other parts of the world.

Slightly more common than mass murder is serial murder, which involves killing a number of people one at a time. But the media has wildly exaggerated the incidence of serial murder by calling it an "epidemic." This exaggeration originated from the claim by a Justice Department official that serial murder accounts for about 20 percent of all homicides. Actually, the most credible figure, based on careful analysis by sociologists, is only 2 or 3 percent. Another myth about serial murder is that its perpetrators roam from one city to another to carry out their killing. The fact is that most (70 to 75 percent) serial murderers commit their crime in one city alone (Kappeler, Blumberg, and Potter, 1993).

While mass murderers are nearly always caught, serial killers are far more elusive because they are practiced and accomplished at what they do. First, they stalk their victims from a distance, studying the victims' routine activities and habits. Then they win the victims' confidence by befriending them, or gain entry into the victims' house that they have staked out for days. Next, they lure the victims into a trap or simply hold them captive by closing off all possibility of escape. Finally, they kill the victims. In the process of killing, they "often torture their victims, taking delight in the victims' agonies, expressions of terror, cries of despair, and reactions to pain" (Norris, 1989). This should not be surprising, because most serial killers have in their childhood tortured dogs and cats for the thrill of watching them suffer. They have also been subjected to a lot of physical and emotional abuse by their parents. Such experiences have apparently taught the serial killer to become a sociopath, incapable of feeling remorse or guilt for hurting others. Nonetheless, the vast majority of serial killers are not mentally ill. They appear as normal people who go to school or work, come home, and blend into their immediate neighborhood (Hickey, 1991; Norris, 1989).

Generally, the mass murderer is demographically similar to the serial killer: Both are typically white males in their late twenties or thirties. The mass murderer usually knows the people he kills but the serial killer tends to target strangers and is more likely to be sociopathic (Fox and Levin, 1998).

School Violence

Over the last several years, boys as young as 11 have gunned down classmates or teachers in the public schools of such little-known places as Littleton, Colorado; Edinboro, Pennsylvania; Jonesboro, Arkansas; Pearl, Mississippi; West Paducah, Kentucky; and Stamps, Arkansas. It appears that school violence, long known as a phenomenon of large and noisy cities, has now spread to small and tranquil towns, suburbs, and rural areas.

The recent surge of juvenile killing in schools can be attributed to roughly the same factors as those that sociologists have often cited to explain youthful homicides in the larger society. One of these factors is the increased availability of *guns*. Another factor is the glamorization of violence in such *media* as movies, television, and video games. Media violence may not cause actual violence among the overwhelming majority of young men, but it is likely to turn a few susceptible, violence-prone youngsters to violence. A third contributing factor is the *culture* of violence, which favors the possession of guns and accepts the use of force for settling interpersonal conflict. This may explain why every Southern state, with their strong historic culture of violence, has more firearm deaths among children under age 18 than do many Northern states such as New York and New Jersey (Blank, Vest, and Parker, 1998). Under the influence of at least these three factors, youngsters are more likely to commit violence if they have been abused by parents or rejected, taunted, or ostracized by peers (Begley, 1999; Baker, 1998).

Despite its horror, schoolboy homicide remains extremely rare. According to the Centers for Disease Control and Prevention, fewer than 1 percent of all youthful homicides take place in or around the school. Moreover, according to the National Center for Education Statistics, the most common form of school violence is not killing but fist fights—or fights without a weapon. Even when physical attacks with weapons occur, firearms are rarely used (Stolberg, 1999).

Does the Death Penalty Deter Murder?

Nowadays, most people believe that the death penalty is an effective deterrent to murder. Not surprisingly, to win an election, most politicians vow that convicted killers shall be put to death. Many sociologists, however, have observed that the death penalty does not have its hoped-for effect. The evidence supporting this observation has come in several forms.

The first indication is the homicide rates in *states that have retained* the death penalty law are generally much higher than in *states that have abolished* it. (See examples in Figure 4.4.) This clearly suggests that the death penalty does not deter homicide. It might even suggest to some observers that the death penalty causes more homicides. It could be the other way around: That is, the higher homicide rates cause the states to bring back the death penalty. Moreover, the

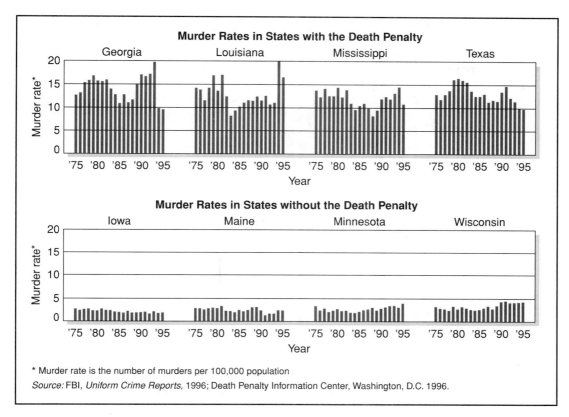

FIGURE 4.4   The Death Penalty and Murder. Murder rates are generally much higher in the 40 states that still retain the death penalty than in the 10 states that have abolished it, as exemplified above.

South, where all the states practice the death penalty, has a very large black population and a culture of violence, as reflected by its traditionally high rate of criminal violence and high level of gun ownership. Thus the distinctive population and cultural characteristics of the South, rather than its death penalty, may be responsible for its higher homicide rate.

In view of this, some sociologists have excluded the southern states from analysis of the relationship between capital punishment and murder. Instead, they focused on northern and western states that have about the same population composition and cultural tradition. The result has consistently shown that the death penalty states still have higher homicide rates than their neighboring states without the death penalty. Although this finding does not prove that capital punishment encourages murder, it does show that the death penalty does not deter murder.

A second type of evidence comes from comparing the homicide rates that occurred *before and after abolition* of the death penalty within the same states. Such comparisons have shown no significant difference in homicide rates before and after the states abolished capital punishment. Furthermore, the *restoration* of the death penalty in states that had earlier abolished it had *not* led to any significant decrease in homicides. This further suggests that the death penalty does not deter people from committing murder.

A final piece of evidence comes from comparing the numbers of homicides *shortly before and shortly after executions* of convicted murderers that have been widely publicized. If the death penalty has a deterrent effect, the execution should so scare potential killers that they would refrain from killing, and the number of homicides in the area should decrease. Apparently, this is not the case. In Philadelphia during the 1930s, for example, the number of homicides remained about the same in the period from 60 days before to 60 days after a widely publicized execution of five murderers. This finding, among others, suggests that the death penalty, even when the state shows people that it means business with it, apparently does not frighten potential killers from killing.

In fact, publicized executions may have the opposite, *brutalizing effect* on potential murderers, indirectly encouraging them to kill, possibly by diminishing respect for human life or by stimulating imitative violence. In California between 1946 and 1955, the state always chose Friday mornings to carry out executions, and there were more murders during the weekends following executions than during the weekends without the Friday-morning executions. Also, in New York between 1907 and 1963, there was an average increase of two homicides in the month after each execution. The brutalizing effect took place in 1990s in Oklahoma (Bailey, 1998; Bowers and Pierce, 1980; Graves, 1964). In a few other cases, the brutalizing effect did not exist, but there was no indication of the deterrent effect either, because the number of homicides remained about the same whether there was a publicized execution or not (King, 1978).

What we have discussed can be summed up by the conclusion from a 14-nation analysis of the death penalty: "If capital punishment is a more effective deterrent than the alternative punishment of long imprisonment, its abolition ought to be followed by homicide rate increases. The evidence examined here fails to support and, indeed, repeatedly contradicts this proposition. In this cross-national sample, abolition was followed more often than not by absolute *decreases* in homicide rates, not by the increases predicted by deterrence theory" (Archer and Gartner, 1984).

Nevertheless, a few studies appear every now and then to challenge that conclusion. The most well-known is economist Isaac Ehrlich's (1975) conclusion from his statistical analysis that one execution can prevent about eight murders. This particular analysis has been criticized for its methodological problems, such as the use of unreliable data on homicides (Bailey, 1980; Kleck, 1979). More devastating to Ehrlich's conclusion is another economist's analysis that uses the same statistical method as Ehrlich's but produces essentially contrary results (Avio, 1979). Like Ehrlich, sociologist David Phillips (1980) also claims to have found the deterrent effect of capital punishment. In analyzing 22 cases of execution that occurred in London between 1858 and 1921, he found that homicides dropped by 35.7 percent within two weeks following an execution that was widely publicized in the city's leading newspaper. But Phillips has been criticized for analyzing only 22 executions, which can hardly represent the many hundreds of executions that took place between 1858 and 1921 (Zeisel, 1982). Phillips has argued that he analyzed only these few executions because they were heavily publicized in the *Times* of London, but it must be said that the poor and uneducated, who were more likely than others to commit murder, were hardly the readers of that newspaper.

We may conclude that the death penalty does not deter murder, or, more precisely, is no more effective than life imprisonment in deterring murder. But why not? One reason is that murder is a crime of passion, most often carried out under the overwhelming pressure of a volcanic emotion, while capital punishment would more likely be effective if murder were a calmly calculated act. Another reason is that the causal forces of murder, such as exposure to brutality and abuse and economic deprivation, are simply too powerful to be neutralized by the threat of capital punishment.

However, despite its lack of deterrence to murder, capital punishment can be effective for other purposes. It is obviously effective in preventing the murderer from doing harm to others again. It is also effective in satisfying the emotion of outrage against murder. Many people seem to advocate capital punishment for these reasons. As public opinion polls have shown, more than half of the U.S. population would still favor the death penalty even if they know that it does not deter murder (Gallup, 1985). This is particularly true today, as suggested by the growing number of executions in recent years (see Figure 4.5). Nonetheless, our society likes to appear civilized in doing away with convicted

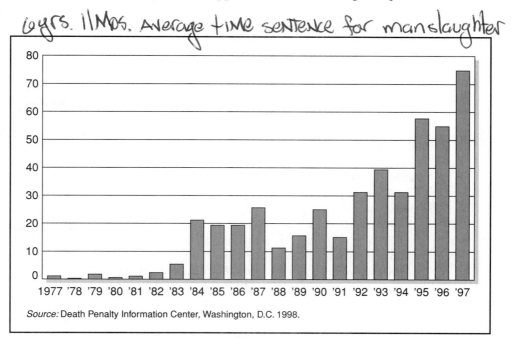

6 yrs. 11 Mos. Average time sentence for manslaughter

Source: Death Penalty Information Center, Washington, D.C. 1998.

FIGURE 4.5   The Rising Number of Executions

murderers. Barbaric methods of execution, such as hangings and firing squads, are for all intents and purposes no longer used; they are replaced by the "more humane" electric chair, gas chamber, and, most recently, lethal injection. Such humane appearances notwithstanding, we remain the only industrialized nation that still executes murderers as well as having the highest murder rate in the industrialized world.

Why Do People Kill?

In general, there are three kinds of theory for explaining why some people commit murder. They differ in telling us *where* the cause of murder can be found. Biogenic theories say that it can be found inside the human *body*. Psychogenic theories maintain that it can be located within the human *psyche*. And sociogenic theories argue that it can be tracked down in the *social environment*—outside both the human body and the psyche. Let us visit each of these three locations and see how murder is supposed to be produced.

Biogenic Theories

There are at least two biogenic theories of murder that are relatively popular today. They are more specifically referred to as the ethological theory and the genetic theory.

Ethological Theory.   This theory has been put forth by ethologists, who are for the most part zoologists specializing in the study of animal behavior. According to these scientists, humans are not biologically just the same as other animals in having the instinct to kill. Humans are far more homicidal. This is evidenced by the fact that while other dangerous animals *rarely* kill other animals of the same species (e.g., tigers rarely kill other tigers, and wolves rarely kill other wolves), humans *often* kill other humans. At least 100 million humans have been killed by other humans in various wars since the First World War in 1914—and this figure is in addition to the number of interhuman killings carried out by private citizens in predominantly lower-class neighborhoods. Ethologists have attempted to explain why this intraspecies aggression is so much more common among humans.

Their explanation is that while such ferocious animals as tigers, wolves, and ravens are endowed with the *instinct to inhibit* their killing instinct, humans are not. Why not? Because, unlike ferocious animals that can easily kill other members of their own species, unarmed humans are more like such harmless animals as doves and rabbits in not being physically capable of killing their own kind. In prehistoric times, then, it was difficult for humans to kill with their teeth and claws as ferocious animals did. Thus, there was no natural selection pressure at work to breed into humans the instinctual mechanism for inhibiting their instinct to kill their own kind. Suddenly, however, humans developed artificial weapons (such as knives and firearms), analogous to, and even far more dangerous than, the built-in bodily weapons (such as sharp teeth and claws) of the ferocious animals. This artificial-weapon development was just too sudden for evolution to cope with it. As a result, the mechanism of inhibition against their killing instinct failed to evolve in humans. Without this inhibiting mechanism, humans have often used their artificial weapons such as knives and guns and bombs to kill each other (Lorenz, 1966).

All this may explain why the human race as a whole is the most homicidal in the animal kingdom. But it cannot explain why some humans are more homicidal than others. Suppose all of us, as the ethological theory implies, have the same evolutionary past, the same killer instinct, and the same lack of instinctual inhibition against killing. Then, if the theory is consistent, all of us should have the same likelihood of killing others. Yet this is not the case. As we have observed, the poor, for example, are more homicidal than the rich. Also, the theory fails to take into account the power of human civilization to curb killing.

Genetic Theory.   Most genetically normal people are born with 23 pairs of chromosomes—46 in all—in each of our body cells. Twenty-two of these pairs are called autosomes, while the remaining pair are referred to as sex chromosomes. In normal males, there are two sex chromosomes, named X and Y. The X is inherited from the mother, the Y from the father. The X is believed to be gentle and passive and the Y tough and aggressive. Normal males are described as XY—those whose gentle and tough characteristics supposedly balance each other.

Now, a tiny percentage of our male population (about one-seventh of one percent) is born with an extra Y chromosome; those in this category are called XYY males. With the extra Y, which is supposed to make a man overly tough and aggressive, the XYY males are considered genetically abnormal. The major characteristics of these abnormal males are that they are somewhat mentally challenged, have much acne on the face, stand taller than average men, and—most important—have a strong tendency to be unusually aggressive. It has been theorized, therefore, that the extra Y chromosome can drive the XYY male into committing a dangerous, violent crime, such as murder. To test this theory, some geneticists have studied violent inmates in prisons as well as hospitals for the criminally insane and have found an unusual number of them to have the extra Y chromosome (Fox, 1971; Montagu, 1968).

The validity of this theory is, however, quite limited, for at least two reasons. One, most XYY boys do not grow up to become murderers, and most murderers do not have the XYY. Two, the XYY may at best serve only as a potentiator, not a determinant, of violence. Even though an extra Y chromosome has the potential of leading its carrier to violence, sociocultural factors may largely determine whether the potential will turn into actuality. As one geneticist admits:

> A social mechanism is entirely possible. Large, possibly slightly retarded, males [with XYY chromosomes] may be ridiculed for their height and may respond aggressively. In any case, it would appear that of the total amount of violence in our society only a very small part is contributed by XYY individuals. (McClearn, 1969)

Psychogenic Theories

There are at least two psychogenic theories of murder. One is the psychoanalytic theory; the other is the psychological theory of frustration-aggression.

Psychoanalytic Theory.   According to psychoanalysts, our psyche consists of three parts: the id, the ego, and the superego. The id, which has been variously referred to as eros, libido, or sex drive, includes the basic drives that we are born with. Very simply, the id is our inborn desire to live, enjoy ourselves, make love, or celebrate life. But such desires cannot be successfully fulfilled unless we have learned *how* to fulfill them. Thus we have learned innumerable ways to live as best we can. The knowledge that results from this learning becomes our ego. In trying to help us enjoy ourselves, our ego tells us that there is a limit to our id satisfaction—that is, self-enjoyment. If we want to satisfy our sexual desire, we cannot simply grab a man or woman in the street and make love right there. This limit to our self-enjoyment is imposed on us by society in the form of rules and injunctions: "You should not do this. . . . You should not do that." Our acceptance of these rules and injunctions becomes the cornerstone of our superego, which is in a way similar to our conscience.

Our id and superego are always at war with each other—both, after all, are equally emotional and quite often unreasonable. Our id wants us to satisfy *all* kinds of sexual fantasies, but our superego says no to *any* kind of sexual fantasy. If we fail to satisfy our id, we feel unhappy; if we fail to obey our superego, we feel guilty. So we are always caught between these two conflicting parts of our psyche, with a good chance of feeling unhappy or guilty. Fortunately, though, the rational part of our mind, the ego, can resolve the conflict between the id and the superego. The ego, then, serves as a mediator, attempting to find a way to satisfy the id without disobeying the superego or to obey the superego without frustrating the id. If the ego often fails in this mission, unhappiness or guilt feelings may so overwhelm the individual that the individual will become mentally ill. This in turn may lead to such violent acts as murder. Thus, many psychiatrists attribute homicide to mental disorder.

The ego has yet another problem to cope with, the failure of which may also lead to violence. According to Sigmund Freud (1961), we are born with not only eros (the life instinct) but also thanatos (the death instinct). These two instincts, in effect, compose our id. Part of the death instinct is an aggressive drive directed against other people rather than oneself. Since this aggressive drive is as normal as the sex drive, it too demands to be expressed. But the superego also demands that the aggressive drive be suppressed as much as the sex drive is. Here we see once again a war threatening our psychic land. If our aggressive drive wants us to cut up a man's body or to defeat him by taking away his life, our superego will prevent us from doing it. Our ego has to step in and play the mediating role. To reconcile the two warring sectors, our ego usually employs the *sublimation* approach, which enables us to satisfy our aggressive drive in a socially acceptable way. In this way both our aggressive drive and superego are satisfied when our ego tells us to cut the man's body as a surgeon or to defeat him in sport, politics, business, or intellectual activity. Through sublimation, then, we turn out to be normal.

However, if we were deprived of love or subjected to brutal attacks during our childhood, our aggressive drive would become too irrational for our ego to cope with—and too powerful for our superego to subdue. Consequently, we could engage in an extremely violent and bizarre murder. A case in point is Edmund Emil Kemper III, who, as an emotionally abused child, bitterly resented the separation between his parents and hated living with his quarrelsome mother. At the age of 21, Kemper murdered eight young women by shooting, stabbing, and strangulation, then cut off their heads and hands, had sexual intercourse with the corpses, and ate flesh from some of them. Finally, he went home and killed his mother. He chopped off her head, and then cut out her larynx and dumped it down the garbage disposal. "This seems appropriate," he said later, "as much as she'd bitched, screamed, and yelled at me over the years" (Lunde, 1975; see also Post, 1982).

On the other hand, if our parents were too strict with us, severely punishing us for even minor misconduct, we would have developed a superego so powerful that it would completely suppress our aggressive drives. Without the normal release of aggressive energy, we would gradually build up a reserve of that energy until it reaches such a high-pressure point that it blows off the heavy lid of the superego. This may explain why a normally "very nice" person suddenly commits murder—to the great shock and disbelief of family, friends, and neighbors. Such a murderer is overcontrolled, with overcontrolled hostility (Quinsey, Maguire, and Varney, 1983). A good example is Anthony Barbaro. At age 17, he "was the kind of son parents brag about. Quiet, considerate, a former Little Leaguer, altar boy and Boy Scout, he studied hard, worked twenty hours a week as a busboy and still managed to make it into the top 2 percent of his high-school senior class." He was, according to one of his friends, "very straight. . . . He didn't drink, he didn't take drugs, he didn't smoke—he mostly just studied all the time." His neighbor said he indeed came from a good family. During a Christmas holiday, this nice boy took a rifle and shotgun to the top floor of his high school building. From there he opened fire on the people in the street. Within two hours, 3 people lay dead and 11 were injured (*Newsweek*, 1975). A study on 13 "sudden murderers" like Barbaro concludes: "There are consistent patterns in their life histories and offenses. Such persons appear to be quite different from the usual delinquent or criminal. *They come from cohesive family backgrounds, where conformity to the rules of the social system was emphasized*" (Lamberti, Blackman, and Weiss, 1967).

There are two basic problems with the psychoanalytic theory. First, it is applicable to only a small, unusual sample of murderers rather than to the majority of the murderers. Second, the theory cannot be empirically tested. It is impossible to observe and measure the so-called id, ego, and superego, as well as the aggressive instinct. But psychiatrists find the theory convincing because of its logical reasoning, with support from anecdotal illustrations.

Psychological Theory.   Although they do not necessarily reject the psychoanalytic theory as false, psychologists prefer to offer their own theories that are more amenable to empirical testing. Examples of these theories are the frustration-aggression theory, the behaviorist or social learning theory, and the personality theory. The most popular and pertinent to murder is the theory of frustration-aggression.

The frustration-aggression theory was first proposed by John Dollard and his fellow psychologists at Yale University in 1939. It was stated as follows:

> This study takes as its point of departure the assumption that *aggression is always a consequence of frustration*. More specifically the proposition is that the occurrence of aggressive behavior always presupposes the existence of frustration and, contrariwise, that the existence of frustration always leads to some form of aggression. (Dollard et al., 1939)

This classic theory was later rephrased by another psychologist as follows: "A frustrating event *increases the probability* that the thwarted organism will act aggressively soon afterward" (Berkowitz, 1969).

These psychologists define *frustration* as the blockage of one's attempt to achieve a goal, whatever the goal may be. Suppose a man wants to have sex with his female date, but she refuses; he can be said to have been frustrated. If she expects to turn him away from sex by firmly saying "No!" but he still strongly insists, then she can be said to have been frustrated, too. As for aggression, it can be any act that hurts a person in any way. Thus, the man and his date may be led by their frustration to behave aggressively. They may call each other names or hit each other.

Although the theory has been generally supported by various kinds of research evidence, it has rarely been applied to murder (Tedeschi and Felson, 1994). Sociologist Stuart Palmer (1960), however, has tested the theory by comparing 50 convicted murderers with their brothers who had not committed murder. He found that the murderers had suffered a greater amount of frustration in their early lives than their nonmurderer brothers. The frustrations include frequent abuse by parents, beatings by others outside the home, and general frustration with peers in school and recreational situations. However, these data were mostly based on interviews with the subjects' mothers, who might have distorted what actually happened in their sons' childhoods. Besides, we should point out that frustration *rarely* leads to murder. Frustration can be expressed in many nonmurderous ways: fast driving, fierce competition in sports and academic work, active vying for attention from the opposite sex, high-pressure selling, relentless politicking, and so on. Compared with these relatively harmless expressions of frustration, murder is, indeed, extremely rare.

Sociogenic Theories

There are many sociogenic theories of violence formulated by sociologists. We will discuss here only two theories that are more specifically designed to explain homicide. One has been called the external restraint theory; the other has been referred to as the subculture of violence theory.

External Restraint Theory. The psychological theory of frustration-aggression is useful only for suggesting aggression as a possible consequence of frustration. The theory does not specify what kind of aggression. Palmer did show murder as a specific kind of aggression that frustration is likely to bring about, but he did not say *why* frustration may lead to murder rather than to other forms of aggression, such as suicide. The reason for murder as a result of frustration can be found in Andrew Henry and James Short's (1954) theory of external restraint.

The external restraint theory is intended to show why some people who are frustrated commit suicide, whereas others who are just as frustrated turn to homicide instead. Henry and Short consider suicide and homicide to be basically the same—both are acts of aggression resulting from frustration. Yet, the sociologists point out, the two acts are different in that suicide is aggression directed inward against oneself, while homicide is aggression directed outward against another person. This theory attempts to explain why intensely frustrated people are likely to choose one type of aggression rather than the other. The explanation is that intensely frustrated people would choose *self*-directed aggression (suicide) if they experience *weak* external restraint, but would choose *other*-directed aggression (homicide) if they suffer *strong* external restraint.

Henry and Short define the *strength of external restraint* as "the degree to which behavior is required to conform to the demands and expectations of other persons." In other words, the strength of external restraint is the amount of social control imposed on people so as to limit their freedom and range of behaviors. According to the theory, people who suffer a great amount of that kind of social control are more inclined toward homicide than suicide because they can legitimately blame others for their frustration.

Martin Gold (1958) has extended the theory of external restraint to include a factor that mediates between strong external restraint and murder. The mediating factor is the *socialization in aggression by physical punishment.* Gold believes that there are two types of socialization—that is, techniques of bringing up a child. One involves the parents using *physical* punishment (spanking, slapping, hitting, or punching) to deter their misbehaving child from further misbehavior. The other involves the parents employing *psychological* punishment (e.g., threatening withdrawal of love, or lecturing to induce guilt) to correct their child's misconduct. Gold theorizes that physical punishment leads to outward aggression against another person, while children psychologically punished turn their aggression against themselves. When they become frustrated adults ready for aggressive action, those who have been physically punished will likely choose murder over suicide, while those who have undergone psychological punishment would choose suicide.

There is some evidence to suggest that strong external restraint is associated with homicide. As we have observed, the lower classes and blacks have significantly higher homicide rates than the middle classes and whites. Such a finding can be said to support the theory because the lower classes and blacks suffer stronger external restraint. There is also evidence to support Gold's theory that physical punishment received in childhood increases the likelihood of homicide in adulthood (Straus, 1991). Still, all this does not mean, as the theories imply, that external restraint or physical punishment has a direct, causal impact on homicide. Instead, as more recent studies suggest, external restraint can lead to homicide only through a third variable called "external attribution of blame"—blaming others rather than oneself for one's own frustration (Unnithan, Huff-Corzine, Corzine, and Whitt, 1994). In other words, excessive external restraint or physical punishment encourages people to blame others rather than themselves for their own problems in life, which in turn causes them to engage in physical violence against others.

Subculture of Violence Theory.   After analyzing his abundant data on homicide, Marvin Wolfgang (1958) concludes:

> There may be a subculture of violence which does not define personal assaults as wrong or antisocial; in which quick resort to physical aggression is a socially approved and expected concomitant of certain stimuli; and in which violence has become a familiar but often deadly partner in life's struggles.

Wolfgang then theorizes that the subculture of violence is the basic cause of high homicide rates in poor neighborhoods.

According to Wolfgang, the violent subculture has such a grip on the poor that they engage in a wider range of violent behavior than the nonpoor. This is because they associate and identify with the model of violence as provided by their parents, peers, and others in the poor neighborhood. At the same time they are discouraged from following the countermodel of nonviolence from the larger society. Consequently, violence becomes a part of their lifestyles and their way of solving interpersonal problems. Not surprisingly, they consider the use of violence not only normal but necessary for survival. They do not feel guilty about their aggression at all (Wolfgang and Ferracuti, 1967).

Critics, however, have questioned the implication that a violent act necessarily reflects the actor's placing a high value on violence. In fact, studies have shown that people who engage in violence do not value violence any more than those who refrain from violence, and that prisoners convicted of murder and other violent crimes do not value violence any more than other inmates convicted of burglary and other nonviolent crimes (Erlanger, 1974; Ball-Rokeach, 1973). Other studies have suggested that the cause of high homicide rates among the poor and African Americans is not the subculture of violence but rather poverty, relative deprivation, or social inequality (Williams, 1984; Blau and Blau, 1982; Messner, 1982). Nevertheless, as it propagates the belief in using violence to solve interpersonal problems, the subculture of violence does encourage—though not cause—homicide, especially among those frustrated by the structural problems of poverty and inequality (Huff-Corzine, Corzine, and Moore, 1986; Messner, 1983).

Assault and Aggravated Assault

Considerably less serious than murder, assault is understandably far more prevalent. Assault involves the unlawful use of physical force against another person. It can be legally divided into two types: aggravated and simple. Aggravated assault involves an atrocious attack with the intent to kill or the use of a deadly weapon. It is considered a felony carrying a relatively severe penalty. All other forms of assault are simple, hence considered a misdemeanor, for which the punishment is less severe. As an act, aggravated assault is basically similar to murder. Aggravated assault differs mostly in consequence: The victim survives rather than dies.

Since assault is behaviorally similar in some ways to homicide, most of the research findings about homicide that we have discussed also hold true for assault. Thus it is true that assaulters are more likely to be poor than nonpoor, to be black than white, to victimize people of the same race than of a different race, to be from the South than other regions, to live in large cities than small towns, to be men than women, to have a violent past than not, to commit the crime during the weekend than during the weekday, and so on. At the same time, assault also differs behaviorally in some ways from homicide. For example, shooting the victim just once, which may result in the offender being charged with assault, is different from shooting three or four times, which is more likely to result in the offender being charged with murder. Given the behavioral differences between assault and murder, some of the data about homicide are understandably not applicable to assault. Research has suggested at least two ways in which assault differs from homicide.

First, for obvious reasons, assaulters are less likely than murderers to use firearms in committing the crime. Second, in the summer, the number of homicides increases only slightly, but assault rises significantly. In the hot season, people tend to go out more, especially the poor whose homes are not comfortably air-conditioned. Going out increases social interaction, especially among strangers, who are likely to get involved in assault. Heat stress and increased consumption of alcoholic beverages further heighten aggression. A combination of all these factors enhances the likelihood of assault (Parker with Rebhun, 1995; Harries, 1990).

Terrorism

The physical violence that we have so far discussed is personal in nature, aimed at specific individuals. In contrast, the violence committed by terrorists is intended for a government, though the victims are usually innocent citizens.

Terrorists are basically powerless individuals futilely fighting a government. Some are international terrorists, who leave their country to attack a foreign government. An example is the Islamic radicals from the Middle East who bombed

New York's World Trade Center in 1993 because of U.S. support for Israel. Other international terrorists, however, carry out policies of their own governments. Examples of such governments are the militant regimes in Libya, Syria, and Iran—known to the U.S. State Department as the "League of Terror"—which have sent terrorists to foreign countries to assassinate their opponents. Other terrorists fight their own governments. Examples of these domestic terrorists include Timothy McVeigh and his associates, who were convicted or accused of bombing the federal office building in Oklahoma City in 1995.

The goal that terrorists seek through violence is either instrumental or expressive. In 1996 when twenty Túpac Amaru rebels in Peru took over the Japanese Embassy and held hundreds of people hostage, their goal was *instrumental,* demanding that the Peruvian government free their imprisoned comrades (Hammer and Larmer, 1997). In seeking an instrumental goal, terrorists are primarily rational and therefore tend to minimize violence. They know that too much violence will provoke the government to concentrate only on destroying them, with the approval of the general public. The restrained use of violence is assumed to enhance their chances of getting a concession from the government or receiving support for their cause from the general public (Hoffman, 1998; Knutson, 1996).

On the other hand, the violence perpetrated by some antigovernment militias in the United States or by religious extremists in the Middle East is *expressive,* serving to vent their frustration with their government. With expressive goals, terrorists are more irrational and more dangerous, taking many more lives. Today, terrorist violence has become more expressive than instrumental (Abu-Sharif, 1996). One reason is the growing frustration from the increased difficulty of achieving instrumental goals. The increased difficulty, in turn, stems largely from changes in government response to terrorism.

Since 1986, the United States and European governments have generally adopted hard-line, "no ransom, no concessions" policies on *international* terrorism. They have also stepped up their cooperative efforts against terrorism. They have further imposed arms embargoes, improved extradition procedures, reduced the size of diplomatic missions of terrorism-supporting countries, and refused to admit any person expelled from another country because of suspected involvement in terrorist activities.

In dealing with *domestic* terrorism, many countries have given considerable powers to law enforcers to prevent terrorist acts. In Britain, for example, the police have the legal authority to detain suspects for seven days without charge, which would probably violate U.S. law. Lately, similar authority has been given to U.S. law enforcement agencies. According to the antiterrorism law passed in 1995, several months after the 1995 Oklahoma bombing, the FBI has the power to obtain phone and travel records without having to establish that the suspect seems to be engaging in criminal activity. The Clinton administration has even proposed that the FBI be granted more power in dealing with suspected terrorists, such as monitoring their telephone calls or infiltrating their organizations.

But this has caused concern that it may unintentionally end up infringing the civil liberties of innocent citizens (Klein, 1996; Lacayo, 1995; Lewis, 1995).

Summary

1. What kinds of people are more likely than others to commit murder? They include the poor, African Americans, men, and young adults. They are also more likely to live in poor countries, in the culture of violence, in the southern region of the United States, in large cities, and in rural areas.

2. Are there any patterns to the occurrence of homicides? Yes. Homicides are somewhat more likely to occur during the hot summer months than the cold month of February. They are most likely to occur on Saturday night. They are about as likely to take place in the home as outside if the killers are male, but tend more to happen at home if the murderers are female. Firearms are more often used than any other weapon for committing homicide.

3. What are the various types of murder? The most common type is the warm-blooded murder, which involves killing a relative, a friend, or an acquaintance. In the second type, the victim helps bring about the murder. The third type is killing for trivial reasons. The fourth is homicide-suicide, in which the killer first does away with the victim and then finishes himself off. The fifth is mass or serial murder, which involves killing a number of people at the same time or different times. And the sixth is mass murder carried out in schools by students.

4. Is the death penalty an effective deterrent to murder? No, at least no more effective than the life sentence. Nevertheless, it enjoys more popular support in those states that have higher homicide rates.

5. Why do some people kill? Various theories have been offered to explain murder. The ethological theory attributes intraspecies killing among humans to the killer instinct along with the lack of an inhibiting instinct; the genetic theory posits the XYY chromosome pattern as the cause of violent crimes like murder; the psychoanalytic theory views murder as the consequence of unresolved psychic conflict; the psychological theory traces violence to frustration; and one sociological theory points to strong external restraint as the cause of murder, while another indicates the subculture of violence as a breeding ground of homicides.

6. Are assaults different from homicide? Assaults differ in that the victim survives, but assaulters share similar characteristics with murderers.

7. What is the nature of terrorism? Terrorism is violence aimed at a government but usually victimizing innocent citizens. It can serve an instrumental or expressive function, and terrorists can go after foreign or domestic targets. But the United States and European governments have generally adopted a hard-line policy to thwart both international and domestic terrorism.

SUGGESTED READINGS

Archer, Dane, and Rosemary Gartner. 1984. *Violence and Crime in Cross-National Perspective*. New Haven: Yale University Press. A remarkable comparative analysis of homicide, critically examining its relationship to wars, urbanization, and capital punishment.

Baker, Jean A. 1998. "Are we missing the forest for the trees? Considering the social context of school violence." *Journal of School Psychology, 36* (Spring), 29–44. Showing how school violence derives from a breakdown of community in schools where students do not feel a sense of belonging.

Bowers, William J. 1984. *Legal Homicide: Death as Punishment in America, 1864–1982*. Boston: Northeastern University Press. A comprehensive, detailed analysis of capital punishment showing why it is unconstitutional as well as how it fails to deter murder.

Hickey, Eric W. 1991. *Serial Murderers and Their Victims*. Pacific Grove, Calif.: Brooks/Cole. A detailed theoretical and empirical analysis of serial murder, including many interesting case studies.

Holmes, Ronald M., and Stephen T. Holmes. 1998. *Serial Murder*. 2nd ed. Thousand Oaks, Calif.: Sage. Presents various types of serial killers, their behavioral patterns, and the motivations behind their killings.

Huff-Corzine, Lin, Jay Corzine, and David C. Moore. 1986. "Southern exposure: Deciphering the South's influence on homicide rates." *Social Forces, 64* (June), 906–924. An empirical analysis that supports the theory of subcultural violence among blacks and white Southerners.

Levin, Jack, and James Alan Fox. 1985. *Mass Murder: America's Growing Menace*. New York: Plenum Press. Provides a deep, uncommon insight into the reality of mass murder.

Mann, Coramae Richey. 1996. *When Women Kill*. Albany, N.Y.: State University of New York. An analysis of both qualitative and quantitative data on nearly 300 women arrested for homicide in six large U.S. cities.

Martinez, Ramiro, Jr. 1996. "Latinos and lethal violence: The impact of poverty and inequality." *Social Problems, 43,* 131–146. An analysis of how a large income gap within the Hispanic population is linked to a relatively high rate of homicide.

Norris, Joel. *Serial Killers*. 1989. New York: Anchor Books. A deep exploration into the lives and minds of serial killers.

Oliverio, Annamarie. 1998. *The State of Terror*. Albany, N.Y.: State University of New York Press. A critical analysis of how the state such as the U.S. government defines as terrorist the destructive acts committed by certain countries and groups but not those by itself.

Rhodes, Richard. 1999. *Why They Kill: The Discoveries of a Maverick Criminologist*. New York: Alfred A. Knopf. An interesting report on sociologist Lonnie Athens's study of criminal violence, showing how "violentization," or violent socialization, causes people to kill.

Straus, Murray A. 1991. "Discipline and deviance: Physical punishment of children and violence and other crime in adulthood." *Social Problems, 38* (May), 133–154. A theoretical and empirical analysis of the relationship between physical punishment and adult violence.

Van den Haag, Ernest, and John P. Conrad. 1983. *The Death Penalty: A Debate*. New York: Plenum Press. A useful debate between a legal scholar who supports capital punishment and a sociologist who opposes it.

CHAPTER

5 Rape and Child Molestation

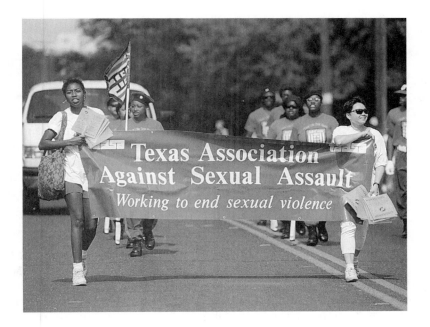

On one afternoon in Kosovo, Yugoslovia, Serbian paramilitary forces pulled 10 young Albanian women out of a refugee convoy of trucks, cars, and tractors that were fleeing the civil war between Albanians and Serbs. Then 10 Serbian soldiers raped the women in an open field about 30 feet from the road, which the victims' families could see with horror and helplessness while they themselves were held at gunpoint by other soldiers. An hour later the Serbians slashed the victims' pants around their thighs and put the women on a truck with their families. Crying, the women said, among other things, "Better dead than what they did to us" (Bumiller, 1999).

As in other wars in the past, sexual violence against women was relatively common in Kosovo. The problem is also prevalent in peacetime in other countries.

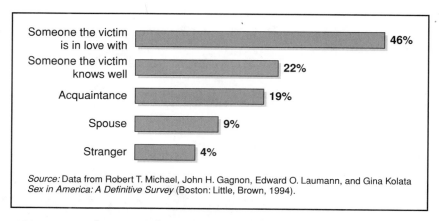

Source: Data from Robert T. Michael, John H. Gagnon, Edward O. Laumann, and Gina Kolata *Sex in America: A Definitive Survey* (Boston: Little, Brown, 1994).

FIGURE 5.1   The Men Who Force Sex on Women

According to a nationwide survey in the United States, 22 percent of women ages 18 to 59 reported having been forced to have sex at least once since age 13 (Michael et al., 1994). In other studies, rape victims were found to make up less than 22 percent of U.S. women. Still, the most conservative estimate has put the average woman's chance of being raped at "an appalling 1 in 10" (Berthelsen, 1999; Koss, 1995; Dowd, 1983). Also significantly, the overwhelming majority of these women know their rapists, as Figure 5.1 indicates.

In this chapter we will first explore the patterns of rape, seeking answers to such questions as: Who is likely to rape? How are rapes generally planned and executed? What is involved in different forms of rape? Why can't the victim be blamed for the rape? We will in turn examine the reactions of both victims and law enforcers to rapes, analyze the pervasive culture that encourages men to assault women sexually, discuss the major explanations for rape, and look at the issue about men being victims of rape. Finally we will analyze the problem of child molestation.

Patterns of Rape

Certain patterns can be detected in rape. Let us first see what kind of men are likely to rape and how they plan and carry out such a crime. Then we will take a close look at the nature of gang rape, acquaintance or date rape, and rape on the college campus along with the controversial issue of victim-precipitated rape.

Racial, Age, and Situational Factors

In his classic analysis of 646 rape cases from the Philadelphia police files for the years 1958 and 1960, sociologist Menachem Amir (1971) found that most of the rapists were poor. He also found that blacks were more likely than whites to be both rapists and victims. Amir further discovered that, contrary to the then wide-spread white fear of black men being more likely to rape white women than black, rape was mostly *intraracial*—black men raping black women and white men raping white women. In about 95 percent of the rapes in Philadelphia, both offenders and victims were of the same race; in only 3 percent were the rapists black and their victims white. In other words, rape was as intraracial as murder. The intraracial nature of rape can be attributed to at least two factors. One is the unusually severe legal penalty against blacks who raped white women. Another reason is racial segregation, which made black women more accessible than white women to those black men who are inclined to express their aggression in rape.

But today rape has become considerably less intraracial—or more interracial. Already by the early 1980s black-against-white rapes had soared to 19 percent (from 3 percent in late 1950s and early 1960s) of all rapes committed by both blacks and whites (Wilbanks, 1985). This may have resulted from increased racial integration and hence more contact between potential offenders and victims of different races. But at least two other factors continue to operate in such rapes: (1) as members of an oppressed minority, some African American men may want to "get even" at the white society by raping its women, and (2) the white-dominated society has enshrined the white female as the ideal of sexual attractiveness (LaFree, 1982). It should be pointed out, though, that most rapes still involve members of the same race.

Age is another factor in the relationship between rapists and their victims. Females from the age of 1 year all the way up to above the age of 80 are subject to rape. The age group most vulnerable to rape, however, is 16 to 20 years of age. In intraracial rapes, offenders are generally somewhat older than their victims. But in *inter*racial rapes, black offenders tend to be *younger* than their white victims. This does not mean that the black offenders prefer older white women. Instead, it is largely a matter of availability, because many of these black–white rape episodes involve the commission of burglary or robbery in addition to rape (Russell, 1984). While this may reflect black hostility toward white society, as suggested, it may also reflect the influence of a sexist society. Burglars and robbers usually feel that "if you rob a woman, you might as well rape her too—the rape is free" (Lear, 1972b). Such criminals simply consider rape "an added bonus" to their property crime (Scully, 1990).

There is also a situational factor in rape. The number of rapes, especially gang rapes, tends to increase during the hot summer months. Most significant is the finding that most rapes occur on weekends (Zeiss, 1984; Michael and Zumpe, 1983). Does summer increase the heat of passion and hence the likelihood of rape? No, summer merely increases the social interaction between potential offender and victim that makes rape more likely to happen (Zeiss, 1984). Most rapes also involve drinking on the part of offenders, just like most homicides (Nicholson et al., 1998; Richardson and Hammock, 1991; Scully, 1990). The use of alcohol serves as an excuse for sexual aggression ("It wasn't my fault; I was drunk"). Because this excuse is to a significant degree socially acceptable, it helps reduce the inhibition against raping as it does against killing. But compared with murderers, rapists are generally less violent, less likely to have previous arrest records for aggravated assault. Since rapists are not as violent as murderers, most rapes do not happen as explosively or impulsively as murders do; they do not spring from a sudden, uncontrolled sexual desire. Instead, rapes are mostly planned.

Planning and Execution

Since most rapes involve acquaintances, friends, or lovers, as Figure 5.1 shows, the planning largely entails the offender using sweet talk, romantic moves, alcoholic beverages, or some other means to induce the woman to have sex, and then single-mindedly striving to achieve his aim without paying any attention to her wishes. A typical example of this was already presented in the story at the beginning of this chapter.

But rapists operate differently if they do not know the victim well or at all. In such cases, offenders tend to choose women who, they believe, are vulnerable to attack. Such targets are in a disadvantaged situation so that they cannot react appropriately or swiftly to the threat of rape. Examples include a mentally challenged girl, a sleeping female, an old woman, or a young woman under the influence of alcohol or drugs. Other women are also more vulnerable to rape if they appear passive or submissive, lacking in assertiveness or confidence. A woman is said to suggest submissiveness to a potential rapist if she "walks slowly and tentatively, stares at the ground and moves her arms and legs in short, jerky motions." Yet some rapists prefer the opposite type of women—those who appear too aggressive or domineering. As many convicted rapists in one study indicated, "they wanted to put a particular uppity woman in her place" (Bart and O'Brien, 1985; Meer, 1984; Myers, Templer, and Brown, 1984). Apparently, women who project confidence without appearing too aggressive are less subject to rape.

If they cannot easily determine the vulnerability of a woman, rapists will likely work out a strategy to test her. They might first try to determine whether or not their selected target is a friendly and helpful person. A rapist might approach a woman on the street and ask her for a light or a street direction. If she provides it, he may proceed to ask her an intimate question, make some sexually suggestive remarks, put his arm around her, or touch her in a sexually provocative place to see how she reacts. If she reacts submissively or fearfully, he knows that she can be intimidated into submitting to his sexual demands. Another rapist might ask a woman to let him in her house to make an emergency phone call or for any other bogus reason. If the woman falls for such a ploy, the rapist may establish her as a prospective victim. An example follows:

> The rapist would walk into an apartment house and ring several doorbells asking for "Sally." When he found a woman who was helpful, attractive and presumably alone, he would explain how hot and tired he was and ask for a drink of water. Then he asked to use the bathroom so he could look around and make sure the victim was alone. Finally he would ask for a second drink of water and then approach the victim as she stood at the kitchen sink. With a knife at her throat and cut off from help, the victim usually capitulated. (Selkin, 1975)

After they have successfully identified a target for rape, the offenders initially do not resort to intimidation with such violent means as brandishing a weapon or administering a brutal beating. The majority of rapes involve only verbal coercion and nonphysical aggression, such as "Don't scream or I'll cut you to pieces," and "If you don't take your clothes off, I'll kill you!" (Kleck, 1990; Amir, 1971). Rapists ordinarily become more violent only when they are ready to carry out the crime. According to Pauline Bart and Patricia O'Brien (1985), the majority of the rapists in their study were rough—pushing, shoving, slapping, or choking their victims. Some rapists would not merely subject their victims to forced intercourse; they would also force them to submit to oral or anal sodomy and repeated vaginal assault. Sometimes rapists make jokes at their victims' expense. After he was through, one rapist proclaimed to his victim: "I'll marry you if you get pregnant" (Macdonald, 1995, 1971).

Gang Rape

Of all the rapes studied by Amir (1971), 43 percent were gang rapes. The most significant fact about these rapes is that the perpetrators are largely adolescents aged 10 to 19. Most of these young rapists come from lower-class families, and are members of street gangs. They find their victims in several ways. First, they may cruise an area looking for a female hitchhiker to pick up and driving the unsuspecting victim to a deserted area to rape her. Second, they may use a knife or gun to kidnap a woman from the street at night. Third, a member of the gang may make a date with a woman and then drive her, without her knowledge or consent, to a predetermined location where he and other members will rape her (Scully, 1990).

Occurring less frequently are gang rapes on college campuses, committed by middle- and upper-class youths. Gang rape takes place at various kinds of schools: large state universities, well-known liberal arts colleges, religious schools, and Ivy League institutions, where gang rape is often referred to as "running a train" on the victim. There is a pattern to the way campus gang rapes occur: At a party, the men encourage a woman to drink or take drugs and rape her when she gets drunk or high on drugs (Sanday, 1990; Brozan, 1986; Mann, 1985).

Why do those lower-class adolescents and college men participate in gang rapes? Psychiatrists generally interpret gang rape as an expression of latent homosexuality, arguing that the fellow rapists have an unconscious wish to have sex with each other (Sanday, 1990). Such an interpretation, however, makes as much sense as the suggestion that several men who rob a store together unconsciously want to rob each other or that a bunch of guys who go hunting together have a latent wish to kill each other. It seems more convincing to theorize that participation in a gang rape fulfills a social need more than a sexual desire, particularly for young boys who feel peer pressure to prove that they are not "chicken" (Groth and Birnbaum, 1979).

Similarly, college men who share a close relationship may find it hard to resist the pressure to participate in a gang rape because they are afraid of having their masculinity questioned. Moreover, through their camaraderie, they can playfully urge each other to participate in a gang rape without seeing it as a serious crime. This may explain why fraternity brothers and college athletes on some campuses are more likely than other students to engage in gang rape (Schwartz and DeKeseredy, 1997; O'Sullivan, 1991). In fact, the likelihood of committing gang rape is relatively great in other similarly cohesive or tightly knit groups. Examples are the Serbian soldiers gang-raping Muslim women in Bosnia in the early 1990s, Japanese soldiers gang-raping women in China and other Asian countries during World War II, and U.S. soldiers gang-raping women in Vietnam during the Vietnam War.

Acquaintance Rape

Compared with their counterparts in stranger rape, the offenders in acquaintance or date rape are more likely to use verbal or psychological coercion and less likely to resort to guns or knives. Verbal coercion may involve pressuring the victim by saying "C'mon, I know you really want it"; psychological coercion may involve making the victim feel inadequate as an object by ignoring her wishes when she says "Stop it!" Also, while stranger rapists typically premeditate the rape, acquaintance rapists tend more to premeditate only a sexual relation, which leads to rape when the victim refuses and the offender brushes her refusal aside, often assuming that she means yes when saying no (Jasper, 1992). Most victims of acquaintance rape see themselves as victims, but they are more likely than victims of stranger rape to blame the rape partly on themselves, such as for being careless or trusting the man too much (Bechhofer and Parrot, 1991). As one victim of acquaintance rape said,

> One summer while I was in college, I worked at a hamburger stand. There was a regular there. He seemed like a nice guy, and we'd gotten to know each other pretty well. He asked if I wanted to come over to his apartment that afternoon when I got off work and listen to a record he'd been telling me about. Once we were up there, he grabbed me, and when I pulled away, he turned up the music really loud and said I'd better not fight unless I wanted to lose some teeth. The music was blasting away—no one could have heard me if I yelled—and I knew he wasn't kidding, so I just let him do it. Afterward I told him what a jerk he was and tried to make him feel bad, but *I was the one who felt awful—how could I have been so stupid to let something like that happen, how could I have been so dumb?* (Mithers, 1980)

Acquaintance rape has always been a common offense. In the 1950s Clifford Kirkpatrick and Eugene Kanin (1957) asked a representative sample of 291 college women whether they had been sexually assaulted during the academic year. More than half (55.7%) replied that they had—at least once. Their experiences ranged from forced necking to forced petting to forced vaginal penetration. In the late 1970s, Kanin and Stanley Parcell (1981) did a follow-up study and found about the same result. In the mid-1980s *Ms.* magazine also found a similarly high incidence of sexual offense in its nationwide survey of more than 7000 college students on 35 campuses: 52 percent of all the women surveyed had encountered some form of sexual assault. The *Ms.* survey further showed that 15 percent were actually raped—forced to have sexual intercourse. Similar studies in the 1990s can be expected to show about the same result. In short, of all college women, *more than half* are sexually assaulted in one way or another and about *15 percent* are forcibly raped by their dates (Jackson, 1996; Koss et al., 1987; Sweet, 1985).

Acquaintance rape is this common because it appears to be an extension of, rather than a departure from, the conventional pattern of male sexual behavior (Schur, 1984). In our culture, where men are expected to be aggressive rather than shy in dealing with women, young men can easily go too far and use too much force to execute a sexual conquest. Not surprisingly, as suggested by one study, the more sexually active they are, the more likely they are to commit date rape (Kanin, 1985). Moreover, most of the rapists and even many of their victims do not regard date rape as real rape. In the *Ms.* survey, about 8 percent of the college men admitted to committing the sexual offenses that can be legally defined as rapes or attempted rapes, but virtually none of these men identified themselves as rapists. In the same survey, of the women who had been raped, nearly 75 percent did not identify their experiences as rape. They simply found it hard to believe that someone they knew could have raped them (Koss, 1995; Jasper, 1992; Sweet, 1985; Shotland and Goodstein, 1983).

Campus Rape

As we have observed, rape is particularly prevalent on college campuses, with about 15 percent of college women having been sexually assaulted. But most of the campus rapists, and even the majority of their victims, do not see the offense as forcible rape (Gilbert, 1995; Koss, 1995). Why not? The reason, as has been suggested, lies in the culture of the larger society that defines aggressiveness with women—rather than gentleness—as a highly desirable quality for young men to have. Campus rape, in other words, represents an extension of this culturally idealized male behavior. Thus the more sexually active men, who can be said to have acquired the highly desirable masculine trait as proven by their great success with women, are more likely than other men to commit date rape (Kanin, 1985).

While the larger society exerts its cultural influence on the college campus, is there something unique about the campus itself that also encourages sexual aggression? The answer from researchers on campus rape is yes. In her analysis of small tribal societies Peggy Sanday (1981) found that many are "rape-free" and a few "rape-prone." Rape-free societies have a culture that discourages sexual aggression while rape-prone societies have a culture that encourages it. More recently, Sanday (1996b) observed that there are also rape-free campuses and rape-prone campuses. On a rape-free campus, sexual assault is treated as a serious offense punishable by expulsion, fraternities discourage heavy drinking, women are respected as friends rather than used as sex objects, and gays and lesbians are accepted in the same way as straights. But on a rape-prone campus, sexual assault is not seriously dealt with, heavy drinking is encouraged, taking advantage of an intoxicated woman is accepted, bragging about sexual conquests is prevalent, homophobia is rampant, and pornography is a popular guide to female sexuality. Thus we can expect a higher incidence of sexual offense on rape-prone campuses.

Other researchers have made similar observations about what causes the high incidence of campus rape. Patricia Martin and Robert Hummer (1995) conclude from their study of fraternities that such student groups contribute heavily to campus rape in a number of ways through their unique norms and practices. First, the brotherhood norm requires "sticking together," which discourages anyone's stopping rapes when they occur or reporting them to outsiders. This form of "participation" effectively condones and encourages sexual violence. Second, fraternity norms emphasize the value of maleness and masculinity over femaleness and femininity, causing members to devalue women by using them as mere sex objects, which can lead to rapes when women resist. Third, certain fraternity practices that often lead to coercive sex include excessive use of alcohol and pressure from fellow members to prove one's masculinity through sexual conquests.

It must be said that not all studies have found these norms and practices to be unique to fraternities, or fraternity brothers to be more rape-prone than other college students. Martin Schwartz and Carol Nogrady (1996), for example, found that excessive alcohol use and peer pressure toward sexual aggression are just as prevalent among other college men (see also Schwartz and DeKeseredy, 1997). Studies on male athletes, though, have so far offered a more consistent conclusion: They are more rape-prone than other students because they subscribe more to the norms and practices presented above (Benedict, 1998; Crosset et al., 1996; Nelson, 1994; Koss and Gaines, 1993). Additional research is needed to determine which campus group is more rape-prone. For our purposes here and now, we may conclude that rape-prone culture exists in the larger society as well as on the college campus, which explains the relatively high incidence of sexual violence on campus.

The Myth of Victim Precipitation

In his classic study of the rapes in Philadelphia, Amir (1971) found that 19 percent were precipitated by the victims themselves. He refers to this kind of offense as "victim-precipitated rape," explaining that "the victim actually—or so it was interpreted by the offender—agreed to sexual relations but retracted before the actual act or did not resist strongly enough when the suggestion was made by the offender." A common victim behavior that Amir interprets as an invitation to sexual intercourse occurs when a woman agrees to have a drink or ride with a stranger. The implication here is that the victim is as much to blame as her offender. The following case has been given as an example of victim-precipitated rape:

An 18-year-old girl was standing in the parking lot of a hamburger drive-in when some men in a car called to her to come over to the car. When she reached the car, she thought she recognized one of the men so she sat in the front seat and started talking to them. Suddenly the driver started the car and drove off. They explained that they were looking for a friend. As they were driving, one of the men asked, "Do you want to fuck?" She laughed and said no. After stopping briefly at another drive-in, the man sitting alongside her put a gun to her head and said, "Are you scared?" She replied, "I don't like having a gun to my head and I am scared shitless, but I don't feel like crying and begging you because I don't feel like hassling you. You won't get any enjoyment out of being sadistic to me." The man turned to the men in the back of the car and said, "Well, what about it, do you want to or not?" They agreed to go ahead and rape her. (Macdonald, 1971)

The concept of victim-precipitated rape reflects a *biased,* male-centered view rather than an accurate description of the crime, and it has drawn criticisms for being a sexist myth. In the example quoted above, the young woman can be said to have "asked for it" only from a biased or rationalizing perspective. As attorney Camille LeGrand (1973) says, "Hitchhiking and walking alone at night in a rough neighborhood may be considered behavior encouraging a sexual attack. This view of what a *man* can assume to be a sexual invitation is unreasonable, because when the female hitchhiker first sets out to get a ride, she normally is not expecting—or hoping for—a sexual encounter."

Sociologist Eugene Kanin (1984) also argues that the concept of victim precipitation, which has been applied to some homicides as discussed in the preceding chapter, is not applicable to rapes. But Kanin contends that some victims do "contribute" in some way to being raped, in the same way as a man contributes to the burglary of his house by failing to stop newspaper delivery while away on vacation. Thus Kanin suggests using the term "victim contribution" to describe those cases of rape in which the victims have willingly engaged in deep kissing or some other form of advanced intimacy prior to the occurrence of the assault.

There could also be problems, however, with the concept of victim contribution. Most important, it amounts to suggesting that virtually all dating women contribute to rape because they usually engage in uncoerced intimacy with their dates. We should note that rape victims only contribute to the *pre*rape intimacy, comparable to the way the man whose house is burglarized contributes to the burglary by failing to stop newspaper delivery while away on vacation. The rape victims cannot be said to contribute to the rape itself because they try to stop it at the moment of the crime, just as the burglary victim cannot be said to contribute to the burglary if he had come home and tried to stop it. In brief, a fundamental difference exists between prerape intimacy, which does not involve the use of force and hence is not a crime, and rape itself, which involves the use of force and therefore is a crime.

Many men, however, do not seem to recognize this difference between consensual prerape intimacy and forced sex. According to one study, 50 percent of the young men interviewed consider it "acceptable for a man to force a girl to have sexual intercourse when she initially consents but then changes her mind, or when she has sexually excited him" (Shotland and Goodstein, 1983). A more recent study found that 76 percent of high school male students regard forced sex as acceptable under similar circumstances (White and Humphrey, 1991). These young men, in effect, blame the victim. It reflects the popular myth that it is her fault if she is flirting, if she is attractively dressed, if she is in the man's perception "a tease," if she joins him for a drink, if she invites him to her apartment for coffee after having gone to a movie with him, or, sometimes, even if she only says "hello" to him at the office (Norris and Cubbins, 1992; Burt, 1991).

Consequences of Rape

Rape is in a way unique, different from murder, robbery, and most other crimes. While each of these other crimes is largely a finished act after it has occurred, rape is more likely to be a continuing process, in which the survivor keeps on suffering after the rape is over. Let us examine the survivor's experiences in the aftermath of the sexual assault.

The Rape Survivor's Response

The response to rape varies from one survivor to another. At one extreme are the survivors who show a lack of concern. One such survivor, when asked what happened between the two attacks of rape by her assailant, replied, "We went out for hamburgers." Some fall asleep after the rape; others are more upset over the theft of a purse, a ring, a transistor radio, or similar property than over the rape; some survivors may voluntarily engage in sexual relations with their assailant when they meet him again after the rape; other survivors may later marry their rapists, whom they may or may not have met prior to the rape (Macdonald, 1995, 1971). At the opposite extreme are the survivors who are so traumatized that they sink into deep depression, attempt to commit suicide, or actually kill themselves. In between these two extremes are the great majority who initially experience shock, disbelief, anger, anxiety, or depression, but eventually pull themselves out of it.

This diversity of reactions to rape is apparently related to such factors as the degree of violence, the age of the survivor, her social class or cultural background, and prior sexual experience. If she has been violently raped, is relatively young, comes from a middle- or upper-class family, or has had no or little previous sexual experience, she is likely to suffer relatively severe consequences. Other factors also have a significant impact on how rape survivors feel. The trauma will be much greater, for example, if the survivor has experienced a major life change (divorce, separation, or unemployment) within a year prior to the rape (Ruch, Chandler, and Harter, 1980). Similarly, survivors of stranger rape are far more likely than survivors of acquaintance rape to have the most persistent depression, fear, and interpersonal problems because stranger rapes are generally more violent (Ellis, Atkeson, and Calhoun, 1981). But survivors of acquaintance rape suffer more from self-blame, primarily because society holds them responsible in some way. They also distrust men more and longer, because their earlier trust in men has been betrayed through rape (Gidycz and Ross, 1991; Katz, 1991; Mandoki and Burkhart, 1991).

Most rape survivors go through two phases of disorganization before they gradually and finally regain their ability to live normally. From the time immediately following the rape to a few days or weeks thereafter is the *acute phase* of disorganization. During this phase most survivors succumb to *extreme* fear, shock, humiliation, embarrassment, self-blame, or anxiety. After this initial, acute phase is over, survivors generally go through a *longer, lingering phase* of disorganization, which often lasts for a few months, but may persist for several years. In this phase survivors experience a variety of phobic reactions, including the fear of being alone and fear of sex. Understandably, survivors suffer from an increased risk of divorce, reduced income, and unemployment (Byrne et al., 1999; Burgess, 1995; Holmstrom and Burgess, 1983).

You may notice the nature of the survivors' feelings: Fear, depression, anxiety, and self-blame are inward-directed. Other possible feelings are outward-directed, such as anger, revenge, and the courage to have the rapist kept behind bars. While most rape survivors are gnawed by the passive, inward-directed feelings, a few others express the outward-directed feelings. One rape survivor with these feelings said, "I have fantasies about cutting off his dick and balls," and another said, "Never in my life had I felt such hate for another human being. I wish I had jammed my fingers into his eyes" (Madigan and Gamble, 1991). Interestingly, such active, angry survivors tend to feel better about themselves and swing back faster to their normal lives. As Pauline Bart and Patricia O'Brien (1984) have found, rape survivors who have resisted their attacker by screaming and kicking readjust more easily to life than passive survivors who have yielded to crying and pleading. Survivors of acquaintance rape can also recover faster if they learn to see the rape as totally their attacker's fault (Gidycz and Koss, 1991).

Since the early 1970s, primarily due to the women's movement, an increasing number of rape survivors not only have expressed their outward-directed feelings, they also have actively tried to combat rape by setting up such antirape organizations as Anti-Rape Squad, WAR (Women Against Rape), Rape Crisis Center, Rape Hot Line, and Rape Action Coalition. The function of these organizations is to help the rape survivor, organize Speak Out on Rape conferences, teach self-defense classes, get special rape squads established in police departments, encourage rape survivors to report offenders, and pressure legislatures to pass laws that would make it easier to convict the rapist, who is still likely to go scot-free. This movement against rape got its major impetus in 1971 when a topless dancer in California came to a local feminist meeting with a complaint: She had been hired to dance at a stag party given in honor of a man about to be married. After the performance, all the men raped her and then threw her out. The feminists later picketed the wedding with signs that read: "THE BRIDEGROOM IS A RAPIST." Word of this incident traveled across the country (Lear, 1972b).

Since then organized women have been offering such postrape services as getting the survivor to the hospital, providing venereal disease and AIDS prevention, pregnancy tests, and, if necessary, abortion and psychiatric help, as well as offering moral support at the police station and legal aid in the courtroom.

Antirape organizations also offer courses in self-defense. These courses may require formal training in one of the martial arts, such as judo, karate, or kung-fu, and they usually also instruct women on how to deal with potential and actual rapists. Thus, a woman might use an object in her purse or on her person—such as a comb, a nail file, an umbrella, high-heeled shoes, hairspray, or perfume—to stun or blind the rapist temporarily to give herself time to flee. A woman should scream, bite, claw with fingernails, pull the rapist's hair, or kick his crotch.

It may reasonably be expected that the impact of rape will change in the future. More and more women who are raped will likely stop plunging into the traditional self-destructive feelings of fear, anxiety, and guilt and will, instead, take the active, constructive steps to give peace to themselves but none to the rapist.

The Feeling of Being Raped Again

In the 1960s and 1970s both popular writers and social scientists published many horror stories about how police officers were grossly insensitive in dealing with rape survivors. For example, when a survivor gave a calm, rational account of the rape, she was asked, "What are you, some kind of sociologist?" If the woman was not physically attractive, her report of rape was dismissed as just another fantasy of a sex-starved woman. A middle-aged mother who reported having been raped might be asked by a young policeman: "Did he come?" (Geis and Geis, 1979; Sheehy, 1971b).

When those blatant insults from the police were added to the physical and psychological injury from the rapist, survivors of sexual assault could not help feeling that they were being raped again. Although the "second rape" by the police described above is only psychological, the impact can be just as painful or traumatic as that of the first rape by the criminal (Madigan and Gamble, 1991). Today, in the 1990s, police officers are generally much more polite and respectful to rape survivors, but many survivors continue to suffer the second rape because the police tend to make them feel responsible for the first rape by questioning their moral character. In many cases police officers ask a woman who comes to report being raped whether, for example, "she agreed to have drinks with the man, accepted or offered him a ride, or left with him after a party," whether she "has ever been arrested for soliciting or is a known prostitute," or whether she has resisted by squirming, struggling, and screaming even if the rape was carried out with a gun or knife (Madigan and Gamble, 1991). The presumption behind these questions is that the rape survivor might have "asked for it." The police in effect blame the victim rather than the criminal.

If the police find their "blame the victim" presumption proven wrong, they will proceed to file a complaint against the alleged rapist. In the court, however, the woman is likely to suffer another psychological rape. In the not-too-distant past, many rape survivors described their courtroom experience as "worse than the rape itself."

A case in point is a woman who brought charges against a 36-year-old man in a San Francisco superior court in the late 1960s. According to the victim, the accused, along with three other men, forced her into a car at gunpoint. She was taken to the accused's fashionable apartment where he and the three other men first raped her and then subjected her to other forms of sexual humiliation. The police, who later searched the apartment, discovered four address books containing the names of hundreds of women. One of those names was the accuser's, which had been crossed out. In court several women testified that the accused had lured them to his apartment and then forced intercourse on them. But the defense attorney argued that his client was a playboy who often picked up girls in bars and took them to his house where sexual relations took place with their consent—and that the accuser was simply one of those willing playmates. Then the same attorney, through clever questioning, portrayed her as a loose, sex-crazed woman. He accused her of "being familiar with liquor," "having left her job as a secretary after it was discovered that she had sexual intercourse on a couch in the office," "having a sexual affair with a man while she worked as an attendant at a health club," "living with a married man," "having spent the night with another man who lived in the same building," and "encouraging her two children to have a sex game in which one gets on top of another." The rape victim protested, "Am I on trial? . . . I did not commit a crime. I am a human being." Although she also protested that all those accusations by the defense attorney were lies, the jury did not believe her. Instead, they believed the defense lawyer's portrayal of her as a "bad" woman, and so acquitted the rapist of both charges— rape and kidnapping. The courtroom experience thus made the woman a victim of another rape. As a leaflet passed out by women in front of the courtroom pointedly stated, "Rape was earlier committed by four men in a private apartment; now it has just been done by a judge and a lawyer in a public courtroom" (Landau, 1974; Griffin, 1971).

Similar cases can be found today (Sanday, 1996a; Vachss, 1994). Essentially, defense attorneys focus on the victim's sexual history or reputation in order to discredit her. In effect, they put her on trial, accusing her of having "asked for it." Since the mid-1970s there have been some legal reforms. At least eight states have renamed rape "criminal sexual assault" or some other term designed to focus the law on what the alleged criminal rather than the victim did. Nearly all states have tried to make the rape survivor's day in court less horrendous by enacting "rape shield" laws, which ostensibly prohibit the admissibility of evidence regarding the victim's previous sexual experience (Spohn and Horney, 1992). Nevertheless, defense lawyers can still get around the rape shield laws by subtly revealing the rape survivor's sexual history.

In one typical case, for example, the defense called the jury's attention to the fact that the rape survivor's address was the same as that of her boyfriend, whom she had known for just one week. This was obviously meant to suggest that she was sexually immoral. The tactic worked, as one juror later admitted, "We weren't supposed to judge her as to her past relations, but it came out that she was living with her boyfriend of 1 week. It was hard not to judge her"

(LaFree, Reskin, and Visher, 1985). Many defense lawyers continue to use similar tactics to put the victim on trial. They will dig out testimony about the victim's drinking, drug use, extramarital sex, birth of an illegitimate child, prior acquaintance or sex between her and the alleged rapist, or some other aspect of her lifestyle that can be used to make jurors question her character and credibility (Sanday, 1996a; Vachss, 1994).

Many judges allow such evidence to be presented to the jury because they believe that without it the defendant cannot get a fair trial. This is what a judge did in 1993 at the trial of four young men in Glen Ridge, New Jersey, who were charged with raping a 17-year-old woman. The judge allowed evidence of the woman's sexual history on the ground that the defendants could only get a fair trial if they were allowed to use the evidence. In presenting the evidence, the defense argued that the woman had willingly performed the sex acts with the young men (Lewin, 1993b). Such an argument actually reflects the popular myth that the rape victim asked for it, and this myth is one of the components of the rape culture.

The Culture of Rape

Obviously many societies openly condemn rape as a serious crime. Less obviously, however, those same societies have a hidden culture of rape—a culture that encourages men to sexually assault women. Of course, the rape culture does not affect all men in the same way; otherwise, all men would rape. Some men are more inclined than others to rape, though they all live under the influence of the same culture. Research has suggested that those who are immature, irresponsible, and lacking in social conscience are more influenced by the rape culture (Sapp et al., 1999; Rapaport and Burkhart, 1984). But what is the nature of this rape culture? We can see it through the prevailing attitudes toward women as well as through the popular concept of male and female sex roles.

Treating Women Like Men's Property

On the face of it the law against rape appears to protect the interests of the female. Actually it protects to a larger degree the interests of the male. This is because the female is treated like a piece of property that before marriage belongs to her father and after marriage belongs to her husband. If a man rapes an unmarried girl, he is, in effect, considered to be committing the crime of vandalism against her father. If a man rapes a married woman, he is considered to be committing the crime against her husband. Thus statutory rape laws "help preserve the 'market value' of virginal young women as potential brides, rather than [protect] the naive girls from sexual exploitation" (LeGrand, 1973). As for forcible rape laws, Susan Griffin (1971) explains:

> The laws against rape exist to protect rights of the male as possessor of the female body, and not the right of the female over her own body. Even . . . the laws them-

selves are clear: [In some states a man cannot be] accused of raping his wife. How can any man steal what already belongs to him? It is in the sense of rape as theft of another man's property that Kate Millett writes, "Traditionally rape has been viewed as an offense one male commits against another—a matter of abusing his woman." In raping another man's woman, a man may aggrandize his own manhood and concurrently reduce that of another man. Thus a man's honor is not subject directly to rape, but only indirectly, through "his" woman.

In marriage men traditionally feel entitled to use their wives as a sexual commodity in any way they want. As one senator opposed to making marital rape a crime said, "When you get married, you kind of expect you're going to get a little sex" (Blakely, 1983).

The absence of marital-rape laws in some states, and the rarity of husbands being imprisoned for raping their wives in all the other states, reflects the treatment of women as men's property. This component of the rape culture also comes across in other ways: For example, when a woman has been raped, it is often said that she has been "ravaged," "ravished," "despoiled," or "ruined." These words connote the idea that a raped woman is like a piece of property that has been damaged. Further, when a man's wife has been raped, he tends to feel as if she is less "lovable" than before—in about the same way as he would feel about a piece of damaged property. If he regarded her as a human being who has feelings rather than an object that does not have feelings, logically the husband should show her more love, affection, or understanding—particularly because, after being raped, she needs emotional support as a human being the most. Instead, her husband tends to show her less love than before, as if she had turned into a piece of damaged property with no feeling and very little value. This is why many men say something like "I can't see how I can face my wife again if she has been raped." It is not surprising that rape has the tendency to wreck or strain the victim's relationship with her husband, fiancé, or boyfriend. In fact, 75 to 85 percent of the marriages in which the wife has been raped end in divorce within two years following the sexual assault (Gordon and Riger, 1989).

Continuing to uncover these parallel assumptions, it is accepted that the more often an object has been used, the less valuable it is considered. Similarly, in a society where women are treated as sex objects, the more often a woman has engaged in sex with various men, the less valuable a property she is judged to be. A woman with very little value is referred to as a "cheap woman," "loose woman," "easy lay," "slut," or "whore." Thus, just as a man who steals or damages another's relatively worthless property can easily get away with it, so a man who ravages a relatively "cheap" woman—"common" property—can get away with it. This may be why it is difficult for a rapist to be convicted if his victim is known to have engaged in sex relations with more than two men—and it is virtually impossible for the rapist to be convicted if his victim is a known prostitute. Also, since black or poor women are considered as less valuable sex objects than white or rich women, raping the former carries a lesser risk of conviction than raping the latter. Raping a woman who is simultaneously African American, poor, and sexually experienced is especially unlikely to result in conviction. This is why, in a case involving the rape of a young, poor, black woman, a juror argued for acquittal by saying that "a girl her age from 'that kind of neighborhood' probably wasn't a virgin anyway" (LaFree, Reskin, and Visher, 1985). In fact, many convicted rapists themselves do not feel guilty for having raped known prostitutes, "loose" women, "promiscuous" women, or women with an "illegitimate" child. The rapists apparently see these women as cheap ("available") sexual commodities that men are entitled to use (Scully and Marolla, 1984).

To take up a broader indication, throughout human history, when conquering armies confiscated or destroyed the conquered population's property, they also raped the women as if they were part of that property. During World War II, German soldiers raped massive numbers of Jewish and Russian women after occupying many villages and cities in Europe, and the Japanese army systematically raped women and girls as it invaded Korea, China, and various Southeast Asian countries. In 1971, when the Pakistani army marched into Bangladesh, soldiers were first shown pornographic movies and then were allowed to rape at least 200,000 women. In 1992 Serbian soldiers in Bosnia raped thousands of Muslim women as part of their "ethnic cleansing" campaign. In 1994 the Hutus in Rwanda, who at that time dominated the country, raped massive numbers of Tutsi women. In 1999 when the Serbian forces took over Kosovo they raped ethnic Albanian women. After having been raped by foreign soldiers, women tended to be regarded as irreparably damaged property and therefore valueless. In some countries their husbands and other relatives would throw them out of their homes as they would junk (Bumiller, 1999; Brownmiller, 1993; Post, 1993; Swiss and Giller, 1993; Medea and Thompson, 1974).

Lastly, the widespread availability of pornography, especially the type that shows violence against women, reinforces the popular image of women as men's sex objects. By degrading women in this way, pornography increases men's callousness toward women. As several studies have shown, extended exposure to pornography tends to cause men to trivialize rape. After viewing pornography for some time, the men in these studies advocated less severe punishment for rapists and expressed less sympathy for the victims (Segal, 1993; Linz, Donnerstein, and Penrod, 1984; Zillman and Bryant, 1982). Pornography apparently encourages rape by producing sexual callousness toward women. This does not mean that pornography by itself causes rape, as it does not have the same impact on all men. But it does make certain men dangerous to women. As research has demonstrated, pornography tends to incite violent, angry men to rape (Gray, 1982).

Since women are culturally defined as men's property, men may find it difficult to respect women as human beings. It is through a lack of respect for women that men are encouraged to rape women, as rape expresses the very essence of this lack of respect for women. Not surprisingly, as sociologists Diana Scully and Joseph Marolla (1985) found in their interviews with 114 convicted rapists, "the overwhelming majority of these rapists indicated they never thought they would go to prison for what they did." These men regard women as sexual objects that they are entitled to use for pleasure, or as one young rapist confided to Scully, "Rape is a man's right. If a woman doesn't want to give it, the man should take it. Women have no right to say no. Women are made to have sex. It's all they are good for. Some women would rather take a beating, but they always give in; it's what they are for" (Scully and Marolla, 1985).

Using Women in Men's Masculinity Contests

In a society that places a high premium on competition, men are pressured to engage in what may be called a masculinity contest to prove their male prowess and to earn a macho reputation among peers (Fields, 1993). To come out a winner, a man has to make out with the largest number of women possible.

> And that means sex under whatever conditions the particular man can stand. Whether in a whorehouse or the backseat of a Toyota, the object is to score. However, your score counts more if you don't pay for it in cold hard cash. The most respected player in the game is the one who best outwits the most females by coaxing, lying, maneuvering; the one who, with the least actual cost to himself, gets the most females to give him the most sex. (Medea and Thompson, 1974)

This masculinity contest is comparable to such competitive sports as football, baseball, soccer, and tennis. In any one of these sports, the players need an object—say, a ball—to grab, hit, kick, or smash. Their goal is to score, and they couldn't care less whether they hurt the ball. Similarly, in the masculinity contest, the male participants need an object—namely, a woman—to play with. They don't care whether they may end up humiliating, degrading, hurting, or terrifying her as a human being. Their goal is to score, as was well illustrated in 1993 by the Spur Posse, a gang of high school boys in the Los Angeles suburb of Lakewood. Members of this group competed with one another to score points for sexual conquests, one point for each sexual encounter, whether the girl consented or not. In such a masculinity contest, men see the woman as merely an object, often referring to her as a "piece of meat," a "piece of ass," a "box," or a "whore." A victim of a gang rape reported that she was indeed treated that way; after they had finished with her, one of the rapists said, "Let's dump this one and find another piece of meat" (Medea and Thompson, 1974).

Such a dehumanizing attitude toward women can further be found in the language that men use to refer to sexual intercourse as if it were a manly game of violence and conquest. American soldiers in Vietnam used to speak of dragging women into the woods for a little "boom boom," as if the penis—the rape weapon—sounded like a gun. To "bang" a woman—to have sex with her—also has the violent sound of a gun. Words, such as "whacking off, screwing, fucking, scoring, shooting off, and knocking up," also give off the tough sound of conquest (Blakely, 1983). This dehumanizing language and attitude toward women may encourage men to play the masculinity game. Whether they will actually do so depends on at least two things: (1) the social pressure to play the game and (2) learning some basic pointers for playing it.

The social pressure often comes from friends who ask something like "Did you score?" "Had any lately?" "Does she put out?" If you answer no, they may say, "What's the matter? You ain't got no balls?" Such social pressure tends to make men, especially teenage males, afraid of showing any sign of "femininity"—being soft, gentle, and considerate. It also tends to make them want to show off their "masculine" qualities—being aggressive, forceful, and violent. A likely consequence is that these men will engage in sexual violence, of one degree or another, against women at some point. As research has shown, the most important factor that distinguishes sexually aggressive males from others is the peer pressure, which comes from sexually aggressive friends (Alder, 1985).

As to the pointers for playing the masculinity game, they come with the masculine role that men have been taught to play. This role requires that the man take the active part in achieving the social and then the sexual relations with a woman. He should be as aggressive as possible to carry out his sexual conquest. He need not concern himself with how much force he is allowed to use. Our culture puts that burden on the woman, who is held responsible for determining the limit of the force he is allowed. But even when the woman bluntly tells him to stop or puts up a fight to ward off his sexual advances, he may still ignore her resistance (Sanday, 1996a; Fillion, 1991). Men often get this lesson in sexual conquest from the stereotype of the television or movie hero who forcefully, persistently embraces and kisses the heroine despite her strong resistance and is finally rewarded by her melting in his arms. In real life such sexual aggression may lead to forcible rape.

The Myth That Women Ask for It

There is a popular myth that women have a secret wish to be raped. As shown by various studies, most people believe that women have an unconscious rape wish. This myth is expressed in various ways and often: "She asked for it," "She actually wanted it," "She lied about it (or consented to sex but later decided to "cry rape")," and "She was not really hurt (or it was only a form of sex, though without her consent)" (Lonsway and Fitzgerald, 1994; Brinson, 1992). In essence, many people—particularly men—hold the victim responsible for the rape. They assume that the victim did something that provoked the man to rape her. That "something" involves being in the "wrong" place (going to a bar or walking alone at night), wearing the "wrong" clothes (short shorts, miniskirts, or some other sexy dress), or turning the man on (letting him kiss or pet her) (Vachss, 1994; Brinson, 1992).

These blame-the-victim rationalizations reflect society's sexist attempt to "put women in their place," denying them the freedom that men enjoy. The rationalizations also stem from the popular assumption that rape is only sexually motivated. This explains why men tend to blame physically unattractive women more than attractive ones for rape. They find it difficult to believe that a man would try very hard to have sex with an unattractive woman if she keeps on resisting. They assume that, since it is less easy for unattractive women to attract men, they would be more inclined to encourage rapes by flirting, dressing sexily, or in some other way presenting a sexually provocative appearance. In short, men tend to consider unattractive women more likely to fantasize about rape and ask for it when a rapist appears (Vachss, 1994; Deitz et al., 1984; Thornton and Ryckman, 1983).

The myth about women wanting to be raped is understandably popular with rapists, which may help explain why they committed the crime in the first place. According to various studies, most convicted rapists, even those serving long prison terms, deny their culpability. Stubbornly, they insist that their victims have encouraged and enjoyed the experience, or that their victims have seduced them, meant yes while saying no to the sexual assault, and eventually relaxed and enjoyed the rape (Vachss, 1994; Scully and Marolla, 1985; Selkin, 1975). The willing-victim myth also prevails in the courtroom. While a man charged with rape is presumed innocent until proven guilty, the rape victim is often presumed guilty until proven innocent of provoking the rape. In the past, defense lawyers often argued to the court how impossible it is to rape a woman if she resists with statements such as "You can't thread a moving needle" or "You can't put a pencil through a moving doughnut." Today, most defense lawyers have abandoned such crude tactics to suggest that the victim "has asked for it." But they manage to convey the same message by emphasizing that she has willingly danced with him at a bar, accepted his invitation to go to his apartment, or asked him to wear a condom before the intercourse. These less blatant tactics often result in the acquittal of the accused rapist because many jurors are influenced by the same popular myth (Vachss, 1994; LaFree, Reskin, and Visher, 1985).

Because of the willing-victim myth, when a woman declines a man's sexual invitation, he is likely to keep on pressuring her: "What's the matter, are you frigid? Oh, come on, you know you really want to." If he eventually rapes her, he will assume that she has consented, even though she has strongly resisted all along (Sanday, 1996a; Vachss, 1994).

Socializing Girls to Be Victims

To make it easier for men to rape women, the rape culture teaches girls to play the stereotypically feminine role. In contrast to boys, who are taught to be "snips and snails and puppy dogs' tails," girls are taught to be "sugar and spice and everything nice." In other words, while boys learn to be tough and active, girls learn to be sweet and passive. Girls also learn from the movies and other mass media that women like macho men and expect such men to be rough with them. Slasher films and rock videos, in particular, teach young women to associate sex with violence. In learning all this as part of the feminine role, the girl acquires two tendencies that make her a potential victim of rape. One is to be "feminine"—passive, gentle, weak, childlike, and dependent on men. The other is to be submissive to aggressive or violent men (Graham with Rawlings and Rigsby, 1994; Warshaw and Parrot, 1991).

To be feminine means that she is physically unaggressive and psychologically unprepared to defend herself in hand-to-hand combat. Thus, when she encounters her would-be rapist, especially one who is her acquaintance or date, she is unlikely to gouge his eyes, kick him in the groin or genitals, or otherwise blind, maim, or kill him. Being ladylike also involves being submissive to men. A "lady" does not shout, scream, scratch, hit, or otherwise make a scene when she is offended by a man. In public places such as buses, subways, elevators, and theaters, she is not supposed to react aggressively to sexual harassment. She is expected to find it too embarrassing to make a public scene in response to such "sex grabs" as the touching of her legs or behind by a molesting male (Weis and Borges, 1973). It is, therefore, not surprising that, as studies have suggested, traditionally passive or submissive women are the ideal victims for rapists. They are more likely than assertive women to be chosen as potential victims, and when they are approached by a potential rapist, they are also more likely to end up raped (Bart and O'Brien, 1985; Myers, Templer, and Brown, 1984).

Why Men Rape

Various researchers have tried to explain why some men are more likely than others to rape women or why some groups or societies have a higher incidence of forcible rape. Psychologists generally attribute rape to some psychological problem in the offender. Sociologists, on the other hand, see rapists as basically normal, psychologically no different from the average population. Various sociologists, however, explain rape differently: Some use a social-psychological theory to attribute rape to sexual permissiveness in society and others rely on a feminist theory to view rape as an expression of gender inequality.

Psychological Theory: Sexual Inadequacy

Generally, psychologists, psychiatrists, and psychoanalysts agree that rapists suffer from some personality defects or emotional disturbance. "The majority of such offenders are not insane," write two psychologists, "nor are they simply healthy and aggressive young men 'sowing some wild oats.' The rapist is, in fact, a person who has serious psychological difficulties which handicap him in his relationships to other people and which he discharges, when he is under stress, through sexual [violence]" (Groth, 1983; Groth and Birnbaum, 1979). And a group of psychiatrists state, "It is true that classic neurotic symptoms are a rarity, but all types of character neuroses, character disorders, and more severe borderline and psychotic states are represented in rapists. It is equally clear that there are some specific characteristics present in rapists which differentiate them from other criminals and from other sexual offenders" (Cohen et al., 1971). One psychologist sums up all this by saying, "What's wrong with a sex offender is what's between his ears, not his legs" (Gelman et al., 1994).

Disagreement abounds over what the *specific* psychological problem is. The problem that has been theorized to reside in rapists ranges from feelings of sexual inadequacy to fear of homosexual tendency to sexual addiction (Herman, 1995; Goldner, 1972). According to a typical psychological theory, the rapist is a man who, as the result of his unpleasant childhood experiences, has developed such a personality defect that he cannot relate successfully to women—a defect called "sexual inadequacy." This inadequacy drives the rapist to indulge in fantasy and then act out this fantasy by raping a woman. Here is how a rapist describes his fantasy:

> I had a complete fantasy life that involved my being stronger than all men, irresistible to all women, a doer of great things. . . . I had fantasies about the woman I was raping, how she felt physically, where she had been in life, some resentment that she's done things in life without me. I had a longing to do things in general with people. Sometimes I'd verbalize these fantasies if the woman was quite submissive, otherwise I'd just take the trip within myself. (Selkin, 1975)

But psychological theories such as this can explain only a few cases of rape. True, there are some rapists who, because of their psychological problems, cannot relate to women well. However, they make up only a small minority of rapists. In prisons, for example, the majority of rapists appear quite normal, no different from other convicts who have committed robbery, theft, or some other nonsexual crime. In an experimental study in which the subjects were asked to chat with a woman for as long as they wanted, the convicted rapists were just as skilled and relaxed as the nonrapists (Scully, 1990; Alder, 1984).

The psychological theory of sexual inadequacy is even less applicable to the countless rapists, especially acquaintance rapists, outside of prisons. Far from sexually inadequate, most of these rapists are highly skillful in dealing with women. In fact, as indicated by Eugene Kanin's (1985) study, the date rapists in college are far more heterosexually successful than other male students—they have had more dates and more consensual sexual experiences (see also Rapaport and Posey, 1991).

Social-Psychological Theory: Sexual Permissiveness

Sociologist Duncan Chappell and his colleagues (1971) ask why the rate of rape is higher in some societies than in others. The reason, they theorized, is that the society with a higher rape rate is, ironically, more sexually permissive—full of opportunities for men to have consensual nonmarital sex with women. Why would more men resort to force to get sex in a society where it is relatively easy to get sex without the use of force? The answer, according to the theorists, lies in the concept of relative frustration: When encountering the *same* experience of being rejected by a woman, the men in a sexually permissive society feel *more frustrated* than the men in a sexually restrictive society in which premarital and other nonmarital sex is prohibited. But why?

In a sexually restrictive society, a man is more able to take a woman's rejection in stride. This is because he can protect his ego by rationalizing that she has rejected him not because he is in some way undesirable but because the restrictive society prevents her from accepting his sexual invitation. He may take comfort from the fact that women are too sexually conservative, too afraid to engage in nonmarital sex, that their religion condemns such sex, or that laws against nonmarital sex are too stringent. In a sexually permissive society the rejected man cannot use this kind of rationalization. Instead, he is more likely to take the woman's rebuff personally, seeing that it is he himself who is responsible for his own failure to win the woman's favors. As a consequence, he is likely to feel hurt, thereby experiencing sexual frustration. This sexual frustration is said to drive many men in a permissive society such as the United States or Sweden to rape women (Geis and Geis, 1979; Chappell, Geis, Schafer, and Siegel, 1971).

In short, the social atmosphere of sexual permissiveness produces a great number of rapes because it generates a great deal of relative frustration by causing men to take a woman's rejection personally. This theory may explain why modern societies such as the United States and Sweden have higher rates of rape today than a century ago or why modern societies have higher rates than traditional societies. It seems obvious that modern societies are more sexually permissive than traditional ones. Feminists, however, question the theory's assumption that rape is mostly sexually motivated. To feminists, rape is primarily motivated by the man's desire to dominate the woman because of gender inequality.

Feminist Theory: Gender Inequality

The social-psychological theory of sexual permissiveness seems to suggest that gender equality produces more rapes than does sexual inequality. This is because relative gender equality is more prevalent in the more sexually permissive societies such as Sweden and other industrialized Western societies than in the more sexually restrictive, traditional societies in the developing world. But feminist theorists blame rape on sexual inequality. To feminists, rape is primarily an expression of men's dominance over women, which in turn is a reflection of society's sexual inequality. Rape, then, serves to intimidate women, keeping them in their place to maintain sexual inequality (Edwards, 1993; Peterson, 1992; Schwendinger and Schwendinger, 1983; Brownmiller, 1975).

The evidence on rape as an expression of male dominance exists everywhere. All over the world, no matter which society we go to, we are bound to find that the overwhelming majority of rapes involve men raping women rather than women raping men. At the same time, men generally have greater physical, political, or economic power than women. We may therefore conclude that rape is largely an expression of male power over women. An abundance of more specific evidence also exists to support the feminist theory. In her study of tribal societies, for example, Peggy Sanday (1981) finds that some of these societies are relatively free of rapes while others are full of rapes. She discovers that male dominance is a key feature of rape-prone societies, defined as societies in which rape is treated as a ceremonial expression of masculinity or where men are allowed to use rape to punish or threaten women. Other researchers have further found that the incidence of rape is high in colleges where masculinity and male dominance are highly valued (Schwartz and DeKeseredy, 1997; Martin and Hummer, 1995; Schwartz, 1995).

Nevertheless, the feminist theory of gender inequality has drawn fire for exaggerating the influence of male dominance on rape. As the major inspiration of the theory, Susan Brownmiller (1975) has often been faulted for arguing that "from prehistoric times to the present, I believe, rape has played a critical function. It is nothing more or less than a conscious process of intimidation by which *all men* keep *all women* in a state of fear." But critics have observed that not all men would use rape to intimidate all women, and that it is easy to think of numerous men who do not want to dominate women by raping them, especially if the women are their mothers and daughters. Through her forceful statement, however, Brownmiller probably means to say that rape is a primary expression—rather than the sole expression—of male dominance.

Males as Victims

According to popular belief, men are simply "too big," "too strong," or "too much in control" to be sexually assaulted. But there is growing evidence in the 1990s that at least 10,000 American men are raped every year. The risk of a man being raped by another man or by a woman is still far less than the risk of a woman being raped by a man. According to surveys in several large cities, males make up only 1 to 10 percent of rape victims. Surveys on U.S. campuses, however, reveal considerably more male victims: 12 to 48 percent of male college students are forced or pressured to have nonconsensual sex. Most of these sexual assaults involve women using verbal pressure such as pleading, demands, or blackmail rather than physical force. In the fewer cases where men are raped by men, though, most offenders use physical force, with sodomy being the most common mode of assault (Gillespie, 1996; Struckman-Johnson, 1991; Kaufman et al., 1980; Groth and Birnbaum, 1979). Male assailants are more likely than female assailants to use physical force because the men's victims are much more likely than the women's victims to be strangers. By contrast, female assailants are more likely to use verbal pressure because their victims are more likely to be their acquaintances (see Table 5.1). Let us take a closer look at these two types of rape: man raping man and woman raping man.

Same-Sex Rape

Although male assailants are far more likely than their female counterparts to be strangers to the victim, nearly half the male assailants know their victim as their peer, coworker, subordinate, or date. These acquaintance rapes include attacks by men meeting their victims at parties or bars, gang rapes in the Navy and other military settings, and seduction with pressure by trusted men such as doctors, psychotherapists, priests, and teachers. Most victims are in their late teens or early twenties. Slightly more than half of the victims are heterosexual. More than half of the offenders are also heterosexual. The rapist assaults his victim mostly out of anger, with the intent to punish or dominate, rather than sexual pleasure (Scarce, 1997; Struckman-Johnson, 1991).

TABLE 5.1   Assailant's Sex and Relation to Male Victim

Assailant's Relation to Male Victim	Sex of Assailant	
	Percent Male	Percent Female
Stranger	39.4	6.7
Acquaintances	48.9	57.6
Relative	2.7	0.7
Lover/Spouse	2.1	32.7
Other*	6.8	2.3
TOTAL	100%	100%

*This includes "employer, teacher, and unspecified."

Source: Data derived from Cindy Struckman-Johnson, "Male Victims of Acquaintance Rape," in Laurie Bechhofer and Andrea Parrot (Eds.), *Acquaintance Rape: The Hidden Crime* (New York: John Wiley & Sons, 1991), p. 195.

Same-sex rape can be illustrated with a few actual cases of a man sexually assaulting a man: (1) A heterosexual man became intoxicated at an office party. He let his boss drive him home. He passed out in the car, but he soon woke up to find himself in the backseat, with his pants down, being anally entered by the boss. (2) A college male student, who was gay, met an older man at a bar. He went to the older man's apartment, where he was sodomized despite his protests. (3) Three Navy men overpowered, beat, and dragged a shipmate to a secluded area of the ship to rape him, but the victim escaped. Three weeks later the same attackers overpowered the victim and then two of the assailants held him down while the third raped him anally (Struckman-Johnson, 1991).

The male victim reacts in about the same way to same-sex rape as the female victim does to heterosexual rape. The reactions include shock, self-blame, shame, anger, and depression. But, due to male-role socialization, the male victim is more likely to control his emotion by denying or minimizing the trauma of rape. Moreover, unlike the female victim, the male victim tends to feel a loss of masculinity. As one victim said, "Hell, I've got no manhood left. He's made me into a woman" (Pelka, 1995; Struckman-Johnson, 1991).

 Such experiences are far more common in prison. Also, same-sex rape is more prevalent in prison than heterosexual rape is outside. About 1 out of 5 inmates in U.S. prisons have been raped, compared with 1 out of 10 females having been raped in the larger society (Cahill, 1985; Lockwood, 1985). In a state prison system, virtually every slightly built young man is sexually approached within 1 or 2 days after arrival. Many of these young men are repeatedly raped by gangs of inmates. Some of these victims commit suicide; others manage to escape gang rape by seeking protection from a more powerful inmate. However, they have to pay for that protection by serving as the protector's "punks"—slaves who provide sexual services as well as keeping house for their "masters." Sometimes punks are forced into prostitution so that they can earn such goods as cigarettes for their keepers. Some new inmates are lured into a trap for forced sex. They are offered goodies such as cigarettes, drugs, or extra food stolen from the kitchen, and after a day or so the gift giver will demand sexual repayment. Sometimes the new inmate is lured into gambling, rolling up large debts, and then being told to "pay or fuck" (Davis, 1982). This stratagem for forced sex is basically the same as that often used by male rapists on their prospective female victim in the larger society: offering her a drink at a bar, a dose of sweet talk, and an invitation into his apartment, and then forcibly demanding sex from her.

Male rapists and their male victims in prison are comparable to male rapists and their female victims in the larger society in several ways. The rapists within the prison, like the rapists without, are heterosexual. Moreover, the prison rapists are like the men who rape women outside the prison (and the male victims in prison are like the female victims outside) in that both types of rapists are generally older, heavier, taller, and more violent than their victims. However, compared with heterosexual rapes outside the prison, same-sex rapes in prison are much more likely to be interracial—blacks raping whites. Still, the two types of rape are similar in the sense that both involve members of the *dominant* group (the males outside the prison and the blacks inside) raping members of the *subordinate* group (the females outside and the whites inside).

Common sense may suggest that the rape in prison is intended to relieve one's sexual deprivation. But that is not the primary motive for prison rape. If an inmate simply wants to relieve his sexual deprivation, masturbation would be a much more convenient and normal method of relief than same-sex rape. Instead, the primary motive for same-sex rape is the need to subjugate and humiliate the victim, as evidenced by the fact that the prison rapists often use such language as "Fight or fuck," "We're going to take away your manhood," "You'll have to give up some face," and "We're gonna make a girl out of you." Of course, this does not mean that the rape serves *only* to express the need for dominance—if it did, the offenders should be content only to bully or beat up others. The rape, then, is also sexually motivated. But the drive for power appears to be a stronger motivation for the rape in prison (Davis, 1982). The same is true of the majority of the men who rape other men in the larger society. As one such rapist says:

> I had the guy so frightened I could have made him do anything I wanted. I didn't have an erection. I wasn't interested in sex. I felt powerful, and hurting him excited me. Making him suck me was more to degrade him than for my physical satisfaction. (McMullen, 1990)

Can Men Be Raped by Women?

Men can be raped by women, because rape, as feminists emphasize, is basically an expression of power. The male prison rapists are more powerful than their male victims. Similarly, the rapists in the larger society are more powerful than their female victims. Since men are typically in a position of power in relation to women, rapes characteristically involve men as the aggressors and women as the victims. But men are not always in the power position; neither are women always vulnerable. Therefore, to the extent that a woman can overpower a man in a sexual encounter, she is able to rape him.

If it is sociologically possible for a woman to rape a man, is it physiologically possible? To the general public, the answer may appear to be "no," because it is assumed that men cannot perform sexually if frightened or anxious. But medical doctors have observed that "all anxieties are not the same. Neither are all men the same. Some men can and do have erections while they are anxious" (Sarrel and Masters, 1982; Sarrel and Sarrel, 1981). Further, even if some men cannot engage in sexual intercourse under stress or duress, they still are vulnerable to rape because they can be forced to perform oral sex or other sex acts that are meant to humiliate them but fulfill their attackers' need for asserting power and dominance.

Therefore, it should not be surprising that there are actual cases of women using physical force to rape men, but such rapes are *extremely rare*. Presumably, if there is a trend for women to become increasingly powerful, there may well be more women raping men. The cases that have occurred so far usually involve a single victim and two or more offenders—an apparent attempt on the part of the women to compensate for their traditional lack of power. As John Macdonald (1995) reports:

> A 37-year-old man was accosted late one evening by two women who forced him at gunpoint inside an abandoned building. They made him undress, tied his hands, manipulated him to erection and had intercourse with him a number of times. When he could no longer maintain an erection, they abused his genitals and rectum. When he fainted, they untied his hands and left him.

However, instead of using physical force as illustrated here, most female offenders resort to verbal persuasion and other nonviolent methods. Examples include an older woman seducing a teenage boy or younger man, a female babysitter sitting on a younger boy and forcing his penis into her vagina, and a female college student persistently "getting fresh" with her date until he gives in to intercourse (Struckman-Johnson, 1991). We may argue, though, that the use of verbal persuasion alone does not legally constitute rape if the victim is no longer under the age of consent.

The use of physical force is a different matter. It is rape and may traumatize the male victim as much as it does the female victim. He is likely to feel a loss of masculinity and consequently suffer such sexual dysfunction as impotence, premature ejaculation, or loss of sexual desire. But since most female offenders do not resort to physical force, most male victims are far from being traumatized. Therefore, the most common effect is avoidance of aggressive women and pressured sex (Struckman-Johnson, 1991). As things stand now, even those male victims who are badly shaken by the more violent assault may not get much sympathy. "A former police officer in San Diego," report Philip Sarrel and Lorna Sarrel (1981), "told us that a few years ago a sailor came into his precinct house to report that he had been raped by a woman. The police in the station house thought he must be drunk, out of his mind, or simply weaving a good tale. They laughed him out the door."

Child Molestation

Child molestation can be considered a form of rape because the victims are too young and hence not legally capable of giving their consent.

Some Basic Facts

There are all kinds of studies giving vastly different estimates of how common child molestation is. It is impossible, therefore, to know with any certainty the true incidence of this sex offense. But we can have more confidence about the accuracy of these basic facts: (1) Girls are far more likely than boys to be molested. (2) The overwhelming majority of child molesters are men rather than women. (3) Molesters are more likely to be acquainted with, than to be strangers to, their victims. (4) The molester is usually unmarried; never or rarely dates; and lives alone or with his parents (Macdonald, 1995; Lanning, 1992; Finkelhor, 1984).

Another basic fact concerns the effects of child molestation on the victim. A review of 45 such studies has clearly demonstrated that molested children are more likely than other children to suffer from various problems. The problems include posttraumatic stress disorders (such as nightmares or nervousness), behavior problems (hyperactivity, immaturity, delinquency, or running away), sexualized behaviors (putting objects in vaginas or anuses, or excessive masturbation), and poor self-esteem (Bruni, 1997; Kendall-Tackett, Williams, and Finkelhor, 1993).

A Profile of Child Molesters

Who are the child molesters? We can construct a profile of these offenders by comparing them with rapists who victimize women: (1) Molesters are considerably older; most molesters are over 35 years of age, while most rapists are under 20. (2) Molesters are more gentle and passive, while rapists are tougher and more aggressive. (3) Molesters are less likely to resort to physical force or vaginal penetration and more likely to restrict themselves to fondling the victim. (4) Molesters are much less capable than rapists of getting along with adult members of the opposite sex—less skilled, more anxious, and less assertive in talking with women. (5) Most molesters commit the offense against the same child for a certain length of time, while rapists attack different victims. (6) Most molesters admit their guilt, while most rapists refuse to do so (Lanning, 1992; Groth and Birnbaum, 1979; McCaghy, 1968; McCaldon, 1967).

All this suggests that child molesters disastrously fail to meet the sexist cultural standard of "masculinity" or male dominance over women. This may explain why they are scorned and, if young enough, are raped by their tougher fellow inmates in prison. Their lack of masculinity may also explain why, unlike rapists who resort to rape to dominate women, child molesters feel inadequate with adult women but dominant over children. Moreover, while the culture of rape—which is related to the ideal of masculinity and male domination over females in society—encourages rapists to blame their adult victims, this same culture fails to have the same impact on molesters. This is why, unlike rapists, most molesters fully and frankly admit their guilt. Nonetheless, child molesters are at bottom similar to rapists: Both victimize a person who is less powerful than they are.

Less Common Types of Child Molestation

We have largely discussed men who molest young girls. What about the far less common type of molester—men who molest young boys? There is some evidence that most of these molesters are not really gay. Although they molest children of their own sex, they are usually married, have no sexual interest in other men, and do not identify themselves as gays. Their boy victims, though, are more likely than other boys to grow up to become child abusers themselves (Finkelhor, 1984).

What about women who molest young boys? This type of molester is even rarer. Perhaps due to their extreme rarity, they have not become a popular subject of scholarly investigation. It is also quite possible that, like the general public, researchers feel that if a woman molests a young boy she could hardly do any harm without a penis or, related to this attitude, that he should consider himself "lucky" (Mathis, 1972). In fact, this kind of sex can anger the boy so much that he may later as an adult take it out on other women by raping them. In an investigation of 83 rapists in a California prison, two researchers found that 59 percent of them had been molested as children by older women, as compared with another study of college students, only 3 percent of whom had been molested by older women (Petrovich and Templer, 1984).

There is, however, a gender difference in the way victims deal with the anger caused by their victimization. Men who have been molested as boys by older women or men are likely to *act out* their smoldering anger from the sexual traumas by becoming rapists or child molesters themselves. In contrast, women who have been molested as children appear more likely to *internalize* their anger by becoming victims of additional abuse, such as rape victims, wife-abuse victims, drug addicts, or prostitutes (Finkelhor, 1984; Russell, 1984). This gender difference can be attributed to traditional sex-role socialization, which encourages boys to be aggressive and girls to be passive.

Summary

1. What are the major patterns of rape? Blacks are more likely than whites to commit rape. Rapes are mostly intraracial, though interracial rapes are more common today than before. Females between ages 16 and 20 are most vulnerable to rape. Most rapists plan their assault rather than act it out impulsively. Gang rape involves mostly young men pressuring each other to prove their masculinity by raping the same woman. More common than stranger rape, acquaintance rape is an extension of men's socially accepted aggressive sexual behavior. Campus rape is relatively prevalent because of the influence of the rape-prone culture. The myth of victim precipitation in effect blames the rape survivor for having asked to be raped.

2. What consequences does rape have for its survivors? Most survivors are beset with anxiety and guilt. A few, but increasingly more, survivors feel outraged and revengeful, and they have also stimulated the growth of organizations for helping rape survivors and other women fight sexual attack. There have been legal reforms to treat rape survivors better, but they are still made to feel that they have "asked for it."

3. What is the culture of rape? It is made up of the prevailing male attitudes toward women as well as the traditional ideas of appropriate sex roles. In such a culture, women are treated as if they were men's property; women are used as objects to enable men to prove their masculinity; women are believed to have a secret desire to be raped; and girls are taught to play the feminine, submissive role. All these jointly encourage men to rape.

4. Why do men rape women? Psychological theory attributes rape to a psychological problem, such as the offender's feelings of sexual inadequacy. Social-psychological theory traces the source of rape to a sexually permissive culture that intensifies the male's feeling of rejection by women and thus increases his sexual frustration. Feminist theory explains that since rape serves to preserve male dominance in a sexually unequal society, men are likely to assault women.

5. What is the nature of same-sex rape? Such rape is relatively rare in the larger society but very common in prison. In many respects, male-against-male rape inside or outside prison is comparable to male-against-female rape in the larger society. It is basically a phenomenon of a more powerful person raping a smaller, weaker person; it is an expression of dominance more than sexual desire. **Can men be raped by women?** Yes. To the extent that some men are weak and submissive and some women are powerful and aggressive, men can be raped by women. But most such rapes involve verbal pressure rather than physical force.

6. What are some of the common characteristics of child molestation? Most victims are more likely to be girls than boys; most child molesters are men; molesters are more likely to be acquainted with, than to be strangers to, their victims; and molesters differ from rapists who assault adults, for example, in being more likely to lack heterosexual social skills.

SUGGESTED READINGS

Bart, Pauline B., and Patricia H. O'Brien. 1985. *Stopping Rape: Successful Survival Strategies.* New York: Pergamon. An empirical analysis of how some women avoid being raped and how others do not.

Benedict, Jeffrey R. 1998. *Athletes and Acquaintance Rape.* Thousand Oaks, Calif.: Sage. A detailed analysis of three court cases involving athletes charged with committing acquaintance rape, showing why such rape is relatively common in sports.

Brownmiller, Susan. 1975. *Against Our Will: Men, Women, and Rape.* New York: Simon & Schuster. A hard-hitting classic on how men use rape to intimidate and keep women in their place.

Ellis, Lee. 1989. *Theories of Rape: Inquiries into the Causes of Sexual Aggression.* New York: Hemisphere. An analysis of the feminist, social learning, and evolutionary theories of rape.

Fairstein, Linda. 1993. *Sexual Violence: Our War Against Rape.* New York: William Morrow. An analysis of rape from the author's vantage point as chief of New York's Sex Crime Prosecution Unit for nearly 20 years.

Finkelhor, David. 1984. *Child Sexual Abuse: New Theory and Research.* New York: Free Press. Providing a sociological explanation for child molesting, along with data from a survey of Boston parents.

Jackson, Thomas L. (Ed.). 1996. *Acquaintance Rape: Assessment, Treatment, and Prevention.* Sarasota, Fla.: Professional Resource Press. A collection of articles on various aspects of acquaintance rape, including its impact on victims, treatment of victims, and prevention of the sexual assault.

Kendall-Tackett, Kathleen, Linda Meyer Williams, and David Finkelhor. 1993. "Impact of sexual abuse on children: A review and synthesis of recent empirical studies." *Psychological Bulletin, 113,* 164–180. A review of 45 studies that challenges conventional assumption about the traumatic or long-term effects of sexual abuse on children.

LaFree, Gary D., Barbara F. Reskin, and Christy A. Visher. 1985. "Jurors' responses to victims' behavior and legal issues in sexual assault trials." *Social Problems, 32,* 389–407. A unique study involving courtroom observations of rape trials, suggesting that the victims are put on trial.

Madigan, Lee, and Nancy C. Gamble. 1991. *The Second Rape: Society's Continued Betrayal of the Victim.* New York: Lexington Books. A critical analysis of the various ways society makes the rape survivor's life worse.

Sanday, Peggy Reeves. 1996. *A Woman Scorned: Acquaintance Rape on Trial.* New York: Doubleday. Illustrates how the U.S. culture and legal system help make victims of acquaintance rape responsible for their own victimization.

Scarce, Michael. 1997. *Male on Male Rape: The Hidden Toll of Stigma and Shame.* New York: Insight Books. The first-ever book-length analysis of male rape outside of prison settings.

Schwartz, Martin D., and Walter S. DeKeseredy. 1997. *Sexual Assault on the College Campus: The Role of Male Peer Support.* Thousand Oaks, Calif.: Sage. Provides a critical review of various theories and studies on campus rape, and shows how male peer groups encourage college men to engage in sexual aggression.

Scully, Diana. 1990. *Understanding Sexual Violence: A Study of Convicted Rapists.* Boston: Unwin Hyman. An insightful analysis of how rapists see themselves and their crime.

CHAPTER

6 Family Violence

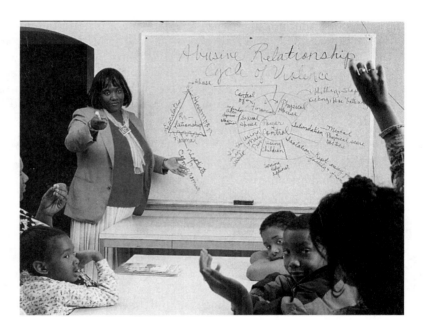

During a summer before entering college as a freshman, Jennifer worked in a bakery where she met Jack, a coworker. She got pregnant by him, and soon they got married. But he turned out to be a heavy drinker and often subjected her to physical violence. Several times, Jennifer moved out, but returned after Jack showed remorse. Still, the abuse got worse. He would tie her up and vaginally and anally rape her, sometimes burning parts of her body with a lit cigarette. Finally, she bought a gun and killed him, after suffering another episode of violence (DeKeseredy and Schwartz, 1996).

Every day, like Jennifer, thousands of women in the United States, along with many children and older persons (mostly over age 75), are targets of family violence. In fact, Americans are so much more likely to be attacked by family

119

members than strangers that two researchers on the subject have called the family the "most violent institution, with the two exceptions of the police and the military" (Gelles and Straus, 1988). In this chapter we will examine some popular myths about family violence, then analyze various forms of family violence and the effects of the violence on the victims, construct a social profile of family abusers, and look at social responses to the problem.

Myths About Family Violence

Because family violence involves the most cherished and intimate social institution in our lives, we may find it difficult to see the discomforting subject with neutrality or objectivity. We may think, for example, that violence happens only in poor, disorganized, and dysfunctional families, not in middle-class or richer homes. Let's take a closer look at this myth and others that have been discussed in a text on family violence (Barnett, Miller-Perrin, and Perrin, 1997).

Myth 1: Family Violence Hits the Poor Only

A great deal of evidence does indicate higher rates of family violence among lower-income people. According to one survey, for example, there is five times as much marital violence in families at or below the poverty level as in families above the poverty level. This means merely that poor people are *more likely* to experience family violence; it does *not* necessarily mean that *most, let alone all,* poor families are violent. In fact, most studies suggest that only a minority of poor families are violent. Take a careful look at this typical finding: 13.4 percent of blue-collar husbands were violent in the past year, compared with 10.4 percent of white-collar husbands (Kantor and Straus, 1990). Findings such as this are often reported to mean that blue-collar husbands are more likely than their white-collar counterparts to be violent, but only a *minority* (13.4 percent) of blue-collar husbands are violent.

Myth 2: Violence and Love Cannot Happen Together

Many people assume that violence and love are so totally opposite they cannot exist together in marriage and the family. But parents do often resort to violence as a way of disciplining their children, whom they love dearly. While married persons may not inflict violence on their spouse in the name of love, couples with one partner battering another do stay together for about the same length of time (6 years) as the average marriage lasts (Walker, 1990; Browne, 1987). This is because violent spouses often express love for their victim, along with apology or remorse for their bad behavior, and most victims do not leave immediately every time their violent spouses become abusive. All this, of course, does not imply that violence is good for marriage, as most battered wives do eventually leave their husbands. It only means that violence does occur in many love relationships.

Myth 3: Most Abused Children Grow Up to Be Abusive Parents

Having been abused as a child is associated with being a child abuser. As research has consistently shown, parents who abuse their child are more likely than nonabusive parents to have been victims of child abuse themselves, but this does not mean that abused children will necessarily become abusive parents. In fact, as will be discussed later, the majority of child-abuse victims do *not* grow up to abuse their children (Kaufman and Zigler, 1993; Widom, 1989; Gelles, 1985).

Myth 4: Alcohol and Drugs Are Involved in Most Family Violence

It is true that users of alcohol and drugs are more likely than nonusers to get involved in family violence. As one study (Kantor and Straus, 1990) shows, for example, the proportion of male binge drinkers who abuse their wives (19.2 percent) is nearly three times higher than that of nondrinkers (6.8 percent). This finding can be taken to mean that heavy drinking plays a role in, but is not the real cause of, family violence. After all, only a minority (19.2 percent) of men who engage in binge drinking beat their wives—the large majority do not. Moreover, even among many of those who drink or use drugs and then hit their spouses, the real reason for spouse abuse is not the psychoactive substance but some personal or financial problems. For men with such problems, alcohol and drugs are often used as an excuse for abusing wives, because, as suggested in Chapter 12, the substance by itself cannot diminish the user's moral competence.

The Extent of Family Violence

There are many different forms of family violence, ranging from fights among siblings to killings of parents by children. Here we will focus on the types that have so far interested sociologists the most: marital rape, wife beating, child abuse, and elder abuse.

The extent of family violence varies from one research report to another. Researchers who define the problem broadly would report a very high incidence of family violence, while those who define it more narrowly would find a lower incidence. For example, if child abuse is broadly defined to include spanking, slapping, cursing, or threatening to send a child away as a traditional way of disciplining a misbehaving child, at least 85 percent of all U.S. parents are found to be child abusers. But if the abuse is defined more narrowly to comprise only such physical violence as punching, hitting, kicking, or throwing the child down, then the proportion of child abusers drops sharply to 5 percent (Lewin, 1995).

If we settle for the more narrow definition of family violence as relatively severe physical or sexual violence—severe enough to cause injury—we will find from various surveys the following percentages of Americans who fall victim to family violence (Lewis, 1995; Russell, 1990; Pillemer and Finkelhor, 1988; Finkelhor and Yllö, 1987; Gelles and Straus, 1987):

- Marital rape: 10 to 14 percent of wives since marriage
- Wife Beating: 3 percent of wives every year
- Child abuse: 6 percent of children every year
- Elder abuse: 2 percent of older people every year

It should be noted that these figures are only the minimum, most conservative estimates of the prevalence of family violence.

The real extent of serious family violence may well be *much higher* than suggested by these percentages because people are generally reluctant to reveal their family problems to researchers. Moreover, even though these percentages appear relatively small, the numbers of women, children, and older people suffering from severe family violence run to millions. Six percent of child-abuse victims, for example, means that more than 4.5 *million* children are sexually or physically abused every year. We should also remember that family violence is considerably more common if many forms of abuse short of severe physical violence are taken into account, such as slapping, verbal abuse, or child neglect. In addition, if financial exploitation is included in the definition of elder abuse, a much greater percentage of older people are victims. Considering all this, we may say that family violence is a common, serious social problem.

Marital Rape

In early 1994 the well-publicized case of Lorena Bobbitt, who cut off her husband's penis after he raped her and then went to sleep, made many people aware of marital violence. But still unknown to the general public, marital rape—the raping of a woman by her husband—is probably the most prevalent form of forced sex, more common than stranger or acquaintance rape. Of the representative sample of women in San Francisco studied by Diana Russell (1990), 8 percent have been raped by their husbands, as opposed to 3 percent by strangers and 5 percent by acquaintances. By focusing on married women rather than all women, Russell and other researchers have found that 10 to 14 percent of wives have suffered marital rape.

The Nature of Marital Rape

Most of the rapes in marriage involve physical violence or the threat of it. A typical example is reported by a victim as follows: "He wanted to make love with me, and I didn't want to. He got mad and tried to force me to take off my panties. He actually did it himself, so I fought back. I pushed him away, but he was stronger than me, so he forced me down, spread my legs, and forced penetration." Some of these rapes result in serious injury to the victim; as one woman said, "He'd hold me so hard I'd have black and blue marks on my throat. And he gave me black eyes too. . . . One time I was so full of blood, the neighbor called the police." Marital rapes also include those accomplished with threats of physical harm ("He said if I didn't do what he wanted he'd choke me"), with coercive, nonphysical threats ("He said, 'You have sex now or I'll get sex elsewhere. I'll leave you'"), and by forcing sex on the victim when she is asleep, extremely drunk, or helpless from drugs (Russell, 1990).

Contrary to what you may assume, the majority of marital rapes do not involve vaginal penetration. Vaginal rapes account for less than half of marital rapes, while forced anal intercourse occurs slightly more often. Other forms of extremely degrading rapes in marriage include inserting objects into the wife's private parts, coercing her to have sex in front of children, or forcing sex on her right after she is discharged from a hospital—usually after giving birth (Barnett, Miller-Perrin, Perrin, 1997; Campbell, 1989).

Most offenders assume that they are entitled to have sex with their wives whether the spouses want to or not. But marital rape is as traumatic to the victim as stranger rape, striking tremendous fear into the raped wife. As one victim said, "It was as though he wanted to annihilate me. More than the slapping, or the kicks . . . as though he wanted to tear me apart from the inside out and simply leave nothing there" (Browne, 1987). After the assault, victims who are employed or able to be economically independent tend to get a divorce, while those who are not employed tend to stay married. Those who stay married, however, usually avoid sex or develop a negative attitude toward sex (Barnett, Miller-Perrin, and Perrin, 1997; Bergen, 1996).

Causes of Marital Rape

Marital rape can be attributed to at least three causes (Bergen, 1996). One is the sexist belief that husbands are *entitled* to have sex in any way they want with their wives. This belief is part of the popular patriarchal myth that wives cannot be raped because they are considered as "belonging" to their husbands—that is, as their husbands' property. Not surprisingly, although almost all the states have finally made marital rape a crime, it is still rare for a man to be charged with raping his wife.

A second cause of marital rape could be the husband's attempt to *punish* the wife for what he considers her unfaithfulness or some other "sin." Here is how a victim describes why her husband raped her:

> A lot of times it [rape] happened because he was so jealous. He always thought that I was looking at other men. Like the time my brother and his friend—who I grew up with—were over, and he thought I was looking at his friend, and he was really mad. He started hitting me and then forced me to have sex (Bergen, 1996).

A third cause of marital rape is the husband's attempt to use rape as a form of *control* over the wife. As one victim reports on what happened to her:

> The more control he thought he was losing, the worse it got. If I got a job or I was doing good, he would take it away. He would beat me up and force me [to have sex] just to get that control back (Bergen, 1996).

These three causes of rape are an integral part of the patriarchal society that encourages men to dominate women, with marital rape the essence of male dominance over women. Presumably, the more strongly a husband believes in patriarchy, the more likely he is to rape his wife as an entitlement to sex, a punishment for her "sin," or a control over her. Due to the paucity of research on the subject, though, it is difficult to explain adequately why, under the same patriarchal, rape-inducing culture, some men are more likely than others to accept patriarchy in the first place.

The same culture that justifies marital rape also tends to lead the victim to blame herself. Here is an example of self-blame as expressed by one victim: "I'm not the most sexual person in the world and there was some unwanted sex. When I tried to say no, he would make me say yes. I'm really a very tight person. I don't send out signals about sex. I was not sexually communicative" (Russell, 1990).

Wife Beating

It has been estimated that about one-third of all U.S. married persons assault their spouses every year, and that two-thirds do so at least once during their marriage. The researchers who came up with these estimates have found that wives are as likely as, if not more likely than, husbands to be the offenders (Straus, Gelles, and Steinmetz, 1980). The problem is that these researchers lumped together violent and nonviolent acts as if they were the same. They defined all acts of slapping, for example, as violence, ignoring the fact that some slaps, particularly those often carried out by women, are not violent at all, while other kinds of slaps, especially those more likely to be perpetrated by men, are violent. Consequently, a wife playfully slapping her husband on the hand to chastise him for trying to steal her dessert was regarded as a violent act, no different from a husband angrily slapping his wife on the face and knocking out several teeth (Dobash et al., 1992). To avoid trivializing the problem, we will focus here on really violent acts, namely, acts serious enough to cause injury, which annually occur to at least 3 percent of wives at the hands of their husbands (Gelles and Straus, 1987).

The Nature of Wife Beating

Of the people who are involved in spouse abuse, husbands are overwhelmingly more likely to severely assault their wives than the other way around. As Martin Schwartz (1987) has found in an analysis of several national surveys on crime victimization, 1,641 women said they had been assaulted by their husbands, while only 102 men claimed to be have been assaulted by their wives. While the percentage of wives being beaten by husbands every year is relatively small (3 percent), the number reaches about 2 million, a figure large enough for wife beating to be considered a serious social problem (Browne, 1993; Gelles and Straus, 1987).

In committing the offense, abusive husbands usually act as if they had the license to batter their wives. This is why, after they commit the violence, they usually do not show genuine remorse by fully admitting guilt. Instead, they often attempt to neutralize or rationalize their violent act in one of three ways (Barnett, Miller-Perrin, and Perrin, 1997; Dutton, 1986):

- Blaming the victim for provoking the offense ("She kept yelling at me; she didn't want to shut up after I told her to.")
- Minimizing the harm done to the victim ("I didn't really hurt her; I just gave her a little slap.")
- Attributing the violence to some problem beyond their control ("I drank a little too much; I had a bad day in the office.")

The effects of wife beating on the victim go beyond physical injury. Generally, the victim tends to develop what psychiatrists call "posttraumatic stress disorders" (more widely known as *posttraumatic syndrome*), similar to the disorder that some U.S. soldiers have developed from their combat experiences in Vietnam. The syndrome consists of feelings of depression, anxiety, and helplessness. Here is an illustration of posttraumatic syndrome suffered by a typical wife-beating victim named Ginger:

> Ginger closed herself off from friends and family. She lost interest in her life and avoided any situation that could "put her in jeopardy." In fact, Ginger appeared more depressed and anxious than many of the patients in the psychiatric unit of the hospital. (Barnett and LaViolette, 1993)

Some victims with this disorder develop *battered woman syndrome,* a specific deadly pattern of losing self-esteem, feeling trapped, expecting constantly the terror of violence, but eventually striking back by killing their abusive husbands (Barnett and LaViolette, 1993).

Why Don't Battered Wives Leave?

It has been widely assumed that most victims of wife beating continue to put up with the abuse and continue to live with their husbands. On the contrary, however, the overwhelming majority of abused women *do* leave the abusive relationship (DeKeseredy and Schwartz, 1996). They leave their homes to seek help or refuge from police, social workers, mental health agencies, shelters, parents, or friends. The victims, nevertheless, continue to show some symptoms of the posttraumatic syndrome while finding themselves at some risk of being stalked and killed by the abusive husbands (Gelles, 1995; Gibbs, 1993b; Wilson and Daly, 1992).

Nevertheless, why do some women continue to live with their abusive husbands? One reason is that they are for the most part *the most socially and economically isolated* of all women as a result of having too little education and not being gainfully employed. The lack of education and employment, coupled with the isolation, forces them to be economically dependent on their abusive husbands as well as discourages them from seeking help from others outside their home. Another reason for remaining in an abusive relationship is the victims' *fear that their husbands will retaliate* if they leave. By staying, however, these women are also more likely to end up getting killed by their husbands or being forced into a corner where they struggle desperately to survive by killing their husbands (Mann, 1996; Goetting, 1995; Gibbs, 1993b; Wilson and Daly, 1992).

Causes of Wife Beating

According to feminist theorists, a major cause of wife beating is *the sexist, patriarchal nature of society,* which treats women as if they were their husbands' property. This kind of patriarchy can be seen, for example, in the fact that in many states an aggravated assault against a stranger is a felony but assaulting one's own wife is a misdemeanor, for which the husband is rarely arrested, much less jailed (Gibbs, 1993b). There is evidence to suggest the impact of patriarchy on wife beating. For example, husbands who hold patriarchal beliefs are more likely to assault their wives than those who do not, and wife beating is generally more prevalent in patriarchal societies than in those with greater gender equality (Brown, 1992; Smith, 1990; Levinson, 1988).

Obviously, however, patriarchy is not the only cause of wife beating. If it were, every husband would become a wife beater. In fact, only about 30 percent of U.S. husbands have ever physically abused their spouse in the entire course of their marriage (Dutton, 1994). In other words, patriarchy influences some husbands more than others, encouraging some more than others to abuse their spouses. But what kinds of husbands are more vulnerable to the influence of patriarchy? Possibly, it is those who have *lost control of their lives* to poverty, unemployment, drug abuse, and alcoholism. Deprived of the sense of power over their lives, those men are understandably more receptive to the patriarchal idea that men may dominate and control their wives. And since they do not have money and other precious resources that rich men can use to control their wives, poor men are compelled to resort to violence as a way of controlling their wives. This may explain why research has often shown poor or unemployed men to be more likely than other men to beat their wives (Cazenave and Straus, 1990).

Child Abuse

Of the different forms of family violence, child abuse seems to be the most serious or shocks people the most. Yet it is not confined to "sick" families; it is quite prevalent, victimizing millions of children every year. Not surprisingly, child abuse has been called a national emergency (Barnett, Miller-Perrin, and Perrin, 1997). There are two broad types of child abuse, one sexual and the other physical.

The Nature of Child Abuse

Some children suffer sexual abuse at the hands of family members, mostly their fathers and stepfathers. Such abuse is popularly called incest. According to one study, anywhere from 10 to 20 percent of women have been victimized this way during their childhood and adolescence, while 1 to 3 percent of men have had the same experience (Meiselman, 1990). These figures appear quite large in part because they include what has happened both in childhood and in adolescence, a long span of 17 years. According to another survey, which focuses on what has happened within the past 12 months only, about 2 percent of all children are sexually abused every year.

Researchers have found a few significant facts about this kind of deviance: Most cases of incest involve fathers as offenders and daughters as victims. Stepfathers are much more likely than biological fathers to commit incest. Incestuous fathers are more likely than average fathers to be isolated from others outside their home. There is, however, no significant difference in incest rates among social classes and racial or ethnic groups—various classes and groups have about the same rate. Incest usually gives rise to a strong sense of shame and guilt as well as anxiety, depression, and isolation among the young victims. When they become adults, the victims are more likely than other people to be dissatisfied with sexual relationships and to encounter marital problems (May, 1991; Finkelhor et al., 1989; Russell, 1986).

Nevertheless, the majority of child abuses in the family involve the parents *physically* abusing their children. The entire gamut of this kind of child abuse exists, ranging from assaults on the child that cause minor bruises to severe battering that results in death. About 3 million children, or 4 percent of all children age 17 or younger, are severely assaulted every year (Lewin, 1995). An enormous increase in child abuse has often been reported in various media over the last 20 years. Much of the reported increase, however, is a result of the 1974 federal law, the Child Abuse Prevention and Treatment Act. Until that year, it was seldom that anyone came to the aid of child-abuse victims because the crime was rarely reported and routinely covered up.

The 1974 law requires professionals, such as health-care providers, law-enforcement officials, teachers, and school administrators, to report suspected child abuse to the appropriate child protection agency. Failure to report may subject such professionals to fines, or even prison sentences. To avoid violating the law, many have tended to report child abuse as more common than it is. The same federal law has encouraged child protection agencies to overreport because the more people they report as child abusers, the more money they receive from the government. Thus they have developed a foolproof technique for "proving" child abuse: It involves routinely defining suspects as "noncredible" witnesses, accepting their testimony as true only when they agree with the allegations, and routinely seeing victims as "credible" witnesses, rejecting their testimony only when they say suspects are innocent (Margolin, 1992b). In reality, according to one survey, very severe violence toward children has declined, thanks to increased publicity about child abuse and prevention programs for child abuse (Gelles, 1995).

Nonetheless, the number of children being severely physically abused (3 million a year) remains disturbingly large. More disturbing is the real 48 percent *increase* of children killed by parents since the mid-1980s, with at least 1200 such deaths occurring in 1994, the year when a young mother in South Carolina, Susan Smith, shocked the nation by drowning her two children, one age 3 years and the other 14 months (Barnett, Miller-Perrin, and Perrin, 1997).

Sociologists have discovered a few significant facts about child abuse: Very young children, under age 5, are at higher risk than older ones for being physically abused, principally because they are more dependent and powerless. Child abuse occurs more frequently in lower-income families than in higher-income ones. Child abusers are more likely than nonabusers to have some emotional, behavioral, familial, or interpersonal difficulties. Examples of these difficulties include depression and low self-esteem, being quick to anger and to lose self-control, and marital problems and isolation from relatives and friends (Barnett, Miller-Perrin, and Perrin, 1997).

In addition to suffering physical injury, children who have been abused are more likely than their nonabused peers to experience many social and psychological problems. These problems include emotional and social difficulties, learning disabilities and poor academic performance, and running away from home, as well as delinquency, criminality, and violent behavior. When they become adults, they are more likely than others to abuse drugs and alcohol, engage in criminal activities, suffer from psychiatric disturbances, and become child abusers themselves (Goode, 1999; Gelles, 1995).

Causes of Child Abuse

Sociologists have discovered a number of causal factors in child abuse. One is the *intergenerational transmission of violence:* Parents are likely to abuse their children if they have learned in childhood that it is all right to use violence in dealing with child-rearing problems. This learning may come from *the experience of being abused as children.* Indeed, research has shown that child-abusing parents are more likely than nonabusing parents to have been abused themselves as children. But this should not be taken to mean that receiving early abuse inevitably leads to later abuse-giving because, contrary to popular belief, the *majority* (about 70 percent) of child-abuse victims do *not* grow up to become abusers (Kaufman and Zigler, 1993; Widom, 1989; Gelles, 1985). A history of the abuser being abused is only one of the causal influences on child abuse, and not its only cause. The other learned influence—the legitimacy of using violence to deal with problems—also comes from *having observed as children how parents and other significant adults use violence* to express anger, to react to stress, or to deal with marital problems. This explains why researchers often find that child abusers are more likely than nonabusers to have been raised in homes with a great deal of marital conflict and violence (Barnett, Miller-Perrin, and Perrin, 1997).

Another contributing factor to child abuse is the *acceptance of the popular view of physical punishment as a proper way of disciplining children.* Nearly half of all U.S. parents resort to physical punishment in an attempt to correct a child's misbehavior. But there is a tendency for physical punishment (say, spanking or slapping) to spill over into child abuse (punching or kicking). As a researcher has found, parents who approve of physical punishment are four times more likely to abuse their children than are parents who disapprove of such physical discipline. Because of the social acceptance of physical punishment, child abusers tend to see their abusive behavior as good and proper. This can be illustrated by the case of a father who had severely beaten his two boys, one 5 years old and the other only 18 months old. In the hospital where the boys were brought in for treatment of multiple bruises, lacerations, and fractures, the father said to the examining physicians, "Children have to be taught respect for authority and be taught obedience. I would rather have my children grow up afraid of me and respecting me than loving me and spoiled" (Lewin, 1995; Straus, 1991).

Other social factors that have been found to contribute to child abuse include *poverty, unemployment, family problems, and lack of education.* Poverty, unemployment, and family problems are likely to cause considerable stress for parents, and stress, as research has shown, is a major factor in child abuse. Moreover, the parents, due to their lack of education, will find themselves less able to cope with the enormous stress that weighs on them, and as a result, they are likely to explode by assaulting people in their immediate environment, including their children (Gelles, 1985). The stress that triggers violence against children can be defused if social and emotional support is available from friends and relatives. But child abusers are more likely than nonabusers to be socially isolated and without a telephone in the house (Barnett, Miller-Perrin, and Perrin, 1997).

Finally, *problematic interaction between parent and child* has been found to increase the risk for child abuse. Interaction becomes problematic if parent, child, or both have problems that make child care demanding, difficult, or stressful. Parent problems include lack of parenting skills, lack of knowledge about normal childhood behavior, unrealistic expectations for the child, or punitive parenting. Child problems comprise antisocial behavior, aggressive behavior, or mental and physical disabilities. Parents with problems, when interacting with children with problems, can feel so frustrated and angry that they become violent and abusive toward the helpless youngsters (Barnett, Miller-Perrin, and Perrin, 1997; Denham, Renwick, and Holt, 1991; Anderson, Lytton, and Romney, 1986).

Elder Abuse

The majority of older people are capable of taking care of themselves, but a significant minority have difficulty doing so. Today, about 25 percent of elders require long-term care. A few live in nursing homes, but the vast majority live at home, often cared for by their spouses or other relatives (Dobrzynski, 1996; Kart, 1990). Some of these older dependents suffer abuses at the hands of their caretakers.

The Nature of Elder Abuse

Older people are more likely to be abused if they live with relatives than if they live alone. This is probably because the full-time care administered to live-in elders is more stressful to the caregiver than the part-time care rendered to live-alone elders. Since older men are more likely than older women to live with relatives, older men are more vulnerable to abuse (Paveza et al., 1992). Older persons are also more likely to suffer abuses if they are socially isolated, with relatively few contacts with friends and relatives other than the caregiver. Without the support of friends and relatives, elders are more liable to become sitting ducks for abuse by the overstressed caregiver. Research has so far found no class difference in rates of elder abuse: Middle-class elders are just as likely as their lower-class peers to be abused (Bachman and Pillemer, 1991).

Abused elders generally suffer from a variety of psychological problems, especially depression and sleep disorders. They are also likely to be withdrawn, shrinking from contact with younger adults like those who have abused them (Wallace, 1996). But not enough research has been done to provide more detailed data on the consequences of elder abuse.

Causes of Elder Abuse

Helping elders is for the most part a highly stressful job. It is particularly hard on the female members of the *sandwiched generation,* the middle-aged group squeezed between raising children of their own and taking care of their parents. For many of these women, the trap between child care and elder care prevents them from working outside the home. Having been on the "mommy track" with the expectation of eventually returning to their careers, they now find themselves on an even longer "daughter track," taking care of older parents with chronic and disabling conditions.

Given the enormous stress from elder care, we may expect, as research has shown, that caregiving daughters are more likely than their noncaregiving peers to abuse parents (Hinrichsen, Hernandez, and Pollack, 1992). We should emphasize, though, that the majority of stressed caregivers do not abuse their elders. Elder abusers are distinguishable for having *severe personal problems,* including alcoholism, drug addiction, unemployment, antisocial behavior, arrest records, or emotional instability. In addition, abusers are generally *beset with money problems or financially dependent* on their victims, which may explain why elder abuse differs from child abuse in that elder abuse often involves financial exploitation and rarely takes the form of physical abuse.

In general, we may conclude that stress from the burden of caregiving tends to trigger elder abuse, and this is usually related to the fact that the abuser has personal and financial problems (Barnett, Miller-Perrin, and Perrin, 1997; J. Shapiro, 1996). Some studies show that elder abusers are more likely to be sons or other male relatives than daughters or other female relatives, but other studies suggest the reverse. Regardless of whether the abusers are male or female relatives, they usually have personal and financial problems (Barnett, Miller-Perrin, and Perrin, 1997; J. Shapiro, 1996).

Ironically, though, a famous study of a random sample of people in the Boston area indicates that older persons themselves are more likely to abuse their spouses than to be abused by their children (Pillemer and Finkelhor, 1988). In other words, most elder abuses turn out to be *spouse* abuses. Again, most of these older abusers are financially dependent on the victim or suffer from some physical or emotional disabilities that prevent them from properly caring for their spouses. But older people are much less likely than younger people to abuse their spouses (Suitor, Pillemer, and Straus, 1990; Pillemer and Finkelhor, 1988).

As for most of the caregiving daughters, who are free of personal and financial problems but overburdened with the stress of taking care of their parents, why are they not likely to abuse their elders? A major reason may be that women have been socialized to feel close to their parents and to take family responsibilities more seriously than men. As caregivers they may "see their efforts as a chance to repay the time and care their parents gave them—a chance to say, again, *I love you*, before it's too late" (Beck, 1990). More generally, women are more likely than men "to respond to the interdependencies of lives by altering their own situations to fit the needs of others" (Moen, Robison, and Dempster-McClain, 1995).

In short, elder abuse arises from problems that plague caregivers: stress, severe personal problems, financial difficulty and dependence. An additional explanation suggested by social exchange theory, which has empirical support, is that the cost of caregiving exceeds the benefit the caregiver expects to receive. As Ola Barnett and her colleagues (1997) observe:

> Taking care of an elder can be very time consuming and unpleasant and offers few benefits to the caregiver. Imagine the frustration of a wife who spends several hours cooking a birthday meal for her husband who is suffering from a severe memory impairment and decides that it is not his birthday, so he will not eat any dinner at all.

But the frustration of this caregiver should not be exaggerated, because she does receive some benefits from her caregiving role that make the frustration bearable. To understand this, we should know that the social exchange between the giver and the recipient of elder care differs from an economic exchange. The benefits in economic exchange are material in nature—only money as we say—but the benefits that providers of elder care often receive are emotional or even spiritual in nature, such as the feeling of satisfaction from being able to repay the material and emotional support received in the past. Another benefit is the caregivers' expectation of receiving aid in the future when they become old and dependent themselves. Such benefits are made possible by societal norms of reciprocity in families (Horwitz, Reinhard, and Howell-White, 1996).

A Social Profile of Family Abusers

Research on family violence, particularly spouse and child abuse, has produced enough data to suggest what the average abusers in the family are like. They are more likely than nonabusers to have the following characteristics.

Age

Young husbands and parents, particularly those under age 30, are more likely than older ones to assault wives and abuse children. This may reflect the greater tendency among young men to commit violence in general (see Chapter 4). In fact, the percentage of young men committing family violence may even be higher than shown in research reports if we also take into account the many young men who are currently unmarried but who have been left so by their abused wives (Gelles, 1993; Suitor, Pillemer, and Straus, 1990).

Class

Family violence cuts across all income levels, but it occurs more frequently among lower-income people. It also takes place more often among individuals without a college education (Sedlak, 1991; Schwartz, 1988). Why is family violence more common in the lower classes? One reason is that, compared with others of higher social classes, lower-class individuals have less ability, resources, or opportunities to demonstrate personal power outside the home. But in their own home, they find themselves in a position of dominance as husbands over their wives or as mothers over their children. Thus lower-class men tend more to abuse their wives and lower-class women their children (Schwartz and DeKeseredy, 1996; Gelles, 1995).

Gender

Outside the home, men are clearly more violent than women, whether the violence involved is serious or minor. Inside the home, men are also more violent when serious injury to the victim is measured, but as we have observed, women are as likely as, or more likely than, men to abuse the spouse without seriously harming the victim.

When physical abuse of children is measured, whether serious or minor, and with the exception of incest, women are slightly more likely than men to victimize children. One obvious explanation, according to Richard Gelles (1995), is that mothers have greater responsibility for child care or spend more time with children and therefore have more opportunity to be abusive. Understandably, in families where men have more responsibility for child care, they are more likely to be abusive (Margolin, 1992a). But there is also a difference between female and male abusers of children: The mothers usually are themselves victims of abuse by their husbands (Jones, 1994).

Stressful Life

People with a more stressful home life are more likely to commit family violence. As research has consistently shown, the greater the number of stressful events besetting the individuals in their home, the greater the likelihood of violence against wives and children. The stressful events include having financial problems, being pregnant, being a teenage mother, being a single parent, and having sexual difficulties (Gelles, 1995).

Social Isolation

To reduce stress and thus the likelihood of family violence, most people are able to call for help from relatives other than those at home or from neighbors, friends, and other members of their community. But those who are likely to get involved in family violence tend to be socially isolated (Gelles, 1995).

Social Responses to Family Violence

U.S. society is caught in a bind in its battle against family violence. On the one hand, violence by strangers against women, children, and elders is widely condemned as a serious crime for which the offender is often severely punished. On the other hand, the same violence by a family member is more likely to be treated leniently or even ignored because of the traditional belief in the sacredness and privacy of the family. It is thus very difficult to protect vulnerable women, children, and elders against family violence with fully satisfying results (Gelles, 1995).

Protecting Women

Today virtually all the states have passed laws against marital rape, but these laws are rarely enforced. Still, too many people refuse to treat marital rape as "real" rape. It is often said of the victim: "She has had sex with him a thousand times before. What is one more time?" Some apparently find it hard to tell the difference between consensual sex and forced sex in marriage (Barnett, Miller-Perrin, and Perrin, 1997). As a result, very few victims succeed in having their offending husbands convicted and sent to prison. Victims can, nonetheless, get help from advocacy groups such as the National Clearinghouse on Marital and Date Rape. Since victims of marital rape are also often beaten by their husbands, some victims can further find protection as battered women.

A battering victim can call the police and have the husband or boyfriend taken away. Since the late 1980s, most states have required or encouraged the arrest of husbands for wife assault. Thus many offenders today are arrested. Another solution to the problem is for the battered woman to obtain a civil order of protection, which empowers the police to evict the offender from the house—and to arrest him only if he returns. This kind of police intervention effectively deters most abusive husbands, but it can backfire in cases in which the offender is unemployed, alcoholic, or has other deep-seated problems. These offenders usually become more violent toward their victims (Gelles, 1995; Zorza and Woods, 1994).

Another way for battered women to seek protection is to go to a shelter or safe house. There they can receive not only physical protection and social support but many important services such as counseling, legal aid, or even occupational counseling. Occupational counseling is ultimately the most useful assistance because it helps the victim obtain employment. Holding down a job, she can free herself from her abusive husband by ending her social isolation and her economic dependence on him (Barnett, Miller-Perrin, and Perrin, 1997; Gelles, 1995).

Finally, the criminal justice system helps to protect women by requiring their abusers to participate in some counseling programs. Generally, as confirmed by research, abusive husbands who have completed a counseling program are significantly more likely to stop beating their wives when compared with those who have not received any counseling. Unfortunately, only a minority of wife beaters are court-mandated to complete the program. Most who are arrested are not prosecuted or convicted, and thus they are not required to seek counseling. Some batterers voluntarily seek counseling, but most drop out before completing the program (Barnett, Miller-Perrin, and Perrin, 1997; Gelles, 1995).

Protecting Children

Since the mid-1970s every state has passed laws requiring teachers, health-care providers, and other professionals to report child abuse to a government agency called Child Protective Services. When the protective service agents determine after investigating the report that a child has indeed been abused, they are empowered to do one of two things: (1) to provide the family with social support, such as counseling, day care services, and food stamps, or (2), if the parents are dangerous, to remove the child from the parents and place the child in a foster home, in the care of relatives, or in a residential treatment center. The majority (about 75 percent) of identified children are placed in foster care (Gelles, 1995; George, Wulczyn, and Funshel, 1994).

Neither solution is ideal. There is risk in providing the family with social support while leaving the child with the abusive parent. The child may continue to be abused, even to the point of getting killed. In fact, it does occur that a child is killed *after* abuse of the child has been reported to Child Protective Services. This is because the agency is usually so understaffed and overworked that some reports of child abuse are left uninvestigated or in some way pending further action. There are also risks in removing the child from the abusive parents. For one, children may not fully comprehend why they are taken away from their parents; they may think that they are being punished for having done something wrong. A second problem is that since mistreated children require special care because of the physical and emotional damage done to them, it may be too heavy a burden for foster parents to care properly for them, so that their condition may become worse. Child advocacy groups have often criticized protective service agencies for failing to adequately protect abused children either in the home or out of it. Still, most analyses conclude that the children would have been in a worse shape without the child protective services (Barnett, Miller-Perrin, and Perrin, 1997; Gelles, 1995).

Sometimes, though, protective service agents can become so zealous in their mission that innocent parents are hauled into court or jail. The most notorious case involved the Child Protective Services in East Wenatchee, Washington. This agency used "intense recovered-memory therapy" to encourage suspected child victims to confirm having been sexually abused by their parents or other adults. In 1994 and 1995 more than 80 adults in the small town were charged with child sexual abuse. Of the 80 accused, more than 20 were convicted and sent to prison. Of those in prison, most are poor and functionally illiterate—and nearly half are women, which is very unusual in such cases. No one who could afford to hire a lawyer and fight the charges has gone to jail (Carlson, 1995; Nathan, 1995). But such a blatant abuse of recovered-memory therapy to accuse innocent parents of child abuse seems relatively rare.

Protecting Elders

There are no formal government protective services agencies for vulnerable elders as there are for children, but all states have some type of elder protection program. In addition, most states have mandatory elder reporting laws similar to the reporting laws for children. According to critics, however, such laws demean elders by treating them like children. This criticism has some validity, as many older individuals (at least one-fourth) refuse intervention or services from outsiders after they have been abused by their relatives (Mixson, 1995; Fredriksen, 1989). Nonetheless, the laws require most health and mental health professionals and law-enforcement officers to report elder abuse to social service departments.

Social service departments provide a wide spectrum of services to abused elders, including homemaker assistance, legal services, medical care, counseling, meals and income assistance, housing or relocation assistance, and guardianship among many other forms of assistance. Two types of service seem most useful to abused elders (Barnett, Miller-Perrin, and Perrin, 1997):

■ Medical services: providing doctors, nurses, physical therapists, and community health nurses (who visit patients' homes).

■ Legal services: obtaining restraining orders to remove abusers, providing guardianship of elders and their estates, safeguarding elders' Social Security and other incomes, and protecting elders against involuntary commitment.

Summary

1. What myths are there about family violence? There are myths that family violence hits the poor only, that violence and love cannot happen together, that most abused children grow up to be abusive parents, and that alcohol and drugs are involved in most family violence.

2. How common is family violence in U.S. society? The extent of family violence depends partly on the definition of the problem. If family violence is defined as severe enough to cause injury, the percentages of Americans victimized are as follows: 10 to 14 percent of wives raped by husbands since marriage, 3 percent of wives beaten by husbands annually, 6 percent of children sexually or physically abused every year, and 2 percent of elders abused every year.

3. What is the nature of marital rape? Most of the rapes in marriage involve physical violence or the threat of it, and include, aside from anal and vaginal rapes, extremely degrading sex acts. Most offenders feel entitled to have sex with their wives regardless of the latter's wishes. But, like stranger rapes, rapes by husbands have a traumatic effect on the victims. **What causes marital rape?** Such rape can be attributed to: (1) the belief in entitlement to sex, (2) the use of rape as punishment, and (3) the use of rape as control.

4. What is the nature of wife beating? Husbands are more likely to severely assault their wives than vice versa. Abusive husbands act as if they had the license to batter their wives, hence are unlikely to show genuine remorse afterward. Wife beating causes not just physical injury but posttraumatic stress disorders or, more specifically, the battered woman syndrome. **Do most battered wives leave their husbands?** Yes, most do leave. But some remain because of social and economic dependence on the husband as well as fear of retaliation from the husband for leaving. **What causes wife beating?** Causes of wife beating can be traced to the sexist, patriarchal nature of society and to the abusers losing control of their lives to poverty, drug abuse, and the like.

5. What is the nature of child sexual abuse in the family? Child sexual abuse in the family, also called incest, mostly involves fathers as offenders and daughters as victims. Stepfathers are more likely than natural fathers to commit incest. Offenders are more likely than nonoffenders to be socially isolated outside the family. Incest usually causes victims to suffer many problems, especially a strong sense of shame and guilt, anxiety and depression, and social isolation. **What is the nature of child physical abuse?** In the family, physical abuse of children is far more common than sexual abuse. A wide gamut of child physical abuse exists, ranging from abuse that causes minor injury to abuse that causes death. Very young children are more likely than older ones to be abused; child abuse occurs more often in lower-income families; abusers have more problems than nonabusers; and victims suffer, in addition to physical injury, many social and psychological problems.

6. What causes child abuse? Factors that have been found associated with child abuse include intergenerational transmission of violence; acceptance of the popular view of physical punishment as proper for disciplining children; poverty and other problems that cause considerable stress for parents; and problematic interaction between parent and child.

7. What is the nature of elder abuse? Elder abuse is more likely to happen to older persons who live with relatives, are male, and are socially isolated outside the family. Elder abuse tends to cause psychological and social problems for the victim. **What causes elder abuse?** Causes of elder abuse include such caregiver problems as stress, severe personal problems, financial difficulty and dependence, as well as the imbalance between the cost and benefit of caregiving.

8. What is the social profile of family abusers? Compared with non-abusers, abusers are more likely to be under age 30, to be lower-class, to be men in the case of spouse abuse and women in the case of child physical abuse, to have a stressful home life, and to be socially isolated.

9. How are vulnerable women protected against sexual and physical abuse? Virtually all states have laws against marital rape but the laws are rarely enforced. Victims of marital rape, however, can find protection as physically abused wives do in several ways: calling the police to have the husband taken away, going to a shelter or safe house, and expecting the court to require the abusive husband to get counseling. **How are children protected?** Mandatory reporting laws require professionals to report child abuse to government agencies, which can either provide the family with social support or remove the abused child from the dangerous home and place the child in foster care. **How are elders protected?** Most states have mandatory reporting laws for elders like those for children. Government departments of social services provide victims with a wide range of services, such as medical and legal services.

SUGGESTED READINGS

Barnett, Ola W., and Alyce D. LaViolette. 1993. *It Could Happen to Anyone: Why Battered Women Stay*. Newbury Park, Calif.: Sage. A critical analysis of various theoretical, empirical, and policy issues on why some battered wives do not leave their abusive husbands.

Barnett, Ola W., Cindy L. Miller-Perrin, and Robin D. Perrin. 1997. *Family Violence Across the Lifespan: An Introduction*. Thousand Oaks, Calif.: Sage. A wide-ranging review of numerous studies on abuses against children, spouses, and elders.

Bergen, Raquel Kennedy. 1996. *Wife Rape: Understanding the Response of Survivors and Service Providers*. Thousand Oaks, Calif.: Sage. Covers all aspects of wife rape, including the nature of the offense, the survivor's reactions, and services for survivors.

Buzawa, Eve S., and Carl G. Buzawa. 1996. *Domestic Violence: The Criminal Justice Response*. 2d ed. Thousand Oaks, Calif.: Sage. A review of various law-enforcement approaches, such as mandatory arrest and protective orders, for dealing with the problem of family violence.

Dobash, Russell P., R. Emerson Dobash, Margo Wilson, and Martin Daly. 1992. "The myth of sexual symmetry in marital violence." *Social Problems, 39,* 71–91. An analysis of the faulty methods and interpretations that have led to the creation of the myth that women assault their husbands as often as men assault their wives.

Gelles, Richard J., and Murray A. Straus. 1988. *Intimate Violence*. New York: Simon and Schuster. Discussing the nature of intimate violence with ample survey data interspersed with the subjects' personal experiences.

Horwitz, Allan V., Susan C. Reinhard, and Sandra Howell-White. 1996. "Caregiving as reciprocal exchange in families with seriously mentally ill members." *Journal of Health and Social Behavior, 37*, 149–162. An illustration of caregiving as a process of mutual exchange rather than as support that a care-provider gives to a dependent recipient.

Jones, Ann. 1994. *Next Time, She'll Be Dead: Battering & How to Stop It*. Boston: Beacon. A critical, powerful presentation of the various aspects of wife beating.

Kantor, Glenda Kaufman, and Jana L. Jasinski (Eds.). 1997. *Out of the Darkness: Contemporary Perspectives on Family Violence*. Thousand Oaks, Calif.: Sage. A collection of articles dealing with the extent, severity, nature, and causes of family violence including child abuse and wife abuse.

Kirkwood, Catherine. 1993. *Leaving Abusive Partners: From the Scars of Survival to the Wisdom for Change*. Newbury Park, Calif.: Sage. An analysis of how victims of marital abuse learn to overcome their dependence on their abusive partners.

Margolin, Leslie. 1992. "Deviance on record: Techniques for labeling child abusers in official documents." *Social Problems, 39*, 58–70. An interesting analysis of 120 official records that reveals how social workers "prove" someone to be a child abuser.

Pryor, Douglas W. 1996. *Unspeakable Acts: Why Men Sexually Abuse Children*. New York: New York University Press. Analyzing the views of men who sexually abuse their sons, daughters, stepdaughters, nieces, and nephews in order to find the reasons for the abuse.

Wallace, Harvey. 1996. *Family Violence: Legal, Medical, and Social Perspectives*. Boston: Allyn and Bacon. Discusses many forms of family violence, including sibling abuse and gay/lesbian abuse, along with related issues such as stalking and victims' rights.

Websdale, Neil. 1999. *Understanding Domestic Homicide*. Boston: Northeastern University Press. A study of how and why husbands kill wives and vice versa, and why they kill children, with special attention to the ways cultural influences and everyday interactions are involved in the killings.

CHAPTER

7 Suicide

In the afternoon of December 2, 1997, 15-year-old Kenny White took his father's pistol, aimed it at his head, and pulled the trigger. He had lived his short life in a small town in South Dakota. The day he killed himself he had not shown to others any sign of suicide in the making: He had eaten lunch with his school buddy, ridden around town in a pickup truck, and bought Christmas presents with his pocket money. Yet he had apparently planned to take his own life. Next to his slumped body in his bedroom was a note he had scribbled: "I really don't know what to say in these dam things, but I want you to know that I love you mom and dad. I'm not in English class so my spelling doesn't have to be perfect." He also asked his mother to quit smoking and his parents, separated for 10 years, to remarry. He further wrote his will, bequeathing his baseball cards, bee-bee gun collection, and Minnesota Twins jersey to various friends (Belluck, 1998).

Like Kenny White, about 30,000 Americans die by their own hand every year. As a cause of death, suicide ranks eighth among adults, but second among adolescents. There is something ironical about suicide. In a highly individualistic society, we are supposed to be more concerned with ourselves than others, to like ourselves more than others. Yet every year we are far more likely to kill ourselves than others as indicated by the fact that the U.S. suicide rate is more than 50 percent higher than the homicide rate (U.S. Census Bureau, 1999).

Since suicide seems such an unnatural act, many people assume that those who kill themselves must be abnormal, mentally ill. The most widely held assumption is that suicide victims have suffered from mental depression. But it is not the depression itself that causes suicide. It is instead the inability to cope effectively with the depression, and this inability has to do with certain social forces in American society. In other words, the overwhelming majority of depressed Americans do not kill themselves. Those extremely few who do commit suicide do so usually because they have been under the influence of certain social forces in their lives. One of these forces is lack of social support. In White's case, he lived in a sparsely populated place where social support seems hard to come by, as many residents have shallow roots in the town and few relatives close by. Other social factors such as race and gender—White's being a white male—also play a role in such a suicide. In this chapter we will take a closer look at race, gender, and other social factors associated with the act of suicide. We will also discuss various forms of suicidal experience, social responses to suicide, and theories that explain why and how some people commit suicide.

Varieties of Suicidal Experiences

On the tragic road to suicide can be found different types of sad travelers with a distinctive kind of experience. Some *threaten* to kill themselves but do not make good their threats. Others *attempt* to take their own lives but do not succeed. And still others actually *commit* suicide. Although they all share the same feeling that their lives are unbearable, these three types of individuals differ in their approaches to suicide.

Threatening Suicide

Those who threaten suicide do so explicitly, directly, or clearly. They clearly want to live rather than die, since their suicide threats are intended as a means of

[handwritten: egoistic suicide - lack of attachment - intimacy]

achieving some objective in life. This does not necessarily mean that they will never carry out their threats. They may do so if the threats fail to achieve their objectives. Given the lack of knowledge about them, it is not possible to determine the percentage of suicide threateners who successfully carry out their threats (Stephens, 1995; Lester, 1988). Obviously, those whose threats are heeded will more likely refrain from killing themselves than those whose threats are ignored. One classic study has indicated various ways in which suicide threats have traditionally been used to produce positive results for individuals:

[handwritten left margin: Fatalistic - intense social controls]

> The threat of suicide forces persons to marry, prevents marriage dissolution, coerces companionship between persons despite their mutual infidelity, prevents marriages, forces parents to acquiesce in their offspring's vicious habits, precludes institutionalization, is rewarded by escape from further military duty, is used to obtain favored treatment over siblings, is employed as a device to avoid military induction. (Siegal and Friedman, 1955)

[handwritten: Altruistic - overly strong, intense attachment]

Attempting Suicide

[handwritten: ANOMIC - conditions in society]

Unlike the threateners, who clearly want more to live than to die, suicide attempters are ambiguous in their intent. They are often seized with the mood of "I don't care whether I live or die." Thus, compared with those who issue threats in unmistakable terms, the attempters are less explicit in communicating their suicidal feelings. They may simply show others how depressed they are, or tell others that they cannot sleep, but generally avoid using the word *suicide*. As a result, most of them do not succeed in conveying their distress signals to others. Only somewhere between 14 and 53 percent of suicide attempters are known to have forewarned others of even an ambiguous intention to die (Bettridge and Favreau, 1995; Wilkins, 1967). When they succeed in communicating their message, others tend not to take it seriously because of its vagueness. This is why suicide attempters eventually resort to dramatic and dangerous methods to express—still implicitly—their appeal for help.

The methods include wrist cutting, swallowing large amounts of sleeping pills, and gas poisoning in the house or car. Although these methods can be lethal, they are less foolproof than those generally used by real suicides, such as shooting and hanging (Peck, 1985–86, 1984). In addition, most suicide attempts are carried out in a setting or in a manner that makes rescue possible, probable, or even inevitable. Some may remain near others during the attempt, or call up a friend immediately afterward. This reflects their lack of determination to die, and most suicide attempts have therefore been described as "a road to life, not death" (*Psychology Today*, 1976).

Suicide attempters are more likely to be women than men, to be young (ages 24 to 44) than old (ages 55 to 66), and to come from lower classes than upper classes. By contrast, those who *actually* commit suicide are more likely to be men than women, to be old than young, and to come from upper than lower classes. Suicide attempters are also more likely to abuse drugs. (O'Boyle and

Brandon, 1998; Hendin, 1995; Harry, 1983; Stengel, 1969). Since the 1960s, however, the gender difference in suicide attempts has narrowed significantly, thanks to the increased independence among women (Kushner, 1995; Kessler and McRae, 1983). Many women are more able today than before, for example, to cope with the emotional impact of divorce because they have worked outside the home prior to the marital breakup. Traditional women, however, are still more likely to attempt suicide. They are more likely to have been socialized to rely heavily on others for emotional support and to feel helpless when having to deal with crises alone. Aside from this "trained dependency and helplessness," suicide attempters in general are also more likely to be rigid in thinking and to see events with a narrow perspective, when compared with nonsuicidal persons (Clifton and Lee, 1995; Patsiokas, Clum, and Luscomb, 1979; Wenz, 1978).

Committing Suicide

About two-thirds of those who commit suicide are known to have had at least one prior attempt to kill themselves. Also, most have openly or subtly communicated their suicidal ideas to others (Hendin, 1995, 1979). Completed suicides comprise a mixed category, which includes suicide threateners who have failed to get what they desperately wanted, suicide attempters who have not been rescued in time, and individuals who were simply more determined to die. From notes left by suicides and from reports given by suicide attempters, we can discern at least five types of suicidal feeling.

First, most suicides may feel so *depressed* that they withdraw themselves from their past daily activities. A deeply depressed college student, for example, cut classes, slept too much, and ate too little. Just before killing himself, he wrote (Wartik, 1995):

> I sit alone, sad and quiet, contemplating death. My hopes and dreams have turned to dust; inside my soul, emptiness. I look back on the bright, bubbly, always contented child that I was, every day and everything was just so great, nothing could really go wrong. Even as I sit and contemplate the end of my life by my own hand, I'm so empty I can't even cry.

Second, many suicides feel *apologetic* toward their survivors. In the following suicide note, for example, a young man apologizes to his parents (Folse and Peck, 1995):

> Mom and Dad,
>   I was supposed to be the model son, doing the best of everything I did. I let you down all those times. I've really screwed up now. I can never be your model son again. I know I can't say anything to let you know how bad I feel about all this, but please try to accept this humble apology and realize this is what I thought best. See you in heaven.
>
> Gary

Third, some suicides feel *vindictive* toward their survivors or themselves. Blaming others for their misery and death, they seek revenge by punishing those they leave behind. This can be illustrated by the following suicide note from a 38-year-old divorced woman (Shneidman, 1975):

> Bill,
>
> You have killed me. I hope you are happy in your heart, if you have one which I doubt. Please leave Rover with Mike. Also leave my baby alone. If you don't, I'll haunt you the rest of your life and I mean it and I'll do it. You have been mean and also cruel. God doesn't forget those things and don't forget that. And please no flowers; it won't mean anything. Also keep your money. I want to be buried in Potters Field in the same casket with Betty. . . . You know what you have done to me. That's why I did this. It's yours and Ella's fault, try and forget if you can. But you can't . . .
>
> Your wife.

Some suicides may feel genuinely angry with *themselves* for having done a wrongful act and for that reason use self-killing to punish themselves. A common example of this suicidal experience is the man who kills himself after murdering another person. This has been referred to as *atonement suicide*. Here is how anthropologist Raymond Firth (1961) describes a case of atonement suicide involving a man on a South Pacific island:

> About the oddest [form of suicide] was that chosen by Pu Sao, who, having broken wind in a public gathering, in his shame climbed a coconut palm and sat down on the sharp-pointed, hard flower-spathe, which pierced his rectum and killed him—a bizarre case of making the punishment fit the crime.

Fourth, suicides may become *magnanimous* toward the world they choose to leave behind. In their suicide notes, some request that their bodies be donated to medical schools, others bequeath their property and money to charitable organizations, and still others forgive whoever has wronged them, as the following indicates (Shneidman, 1975):

> Mary:
>
> We could have been so happy if you had continued to love me. I have your picture in front of me. I will look at it the last thing. I do love you so much. To think you are now in the arms of another man is more than I can stand . . . I am giving my life for your indiscretion. Please don't let me pay too high a price for your happiness. All your faults are completely forgotten and your sweetness remembered. You knew I would do this when you left me—so this is no surprise. Good-bye darling—I love you with all of my broken heart.
>
> W. Smith

Fifth, suicides usually become suffused with *surrealistic* feelings during the very act of ending their lives. The stormy tension that has initially driven them to suicide dies down, and an overwhelming calm takes over just before they consciously breathe their last breath. In this state of calmness, they experience surrealistic feelings. A number of suicide attempters who have cut their wrists report that wrist slashing was not painful. They felt that the sight and smell of their blood was enlightening, leading them to "return to reality and life from the state of dead unreality" of this world. Some wrist cutters even likened the experience to orgasm, followed by a soothing feeling of relaxation and then deeply comfortable sleep (*Psychology Today*, 1976). This type of suicidal experience, however, is becoming less common today because an increasing number of suicides choose the immediately lethal method—firearms—to end their lives. In fact, the proportion of suicides by firearms has grown so much since the late 1960s that guns have replaced asphyxia (which includes drowning, suffocation, and hanging) as the most popular means of suicide today (Boor, 1981; Lester and Murrell, 1980; Ford et al., 1979; Marks and Stokes, 1976).

Groups with Higher Suicide Rates

In general, sociologists, psychiatrists, and researchers in other fields have ignored suicide threateners and attempters and focused instead on suicides. In their efforts to assess the social characteristics of suicides, sociologists have relied heavily on suicide statistics compiled by coroners and other government officials. Usually these statistics are expressed in the form of a *suicide rate,* which refers to the number of suicides for every 100,000 people of a given population. At the same time, sociologists have recognized, to one degree or another, that the official statistics are not highly reliable. At least two reasons have long been suggested for the relative unreliability of official suicide statistics (Labovitz, 1968; Douglas, 1967).

The first is that officials in different countries, states, and local areas use different procedures to determine what constitutes suicide. Consequently, what is judged suicide in one place is considered a natural, accidental, or homicidal death in another. Even within the same country, state, or local area, coroners sometimes disagree whether a given death is caused by suicide—or by homicide or accident. Thus, when officials report a death as suicide, it may not be a suicide. On the other hand, when officials fail to report a death as suicide, it may actually be a suicide. When a corpse is found floating on a river, for example, it may be reported as a case of suicide when it is actually an accident, or vice versa. Also, deaths from victim-precipitated homicide (as discussed in Chapter 4: Physical Violence) may be considered suicides but are routinely not reported as such but as homicides. In short, official statistics on suicide are far from reliable, not only because different officials define suicide differently, but also because it is sometimes difficult to distinguish a suicide from a homicide, an accident, or a natural death.

Second, even if all the official investigators, using different procedures, found the same suicide rate for a given population, the rate might still be relatively unreliable. The reason is that suicide victims or their relatives may conceal the evidence that the deaths were self-inflicted. They would report the suicide as an accidental death. This is particularly the case if suicide is considered a disgrace for the self-killer and his or her family. Furthermore, many automobile fatalities (about 15%) are actually suicides but are routinely reported as accidents (Madge and Harvey, 1999; Lester, 1985; DenHouter, 1981; Phillips, 1979). Thus, official statistics tend to consistently underestimate the suicide rate.

Although sociologists recognize the relative unreliability of official suicide statistics, there are no data showing the *amount* of the unreliability. Consequently, sociologists differ in their estimations of how unreliable official statistics are. Those who want to search for the social meanings rather than causes of suicide are extremely critical of official statistics, arguing that they are grossly unreliable. In contrast, those who want to seek out the causes of suicide assume that official statistics are fairly reliable or at least the best available for studying suicide. Some sociologists have found that systematic misreporting— consistently underreporting suicides—does exist but that it does not significantly distort the analysis aimed at finding out which social groups are more likely than others to commit suicide (Phillips, 1993; Pescosolido and Mendelsohn, 1986). Let us turn to such an analysis.

Industrialized Societies

In the past, anthropologists referred to the occurrence of suicide in non-European societies as either *common* or *rare,* rather than by giving a specific suicide rate. Generally, suicide was considered common in those societies where ritual suicide was known. Examples of ritual suicide include *suttee* (a Hindu ceremony in which the widow would throw herself onto the funeral pyre of her husband), *hara-kiri* (a Japanese ceremony in which a disgraced nobleman or defeated warrior would plunge a sword into his stomach), and the Inuit custom whereby an old man would do away with himself because he could no longer make an economic contribution. Since these ritual suicides were impressively exotic to Western anthropologists and socially approved in the societies where they occurred, they were thought to be very common.

Today, however, sociologists believe that the suicide rates of non-European peoples have been low on average when compared with the rates of Europeans. For example, the suicide rate for the whole of India in 1907 was estimated to be only about 4.8, as compared with a rate of 32.6 for the north German province of Saxony in the period 1906 to 1910. Suicide also tends to increase among traditional people, such as the Native Americans in Brazil today, after their land has been taken over and their customs disrupted by European immigrants (Schemo, 1996). Since European societies were generally more industrialized, high suicide rates have also been attributed to high levels of industrialization. Indeed, as modern suicide statistics have indicated, the more industrialized countries, such as Denmark and Austria, have higher rates than the less industrialized, such as Mexico and Nicaragua (Lester, 1989; Stack, 1982). But among the more industrialized nations rates also vary. As shown in Table 7.1, countries such as Finland,

TABLE 7.1 **Suicide Rates and Income Inequality**

Country	Number of Suicides per 100,000 Population	Income Inequality*
Finland	26.4	6.0
Denmark	20.4	7.1
Switzerland	19.6	**
Belgium	17.9	4.6
Japan	15.1	4.3
Sweden	14.7	4.6
Norway	13.0	5.9
Germany	13.8	5.8
	Average: 17.6	Average: 5.5
Canada	12.8	7.1
United States	11.8	8.9
Australia	11.4	9.6
Netherlands	9.7	4.5
Britain	9.2	9.6
Portugal	7.1	**
Italy	7.1	6.0
Spain	6.6	4.4
	Average: 9.5	Average: 7.2

*Ratio of highest 20% of national income share. For example, 7.2 means that the income of the rich people (those being in the top 20-percent income bracket) is 7.2 times higher than the income of the poor people (those in the bottom 20-percent income bracket).

**Not available.

Source: Human Development Report, 1996; Statistical Abstract of the United States, 1998.

Denmark, and Belgium have higher rates of suicide than do the United States, Britain, and Australia. The relative lack of income inequality seems to have something to do with high suicide rates. As Table 7.1 also shows, countries with higher suicide rates on average have less inequality.

All this suggests that high suicide rates are associated with both economic affluence and equality. Why this association? Because affluence and equality tend to bring a great deal of individual freedom. Given such freedom, individuals tend to rely on themselves more than on others in trying to solve personal crises. Some people, being far too subjective or emotional when faced with a crisis, will find it difficult to solve the problem and therefore increase their risk of suicide.

For the last 100 years, there has also been a certain pattern of temporal variation in the suicide rates of industrialized countries in North America and Western Europe. The rate peaks in the spring and bottoms in the winter, and rises significantly at the beginning of the week and declines sharply during the weekend (McIntosh, 1991; Massing and Angermeyer, 1985; Lester, 1983; Sanborn and Sanborn, 1978). This temporal variation in suicide apparently has to do with the ebb and flow of social life. In the spring and the beginning of the week, most people tend to be so active and busy that they pay little attention to the few distressed, suicidally prone individuals among them, which makes suicide more likely. But in the winter and on the weekends, people tend more to stay home and relax with relatives and friends, and are therefore more able to render social support to the distressed and forestall their suicides.

Residents in Rural, Wide-Open Areas

In the past, most researchers found a positive correlation between urbanization and suicide. Their studies suggest that during the nineteenth century and well into the twentieth century in practically all countries, urban dwellers were more likely than rural residents to kill themselves. The higher urban suicide rate has been attributed to certain characteristics of city life. The heterogeneous population, conflicting social norms, and fast-changing lifestyles in the city were assumed to weaken the individual's ties to others, thereby increasing the potential for suicide (Gibbs, 1971). But in the 1990s the difference between urban and rural life has greatly diminished because the mass media and other institutions have for the last 40 years spread the urban culture to the rural areas. It is now the rural areas that have higher suicide rates (Zekeri, 1995). As shown by Table 7.2 (p. 148), the five states with the highest suicide rates are considerably more rural and more sparsely populated than the five states with the lowest suicide rates. Why is suicide the most prevalent in states such as Nevada, New Mexico, and Arizona? One reason is that people who live in those wide-open areas tend to be more individualistic, more dependent on themselves or less willing to seek help from others when facing a personal crisis, the type of social characteristic significantly associated with suicide. Another reason is that the share of whites is higher in those areas, and whites have higher suicide rates than blacks.

Whites

Indeed, the rate of suicide is much higher among whites than blacks in the United States (see Table 7.3, p. 149). Among males, whites of all ages have a rate of about 21.4 suicides for every 100,000 whites, compared with only 12.5 for blacks. And among females, whites of all ages have a suicide rate of 5, compared with 2.1 for

TABLE 7.2   States with Highest and Lowest Suicide Rates

State	Suicides per 100,000 Residents	Percent Rural	Population per Square Mile
Nevada	29.79	11.7	30.61
New Mexico	23.29	27.0	12.39
Arizona	19.83	12.5	30.61
Colorado	18.42	17.6	31.71
Montana	18.39	47.5	5.47
Average	21.94	23.3	22.16
D.C.	8.75	0	8942.03
Massachusetts	8.58	15.7	710.89
Hawaii	8.47	11.0	169.68
New Jersey	6.85	10.6	991.52
New York	6.62	15.7	364.69
Average	7.85	10.6	2235.76

Source: National Center for Health Statistics, 1993.

blacks. Of all age groups, whites also have higher suicide rates than Asian and Hispanic Americans. Why do whites have higher suicide rates than minorities? The reason is that whites experience less social regulation or more individual freedom, which is associated with a higher suicide rate. But in the last two decades the suicide rate among *black* youths has risen sharply, though still not approaching the rate for their white peers. The sharp rise in black suicide reflects a significant move to middle-class life, which weakens social regulation as shown by a splintering of community and family support networks and a decline in bonds to religion (Belluck, 1998).

But whites of various younger age groups (ages 15–24, 25–34, and 35–44) have consistently *lower* suicide rates than Native Americans of the same age groups. Only among older age groups (beginning age 45) are whites more likely to kill themselves than Native Americans. Put another way, Native Americans of the younger age groups have the highest suicide rate of all racial groups. The basic reason is that the dominant, white society has largely destroyed their tradition-ally proud culture, creating an identity crisis, self-doubt, and self-criticism, which is particularly likely to lead young people to suicide. Suicide rates are lower, though, among many of the Southwestern Pueblos and the Navajo because these peoples have managed to retain their traditional cultural values and practices (Young, 1991; U.S. Congress, 1990; Committee on Cultural Psychiatry, 1989).

TABLE 7.3   Suicide Rates by Gender, Race, and Age

Age	Male		Female	
	White	*Black*	*White*	*Black*
All ages	21.4	12.5	5.0	2.1
10–14	2.4	2.3	1.0	0*
15–19	18.5	14.4	4.2	0*
20–24	27.4	25.9	4.4	3.9
25–34	25.9	21.5	5.5	3.1
35–44	25.5	16.2	7.1	3.0
45–54	23.9	14.1	7.8	2.2
55–64	25.7	9.7	6.8	2.6
65 & over	31.4	11.7	6.2	2.2

*The number is too small, less than 0.1.

Source: Statistical Abstract of the United States, 1996.

The Less Religious

On the whole, Protestants have higher suicide rates than Catholics, who in turn have higher rates than Jews. Sometimes, though rarely, research reveals no real difference in suicide between Catholics and Protestants (van Poppel and Day, 1996; Breault, 1986). But the type of religion people subscribe to is not as important as the strength of their religious identity or the degree of their religious conservatism. Thus, regardless of what religion people have, the weaker their religious identity or the less religiously conservative they are, the higher their risk of suicide. During the period 1900 to 1910 in the Netherlands, for example, the Jewish suicide rate far exceeded both the Catholic and Protestant rates, apparently because the Jews, unlike those in other countries, did not have a strong Jewish identity. Also, in New Zealand, among the Protestants, Congregational church members have the highest suicide rate, Baptists the next highest, and Church of Christ members the lowest (Stack, 1983; Gibbs, 1971; Labovitz, 1968). This is apparently because the Congregational church is the most liberal and the Church of Christ the most conservative. However, if religious identity or conservatism is held constant, religious type does play a significant role in suicide. Thus in the United States those who adhere to Confucianism, Buddhism, or Hinduism, which have no strong prohibition against suicide, are more likely to kill themselves than those who believe in Christianity or Islam, which prohibit suicide (Ibrahim, 1995).

Most sociologists explain the religious differences in suicide rates by using Durkheim's concept of social integration. Thus the higher Protestant rates are seen as having to do with Protestants' lesser degree of integration into their church, when compared with Catholics or Jews. In essence, weak religious identity, religious liberalism, and lack of religious integration seem to reflect the same thing—inadequate social involvement. Regardless of whether they are Protestant, Catholic, or Jewish, people are apparently more likely to commit suicide if they do not go to church or do not participate in some other religious activities. In fact, as research suggests, nominal Christians are more likely than practicing Christians to kill themselves (Martin, 1984; Stack, 1983).

Males

In virtually all societies, men are much more likely to kill themselves than are women. As Table 7.3 shows, the suicide rate among white males in the United States is much higher than the white female rate. This probably has to do with the social inequality between the sexes. Given their greater freedom and opportunities for success, men may find it harder to blame others when having serious problems in life. Instead, they tend more to blame themselves for their own problems and therefore become more likely to commit suicide as an aggression against themselves. Thus, the greater the sexual inequality, the greater the gender difference in suicide. But many studies have suggested that as sexual inequality has decreased since the 1960s, so has the gender difference in suicide (Steffensmeier, 1984; Stack, 1982). Still, the male suicide rate remains much higher, as we have observed. In contrast, though, the *attempted* suicide rate is considerably higher among women than among men (Canetto and Lester, 1995; Kushner, 1985).

There is also a gender difference in methods of committing suicide. As Table 7.4 indicates, men are more likely than women to use firearms, while women are more likely to use poisoning, including gas and sleeping pill overdose. This gender difference reflects the overrepresentation of men in completed suicides and the preponderance of women in attempted suicides. Most of the completed sui-

TABLE 7.4   Gender and Suicide Methods

Suicide Method	Male	Female
Firearms	66%	39%
Poisoning*	14	35
Hanging	15	13
Other	5	13

*Includes drug overdose and gases.

Source: Statistical Abstract of the United States, 1996.

cides involve using the immediately lethal method, which firearms are. But most attempted suicides involve the use of less immediately lethal methods such as gas poisoning and drug overdose (Miller and Hemenway, 1999; Gunnell, Wehner, and Frankel, 1999).

The Divorced

There are large differences in suicide rates by marital status. In general, divorced persons have the highest rate, married persons the lowest rate, and those who are single or widowed intermediate rates. Married couples are most immune to suicide. Those with children are even more immune to suicide than those without children (Lester, 1991; McIntosh, 1991). All this has been taken to suggest that the more and stronger ties we have to other people, the less likely we are to escape our problems through suicide.

Older People

In the United States the suicide rate tends to rise with increasing age, with the young having the lowest rates and the old the highest. Most notably, the suicide rate starts to increase sharply with age 64 and peaks in the oldest age group. But this relationship between age and suicide holds mostly for white males. For white and black females, suicide rates remain low in old age, while for older African American men the suicide rate rises but much less than for their white peers (see Figure 7.1).

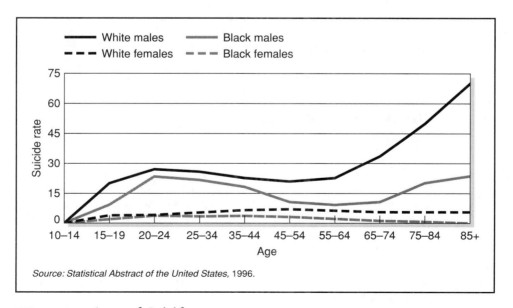

Source: Statistical Abstract of the United States, 1996.

FIGURE 7.1   Age and Suicide

Why does the suicide rate increase so much among white older men? According to a sociological explanation, the social ties that have been formed through marriage, children, work, friendships, community participation, and other social commitments and activities start to diminish with the commencement of old age. The social ties inevitably weaken when "adult children leave home, loved ones die, careers end, and health declines" (Girard, 1993). Without the support of the significant others, older men, when faced with serious life problems, tend more to commit suicide.

Still, as Chris Girard (1993) points out, more women are widowed and living alone in old age but their suicide rate does *not* go up. Apparently, there is something more than the mere lack of social ties that causes high suicide rates. That something more, according to Girard (1993), is the distressing decline in physical and mental capacities. This is conducive to suicide because it threatens men's self-identity as a capable, worthy person. Male self-identity is likely to be threatened in old age because it is oriented to performance—that is, based on demonstration of talent, competence, and accomplishment—in the business or professional world. In contrast, female self-identity is less performance-oriented and more intrinsically oriented—that is, based more on "me as I am, just because I am this way." Thus older women tend to see themselves as a senior citizen, a caring person, a religious person, a person with a hobby, or some other kind of person that is less likely to be threatened by old age. But as more women enter the business world, their self-identity will increasingly be oriented to performance and their suicide rate can be expected to rise in old age (Girard, 1993).

What about older African American men and women? Why don't their suicide rates increase as sharply as those of older white men? Apparently, their self-identity is less performance-oriented, because racism has long denied them entry into business or professional careers. But, again, like white women, their growing participation in the business world can be expected to push their suicide rates upward. This upward push cannot go too far, though, because African American culture strongly condemns suicide (Early and Akers, 1995; Early, 1992).

The Relatively Well-Off

Inconsistencies abound in the observations and findings on the relationship between social class and suicide. Sociologists have long observed that the rich are more likely to kill themselves than the poor because, given their higher status and aspirations, they have farther to fall in times of economic crisis (Henry and Short, 1954; Durkheim, 1897). Supporting evidence can be found in the finding that the richer, more industrialized countries generally have higher suicide rates than the poorer, developing countries, as we have discussed. Within a rich country like the United States, occupations with low unemployment rates and high incomes have been found to have the highest suicide rate (Lester, 1983). Moreover, in developing countries such as Mexico, the more affluent middle class has a higher suicide rate than the lower class (Stack, 1982). Such a positive relationship between class and suicide, however, does not always appear in sociological research. Some studies have shown just the opposite—a negative relationship—with the poor having higher suicide rates than the rich (Stack, 1982). This is consistent with the common finding that unemployment, which is more likely to happen to the poor, is associated with suicide (Platt, 1984). According to the researchers, poverty and unemployment may cause suicide by generating stress or exacerbating a preexisting depression. There is yet a third type of study, which has found no relationship at all between class and suicide (Marks, 1980).

The contradiction in those findings stems largely from the different ways researchers define social class or test the relationship between class and suicide. Some use income and others employ occupation to define social class. Some control for the impact of intervening variables such as race, age, or divorce in analyzing the class–suicide relationship; others do not. Given the conflicting data, we obviously do not know with total certainty whether the rich are more suicidal than the poor or vice versa. But we can be *reasonably* certain that the rich are more suicidal because of the consistent evidence that suicide rates are higher in affluent societies than in poor ones and also higher among whites (a relatively well-off group) than among blacks (whose poverty rate is higher).

Situational Factors in Suicide

We have just observed that individuals with certain social characteristics are more inclined to commit suicide. We also know that they are even more likely to kill themselves if they find themselves in certain social situations or undergoing certain social experiences. These situations or experiences may include going through adolescence, going to college, being in prison, being infected with the AIDS virus, and being exposed to media influences.

Going through Adolescence

Among adolescents, suicide ranks as the second most frequent cause of death after accident. In fact, many accidents, especially car crashes, that take the lives of adolescents, are actually suicides (U.S. Census Bureau, 1999; Phillips, 1979). More significant, while their suicide rate is still lower than that of older adults, teenagers today are much more likely than their peers of the past to kill themselves. Of all U.S. age groups, adolescents have experienced the largest increase in suicide rates over the last 20 years. As shown in Table 7.5, the greatest increase involves ages 10 to 14, followed by ages 15 to 19. By contrast, suicide rates have declined among the older age groups—from age 35 to above 65.

The huge rise in youthful suicide may stem from the fact that adolescence as a life crisis has gotten worse over the last 20 years. It is well known that adolescents are often caught in the transition between childhood and adulthood. Treated simultaneously like children (e.g, being considered too young to drink, to stay out late, or to have sex) and like adults (being old enough to drive, work, or vote), adolescents tend to feel "conflicted" and confused—resentful of being

TABLE 7.5   Changes in Suicide Rates by Age Groups

| Age | Suicide Rate | | % Change |
	1970	1993	
10–14	0.6	1.7	+183
15–19	5.9	10.9	+85
20–24	12.2	15.8	+30
25–34	14.1	15.1	+7
35–44	16.9	15.1	−11
45–54	20.0	14.5	−28
55–64	21.4	14.6	−32
65+	20.8	16.3	−22

Source: Statistical Abstract of the United States, 1973, 1996.

treated like children and fearful of being unable to discharge adult responsibilities adequately. This feeling is often expressed in the form of defiant and rebellious behavior toward parents, delinquency, drug use, reckless driving, or some other action designed to attract attention from others (Hendin, 1995). Such problems are part of the transition from childhood to adulthood, which youths of every generation, with social support from adults, have gone through and come out of without too much difficulty.

However, over the last 20 years, significant changes have occurred in the family as well as in the economic and religious lives of adolescents that make it more difficult to deal with the transition problems. Today there are proportionately more parental divorces, more single-parent families, more two-career families, and more latch-key kids who come home to empty houses after school. Teenagers are also less likely to work part-time during the school year and full-time during the summer than were their peers of 20 years ago. The rate of church attendance and participation in other religious activities is also lower among teenagers today (Stack, 1986). In other words, contemporary youngsters have effectively suffered a decline in social integration and regulation (traditionally provided by the family, job market, and religion), hence an increase in suicide rates among them. Lack of social integration and regulation is associated with a relatively high rate of suicide, as we will discuss later.

Going to College

Research has shown that college students in the United States have higher suicide rates than individuals of the same age group in the general population.

Among college students themselves, those who attend better universities are more likely to kill themselves because of greater pressure to achieve in an intensely competitive atmosphere (Lester, 1983; Peck and Schrut, 1971). At any given institution, suicide-prone students generally do better than others in their studies, but their grades typically drop to Ds and Fs when they begin to think about killing themselves. Most give some warning of their intentions to parents and friends by appearing troubled or depressed (Hendin, 1995).

Since college life appears more stressful than noncollege, working life, the greater stress experienced by students may be an important factor in their higher risk of suicide. But something else also contributes to their suicides, something that makes it difficult to cope with the stress, namely, their lack of social ties or social support, a common problem among suicidal students. As one such student says about his university, "This place is just so damned big! Nobody here really cares what happens. So, nobody here will notice when I'm gone" (Rickgarn, 1994). Another suicidal student says, "Nobody wants to associate with me. I've never felt so alone. I eat alone and no one comes to see me in my room" (Rickgarn, 1994). The significance of the lack of social ties or support as a factor in suicide can also be discerned from the fact that college students are more likely than nonstudents to be single. Without a spouse and children, college students lack the social ties that typically help married couples relieve their stress as well as restrain them from killing themselves.

Being in Prison

Suicide in prison is relatively common. It is, in fact, the leading cause of death among prison inmates. In a number of countries, suicide rates are considerably higher inside prison than outside. As Table 7.6 indicates, prisoners are on average 8 times more likely to kill themselves than free citizens. Moreover, the rate of prison suicides has, over the last 20 years, increased considerably more than the rate of suicides among the general population (Hayes, 1995; Liebling, 1992).

Those who kill themselves in prison are predominantly whites, in their early twenties, and are single, divorced, or lacking stable and supportive relationships. The majority die by hanging, which is the most easily available method. Ironically, proportionately more inmates commit suicide in local jails while awaiting trial or sentencing than in state prisons after conviction or sentencing. Even more ironically, most of the suicides have been charged with relatively minor crimes. Does this mean that they are probably mentally ill or emotionally disturbed? No, because they are far less likely than the suicides in the larger society to have a history of mental depression or psychiatric treatment. The immediate cause seems to be fear of other inmates or imprisonment itself, which arises from the *radical transformation* of a free person in a familiar, safe environment into a confined person in an unaccustomed, dangerous milieu, further compounded by the *uncertainty* of judicial outcome (Hayes, 1995; Lester and Danto, 1993; Liebling, 1992).

During the initial phase of imprisonment the level of stress is the highest; it diminishes only with adjustment to prison life. Not surprisingly, inmates are most

TABLE 7.6   **Prison Suicide Rates in Various Countries**

Country	Prison Suicide Rate	Ratio of Rate in Prison to Rate Outside Prison
Britain	56	4
Belgium	60	3
Italy	80	10
Austria	81	4
France	106	5
Canada	120	6
Australia	135	8
United States	200	14
Switzerland	465	14
Average	145	8

Source: Alison Liebling, *Suicides in Prison* (London: Routledge, 1992). Used with permission of the author.

likely to kill themselves during the first few days of their imprisonment. However, death-row inmates, who are imprisoned for life or awaiting execution, also have a higher suicide rate than the general prison population. But the *immediate* cause of such suicides is an overwhelming sense of despair or hopelessness, paradoxically quite similar to the emotion of the suicides outside the prison (Hayes, 1995; Lester and Danto, 1993; Liebling, 1992).

Being Stricken with AIDS

Research has found higher rates of suicide among people who are stricken with fatal diseases such as terminal cancer. Since AIDS (acquired immune deficiency syndrome) is a fatal disease, it shouldn't be surprising that AIDS patients are more likely than healthy people to kill themselves. As a study shows, the yearly suicide rate of male AIDS patients in New York City is nearly 700 suicides for every 100,000 patients, compared with only 20 for men free of AIDS (Mancoske, 1995; Lester, 1989). The standard explanation is that dying from AIDS produces an enormous sense of hopelessness while the social stigma attached to the disease brings the additional burden of social rejection and isolation (Beckerman, 1995).

But less sick patients, those who are only infected with HIV (human immunodeficiency virus, the virus that causes AIDS) and have a chance of surviving, are even more likely to kill themselves. Why are these less sick HIV-infected patients more suicidal than the dying AIDS patients? One reason has to do with the tremendous tension resulting from the *uncertainty* about the outcome of HIV infection—which may or may not lead to death. By contrast, the certainty of death facing the AIDS patient tends to induce an attitude of resignation or acceptance, which reduces stress and hence the risk of suicide. Another reason is the sudden, *radical transformation* from being a totally healthy person to being a seriously—possibly deathly—ill patient. Being struck with this transformation is bound to be extremely stressful. Such stress tends to diminish when the HIV infection becomes, after some passage of time, full-blown AIDS, because the patient will have learned to master the fear of death. In fact, some terminally ill AIDS patients may have the same low risk of suicide as healthy people (McKegney and O'Dowd, 1992). In other words, the stress that triggers suicide among HIV-infected patients is basically the same as the stress that provokes suicide among newly jailed inmates. In both cases, the stress comes from uncertainty about a new, frightening situation and from failure to cope with the radical transformation of status.

Under Media Influence

Research has demonstrated the mass media's influence on suicide. When the suicide of a famous person, such as the novelist Ernest Hemingway or the movie star Marilyn Monroe or the grunge-rock star Kurt Cobain, is widely publicized, the nation's suicide rate tends to go up (Stack, 1987; Wasserman, 1984; Phillips, 1974). This does not mean that celebrity suicide causes imitative suicide among all kinds of ordinary people. Rather, imitative suicide is more likely to occur among the suicidally inclined persons with the social characteristics (such as being male and white) that we have seen associated with high suicide rates. Why, then, does celebrity suicide encourage imitative suicide among those individuals? Apparently it is because celebrities are regarded as role models, and, by killing themselves, celebrities demonstrate the act of suicide as well as legitimize it as a way of solving a terrible life problem. Note too that the news about an ordinary person's suicide can also raise the country's suicide rate *if* the news is so widely disseminated that it reaches a truly national audience. Such publicity has the same impact on imitative suicide as TV commercials featuring an ordinary person have on consumer purchases (Stack, 1991).

Country music can also exercise a significant influence on suicide. As research has shown, the greater the radio airtime given to country music, the higher the white suicide rate is. Country music tends to promote suicide by reinforcing preexisting suicidal moods in suicidally inclined listeners. This is because country music conveys many suicide-related themes, such as marital strife and dissolution, alcohol abuse, financial strain, and exploitation at work. A content analysis of 1400 hit country songs reveals that nearly three-fourths deal with the travails of love. Hopelessness further pervades most country songs. While country music cannot by itself drive people to suicide, it can increase suicide risk among those with suicidal tendencies (Stack and Gundlach, 1992).

Social Responses to Suicide

Whether suicide is common or rare depends to some degree on how society responds to it. As two sociologists observed more than 60 years ago, "Where custom and tradition accept or condone it, many persons will take their own lives; where it is sternly condemned by the rules of the Church and State, suicide will be an unusual occurrence" (Dubin and Bunzel, 1933). There is much evidence to support this observation. Islamic nations, which condemn suicide more strongly than other societies, usually have lower suicide rates. Similarly, African Americans have a relatively low suicide rate in the United States because their culture strongly condemns self-destruction (Early and Akers, 1995). Also, in Western societies, suicide has become more common in the present century than in previous ones, largely because of the increasingly permissive attitude toward suicide. In the past, those who committed suicide were treated as criminals to be punished; today, suicides are considered victims to be sympathized with. In medieval England and Europe, for example, suicides were punished by denial of Christian burial, confiscation of property, or burial at a crossroads with a stake driven through the heart—presumably to keep the condemned spirit from wandering. Such harsh treatments of suicides are unheard of today. Instead, an upsurge of posthumous love, or at least tender feeling, toward the self-killer typically fills the hearts of the surviving relatives, friends, and others.

Survivors' Reactions

When a loved one, such as a friend or family member, commits suicide, those who are left behind tend to feel guilty. Parental suicide is particularly traumatic to young children, who may be so overwhelmed with guilt feelings that they become seriously disturbed. The children typically think that they were in some way responsible for their parent's death (Carter and Brooks, 1991; Cain and Fast, 1966). Mature adults also can hardly avoid the assault of guilt feelings. They often blame themselves for having failed to perceive the self-killer's suicidal intent, for having been unable to prevent the suicide, or for having done something that might have caused the suicide (Farberow, 1991; Calhoun, Selby, and Walton, 1985–86; Henslin, 1970). Society further intensifies their self-blame by holding them responsible in some way for the death (Calhoun, Selby, and Abernathy, 1984). However, unlike young children, mature adults are capable of neutralizing their guilt. As shown in one study, adults can rationalize their guilt in several ways: (1) They can regard themselves as having been good to the person who committed suicide. (2) They can view the suicide as inevitable, believing that even if they had been extraordinarily nice to the deceased, they still could not have stopped the suicide. (3) They can consider the suicide as a good thing for the person involved because the deceased is no longer suffering in this world (Henslin, 1970).

Most people also suffer from some symptoms of physical illness and emotional disturbance (such as migraine headache, hypertension, crying spells, and depression) subsequent to a close relative's suicide. These symptoms are comparable to, but more prolonged and devastating than, bereavement effects from natural or accidental death. They continue to plague the survivors even six months after the suicide. Within the same period, however, the relationships among the surviving family members are frequently strengthened, largely because the suicide prompts them to feel closer to each other in their common plight. The survivors also receive considerable support from other relatives and friends, who tend to be sympathetic, to listen, and to avoid the topic of death in order to focus on living (Farberow, 1991; Rudestam, 1977). Not surprisingly, health problems tend to remain in those who continue to think about their loved one's suicide and avoid discussing it with friends, keeping it as a "psychological skeleton in their emotional closet" (Pennebaker and O'Heeron, 1984).

While a parent's suicide has the greatest impact on the surviving child, a child's suicide has the most severe effect on the surviving parents. In addition to having the inevitable sense of shock and devastation in the wake of a child's suicide, the parents tend to feel totally responsible for the death, because they are acutely aware of the tremendous stigma society attaches to parents whose child commits suicide. Research has shown that most people blame the parents of a child suicide more than they blame survivors of other suicides. Typically, the general public asks how this tragic event could possibly have happened (Calhoun, Selby, and Faulstich, 1980).

Advocating Suicide

Since the U.S. Supreme Court ruled in 1990 that Nancy Cruzan's parents had the right to remove the feeding tube that kept their comatose daughter alive, a growing number of Americans have come to believe that there is no virtue in heroically prolonging life against the patient's wishes. In fact, most Americans believe that terminally ill patients should be allowed to die with dignity rather than live in a deathlike, vegetative state. In response to this development, Congress has passed the Patient Self-Determination Act, which requires hospitals to inform patients of their right to control their treatment through living wills—advance instructions about what they want their doctors to do in the event of a terminal illness. This in effect allows patients to kill themselves by refusing life-sustaining treatments. More than half of U.S. doctors support this option. Further, increasing determination on the part of the government and general public to cut medical costs can be expected to encourage or pressure more doctors to withhold extremely expensive life-prolonging treatments from terminally ill or permanently unconscious patients (Gibbs, 1995; Davis, 1990).

Such a suicide (if it is a suicide), however, is different from a doctor-assisted suicide, in which the doctor helps the patient die by prescribing a deadly drug overdose or providing the patient with a suicide machine like the one made by Dr. Jack Kevorkian. In about 40 states it is still a crime for a doctor to assist patients in committing suicide (Reibstein, 1997). Primarily because it is illegal, only a small number (less than 5 percent) of U.S. doctors in a national survey said they had helped patients end their lives. If assisted suicide is legal, 24 percent of the doctors said they would help patients commit suicide (Stolberg, 1998).

But this is not the case with their counterparts in the Netherlands and the Northern Territory of Australia. In 1995 the northern Australians passed the world's only euthanasia law, although their national parliament overturned it in 1997. In the Netherlands, euthanasia is technically not legal yet, but doctors who practice it are almost never prosecuted. Although popularly known as "mercy killing," euthanasia as practiced in the Netherlands and Australia is actually doctor-assisted *suicide* because it must be requested by a patient who is doing so voluntarily, is mentally competent, has a disease with no prospect for improvement, and is experiencing unbearable physical or mental suffering (Loff and Cordner, 1998; Mydans, 1997; Simons, 1995). In other countries, particularly Great Britain, the same kind of suicide is illegal but support for it has been growing. In the United States, Oregon has approved of assisted suicide, and two federal appellate courts have struck down laws in the states of New York and Washington that prohibit assisted suicide. The right-to-die supporters believe that the U.S. Supreme Court will eventually legalize assisted suicide, although opponents disagree and the U.S. Congress has in late 1999 passed a bill banning it (Pear, 1999; Kamisar, 1998; Reibstein, 1997).

An apparent reason behind the growing support for assisted suicide is the patient's unbearable pain or suffering. Some critics argue that the medical profession is to blame for this problem because the vast majority of doctors do not know how to treat pain, so that up to 90 percent of patients die in too much pain (Gibbs, 1993a). The critics assume that if the medical profession can eliminate the pain, terminally ill patients would stop requesting suicide. But unrelievable pain is not the only reason for suicide. There is another reason: In the eyes of right-to-die advocates, the quality of life (such as loss of dignity, loss of autonomy, or loss of meaning in life) is more important than merely being alive. It is therefore argued that people should be allowed to die if they find their lives worthless or unbearable. There is also the legal argument that the right to die is the same as the constitutionally guaranteed right to privacy, the right to be left alone (Gianelli, 1999; Stolberg, 1998; McCord, 1995). Such arguments help ensure the continuing practice of assisted suicide for some people.

Preventing Suicide

All this has alarmed right-to-life groups. They are more concerned with the sanctity of life. Considering every life sacred, they argue that it is morally wrong to take one's own life just as it is to take another's, and that it is the state's duty to help preserve rather than destroy life. They fear that doctor-assisted suicide would lead down the "slippery slope" to widespread euthanasia. They picture that, although they would not necessarily want to die, the physically or mentally different, the poor, and others devalued by society, along with many terminally ill patients, would be eliminated in the same way as their counterparts were in Nazi Germany. Their lives would be regarded from the quality-of-life perspective as worthless, and it would be considered justifiable and even merciful to terminate them. If these "worthless" people are not legally required to die, they would still be under great social pressure to commit suicide as an act of love and patriotism, because their death would remove a costly burden on family and society (Emanuel, 1997, 1996; Hendin, 1997; Mauro, 1996; Shapiro, 1995). As an author who opposes mercy killing of the terminally ill sums it up, "From there, it's a hop, skip and a jump to killing people who don't have a good 'quality' of life, perhaps with the prospect of organ harvesting thrown in as a plum to society" (Smith, 1993).

While the right-to-life forces try to stop doctor-assisted suicide, another group is more interested in discouraging large masses of distressed, suicidal people from killing themselves. Since the 1950s, many suicide-prevention centers have appeared in various countries. At least 150 such organizations now exist in Great Britain and over 200 in the United States. Their primary function is to encourage troubled individuals to telephone them for help. They have friendly, compassionate, and dedicated volunteers working around the clock (Hendin, 1995).

There is some evidence that these organizations, using the psychological method of counseling, can effectively deal with a few individual cases of potential suicide. But they cannot substantially reduce suicide rates. Thus, despite the tremendous increase in the number of suicide prevention centers in the United States over the last 20 years, the suicide rate has not declined significantly. One study even shows that there is little overall difference in suicide rates between counties that have suicide prevention centers and those that do not (Miller et al., 1984). The reason is that suicide is basically a sociological problem (caused by larger social factors) rather than a psychological problem (caused by factors within the individual).

It is worth noting that people who are characteristically prone to suicide, such as older men, tend to stay away from suicide prevention centers, and, in the few cases when they do call the centers for help, tend to go ahead and kill themselves anyway. On the other hand, people who are less inclined to commit suicide, such as young white women, constitute the majority of those who call up the centers and are likely to refrain from taking their lives (Hendin, 1995; Greer and Weinstein, 1979). In other words, suicide prevention centers are more useful to people who are *less* likely to commit suicide, but less useful to people who are *more* likely to end their own lives. Apparently the organizations cannot deal with the social forces that cause some older men and other seriously suicide-prone individuals to kill themselves. What exactly is the nature of these social forces? Some of the theories discussed below may give us the answer.

Sociological Theories of Suicide

Efforts to explain suicide can be divided into two broad categories: psychiatric and sociological theories. Psychiatric theories generally assume that there is *something wrong* with the person who commits suicide, whereas sociological theories assume that there is *nothing wrong* with that person. More specifically, a few psychiatrists believe that suicidal people are in one way or another mentally ill—hence, mental illness is considered the cause of suicide. A few other psychiatrists hold the classical Freudian view that the death instinct, thanks to the breakdown of ego defenses, drives individuals to kill themselves. Most psychiatrists, however, theorize that the cause of suicide is mental depression, morbid anxiety, intense hopelessness, deep frustration, or a traumatic experience during early childhood.

Most sociologists find the psychiatric theories useless for not being able to explain why some individuals (who are, say, men, whites, or older persons) are more likely to commit suicide than other individuals (who are women, blacks, or younger persons). If we used the psychiatric theories for an explanation, we would have to insist that men, whites, and older persons are somehow psychologically abnormal, which is, of course, far from the truth. Also, to sociologists, the causes of suicide do not reside within the individual, but within the group to which the individual belongs. This idea underlies the following sociological theories.

Classical Durkheimian Theory

Although French sociologist Émile Durkheim (1897) presented his theory of suicide many years ago, it remains the most influential theory in the field. If we examine it very closely, as we would the trees of a forest, we can get confused by its many ambiguities and inconsistencies. But if we look at it as a whole, as we would the forest, we may see with clarity a very useful theory for explaining various types of group influences on suicide rates. Let us look at the theory as a whole.

According to Durkheim, there are two major causes of suicide: One has to do with *social integration*, the other, with *social regulation*. Social integration involves individuals voluntarily attaching themselves to a group or society of which they are members. Social regulation involves individuals being restrained, constrained, or controlled by a group or society of which they are members. Social integration or regulation varies from one individual to another. Compared with unmarried individuals, for example, married persons experience more social integration by virtue of their being a spouse and parent, an important part of a group called the family. Similarly, compared with males, females are subjected to greater social regulation by a society with gender inequality, as exemplified by girls experiencing greater parental control than their brothers.

According to Durkheim, people who experience *too little* social integration as well as people who experience *too much* integration are more likely to commit suicide, when compared with those who experience *moderate* integration. In like manner, those who are subjected to *too little* social regulation as well as people who are subjected to *too much* regulation are more likely to kill themselves, when compared with those who are subjected to *moderate* regulation. There are, then, four types of suicide, as shown in Figure 7.2: (1) *egoistic suicide*, which is caused by too little social integration; (2) *altruistic suicide*, brought about by too much integration; (3) *anomic suicide*, generated by too little social regulation; and (4) *fatalistic suicide*, produced by too much regulation.

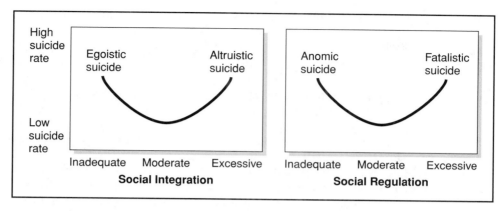

FIGURE 7.2   Schematic Presentation of Durkheim's Theory

A few examples can be used to explain how the theory works. Compared with married persons, unmarried ones are more likely to commit *egoistic* suicide, because they are *less socially integrated,* and are unable to receive love, affection, or moral support from a spouse and children when deeply frustrated with their lives. Compared with ordinary soldiers of a country, members of a small close-knit terrorist group are more likely to commit *altruistic* suicide by becoming suicide bombers, because they are *more integrated* into their organization. Rich countries have higher rates of *anomic* suicide than poor countries. This is because the citizens of rich countries, being *less socially regulated,* are more encouraged to expect too much from life, and thus more liable to greater frustration when their expectations fail to materialize. In ancient societies slaves were more likely than free persons to commit *fatalistic* suicide, for, as Durkheim reasoned, the slaves were *more regulated* in that their "futures were pitilessly blocked and passions violently choked by oppressive discipline" (Durkheim, 1897). Fatalistic suicide is also relatively common today among rural women in China, where the women are often made to feel worthless and helpless because of their gender (Rosenthal, 1999).

Many studies have supported Durkheim's theory. Here are a few examples:

■ In their analysis of 42 nations, K. D. Breault and Karen Barkey (1982) found that social integration in the form of being religious, family-oriented, and patriotic is strongly related to suicide: the greater the integration, the lower the suicide rate.

■ Nick Danigelis and Whitney Pope (1979) found that the married have lower suicide rates than the single, divorced, or widowed, because, as Durkheim's theory suggests, married people are more socially integrated than others.

■ Steven Stack (1979) discovered that a sharp increase in political regulation—indicated by such events as declarations of martial law and banning of a political party—is associated with an increase in suicide.

■ Walter Gove and Michael Hughes (1980) found that living alone, which reveals a lack of social integration, is a powerful predictor of suicide.

Modern Durkheimian Theories

A number of modern theories derive their core concepts from Durkheim's classical theory. The most viable and interesting is the theory developed by Andrew Henry and James Short (1954).

Henry and Short first define suicide as an act of aggression directed against oneself, the aggression having been induced by one's frustration with life. They then theorize that this self-directed aggression results from three different factors, which are (1) sociological, (2) psychological, and (3) economic in nature.

The sociological factor consists of two parts: a *weak relational system* and *weak external restraint*. The first term refers to a lack of involvement with other people, so the term *weak relational system* means about the same thing as Durkheim's *inadequate social integration*. As Durkheim would have anticipated, Henry and Short point out that individuals who are inadequately involved with others are prone to suicide. These suicide-prone people include those who are unmarried rather than married and those who are older (over age 65) rather than younger.

The second term, *weak external restraint*, has the same meaning as Durkheim's *inadequate social regulation*. Like Durkheim, Henry and Short argue that higher-status persons are more likely than lower-status ones to commit suicide, because higher-status individuals have less external restraint so that they tend to blame themselves rather than others for their own problems. By higher-status persons, Henry and Short refer to whites, males, individuals with high income, and army officers. By low-status persons, Henry and Short have in mind blacks, females, individuals with low income, and army recruits.

With respect to the psychological factor of suicide, Henry and Short suggest that a strong superego, which is thought to result from "internalization of harsh parental demands and discipline," produces a high psychological propensity to suicide. This means that if people have been conditioned by their parents to develop a strong conscience, they are likely to blame themselves rather than other people for their problems and frustrations. Since they blame themselves (instead of others), they will likely kill themselves (instead of others).

As for the economic factor of suicide, Henry and Short show that suicide rates rise in times of economic depression and fall in times of prosperity. Economic depression, then, is a major cause of high suicide rates. Henry and Short also observe that, although people of both higher and lower statuses find economic depression frustrating, the frustration is greater for higher-status individuals and therefore more likely to cause them to kill themselves. This is because, during an economic depression, higher-status individuals, who by definition occupy a higher social position than lower-status people, fall harder and hurt more.

These three factors in suicide are interrelated through the concept of social status. In terms of the sociological factor, the higher-status person is more likely to be part of a weak relational system and to experience weak external restraint and therefore to commit suicide. In terms of the psychological factor, the higher-status person is likely to have a stronger superego and consequently a greater tendency toward suicide. Finally, in terms of the economic factor, the higher-status person is likely to experience greater frustration during an economic depression and is thus more prone to suicide. By integrating the sociological, psychological, and economic concepts into one theory, Henry and Short have contributed a great deal to our knowledge about the causes of suicide. Research has also largely supported their theory (Unnithan, Huff-Corzine, Corzine, and Whitt, 1994; Lester, 1990).

Phenomenological Theories

Ultimately the validity of the Durkheimian theories, both classical and modern, depends on the reliability of the official suicide statistics that have been used as the source of empirical support for the theories. Durkheimian theorists assume that these statistics are reasonably reliable; consequently, they consider their theories reasonably valid. Phenomenological sociologists, however, believe that the official statistics are seriously unreliable; therefore, they develop a different perspective on suicide.

Two basic differences exist between Durkheimian and phenomenological theories: (1) Durkheimian theories are etiological, primarily concerned with seeking out the *causes* of group differences in suicide rates. In contrast, phenomenological theories are nonetiological, dealing with the popular *meanings* of suicide or with how the suicidal person acts on these meanings. In a way, though, the meanings may cause the individual to commit suicide. (2) Durkheimian theories look at suicide *from a distance*—through abstract official statistics. On the other hand, phenomenological theories look at suicide *up close*—through actual suicide notes, interviews with the suicide victim's surviving relatives and friends, and interviews with suicide attempters.

Theory of Suicidal Meanings.   According to Jack Douglas (1967), before committing suicide, individuals impute certain meanings to their own prospective suicidal acts. These personal meanings, however, differ from the widely shared meanings that the society attaches to suicide.

Douglas believes that our society attaches to suicide three types of meaning: (1) *"Suicidal actions are meaningful."* This means that many people typically ascribe some motive to suicide, such as depression, hopelessness, or drug abuse. (2) *"Something is fundamentally wrong with the suicidal person's social situation."* The general public often blames a suicide on the victim's parents, spouse, lover, or employer. (3) *"Something is fundamentally wrong with the suicidal person himself."* Most people are jolted with shock, bewilderment, or disbelief on hearing that someone they know has committed suicide. The reason is that the society has conditioned them to view suicide as a very unnatural act. Individuals who kill themselves are consequently thought of as psychologically abnormal.

Unlike these three popular meanings of suicide, the meanings that suicidal people construct to make sense of their prospective self-destruction make it easier for them to end their own lives. Douglas divides these personal meanings into four types: (1) *"Suicide is a way of transporting the soul from this world to the other world."* By killing themselves, people believe that they will leave behind their tumultuous lives for a tranquil, peaceful world. (2) *"Suicide is a way of changing the view of oneself held by others in this world or by God."* Feeling that their family and others have taken them for granted while alive, people expect their suicide to attract a great deal of attention, believing that they will be greatly missed and their fine qualities appreciated after they die. (3) *"Suicide is a way of achieving fellow-feeling."* In a surrealistic, dreamlike way, people expect their suicide to generate a great deal of sympathy, thereby bringing their family and friends closer to them. (4) *"Suicide is a way of getting revenge."* Some people want to use their suicide to get even with others by making them feel guilty for having made their lives miserable.

To suicidal people, these personal meanings of suicide are *positive* in nature, and therefore make it easier for them to commit suicide. While Douglas focuses on the positive types of suicidal meanings that facilitate suicides, the theorist we will turn to now views suicidal meanings as *negative* in that they discourage suicides. Individuals must therefore go through a process of rejecting the negative meanings before they can commit suicide.

Theory of Suicidal Process. Jerry Jacobs (1967) views the meanings of suicide as social prohibitions against the act because suicide is defined by society as "a violation of the sacred, God-given trust of life." Thus, according to Jacobs, suicidal people must overcome the social prohibitions before taking their own lives. This entails going through a series of experiences, conceptualizations, or rationalizations.

1. Individuals find themselves faced with unexpected, intolerable, and unsolvable problems.

2. They view these problems not as isolated incidents, but as part of a long-standing history of problems. At the same time, they expect more problems in the future.

3. They believe that death is the only way to solve these problems.

2. Their belief in the efficacy of death intensifies through increasing social isolation, because they cannot share their problems with others.

4. They now diligently look for ways to overcome the social prohibition against suicide, which they have so internalized that they view suicide as immoral.

5. They succeed in overcoming the prohibition because they already feel isolated from others and therefore feel freer to act on their own.

6. They succeed in overcoming the prohibition by rationalizing their intended suicide in such ways as, "Killing myself doesn't necessarily mean I don't hold life sacred. In fact, I still hold life sacred despite my suicide."

7. They convince themselves that the problem they experience is not of their own making and cannot be solved except through suicide.

8. Defining suicide as the necessary solution, they feel that they do not have the choice not to kill themselves, thereby freeing themselves from a sense of guilt and responsibility for their impending suicide.

9. Finally, just to make sure that they will not be punished in the afterlife, they pray to God for forgiveness or leave a suicide note requesting the survivors to pray for their souls. Then they decisively kill themselves.

Summary

1. How do suicidal people approach suicide? There are three types of suicidal people, each with a different way of dealing with suicide. (1) Suicide threateners are explicit in communicating their suicidal intention to others. (2) Suicide attempters are less explicit with their suicidal messages but more likely to actually try to end their lives. (3) Suicide committers may have threatened or attempted suicide or neither in the past. Suicide committers may feel depressed, apologetic, vindictive toward others, angry with themselves, magnanimous, or surrealistic just before they die.

2. Who are more likely than others to commit suicide? Suicide rates are higher among individuals in industrialized than in traditional societies, among residents in sparsely than in densely populated areas or in rural than in urban areas, among whites than blacks, among the less than the more religious, among men than women, among the divorced than the married, among older than younger people, and among the affluent than the less well-off.

3. How are some social situations or experiences conducive to suicide? The rate of youthful suicide has increased sharply over the last two decades because of declining social integration and control in the teenager's life. College students are more likely than their noncollege peers to commit suicide not only because of the greater stress in college life but also because of socially limited capability for coping with the stress. Prison inmates are more likely than free citizens to kill themselves because of tension and stress resulting from the new, unaccustomed experience of confinement and the uncertainty of what will happen to them. HIV-infected patients are more suicidal than those with full-blown AIDS because of extreme stress from having suddenly become seriously ill as well as from uncertainty about the outcome of their sickness. Ordinary suicidal people tend to kill themselves after a celebrity suicide is widely publicized because the celebrity serves as a role model and lends legitimacy to suicide. The frequent radio broadcast of country music also promotes suicide by reinforcing the suicidal moods of suicidally inclined listeners.

4. How does society respond to suicide? While societal response to suicide was punitive in the past, it is sympathetic today. Consequently, suicide tends to generate guilt feelings and even symptoms of physical and mental illness in the survivors. Further, sympathy toward suicides has generated two different social responses. One involves advocating the right to die with dignity, especially when suffering a terminal illness or unrelievable pain. The other involves preventing suicide either by generally supporting the right to preserve the sanctity of life or by specifically helping suicide-prone individuals to avoid killing themselves.

5. How do sociologists explain suicide? While psychiatrists generally attribute suicide to mental disturbance of one type or another, sociologists view the suicidal person as normal. There are two categories of sociological theories: (1) Durkheimian theories are etiological, designed to explain the causes of group differences in suicide rates. Durkheim's original theory suggests that high suicide rates result from either excessive or inadequate social integration and regulation. Henry and Short's theory includes sociological, psychological, and economic factors as causes of high suicide rates. (2) Phenomenological theories are nonetiological, focusing on the meanings of suicide and on how individual suicides behave in accordance with the meanings. One such theory, developed by Douglas, deals with how society and the suicidal person differ in defining suicide and how the personal meanings imputed to suicide facilitate the process of suicide; another meaning-based theory by Jacobs shows how individuals have to overcome the moral prohibition against suicide through certain experiences, conceptualizations, or rationalizations before they can take their own lives.

SUGGESTED READINGS

Committee on Cultural Psychiatry. 1989. *Suicide and Ethnicity in the United States.* New York: Brunner/Mazel Publishers. A review of many studies on suicides among various ethnic groups including Native, African, Hispanic, and Asian Americans.

Early, Kevin E. 1992. *Religion and Suicide in the African-American Community.* Westport, Conn.: Greenwood. An empirical analysis of how the African-American community and culture keeps the black suicide rate low.

Girard, Chris. 1993. "Age, gender, and suicide: A cross-national analysis." *American Sociological Review, 58,* 553–574. An empirical analysis of how role identities, economic development, and kinship institutions affect the age and gender patterns of suicide—such as highest suicide risks for men in old age and for women in middle age in economically developed countries.

Hendin, Herbert. 1997. *Seduced by Death: Doctors, Patients, and the Dutch Cure.* New York: Norton. A critical analysis of the practice of euthanasia and suicide in the Netherlands.

Lester, David. 1989. *Questions and Answers About Suicide.* Philadelphia: Charles Press. Using findings from various studies to answer questions that people are likely to ask, such as what causes suicide.

Liebling, Alison. 1992. *Suicides in Prison.* London: Routledge. A theoretical and empirical analysis of prison suicides in various countries.

Pescosolido, Bernice A., and Robert Mendelsohn. 1986. "Social causation or social construction of suicide? An investigation into the social organization of official rates." *American Sociological Review, 51,* pp. 80–101. A sophisticated analysis of how systematic misreporting of suicide exists in the official statistics but has no significant impact on the relationship between suicide rates and sociological factors.

Rickgarn, Ralph L. V. 1994. *Perspectives on College Student Suicide.* Amityville, N.Y.: Baywood. An analysis of various aspects of campus suicide, including how suicidal students view college and suicide and how to prevent student suicides.

Stack, Steven, and Jim Gundlach. 1992. "The effect of country music on suicide." *Social Forces, 71,* 211–218. An empirical study of the influence of radio-broadcast country music on white suicide rates in large cities.

Unnithan, N. Prabha, Lin Huff-Corzine, Jay Corzine, and Hugh P. Whitt. 1994. *The Current Lethal Violence: An Integrated Model of Suicide and Homicide.* Albany, N.Y.: State University of New York Press. Reformulating Henry and Short's classic theory to explain how attribution of blame leads to suicide rather than homicide or vice versa.

van Poppel, Frans, and Lincoln H. Day. 1996. "A test of Durkheim's theory of suicide—without committing the 'ecological fallacy.'" *American Sociological Review, 61,* 500–507. Attempts to invalidate Durkheim's theory by offering data on the lack of real difference in suicide rates between Protestants and Catholics in the Netherlands.

CHAPTER

8 Mental Disorder

When he was 16, currently 29-year-old Andrew Goldstein first sensed that something was wrong with him. He felt his life had begun to turn inward and downward. He watched *The Simpsons* and listened to the rock band Pink Floyd and constantly paced the floor in his room. He would often talk about becoming a business executive, though he never got a job better than at a Dunkin' Donuts, where his employment lasted just one day. He yearned to have an adoring wife and family, yet he had no real friends. He would wander through a graveyard and walk the streets before dawn. Then, in early 1999, he pushed a blond and vivacious 23-year-old woman to her death under a subway train. He later described why he did it: "I felt a sensation, like something was entering me. . . . I got the urge to push, shove, or sidekick. As the train was coming, the feeling disappeared and came back. . . . I pushed the woman who had blond hair."

Goldstein was a victim of the mental disorder schizophrenia (Kleinfield and Roane, 1999; Winerip, 1999).

Only about 1 to 2 percent of the U.S. adult population, like Goldstein, have ever suffered from schizophrenia, a very severe form of mental disorder (Andreasen and Black, 1995). A rate of 1 or 2 percent may suggest that schizophrenia is relatively rare, but if other, far less serious psychiatric problems are also taken into account, mental disorder is indeed very common. According to the latest national survey, nearly 50 percent of all adult Americans have experienced at least one episode of psychiatric disorder during their lifetime, and 30 percent within the past year alone (Bower, 1994).

In fact, all of us have been mentally ill at one time or another in the same way as all of us have been physically ill. Of course, most of our mental disorders are not serious, just as most of our physical illnesses are not. But, just as we all have occasionally come down with a minor physical ailment such as the flu, we all have occasionally come down with a relatively minor mental disorder such as mild depression. Indeed, depression is so prevalent that it has been called "the common cold of mental illness" (Cherry and Cherry, 1973).

Yet, because of the stigma attached to mental illness, most people associate it with only the most severe forms of illness such as schizophrenia and major depression. Therefore, if we come down with the flu and call in sick we would say to our boss, "I'm ill today," but if we are too depressed to go to work, our family would be too afraid to tell our boss that we are mentally ill. If we say we are *physically* ill, most people would *not* automatically assume we are suffering from a very serious illness such as heart disease, cancer, or AIDS. But if we say we are *mentally* ill, most people would jump to the conclusion that we need to be sent to a mental institution right away.

While the general public equates "mental illness" only with the relatively severe and uncommon forms of mental disorder, most of the mental illnesses that occur every day are far from severe and extremely common. They are basically problems of everyday life, ranging from being sad, anxious, irritable, or antisocial to being dependent on drugs, alcohol, or coffee to doing poorly in reading, writing, or math as a youngster. Psychiatrists define all such problems as mental disorders (Ratey and Johnson, 1997; APA, 1994), but we would not if we associate mental illness only with its relatively serious forms (Kutchins and Kirk, 1997). In this chapter we will deal mostly with serious forms of mental disorder. First, though, we will discuss a number of popular myths about mental disorder. Then, we will take a look at various types of mental disorder, examine a number of social forces behind mental disorder, analyze a series of societal responses to the problem, and see how different psychiatrists and sociologists view or explain mental disorder.

Some Popular Myths

The mentally ill are popularly believed to be extremely weird. In fact, most are far from greatly disturbed. This is the first of several common misconceptions. Only a few inmates of mental institutions spend their time cutting out paper dolls, screaming and yelling, talking to the air, or posing as kings or queens. Even among the most severely mentally ill—schizophrenics—the flamboyant symptoms of hallucinations and delusions are not the most important characteristics of their disorder. Instead, the less demonstrative symptoms of apathy and inertia constitute the core of schizophrenia (Boffey, 1986).

Mental illness is—to take up a second misconception—commonly regarded as hopeless, as essentially incurable. Even after people are discharged from a mental hospital as recovered, they are likely to be viewed with suspicion. In reality, the majority (some 70 to 80 percent) of hospitalized mental patients can recover and live relatively normal lives if their treatment has been adequate and received in time. Even many schizophrenics, whose illness is probably the most debilitating and devastating, can eventually recover. According to studies in the United States and Europe, about half of all schizophrenics *spontaneously* get better over the course of 20 years, and professional treatment with support from family and friends further makes the recovery easier and faster (Kopelowicz and Bidder, 1992; Boffey, 1986).

A third misconception is that there is a sharp, clear distinction between "mentally ill" and "mentally healthy." This is widely taken for granted, but it is true only if we compare the extremely few mentally ill persons who are extraordinarily disturbed with average "normal" people. Most of the time even a psychiatrist cannot clearly differentiate the vast majority of the mentally ill from the mentally healthy. Thus the dividing line between mental health and illness is mostly arbitrary (Brody, 1997; APA, 1994). This is not only because the behavior of different individuals ranges by imperceptible degrees from normal to abnormal, but also because an individual may shift at different times to different positions along that range, appearing normal at one time and abnormal at another.

The fourth point is that the mentally ill are often portrayed in news media, movies, and television programs as crazed, violent people. In fact, the great majority (about 90 percent) of mental patients are not prone to violence and criminality. They are more likely to engage in behavior harmful to themselves rather than to others. Although they have a higher risk of violence than the general, normal population, the mentally ill are less violent than alcoholics, drug abusers, or young lower-class men (Monahan, 1992; Teplin, 1985).

The fifth popular myth is about midwinter depression, which psychiatrists call SAD (seasonal affective disorder). Many people assume that we are likely to become depressed in the middle of winter because of its coldness and lack of sunshine. Research has shown otherwise: Depression is more likely to strike people in the summer than winter (Smyth and Thompson, 1990; Christensen and Dowrick, 1983). Presumably, the summer is more likely to give us the blues because we spend less time with our loved ones than we do in the winter.

Types of Mental Disorder

Psychiatry has two opposing views on what constitutes mental disorder. One is the medical view, which defines mental disorder chiefly as a _biologically_ caused disorder, similar to a physical disease. This view dominates psychiatry today, and its influence can be found in the current edition of a manual published by the American Psychiatric Association for helping psychiatrists diagnose patients. This diagnostic manual contains a long list of mental disorders with numerous symptoms the same way as a medical manual does for physical diseases. The other view of mental disorder is psychoanalytic, which defines mental disorder primarily as an emotional problem that is *psychological* in origin. This view dominated psychiatry in the 1950s and 1960s and is less popular with psychiatrists today. But its traditional classification of mental disorders into fewer and broader types still provides insight into what it is like to be mentally ill (Wilson, 1993).

Traditional Classification

In the traditional classification system, mental illness is divided into two broad types: *organic* and *functional* disorders. Both types may show the same symptoms, such as hallucination, delusion, impaired judgment, and other behavioral disturbances, but they can be differentiated on the basis of their underlying causes. Organic disorder is caused by damage to the brain, which in turn may have originated from a tumor, head injury, viral meningitis, brain syphilis, lead poisoning, deterioration from old age, drug abuse, or other acute physical damage. Functional disorder, on the other hand, is believed to result from psychological and social factors, such as unpleasant childhood experiences, interpersonal conflict, or social stress. Functional disorder constitutes a much larger category of mental disorders than organic disorder. Psychiatrists, psychologists, and sociologists are primarily interested in the study of functional disorder.

Functional disorder can be further divided into three major categories: *psychosis, neurosis,* and *personality disorder.* (See Figure 8.1). In general, psychosis is typified by losing touch with reality, and neurosis by an inability to face reality. As Freud put it, "Psychosis denies reality and tries to substitute something else for it; neurosis does not deny reality, it merely tries to ignore it" (quoted in Kolb and Brodie, 1982). Since psychotics have lost contact with reality, they do not recognize that they are mentally ill and therefore have no desire to seek treatment. Neurotics, conversely, still know what reality is, keenly feel their suffering, and consciously want to get well. Their problem is an inability to accept reality for what it is, causing them to be unreasonably worried about it, terrified by it, or obsessed with it. A psychotic can be likened to a person who thinks that 2 plus 2 is equal to 10 and strongly believes it, whereas a neurotic can be compared to a person who thinks that 2 plus 2 is equal to 4 but constantly worries about it. What about the third type of disordered person, who has the personality disorder? This individual is basically too self-absorbed, unsociable, or antisocial, and may say, "The hell with 2 plus 2; what a silly game to play." Let us get a closer view of these three categories of functional disorder.

Psychosis.   Psychosis is more serious than neurosis and personality, or character, disorder. More importantly, because psychosis involves the loss of touch with

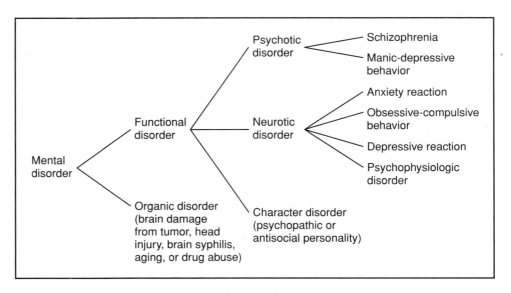

FIGURE 8.1   Traditional Classification of Mental Disorders

reality, the patient cannot attend school or work, or do other things that normal people do. There are many different types of psychosis, but we will discuss only two major ones here for purposes of illustration.

Schizophrenia is the most common type of psychosis. Schizophrenics think and talk in unconventional, illogical, or ambiguous ways; they may say things like "My body is a bottle." They express emotions inappropriately, for example, by laughing in response to sad news and crying in response to happy news. They withdraw from others into their inner selves, often becoming totally unresponsive to their surroundings. They may simply sit, mute, motionless, and emotionless, sunk in deep apathy. Sometimes they engage in such infantile acts as thumb sucking. They have delusions of grandeur (e.g., thinking themselves to be presidents) and delusions of persecution (believing the whole world is plotting to assassinate them). They have hallucinations, hearing voices where there is only silence and seeing things that do not exist. They will talk to themselves, or scream loudly to voices only they can hear. Actually, these experiences of distorted reality are not rare; all of us may have encountered them once in awhile. But psychiatrists would not consider us schizophrenic unless these experiences occur so frequently that our school, job, or family functions are severely disrupted. Because of the severe nature of their mental disorder, schizophrenics are thought to require hospitalization.

Another major type of psychosis is *manic-depressive disorder,* also called bipolar disorder. This involves fluctuating between two opposite extremes of mood. One extreme, called *mania,* is characterized by great elation, exuberance, confidence, or excitement. Individuals in this mood are constantly joking, laughing, and making speeches, although they are far from happy or content. They are continually on the move, not because they enjoy it but because they are driven to it by powerful tension within them. In this hyperactivity, they are enveloped by grandiose delusions, thinking that they are superior or godlike, capable of achieving anything. After going through this manic phase, they suddenly find themselves in the opposite extreme, called *depression*. When brought down to a depressive state, the victims feel an overwhelming despair, experience the delusion of worthlessness, and think of committing suicide. Consequently, they lose the desire to talk, move, eat, and sleep, and spend a lot of time crying.

Neurosis. Neurosis is less severe than psychosis. There is little distortion of reality, and most neurotics are still able to appear normal and do most of the things that normal people do, such as staying in school, keeping jobs, and maintaining family relations. The only problem is that their neurotic symptoms prevent them from being as happy as they want to be. There are various types of neurosis, each characterized by a certain syndrome.

One is *anxiety reaction,* which is a generalized, vague, freely floating apprehension. The object of apprehension cannot be identified. Normal people occasionally experience such anxiety, such as the nervousness we feel before taking an exam, giving a speech, or being interviewed for a job. But the anxiety that attacks the neurotic is far more serious. Consider the case of a 25-year-old secretary: When she was about to leave her office one evening, she suddenly had an intense panicky sensation that something dreadful was going to happen. She had difficulty breathing, feeling as though she was choking. She also felt dizzy. Waves of fear ran through her. Her heart was pounding strongly and loudly, making her think she might be dying. Her legs became rubbery, but she managed to make it outside to get some fresh air. Gradually, the panic subsided. Relieved but still shaky, she made her way home. Later, she described the terror of her anxiety attack: "It could not be worse if I were hanging by my fingertips from the wing of a plane in flight. The feeling of impending doom was just as real and frightening" (Fishman and Sheehan, 1985).

If neurotics can identify a specific object of their anxiety, they are said to suffer from *phobia*. Phobic neurotics may have an extreme, unreasonable fear of animals *(zoophobia)*, fear of heights *(acrophobia)*, fear of closed spaces *(claustrophobia)*, fear of open spaces *(agoraphobia)*, or any of a variety of other specific fears. These are simple, monosymptomatic phobias, triggered by specific animals or situations, such as cats or open spaces. Another type of fear is *social phobia*, brought on by the presence of other people. The neurotic with social phobia cannot speak before an audience, eat in restaurants, or write his or her name when someone else is around.

The second type of neurosis is a combination of *obsession* and *compulsion*. Obsession involves some bothersome idea that keeps interrupting the individual's train of thought. One college student describes his earlier obsession this way: "When I was about eight years of age . . . I thought I was going to cut my throat from ear to ear with a certain large butcher knife in my grandmother's kitchen. I couldn't throw off the idea. . . . I was afraid to go near the knife" (Cashdan, 1962).

A compulsion involves some ritualistic action that neurotics feel they must perform. An example of this can be found in people whose extreme fear of germs and contamination by others drives them to wash their hands repeatedly. Yet the more they wash to get rid of their anxiety about germs, the more anxious they become.

The third type of neurosis is *depressive reaction.* Neurotic depression is distinguishable from psychotic depression, which is much more severe both in degree and in duration. The milder neurotic depression is characterized by the feeling of sadness, dejection, and self-deprecation. Although this depressive reaction may last for weeks or even months, it usually clears up eventually. If it does not, it may become psychotic depression.

The fourth type of neurosis is *psychophysiologic disorder,* also known as *psychosomatic illness.* Its symptoms range from the relatively minor to the very severe, including headaches, ulcer, amnesia, and paralysis. These symptoms have no basis in physical injury or nerve damage; they represent the neurotic's way of solving a psychological problem. This can be illustrated with the case of a young army draftee who had been a dancer and circus acrobat. He found his life in the army too restrictive and monotonous and longed for the travel and excitement he had previously enjoyed. But he could not leave the army for fear of being treated as a deserter. The situation became so intolerable that he developed a psychophysiologic disorder. He could neither walk nor stand, and his legs could not even respond to vigorous prickings by a pin. A few months later, he was discharged from the army on a physician's certificate of disability. Soon his legs began to recover, and in another three months he left the hospital practically well (Kolb and Brodie, 1982).

Personality Disorder. This is a general category for all sorts of deviant behavior the psychiatrist can describe but cannot diagnose as either psychotic or neurotic. This mental disorder has also been called *character disorder* or *sociopathic (psychopathic) disorder.* Its most prominent feature is blatant disregard for society's rules. Its cause is thought to be a lack of moral development—failure to develop conscience, acquire true compassion, or learn how to form meaningful relationships. People with personality disorder include con men, dope pushers, pimps, criminals, unprincipled businesspeople, shyster lawyers, quack doctors, and crooked politicians. Such people come across as merely self-centered nonconformists rather than seriously disturbed patients.

This traditional classification system provides insight into the characteristics of various types of mental disorder by explaining in some detail how they differ. It also encourages psychiatrists to analyze their patient's life in order to find and eliminate the causes of his or her mental disorder. But, to medically oriented psychiatrists, the types of mental disorders presented in the traditional system are too broadly and ambiguously defined, so that they cannot be precisely identified in terms of specific symptoms. Related to this problem, the system presents only a small number of disorders, thereby missing a large number of more specific ones that are often uncovered in psychiatric practice and research.

DSM-IV Classification

A much greater number of mental disorders, totaling over 300, can be found in the DSM-IV, an acronym for *The Diagnostic and Statistical Manual of Mental Disorders, Fourth Edition,* published in 1994 by the American Psychiatric Association (see Table 8.1). Each of the mental disorders is defined as having a list of symptoms. Panic disorder, for example, is defined as having symptoms such as the following:

1. Shortness of breath or smothering sensations

2. Dizziness, unsteady feelings, or faintness

3. Palpitations or accelerated heart rate

4. Trembling or shaking

5. Sweating

6. Choking

7. Nausea or abdominal distress

8. Chest pain or discomfort

9. Fear of dying

Checking a patient against lists of symptoms such as this, psychiatrists can determine what mental disorder their patient is possibly suffering. By using this mechanical, routinized method of diagnosing mental disorders in the same way as physicians diagnose physical diseases, psychiatrists can dispense with the time-consuming psychoanalysis required by the traditional classification system. Psychiatrists can also use the DSM-IV to collect payments for their services from insurance companies or government agencies, which insist that the manual be used (Kutchins and Kirk, 1997).

But the scientific value of DSM-IV falls short. One problem is that the diagnostic manual is merely *descriptive*, describing mental disorders with lists of symptoms without explaining how the disorders differ from one another. DSM-IV also arbitrarily defines disorders in terms of a specific number of symptoms: To be diagnosed as suffering from mania, for example, a patient must have three symptoms from a list of seven, but the manual does not explain why three, not five or six, is required for defining mania (Davison and Neale, 1996). Further, the focus on symptoms in DSM-IV inevitably encourages psychiatrists to eliminate the symptoms rather than the cause of the problem. Influenced by the medical view

TABLE 8.1   The DSM-IV Classification of Mental Disorders

DSM-IV provides a list of over 300 specific disorders. The following are the major types:

1. DISORDERS USUALLY FIRST EVIDENT IN INFANCY, CHILDHOOD, OR ADOLESCENCE. *Examples:* separation anxiety, stuttering, defiance, doing poorly in reading, math, or writing

2. DELIRIUM DEMENTIA, AMNESIC AND OTHER COGNITIVE DISORDERS. *Examples:* delirium from intoxication, substance-induced loss of sanity, amnesia caused by a medical condition

3. SUBSTANCE-RELATED DISORDERS. *Examples:* excessive use of alcohol, cigarette, coffee, cocaine, and other psychoactive drugs

4. SCHIZOPHRENIA AND OTHER PSYCHOTIC DISORDERS. *Examples:* being paranoid, disorganized, catatonic, delusional

5. MOOD DISORDERS. *Examples:* major depression, substance-induced mood swings

6. ANXIETY DISORDERS. *Examples:* panic attack, social phobia, acute stress

7. SOMATOFORM DISORDERS. *Examples:* psychosomatic illness, hypochondria

8. FACTITIOUS DISORDERS. *Examples:* intentional feigning of pains or distress of some physical illness

9. DISSOCIATIVE DISORDERS. *Examples:* multiple personality, amnesia without any medical condition

10. SEXUAL AND GENDER IDENTITY DISORDERS. *Examples:* premature ejaculation, voyeurism, sexual masochism or sadism, transsexualism

11. EATING DISORDERS. *Examples:* anorexia, bulimia

12. SLEEP DISORDERS. *Examples:* insomnia, sleepwalking, having nightmares

13. IMPULSE CONTROL DISORDERS. *Examples:* compulsive gambling, kleptomania (stealing repeatedly), pyromania (being excited about setting fires)

14. ADJUSTMENT DISORDERS. *Examples:* responding to stressful life changes with anxiety or depression

15. MENTAL RETARDATION. *Examples:* Mild, moderate, or severe mental retardation

16. PERSONALITY DISORDERS. *Examples:* antisocial, paranoid, schizoid, dependent personalities

17. OTHER CONDITIONS THAT MAY BE A FOCUS OF CLINICAL ATTENTION. *Examples:* academic problem, marital problem, child abuse

of mental disorder as a biologically caused disease, the elimination of symptoms often involves prescribing medication just as physicians do; however, the mental disorder usually persists because its nonbiological cause remains.

Since its first edition, which was published in 1952, the DSM has been criticized for promoting the medical view of mental disorder as a biologically caused disease. But in its more recent editions, especially DSM-IV, psychiatrists are encouraged to see social factors as possibly additional causes of mental disorder. Thus, after identifying the symptoms of a patient's disorder, users of DSM-IV are instructed to find out if the patient has experienced any "environmental" problems, such as those involving education, occupation, money, or housing. Still, the main emphasis remains on diagnosing mental disorder as a disease with specific symptoms.

DSM-IV has also come under fire for defining too many ordinary problems in our lives as mental disorders. Consider, for example, the "disorder of written expression." According to the psychiatric manual, this so-called mental disorder consists of the poor use of grammar or punctuation, sloppy paragraph organization, awful spelling, and terrible handwriting. It is possible that some students who exhibit these traits may be mentally ill, but it is doubtful that most students with similar problems are mentally ill—they are simply weak or unskilled writers. Also consider the "oppositional defiant disorder," from which children are said to suffer if they often do any four of the following things: lose tempers; argue with adults; disobey adults; annoy people; blame others for their own behavior; or act touchy, angry, or spiteful. It is possible that, in the heat of the moment, some parents may say that their unruly kids are mentally ill. But it is doubtful that most parents believe that those irritating behaviors are signs of mental disorder (Kutchins and Kirk, 1997).

Social Factors in Mental Disorder

Sociologists have long discovered the influence of social factors on mental disorder. We will discuss the more important factors here.

Social Class

Of all the social factors assumed to be related to mental disorder, social class has been most consistently and most clearly demonstrated in various studies to be associated with the disorder. More specifically, people from the lower classes are more likely than those from other classes to become mentally ill. Although the mental illness among the lower classes is more likely to be *reported* to the authorities, surveys on random samples of Americans have consistently found a greater percentage of lower-class people suffering from psychiatric symptoms (Dohrenwend, 1975; Srole et al., 1962; Hollingshead and Redlich, 1958; Faris and Dunham, 1939).

This finding, however, has prompted two conflicting explanations. One, called *social causation,* suggests that lower-class people are more prone to mental disorder because they are more likely to experience social stress (such as unemployment and divorce); to suffer from psychic frailty, infectious diseases, and neurological impairments; and to lack quality medical treatment, coping ability, and social support. This means that low social status is, through those problems, a *cause* of mental illness. The other explanation, called *social selection* or *drift*, suggests that mentally ill people from higher social classes often drift downward into the lower-class neighborhood, helping to increase the rate of mental illness in that neighborhood. This means that the lower-class position is a *consequence* of mental illness among formerly higher-status people. Both explanations have been found to have some basis in fact: Some lower-class people do become mentally ill because of their stressful lives and some middle-class people with emotional problems do drift into the lower-class neighborhood (Jones et al., 1993; Link, Lennon, and Dohrenwend, 1993; Rodgers and Mann, 1993; Kessler et al., 1985).

Gender

There are conflicting findings as to which gender is more likely to become mentally ill. In most studies, women are found to have higher rates of mental disorder. But in some studies, men are the ones with the higher rates. Still other studies fail to find any difference between the sexes (Schwartz, 1991; Dohrenwend and Dohrenwend, 1976).

These conflicting findings, however, concern mental illness *in general*. Studies on *specific types* of disorder do indicate a gender difference. They usually show that women are more likely to suffer from depression and anxiety attacks while men tend more to have antisocial personality, paranoia, and drug and alcohol abuse disorders (Yonkers and Gurguis, 1995; Newmann, 1986; Lewis, 1985). How can we account for this gender difference?

Most sociologists attribute it to the difference in gender roles. The female role is relatively restrictive and oppressive, likely to confine the woman to her inner self, so that she tends to keep her frustration and anger to herself rather than aggressively pour it out on others. Hence women are more likely than men to fall victim to depression and anxiety attacks, which essentially involve the victims hurting themselves. In contrast, the male role is more liberating, more likely to encourage men to be assertive, bold, and aggressive in social relations. If frustrated and angry, they tend more to take it out on others, behaving like antisocial and paranoid individuals. All this can be summarized in Durkheimian terms: Women are more likely to respond to social stress by developing depressive disorders because they are *more* socially integrated and regulated, whereas men are more likely to respond to social stress by developing antisocial personality disorders because they are *less* socially integrated and regulated (Schwartz, 1991).

Research has further suggested that the female role has taught women to value emotional attachment to others, to be sociable, while the male role has trained men to be emotionally detached from others, to be aggressive. Women, then, become more vulnerable to "social loss" such as death of a loved one, while men are more vulnerable to "material loss" such as unemployment (Lewis, 1985; Gove, 1984). However, as more and more women enter the man's competitive world of economic struggle, they would suffer less depression and anxiety. As research has suggested, the increase in women's employment over the last 30 years has caused a decline in their psychiatric distress. During the same period, though, there has been a decline in men's employment, triggering a rise in anti-social personality disorders among men. As a consequence, the gender difference in psychological distress has narrowed in the last several decades (McLanahan and Glass, 1985).

Race and Ethnicity

Like gender, race and ethnicity have not been consistently found to be related to mental illness in general. Many studies have shown higher rates of psychiatric distress among American blacks, Hispanics, and Asians than whites. The standard explanation for this finding is that minorities experience more social stresses stemming from discrimination, poverty, and cultural conflict (Kessler and Neighbors, 1986; Yamamoto et al., 1983). On the other hand, there are studies showing no significant difference in psychiatric problems between minorities and whites. An equally plausible reason has been given for this finding: The minorities' group identification, group solidarity, or social network protects them against those social stresses (Kuo and Tsai, 1986; Kessler et al., 1985). The same explanation has been used to account for the *lower* level of mental illness among Great Britain's minorities, for example, among Pakistanis and Indians. These minorities are the most isolated from Britain's mainstream society because of the whites' prejudice and the minorities' desire to maintain their separate traditions. Yet they are the least vulnerable to psychological disorders because they are said to have strong "community integration," resulting from the very same factors that have brought about their isolation (Shrout et al., 1992; Cochrane, 1983).

More consistent data are available on the relationship between race or ethnicity and specific forms of mental disorder. Among the lower classes, Puerto Ricans and African Americans are more likely than Irish and Jewish Americans to have sociopathic inclinations ("I can easily make people afraid of me and sometimes do just that for the fun of it"), as well as paranoid tendencies ("Behind my back people say all kinds of things about me"). While African Americans are more likely to show paranoid disorders (viewed by researchers as anger expressed outwardly—against others), Jewish Americans tend more to manifest depressive disorders (anger turned inward—against oneself) (Ruiz, 1982; Kaplan, 1972). Asian Americans, particularly those of Korean ancestry, also have more depressive symptoms than whites (Kuo, 1984).

The Urban Environment

Many studies have suggested that the urban environment is a major producer of mental disorders. A community survey, for example, indicates higher rates of mental disorders in urban areas, particularly the inner city, than in rural areas, including the suburbs and small towns (Robins et al., 1984). According to many sociologists and psychiatrists, the urban environment produces a lot of mental problems because it generates an abundance of physical and social stresses—in the forms of traffic congestion, excessive noise, population density, tenuous social relations, loneliness, and lack of social support.

Some community studies also reveal a link between urban living and *specific* psychiatric problems. Generally, urban residents exhibit higher levels of neurotic and personality disorders while the more serious psychotic conditions, especially severe depression, are more prevalent among rural and small-town dwellers (Dohrenwend and Dohrenwend, 1974). Why? Perhaps rural and small-town residents are more likely to find their lives in the nonurban areas too restrictive. They cannot freely express frustration and anger in the presence of relatives, friends, acquaintances, and even strangers—who can easily find out who the troublemakers are. By suppressing their frustration, the ruralites and small-towners may get deeper and deeper into themselves until they become psychotic, totally withdrawing into themselves, breaking the ties between themselves and others, or losing touch with conventional reality. In contrast, urban dwellers can more easily get away from family and friends and are freer to express frustration in the midst of strangers, who tend to tolerate unconventional behavior or anti-social outbursts. If they persist in doing so, the urbanites may become neurotics, who, unlike psychotics, still retain their grip on conventional reality. Otherwise, they may develop an antisocial psychopathic personality, which essentially is an "acting-out" disorder.

Young Age

Many studies before the mid-1980s suggested that in our society older persons are more likely to suffer from mental disorder than younger persons. This was typically attributed to societal neglect of older persons: Older individuals are not given meaningful and satisfying roles to play in society, since these roles are largely allocated to the young, on whom industrial production depends heavily. Deprived of respect by others, older individuals become isolated. As they begin to develop psychopathological symptoms, their families and other close relatives do not bother taking them to a hospital or psychiatrist. By the time their psychopathology becomes hopelessly severe, they are brought to a mental institution where they will be kept out of their families' sight for a long time (Gallagher, 1980; Kaplan, 1972).

However, more recent studies in the 1980s and 1990s show that the elderly are the least likely among all age groups to become mentally ill. According to a national survey published in 1994, for example, relatively young people, aged 25 to 34, have the highest rate of mental illness (Kessler, 1994). Another study by a research team called the Cross-National Collaborative Group (1992) also found a significant increase in major depression among the younger generations, especially over the last several decades. In countries as diverse as the United States, Taiwan, Lebanon, and New Zealand, each successive generation has been growing more vulnerable to depressive disorders. In those countries, people born after 1955 are more than three times as likely as their grandparents to have a major depression. Among Americans, about 6 percent of those born after 1955 have become severely depressed by age 24, while only 1 percent of those born before 1905 have suffered similar depression by age 75.

The increasingly greater prevalence of depression among young people can be attributed to changes in modern society—more specifically, to an increase in social stresses and a decrease in social resources for coping with the stress. Most of the stresses come from family problems, such as divorce, child abuse, or parental indifference to children's needs for love and support. And the difficulty in coping with these stresses comes largely from the loss of the extended family and close-knit, villagelike community in modern society. As research has shown, the lack of parental love and affection as well as the lack of social interaction with parents contributes significantly to the development of depression, heightened anxiety, or other similar kinds of mental disorder. Divorce is also a significant contributor, as indicated by the finding that divorced people generally show a higher degree of psychological impairment when compared with marrieds (Kaplan, 1972).

Societal Responses to Mental Disorder

To understand mental disorder, it is not enough to focus on the problem itself, as we have so far done. It is also important to turn our attention to how various aspects of society respond to mental illness, because these responses can have an enormous impact on the sufferer's life or illness. Let us begin by taking a look at how people in the past dealt with the mentally ill (Cashdan, 1972).

Historical Background

For hundreds of years in ancient Greece, mental illness was viewed with awe. Even the famous philosopher Socrates believed that mental illness was the greatest blessing, for which both states and individuals in Greece should be thankful. Epilepsy, which was then equated with mental illness, was considered sacred—a sign of divine favor. Later, in the Middle Ages, the mental patient was sometimes portrayed by artists and writers as the only one in touch with ultimate reality.

However, for most of human existence, the mentally ill have been badly treated. During the Stone Age, mental illness was attributed to some evil spirit that had somehow entered the body. Archaeological evidence suggests that Stone Age people were the first to perform what is today called *lobotomy* on their mental patients. Their psychosurgical technique, called *trephining*, involved boring a hole in the skull to allow the evil spirit to escape.

With the beginning of the Hebrew and early Greek civilizations, the evil spirit was still considered the cause of mental illness. The fear surrounding the mentally ill is reflected in the Bible: "A man also or woman that hath a familiar spirit, or that is a wizard, shall surely be put to death" (Leviticus 20:27). This pronouncement later provided the rationale for witch burning in medieval Europe, when the church defined the mentally ill as witches who had invited the devil to reside in their bodies. Witch burning took several forms: Some witches were burned alive; others were strangled or beheaded before being burned; and still others were mutilated before being thrown into the fire. In 1636 a man in Konigsberg, Germany, claimed that he was God, and the authorities treated his "demon possession" by cutting out his tongue, chopping off his head, and burning his body.

By the middle 1700s, demonology and witch burning began to disappear, but the mentally ill were still harshly treated. Those who were believed to be dangerous were kept in jails and poorhouses, while those considered less violent were allowed to beg for food on the streets. There were also a few institutions for treating the mentally ill. One such institution, Bethlehem Hospital in London, became widely known as "Bedlam." It handcuffed and chained patients to the walls. It even put patients on display for the amusement of the public. Tickets were sold for a sideshow featuring the wilder, more agitated patients. Similarly, in France not only were the mentally ill treated like animals, but their asylums were much worse than zoos. One French physician of the period reported:

> I have seen them naked, or covered with rags, and protected only by straw from the cold, damp pavement. I have seen them in squalid stinking little hovels, without air or light, chained in caves where wild beasts would not have been confined. There they remain to waste away in their own filth under the weight of chains which lacerate their bodies. Whips, chains, and dungeons are the only means of persuasion employed by keepers who are as barbarous as they are ignorant. (Cashdan, 1972)

In 1793 a revolutionary change in attitude toward the mentally ill occurred when the doctor Phillippe Pinel was placed in charge of a large asylum in Paris. Pinel removed the chains from the inmates. Then he administered to them what has become known as *moral treatment*—treating them like human beings and encouraging them to have hope and confidence in themselves. As a result, instead of acting wild and destructive as they were popularly believed to be, the patients became thankful and docile, and some who had been chained for more than 20 years were able to leave the hospital a few months later. Soon Pinel's moral treatment was adopted in England and the United States. Many mentally ill inmates in jails and poorhouses were moved to new asylums to receive the new humane treatment. But gradually the asylums became overcrowded and served largely as warehouses for the mentally disordered. The conditions in many mental institutions became almost as dismal as before (Gamwell and Tomes, 1995). By 1955, however, new alternatives to mental institutions began to emerge. They included general hospitals that opened outpatient clinics, private psychiatrists, private clinics, and community mental health centers, all of which attempted to be more therapeutic than asylums had been in the past. But even today this therapeutic objective is still far from fulfillment for many mental patients.

The Public

One major difficulty in trying to help the mentally ill lies in the public's negative attitude toward them. Although the public today does not believe in burning the mentally ill as devils, basically the attitude of the past still remains: The mentally ill are stigmatized as moral lepers. Most people, whether they are old or young, highly educated or with little schooling, feel that the mentally ill are somehow dangerous, dirty, unpredictable, or worthless (Trad, 1991; Bissland and Munger, 1985; Nieradzik and Cochrane, 1985; Nunnally, 1961). But unlike the barbaric ancients, who openly showed their intolerance, today's apparently civilized people try to conceal theirs by presenting a front of tolerance, publicly expressing sympathy for the mentally ill. Nonetheless, the intolerance often comes through, as can be illustrated by the experience of a female lawyer who is mentally ill in addition to being a recovering alcoholic. Here is how she describes her experience:

> Several years ago, a nurse told me that she dropped out of a therapy group because there were too many "crazies"—some of them *even took lithium!* (Unknown to her, I take lithium.) Some of my recovering alcoholic brothers and sisters maintain that a person on psychiatric drugs is not "clean and sober." This perverse philosophy is reinforced by social agencies caring for the less fortunate; in my city, most halfway houses willingly accept recovering alcoholics and addicts, but not those taking psychiatric medications. When I told one of my lawyer co-workers about my "problem," he was markedly uncomfortable. (Collier, 1993)

The public's negative attitude about the mentally ill can also be discerned from popular, stereotypical jokes about them. For example, a character in the popular TV show *Roseanne* says that "only murderers, psychos, and schizos can beat a lie-detector test." Even presidential candidate Ross Perot told a cheering crowd during the 1992 campaign: "We're all crazy again now! We got buses lined up outside to take you back to the insane asylum." An award-winning TV commercial for Daffy's, a chain of discount clothing stores, shows a straitjacket with the caption, "If you're paying over $100 for a dress shirt, may we suggest a jacket to go with it?" (Willwerth, 1993; Socall and Holtgraves, 1992).

The negative public attitude toward the mentally ill is so pervasive that it even gets into, of all people, psychiatrists, who are supposed to be compassionate to do their job well. As one psychiatrist observes,

> The curious thing to note about psychiatrists as doctors is in the realm of what they do. They never touch their patients. . . . The exceptions to this are rare and are frowned upon by the profession. I can clearly remember one of my supervisors confiding to me during my training that he sometimes patted his patients on the back on their way out of the office. Horrors! If discovered, he may be branded as an infidel. (Torrey, 1974)

It is indeed difficult for psychiatrists to approach the mentally ill as equals. According to R. D. Laing (1985), most psychiatrists believe that "an unbridgeable gulf," "an abyss of difference," or "a total difference" exists between psychotics and the rest of us. Of course, some psychiatrists do befriend mental patients by spending much time in their company. But their conventional colleagues often call them "the lunatic fringe of the psychiatric profession" (Laing, 1985).

The Court

Since the public does not appreciate having the mentally ill around, the court can oblige by putting them away in mental institutions or prisons. This can be done by using (1) involuntary commitment proceedings, (2) denying the right to trial, and (3) allowing the defense of insanity.

Involuntary Commitment.   The court can hospitalize the mentally ill against their will. This involuntary hospitalization is for an indefinite period; it may be just for a few days or for a lifetime. Individuals can be released only if they can convince the hospital authorities of their recovery from mental illness. In order for individuals to receive involuntary commitment, they need not commit a crime, or be convicted of a crime, or even be charged with a crime. They only have to be judged by a court-appointed psychiatrist as mentally ill or, more commonly, as dangerous to themselves or others.

Since involuntary hospitalization is a serious matter, elaborate safeguards have been set up to protect the rights of the mentally ill. But these safeguards were often sidestepped or ignored in the 1960s. The judge, the psychiatrist, and the attorney were relatively careless in handling commitment proceedings. Usually they took only two or three minutes to decide whether to commit the individual to a mental institution for an indeterminate period. In addition, court psychiatrists were typically incompetent. As a result, many persons who were not really mentally ill or dangerous were coercively committed (Scheff, 1966, 1964; Kutner, 1962).

Since the early 1970s many higher courts have clamped down on the abuse. Most laws today are much more concerned with protecting the civil liberty of the mentally ill than with committing them to psychiatric hospitals for treatment. And many lower-court judges would not commit patients to a mental hospital even if the patients are severely mentally ill. While this judicial approach has greatly enhanced the rights of the mentally ill, it has ironically created a new problem. Many of the patients whom the courts have released into the community suffer from serious mental illness and do not receive any treatment. These released patients tend to end up homeless or in jails and prisons for disorderly conduct, disturbing the peace, or vagrancy (Torrey, 1997; Satel, 1996; Gove, Tovo, and Hughes, 1985).

Denying Rights.   The court can confine in the mental institution presumably mentally ill people by denying them the right to be tried. It is our fundamental right to stand trial if we are charged with a crime. But this right can be taken away from the mentally ill. When individuals are accused of a crime, the court will decide whether to try them or not. If they are found to be mentally ill, the court can rule that they are not competent to stand trial. Thus, without the benefit of a trial and without having been found guilty, the mentally ill defendants can be committed to a mental institution for an indefinite period. In fact, these unconvicted defendants can end up being confined in the institution longer than convicted criminals are in the prison. At one time, over half of nonconvicted defendants—considerably more than convicted criminals—spent the rest of their lives in mental institutions (Hess and Thomas, 1963).

In some states, ex-convicts with a history of violent sex crimes can be judged in court as having a "mental abnormality" that causes them to lose control of their sexual impulses and become sexual predators. They can therefore be sent back to prison to be indefinitely locked up for treatment at its psychiatric facilities. One ex-convict who is thus reincarcerated protests:

> There's a wrong being done here. I served my time and stayed clean during the five months I was out. I'm not a sexual predator. They even talked to girls I dated after I got out and couldn't find anything wrong. (Richards, 1992)

Insanity Defense.   The court can put away a mentally ill person for a crime by allowing a defense of insanity. If judged "insane," the defendant is sent to a mental institution; if judged "sane," the defendant is sent to prison. But the legal concept of insanity is not necessarily the same as the popular or psychiatric notion of mental illness. Consider the 1992 case of Jeffrey Dahmer, who was convicted of murdering 15 young men. Dahmer drugged some of his victims and crudely operated on their brains in an attempt to turn them into zombie-like companions. He had sex with some corpses. And he dismembered bodies, cooking some hands in a kettle and storing a severed head in the refrigerator, where he also saved a heart to be eaten later (Toufexis, 1992b). Given these facts, we will most likely agree with psychiatrists that Dahmer was mentally ill. But the court pronounced him sane, found him guilty, and sent him to prison.

There have been two major rules for establishing an insanity defense. The first is the M'Naghten Rule, according to which the accused are insane and therefore not guilty if at the time of committing the crime they did not know what they did was wrong. Another way of saying this is that they did not know the difference between right and wrong; hence the M'Naghten Rule is also known as the *right-or-wrong test*. This test has been in existence for over 100 years and has been used in about two-thirds of the states in this country. Then in 1954 the U.S. Court of Appeals broadened the definition of the M'Naghten Rule by handing down the Durham Rule. This new rule states that the accused are not guilty if they are mentally ill, because their crime is considered the "product" of their mental illness. Hence this rule is also called the *product test*.

For about 30 years until the mid-1980s, many defense lawyers successfully used the product test to win acquittal for their clients. One reason is that acquittal can be easily won if the defendant is clearly mentally ill—the defendant's behavior is so bizarre that everybody readily agrees that the individual is insane.

Another reason is that in cases where the accused is *not* clearly mentally ill, acquittal by reason of insanity can also be easily won. This is primarily because the burden of proof lies with *the prosecution* rather than the defense. To win conviction, the prosecution must prove *"beyond a reasonable doubt"* that the defendant is *sane*. This is extremely difficult to accomplish because defense psychiatrists, by presenting evidence on the defendant's illness, can easily convince the jury that there is at least some possibility of the defendant's being insane, which in effect will create *some doubt* in the jury's mind that the defendant is sane.

A good example is the case of John Hinckley, who tried to assassinate President Ronald Reagan in 1981. Hinckley was acquitted by reason of insanity because the prosecution failed to prove that he was sane at the time of his crime. Commenting on how difficult it was for the prosecution to prove Hinckley sane, President Reagan said, "If you start thinking about even a lot of your friends, you would have to say, 'Gee, if I had to prove they were sane, I would have a hard job'" (Carrithers, 1985).

Well-known cases like Hinckley's caused many legislators to believe that the insanity defense had helped too many guilty people to get away with murder. Consequently, in 1984, Congress passed a law that shifts the burden of proof from the prosecution to the defense. Now it is *the defense* that must prove the defendant's insanity, which can be easily refuted by the prosecution psychiatrists' testimony about the defendant not being insane all the time. More importantly, the defense must prove that the defendant, if proven insane, did not know right from wrong at the time of the alleged crime. But this, too, can be easily refuted by prosecution psychiatrists' testimony that even severely mentally ill people do know what they are doing most of the time. Thus, since the mid-1980s, it has been extremely difficult for defendants to win acquittal by reason of insanity. Consequently, most of the mentally ill criminals today are sent to prisons rather than mental institutions. Mental patients now constitute about 16 percent of the prison population (Butterfield, 1999; Schmitt, 1996).

The Mental Hospital

The mental hospital is a "total institution," a place of residence and work where a large number of individuals are cut off from the greater society and lead an enclosed, regimented life (Goffman, 1961). The patients' needs and desires are subordinated to the smooth operation of the hospital, and consequently the hospital staff tends to treat the patients as if they were objects rather than humans. Psychiatrist D. L. Rosenhan (1973) and his fellow researchers saw various aspects of this dehumanizing treatment after they had gotten themselves admitted to 12 different mental hospitals by pretending to be psychotic. Rosenhan gives these revealing and telling examples of the dehumanizing attitude toward the patients:

> A nurse unbuttoned her uniform to adjust her brassiere in the presence of an entire ward of viewing men. One did not have the sense that she was being seductive. Rather, she didn't notice us. A group of staff persons might point to a patient in the dayroom and discuss him animatedly, as if he were not there.

Considering patients (who are also called inmates, as prisoners are) as objects that can neither see nor feel, staff people tend to show them no respect. Staff members may enter patients' rooms and examine their possessions at any time. Hospital personnel sometimes even monitor their patients' personal hygiene and waste evacuation in the toilet. The situation is particularly bad in state institutions. The air inside these institutions is often thick with the odor of cigarette smoke and urine. Patients are often lined up like cattle to be showered in succession, or sometimes gang-showered without curtains. Deliberate and systematic physical abuse of patients, including tying patients to beds in isolation rooms, can be found in some institutions. Sexual abuse of female patients, overuse of drugs, and medical neglect are also common. These are part of the "dangerous routine" of state institutions that has been reported in testimony before the U.S. Senate (Weicker, 1985). Moreover, institutional psychiatrists are on the whole incompetent. Ironically, their charges are the most severely disturbed. These patients obviously need the most competent psychiatrists, but such psychiatrists prefer the far easier and more lucrative private practice of treating the "worried well"—mildly neurotic rich people. As a former APA president admits, psychiatry is "one of the few specialties where the most skilled practitioners take care of the least impaired patients" (Boffey, 1986).

The combination of staff incompetence and patient dehumanization tends to produce certain unexpected consequences. First, patients often exhibit symptoms that the staff consider to be indicative of their mental illness, but actually the symptoms result from the staff's action. When staff members strip recalcitrant patients and put them in isolation, for example, the patients may tear up mattresses or write with feces on the wall. The staff will then interpret such behavior as befitting very sick people, but the behavior actually expresses patients' attempt to stand apart from the dehumanizing place forced upon them (Goffman, 1961). Second, some patients develop what has been called "hospitalitis" or "institutionalism," a hospital-caused problem characterized by a deep sense of hopelessness, pervasive loss of initiative, deterioration of social skills, and inability to function in the larger society. Third, the professional staff becomes less capable than many mental patients in diagnosing mental illness. As Rosenhan (1973) discovered, when he and his normal associates had themselves committed to mental hospitals, many of the mental patients quickly found out that Rosenhan and his associates were normal—but the hospital staff did not. Actually, this need not be surprising. The psychiatric staff, aloof from the patients, cannot see the latter as whole, multidimensional persons. In contrast, the patients, living intimately with one another day in and day out, can develop deeper insight into one another's behavior and thus into mental illness in general (Kaysen, 1993).

But this negative view of the mental hospital has not emerged from every study on the subject. According to Raymond Weinstein (1983, 1981), there are two kinds of data about the goings-on in the mental hospital. One is *qualitative* data, which the researcher collects from participant observation, in the same way as Rosenhan and his associates did, observing closely the mental-hospital patients while living or interacting with them. The other is *quantitative* data, which the researcher gathers by taking a representative sample of patients, questioning them about the hospital, using objective tests or scales, and presenting the findings in a statistical format. The qualitative data are overwhelmingly critical of the mental hospital, as we have seen. But Weinstein claims that most (about three-quarters) of the quantitative studies reviewed by him show the mental institution as a nice place for the patients. The basis for this claim is that a majority of the patients in these studies told the interviewers that "hospital personnel understood their problems, helped them to get well, treated them with kindness and respect, took a personal interest in them, and were attentive to their needs" (Weinstein, 1981).

Weinstein's analysis, however, has drawn fire. Critics have argued, among other things, that in most of the quantitative studies where the researchers are detached and aloof from their subjects, as they are professionally required to be, the patients may not reveal their true feelings. As one critic says, the patients' "expressions of a positive attitude [toward the hospital and its staff] may be designed to impress the staff with their 'progress' and thereby secure a quicker release from the hospital" (Essex et al., 1981).

Perhaps as a result of failing to cure their patients, mental hospitals today routinely use tranquilizing, antidepressant, or antipsychotic drugs to alleviate the symptoms rather than eliminate the cause of mental disorder. In addition, over the last 20 years, fiscal problems have forced many communities to cut back on social services for people with disabilities, causing public mental hospitals to "deinstitutionalize" (discharge) their patients sooner than before. Consequently, many mental patients today are homeless on the streets, in jails, or in prisons (Torrey, 1997; Satel, 1996). But the majority of deinstitutionalized individuals live in state-financed group homes, apartments, or single-family homes, receiving treatment in general hospitals, Veteran's Administration hospitals, or outpatient clinics. Much of this treatment is community-based, provided by community mental health centers throughout the country (Sharpe, 1997; Foderaro, 1995).

The Community Mental Health Center

The notion of community mental health care was initiated in the 1950s, and then, in 1963, Congress passed a law to provide funds for helping states and communities to build and staff community mental health centers. Today such centers exist all over the country. Their objective is to offer professional and paraprofessional help to the emotionally disturbed. Resources such as hospitals, courts, police departments, welfare agencies, schools, churches, employers, coworkers, neighbors, and other concerned citizens are integrated in order to provide support to anyone in time of stress. Patients can receive inpatient or outpatient care in their communities. This is a very important option, for individuals already under stress do not have to suffer either the inconvenience of leaving their usual surroundings or the disturbance of being "put away" in some distant, isolated, large, and dehumanizing institution. Patients are free from the stigma usually attached to incarceration in a mental institution, and have a better chance of recovery because of the active participation of family members and others who are genuinely concerned and treat them with respect.

Interestingly, the *nonprofessional* method of treatment provided by a network of family and friends—hence the name *network therapy*—has proven highly effective in bringing deinstitutionalized patients back to normal life. It involves offering a support system to former hospital patients who otherwise would feel lonely and isolated. Relatives, friends, neighbors, and whoever knows the patient get together to discuss what each can do for him or her. Some will promise to call the patient more often, others will volunteer to bring him to church, still others will help him find a job, and so on. In addition, a crisis team is available 24 hours a day, ready to make house calls at any time to resolve crises. Through network therapy even schizophrenics, who are severely mentally ill, are rarely readmitted to mental hospitals. They have lower rates of relapse, show far fewer symptoms of schizophrenia, and are more satisfied with their lives, when compared with those who are hospitalized or under drug treatment alone (Goleman, 1986).

Why do laypersons who provide network therapy seem to do a better job in treating mental disorders than professional psychiatrists? The reason is probably that many psychiatrists, especially the medically oriented ones, are so professional that they cannot relate to their patients on their social level, let alone spend a lot of time with their patients as their friends. To these psychiatrists, being professional often means treating a mental illness as a medical doctor would a heart disease. But treating a mental disorder is radically different. A heart ailment may require only objective professionalism to effect a treatment, but curing a mental illness requires more than that—it demands a great deal of genuine compassion and empathy, as does network therapy (Breggin, 1997).

Perspectives on Mental Disorder

There are three different ways of looking at mental disorder, represented by the *medical, psychosocial,* and *labeling* models. The medical model defines mental disorder as a disease with a biological origin, so that the psychiatrist who embraces this model treats the illness by using physical means such as drugs, electric shock, and surgery. The psychosocial model can be found in many psychological and sociological theories, such as behaviorist, social-learning, cognitive, psychoanalytic, and social-stress theories. Here we will discuss only the two most important ones: psychoanalytic and stress theories. The psychoanalytic theory attributes mental disorder to emotional conflict (developing largely from child–parent interaction) and consequently treats the illness by using talk therapy to resolve the conflict. The stress theory is principally aimed at explaining mental disorder as a result of stressful social experiences rather than suggesting how to treat the disorder. Finally, the labeling model is neither explanatory nor treatment-oriented. It has often been called antipsychiatric because it is a radical critique of what psychiatrists think and do about mental disorder. Let us take a closer look at each model.

The Medical Model

According to this model, mental illness is similar to a physical disease in that its causes are biological; it should be treated, then, in the same way as a physical disease (Gottesman, 1995). This model has been dominating psychiatry since the 1970s when drug treatment emerged as a promising alternative to talk therapy. Advocates of this model, who are known as medical or biological psychiatrists, often point to one of two kinds of evidence to support their belief in the biological causes of mental disorder.

One type of evidence comes from studies on genetically related individuals. According to one of these studies, if one *identical* twin suffers a major depression, the other has a 78 percent chance of suffering the same condition, but the figure is only about 20 percent among *fraternal* twins (Goleman, 1992). Since identical twins are more genetically alike than fraternal twins, it is assumed that mental depression runs in the family. A similar study shows that schizophrenia is three-and-a-half times more common among schizophrenic adopted children's biological relatives than among their nonbiological relatives (Kety, 1974). As a review of such studies concludes, "Genetic factors are at least as important in the etiology of schizophrenia as they are in the etiology of diabetes, hypertension, coronary artery disease, and ulcers" (Kendler, 1983).

Another type of evidence that seems to support the biomedical model comes from numerous cases of successful treatment of mental patients with antipsychotic and antidepressant drugs. In the 1950s hospitalized schizophrenics were first treated successfully with a drug called Thorazine. For the next 20 years, Thorazine and other antipsychotic drugs enabled as many as 500,000 schizophrenics to leave hospitals. Since the 1970s more new psychiatric drugs—including lithium, Clozaril, and Prozac, the most popular antidepressant drug of the 1990s—have been proven relatively effective in treating schizophrenia, depression, and other mental disorders. ("Relatively effective" means that the drugs work in two-thirds to three-quarters of the cases.) Aside from their relative effectiveness, the drugs are so convenient to use that most psychiatrists today routinely prescribe them for their patients (Stone, 1992). The success of these psychopharmacological treatments is taken to suggest that mental illness originates from a chemical imbalance in the brain.

Actually, however, these drugs treat only the symptoms, not the causes, of mental disorders. Since the causes remain, the drug treatment must continue in order to avoid relapse, that is, to prevent the symptoms from returning. Logically, then, the chemical imbalance in the brain cannot be the cause of mental disorder. If it were, the drug treatment alone would have eliminated it. As for the twin and other genetic studies, they do not necessarily mean that mental disorder is genetically determined. If some defective genes were the cause of mental illness, the chance of one identical twin being mentally ill in the event of the other having the same illness would be 100 percent. We cannot ignore, though, the fact that the concordance rate of mental illness is significantly higher among identical twins than fraternal twins. This does suggest that some people may be more genetically vulnerable than others to mental disorder (Begley, 1996; Crossen, 1996). But genetic vulnerability cannot by itself lead to mental disorder. It has to be triggered by some psychosocial forces, such as emotional conflict or social stress.

The Psychosocial Model

One version of the psychosocial model is psychoanalytic theory. The other version is social stress theory, which has in recent years attracted a great deal of attention from sociologists and psychologists.

Psychoanalytic Theory. Presented by Sigmund Freud a century ago, psychoanalytic theory traces mental disorder to some unresolved psychic or emotional conflict in the patient. To Freud, conflict is inevitable within the personality of every human being. This is because personality is made up of three conflicting parts: the id, the ego, and the superego. The id consists of the animal desires for sex and aggression, which all humans are born with. The id is governed by the "pleasure principle." It seeks self-gratification however it can get it, with no regard for reason, logic, or morality. The ego, on the other hand, operates in accordance with the "reality principle." Developed from ages 1 to 3 through interacting with the environment, especially the parents, the ego is rational and logical, able to deal with the environment realistically. It therefore conflicts with the id by setting limits on how far the id can go in gratifying its impulses. The superego also seeks to restrain the id, but for moral reasons. It emerges in ages 3 to 6 when the child internalizes the parent's, or society's, morals in the form of ideals and restrictions. The superego is roughly the same as what is traditionally called "conscience."

But, in Freud's view, the superego is just as completely unreasonable as the id. While the id wants to have, among other things, sex with *anybody* (e.g., one's own parent), the superego prohibits *any* form of sexual pleasure, including sex between husband and wife. Being the only reasonable one, the ego has to mediate between the id and the superego, trying to resolve the conflict between them. The ego may try to persuade the id to stop being completely animal-like while pointing out that the id can still enjoy pleasure in a civilized way, say, having sex with one's spouse. Simultaneously, the ego may try to persuade the superego to give up its total opposition to any form of pleasure seeking and let the id enjoy marital sex, while pointing out that such sex does not destroy the morality upheld by the superego. There are, of course, many other issues for the id and superego to fight over, and each time the fight occurs, the ego will try to settle it. Most of these conflicts take place during childhood. If the ego succeeds in resolving the conflicts, the child will grow up to be normal. But if the ego fails to resolve a conflict, the unresolved conflict will develop into a neurosis or psychosis.

The conflict is usually such a painful experience that the patient "represses" it, pushing it into the unconscious area of the mind. The conflict manifests itself, however, in the form of psychiatric symptoms such as anxiety, depression, or compulsion. To help cure the patient, the psychoanalyst must bring the conflict out into the open, so that the patient can understand and solve the problem (Edmundson, 1999).

Suppose the patient is a male university president suffering from the compulsion of making phone calls to women who advertise child-care services and asking them whether they enjoy having sex with children. After each call, he feels extremely guilty but does not know why he has made the call. To treat this patient, a psychoanalyst would meet with him several times a week for 4 to 6 years, with each meeting lasting about one hour. At each session, the psychoanalyst may encourage the patient to say anything that comes into his mind. Meanwhile, the psychoanalyst analyzes everything the patient says, in order to dig out the unresolved conflict that has long been buried in the unconscious.

Finally, the patient may say something that the psychoanalyst is looking for: when he was 8 years old his mother first asked him to have sex with her, and then when he was 11, she forced him to have sex again and again for many months. This experience, according to psychoanalytic theory, must have been so traumatic that it became repressed, or buried, in the unconscious. But why must the experience be traumatic? Because it involves a conflict between the id's sexual gratification with the mother and the superego's total disapproval of it. The ego obviously has failed to resolve the conflict; otherwise it would not have been repressed. The unresolved conflict later appeared in the form of a neurotic compulsion, which caused the patient to make obscene phone calls to child-care workers. This compulsion involved the patient's "projecting" (unconsciously attributing) his sexual feelings for his mother to those child-care workers. In other words, in the patient's unconscious mind, making the obscene phone calls to the child-care workers was effectively the same as having sex with his mother. With all this out in the open, the patient can resolve the conflict, with the psychoanalyst's help (Berendzen and Palmer, 1993).

Psychoanalytic theory, however, is not empirically testable. It is difficult, if not impossible, to operationally define and measure the key concepts of the theory, namely the id, ego, and superego. One has to rely on faith to accept them as real in the same way as accepting ghosts as real. Once the concepts are accepted as real, though, the theory sounds convincing because there is enough logical reasoning and "talking cure" to support it.

Social Stress Theory.   Since the 1980s there has been an avalanche of studies on social stress as a significant contributor to the development of mental illness (Coyne and Downey, 1991). Various studies on the impact of life crises on the victims, for example, show that a large minority—from 20 to 40 percent—fail to recover fully from depression or other psychiatric problems despite a long passage of time (Kessler et al., 1985). These sufferers usually have gone through life crises such as divorce, unemployment, and death of a loved one. Even less serious experiences can be stressful enough to develop mental problems. Research has shown, for example, that an increasing number of Americans, from school principals to shoe salespersons, are suffering emotional breakdown from their jobs. Blue-collar jobs are particularly stressful because of their unpleasant work conditions—characterized by hazard, noise, heat, humidity, fumes, and cold. These have been found to play an important etiologic role in the prevalence of schizo-phrenia among lower-class people (Link, Dohrenwend, and Skodol, 1986).

While stress can lead to mental disorder, most people exposed to stressful situations do not develop any psychiatric symptoms. The reason is that they have the coping resources for dealing with stress. Several types of coping resources have been found effective in offsetting stress. One is *social support*, otherwise called strong social ties, intimate personal relationships, or social network. Another is *personal skill* in actively solving problems, seeking information, using distraction or humor, or reducing tension. A third type of coping resources is *high self-esteem* (Kessler et al., 1985).

In short, social stress can cause mental illness if the coping resources are inadequate. Since some individuals encounter more stress and have less coping resources than others, they are more likely to develop psychiatric symptoms. Society can be seen as promoting (through, for example, its structure of social inequality) mental illness in two ways: first, by putting some people in more stressful situations and, second, by depriving them of the social and psychologi-cal resources required for dealing with the stress (Cochrane, 1983). Critics, though, have observed that most of the studies on stress and psychopathology have not clearly demonstrated stress as the *cause* of mental disorder. This is because stress is also often the *effect* of the problem—that is, troubled individuals are more likely to experience stresses such as joblessness and divorce (Coyne and Downey, 1991; Mitchell and Moos, 1984).

The Labeling Model

Advocates of the medical or psychosocial model assume that mental illness is real; otherwise they would not bother to look for the causes and cures of the illness. But a few psychiatrists and many sociologists question that assumption. They believe that mental disorder is not a sickness but only a label imposed on some disturbing behavior. Such an argument has appeared in three versions.

Mental Illness as a Myth.   Psychiatrist Thomas Szasz (1994, 1974) has sharply criticized the medical model for assuming that mental illness is just as real and objective as a bodily disease. Psychiatrists who embrace the medical model, according to Szasz, are actually spreading a kind of psychiatric propaganda: "Mental illness is a myth, whose function it is to disguise and thus render more palatable the bitter pill of moral conflicts in human relations." In saying that men-tal illness is a myth, Szasz does *not* imply that the behavior labeled "mental ill-ness" does not exist. Szasz simply objects to the use of the label because it masks as well as distorts the true nature of the behavior by implying that it is similar to physical disease.

"Mental illness," in Szasz's view, can be more accurately referred to as "a problem in living," "a moral conflict in human relations," or "a communication expressing some socially unacceptable idea." All these terms imply that so-called mental illness is not a medical problem, but a social and moral one. It does not originate from within the individual—as physical illness does—but from without.

More precisely, it is a conflict between the "mental patients" and those around them, such as family, neighbors, friends, or the whole society. But, in labeling them mentally ill as if they had a disease *within* them, psychiatrists use such means as drug therapy, electroshock treatment, or psychiatric incarceration to control *them alone*, exempting their family or others involved in the moral conflict with them. As a woman who was committed as a teenager to a mental hospital for being "uncertain about life issues" says, "Often an entire family is crazy, but since an entire family can't go into the hospital, one person is designated as crazy and goes inside" (Kaysen, 1993). To Szasz, those psychiatric treatments violate the sufferers' civil rights—the rights to freedom and privacy. The treatments are, in effect, less for the good of the "patients" than for the good of the others, who end up enjoying the double benefit of freedom from being "treated" and freedom from being disturbed by the "patients."

If mental illness is merely a label imposed on an interpersonal conflict, it should not be surprising that today many normal people are treated as mental patients simply because they have problems with others. When DSM-I (the first edition of the APA's diagnostic manual of mental disorders) came out in 1952, only about 100 types of behavior were listed as mental disorders. That number has jumped to more than 300 with the publication of DSM-IV in 1994. This means that many problems, such as reacting angrily to criticism or losing one's temper, which have never been treated as mental disorders, are now included in DSM-IV and are, therefore, expected to be controlled. Moreover, psychiatrists are recruited by various social and government agencies to treat or control youngsters who behave in some ways like Tom Sawyer or Huckleberry Finn—whose behaviors offend or disturb others, behaviors such as being defiant, using drugs, fighting, hating school, or being disrespectful (Diller, 1998). Actually, many of these youngsters are victims of poverty, child abuse, or family misery, and their behaviors reflect a normal response to their abnormal environment. But, instead of dealing with the abnormal environment that causes those troublesome behaviors, psychiatrists label those normal children "emotionally disturbed," then give them drug treatments or isolate or incarcerate them. In short, kids who stand out as different are labeled mentally ill and controlled accordingly. As one of the victims says, "The Bart Simpsons of this world do not wind up in the cartoons. They wind up in the hatch" (Armstrong, 1993).

The Impact of Labeling.   Sociologist Thomas Scheff (1966) also views mental illness as a myth. More precisely, he sees it as an ambiguous label. He calls mental illness "residual rule-breaking" because it is such a residue of diverse kinds of rule violations that society does not clearly define it as rule-breaking. Society does clearly define as rule-breaking other forms of deviant behavior, such as crime, perversion, immoral acts, and bad manners. As rule violations, these behaviors are punishable in one way or another. But the mentally ill may only appear to violate social norms, but do not exactly or actually do so—not in the same way as criminals and other rule breakers. In other words, most people do not clearly regard the mentally ill as rule breakers who should be punished. Therefore, the mentally ill can be said to belong in the residual, leftover category of deviance, which is ambiguously defined as a sort of rule violation after all the other rule-breaking acts have been clearly defined as such. The ambiguity of mental illness makes it easy for people to label a person as mentally ill. Such labeling, Scheff emphasizes, can lead the person to develop stabilized, chronic mental disorder.

Scheff assumes that psychiatric symptoms arise from diverse sources. These sources may include genetic, biochemical, physiological, and psychological factors, or whatever you can think of—fear of combat, overwork, continuous lack of sleep, ingestion of psychoactive drugs, and so on. Many people, after being influenced by one of these factors, show such psychiatric symptoms as hearing voices, seeing visions, or imagining fantastic events. Yet their families, friends, and others who know them do not label them mentally ill. This is because most symptoms appear in apparently normal people and last only for a short while. However, a small minority of these people do get labeled mentally ill, which will eventually cause them to become chronically mentally disturbed.

According to Scheff, after people are labeled mentally ill, they are encouraged to acknowledge their mental illness. If they refuse to see themselves as mentally ill, they will be forced to enter a mental hospital, where staff and patients will pressure them to admit their illness. If they ask to be admitted to mental hospitals, they will be complimented for "doing the right thing." After release, they may try to resume their normal lives, but, as former mental patients, they are likely to be rejected by others. Consequently, they may become extremely confused, anxious, or ashamed. In such an emotional crisis, they tend to accept their families', psychiatrists', and community's judgment that they are mentally ill. All this leads Scheff to conclude that labeling a person mentally ill is the single most important factor in making that person become a chronic mental patient. Indeed, research evidence can be found to demonstrate the power of such labeling in aggravating the mental patient's condition (Link, Mirotznik, and Cullen, 1991).

Insanity as Supersanity. The British psychiatrist R. D. Laing (1967) also considers mental illness a myth, but his way of attacking the myth differs from Szasz's. Laing criticizes his fellow psychiatrists for believing in the myth that their mental patients' experiences are somehow unreal, invalid, false, perverse, or otherwise inferior to their own and other normal people's experience. He asks rhetorically: How can the so-called insane's experiences be inferior, when it is the normal people who have killed over 100 million of their fellow human beings since the outbreak of the First World War in 1914? He further writes: "The statesmen of the world who boast and threaten that they have Doomsday weapons are far more dangerous, and far more estranged from 'reality' than many of the people on whom the label 'psychotic' is affixed" (Laing, 1965). This is why Laing sees psychotics as more sane than normals—and their psychosis as a sane response to an insane world. He invites us to imagine a single bird that drops away from its flock in midflight. The flock is heading toward disaster while that deviating bird will land safely on the ground. But most psychiatrists see the psychotic unfavorably, assuming that the sufferers are *dis*oriented as to space and time.

Laing, however, criticizes the psychiatrists for failing to understand the nature of space and time. There are, in Laing's view, two types of space and time, one being outer and the other inner. When a psychiatrist prejudicially considers a mental patient disoriented, the patient actually is oriented to *inner* space and time, while the psychiatrist is oriented to *outer* space and time. By inner orientation, Laing refers to the experience of seeing those realities that have no external or objective presence, as in imagination, dreams, fantasies, contemplation, or meditation. If we simply experience God's presence, that's an example of having an inner experience; but if we try to prove rationally or objectively that God exists, we are demonstrating our orientation to the outer world. Mentally ill people are *inner-oriented,* attuned to themselves, not concerned with what others think of them. By contrast, normal people are *outer-oriented,* attuned to others and sensitive to what they think of them. To Laing, inner orientation is superior to outer orientation. As a form of inner orientation, insanity involves entering a state of more rather than less reality, of supersanity rather than subsanity, of mental breakthrough rather than breakdown.

If insanity is supersanity, why do many mental patients appear so unhappy with their experience? Their unhappiness, Laing suggests, can be traced to society's extremely negative attitude toward madness. Due to our society's greater appreciation for outer orientation than for inner, we are conditioned to *respect* individuals who climb Mount Everest, fly a balloon across the Atlantic, rocket to the moon, or embark on other similar adventures. But we do *not* respect the other kind of travelers, who journey into inner space and time. This is why when astronauts return from outer space, they are welcomed back as heroes, but when schizophrenics return from inner space, they are stigmatized as ex–mental patients. Given our far more positive attitude toward outer exploration, highly competent persons from favorable home environments would willingly embark on a voyage into outer space and with such advantages as moral support from others, prevoyage training and preparation, and all the information and apparatus necessary for making the voyage a successful one. By contrast, most mental patients have been forced into inner space and time by being placed in an untenable, unlivable position in the "normal" world. Therefore, unknowledgeable about and unprepared for the voyage into inner consciousness, they do not know how to deal with the terrors, voices, or images to be encountered on the voyage. As a result, they get lost in the inner world, which is why they appear so spaced-out and unhappy.

However, since he regards insanity as supersanity, Laing does not use drugs to dull his psychotic patients' sensitivity to their inner world. Instead, he lets them live freely in his group home, with only minimum psychiatric supervision. In effect, he gives his patients the opportunity to engage in deep thinking, so that they can more effectively explore their inner world, come to terms with the demons, and eventually return to the outer, "normal" world. This unique program has reportedly cured most of the patients who stayed at Laing's unconventional hospital (Mishara, 1983).

Criticisms of the Labeling Model.   A number of sociologists have criticized the labeling model, arguing that mental illness is not a myth but real behavior that exists all over the world. For example, John Clausen and Carol Huffine (1975) argue that "If mental illness is a myth, as Szasz and Scheff and others propose, it is remarkable that the manifestation of the myth should be found in antiquity and in preliterate societies as in modern industrial societies, in the People's Republic of China as in fascist states." Apparently Clausen and Huffine misunderstand what Szasz means by calling mental illness a myth. By "myth," Szasz refers to the use of the *label* "mental illness," not to the *behavior* so labeled. Further, Clausen and Huffine's criticism serves to divert attention from Szasz's reason for calling mental illness a myth, which is to show how the label "mentally ill" unjustly victimizes individuals so labeled.

Scheff also assumes that the label unjustly victimizes the individual. To Scheff, the victimization involves committing individuals to mental institutions, and thereby causing them to become chronic mental patients, even though they may have only mild, harmless psychiatric symptoms. This labeling argument has also been attacked by critics. One of them, Walter Gove (1970), argues that many research studies have refuted Scheff's labeling argument:

> The evidence shows that a substantial majority of the persons who are hospitalized have a serious psychiatric disturbance. . . . Once prospective patients come into contact with public officials, a substantial screening still occurs, presumably sorting out persons who are being railroaded or who are less disturbed. [In addition], the studies reviewed, while in no way denying the existence of the processes outlined by [Scheff], suggest that mental hospitalization does not necessarily or even typically lead to [chronic mental illness].

Therefore, Gove concludes that the evidence supports his own medical model more than Scheff's labeling model. In response, Scheff (1974) claims that the studies that he analyzes give stronger support to his own labeling model. But Gove (1982) argues that many of the studies employed to support labeling theory are methodologically flawed.

Summary

1. What are some popular myths about mental disorder? The myths are: (1) the mentally ill are extremely weird; (2) mental disorder is hopeless, mostly incurable; (3) a sharp difference exists between "mentally ill" and "mentally healthy"; (4) the mentally ill are mostly crazed and violent; and (5) people are likely to be depressed in the coldness of winter.

2. What is the traditional classification of mental disorders? There are two broad types of disorders: organic and functional. Organic disorders are physically caused, while functional disorders are psychologically and socially caused. Functional disorders are further divided into three types: psychosis, neurosis, and personality disorder. Psychosis is the most debilitating, neurosis is less so, and personality disorder is the least. Psychosis is characterized mostly by being out of touch with reality, neurosis by being constantly fearful or worried about apparently unimportant things, and personality disorder by being self-absorbed, antisocial, or a nonconformist. Each of these three types of functional disorder is further divided into various subtypes. **What is the DSM-IV classification of mental disorders?** Over 300 disorders are listed, each defined as having a set of symptoms. In using DSM-IV, psychiatrists can determine what mental disorder their patient is supposedly suffering.

3. What social factors are involved in mental disorders? The lower classes have higher rates of mental disorder than other classes. Women are more likely to suffer from depression and anxiety, and men from antisocial personality, paranoia, and drug and alcohol abuse disorders. Puerto Ricans and African Americans are more likely to have sociopathic and paranoid tendencies, and Jewish and Asian Americans tend more to suffer from depressive disorders. Urban areas have higher rates of mental illness in general than do rural areas, and urbanites also tend more to suffer from neurotic and personality disorders but ruralites tend more to suffer severe depression. Finally, young persons today are more likely than older persons to have psychological problems, particularly depression.

4. How does society respond to mental disorders? In the past, the mentally ill were believed to be possessed with the devil and so were sometimes burned alive. By the mid-seventeenth century, they were chained or otherwise treated like animals. Today, the treatment of the mentally ill is no longer barbaric but remains unpleasant. The public as well as many psychiatrists treat the mentally ill like moral lepers; the courts put them away through involuntary commitment, denial of rights, and granting of the insanity defense; and the mental hospitals dehumanize them. The number of hospitalized mental patients has declined significantly, while increasing numbers receive treatment from community mental health centers.

5. What are the current perspectives on mental disorder? The medical model views mental disorder as similar to a physical disease, attributes its causes to some biological factors, and, therefore, treats it with drugs and other physical means. The psychosocial model, including psychoanalytic and social-stress theories, attributes mental disorder to nonbiological factors such as emotional conflict and stressful social experiences. While both the medical and psychosocial models assume that mental illness is real, the labeling model sees mental illness as only a label that has undesirable consequences for individuals to whom the label is applied. Critics of labeling theory insist that mental illness does involve real behavior, but the labeling model does not question the reality of the behavior, but opposes the unjust imposition of the label "mental illness" on the behavior.

SUGGESTED READINGS

Armstrong, Louise. 1993. *And They Call It Help: The Psychiatric Policing of America's Children.* Reading, Mass.: Addison-Wesley. Shows how the psychiatric profession labels as mentally disordered and treats as mental patients more and more children whose behavior disturbs or offends others.

Cross-National Collaborative Group. 1992. "The changing rate of major depression: Cross-national comparisons." *JAMA (Journal of the American Medical Association), 268* (December 2), 3098–3105. An empirical study showing an overall increase in major depression in widely different countries as well as increasing depression among successively younger generations.

Gamwell, Lynn, and Nancy Tomes. 1995. *Madness in America: Cultural and Medical Perceptions of Mental Illness Before 1914*. Ithaca, N.Y.: Cornell University Press. Presents a historical tour via text and pictures into the past three centuries of how U.S. society viewed and treated the mentally ill.

Karp, David A. 1996. *Speaking of Sadness: Depression, Disconnection, and the Meanings of Illness*. New York: Oxford University Press. A phenomenological analysis of a common type of mental disorder, as experienced by 50 people and the author himself.

Kaysen, Susanna. 1993. *Girl, Interrupted*. New York: Turtle Bay Books/Random House. An interesting account of the author's two-year stay at a private, expensive mental hospital, revealing, among other things, that often the psychiatric staff seems less rational or more insane than the patients.

Kendler, Kenneth S., and others. 1993. "The prediction of major depression in women: Toward an integrated etiologic model." *American Journal of Psychiatry, 150*, 1139–1148. A study of twins that discovers four factors in the causation of major depression (stressful life experiences, genetic factors, temperament, and interpersonal relations), with stressful life experiences being the most powerful risk factor for the mental problem.

Kutchins, Herb, and Stuart A. Kirk. 1997. *Making Us Crazy*. New York: The Free Press. Shows how the DSM (Diagnostic and Statistical Manual of Mental Illness) contains "a strange mix of social values, political compromise, scientific evidence, and material for insurance claim forms."

Link, Bruce G., Mary Clare Lennon, and Bruce P. Dohrenwend. 1993. "Socioeconomic status and depression: The role of occupations involving direction, control, and planning." *Americana Journal of Sociology, 98*, 1351–1387. An empirical analysis of how low socioeconomic status can cause mental depression.

Link, Bruce G., Jerrod Mirotznik, and Francis T. Cullen. 1991. "The effectiveness of stigma coping orientations: Can negative consequences of mental illness labeling be avoided?" *Journal of Health and Social Behavior, 32*, 302–320. An empirical analysis of how attempts to soften the impact of stigmatization on mental illness make the illness worse.

Rosenberg, Morris. 1992. *The Unread Mind: Unraveling the Mystery of Madness*. New York: Lexington Books. An interesting sociological analysis of mental illness as a breakdown in human relations in which the patients and nonpatients each cannot see the world through the other's eyes.

Slater, Lauren. 1996. *Welcome to My Country: A Therapist's Memoir of Madness*. New York: Random House. Offers an intimate look into the world of mental illness with the insight of the author as a former sufferer.

Socall, Daniel W., and Thomas Holtgraves. 1992. "Attitudes toward the mentally ill: The effects of label and beliefs." *The Sociological Quarterly, 33*, 435–445. This research shows that people reject the mentally ill much more than the physically ill.

Szasz, Thomas. 1994. "Mental illness is still a myth." *Society, 31*, 35–39. An updated version of the author's provocative view that mental illness is a myth.

Vaughan, Susan C. 1997. *The Talking Cure: The Science Behind Psychotherapy*. New York: Grosset/Putnam Book. Presents the new view that psychotherapy, like medication, can cure patients by altering their brains.

CHAPTER

9 Heterosexual Deviance

Every Saturday night as many as 300 young women line the sides of a 7-mile stretch of a highway from Prague to Berlin in Eastern Europe. On this so-called Highway of Cheap Love, the world's longest brothel, travelers can stop to buy sex from one of those women for $30. Among the women are Czechs, Germans, Hungarians, Romanians, and Bulgarians. Virtually all of them have been forced into prostitution by poverty, which in turn has largely resulted from the collapse of the Soviet empire. Some have entered the sex trade through gangsters and others through their own parents. On that night, the gangsters can be seen lurking in nearby cars, the fathers sitting in backup automobiles, or the mothers negotiating the deal for their daughters. Every now and then the prostitutes' little brothers appear with a sponge and a bucket of soapy water, offering to wash the customer's car for an extra $5. All this is part of the fast-growing, now multibillion-dollar, global sex business (Specter, 1998; Hornblower, 1993).

This kind of prostitution, which involves women selling sex to men, is an example of heterosexual deviance. In this chapter, we will take a look at various aspects of prostitution. But first we will examine three other forms of heterosexual deviance: pornography, extramarital sex, and sexual harassment.

Pornography

It is against the law to distribute what is called pornography—sexually explicit materials—in the media, but the law is not strictly enforced because the meaning of pornography is subject to different interpretations. A large majority of Americans are also opposed to the distribution as well as the consumption of pornography (Maguire and Pastore, 1996). Yet sexually explicit materials can be found everywhere, and most people, especially men, have used it. The recent film about *Hustler* magazine's founder, *The People vs. Larry Flynt,* raises the interminable controversy over whether the constitutional right to free speech allows even the most vulgar form of expression. Some would endlessly debate this kind of issue, but here we will focus more on what the producers and distributors of pornography sell and what effects the merchandise has on the consumers.

The Porn Industry

Pornography has become an enormous industry today. A major reason is that the demand for sexually explicit materials has soared over the last decade. The number of hard-core video rentals, for example, skyrocketed from only 75 million in 1985 to 665 million in 1996. Today, the United States has become by far the world's leading producer of hard-core videos, churning them out at the astonishing rate of about 150 new titles a week. Also widely consumed, though to a lesser extent than hard-core videos, are sex magazines, adult cable programming, peep shows, live sex acts, phone sex, and computer porn. The amount of money spent on all the adult materials ($8 billion in 1996) is much larger than Hollywood's domestic box office receipts or the entire revenue from rock and country music recordings. Strip clubs alone bring in more money than all the opera, ballet, and jazz and classical music performances combined (Schlosser, 1997).

The porn industry's fantastic growth has stemmed mostly from the invasion of pornographic videos into mainstream society. In the past, most people were too embarrassed to go to seedy movie theaters and adult bookstores, but today they can watch porn videos in the privacy of their homes. Not surprisingly, the number of those traditional suppliers of porn has declined. Now, not only mom-and-pop video stores but also cable-TV companies profit greatly from pornographic videos. Even large hotel chains such as Hyatt, Holiday Inn, and Marriott reportedly earn millions each year by making their guests feel at home with adult films to watch in their rooms.

There is a wide spectrum of hard-core videos to meet every conceivable consumer demand: videos that feature gay, lesbian, straight, transsexual, interracial, or older couples; "cat fighting" videos that show naked women wrestling each other or joining forces to beat up a naked man; videos for sadomasochists, aficionados of bondage or spanking, or people fond of verbal abuse; and other kinds of videos too numerous to list. Other forms of pornography, particularly phone sex and computer porn, have also emerged on the scene, generating significant revenues for long-distance carriers such as AT&T (Schlosser, 1997).

The Effects of Pornography

Research has produced seemingly conflicting findings on the effects of pornography. Some studies seem to support the antiporn feminist and conservative view that pornography is harmful. Other studies appear to confirm the anticensorship, liberal view that pornography is harmless. Let us take a closer look at each of these two views and the studies supporting them.

Pornography as Harmful.   Some feminists support the idea that a woman has the legal right to free expression via pornography even though they may personally find the material distasteful (Carse, 1995; Califia, 1994). But many other feminists are opposed to pornography and want it banned, because they believe that pornography is harmful to women (Ferguson, 1995; MacKinnon, 1993).

To support this view, antiporn feminists usually point out many laboratory studies showing that exposure to violent pornography encourages male aggression against women (Linz and Malamuth, 1993; Donnerstein et al., 1987). In one experiment, for example, male subjects were divided into two groups: One watched a film depicting sexual violence against women; the other watched a nonviolent film. After seeing the movies, the subjects who had watched the violent film were more likely to adminster electrical shocks to women than were those who had watched the nonviolent film (Donnerstein et al., 1987). But we cannot generalize, as some feminists do, from the laboratory finding to what goes on in the larger society by insisting that violent pornography contributes significantly to the prevalence of antiwomen sexual aggression *in the society at large*. The reason is simply that, as research has indicated, *most* of the pornographic materials in the United States are not violent at all (Scott and Cuvelier, 1987; Lynn, 1986), and nonviolent pornography, which merely shows nudity and consensual sex, generally does not cause male aggression against women (Donnerstein et al., 1987).

Nevertheless, many feminists still assume that most pornography is violent—and that it leads to widespread violence against women in society (Itzin, 1993; MacKinnon, 1993; Dworkin, 1982). But many feminists also hold the convincing belief that pornography, if not violent, still degrades women by treating them as pieces of meat. Thus, cities such as Minneapolis, Indianapolis, and Los Angeles have considered or passed tougher laws to stop the spread of pornography, but they have been either defeated by lawmakers or overturned by courts on grounds that they violated the First Amendment guarantee of free speech. Some feminists have, however, argued that pornography should be prohibited because it violates the Fourteenth Amendment guarantee of equal protection of the law. Agreeing with this position, the Supreme Court of Canada has ruled that pornography does harm women by dehumanizing and degrading them. Ironically, though, the feminist fight for tougher antipornography laws receives considerable support from conservatives, who are opposed to the women's movement or gender equality (Wilkerson, 1993).

Aside from supporting the feminist view that pornography degrades women, conservatives believe that sexually explicit materials can destroy traditional family values and, thereby, the entire society. Often cited to support this belief is the research finding that long exposure to explicit depictions of common sex acts often leads men to seek portrayals of less common, more deviant practices such as violent, sadomasochistic, or bestial sex. Such men are then more likely to engage in various deviant sexual activities, which they find exciting. At the same time, however, they become more likely to find conventional, monogamous, or marital sex boring. All this is considered to have "devastating consequences" for traditional monogamy, marriage, family, and society (Linz and Malamuth, 1993). There is, however, no clear-cut evidence that pornography wrecks many marriages, let alone threatens the survival of the society.

Pornography as Harmless.   Liberals may personally find pornography distasteful, but they are opposed to the censorship of sexually explicit material not only because it violates the freedom of expression but also because they view pornography as basically harmless.

To support their belief that pornography is harmless, liberals usually call on studies showing that, in the real world outside the laboratory, exposure to sexually explicit materials does not cause rape or other sex crimes. For example, the availability of pornography in the United States increased substantially between 1960 and 1969 but the incidence of rape did not go up as much during the same period. Similarly, over the last ten years, the advent of the VCR has vastly increased the dissemination of hard-core videos, but the rate of rape has not increased to the same extent. U.S. cities with high circulation of sexually oriented magazines have basically the same rates of rape as cities with low circulation. In Denmark, in the late 1960s, after all legal prohibitions on the sale of pornography were removed, sex crimes did not rise but instead dropped sharply (Linz and Malamuth, 1993). To liberals, all these data strongly suggest that pornography is harmless.

It is more accurate to say, however, that *nonviolent* pornography is harmless because most of the sexually explicit material in the society at large is nonviolent. Considering everything that we have discussed, we may conclude that *nonviolent* pornography is harmless, as suggested by "real world" studies, but *violent* pornography is harmful, as shown by laboratory studies.

Extramarital Sex

Extramarital sex, popularly known as adultery, infidelity, or an affair, is sex that a married person has with "the other" woman or man. An overwhelming majority of Americans frown on extramarital sex: Nearly 90 percent of men and 94 percent of women said in a national survey that they considered adultery "always wrong" or "almost always wrong." Not surprisingly, only a relatively small minority engage in extramarital sex: 25 percent of married men and 17 percent of married women reported having at least one affair. These data, however, can also be taken to suggest that adultery is very common, because the ratios (25 and 17 percent) mean that at least 19 million U.S. men and 12 million American women have committed adultery. "That's a helluva lot of people being unfaithful," said a sex researcher in Florida (Norman, 1998; Michael et al., 1994; Janus and Janus, 1993).

Seductive Myths

Although faithful to their spouses, most married Americans, especially men, wish at one time or another to have an extramarital affair. According to the classic Kinsey Report, over 70 percent of married men had such a wish in the late 1940s. While women tend to associate an affair with love more than sex, men are more likely to think of it as a sexual escapade (Glass and Wright, 1992). As a result, many men seem to believe in the myth that extramarital intercourse is far more exciting or satisfying than marital sex. But data show otherwise. Perhaps because extramarital copulation is mostly carried out in secrecy, and frequently charged with tension and guilt, the experience is far from gratifying. According to one study, two-thirds of married men rated their marital sex "very pleasurable," but fewer than half of the unfaithful husbands gave the same rating to their extramarital coitus. And 53 percent of married women regularly reached orgasm with their husbands, but only 39 percent of the straying wives did so in extramarital intercourse (Katchadourian, 1985).

Another myth about extramarital sex may be equally popular with both men and women: "People have affairs because they are oversexed." Research suggests, however, that those who engage in adultery are far from oversexed. They generally are much less sexually active—having a lot less sex—than monogamous couples (Adler, 1996; Pittman, 1993). If being oversexed is not the cause of infidelity, what is? The cause can be found in a set of social and cultural factors, as suggested by the fact that the incidence of extramarital sex varies from one group to another in the United States as well as from one culture to another in the world.

Cultural Variations

There are legitimate and illegitimate adulteries, and each appears in different forms in different cultures. First, consider the different forms of illegitimate adulteries. Among the Lozi of eastern Africa, adultery does not involve sexual intercourse. If a man walks with a married woman he is not related to, or if he gives her a beer, he has committed adultery. By contrast, in most other societies, illegitimate adulteries always involve copulation. To conservative Christians who interpret the Bible literally, even divorce and remarriage, which involves copulation, is condemned as adultery. As Jesus says in Mark 10:11, "Whoever divorces his wife and marries another commits adultery against her; and if she divorces her husband and marries another, she commits adultery." In various societies, however, women have historically been punished for adultery more harshly than men. In Muslim societies, for example, unfaithful wives could be stoned to death. Generally, because illegitimate adulteries are socially condemned, they do not occur frequently (Fisher, 1992; Lawson, 1988).

Legitimate adulteries, however, take place more often in societies where they are by definition socially approved. Among the Kofyar of Nigeria, a woman who is unhappy with her husband but does not want to divorce may, without seeking his consent, take an extra lover, who lives openly with her in her husband's house. A Kofyar man may do the same for the same reason. In many Italian towns on the Adriatic coast, virtually every married man has a lover whom he visits regularly. Most of these affairs are between men and women who are married to others. Sometimes younger male servants visit rich men's wives, while rich men occasionally copulate with their maids or cooks. But it is taboo for any married person to ever speak of his or her affair. This is because boasting, gossiping, or even whispering to others about one's dalliance can expose the extensive network of extramarital relationships, seriously threatening their highly cherished community cohesion and family life (Fisher, 1992). However, legitimate adulteries such as these do not exist in American society.

All this points to the significant influence of culture on extramarital sex. Whatever form of adultery a culture considers acceptable is likely to be prevalent. Research that focuses on U.S. society alone further suggests the influence of certain social factors on extramarital sex.

Social Factors

Under the influence of the same culture that basically discourages infidelity, some groups of Americans are nonetheless more likely than others to cheat on their spouses. As shown by various studies, extramarital sex is more common among those who have experienced premarital coitus than among those who have not (Janus and Janus, 1993); men are more likely than women to have an affair; the less religious generally have a higher incidence of extramarital sex than the more religious; and lower-income people are more likely than higher-income Americans to be unfaithful to their spouses (see Figure 9.1).

Sociobiologists regard the gender difference in adultery as the most significant finding because it exists in virtually all societies. Sociobiologists trace it to humankind's long evolutionary past when men had to impregnate more women

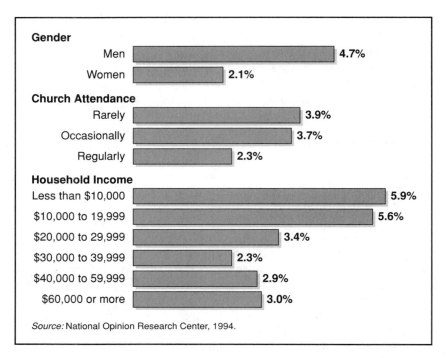

FIGURE 9.1   **The Extent of Extramarital Sex.** Percentages who reported engaging in extramarital sex in the past 12 months.

to produce more young so as to ensure the survival of their genes (Norman, 1998; Fisher, 1992). But the last thing that today's philandering men want is to produce babies. After all, most people, both male and female, now regard the primary purpose of sex as recreation rather than procreation. Far from scientific and valid, the evolutionary theory merely reflects the patriarchal belief that men should prove their masculinity by screwing around. It is this widely shared belief that causes men to philander more than women do. Most male philanderers also differ from their affair partners. The men tend to attach too little significance to the affair, being far from deeply in love with the women. But women tend to attach too much significance to the affair, believing that they no longer love their husband and that their affair partner is the true love of their life (Pittman, 1993).

Many affairs begin accidentally. The straying spouse may have drunk too much, got caught up in the moment, or just had a bad day. Here is how a typical accidental infidelity "just happens" to a 47-year-old college professor:

> I had my first affair with a young faculty member who was divorced. We had known each other for several years, and there was no great passion, but she was a woman and I a man. It was strange how it came about. We were both out of town at a professional conference. . . . The very first night, after some drinks, I

found myself in bed with her. The sex was fine, but the guilt was awful. She kept telling me, "Grow up, we're both adults, and if we can give each other some pleasure, what's the sin in that?" It wasn't easy; I could see my poor sad-sack wife, and the dread of my kids ever finding out. The conference lasted a week but I carefully avoided my colleague for the rest of it. (1993)

Infidelity may lead to divorce, as suggested by a research finding that divorced persons are much more likely to have had an affair while they were still married when compared with their married counterparts (Janus and Janus, 1993). But more often the betrayed wife or cuckolded husband strives to do whatever they can to save their marriage, although they initially feel deeply hurt and outraged. The marriage usually survives if the affair is stopped, brought into the open, and dealt with (Pittman, 1993).

Sexual Deviance in Cyberspace

Since the early 1990s the personal computer has fast become a common sight in many homes. It is now widely known as a remarkable tool for seeking information and entertainment, e-mailing, shopping, and other activities and services. But it has also encouraged deviant sexual activities, especially in the forms of cybersex and cyberporn.

Cybersex

To experience cybersex, most people first find their partners by placing or answering personals on the Internet or by entering an online chat room. Then they exchange erotic e-mails, trade pornographic pictures of themselves, or engage in steamy conversations in the chat room, and in the process get sexually stimulated and, most often, masturbate. Some of these cybersex enthusiasts go offline to meet their partners in person. If the meeting is mutually satisfactory, they will have sex (Wysocki, 1998; Lamb, 1997).

Most of the cybersex participants are white, male, and college-educated. Many, or about half, are married. Whether married or not, why do these people take part in cybersex? At least five reasons have emerged from an empirical study by sociologist Diane Wysocki (1998):

One reason is the need for *anonymity*. Unlike the real world in which sexual partners can see each other, the virtual, cybernetic world enables them to keep their true identities under wraps. They can thus take on whatever persona they want within the comfort of their home. If a man is shy and becomes tongue-tied when meeting partners face-to-face, online he can shed his shyness, feel bold, and turn chatty, projecting himself as the life of the party. Some women feel fat, old, and undesirable in person, but online they feel slim, young, wanted, and sexy—and this is the image they get across to the men on the other side of the electronic connection.

A second reason for participating in cybersex is the relative *ease and convenience* of finding sex partners. Trying to find a person with similar sexual attitudes and desires is difficult and time-consuming in the real world, where most of the people you meet do not share your interest. But it is much easier to find sex partners in the virtual world because it attracts only people with the same interest. This ease and convenience of finding a partner is especially important for people who are too busy to pursue friendships and sexual contacts on the face-to-face basis.

A third reason for engaging in cybersex is *sharing sexual fantasies*. Most people entertain sexual fantasies such as engaging in sexual activities outdoors, having sex with more than one partner, or being a transvestite by wearing the clothing of the opposite sex. Since conventional society frowns on these fantasies, most people find them too embarrassing to share with others or even with their wives or husbands in the real world. But in the virtual world, where people with similar fantasies get together, the fantasies can be freely talked about and can even be easily turned into reality with willing partners.

A fourth reason for seeking online sex is the easy availability of partners as an *outlet for masturbation*. As a woman who is a regular participant in cybersex says, "I love it when the guy gets off . . . it starts with teasing and flirting . . . I usually rub my clit and we eventually get off. I most often am wearing a miniskirt or nude and it goes from there . . . usually the men are online for a hot chat and wanting to come" (Wysocki, 1998).

A fifth reason is the expectation that online sex can lead to *real sex* with a willing partner face-to-face. Most of the online partners find their sexual experience in the real world very satisfactory. But some find the experience disappointing, because either one or both parties have lied online about their physical appearance. One man, for example, complains that some people he has met have not been completely honest: "[They] tell you how good of shape they're in . . . you know like 38-22-36 and 128 lbs . . . when you get there they are more like 180 or so . . . or they will tell you things like yes, I want to do this or that and when you meet it is different" (Wysocki, 1998).

Cyberporn

Cyberporn, or pornography in cyberspace, is not new. Soon after the Internet came on the technological scene, people started to trade dirty pictures on the Net. But amateur swapping has now given way to commercial ventures. By mid-1997, according to an online guide to cyberporn, there were already about 900 sex sites on the Web. Only one year later, this number had soared to somewhere between 20,000 and 30,000. These commercial sites vary in size from small outfits with just a few hundred paying members to major networks with thousands of subscribers (Barnako, 1998; Weber, 1997).

Cyberporn has become big business, raking in some $700 million a year. Sex sites are comparable in popularity to sports or weather sites and have only slightly few visitors than business and travel sites. A onetime stripper's site brings in so much revenue that she has given up stripping for good. In her former profession, she made only $1,500 a month, but right after going on the Web, her monthly earnings jumped to somewhere between $10,000 and $15,000. A 23-year-old man formed a company called Internet Entertainment in 1997 and now makes $20 million annually by offering a wide range of online shows. One type, called "live video," features exotic nude dancers in full color on the computer screens of customers, who can chat on the phone with the gyrating performers. Customers can also click their way to different virtual rooms: In the "bedroom" the visitor can see a naked dancer rolling around on a giant mattress, and in the "health club" the performer works out on a step exerciser with no clothes on (Barnako, 1998; Weber, 1997).

Cyberporn has become so popular primarily because customers can view racy material in the privacy of their homes. They no longer have to sneak into a sleazy adult bookstore or the back room of a video shop. But the popularity of cyberporn has caused some parents to fear that children can easily look up pornographic material when going online. Curious about sex, youngsters may indeed want to do so, and they can find the Web sites that provide what they are looking for. Theoretically, masses of youngsters will likely consume cyberporn, for several reasons: One, they can obtain the material in the privacy of their home, without having to walk into an adult bookstore or cinema. Two, they can download only the portions of the material that turn them on, rather than buy an entire magazine or video. And three, they can explore sex without risking public ridicule or communicable diseases (Elmer-Dewitt, 1995).

This has led the U.S. Senate to pass a bill in 1995 prohibiting anyone from making "indecent" material available to children under 18. But the bill failed to become law, not only because many believed it violated the First Amendment guarantee of free speech but also because many feared it could transform the vast library of the Internet into a children's reading room where only subjects suitable for kids could be discussed (Elmer-Dewitt, 1995). However, the computer industry has come up with programs such as SurfWatch and Net Nanny that can block children's access to questionable material. In addition, most pornographic sites on the World Wide Web require an adult ID and a credit card (Onstad, 1996). Parents, too, can help solve the problem by raising their children to shun pornography.

There is, however, already a federal law that prohibits distributing obscene material across state lines. This law has been vigorously enforced against adults who sell or exchange child pornography via the Internet. For engaging in this kind of cyberporn, a growing number of people have been arrested in various states since 1995 (Labaton, 1995).

Sexual Harassment

Sexual harassment can be defined as an unwelcome act of a sexual nature. The U.S. Supreme Court has provided a more precise, legal definition: Sexual harassment is any sexual conduct that makes the workplace environment so hostile or abusive to the victims that they find it hard to perform their job.

The Supreme Court's definition came with its ruling on the suit that Teresa Harris filed against her former boss, Charles Hardy. In 1987 Harris quit her job in despair because she felt she had been sexually harassed by Hardy. According to Harris, Hardy often asked her—and other female employees—to retrieve coins from the front pockets of his pants. He once asked Harris to go with him to a hotel room to negotiate her raise. And he routinely made such remarks to her as, "You're a woman; what do you know?" She spent six years trying to convince judges that she was sexually harassed in violation of federal law, but to no avail. The judges found Hardy's conduct not severe enough to "seriously affect her psychological well-being." But Harris persisted, and finally the Supreme Court ruled that sexual harassment does not have to inflict "severe psychological injury" on the victim. As the Court said, federal law "comes into play before the harassing conduct leads to a nervous breakdown" (Sachs, 1993). More recently, in 1998, the Supreme Court further broadened the definition of harassment: A female employee can sue her employer even if she gets a salary raise or promotion after resisting unwanted sexual advances from her supervisor (Lavelle, 1998).

The Harris case was the second on sexual harassment to reach the Supreme Court. In the first, in 1986, the Court ruled that sexual harassment was a form of gender discrimination prohibited by the Civil Rights Act of 1964. Since that first ruling, the number of harassment charges has increased substantially. To avoid being sued, many companies as well as universities and colleges have instituted antiharassment policies, guidelines, or educational programs, especially since 1998 when the Supreme Court ruled that companies can protect themselves against lawsuits only if they have a strong and effective program to prevent and discipline harassment (Lavelle, 1998). Even primary and high schools have started to prevent harassment after the Court ruled in 1999 that schools can be sued if they fail to stop a student from "severely" harassing another (Greenhouse, 1999).

The problem, however, is too prevalent to soon go away. According to various studies, about half of all working women have been sexually harassed at some point in their careers, and about 40 percent of college women have been harassed. Examples of harassment range from unwanted sexual remarks to actual rape. Also, among high school and junior high students, close to 70 percent of girls and 42 percent of boys have been touched, groped, or pinched on school grounds (Henneberger and Marriott, 1993; Kantrowitz, 1991).

Generally, sexual harassment reflects men's attempt to preserve their traditional dominance over women. Men are, therefore, more likely to harass a woman if they feel threatened by her "invasion" into their male-dominated world. This may explain why sexual harassment seems to occur most frequently in traditionally and heavily male-dominated occupations, such as the U.S. military (see Figure 9.2). At bottom, sexual harassment is an expression of power, involving a more powerful person victimizing the less powerful. It is possible, for example, for a female boss to sexually harass a male employee. But, given the predominance of men in positions of power, they are the offenders in most cases.

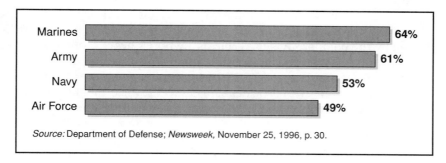

Source: Department of Defense; *Newsweek*, November 25, 1996, p. 30.

FIGURE 9.2   Sexual Harassment in the Military. Percentage of women in each service reporting harassment.

Popular Myths about Prostitutes

Prostitution, the exchange of sex for money, is legal in many countries in Europe and elsewhere. By contrast, it is not legal in the United States, except in some counties of Nevada. Nonetheless, prostitution has long been big business here. Every year billions of dollars are spent on the sexual favors of prostitutes, whose profit amounts to at least ten times the annual budget of the U.S. Department of Justice. The number of prostitutes has been estimated to range from 84,000 to 336,000 (Potterat et al., 1990). But such estimates grossly underrepresent the real number of prostitutes because the figures are almost entirely derived from sex workers who are known to the police and fail to take into account those who are not. According to one survey that asked a nationwide sample of American women ages 18 to 64 whether they had ever had sex for money, nearly 6 percent said yes. This seemingly small percentage translates into a huge number—at least 4.2 million women (Janus and Janus, 1993).

Although there are many prostitutes, we know very little about them. We often hear, for example, that prostitution is the oldest profession in the world. This is a myth, however, because priesthood is the oldest profession. We frequently encounter other myths about prostitutes such as those that follow.

First, it is often mentioned in both folklore and sometimes even in scientific literature that prostitutes typically are nymphomaniacs, having an insatiable desire for sexual intercourse with many men. This is male fantasy, not substantiated by facts. Before going into the sex business, most prostitutes did not have many more sex partners than other, average women. What is true is that prostitutes have started having sex at a younger age than other women (Perkins, 1991).

Second, some clinical psychologists assume just the opposite of the first myth: Prostitutes are sexually frigid. Actually, when they have sex with their husbands or boyfriends, prostitutes as a group are more responsive than other women—more able to achieve orgasm.

Third, there are two contradictory beliefs about how prostitutes treat their clients: On the one hand, they are believed to be nasty and hard-hearted—as evidenced by the popular saying "as cold as a whore's heart"—and on the other, they are romanticized as sweet and warmhearted—"a woman with a heart of gold." In reality, however, the average prostitute's attitude toward her clients is quite similar to that of anyone who provides services to a diverse clientele. Some clients she likes, a few others she dislikes, and toward most of them she simply feels neutral.

Fourth, according to popular belief, most prostitutes are drug addicts or have turned to prostitution to support their drug habits. It is true that the percentage of prostitutes who are drug addicts before or after entering the sex business is higher than the percentage of conventional women addicted to drugs. Young streetwalkers are particularly likely to be addicted to drugs, but the *majority* of prostitutes are not drug addicts (Perkins, 1991).

Fifth, it is widely believed that most prostitutes have been sexually abused as children. Indeed, as shown by many studies, most of the streetwalkers who start prostituting at a young age or prostitutes who have often been arrested by police or helped by social agencies have been victims of child abuse. But, unlike these prostitutes, most sex workers do not have a history of child abuse (Perkins, 1991).

Types of Prostitutes

There is a great variety of prostitutes. Some researchers have found as many as 18 different types (Benjamin and Masters, 1964). Most of these kinds are relatively rare, however, so we need to know only the more common types, namely, streetwalkers, child and adolescent prostitutes, house prostitutes, and call girls. These sex workers are employed in a highly stratified occupation, so that they vary from one another in their status in prostitution, the price they charge, or the quality of their social and work life. The status, price, or life quality rises as one goes from streetwalkers, who occupy the lowest status, to call girls, who have the highest status.

Streetwalkers

In prostitution, soliciting customers on the street is probably the most ancient method. Generally, compared with most other types of prostitutes, streetwalkers are less educated, more likely to shoot drugs and get AIDS, and more often arrested by the police.

Streetwalkers normally use a standard method of soliciting. When a streetwalker sees a potential customer strolling on a sidewalk, she is likely to smile at him. She may then say to him such things as: "Hi. How are you today?" or "Which direction are you heading?" If the man responds, she may ask, "Do you want company?" or "Want a date?" or "Wanna do something?" Then she tells him her price, although very often, the man himself takes the initiative and simply asks, "How much?" Once a deal is struck, she typically takes him to a hotel room.

Increasingly, streetwalkers solicit business from cruising motorists. For most of these transactions, the service is rendered in the car. Because many customers find their cars too cramped for intercourse, a large number of "car jobs" involve oral sex only. By contrast, virtually all the sexual services in hotel rooms involve vaginal intercourse. Wherever and however the sexual act is carried out, most streetwalkers, not being well paid, strive to minimize its duration. Thus, most of the sexual services in the room last 15 to 30 minutes, while most of the car jobs only 4 to 15 minutes (van Gelder and Kaplan, 1992; Freund et al., 1991). Many car customers may whine about the shortness of the service, but most streetwalkers consider their job finished when the customer ejaculates. And it does not take long for this to occur, as a streetwalker says, "The men who are driving around here are so excited and horny. When you touch that thing, well, it almost happens right away" (Gelder and Kaplan, 1992). That's why, despite the complaint, most customers repeatedly return for the same kind of service.

Traditionally, streetwalkers tend to ply their trade in lower-class areas, where they can afford to solicit blatantly and openly, without much fear of getting arrested by the police. But in many suburban areas today streetwalkers are more careful to avoid arrest. This presents a problem, though. How can customers know the identity of a streetwalker if she camouflages it to avoid being too obtrusive to the general public? To solve this problem, streetwalkers resort to a unique strategy: alternating between actively soliciting when spotting a potential customer and discreetly blending into the street scene when seeing a police officer. Thus, most streetwalkers tend to stand near a bus or taxi stop, a public telephone booth, street corner, or hotel entrance. This enables a customer to distinguish a streetwalker from other pedestrians, and when she sees him approaching her she will know him to be a customer. At the same time, such public places enable a streetwalker to loiter like any other pedestrian when a police officer appears (Riccio, 1992).

The prospect of being arrested is not the only problem facing streetwalkers. More than other types of prostitutes, streetwalkers are often abused by customers, pimps, and even police. Customers frequently force them to engage in kinky sex, rape them, refuse to pay them, rob them, or beat them. Pimps regularly beat them, too. Policemen sometimes beat them or demand free sex. Serial killers often murder them one after another, while their families would not miss them and the police would not find them. Young streetwalkers, particularly those under age 16, are most likely to suffer these forms of victimization (Silbert and Pines, 1981). Older streetwalkers are more able to protect themselves. They know how to "manipulate anonymity" before soliciting, concealing their true identity while trying to determine which customers are trustworthy or dangerous (Merry, 1980).

Child and Adolescent Prostitutes

Some prostitutes are only 8 to 12 years old. These child prostitutes are often called "baby pros." Most have been brought up in poor and chaotic families, where they are accustomed to seeing their mothers or older sisters engaged in sex with different men, in pornography, or in prostitution. Many have suffered physical or sexual abuse at the hands of their parents or other adults. Consequently, when first approached by a man with an offer to pay them for sex, they were "ready" to accept. Still too young, though, they continue to live with their parents and attend school, working as prostitutes only on a part-time basis.

Somewhat older than these children are adolescent prostitutes, aged 13 to 17. Most have also been brought up in disorganized families. They, too, have suffered physical or sexual abuse in childhood. But, unlike their younger counterparts, many adolescent prostitutes have run away from home and most have become heavy drug users. The need to support themselves, further intensified by the craving for drugs, is the most common motivation among the adolescents to sell sex for money (Weisberg, 1985). But often the pimp plays a significant role in their entry into prostitution. Alone in a large city, many young runaways from small towns or rural areas are fair game for pimps, who frequently look for new prey to entice or force into prostitution. Here is an account by a 14-year-old girl of her forced induction into prostitution:

> I was grabbed in a store by this guy and this chick who said they were taking me for a ride. They said they wanted me to meet a friend. He was a pimp. They sold me to him. He locked me up in this hotel room and ran in cheap tricks. I got away after a week, but he followed me and gave me a line I fell for, so I went back with him. He grabbed my hair, so I kicked him between the legs—boom! He called in another guy and they took my clothes off. They began to heat up this coat hanger with matches and burn my ass with it. Then the pimp put his foot on my face and stomped it. I figured, well, you've got to take some bad things in life. (*Time*, 1972)

Being coerced into prostitution is, however, relatively rare in the United States. It hardly ever happens to adult women, who make up most of the prostitutes in our society. It may occur to young girls, but not frequently, which explains why adolescent prostitutes compose only a small minority of prostitutes in the United States and other Western societies. The situation is different in poor countries, where far greater numbers of youngsters are forced or tricked into prostitution by pimps, parents, or poverty. In many poor villages in Thailand, many young girls are sold by penniless parents to brothel operators, or are tricked into coming to big cities where they are forced to work in whorehouses, or are enticed to marry German tourists and then brought to Germany to serve as house prostitutes. In Nepal's poor Himalayan villages, some 7000 adolescents are sold every year to the brothels in the Indian city of Bombay. In Brazil, about 25,000 girls from poor families have been forced into prostitution in remote Amazon mining camps. In Eastern Europe, many poor parents have forced their young daughters to sell sex, and those who work in brothels are often beaten to make them submit. As one official in a European aid group observes, "Many of the girls have broken teeth. They say they fell downstairs. But there are so many of them that either this business has the worst-maintained stairs in the world or these girls have been punched" (Kristof, 1996a; Hornblower, 1993).

Poverty is not the only driving force behind the prevalence of adolescent and child prostitution in those countries. A great demand for this kind of prostitution is another important factor. In recent years, the widespread belief among customers that very young sex partners are less likely to have AIDS has fueled a surging demand for youthful prostitution. In addition, many more tourists from rich, Western countries and Japan today flock to those poor countries for sex with children. These tourists know that they can exploit the children without any fear of being arrested for child abuse, as they would be in their home countries (Kristof, 1996a; Serrill, 1993; Simons, 1993).

House Prostitutes

A brothel is a place where prostitutes meet their customers and share their earnings with its operator. It has been variously referred to as a cathouse, whorehouse, parlor house, and bordello. Very often it is simply called a "joint" or "house." In the 1920s and 1930s many brothels existed in this country. Since 1945, most of them have been forced to shut down. Some houses today still operate openly in Nevada and clandestinely in other parts of the country.

In Nevada, where prostitution is legal, brothel prostitutes are fingerprinted and carry prostitute identification cards issued by the police or district attorneys. The women are generally required to have a weekly medical checkup. When a customer enters the house, the madam (proprietor) will direct a young woman to him. The following account by a visitor to a Nevada brothel is fairly typical of how the woman conducts her business:

> She said, "I'll sit with you, . . . Where are you from? . . . I'm from Los Angeles . . . Let's go to my room, so we can talk . . . " In her room she continued: "I can give you a nice date . . . I can give you French [fellatio] . . . or a straight [coitus] . . . you could have a real good time . . . You don't need to be afraid . . . We get a blood test once a month . . . You won't have to worry—the doctor makes sure." (Winick and Kinsie, 1971)

Before the sex act, most prostitutes in Nevada always make sure their clients wear condoms, though their counterparts in other states are less likely to do so (Hilts, 1987).

In many states where the brothel is covertly operated, the madam usually ensures that the potential client is not from the "pussy posse," which is what the vice squad is called in the sex industry. The madam will, of course, readily admit a regular customer. In cases in which she does not know him, she will first meet him at a nearby bar or send a cooperating cab driver to size him up. Only when convinced he is a genuine customer will the madam admit him into the brothel. Some prostitutes wait in the brothel, while others wait in their own apartments for phone calls from the madam, to whom she typically gives half her earnings. Since the clients often look for variety, the house prostitute usually does not work in a brothel for an extended period—the longest she will stay in one brothel is four or five years. To minimize the risk of arrest, many houses simply operate as escort agencies (Potterat et al., 1990).

Most house prostitutes find that they have a distinct advantage over streetwalkers: Working in the house is safer and more secure. For lonely women, the brothel can offer opportunities for regular contact with other women, which may further blossom into friendship. Similar opportunities are rare for streetwalkers, because they have to work alone. But there are also disadvantages to working in a brothel. House prostitutes are not free to set their own working hours and must give half of their earnings to the house. These are restrictions that streetwalkers do not have. House prostitutes who work as escorts seem to have the best deal. Although they have to split the take 50/50 with the house, there are better opportunities for receiving a fat tip from a satisfied customer after a good night out. There is a downside to escort work, though, as one prostitute explains: "You are very vulnerable in the client's room and have no control over the situation, which can be pretty frightening if things get nasty . . . you could be dead" (Perkins, 1991).

Call Girls

Occupying the highest status in the sex business, call girls have been referred to as "the aristocrats of prostitution" (Greenwald, 1970). As befitting this title, they usually charge from several hundred dollars for each sexual intercourse to, occasionally, even more. Every year they can earn as much as or more than a successful lawyer or doctor. They are generally better educated or more sophisticated than other types of prostitutes. They dress expensively, and they live in affluent neighborhoods. Call girls are acutely aware of their high status and will feel insulted if they are treated like an ordinary streetwalker or brothel prostitute. In fact, many call girls will not apply the term *prostitute* to themselves.

It is typical for a call girl to wait for customers to telephone her. Initially she gets a few clients through other call girls and advertisements. Later, and more important, her previously satisfied clients often recommend her to their friends, so she often receives calls from prospective customers who say, "I'm a friend of so-and-so; he gave me your number." Many call girls do not use personal telephones, though. They receive their calls from an answering service or machine, and this is the number they give to their clients. Such an arrangement is said to serve two purposes. One is to minimize the risk of arrest or of being traced by police; the other is to maximize the volume of business. As one call girl explains:

> The first prerequisite is a telephone in good working order, with an answering service connected so that business can continue even when the proprietor is out on a call—away from home. Usually as soon as "business has been completed," the girl will call her answering service for messages, thus enabling her to hop from one address to another without wasting expensive time. If there has been a call at her residence while the present job is in progress, and the phoned-in customer has left a message or number with the girl's answering service, it is not unusual for the amenities of the current business to be completed quickly and a hasty departure for the next destination made by the busy young lady. (Greenwald, 1970)

Compared to lower-paid prostitutes, the call girl tends more to dress in good taste rather than poorly or garishly. She is skilled in making her commercial transaction appear noncommercial by, for example, acting like her clients' girlfriend in public. She may adhere to a professional code of ethics. For example, if a client is a prominent person, she would not even mention his name in her conversation with other call girls. She would not steal from her customers or let them overpay her when they are drunk and thus temptingly exploitable. She would do her best to satisfy her clients, even in cases where a client has difficulty getting an erection.

Most call girls claim that they fare much better than housewives and women with legitimate employment. They crow that they can afford to live in style because of the huge sums of money they are making. They also contend that they have found fulfillment of their desire for independence in their profession: "The difference between being a prostitute and being a wife is the security a wife's got. But it's also the difference in having a lot of men versus having just one. If you have a lot of men—like if you have ten a day—then you're not dependent on any one of them. They can always be replaced . . . that's the thing I wanted— never to be dependent" (Rosenblum, 1975). While it is easy to accept their claim to the big buck and high living, it is harder to agree with their claim to independence. This is because call girls are heavily dependent on their customers for the high income they get, which requires taking orders from customers. Even in the case of a masochistic client, who likes to follow orders himself, the call girl still has to follow *his* order to give him orders (Rosenblum, 1975).

The World of Prostitution

Although they can be divided into different types, prostitutes as an occupational group do have something in common. They have basically similar social and working lives. Let us take a close look at various aspects of these lives.

Social and Sexual Backgrounds

According to sociologist Roberta Perkins (1991), many studies give a distorted picture of prostitutes as child-abuse victims, heavy drug users, victims of low self-esteem, or as being socially immature, emotionally disturbed, or pitifully abnormal in some other way. These studies are biased, Perkins contends, because they have focused mostly on adolescent streetwalkers or prostitutes who have been arrested by police or helped by social agencies. Such prostitutes indeed have more problems in their lives than other sex workers. But they are a minority, representing only about 5 to 30 percent of all prostitutes, and they differ significantly from most other prostitutes (Perkins, 1991).

The prostitutes in Perkins' study, however, are a reasonably representative sample of the women in the sex business. Although these prostitutes are Australians, they are comparable to their counterparts in the United States and other Western societies. Perkins found that most prostitutes do not differ

TABLE 9.1   Reasons for Entering Prostitution

To earn more money than at the time	44.5%
Unemployed at the time	36.7
To satisfy curiosity about self or prostitution	25.8
To support a family	18.7
For a specific purpose (education, debt, holiday)	15.6
To support a drug habit	9.4
To seek excitement in own life	5.5
To support a man	5.5
Freedom from home; to be independent	3.9
For sexual enjoyment or experiment	3.1

Note: Percentages add up to more than 100% because many prostitutes in the survey gave more than one reason.

Source: Adapted from Roberta Perkins, *Working Girls* (Canberra: Australia Institute of Criminology, 1991), p. 256.

significantly from conventional women in their social and sexual backgrounds. For example:

■ They have the same desire as conventional women to be married and have a traditional family life. Among those who already have young children, there is a plan to quit turning tricks when the children are old enough to begin catching on to their mothers' stigmatized occupation. As one prostitute says, "My oldest son will be 13 this year and I don't want to be at work much after that."

■ Prostitutes have about the same level of education as the general population of women. The percentages of prostitutes having been brought up in white-collar and blue-collar families are similar to those of conventional women.

■ Most prostitutes are not friendless, loveless, or particularly "promiscuous" in their private lives. Like most women, they live with their husbands, lovers, or children, or share apartments with friends. But since their occupation is highly stigmatized, they are significantly more likely than other women to be raped.

Reasons for Becoming Prostitutes

According to public opinion, the common reasons for entering prostitution are drug addiction, severe poverty, low self-esteem, and emotional problems. Most of these reasons have to do with personal, social-psychological deficiencies. Such problems have indeed driven most teenage streetwalkers into prostitution, but these young hustlers differ from the large majority of prostitutes. Thus, when prostitutes in a representative sample were asked why they become prostitutes, a different set of reasons emerged. As suggested by Table 9.1, the most common reasons are economic, such as wanting to make more money, being unemployed, supporting a family, or paying for an education, an overseas trip, a car, or some other specific thing. Money, then, is the most important reason for going into the sex business. This is no different from the reason that most other people have for working in conventional businesses.

Those economic reasons, however, merely serve as a predisposing factor in entering prostitution. They are not enough for a woman to become a prostitute— she needs to know something about the business before entering it. Necessary knowledge usually comes from an acquaintance, as illustrated by the following accounts from two prostitutes (Perkins, 1991):

■ I needed some money because I was having legal hassles and my present job wasn't bringing in enough to pay for this. A girlfriend of mine had an escort agency and this seemed the quickest way to get the amount of money I needed.

■ I met an old school friend and we had lunch together. She told me she was a prostitute and how much money she made. She asked me if I would [go out with] her one night. But the fellows kept asking for me, not her. So, I thought, I must be sitting on a gold mine. And that's how I started.

The Threat of AIDS from Customers

Although they are more likely than others to be infected with the AIDS virus, prostitutes in the United States and other Western countries do not have as high an incidence of AIDS virus infection as popularly believed. In a massive national survey of prostitutes in the early 1990s, the U.S. Centers for Disease Control found that the incidence of being diagnosed with the AIDS virus varied from zero percent among the house prostitutes in Nevada to 6.2 percent in San Francisco. The incidence was considerably higher, though, among prostitutes who used drugs intravenously. Fifty-seven percent of the drug-using prostitutes in New Jersey, for example, had the AIDS virus (Perkins, 1991). These prostitutes obviously contract the deadly virus from intravenous drug use, not from sex with customers. Most other prostitutes do not get the AIDS virus, not only because they do not use drugs but also because they often practice safe sex by having their customers wear condoms (Jackson et al., 1992; Modan et al., 1992).

The use of condoms is particularly critical to prostitutes because women are ten times more likely to get the AIDS virus from men than men are to get it from women. But in many poor countries, where women are far more oppressed, most men refuse to wear condoms when having sex with prostitutes because of the belief that condoms diminish the pleasure. Consequently, the percentages of prostitutes infected with the AIDS virus are much higher in many poor countries than in the United States (Kristof, 1996a; Shenon, 1996). Here is a typical case of how those prostitutes get infected with the deadly virus:

When Pon and Tai were 15, a woman showed up one day in their village in Burma, just across the Thai border. She promised to take the two girls on a sightseeing tour of Bangkok. When they got there she dropped them off at a brothel. They were locked up, and their virginity was quickly sold for $40. Soon, they were forced to service four or five customers a day—up to a dozen on weekends—without payment. Fearful of AIDS, about which they learned from Thai television, they offered to buy clients condoms out of their meager tip money. Most men refused. Now both girls have tested HIV-positive . . . Pon, now 17, says, "The men knew about AIDS but didn't care. They certainly didn't care about us." (Moreau, 1992)

Recently, however, many prostitutes in the poor, developing countries of Asia, Africa, and Latin America have begun to insist that their customers wear condoms. If the men refuse, they are sent away. But in order to avoid rejecting customers who refuse to use a condom, an increasing number of prostitutes in these countries have begun to use the female condom, which is still rarely used in the United States and other Western countries (McNeil, 1999; Dugger, 1999).

The Subculture of Prostitution

Like any other profession, prostitutes hold certain beliefs about themselves and their work. One belief is that prostitutes are morally superior to conventional people. This is because prostitutes see themselves as honest and others as dishonest. To prostitutes, conventional women who marry so they can depend on their husbands for lifelong financial support—especially the young women who marry wealthy older men—are, in effect, prostitutes, except that they are not honest enough to regard themselves as such. Prostitutes also see their so-called respectable customers as hypocrites. As one prostitute says, "We come into continual contact with upright, respected citizens whose voices are loudly raised against us in public, and yet who visit us in private" (Hirschi, 1962). If most customers do not publicly condemn prostitutes, they in essence cheat on their wives by patronizing prostitutes. Many prostitutes, therefore, despise their customers, and try to exploit them by maximizing the fee and minimizing the service. Such an attitude and behavior is common among streetwalkers and other low-paid prostitutes who immerse themselves in the prostitution subculture by associating only with one another. Other prostitutes are less contemptuous and exploitative toward their customers. They include call girls and other higher-priced prostitutes who are less alienated from conventional society because their circle of friends includes straight people. These prostitutes are more likely to accept another, more positive aspect of the prostitution subculture to be true.

The more positive aspect of the subculture is the belief that prostitution is good for society because it performs many important services. One service is believed to involve preventing sex crimes; as one prostitute puts it, "I believe that there should be more prostitution houses and what have you, and then we wouldn't have so many of these perverted idiots, sex maniacs, all sorts of weird people running around." Another service is believed to involve contributing to marital success: "I could say that a prostitute has held more marriages together as part of her profession than any divorce counselor . . . the release of talking about an unhappy home situation may well have saved many a marriage, and possibly even lives, when nerves have been strained to a breaking point." Prostitutes liken themselves not only to marriage counselors but also to humanitarians, social workers, psychologists, or psychiatrists. One prostitute explains, "I don't regret doing it because I feel I help people. A lot of men that come over to see me don't come over for sex. They come over for companionship, someone to talk to. . . . They talk about sex. . . . A lot of them have problems" (Bryan, 1966; Hirschi, 1962).

This professional self-image has fueled civil rights movements among prostitutes in Western societies. In Great Britain, for example, prostitutes have long campaigned against the laws that prohibit public solicitation, as in streets, hotels, and bars, arguing that peaceful soliciting should be as lawful as peaceful picketing (*The Economist,* 1979). In the United States, prostitutes have formed unions in various cities with the aim of decriminalizing prostitution so that their working conditions can be improved and their sex work can be respected like any other legitimate profession. The most famous prostitutes' rights organization is COYOTE (Call Off Your Tired Ethics). It fights for full decriminalization and the elimination of all legal restrictions on prostitution. COYOTE argues that prostitutes have the right to sell sex because selling sex is no different from other kinds of work women do:

> A woman has the right to sell sexual services just as much as she has the right to sell her brains to a law firm where she works as a lawyer, or to sell her creative work to a museum when she works as an artist, or to sell her image to a photographer when she works as a model, or to sell her body when she works as a ballerina. (Jenness, 1990)

COYOTE asserts that arresting or jailing prostitutes violates their civil rights, and that their sex work should be respected and protected like other legitimate professions. However, most feminists have rejected COYOTE's crusade to turn prostitution into a legitimate, respectable profession, because they consider prostitution a form of sexual slavery—which they want prostitutes to get out of, not into. COYOTE has also failed to get support from most of the general public, legislators, and law enforcers (Weitzer, 1991).

Other Participants in Prostitution

Aside from prostitutes, three other kinds of people are involved in the so-called skin trade. They are the madam, the pimp, and the customer.

The Madam. The general public uses the term *madam* to refer to the owner or manager of a brothel; brothel owners themselves call one another "landlady." Most are former prostitutes with a great deal of experience "in the life" behind them. They run their establishments in about the same way as legitimate businesspeople run theirs, except that they must deal with problems arising from the illegal nature of their trade. There are three major forms of activities that the madam characteristically engages in. The first has to do with the employees, the second the customers, and the third the police.

The madam recruits her prostitutes largely through her current employees, but also from pimps and other madams. She trains the new employee to be clean, develop social skills, and observe such old customs of prostitution as asking for payment before giving the sexual service and refraining from getting emotionally involved or spending too much time with a customer. After the employees become professional, the madam supervises their work, keeps them happy, prevents quarrels and jealousy among them, and makes and enforces rules governing their behavior. The nature of her work is such that she usually functions as if she were the employees' mother. Some madams even insist that they are in effect running a charm school—where they teach social graces (*Time*, 1980).

The madam is responsible for finding customers. She keeps a "john book," which contains the customers' names and telephone numbers; she uses it when there is not much business in the house. Usually, customers call her. The madam's main concern is to make the client happy so that he will become a regular visitor. This means, among other things, that she has to find and hire new women constantly, because it is the variety of women that many customers look for in prostitution.

To avoid arrest, the madam must know how to deal with the police. She is usually skilled in recognizing a police officer disguised as a customer. As one madam says, albeit boastfully, "I could spot a copper a mile away—if I don't see him I can smell him" (Winick and Kinsie, 1971). Nonetheless, madams often have to work out some stable arrangements with the law officers. One arrangement involves bribing them. But more often the madam develops an understanding with the police that they will go through the motion of arresting her every now and then—thereby keeping up the appearance of performing their duty to appease the public's moral outrage against prostitution—while allowing her to continue her business. If all this cannot be done, a madam would ask her employees to wait for her calls at their own residences. Such a madam essentially runs a "call house"—euphemistically referred to in the sex business as "escort agency"—by maintaining a list of prostitutes on call. She simply sits by a telephone, gets calls from customers, and then sends prostitutes to customers, or sends customers to prostitutes, or arranges for both to meet in some other place.

The Pimp.   Many of the prostitutes who do not work for a madam work for a pimp. While the madam gets a large portion—usually about half—of her employees' earnings, the pimp typically gets all of them. Also, unlike the madam, who has to find customers for her prostitutes, the pimp generally just tells his prostitutes to go out in the street and hustle. He does not want to be bothered with the details of their working life. The pimp, then, is *not* what many dictionaries say he is—"a pander, a procurer, or a man who solicits customers for a prostitute in return for a share of the proceeds." Rather, he is simply a man who lives off the entire proceeds of one or more prostitutes. For this reason, most people in conventional society would consider him "the lowest of the low."

A pimp may have anywhere from 1 to 20 women, his "stable," but most pimps have only one or two women. Pimps and their stables live in a subculture that is in many ways the opposite of conventional culture. In the pimping subculture, men are extremely dominant, women are extremely submissive, and the ideal union is between a black man and several white women. Also, the men are obsessed with their own appearance, spending many hours a day on their hair, clothes, and jewelry in order to make themselves look beautiful. The women, who consider themselves "wives-in-law," are the real economic providers, working hard to support the household. Since the women routinely have sex with other men—their customers—paternity of their children often comes from outside the subcultural group. In this subculture, then, men are expected to demonstrate great style and creativity in the way they dress and groom themselves; women generally sleep during the day and work at night; money is worshiped as a god; conspicuous consumption is indulged in every day; and there is little concern for future security (Milner and Milner, 1972).

The pimp often resorts to violence to control his women. As a former prostitute says, "I saw a girl walk into a bar and hand the pimp a $100 bill. He took it and burned it in her face and turned around and knocked her down on the floor and kicked her and said, 'I told you, bitch, $200. I want $200, not $100.' Now she's gotta go out again and make not another hundred, but two hundred" (Millett, 1973). The pimp's violent method of controlling his women is apparently effective. According to one study, over 50 percent of the prostitutes who had been beaten by their pimps "accepted it as a way of life, felt they deserved it, or were flattered by it as a sign of caring" (Caplan, 1984; Silbert and Pines, 1981). According to another study, a pimp's women generally worship him as if he were a god. They invest in him all their hopes, dreams, and goals for the future. They wear his beatings proudly as symbols of his love. Everything that he does to them is considered right, proper, or admirable. When a prostitute was asked what her pimp did to deserve all her earnings, she replied, "He doesn't do *nothing*. But the way he does nothing is *beautiful*" (Sheehy, 1971a). In short, as Kathleen Barry (1995) suggests, the prostitutes are so emotionally entangled with their pimp that they cannot see themselves being controlled by him.

The John. In the argot of the sex trade, the prostitute's customer is called "john" or "trick." According to a national survey, men who have slept with different women are more likely than monogamous men to become a john (Michael et al., 1994). If sexually active men can get sex with conventional women for free, why would they want to buy sex from prostitutes? One reason, according to feminists, is that prostitution gives the customer the benefit of being a sexual master and the prostitute his sexual servant. As one prostitute says, "What they're buying, in a way, is power. You're supposed to please them. They can tell you what to do, and you're supposed to please them, follow their orders" (Overall, 1992). In this structure of power inequality between the sexes, the johns are, in effect, the prostitute's oppressors or victimizers.

Men also have other reasons for buying sex (Winick and Kinsie, 1971; Benjamin and Masters, 1964). First is the desire to get *quick, easy sex*. Finding a willing woman for sex requires time, effort, or ability. There are men who do not have the time to find such a woman, particularly if they are too busy pursuing a career or if they are strangers in a city far away from their wives or girlfriends. There are also men who simply want to have sex—not conversation, not companionship, not cultivation of friendship or love. For these individuals, the ritual of dating—taking a woman to a restaurant, a movie, a bar, and possibly a bedroom—demands too much effort. They prefer a prostitute from whom they can effortlessly get what they want. There are yet other men who are too shy or are otherwise lacking the ability to attract and persuade a woman to go to bed with them. For such men, a prostitute can be easily gotten without risking rejection.

A second reason for going to a prostitute is the desire to get *untangled sex*. There are men who do not want to get seriously involved with women. They want to dodge emotional entanglements, obligations, or interpersonal conflict. More specifically, they want to avoid getting entangled with a woman in courtship or marriage; avoid being obligated to her if she becomes pregnant; or avoid the risk of breaking up a marriage—their own or the woman's if she is married. What these men want is impersonal, untangled sex, which can free them from the conventional strictures regarding the responsibility of sex. Sex of this kind is characteristically available from the prostitute. Here's how a john describes the straightforward, no-strings-attached sex: "I like the basic rawness of it . . . the basic honesty of it. There's a lot of honesty in that. You girl, me have sexual desire, you have the object of my sexual desire, me give you money, you give me what I want, no bullshit, no play, no games. . . . It's raw, honest, and it's good" (Holzman and Pines, 1982).

A third reason for patronizing prostitutes is the desire to get a *variety of sexual experiences*. There are men who want to have sex with a variety of women rather than with the same one only. Some men may want to engage in certain types of sex, such as oral sex, anal sex, or sadomasochistic sex, that turn off their wives or girlfriends. All these needs can be easily met with a visit to prostitutes.

The majority of the men who buy sex are *occasional johns,* while a few are *habitual* and *compulsive johns* (Greenwald, 1970). Occasional johns, who buy sex only occasionally, are psychologically normal. But habitual and compulsive johns are less normal. Habitual johns want to get emotionally attached to one special prostitute. They are fond of asking the prostitute many questions, telling her about their lives, offering to help her in whatever way they can, or trying to make her enjoy having sex with them. Compulsive johns also seem a little abnormal: They cannot keep away from prostitutes. Generally, compulsive johns feel that sex is dirty and would not want to defile a "good" woman, so that they will copulate only with "bad" ones—namely, prostitutes. Some compulsive johns can be sexually potent only with prostitutes; they cannot have an erection with their wives or other conventional women.

Societal Reaction to Prostitution

In ancient civilizations, prostitution was not condemned as evil. It was even considered sacred by some religious sects, so that only priestesses had the privilege to practice it. Nowadays, it is regarded as an evil in virtually all societies; but in most societies, it is recognized as an evil that cannot be eradicated. Consequently, one of two situations usually prevails: (1) prostitution is legal but public solicitation for it is not, as is the case in many European and Asian countries (Davis, 1993), or (2) prostitution is illegal but the law is not strictly enforced, as is the case in the United States.

Before the turn of this century, prostitution was illegal but practiced openly in the United States, particularly in the Wild West, where prostitutes were as much a part of the new frontier as miners, cowboys, town preachers, and small merchants (Symanski, 1974). In the early part of the twentieth century, various organizations, such as the YMCA and the American Purity Alliance, mounted an increasingly powerful campaign against prostitution. These vice crusaders eventually won; most brothels that had openly operated were closed down by the mid-1940s. Today, the few houses that continue to do business openly exist in several sparsely populated counties of Nevada, where prostitution is legal. In other parts of the country, where prostitution is not legal, the majority of prostitutes find their customers outside the house. The streetwalkers, who bear the brunt of law enforcement against prostitution, are periodically arrested. Soon after they pay a fine in court or are released from jail, however, they go right back to hustling on the street.

If prostitution is so tough to wipe out, why bother trying to enforce the antiprostitution laws? Conservatives have over the years developed the following rationales for the continued attempt at enforcement: (1) Prostitution often brings about mugging, robbery, or assault. (2) Prostitution provides a breeding ground for organized crime activities. (3) Prostitution helps spread the AIDS virus and other sexually transmitted diseases. (4) Prostitution often subjects innocent citizens to offensive public solicitation. (5) Prostitution is destructive to public morals, which enforcement of the laws helps to preserve (Bryant, 1977). Many feminists also condemn prostitution as degrading to women, robbing them of their dignity and worth as human beings. One feminist regards prostitution as "female sexual slavery" because she believes that most prostitutes, being controlled by pimps, cannot get out of it (Barry, 1995; Farley, 1994).

On the other hand, liberals have argued for the legalization of prostitution. They contend that most problems associated with prostitution stem largely from antiprostitution laws themselves. Treated as criminals, prostitutes are bound to operate secretly and stay as far away from the watchful eye of the law as possible. As a result, they and their customers are likely to commit crime against each other or transmit VD (venereal diseases) or AIDS to each other. If prostitution is legalized, liberals argue, those problems will disappear because specific statutes can be enacted to control prostitutes' activities. Prostitutes will be required to undergo regular medical checkups, be made to confine their business activities within a specified area, or be prohibited from soliciting on the street. Some liberals also argue that antiprostitution laws do not necessarily uphold national moral standards but instead encourage corruption among the police as well as moral hypocrisy and disrespect for the law among the general public. It is further argued that it costs too much to prosecute prostitutes and that precious law-enforcement efforts would be better employed against more serious crimes (Quindlen, 1994; Bode, 1978; Anderson, 1977).

The general public favors the conservative position over the liberal one. According to a survey, when Americans were asked whether they support or oppose the legalization of prostitution, 72 percent said "oppose" and only 23 percent said "support." Another survey also found significantly more people who want the current antiprostitution laws strictly enforced (Weitzer, 1991). However, no matter how strictly enforced the laws are, prostitution cannot be eradicated because of the substantial demand for it on the part of large numbers of ordinary men.

Prostitution in Global Perspective

In recent years, prostitution has become a fast-growing global industry. The sex workers in Eastern Europe and Asia, however, generally suffer more than their counterparts in the United States and other Western countries.

Due to the collapse of the Soviet Union, many unemployed women in the former communist world have drifted into more prosperous countries to sell their bodies. Women from Russia, Poland, Romania, Hungary, and other Eastern European countries can be found selling sex in Western Europe. Those women now make up at least a quarter of Germany's prostitute population. In Israel, many newspaper ads offering "entertainment services" brag about "hot new Russians." In Japan, blond and blue-eyed Russian women have become the latest addition to fancy "hostess" bars. Even in deeply religious Saudi Arabia, many Russian women have arrived to work as prostitutes. Many of these women have chosen to enter the skin trade. But others have been tricked or forced into it after arriving in the foreign countries with promises of singing, dancing, modeling, or waitressing jobs—the promises having been given earlier by pimps posing as businessmen in their home countries (Hornblower, 1993). In short, many women in Eastern Europe have chosen to become prostitutes while others have been tricked or forced into prostitution in foreign countries.

Many more women from Asia have been lured into Western Europe with promises of legitimate jobs only to be sold to brothels. Similar job promises have also enticed numerous women in Thailand and the Philippines to go to Japan, where they are turned into virtual sex slaves in bars mostly controlled by *yakuza*, Japanese organized crime syndicates. In the United States some "nude-modeling studios" pay U.S. soldiers in South Korea to marry Korean women, bring them here, and then divorce them. Unable to speak English, these women are finally forced into brothels in Houston, Detroit, and other cities. There are also large numbers of prostitutes in Thailand and the Philippines, catering not only to local men but also to hordes of Japanese and Western European men on organized sex tours. Most of these Asian prostitutes have come from poor villages to work in large cities, and after having been tricked or sold into brothels, they serve as virtual sexual slaves (Human Rights Watch, 1995; Hornblower, 1993).

A typical example is 20-year-old Manju, a brothel prostitute in the Indian city of Bombay. She originally came from a poor village in Nepal. When she was 12, her father let two strangers take her to Bombay, after being told that she would work as a housemaid. Then the two men sold her to a brothel for $1000. "There was nothing I could do," she says, "I was trapped." She would be set free only if she could repay her full purchase price. Every day she services an average of seven customers. Her fee is only $1 each, and the brothel owner takes more than half. Moreover, rent, food, and clothing are deducted from her wages. Now, having worked for more than 7 years, she is told that she still owes $300 (Hornblower, 1993).

Prostitution is far more prevalent in the developing world than in the West, and attempts have been made to explain it. One popular explanation is the abject poverty in the rural areas of developing countries. As Manju, the Nepalese prostitute in Bombay, whose father is an extremely poor farmer, says, "Even if you work 24 hours a day in Nepal, you do not get enough to eat. One can endure anything except hunger. If I were a man, maybe I would have committed murder to fill my stomach. But as a woman, I became a prostitute" (Hornblower, 1993). Marxist theorists take this explanation a step farther by blaming the rural poverty in some Asian countries on neocolonialism. Behaving like colonial powers, Western countries have in the last four decades destroyed the traditional system of agriculture on which most people in the Third World depended for their livelihood. For example, large U.S. agribusinesses such as Dole and Del Monte used up a huge expanse of farmland in the Philippines to plant pineapples and bananas for export, which drove many peasants out of their farms and caused widespread poverty in the rural areas (Sturdevant and Stoltzfus, 1992).

However, rural poverty by itself cannot explain why the overwhelming majority of prostitutes are women. Feminist theorists explain this in terms of gender inequality: Being heavily dominated or oppressed by men, poor women are said to be forced to sell their bodies as commodities. Poor women are also said to have been socialized to feel, with resignation, that they have to sell sex to support their families. This is because the Third World's patriarchal culture imposes a much heavier burden of filial and familial duty on daughters than on sons (Muecke, 1992). The same patriarchal culture further encourages young men of higher social classes to visit prostitutes as a way of confirming their manhood. In Thailand, for example, male college students often go to a brothel together. "If you refuse to go along," a young man says, "they call you gay or reject you" (Erlanger, 1991).

Theories of Prostitution

There are at least three major theories about prostitution: functionalist, feminist, and social-psychological theories. Functionalist and feminist theories focus on prostitution, explaining why prostitution exists despite efforts to eradicate it. But social-psychological theory zeroes in on the individual prostitute, explaining why some women are more likely than others to become prostitutes.

Functionalist Theory

According to sociologist Kingsley Davis (1971), there are two reasons why prostitution exists. The first is the very system of *sexual morality* that ostensibly condemns prostitution but unintendedly or ironically causes prostitution to exist as a social institution. The moral system causes prostitution by creating advantages for it in at least two ways. First, the moral system divides sex into two types: Sex with one's spouse is part of a "meaningful" relationship and sex with a prostitute is "meaningless." This has the effect of encouraging men to go to a prostitute if they want to have "meaningless" sex. Second, by defining certain sex acts such as oral or anal sex as immoral and hence not to be indulged in with one's "moral" wife or girlfriend, the moral order encourages men to turn to "immoral" women—namely, prostitutes—for these sex acts. The moral system, in effect, creates a demand for prostitution.

Another reason for the existence of prostitution is also ironic: *prostitution's function of strengthening sexual morality*. More specifically, prostitution exists because it serves to strengthen sexual morality by "keeping the wives and daughters of the respectable citizenry pure" (Davis, 1971). In other words, the sex industry encourages men to go to prostitutes for premarital sex, extramarital sex, or other "immoral" sex so that they do not have to persuade or pressure "respectable" women to engage in the same "immoral" sex. By thus preserving the sexual morality of conventional women, who constitute nearly half of humankind, the level of a society's morality should be higher than if many women engage in the same sexual "immoralities" as prostitutes and men do.

In short, Davis's theory suggests that prostitution exists because the moral system paradoxically encourages it, and it in turn serves the important function of protecting "feminine virtue." This theory runs counter to the popular belief that "an evil such as prostitution cannot cause a good such as feminine virtue, or vice versa" (Davis, 1971).

There is some evidence to support the theory. In traditional Asian societies where prostitution is prevalent, "respectable" women are relatively unlikely to engage in "immoral" sex, while in modern Western societies where prostitution is less common, "respectable" women are more likely to get involved in "immoral" sex. Also, on many U.S. campuses, male students are more likely to think of having sex with college women than with prostitutes, so that they are more likely than their counterparts in Thailand to persuade or pressure college women to engage in premarital sex. There is, however, a basic problem with functionalist theory. It defines sexual morality and feminine virtue in sexist terms, implying that only women, particularly prostitutes, are immoral and virtueless when committing "meaningless" or "immoral" sex. That's why functionalist theory does *not* regard sexually "promiscuous" men, especially those who often patronize prostitutes, as a threat to the moral order.

Feminist Theory

To feminists, functionalist theory merely reflects a sexist society's view that "promiscuous" men are not a threat to the moral order, only "promiscuous" women such as prostitutes are. This explains why in a sexist society prostitutes are far more likely to be arrested than their male customers for committing the same sexual act. But why are "promiscuous" men not considered a threat to the moral order in the first place? Because the moral system reflects the larger patriarchal, gender-stratified system in which men dominate and exploit women.

According to feminist theory, the patriarchal system encourages prostitution by creating both demand and supply for it. On the demand side, boys are socialized under the influence of patriarchy to be dominant over girls and, when boys become adults, they are expected to desire sexual domination of women, which can be easily realized through sex with prostitutes. If a young man does not want to visit a prostitute, his peers will pressure him to do so, as we have observed in regard to college men in Thailand. On the supply side, girls are socialized to be submissive to boys and, later as adults, to men in work, play, or sex. At the same time, women are relegated to predominantly low-status employment, including prostitution. All this explains why prostitution is usually more prevalent in traditional societies marked by great gender inequality, when compared with more modern societies with less gender inequality.

While the patriarchal system with its gender inequality encourages prostitution, prostitution in turn reinforces patriarchy. Some feminists have observed that prostitution "serves to perpetuate women's social subordination" (Overall, 1992) or "perpetuates socially hegemonic belief which oppresses all women in many domains of their lives" (Miller, 1991). In other words, by selling their bodies as a commodity, prostitutes convey the message that women can be bought or used as an object. This directly reinforces the prevailing patriarchal "notion that all women are whores at heart; all women have a price" (Overall, 1992). Consequently, many men, for example, find this sexist joke funny: A man asks a woman, "Would you sleep with me for a million dollars?" The woman answers, "I guess I would." Then the man asks, "Would you sleep with me for five dollars?" The woman turns angry, saying, "What do you take me for?" But the man responds, "We've already established that; now we're just negotiating your price" (Overall, 1992). Learning from prostitutes that women can be bought like an object, as implied in this joke, many men will continue to support the patriarchal structure of gender inequality, which in turn encourages prostitution.

Social-Psychological Theory

According to this theory, a combination of social and psychological factors causes some women to become prostitutes. These factors include the following:

- *Predisposing* factors—exemplified by such unpleasant experiences as struggling with parental "promiscuity," parental neglect, child abuse, or other traumatic events that cause psychological problems.

- *Attracting* factors—exemplified by the expectation based on popular belief that a woman can have an easy life or lots of money as a prostitute.

■ *Precipitating* factors—exemplified by such social situations as being unemployed, meeting a prostitute friend, or being pressured by a pimp to sell sex (Brown, 1979; Benjamin and Masters, 1964).

Most psychologists and psychiatrists stress the predisposing factors as the key to entering prostitution. According to Harold Greenwald (1970), for example, prostitutes sell their sexual service because they have suffered parental neglect, rejection, or abuse in childhood and consequently have developed such abnormal symptoms as feelings of loneliness and unworthiness, lack of self-control, and inability to establish stable relations with others. This implies that a woman must be psychologically abnormal to become a prostitute.

From the sociological perspective, however, we need not assume that prostitutes are abnormal even if they have been abused by their parents. It seems largely a matter of emotional socialization that teaches the victim to be a normal prostitute, one who is able to detach herself emotionally from her johns. This is because parental abuse teaches the victim to detach herself emotionally from her parent and, by extension, anyone who treats her like an object in the same way as her parent does. With this emotional detachment, the victim may later find it easier to enter into prostitution, detaching herself emotionally from her customers, who in a way treat her as her abusive father has done, that is, as an object. In short, some women are more likely than others to become prostitutes not because they are abnormal, but because they are *normal* for being able to withhold affection from their customers in the same way as a normal child-abuse victim withholds affection from her parent. But this capacity for emotional detachment may only *predispose* a woman toward entering prostitution; it is not enough to cause her to sell sex. She is more likely to do so if the attracting and precipitating factors also appear in her experience, as has been suggested by the theory and some research (Perkins, 1991; Heyl, 1977).

Summary

1. How is the pornography industry today? It has grown to be an enormous industry today, much more profitable than all the Hollywood movies distributed in the United States. **What are the effects of pornography?** Some argue that pornography is harmful, but others say it is harmless. Evidence suggests that while the erotic, nonviolent type of pornography is generally harmless, the violent type is harmful.

2. What are the myths about extramarital sex? One myth is that extramarital sex is more exciting or satisfying than marital sex. Another myth is that people have affairs because they are oversexed. **How does adultery vary from one culture to another?** Adultery is socially approved in some societies but not so in others. Legitimate adultery varies in form from one culture to another and so does illegitimate adultery. **Which groups of Americans are more likely**

than others to engage in extramarital sex? The groups that are more likely to have an affair include men, the less religious, and lower-income persons.

3. Why do some people engage in on-line sex? The reasons include being anonymous, the ease and convenience of finding sex partners on-line, being able to share sexual fantasies and turn them into realities, and seeking real sex with partners that one has met on-line. **What is cyberporn?** Cyberporn is sexually explicit material accessible via the Internet. It has become very popular today, and some parents fear that their children will be exposed to cyberporn, but there are ways to block children's access to it.

4. What is sexual harassment? It is an unwelcome act of a sexual nature, but if it involves workers it means, according to the U.S. Supreme Court, any conduct that makes the workplace environment so hostile that the victim finds it harder to perform her job. **What causes sexual harassment?** An apparent cause is the threat posed by women to male dominance, which may explain why sexual harassment often occurs in traditionally and heavily male-dominated occupations.

5. What are the popular myths about prostitutes? The myths are that prostitutes are nymphomaniacs, that they are sexually frigid, that they are nasty and hard-hearted or sweet and warmhearted, that they are mostly drug addicts, and that they have been sexually abused as children. **Are all prostitutes largely the same?** No, there are many different types of prostitutes. They include—in ascending order of status, price, or life quality—streetwalkers, child and adolescent prostitutes, house prostitutes, and call girls.

6. What kinds of backgrounds do prostitutes come from? Most prostitutes have about the same social and sexual backgrounds as conventional women, such as desiring marriage and traditional family life, having the same level of education as other women, and being not particularly "promiscuous" in their private lives. **What have been their reasons for becoming prostitutes?** The most common reasons are economic, such as wanting to make more money, being unemployed, or supporting a family. **Are prostitutes very liable to get AIDS?** Yes, but prostitutes in Western countries are far less likely than those in Third World countries to get the disease because condoms are often used. **What is the subculture of prostitution?** Prostitutes believe that they are morally superior to straights and that their so-called respectable customers are hypocrites. Prostitutes also regard their work as good for society because they compare it to the service rendered by a marriage counselor, social worker, or some other helping profession.

7. Who are the prostitute's coparticipants in prostitution? They include madams, pimps, and johns. The madam is a brothel owner or manager who employs prostitutes to serve her customers. The pimp is primarily the prostitute's nonworking lover or husband, who often uses violence to keep her under his thumb. The john visits prostitutes to enjoy being a sexual master or to seek quick and easy sex, untangled sex, and sexual variety. **How do conservatives and**

liberals want to deal with prostitution? Conservatives want strong enforcement of antiprostitution laws, believing that prostitution causes many problems, such as crime and disease. Liberals want to legalize prostitution, arguing that legalized prostitution can be more effectively controlled and that the very problems currently associated with illegal prostitution will disappear.

8. How do prostitutes in Eastern Europe and Third World countries differ from their peers in Western countries? Eastern European prostitutes are more likely than their Western counterparts to have been tricked or forced into the skin trade. Asian prostitutes too are more likely to have the same experience, but they are also more likely to have come from poor villages to work as virtual sex slaves in cities. **Why is prostitution more prevalent in the developing world than in the West?** One reason is abject poverty in the rural areas of developing countries. Other reasons include Western colonialism and local patriarchal culture.

9. How do various theories explain prostitution? According to functionalist theory, prostitution exists because it is encouraged by society's system of sexual morality, and prostitution in turn serves the function of strengthening sexual morality. According to feminist theory, the patriarchal system encourages prostitution by creating demand and supply for it, and prostitution in turn reinforces the patriarchal structure of gender inequality. Social-psychological theory offers three factors—predisposing, attracting, and precipitating factors—to explain why some women are more likely than others to become prostitutes.

SUGGESTED READINGS

Barry, Kathleen. 1995. *The Prostitution of Sexuality.* New York: New York University Press. An analysis of how prostitution represents the essence of sexual exploitation that serves to oppress womankind.

Davis, Nanette J. (Ed.). 1993. *Prostitution: An International Handbook on Trends, Problems, and Policies.* Westport, Conn.: Greenwood. A collection of articles on the problems of prostitution in various countries, showing the importance of outlawing and abolishing the sex business.

Fisher, Helen E. 1992. *Anatomy of Love: The Natural History of Monogamy, Adultery, and Divorce.* New York: Norton. A sociobiological attempt to explain the universality of adultery, though providing data on cultural differences in form and frequency of adultery.

Gibson, Pamela Church, and Roma Gibson (Eds.). 1993. *Dirty Looks: Women, Pornography, Power.* London: British Film Institute. A volume of articles that deal mostly with nonviolent, erotic pornography, showing the harmlessness of pornography and the harmfulness of censorship.

Hicks, George. 1995. *The Comfort Women: Japan's Brutal Regime of Enforced Prostitution in the Second World War.* New York: Norton. A documentation of how the Japanese army forced massive numbers of young women in Korea, China, and other Asian countries to become sex slaves for Japanese soldiers.

Itzin, Catherine (Ed.). 1993. *Pornography: Women, Violence, and Civil Liberties: A Radical View.* New York: Oxford University Press. Presents a collection of articles showing how pornography causes violence against women and children as well as reinforcing male dominance.

Jenness, Valerie. 1993. *Making It Work: The Prostitutes' Rights Movement in Perspective.* Hawthorne, N.Y.: Aldine de Gruyter. An analysis of how the prostitutes' rights movement attempts to have prostitution publicly recognized as freely chosen work so that it can be decriminalized.

Linz, Daniel, and Neil Malamuth. 1993. *Pornography.* Newbury Park, Calif.: Sage. Presenting the conservative, liberal, and feminist views of pornography as well as the data employed to support them.

Overall, Christine. 1992. "What's wrong with prostitution? Evaluating sex work." *Signs, 17,* 705–725. Explaining that prostitution is a form of sexual slavery not because of the rendering of sex service itself but because of the power imbalance involved in sex service.

Prus, Robert, and Styllianoss Irini. 1988. *Hookers, Rounders, and Desk Clerks: The Social Organization of the Hotel Community.* Salem, Wisc.: Sheffield. A rich source of information about prostitutes working in the bar and hotel.

Sturdevant, Saundra Pollock, and Brenda Stoltzfus. 1992. *Let the Good Times Roll: Prostitution and the U.S. Military in Asia.* New York: The New Press. Analyzing the oppressive life and work of bar girls in the Philippines, South Korea, and Okinawa under the dehumanizing shadow of the U.S. military.

CHAPTER

10 Homosexuality and Homophobia

Kelli Peterson, a 17-year-old senior at East High School in Salt Lake City, had felt lonely as a lesbian student for at least two years. "I thought I was the only lesbian student in East High," she said. "As a sophomore I was really pressured by my friends to date. I came out that year, and immediately lost all my friends. I went through the cycle of denial, trying to hide, acceptance, then your friends abandoning you." Therefore, she and two other gay students formed an extracurricular club called the Gay/Straight Alliance. But this touched off a furor among national conservative leaders, the State Legislature, and the local school board. Apparently possessed with the unfounded fear that the club could turn straight students into gays or lesbians, one antigay leader proclaimed: "Homosexuals can't reproduce, so they recruit. And they are not going to use Utah high school and junior high school campuses to recruit." Eventually, a state law was passed banning all gay clubs in high schools (Brooke, 1996; Smolowe, 1996).

Such a negative reaction toward lesbians and gays is an example of *homophobia,* prejudice and discrimination against people with the same-sex orientation. In this chapter, we will take a look at various aspects of homophobia. But we will first analyze different facets of same-sex orientation (traditionally called "homosexuality"), including the popular myths about it, the lives and activities of the sexual minority (gays and lesbians), same-sex practices among straights and bisexuals, and various controversial theories for explaining same-sex orientation.

Myths about Homosexuality

According to one popular myth, gay men are typically effeminate and lesbians masculine. Gays are believed to walk like women, talk like women, or look like women, and lesbians are believed to walk, talk, or look like men. In reality it is difficult to differentiate most gays and lesbians from straights. Most gays look and behave just like most heterosexual men, and most lesbians look and behave just like most heterosexual women (Marcus, 1993; Dunkle and Francis, 1990).

A second myth is that gay men like to molest or seduce young children. The fact is that the great majority of gay men have no more sexual interest in young boys than the great majority of straight men have in little girls. Actually, most child molesters are male *heterosexuals.* For one year, between 1991 and 1992, at the Children's Hospital in Denver, Colorado, there were 387 cases of suspected child molestation. Only one perpetrator was gay; all the rest were heterosexual men (Marcus, 1993).

A third myth is that gays and lesbians consistently play one specific role—either as an active or passive partner—in their sexual activities. The active partner is assumed to perform oral sex on the passive partner. The truth is that most gays and lesbians engage in a lot of alternation between those two roles. Same-sex couples are also popularly expected to behave like traditional couples, one mate playing the role of dominant husband, the other the submissive wife. Again the reality is quite different: Partners in a same-sex relationship often resemble best friends, who, being equal, "share and share alike" so that *both* may cook, make money, or disclose deep feelings (Peplau, 1981).

According to a fourth myth, same-sex orientation is a symptom of mental illness. Some gays and lesbians, particularly those who go to psychiatrists, are perhaps emotionally disturbed, but so are some straights, especially those who go to psychiatrists. Therefore, just as it is wrong to conclude that straights are mentally ill, it is wrong to conclude that lesbians and gays are. This is one reason why the American Psychiatric Association has, since 1973, removed "homosexuality" from its *Diagnostic and Statistical Manual* as a mental illness. There are still some psychiatrists, psychoanalysts, and psychologists, though, who continue to believe that same-sex orientation is a mental illness that can be cured (Socarides et al., 1997).

A fifth myth is that lesbians and gays cannot be expected to have a satisfactory sex life because it is abnormal or unnatural. Research, however, has shown no real difference between gays/lesbians and straights in their physical capacity to enjoy sex. The basic difference involves styles of making love. Same-sex couples tend to treat sex as play, spending much time on foreplay—focusing on kissing and caressing various parts of the body—before directing attention specifically to genitals for reaching orgasm. Heterosexual couples are more likely to treat sex as work, bent on a quick attainment of orgasm (Masters and Johnson, 1979).

According to a sixth myth, gays and lesbians are obsessed with sex, having sex all the time. In reality, gay men have about as much sex as their heterosexual peers—two or three times a week. As for lesbians, they seem less interested in sex when compared to heterosexual women: no more than once a week for lesbians but two or three times a week for married heterosexual women (Blumstein and Schwartz, 1990).

Finally, a seventh myth suggests that most people are either completely gay or completely straight. In reality, as biologist-turned-sexologist Alfred Kinsey (1948) wrote,

> [People] do not represent two discrete populations, heterosexual and homosexual. The world is not to be divided into sheep and goats. . . . It is a fundamental of taxonomy that nature rarely deals with discrete categories. Only the human mind invents categories and tries to force facts into separate pigeon holes. The living world is a continuum in each and every one of its aspects.

The difference between the sexes is mostly a matter of *kind:* People are either male or female. But the difference between sexual orientations is a matter of *degree:* Some people are more, or less, heterosexual (or homosexual) than others. Thus Kinsey assigned people varying positions on a scale from one extreme of being exclusively heterosexual to the other extreme of being exclusively homosexual (see Figure 10.1).

Gay and Lesbian Life

Due to their same-sex orientation, gay and lesbian life differs in some ways from straight life. But most gays and lesbians live a normal, happy life, as most straights do.

The Numbers of Gays and Lesbians

How many gays and lesbians are there in the United States? The answer depends first on the definition of what constitutes being a gay or lesbian. It appears from various studies that a lesbian or gay is a person with one or more of these characteristics: *same-sex feeling*—being attracted to a person of the same gender, (2) *same-sex behavior*—having sex with a same-gender person, and (3) *identifying oneself as gay or lesbian.*

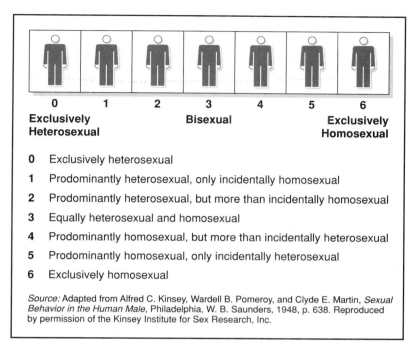

0   Exclusively heterosexual

1   Prodominantly heterosexual, only incidentally homosexual

2   Prodominantly heterosexual, but more than incidentally homosexual

3   Equally heterosexual and homosexual

4   Prodominantly homosexual, but more than incidentally heterosexual

5   Prodominantly homosexual, only incidentally heterosexual

6   Exclusively homosexual

Source: Adapted from Alfred C. Kinsey, Wardell B. Pomeroy, and Clyde E. Martin, *Sexual Behavior in the Human Male,* Philadelphia, W. B. Saunders, 1948, p. 638. Reproduced by permission of the Kinsey Institute for Sex Research, Inc.

FIGURE 10.1   The Kinsey Heterosexual–Homosexual Continuum

Keeping in mind these different definitions of same-sex orientation, let us consider the following data from a study of a representative sample of the U.S. adult population (Laumann et al., 1994; Michael et al., 1994):

■ Persons with same-sex feeling: 6 percent of men; 4 percent of women

■ Persons who have ever engaged in same-sex behavior: 9 percent of men; 4 percent of women

■ Persons with gay or lesbian self-identification: 2.8 percent of men; 1.4 percent of women

Most of these numbers fall significantly below the 10 percent that gay activists have long cited from Kinsey's classic studies as the proportion of gays and lesbians. In the late 1940s and early 1950s, Kinsey found that 10 percent of the U.S. adults were "predominantly" or "more or less exclusively homosexual." However, he discovered that only 2.5 percent were "exclusively homosexual," which is quite similar to the proportion of today's Americans identifying themselves as gay or lesbian, even though the people in Kinsey's survey were a not representative sample of the U.S. adult population (Voeller, 1990; Kinsey et al., 1953, 1948). Nonetheless, the real number of gays and lesbians must be higher than 2.5 percent because the homophobia in our society discourages identifying oneself as "homosexual," particularly among young people with same-sex orientations.

Some Gay Characteristics

Compared with male heterosexuals, gay men are more likely to be "promiscuous"—sexually active (Blumstein and Schwartz, 1990). Contrary to popular belief, though, the greater likelihood of promiscuity among gay men does not originate from gayness itself. It is in the main a product of *heterosexual* society, which socializes men to be more sexually active than women. Through its male-dominated culture, heterosexual society imposes a double standard of sexual behavior on men and women. If a woman is very sexually active, she is likely to be scorned as a "slut," but a man with the same experience is more likely to be praised as a "stud." Men, then, are encouraged to be more sexually active. Since they have been brought up in the same heterosexual culture as straight men, gay men equally have learned to be sexually active. Not surprisingly, just as heterosexual men are more sexually active than heterosexual women, gay men are more sexually active than lesbians. But why are *gay men* more sexually active than *heterosexual men*? Because the prospect of a heterosexual encounter involves only one person (a man) eager for casual sex—the other person (a woman) less interested—but the prospect of a same-sex encounter involves two persons (both men) equally eager for casual sex.

Casual sex was extremely common among gay men during the heyday of the sexual revolution in the 1960s and 1970s. Since the AIDS crisis struck the gay community in the early 1980s, however, there has been a drastic shift from casual sex to monogamy. Afraid to play sexual "Russian roulette" by putting their lives on the line, gay men have greatly reduced the number of partners they have sex with. The streets and parks that used to bustle with men "cruising" for sex partners are nearly deserted. In gay newspapers and magazines, classified advertisements placed by men seeking "sex only" have declined significantly, while ads looking for "relationships" have increased. Ads for models or escorts have also decreased substantially, and gay men are more likely to seek out other men for baseball, soccer, choral groups, and other social activities as alternatives to bars, heavy drugs, and sex. Walking on the street, they are less likely to eye each other as potential sex partners and more likely to greet each other by saying hello and smiling (Feldman, 1985; Morin et al., 1984).

Today, while gay men are still more likely than straight men to be sexually active, the majority of gay men are involved in a steady, long-term relationship. In fact, most male couples are as satisfied with their relationships as most heterosexual couples are with theirs (Peplau and Cochran, 1990). Given the homophobic society's opposition to same-sex marriages, it seems remarkable for male couples to pull off the same level of love and happiness that heterosexual couples enjoy. What is the secret? Some researchers have analyzed gay couples' various personal and social characteristics, such as age, education, income, religion, ethnicity, or living arrangements. None of these was found to be associated with male couples' satisfaction. But researchers did find greater satisfaction among couples with one partner's income being about equal to another's. This finding is similar to the evidence from several other studies that male couples are happier when they perceive their relationships as egalitarian (Peplau and Cochran, 1990). In an egalitarian relationship, both partners make decisions together as equals, which is likely to occur if their incomes are roughly similar rather than widely different. In short, it is *power equality* that helps ensure "marital" happiness among male couples.

Some Lesbian Characteristics

Brought up in the same heterosexual society, lesbians are in some ways *like other women*, which therefore makes them appear different from gay men. On the other hand, having the same sexual orientation, lesbians are in some ways just like gay men, which makes them *unlike other women*.

Like Other Women. Like straight women, lesbians have been socialized to be less interested in casual sex and more interested in relationship and love. Thus they rarely look for one-night stands in gay bars, let alone "cruising" in the streets or parks. Lesbians are far more interested in making friends in the context of social gatherings, parties, mutual friends, and school. The relationship grows slowly, through a long process of knowing the other person, becoming good friends, dating, and cultivating deep affection. Usually, only after a fairly stable, prolonged, and affectionate bond has formed does sexual involvement take place (Nichols, 1990).

Also, like heterosexual women, a majority of lesbians carry on a comfortable relationship with straights by passing as one of them. The posture of heterosexuality is easy for lesbians to put on, because they—like other women—have been socialized to play the conventional female role. Some lesbians may look like men because of their severely tailored clothes, short hair, and masculine mannerisms, but the vast majority look like other women. Being a part of the straight community's social and occupational scene, lesbians can slip into its sexual scene as well. Thus, more than a third of lesbians exhibit a "partial bisexual style" by having sex with men, and about two-thirds are attracted to men (Rust, 1995; Nichols, 1990).

Finally, many lesbians have the same desire as heterosexual women to be mothers. They may decide to adopt a child or to bear one through artificial insemination. If they are already mothers by an earlier heterosexual marriage, they may fight for custody of their children. Stumbling blocks, however, are sometimes thrown in their way. In 1995, for example, the Virginia Supreme Court ruled in favor of a lower court that took away a child from his mother after declaring her "an unfit parent" simply because she is a lesbian. Nevertheless, today, lesbians are already almost as likely to be mothers as heterosexual women (Kantrowitz, 1996; Henry, 1993).

By sharing those characteristics with heterosexual women, lesbians appear different from gay men: less interested in casual sex, more involved socially and sexually with straights, and more interested in raising children—67 percent of lesbians are mothers, while only 27 percent of gay men are fathers (LeVay and Nonas, 1995).

Unlike Other Women.   Lesbians are more likely than heterosexual women to reject the traditional female role. In a study of lesbians and a control group of heterosexual women, only one-third of the former said that they saw themselves as "appropriately feminine" (passive, dependent, or nonassertive) while most of the latter considered themselves "feminine" (Saghir and Robins, 1980).

While still teenagers, lesbians are far and away less likely than their straight peers to know their sexual identity. While virtually all heterosexual youths know they are heterosexual, most adolescent lesbians are not aware or certain of being lesbian. They therefore tend to see their same-sex attraction in a nonsexual way, as the following description by a lesbian of her adolescent experience suggests.

> We started out just being friends and then it became something special. She taught me a lot of things. I love music and she taught me how to listen to it and appreciate it. She liked things I liked, like walking. We read a lot together. We read the Bible, we read verses to each other. We shared things together. We caressed each other and kissed. *I think it was a need to have someone there. And I was there and she was there and we just held on to each other.* (Simon and Gagnon, 1974)

By being different from heterosexual women in these ways, lesbians appear similar to gay men. Just as lesbians are more likely to reject the traditional female role, gay men are more likely to reject the traditional masculine role—by being, for example, both tough and gentle rather than tough only. And like lesbians, gay men are less likely than heterosexuals during adolescence to be aware of their sexual orientation. But since males generally have sex at a younger age than females, gay men identify themselves as gay earlier than lesbians do, as we will see in the next section.

Coming Out

In the argot of the gay community, becoming openly gay is called "coming out," because it involves people *publicly* identifying themselves as gays or lesbians. It is difficult for most gays and lesbians to come out by revealing their sexual orientation to parents, friends, or coworkers, because the latter may react with shock, rejection, or worse.

Before coming out, many young gays and lesbians do not even *privately* identify themselves as being gay, even though they feel attracted to a person of the same sex. In his classic study of same-sex orientation, sociologist Barry Dank (1971) asked his subjects whether, prior to their graduation from high school, they knew they were gay. Some of their typical responses follow:

SUBJECT 1: I think I did but I didn't know how to put it into words. I didn't know it existed. I guess I was like everybody else and thought I was the only one in the world. . . I probably would have said I didn't know. I don't think I really knew what one was. I would have probably asked you to explain what one was.

SUBJECT 2: I would have said, "No. I don't know what you are talking about." If you had said "queer," I would have thought something about it; this was the slang term that was used, although I didn't know what the term meant.

SUBJECT 3: I don't think I would have known then. I know now. Then I wasn't even thinking about the word. I wasn't reading up on it.

Young people like these fail to develop a gay identity because their parents and other socializing agents of society have taught them the meaning of heterosexuality but nothing about gayness and lesbianism. There are, however, a number of social contexts where they can learn the meaning of gayness or lesbianism, which leads them to privately or publicly identify themselves as being gay or lesbian. As Dank points out, they may acquire the knowledge about same-sex orientation through meeting self-defined gays or lesbians, from straight persons who are knowledgeable about the subject, by reading about it, or watching TV news about gays and lesbians. The gay identity, especially for men, is also likely to emerge in one-sex environments, such as YMCAs, prisons, the military, school dormitories, and gay bars (Dank, 1971).

Sociologist Richard Troiden (1979) presents a more detailed analysis of how most of the gay men he studied came to acquire their gay identity. The identity acquisition involved going through four stages of experience.

In the first stage, *sensitization*, the gays felt that they were different from their peers. As one recalled, "I never felt as if I fit in. I don't know why for sure. I felt different. I thought it was because I was more sensitive." Another expressed a similar feeling: "I felt different due to my interest in school, ineptness at sports, and the like." Most gays had these feelings when their puberty began, that is, at about age 13. A few, though, knew they were gay when they were as young as 6 or 7, but such men tend to have been "sissy boys" who always identified with women (Bawer, 1993).

In the second stage, *dissociation*, the gays, about 17 years of age, began to feel that they might be gay but refused to define themselves as such. One described how he was in this stage: "Before I was publicly labeled a faggot, I realized that I wasn't very interested in women. I had had enough experiences with girls to realize that while I was aroused by them, I was also aroused by males and wanted to have sex with them. However, I thought this was something I'd outgrow in time, something that would straighten itself out as I matured." In this stage of dissociation, they might deny their own gayness by being hostile to gays, calling them "faggots."

In the third stage, *coming out*, the gays, roughly at age 19, regarded their sexual feelings as definitely gay, got involved in the gay subculture, and redefined gayness as a positive and viable lifestyle. While the very act of coming out is usually very painful, frightening, or overwhelming, the resulting experience is often highly positive. It has been described as "an incredible sense of relief and renewal . . . like being born. The burden had been lifted from my shoulders. For the first time I felt like I had a life" (Marcus, 1993).

In the final stage, *commitment,* the gays, now mature adults, are committed to gayness as a way of life. They insist that they are happy being gay, that they would not change even if given the opportunity, and that they cannot see any benefit in choosing heterosexuality. Such a positive feeling even prevails among those who have lost their jobs or have been rejected by their families and children (Marcus, 1993).

More recent studies have found largely the same sequence of stages that gay men and lesbians go through in coming out of the closet (Blumenfeld and Raymond, 1993). There is one exception: compared with gay men, lesbians generally take several years longer to become aware of their same-sex orientation or to come out of the closet. For example, while the men usually come out in their late teens, the women do so in their early twenties (Blumenfeld and Raymond, 1993). Societal reaction also influences the process of coming out. In many upscale high schools throughout the country today, the increased acceptance of same-sex orientation by straight students seems to have caused teenagers to come out younger (Gelman, 1993).

Even after gays and lesbians have publicly revealed their sexual orientation, the process of coming out never ends. "Coming out is not something you do just once and then forget about," observes gay writer Eric Marcus (1993). "For gay and lesbian people who choose to live out of the closet, coming out is something you may do almost every day. There are all kinds of chance encounters and conversations that force gay people to decide whether to answer honestly or not." Every time somebody at a party or some other place asks questions such as "Are you married?" openly gay men and women are forced to come out again by saying something like, "No, because I am gay." This is likely to occur to gays and lesbians all the time simply because the society in which they live is predominantly heterosexual—so that most people routinely assume others to be heterosexual like themselves, and ask questions based on that assumption. Thus, even though they have come out, openly gay men and lesbians continue to face the same challenges from heterosexual society as those who remain in the closet.

Family and Children

Lesbians and gays encounter the same prejudice and discrimination as other minority groups. But there is a basic difference. In nearly all cases, the parents of African Americans are African American, the parents of Hispanics are Hispanic, or the parents of Jews are Jewish. In contrast, virtually all the parents of gays and lesbians are *heterosexual.* Unlike the other minorities, gays and lesbians cannot always count on their families for support in dealing with society's homophobia. In fact, practically all parents are upset when they find out their son or daughter is gay. Some react with tears but eventually manage to deal with it in a loving way; others react with anger, refusing to have anything to do with the gay child. Actually, these parents are not to blame for their negative reaction. Because of societal homophobia, parents with a gay child are typically afraid of what friends, neighbors, relatives, or even strangers will think if they find out. The parents are in effect victims of society's antigay culture. Therefore, ironically, while their gay child has come out of the closet, they themselves go into the closet, hiding from others the fact that their child is gay. All these problems are less common today, thanks largely to groups such as Parents and Friends of Lesbians and Gays (P-FLAG), which help parents accept their child's same-sex orientation without fear or embarrassment (Marcus, 1993; Blumenfeld, 1992).

What about grandparents? Do they often react in the same negative way when hearing about their grandchild being gay? If they have learned to accept a son's or daughter's same-sex orientation, parents often advise the child against sharing the truth with the grandparents. The parents may say something like: "Whatever you do, don't tell Grandpa or Grandma you're gay!" Or "They're old. They'll never understand. Why upset them? Let them die in peace." Interestingly, compared with parents, grandparents turn out to be more resilient and more accepting of the child's same-sex orientation. This should not be surprising, though. Suffering some prejudice and discrimination in our youth-oriented culture, grandparents are closer to the fringe of society on which gays and lesbians find themselves (Marcus, 1993).

What if parents are gay? How do their heterosexual children react? In cases where children have been raised since birth or early childhood in a household with two gay parents, there is no real news for them to react to. The child has learned to accept the fact that they have two daddies or two mommies at home. As they grow older, particularly in adolescence, they may face teasing or even ridicule. But most studies show no psychological disadvantages for children raised by lesbians or gays. Such children do not differ from others in their social adjustment or in their identity as a boy or girl. Further, they are no more likely than other children to become gay (Kantrowitz, 1996; Marcus, 1993). Today, children of gay parents find it easy to live normal lives like everybody else. They have even formed their own networks such as Colage (Children of Lesbians and Gays Everywhere).

Dating and Marriage

It is easier for gays and lesbians to find a date in a relatively large city than in a small town simply because there are many more gays and lesbians in the city. The places where they hang out include bars, restaurants, clubs, and organizations that cater to lesbians and gays. But, like straights, gays and lesbians can also meet in any place imaginable, such as at work, at social events, at the grocery store, or at the mall. At such places, though, most people are straight rather than gay. It is usually quite a challenge for people with same-sex orientation to differentiate gays from straights, but occasionally they can spot each other by such clues as the style of clothing or haircut popular among gays and lesbians.

When having dates, lesbians and gays mostly do what straights do. They may go to a restaurant, a movie, or some other social place. They tend, though, to avoid holding their date's hand or some other intimate act in public unless they are in a predominantly gay neighborhood. Since they, like straights, have been socialized to the standard boy–girl roles, they may initially be uncertain as to who should, for example, make the first move in getting a date. But most gays and lesbians quickly learn to do what a specific situation calls for, rather than rigidly acting out the traditional gender roles. Thus, who asks for a date depends on who is more interested or bold, who pays for dinner depends on who asked for the date or who makes more money, and so on. Interestingly, such disregard for traditional gender roles in dating has become increasingly common among heterosexuals.

When they fall in love, they will get married. There are a variety of gay weddings, ranging from simply exchanging rings in private to pulling out all the stops—"including the church ceremony, matching tuxedos or dresses, traditional vows, formal reception for two hundred, and a four-tiered wedding cake topped with two grooms or two brides" (Marcus, 1993). Sociologically, the union ceremony serves to strengthen the couple relationship. By expressing their vows and love for each other in the presence of their significant others, the same-sex couple tend to feel a stronger sense of commitment and security. But, since they cannot get a marriage license, same-sex couples do not have the same legal protections and financial benefits as heterosexual couples, such as the right to be on each other's insurance and pension plans or receive the Social Security survivor's benefits. In recent years, though, several cities such as San Francisco have granted unmarried couples, both gay and straight, a legal document called a "domestic partnership agreement," which can be used to gain family benefits from employers, insurance companies, health clubs, and other commercial establishments. But no states have legalized same-sex marriage (Cloud, 1998).

Where They Live and Socialize

Lesbians and gays live everywhere, from rural areas to urban centers. But they are much more likely to live in urban than rural areas because, in the last 30 years, massive numbers have moved to metropolitan areas such as San Francisco and New York in search of people like themselves. These cities have developed huge gay communities, with their own bars, restaurants, stores, doctors or lawyers, community centers, softball teams, choruses, and numerous social, religious, and professional organizations. Northampton, Massachusetts, has the largest concentration of lesbians in the United States, who constitute at least 10 percent of the town's women. There are also resort areas lesbians and gay men like to visit. They include Provincetown on Cape Cod in Massachusetts; Palm Springs, California; Rehoboth Beach, Delaware; Key West and Miami Beach, Florida; and The Pines and Cherry Grove on Fire Island in New York (Drummond, 1995; Marcus, 1993). In these communities there are opportunities galore for gays and lesbians to socialize. They can also feel free to be themselves, doing things that heterosexuals do in the larger society, such as holding a partner's hand in public. They talk about all the things that heterosexuals talk about, though they also talk about their gay and lesbian lives and about the latest news on the sexual minority.

Politics, Education, and Religion

Because the Democratic Party has often espoused policies sympathetic to the sexual minority, gays and lesbians are most likely to be Democrats. According to one poll, lesbians and gays are 45 percent Democrat, as against 27 percent Republican and 21 percent Independent (LeVay and Nonas, 1995). Straights have about the same distribution of party affiliations. But gays and lesbians are much more politically active than straights: While straight Democrats are somewhat less likely than straight Republicans to vote, gay/lesbian Democrats are much more likely than gay/lesbian Republicans to vote (LeVay and Nonas, 1995). Apparently, homophobia makes the sexual minority more eager than the sexual majority to vote for gay-friendly candidates.

Lesbians and gays are generally better educated than straights. According to a national survey, for example, 49 percent of gays and lesbians have some college education, compared with 37 percent of heterosexuals. Some scholars attribute this to higher IQ among gays and lesbians. According to others, the stress of belonging to a stigmatized group drives many gay and lesbian teenagers into an "overachiever" mode (LeVay and Nonas, 1995). Perhaps, with few or no friends to socialize with because of antigay ostracism, lesbian and gay youngsters spend more time reading and studying than their straight peers do. Homophobia has also made the suicide rate among gay youth much higher than among straight youth. In response to this problem, some high schools in a few cities have set up counseling programs, such as Project 10 in Los Angeles, for gay and lesbian students, as well as programs designed to reduce the fear, prejudice, or hostility that straight students have toward gay people (Marcus, 1993).

Although many churches and synagogues condemn same-sex practices, gays and lesbians belong to various major faiths and denominations in about the same proportions as heterosexuals. For example, about 25 percent of gays and lesbians are Catholics, compared with 22 percent of heterosexuals. Moreover, lesbians and gays are no more unreligious than straights (LeVay and Nonas, 1995). But gays and lesbians usually attend churches and synagogues that they know will welcome them. These gay and lesbian worshipers, along with their pastors and rabbis, believe that God loves them as much as anybody else. They do not regard their own sexuality as sinful in the same way that straights do not consider their own sexuality as sinful (Marcus, 1993). An increasing number of pastors and other religious officials agree, to such an extent that they are willing to perform same-sex marriage ceremonies (Niebuhr, 1998).

Work, Sports, and the Military

Lesbians and gays work in every occupation, as do straights. But certain occupations seem to have a larger share of gays and lesbians. For example, gay men are more likely than straight men to work as nurses, flight attendants, dancers, actors, and musicians, and lesbians are more likely than straight women to be athletes, gym teachers, and military personnel. Generally, the jobs that tend more to attract gay men are traditionally female occupations, and the ones that tend more to attract lesbians are traditionally male occupations. According to one explanation, gays and lesbians are more likely than heterosexuals to feel comfortable about crossing traditional gender lines. According to another, gays and lesbians are more attracted to occupations, such as the arts, that are more accepting of the sexual minority (Marcus, 1993). Most gays and lesbians, however, work in various companies that do not offer any of the jobs cited above. An increasing number of such companies, such as AT&T and IBM, have made an effort to welcome sexual-minority workers. But homophobia is still prevalent, forcing many gays and lesbians to stay "in the closet" at work.

An even greater number of gay professional athletes stay in the closet. Very few come out during or after their careers. Gay athletes are generally afraid, if they come out, of risking their careers as well as lucrative product endorsements. Their fears are far from groundless. According to former tennis superstar Martina Navratilova, who is a lesbian, she received fewer offers for product endorsements after she publicly revealed her sexual orientation. Thus, gay professional athletes, especially the male ones, keep their same-sex orientation a secret. This tends to reinforce the popular stereotype that gay men do not like sports. Actually, gay men as well as lesbians are no different from others in their enjoyment of sports. Gays can be found not only in professional sports but in amateur sports as well, as long as they are provided with the opportunity to participate, as evidenced by the popularity of the Gay Games (Gay Athletic Games) among the sexual minority (Marcus, 1993).

The pressure to hide one's same-sex orientation is even greater for gay soldiers. The same-sex feeling itself, let alone the behavior, has, until 1993, been banned in the military. If soldiers were discovered to be gay, they could be discharged. Consequently, most gay soldiers resorted to various methods of camouflaging their sexual orientation, such as pretending to be straight, laughing at jokes about gays, and telling bogus stories about heterosexual escapades. Some lesbians were forced to "prove" themselves to be straight by having sex with men.

In 1993, however, President Clinton lifted the ban on gays and lesbians in the military, but with a condition: They must be celibate by not engaging in same-sex acts and must keep quiet about their sexual orientation. This means that they must continue to stay in the closet. Military leaders are afraid that if gay soldiers are allowed to come out, they would create an "unacceptable risk" to morale, discipline, and unit cohesion. Such fear is groundless, though. Numerous studies have shown that gays and lesbians perform their military duty as well as heterosexuals and that gay and straight soldiers can work together effectively (Shenon, 1997; Jones and Koshes, 1995; Shilts, 1993). At any rate, the Clinton policy, known as "don't ask, and don't tell," has *failed* to achieve its purpose of allowing gays to serve in the military as long as they "don't tell" others their sexual orientation. Gay troops have been discharged from the military at higher rates than before, because they were forced to reveal their homosexuality by their commanders illegally "asking" them if they were gay (Shenon, 1999; Weiner, 1998).

Same-Sex Practices among Straights and Bisexuals

As Kinsey suggested, many straights are not exclusively heterosexual, so it should not be surprising that some straights and all bisexuals do engage in same-sex activities. Although they may not see themselves as gays or lesbians, homophobes generally regard this kind of straight as "homosexual."

Trades

The straights whose sexual feelings and experiences are predominantly heterosexual and only incidentally gay are called trades. All trades are males. They are, or have been, married, and seek same-sex experiences mostly as a means of releasing tension. Were cheap brothels easily accessible to them, they would frequent them. They want other men to go down on them but refuse to reciprocate. They will not fellate other men because they consider themselves straight and have a masculine self-image. Defining themselves as straight and masculine, they tend to treat their partner's mouth as if it were a woman's vagina. Many trades find their male sex-objects in public parks and rest rooms. In his classic study of same-sex activities in public rest rooms, Laud Humphreys (1970) found that most trades come from lower classes, are Roman Catholics, and do not get enough sex with their wives.

Street Hustlers

This type of straight resembles the trade in having predominantly heterosexual feelings, but engages in a greater volume of same-sex activities. Like trades, all street hustlers are males. They are usually lower-class teenage boys who consider themselves heterosexual and masculine. But they frequently make money from letting adults perform oral sex on them, although, like the trade, they often refuse to reciprocate sexually. Many street hustlers have grown up in broken homes, could not get along with parents, or have run away from home. They are lonely and penniless at the time of their initial hustling experience. They generally do not take the initiative to start hustling; it is, instead, some older men who encourage them to do so. Here is how a young runaway, Eddie, got his first trick:

> After arriving in the city by bus, Eddie was standing in the bus terminal, "getting my bearings," when the customer approached....The man inquired, "Where are you staying?" "No place. Actually, I'm looking for my uncle." He suggested that they go to his place so they could look in the telephone book for the uncle's address. Shortly after they arrived at the customer's home, the man asked, "Have you ever had your dick sucked?" Eddie replied, "What? No!" He was shocked by the query, for "that was something I never heard of down in Selma, Alabama." The man said, "Well, how would you like to make $100?" Eddie accepted the offer. (Luckenbill, 1985)

Once youngsters such as Eddie are introduced into prostitution, they would search for customers by standing around particular streets, parks, bus stations, or bookstore entrances. Since they are basically heterosexual, they are likely to abandon homosexual prostitution when they reach adulthood (Pieper, 1979; Reiss, 1961). There are, of course, street hustlers who continue prostituting themselves by finding customers in the gay bars or through escort agencies, but they are likely to have seen themselves as gay in the first place (Luckenbill, 1986, 1985).

Situationals

Some straight men and women would engage in same-sex acts in situations in which the opportunity presents itself. These situational "gays" and "lesbians" can be found among prison inmates, priests, stripteasers, and others in one-sex situations (Blumenfeld and Raymond, 1993). They are predominantly heterosexual, see themselves as heterosexuals, and are able to abandon same-sex activities if circumstances permit. But they are compelled or tempted by their life in a unisexual institution to resort to sexual release with same-sex others. Among strippers, for example, the availability of opportunities for same-sex contacts is considered comparable to having a martini after a hard day's or night's work. As one stripper says, "I usually don't get kicks out of other women, not really, but there are times. Sometimes you come home and you are just too tired to work at it. Then it's nice to have a woman around. You can lay down on the floor, relax, watch TV and let her do it" (McCaghy and Skipper, 1969).

However, opportunities for same-sex involvement are not only available in one-sex institutions. Straight women who find something lacking in their marriage may have a lesbian lover on the side, although they do not see themselves as lesbians. As one such a woman says, "I don't consider myself gay. I simply can't relate to that for me. I need a romantic involvement in my life and it happens to be with Victoria, but I was with a man before this. I love my husband in a way. I need the kind of anchoring or stability he gives me . . . But I also have a romantic side" (Ponse, 1984). In fact, situational lesbianism has recently become an "in thing" at some colleges. It involves a straight female student experimenting sexually with a member of the same sex. Such students are known as "LUGs" (lesbians until graduation) or "four-year lesbians," because they give up their same-sex activities when leaving college. As a 25-year-old woman who has been a LUG at Wellesley College explains, "It was a real lesbian experience. It was a unique, phenomenal experience. Now it's not an issue anymore. I'm going to marry Richard" (Rimer, 1993).

Bisexuals

Bisexuals can be found among men as well as women. The bisexual is about equally straight and gay. Most bisexuals are married to members of the opposite sex, but also have sexual relations with others of the same sex. In some cases only one spouse, most likely the husband, is bisexual. In other cases both husband and wife are bisexual:

> Happily married for 10 years, Richard Sharrard, a dance instructor, and Tina Tessina, a psychotherapist and writer, blend in nicely enough with their neighbors in the middle-class community of Long Beach, California. But the couple's lifestyle is far from ordinary: Richard and Tina are openly and unapologetically bisexual. During their unusually flexible marriage, Richard has enjoyed liaisons with half a dozen men, while Tina has taken two female lovers. (Toufexis, 1992a)

According to popular belief, bisexuals are *basically straights* with a taste for exotic adventure or *essentially gay* and unwilling to acknowledge their true sexual orientation. However, most of these individuals do not see themselves as either straight in some ways or gay in other ways but as *totally unique persons with a third kind of sexual identity.* Thus they do not consider their bisexuality "a walk on the wild side" or "a run from reality" but a legitimate and healthy identity (Leland, 1995; Rust, 1995). As lovers, bisexuals appear to be more sensitive and empathic than others because their bisexual orientation enables them to see things from more than one perspective. Nonetheless, many bisexuals still cannot transcend the societal expectation that they are either basically straight or gay. Not surprisingly, they are racked by discomfort and conflict. As a bisexual explains, "Your feet are in both camps, but your heart is in neither. You have the opportunity to experience a kind of richness, but you constantly feel you have to make a choice" (Toufexis, 1992a).

This problem is likely to continue because bisexuals usually have sex with either straights or gays rather than with other bisexuals. The problem will diminish, though, if bisexuals develop their own bisexual community to the same extent as gays and lesbians have formed their own. Like the gay community, the bisexual community will be able to strengthen its members' unique sexual identity so that they can enjoy sex with one another without being torn with guilt and other psychological problems. The bisexual community will also bring social harmony to our multicultural society because bisexuals are uniquely qualified to mediate between the lesbian and gay community and the larger heterosexual society (LeVay and Nonas, 1995).

Homophobia

The word *homophobia* originally meant only the fear of same-sex orientation, but now it refers more broadly to antigay prejudice and discrimination. Homophobia is also called "heterosexism" for being comparable to racism and sexism. This is because the sexual minority often encounters prejudice and discrimination for their same-sex orientation in about the same way as racial minorities and women do for their skin color and gender.

The Homophobic Definition of Same-Sex Orientation

In the United States and other Western societies, the definition of same-sex orientation as deviant can be traced to the Judeo-Christian scripture, where same-sex practices are strongly condemned:

> You shall not lie with a male as with a woman; it is an abomination. (Leviticus 18:22)
>
> If a man lies with a male as with a woman, both of them have committed an abomination; they shall be put to death, their blood is upon them. (Leviticus 20:13)

It is from these biblical passages that many ultraconservative, fundamentalist Christians get their idea about same-sex orientation as an "abomination" that should be punished by death. But most homophobes today presumably would not go that far by interpreting the Bible so literally. If they do, they would have to condemn many heterosexuals to death for committing adultery or engaging in sex when the wife is menstruating, because in the same book of Leviticus these sex acts are also condemned as abominations punishable by death. Nonetheless, all homophobes still regard same-sex orientation as deviant in some way. Why? Usually, an act is considered deviant if it deviates from a *norm*. What, then, is the norm that most homophobes use to define same-sex orientation as deviant?

On the face of it, the norm may appear to be simply that sex should only involve persons of different genders. But the norm that is often used to condemn same-sex practices is more than simply gender-related, as can be discerned from standard arguments that oppose same-sex marriages. In 1996, for example, the Hawaiian legislators who opposed same-sex marriage argued that marriage is "intended for the *propagation* of the human race by man-woman units." And former Vice President Dan Quayle's speechwriter, Lisa Schiffren (1996), contends, "'Same-sex marriage' is inherently incompatible with our culture's understanding of the institution. Marriage is essentially a lifelong compact between a man and woman committed to sexual exclusivity and the *creation* and nurture of offspring." Even if Schiffren is persuaded that gay couples can have "lifelong sexual exclusivity" and "nurture" children just as heterosexual couples can, she still will consider same-sex marriage deviant, because such marriage *cannot create* offspring. It is, therefore, clear that procreation or reproduction is often used as the norm for defining same-sex marriage—and, by extension, same-sex orientation—as deviant.

The reproductive norm is a holdover from the past when the purpose of marital sex was widely believed to be procreation. Logically, according to this anachronistic norm, any sex engaged in without any intention of producing a baby is deviant. This means that the vast majority of married heterosexual couples today are deviant because they routinely engage in sex for *pleasure* or *love* alone rather than for procreation. Among the married heterosexuals who violate the reproductive norm are not only average couples but also infertile or childless couples, couples who marry past childbearing age, couples who use birth-control methods, and couples who engage in oral or other nonreproductive sex. If premarital sex, extramarital sex, or masturbation committed by countless other heterosexuals are also taken into account, it seems clear that all of the straights violate the reproductive norm as lesbians and gays do. Nevertheless, homophobic society illogically uses the same norm to define the sexual minority as deviant and the sexual majority (heterosexuals) as normal.

The Nature and Extent of Homophobia

Homophobia is both a negative *attitude* (hence prejudice) toward gays and lesbians and an unjust *action* (discrimination) against them. As an antigay attitude, homophobia is therefore covert and invisible. It may be in the form of an unfavorable *belief* about same-sex orientation—as, for example, abominable, evil, or unnatural. It may also be in the form of a negative *feeling* (such as fear, disgust, or hatred) toward lesbians and gays. Antigay discrimination, however, is overt and observable, in the form of an unfair action against the sexual minority (such as denying them jobs, calling them names, or assaulting them).

It is difficult to assess the extent of homophobia in U.S. society, but if homophobia involves condemning same-sex orientation as morally wrong, then nearly half of Americans may be considered homophobic. Asked in a national poll whether same-sex relationships between consenting adults are morally wrong, 48 percent indicated yes (Lacayo, 1998). Most Americans are, however, antigay in regard to other highly emotional issues. According to other surveys, 58 percent do not want the sexual-minority members to be legally married, and 56 percent do not want them to raise children (Berke, 1998; Kantrowitz, 1996; Kaplan and Klaidman, 1996).

However, if homophobia involves denying the sexual minority the same civil rights enjoyed by the sexual majority, then most Americans do not appear to be homophobic: Over 80 percent say that gays and lesbians should have equal rights in job opportunities, health insurance, inheritance, and social security (Berke, 1998; Kantrowitz, 1996; Kaplan and Klaidman, 1996).

In short, U.S. society is deeply ambivalent about its sexual minority, torn between an uneasy feeling about their same-sex orientation and a democratic tolerance for them as citizens (Wolfe, 1998). All this, however, deals with homophobia

TABLE 10.1 Frequency of Antigay Action

Percentages of gays and lesbians saying they have been a victim of the following:

65%	An antigay slur
64%	An antigay joke
16%	A beating or other physical attack motivated by dislike of gays

Source: Newsweek, June 27, 1994, p. 47.

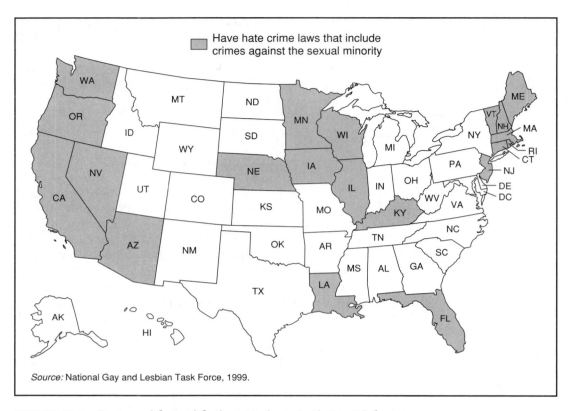

FIGURE 10.2   States with Legislation Against Anti-Gay Violence

as an antigay attitude. As for homophobia as an antigay action, it varies in its degree of harmfulness to gays and lesbians, as Table 10.1 indicates. Assaults on the sexual minority constitute at least 11 percent of all hate crimes but only 21 states include crimes against gays and lesbians in their hate crime legislation (see Figure 10.2).

A Profile of Homophobes

Not all straights are homophobic, but some are more so than others. The more homophobic ones have been found to have certain characteristics that distinguish them from others (Kite and Whitley, 1996; Blumenfeld and Raymond, 1993; Berrill, 1992). They are generally:

1. less educated and less well-off;

2. more conservative—socially, politically, religiously, and sexually;

3. more negative toward racial or ethnic minorities;

4. more supportive of traditional gender roles, in which men are supposed to be aggressive and women gentle;

5. men who see themselves as "masculine" and women who see themselves as "feminine";

6. more likely to stereotype as "homosexual" a man whom they consider to be "feminine" in some way and a woman whom they consider to be "manly";

7. more likely to be men than women;

8. older, except in cases of extreme violence against gays, known as "gay bashing" or "hate crime," which are more common among young men;

9. less likely to personally know someone who is gay or lesbian;

10. more likely to be influenced by peers.

Why are heterosexual men more homophobic than women? According to one explanation, men are more likely to feel pressured by traditional gender roles to be "masculine" and to avoid being "feminine." Since gay men are stereotyped as "feminine," straight men are more likely to display antigay prejudice as a way of assuring themselves that they are "masculine" (Kite and Whitley, 1996). According to another explanation, straight men, accustomed to playing the stereotypically masculine role, do not want other men to look at them the way they themselves look at women. They are afraid of becoming what women in a sexist society often are: an object of unwanted sexual attention, or a victim of sexual assault, harassment, lusting, or just plain ogling. Explaining why he fears the presence of gays in the military, a homophobic man said, "Some of the gays are not little pansy guys but big hulking guys and if a small man said no, what is to stop him?" (Graham with Rawlings and Rigsby, 1994). Both explanations share the same assumption: Male homophobes are afraid of being treated like women. This not only explains why heterosexual men are more homophobic than heterosexual women, it also explains why straight men are much more prejudiced against gay men than against lesbians (Kite and Whitley, 1996).

The Impact of Homophobia

Homophobia strongly affects virtually all aspects of gay and lesbian life. The problems that homophobia creates for its targets can be social or psychological in nature.

Social Problems. The social problems caused by antigay forces in the lives of gays and lesbians have recently become well known because they are often presented in the media. To cite just a few examples: Gays and lesbians cannot get

TABLE 10.2   Many Gays/Lesbians Remain in Closet

Percentages of gays and lesbians give the following answers to "How many of your gay friends or acquaintances are 'out'?"

37%	Nearly all
18%	More than half
16%	About half
10%	Less than half
12%	Very few or none

Source: Newsweek, June 27, 1994, p. 48.

legally married; same-sex couples are denied health, insurance, and other benefits enjoyed by heterosexual couples; and people with the same-sex orientation are often rejected by straight family members and friends, shunned or ostracized by fellow employees, discharged from the military for revealing their sexual orientation, and prohibited from discussing same-sex orientation with students in public schools. Indeed, there are countless other problems suffered by gays and lesbians as victims of antigay prejudice and discrimination (Blumenfeld, 1992). Due to the prevalence of homophobia, then, lesbians and gays have to struggle harder than straights to succeed and live a happy life in the same society. Not surprisingly, large numbers of gays and lesbians remain "in the closet," keeping their sexual orientation to themselves in order to be treated like heterosexuals, as Table 10.2 suggests.

Psychological Problems.   Homosexuality does not cause mental health problems, just as heterosexuality does not. But the homophobic nature of society does make lesbians and gays more likely to develop some psychological problems, such as constant tension, self-hatred, and depression, which in turn lead to higher rates of suicide and alcohol and drug abuse among gays and lesbians than among straights. Running through these problems is the failure to achieve a harmonious integration of one's diverse identities (O'Hanlan, 1996; LeVay and Nonas, 1995).

Raised in a predominantly heterosexual and homophobic society, gays and lesbians, like straights, usually grow up identifying themselves as loving sons or daughters to their heterosexual parents, as fun-to-be-with persons to their heterosexual friends, and as productive or respected members to various heterosexual groups and organizations. But all these self-identities are based on conformity to the heterosexual way of life, and are therefore in conflict with their sexual self-identity as gays and lesbians. The conflict itself creates tension and restlessness. Some gays and lesbians try to resolve the conflict by assimilating into the straight world and outwardly carrying on like heterosexuals, but they tend to feel miserable for living a lie, for betraying their true self, or for deceiving their significant others. Other lesbians and gays try to resolve the identity conflict by leaving the straight world for the gay community, but many still feel the need to commute, physically or emotionally, between their new gay and old straight worlds (LeVay and Nonas, 1995). Thus the identity conflict that causes tension and other psychological problems is likely to remain as long as homophobia continues to hold sway in society. But through constant support from fellow gays and lesbians as well as from sympathetic straights, most members of the sexual minority manage to transcend those psychological problems and to live a relatively normal, happy life, like most heterosexuals do.

A Global View of Homophobia

While the problems created by homophobia are serious in the United States, they are even more so in less affluent societies. The International Gay and Lesbian Human Rights Commission has documented many cases of abuse committed by non-Western governments against people with the same-sex orientation. The cases include gays or lesbians being beaten, raped, imprisoned, and institutionalized. One gay man in Romania, for example, reported that he and his partner were arrested after the police were told about their gay love. While in jail, other inmates raped him, and when he disclosed the rapes in court, the warden beat him (Dunlap, 1995).

In Russia, since the law against sodomy was abolished in 1993, personal ads in newspapers under sections labeled "Man to Man" have become as frank and easy to find as they are in New York City. But homophobia among the general public remains stronger in Russia than in the United States. In a 1994 poll, 47 percent of the Russian population said that gays should be executed or isolated, while only 29 percent said they ought to be left alone. Most Russian gays and lesbians know that their government no longer locks them up, let alone having any plan to kill them, but they are acutely aware of the profound hatred the public has for them. They are fearful of being beaten up by straights and of losing their jobs if they are known to be gay. As a result, Russian gays and lesbians are much more likely than their U.S. peers to stay in the closet (Specter, 1995).

In the African nation of Zimbabwe, formerly called Rhodesia, the president has publicly announced that gays and lesbians have no legal rights, calling them "sodomists and perverts" and "worse than dogs and pigs." When 70 U.S. Congress members signed a letter of protest, the Zimbabwean president said, "Let the Americans keep their sodomy, bestiality—stupid and foolish ways" (McNeil, 1995). There is more tolerance among the general public, but popular knowledge about same-sex orientation is abysmal. When confronted with a gay man, ordinary Zimbabweans would ask questions like, "How many organs do you have?" Because the society is heavily male-dominated, lesbians suffer more than gays. The family of a lesbian, for example, "locked her up and had a man rape her so she would get pregnant. After she ran off and had an abortion, they caught her and did it again. Now she has the baby and is forced to live with the man" (McNeil, 1995). Since the president often verbally attacks the sexual minority, the Zimbabwean society has become more homophobic (McNeil, 1998).

AIDS, Gays, and Straights

When AIDS first broke out in the early 1980s, virtually all the victims were gay men. Today, notably, gay men are much less likely to get AIDS, thanks to dramatic increases in safer sex practices such as monogamy and condom use (Altman, 1999; Gagnon, Levine, and Nardi, 1997). The majority of *new* AIDS cases do not appear among gay men but among intravenous drug users, who often share contaminated needles when shooting drugs and consequently pass the AIDS virus on to one another. But, having been exposed to the virus longer, gay men still make up the largest proportion of infirm AIDS patients today.

In the 1980s, the homophobic society blamed the emergence of AIDS on "promiscuity" among gay men. AIDS was then associated with the same-sex orientation itself, and the disease was called the "gay plague." Discrimination against gays visibly soared. Suspected of being infected with the AIDS virus simply because they were known as gays, gays were often denied insurance coverage, fired from their jobs, and evicted from their apartments. Those who were actually infected with the virus or ill with AIDS also received shabby treatment from society. Even the U.S. Justice Department said it was legal for employers to discriminate against AIDS-infected employees if the discrimination was based on fear of contagion. Often, those who were ill with AIDS could not even see their gay lovers or have them attend their funerals because their families prohibited it. Physical attacks on gays also became more common.

Some well-known conservatives fanned the hostility toward gays further with inflammatory public statements. Patrick Buchanan, a conservative columnist, made the argument that AIDS is a fitting punishment for gays: "They have declared war upon Nature, and now Nature is exacting an awful retribution." Some conservatives even demanded that gays be incarcerated "until and unless they can be cleansed of their medical problems" (Bayer, 1985). Because they wanted to see gays punished with AIDS, many conservatives were opposed to any government attempt to develop a vaccine against the deadly disease. They declared that by showing compassion in developing the vaccine the government was in effect approving and supporting gayness as a normal, legitimate lifestyle (Marcus, 1993).

But today the general public has become less condemnatory toward gays and more sympathetic to those with AIDS. The Clinton administration, which is more friendly to gays than its predecessors were, has greatly increased federal funding for fighting the disease. Most states have passed laws protecting AIDS victims against job dismissal and other discriminations. A number of factors have caused this turnaround in public sentiment: (1) A growing number of *heterosexuals*, including not only drug addicts but children and babies, have been afflicted with AIDS. (2) Many widely admired and loved celebrities, such as actor Rock Hudson and dancer Rudolf Nureyev, were brought to light as gay when they died of AIDS. (3) The media have often portrayed AIDS-infected gays and their gay companions and friends in a positive way, as courageous, compassionate, and hardworking people. (4) The AIDS crisis has galvanized thousands of otherwise apathetic gays and lesbians into joining the fight against the disease, thereby gaining respect from the general public—because the gays' anti-AIDS crusade also helped slow the spread of the disease among *heterosexuals* (LeVay and Nonas, 1995; Marcus, 1993).

The Lesbian and Gay Rights Movement

For nearly 50 years now gays and lesbians in the United States have been fighting for equal rights in a homophobic society. The gay rights movement began in the late 1940s with the discovery among many individual gays and lesbians that they were not alone. This "gay awakening" resulted in large part from the widely publicized Kinsey report that millions of men and women had engaged in same-sex activities. The first major gay organization was soon established in San Francisco. It was called the Mattachine Society, named after medieval court jesters who told the truth while hiding behind masks. True to its name, the Mattachine Society was at first an essentially secret organization concerned primarily with teaching gays and their straight sympathizers about the nature of same-sex orientation. Soon afterward the first lesbian organization, the Daughters of Bilitis, or DOB, was formed in San Francisco. Then chapters of these two organizations, along with other new same-sex groups, were established all over the United States. By 1969, the number of same-sex organizations had soared to about 150 (Sagarin, 1969). These organizations differed in their goals and activities, but were all basically alike in being nonmilitant. They were concerned with educating the public about same-sex orientation, counseling gays and lesbians in trouble, and providing them with recreational services.

Then, in June 1969, the police raided the Stonewall Inn, a gay bar in New York, simply for being gay. The patrons, who used to be cowed by such raids, reacted by throwing bottles and stones at the police. This violent reaction against police harassment soon led many young gays and lesbians to form militant organizations. They tried to confront the country with the fact that gays are an oppressed minority group, whose aspiration for respectability is no different from that of African Americans, Hispanics, women, migrant farm workers, and the like. They marched in great numbers, shouting such slogans as "Two-four-six-eight, gay is twice as good as straight!" "Three-five-seven-nine, Lesbians are mighty fine!" and "Gay Power!" They also resorted to dramatic confrontation tactics in dealing with antigay political figures. One such tactic was "zapping"—disrupting, for example, a Foran for Governor rally in Chicago in 1971 by marching, dancing, and chanting "Ho, ho, hey, hey, freaking fags are here to stay" as well as "Foran is a macho pig" (Humphreys, 1972). By the mid-1970s the militant fervor had cooled, and there was renewed concern with providing counseling and other social services to gays who needed them.

The cooling of the gay militancy apparently resulted from the many victories achieved by the gay power movement between the early and mid-1970s.

Some of the victories are as follows: A dozen states legalized consensual sex between same-sex adults. The school boards in some cities banned discrimination in the hiring of gay teachers, and a number of court decisions upheld the gay's right to teach. The Bank of America, IBM, NBC, AT&T, and other big corporations, as well as the Civil Service Commission, announced their willingness to hire gays and lesbians. The American Psychiatric Association stopped listing same-sex orientation as a psychiatric disorder. And more than 300 same-sex marriages were performed in a church in Los Angeles.

With the outbreak of AIDS in the early 1980s, the lesbian and gay rights movement began to shift into high gear again. At first, efforts were focused on fighting the disease. Gays and lesbians provided care for the sick and dying, presented AIDS education programs, lobbied for increased government funding for AIDS research, pressured medical researchers and drug companies to go all out searching for treatments and a cure, and fought discrimination against people with AIDS or HIV. Then, in the early 1990s, a few young people at the forefront of the AIDS battle began to reinvigorate the lesbian and gay rights movement with confrontational tactics. Giving themselves such militant names as "Queer Nation" and "Queer Action," they shouted their demands for equal rights in the streets, city halls, and suburban shopping malls. They staged gay-pride marches, with some appearing in drag, wearing nipple rings, kissing each other ostentatiously, or exhibiting some other anticonventional behavior. They even organized a massive march on Washington in 1993, shouting slogans like "We're here! We're queer! Get used to it!" (Marcus, 1992). But given today's conservative climate, those gay militants may have hurt rather than helped the cause of equal rights for gays. As gay writer Bruce Bawer (1993) explains, the confrontational and exhibitionist derring-dos in gay-pride marches helped "perpetuate the widespread view of homosexuals as freaks, outlaws, sex addicts, and sexual exhibitionists."

However, the majority of gay-rights activists are far from militant. Consider, for example, the Human Rights Campaign, the largest lesbian and gay organization. Its members are moderate, engaging in the same campaigning, fund-raising, and lobbying tactics as conventional interest groups. They also emphasize the importance of equal rights in the same way as other minority groups. They have, in a word, mainstreamed (Lacayo, 1998; Vaid, 1995). Thus gays and lesbians have become an important, powerful political force. They can now count on the White House and an increasing number of leaders from both political parties to take their equal rights seriously. Eight states and more than 135 local jurisdictions have passed laws that protect the sexual minority against discrimination. Many more states and cities are expected to follow suit. But homophobia remains throughout the society, and antigay forces continue their efforts to oppose gay rights by arguing that gay-rights laws not only give the sexual minority special treatment but also encourage gay lifestyles and threaten traditional marriages (Lacayo, 1998; Levay and Nonas, 1995; Fineman, 1993; Lewin, 1993a). Actually, the sexual minority only wants the same rights as other Americans, not wanting to attempt the impossible task of turning straights into gays and destroying traditional marriages (see Table 10.3).

TABLE 10.3   What Gays and Lesbians Want

In response to the question, "How important are the following goals for gay people?" percentages of lesbians and gays saying "very important" are:

91%	Equal rights in the workplace
77%	Health-care and Social Security benefits for gay partners
62%	Serving openly in the military
42%	Legally sanctioned gay marriage

Source: Newsweek, June 27, 1994, p. 48.

Theories of Same-Sex Orientation

Scholars and researchers in various disciplines have tried to explain why some individuals become gays or lesbians. Their explanations may be classified into three major types: biological, psychoanalytic, and sociological theories.

Biological Theories

Same-sex orientation has been linked to at least three kinds of biological factors: hormones, genes, and the brain.

According to the *hormone theory,* gay men have lower levels of male sex hormones than straight men, and lesbians have fewer female sex hormones than male sex hormones, while straight women have more female sex hormones. But most studies have found no hormonal difference between gays and straights (Burr, 1996; Porter, 1996).

According to the *genetic theory,* people are born, rather than bred to be, gay. Studies have suggested that the probability of two siblings becoming gay together is significantly higher among *identical* twins than among *fraternal* twins. This is taken to mean that same-sex orientation is largely determined by genes, because identical twins are more genetically alike than fraternal twins. But the findings, critics point out, do not necessarily mean that same-sex orientation can be traced to genes. According to critics, social environment may contribute to the development of same-sex orientation because, when compared with fraternal twins, identical twins are more likely to elicit similar reactions from others. If parents react to an identical twin boy by treating him as if he were a girl, they will most likely treat his twin brother in the same way. Given similar experiences, identical twins are likely to develop similar behavior patterns, including same-sex orientation (Wickelgren, 1999; Alessio, 1996; Burr, 1996; Porter, 1996).

The *brain theory* comes from a study in which Simon LeVay (1996) examined brain tissues from deceased gay and straight men. The researcher found, among other things, a difference in the size of the hypothalamus, the cluster of neurons, or nervous tissues, in the brain's lower area, which controls sex drive and body temperature. The gays' hypothalamus was less than half the size of the straights'. Le Vay concluded that a relatively small brain could make a person gay. Critics of this theory argue that it could be the other way around, that is, that AIDS (which killed all the gay subjects that LeVay studied) or same-sex activities may change brain size, as suggested by the evidence that the brain's neural networks can change in response to certain experiences. In people who read braille after becoming blind, for example, the area of the brain controlling the reading finger usually grows larger (Ridley, 1996).

Psychiatric Theories

For many years, most psychiatrists regarded same-sex orientation as a form of mental disorder. But, in 1973, the American Psychiatric Association (APA) decided to define "homosexuality" as normal. Still, today the APA continues to find some, though not most, gays and lesbians to be suffering from what it calls *sexual orientation disturbance*. Most psychiatrists would help these troubled gays to accept their same-sex orientation and feel comfortable with themselves. But some psychiatrists would try to "cure" the "patients" of their same-sex orientation. Such psychiatrists continue to hold the belief that same-sex orientation is characterized by "hidden but incapacitating fears of the opposite sex" (Socarides et al., 1997; Berger, 1994; Bayer, 1987).

This pathological fear is often attributed to an abnormal parent–son relationship. A young boy is said to become gay later in life if he has a domineering, overprotective, or seductive mother and a weak, detached, or hostile father. Alienated from his father, the boy will not look upon him as a model for learning the masculine role. Instead, being driven by his hostile father into the arms of his loving mother, the boy will cling excessively to her, identify himself with her, and fail to develop a strong masculine identity. As a consequence, the theory argues, the boy will likely grow up to become gay (Socarides et al., 1997; Herman and Duberman, 1995).

Many psychiatrists have found most of their gay patients to have had disturbed relationships with their parents, but these patients do not represent the majority of the gay population. Numerous studies on average, *non*patient gays have found them to be no different from heterosexuals in parent–child relationships (Ross and Arrindell, 1988).

Sociological Theories

A basic problem with biological theories is their assumption that same-sex orientation is universally the same. Were this true, we should expect different societies to have about the same incidence of gayness or lesbianism. The reality is that same-sex orientation varies greatly in form and frequency from one society to another.

Though relatively rare in many Western societies today, same-sex practices have been and are common in other societies, from ancient Greece and ancient Japan to the present-day Azande of Africa and various New Guinea societies. In some of these societies, male teenagers have sex regularly with older men as a normal way of growing up but later in their adulthood marry women and have children (Herdt, 1990). This suggests that society has much to do with the development of same-sex orientation. To most sociologists, then, same-sex orientation is just like heterosexuality, both developing from past social experiences. Only the specific nature of their social experiences differs.

While they do not believe that certain hormones, genes, or brain size causes same-sex orientation, many sociologists assume that gays and lesbians may be born with a biological *predisposition* that makes them more likely than other children to be attracted to members of the same sex. By itself, however, this biological predisposition does not automatically cause a person to become gay or lesbian. As suggested by societal variations in the incidence of same-sex orientation, society can check—or encourage—it through some social forces such as *socialization* and *social approval* (Dickermann, 1995; Bullough, 1993).

Socialization may involve children acquiring sexual orientation from physical contact with parents during the sensitive period between birth and age 3. As research has suggested, if a mother kisses, touches, or caresses her little girl much more than her little boy, as expected by the predominantly heterosexual society, then both the girl and the boy are likely to become heterosexual. If, contrary to the expectation of heterosexual society, the mother has much more physical contact with the boy than the girl, the boy will likely grow up to be gay and the girl, lesbian. Thus, parents can socialize, though often unintentionally, their children to feel like members of the opposite sex by treating them as such. Parents can also *intentionally* socialize children toward becoming gay or, for that matter, straight. But since their society condemns homosexuality and supports heterosexuality, parents are pressured to socialize their youngsters to become straight much more than gay, which explains why heterosexual adults far outnumber their homosexual counterparts (Fleishman, 1983).

In short, the origin of homosexuality is both biological and sociological. Growing up to become gay is like growing up to become left-handed. To grow up left-handed, one is usually first born with the *tendency* to be left-handed but, in order to become a lefty *as an adult*, the child must be socialized or allowed to use the left hand. Thus in societies such as the United States where left-handedness is socially approved there are relatively many left-handed adults. But left-handedness among adults is much less common in societies such as China where left-handedness is frowned on and left-handed children are taught or pressured to stop using their left hand. About the same social force can cause children born with the homosexual *tendency* to grow up gay—or straight.

The sociologists who basically agree with what has just been discussed are *essentialists,* who regard same-sex orientation as real and therefore seek to explain how it has come about. Other sociologists may be *social constructionists,* who are *not* interested in seeking the cause of same-sex orientation because they see the phenomenon not as real in and of itself but only as a social construct—society's definition of same-sex orientation as undesirable. To constructionists, then, how gays and lesbians live their lives depends on how society treats them, not on their sexual orientation. Constructionists are, therefore, mostly interested in studying societal responses to same-sex orientation, such as various expressions of homophobia, and how those responses affect the lives of gays and lesbians, as we have discussed in the second section of this chapter.

Summary

1. **What are the popular myths about the sexual minority?** One myth is that gay men are effeminate, while lesbians are manly. Other myths hold that gay men often molest young children, that gays and lesbians are restricted to either the active or passive role, are mentally ill, have an unsatisfactory sex life, and are obsessed with sex.

2. **How many gays and lesbians are there in the United States?** About 2.5 percent of U.S. adults see themselves as gay or lesbian. **What are some of the characteristics of gays and lesbians?** Gay men are more likely than straight men to be sexually active, but the majority of gay men are involved in long-term relationships characterized by power equality between partners. Lesbians resemble heterosexual women in having been socialized to desire long-term relationships, in having a comfortable relationship with straights, and in having the desire to be mothers. But compared with conventional women, lesbians are less likely to play the traditional female role and less aware of their same-sex orientation during adolescence.

3. **What is "coming out"?** It involves people revealing to others that they are gay or lesbian. **What does the process of coming out entail?** It entails going through four stages of experience: sensitization, dissociation, coming out, and commitment. **What are the other aspects of the gay and lesbian life like?** Despite the homophobia around them, lesbians and gays manage to live a relatively normal, happy life. They get along well with their straight parents, grandparents, and children. They date and get married like straights except that their marriage is not legally recognized. They can easily participate in social activities, especially in many large cities where there are large gay communities. They are mostly Democrats, better educated than straights, and belong to religious organizations as straights do. They work in all kinds of occupations, but are more likely than straights to be in those that traditionally attract members of the opposite sex. They participate in sports wherever there is an opportunity to do so, but the professional athletes among them, due to public and commercial attitudes, tend to stay in the closet, as do gays in the military.

4. **Do people who do not identify themselves as gay or lesbians engage in same-sex practices?** Some do. They are called trades, street hustlers, situationals, and bisexuals.

5. How does homophobic society "deviantize" gays and lesbians? By using the anachronistic norm that people may only engage in reproductive sex. **What is homophobia and how widespread is it in the United States?** Homophobia is antigay prejudice and discrimination. The general public is deeply ambivalent about gays and lesbians. While it opposes their lifestyle, it nonetheless supports most equal rights for the sexual minority. **Who are the homophobes?** They are distinguishable from others for having such characteristics as being less educated, less well-off, more conservative, and more negative toward racial/ethnic minorities. **What is the impact of homophobia on the sexual minority?** Homophobia creates some social and psychological problems for gays and lesbians. **How does homophobia in other countries compare with that in the United States?** The homophobia seems more serious in less affluent societies than in the United States.

6. How has the AIDS crisis affected gays and lesbians? The sexual minority is more likely to practice safer sex now than before. When AIDS first emerged in the 1980s, however, homophobia grew more intense and gross insensitivity toward AIDS victims became common. However, today the general public has become more sympathetic due to factors such as the growing number of heterosexuals being afflicted with AIDS and the effort of gays and lesbians to fight the disease for everybody.

7. What is the nature of the gay and lesbian rights movement? Most gay organizations were initially service-oriented, counseling gays in trouble or providing them with recreational activities. But in the late 1960s and early 1970s, they became militant, aiming to end antigay discriminations in all aspects of life. This brought some victories for the sexual minority, which cooled the militancy. Since the outbreak of the AIDS crisis led to greater homophobia in the 1980s, some gay activists have became militant again, but the majority have remained moderate, engaging in antihomophobic activities much like any conventional interest group.

8. What are the theories of same-sex orientation? According to biological theories, same-sex orientation can be traced to hormones, genes, and the brain. According to some psychiatrists, "homosexuality" is a form of mental illness that stems from strained parent-son relationships. Sociologists who hold the essentialist view of deviant behavior attribute the development of same-sex orientation to cross-gender socialization in childhood, but sociologists who embrace the constructionist view are more interested in studying homophobic reactions to gays and lesbians.

SUGGESTED READINGS

Beemyn, Brett, and Mickey Eliason (Eds.). 1996. *Queer Studies: A Lesbian, Gay, Bisexual, and Transgender Anthology.* A collection of articles on various dimensions of same-sex attractions and practices.

Blumenfeld, Warren J. (Ed.). 1992. *Homophobia: How We All Pay the Price*. Boston: Beacon. A collection of articles on various aspects of homophobia, ranging from sources and manifestations of the problem to ways of breaking free from it.

Blumenfeld, Warren J., and Diane Raymond. 1993. *Looking at Gay and Lesbian Life*. Boston: Beacon. Discusses many different issues about homosexuality, including gay sex, causes of homosexuality, homophobia, the gay rights movement, and AIDS.

Byne, William, and Bruce Parsons. 1993. "Human sexual orientation: The biologic theories reappraised." *Archives of General Psychiatry, 50* (March), 228–239. An examination of various biological theories, which concludes that genes or hormones per se do not directly influence sexual orientation.

Harris, Daniel. 1997. *The Rise and Fall of Gay Culture*. New York: Hyperion. A critical analysis of how the increasing assimilation of gays into meanstream society robs the gay culture of its distinctive sensibility and other values.

Katz, Jonathan Ned. 1995. *The Invention of HeteroSEXUALITY*. New York: Dutton Book. A social constructionist analysis of how the concept of heterosexuality—the basis for defining homosexuality as deviant in psychiatry and society in general—did not exist until about a century ago.

LeVay, Simon, and Elisabeth Nonas. 1995. *City of Friends: A Portrait of the Gay and Lesbian Community in America*. Cambridge, Mass.: The MIT Press. A highly informative guide into the community and lives of gay and lesbian Americans.

Marcus, Eric. 1992. *Making History: The Struggle for Gay and Lesbian Equal Rights*. New York: HarperCollins. An interesting and enlightening collection of autobiographical accounts of various stages of the gay rights movement.

McWhirter, David P., Stephanie A. Sanders, and June Machover Reinisch (Eds.). 1990. *Homosexuality/ Heterosexuality: Concepts of Sexual Orientation*. New York: Oxford University Press. A collection of articles by researchers from various academic disciplines that presents their perspectives and data on homosexuality and heterosexuality.

Miller, Neil. 1992. *Out in the World: Gay and Lesbian Life from Buenos Aires to Bangkok*. New York: Random House. A close-up view of same-sex experiences in twelve countries, most quite different from the gay life in the United States.

Vaid, Urvashi. 1995. *Virtual Equality: The Mainstreaming of Gay and Lesbian Liberation*. New York: Anchor Books. Shows how mainstreamed gays and lesbians are only virtually—but not really—equal to straights.

CHAPTER

11 Drug Use

A successful, extremely well-paid advertising executive, David, aged 25, smokes marijuana every day, usually at night, after work. "I use marijuana to relax," he explains, "to contemplate, and to enjoy myself. It makes me feel good, and I get a lot of insight from it. I'm more able to perceive who the other person is, and suspend all of life's petty 'games.' Anyway, I feel good when I'm stoned. That's why I do it. That's why I do it *regularly*. . . . It's fun. Food tastes better, sex is more expressive and enjoyable—yes, pot is an aphrodisiac, at least it is for me—I enjoy music more, I use my imagination more listening to music. . . . When someone asks me, why do I smoke dope, I answer, why not? There are no negatives, only positives. Really. Why not?" (Goode, 1999).

Is David a drug abuser? Objectively, he is not, because he does not use the drug to the extent of losing his job, his health, or his life. But the general public would consider him a drug abuser, simply because the drug in question, marijuana, is *illegal*. If David were regularly smoking cigarettes or drinking wine rather than using marijuana, he would *not* be considered a drug abuser, because tobacco and alcohol are *legal* drugs. The public also assumes that illegal drugs are always more dangerous than legal drugs, and that most users of illegal drugs are hopelessly hooked on the substances. Thus, in this chapter we will first discuss why this is not the case. We will then analyze the effects of various illegal drugs and the connection between such drugs, on the one hand, and AIDS and crime, on the other. We will also examine the extent of illegal drug use, the characteristics of the drug users, the process of becoming a drug user, the war on drugs, and theories of drug use. Finally, we will zero in on use of tobacco as an example of legal drugs.

Drug Use in Perspective

Contrary to popular belief, *legal* drugs may in some ways be more dangerous than illegal ones. First, the use of such legal drugs as alcoholic beverages and tobacco cigarettes is considerably more prevalent than the use of such illegal drugs as marijuana, heroin, and cocaine. Some 18 million Americans are alcoholics and 55 million are regular smokers, compared with only 5.5 million users of illegal drugs. Other legal drugs, such as sedatives, tranquilizers, and stimulants, though less popular than alcohol and tobacco, are still more widely used than such illegal drugs as heroin and cocaine. Not surprisingly, the use of legal drugs, particularly alcohol and tobacco, causes far more death, sickness, violent crime, economic loss, and other social problems than the use of illegal drugs. For example, every year about 200,000 Americans die from alcohol-related diseases and accidents, and more than 430,000 die from smoking, while only 5,000 to 10,000 die from illegal drugs. In other words, just two legal drugs—alcohol and tobacco—every year kill at least 60 times as many Americans as do all the illegal drugs combined (Falco, 1992).

Contrary to popular assumption, then, legal prohibition—or, more generally, societal disapproval—of a drug does not necessarily indicate how dangerous the drug really is. Instead, the disapproval reflects more the temper of the time and place. Opium is today an illegal drug and is widely condemned as a panopathogen (a cause of all ills), but in the last two centuries it was a legal drug and was popularly praised as a panacea (a cure for all ills). In contrast, cigarette smoking is legal in all countries today, but in the seventeenth century it was illegal in most countries and the smoker was harshly punished in some. The penalty for smoking, for example, included death in Turkey and China, removal of noses in Russia, and slitting of lips in Hindustan (Goode, 1999).

In assuming that illegal drugs are more dangerous than legal ones, the general public also believes that people who use illegal drugs typically become addicted, compulsive, or heavy users. But empirical evidence suggests that most people who use illicit drugs do so only experimentally, occasionally, or moderately, without sliding down the slippery slope to compulsive and uncontrollable use. This is because the majority of drug users have the ability to draw the line on what they do. Drugs by themselves do not have the power to pull users down the slippery slope. There are, of course, real horrors in drug use, but they befall only a few, not most, users (Goode, 1999).

Illegal Drugs: Their Effects and Users

Most drugs can be differentiated into three categories according to their effects on the user's central nervous system—the brain and spinal cord. One category includes *stimulants* ("uppers") such as cocaine, crack, caffeine, and nicotine. These drugs can stimulate the activity of the central nervous system, temporarily producing alertness and excitation as well as suppressing fatigue and sluggishness. Another category consists of *depressants* ("downers") such as heroin, PCP, morphine, and aspirin. In direct contrast to stimulants, depressants reduce the activity of the nervous system, so they can relax muscles, relieve anxiety, alleviate pain, create euphoria, or induce sleep. The third category comprises *hallucinogens* (psychedelics) such as LSD and MDMA ("ecstasy"). These drugs can disturb the nervous system, distorting the user's perception of reality. Most illicit drugs belong in only one of these three categories of drugs, but marijuana does not. Marijuana is in a class by itself, because it can affect the user in the same way as each of the three types of drugs. Thus some experts have classified marijuana as a stimulant, others have categorized it as a depressant, and still others have regarded it as a hallucinogen (Goode, 1999).

No matter what kind of drug they are, they do not by themselves produce the effects mentioned above. Certain factors also influence the effects of drugs. One factor is the *dosage:* The higher the dosage or amount of a drug, the stronger its effect on the user. A second factor is the *purity* (or *potency*) of the drug: The more psychoactive substance (such as the chemical THC in marijuana) there is in the drug—or the more actual heroin or cocaine there is in a batch of heroin or cocaine—the easier it is to get "high." A third factor is *drug mixing:* Snorting cocaine while high on marijuana, or taking an injection of "speedball" (a combination of cocaine and heroin) has a synergistic or multiplier effect, which is many times more powerful than either of the two drugs taken separately. A fourth factor is the method of *administration:* Intravenous injection ("mainlining")—putting a drug directly into the bloodstream—produces a stronger effect than intramuscular injection ("skin popping"), which involves injecting the drug into the arm or leg muscles. Smoking cocaine in the form of crack also has a more powerful effect than snorting it. And a fifth factor is the degree of *habituation:* A drug has a greater effect on occasional users than chronic users (Goode, 1999). Keeping in mind these factors that influence drug effects, let us now take a closer look at the effects and users of today's three most-often-used illegal drugs and two newly popular ones.

Marijuana

Marijuana is the most widely used illegal drug in the United States. It is derived from the Indian hemp plant called *Cannabis sativa.* The top of the plant produces a sticky resin containing a psychoactive substance. A small portion of this psychoactive resin flows downward and coats the lower part of the plant. What is typically sold and bought as marijuana ("grass," "weed," "pot," or "dope") in the United States comes from the entire plant. But when only the top of the plant is harvested, the product is *hashish,* which is far more psychoactively potent than marijuana. Both marijuana and hashish can be eaten or drunk, but are more commonly smoked in the form of cigarettes ("joints" or "reefers"). The cannabis plant can grow all over the world, but the better grades come from the United States, Mexico, Jamaica, and Thailand.

When it was first used in ancient times, marijuana was considered a sacred and useful drug, as suggested by the following passages from ancient Indian literature:

> To the Hindu the hemp plant is holy. A guardian lives in bhang [marijuana]. . . . Bhang is the joy giver, the sky flier, the heavenly guide, the poor man's heaven, the soother of grief . . . No god or man is as good as the religious drinker of bhang. The students of the scriptures of Benares are given bhang before they sit to study. At holy places, yogis take deep draughts of bhang, that they may enter their thoughts on the Eternal. . . . By the help of bhang, ascetics pass days without food or drink. The supporting power of bhang has brought many a Hindu family safe through the miseries of famine. (quoted in Szasz, 1974)

Yet there has been a great deal of opposition toward using marijuana in our society. This has distorted the judgment of both lay and scientific people about its effects. In the early 1950s, the former head of the Bureau of Narcotics expressed the popular view of the effects of marijuana this way: "In the earliest stages of intoxication the willpower is destroyed and inhibitions and restraints are released; moral barricades are broken down and often debauchery and sexuality result. Where mental instability is inherent, behavior is generally violent" (Anslinger and Thompkins, 1953). But later many researchers found that marijuana tends to inhibit rather than induce aggressive behavior. In an experimental study by two of these researchers, subjects who had taken relatively high doses of marijuana responded less aggressively to provocation than did those who had taken a lower dose (Myerscough and Taylor, 1985).

In the 1970s and 1980s a number of scientists claimed that there are serious health hazards in smoking marijuana. The scientists claimed to have found that marijuana damages the brain and the lungs, causes the user to age prematurely, lowers the body's resistance to infectious disease and cancer, causes severe chest pain, produces respiratory disorders (e.g., bronchitis and asthma), brings about precancerous changes in the lung cells, increases the likelihood of sterility or impotence, and contributes to birth defects and hereditary diseases in the user's children. But careful checking of these findings—either by repeating the experiment or by devising a better one—has largely found no damage from marijuana use (Brecher et al., 1975).

However, if smoked in large doses for an extended period, marijuana can be *physically* addictive. If marijuana use is discontinued, the user will suffer withdrawal symptoms such as mild nausea, restlessness, and loss of appetite, though not as serious as those caused by addiction to heroin and other hard drugs. Marijuana can also be *psychologically* addictive, but only mildly so, because it is not as immensely pleasurable as cocaine or heroin. If used to the point of intoxication, marijuana can create problems in the same way as alcoholic beverages. It can, for example, impair intellectual judgment, short-term memory, and human psychomotor function. It can thus hamper reading or studying. It can also undermine the performance of car drivers and airline pilots (Murray, 1986; Yesavage et al., 1985). But when used moderately, marijuana can create euphoria, heighten sensitivity, improve perception, and increase appetite (Falco, 1992). Marijuana can also be used for medical purposes, particularly for the benefit of the very ill. In the purified form under the trade name Marinol, or when smoked like a cigarette, marijuana has proven effective for controlling nausea and relieving pain in seriously ill patients with AIDS, cancer, and other diseases (Conant, 1997; Cowley, 1997; Doblin and Kleiman, 1993).

Many people believe that marijuana is a "gateway" to harder drugs. Indeed, considerable research has shown that almost all heroin and cocaine users started out with weed (Morganthau, 1997). But such a finding does not mean that marijuana use inevitably leads to hard drugs in the sense of marijuana itself being the cause of the drug escalation. The cause more likely lies in the marijuana user's involvement with friends who use hard drugs. In other words, pot smokers use heroin or cocaine largely because they have friends already using the hard drug (Goode, 1999).

Heroin

This drug, also called "P-dope" on the street, was first produced in 1898 from morphine, which was in turn first derived in 1803 from opium. Both morphine and heroin are analgesics (painkillers) and have been used as such. But heroin use is now a major source of our society's concern with the problem of drug abuse. Most of our heroin comes from opium poppies harvested in the Golden Triangle of Southeast Asia (Burma, Thailand, and Laos), the Golden Crescent of South Asia (Pakistan, Afghanistan, and Iran), Mexico, and Colombia.

Heroin can be smoked, sniffed through the nose, taken orally, or injected into the skin, a muscle, or a vein. Injection of the substance into a vein, or mainlining, produces the quickest and most intense high. Traditionally, mainlining has been by far the most common method of ingestion. But fear of AIDS and the greatly increased potency of today's heroin have made smoking or snorting increasingly popular. Taken in moderate doses, heroin not only can dull pain but also diminish anxiety and tension. Most important, heroin can induce euphoria—the feeling of a "flash," "rush," or intense orgasmlike sensation. Actually, heroin itself does not bring about the euphoric feeling; the user has to *learn* to achieve the sense of pleasure from heroin injection. The novice user typically encounters an unpleasant experience from the first shot. Yet the negative experience can easily be rationalized, thus opening the way for taking more heroin trips. Here's how a young woman described her first heroin experience with her boyfriend:

> The rush was so powerful that he almost fell down. He turned white and began to sweat profusely. . . . I, too, began to sweat and tremble. If anyone had seen . . . us walking out of the house, he would have called an ambulance, we could barely walk. For some insane reason, we had decided to drive home immediately after shooting up . . . I had to keep pulling over to throw up on the side of the road . . . I was truly surprised that we both didn't die that very first night. I was more physically miserable than I had ever been before. The whole night was spent vomiting. The thing that surprises me is that we didn't forget about heroin right then and there. It was horrible! But we later decided that our dear friend had given us too much. So I decided to give it another chance. (Goode, 1999)

Once users try heroin several times, as this woman did, they feel an extreme pleasure from the drug experience. Many heroin users, both male and female, claim that the heroin rush is more satisfying than orgasm and the heroin high far more glorious and pleasurable than anything the nonuser could possibly experience. This, however, can easily lead to psychological dependence on the drug. Furthermore, heroin is physically addictive. If deprived of it for just one day, the addict may suffer withdrawal sickness. Those symptoms include profuse sweating, running nose, watering eyes, chills, cramps, nausea, and diarrhea (Chase, 1996).

To relieve or avoid these withdrawal symptoms, the addict obviously has to keep on using heroin. This has led many researchers to believe that once people become addicted, they can no longer experience the pleasurable effects of preaddiction drug use—that addicts use heroin only for *avoiding* the withdrawal distress. As the influential drug researcher Alfred Lindesmith (1968) wrote, "The critical experience in the fixation process is not the positive euphoria produced by the drug but rather the relief of the pain that invariably appears when a physically dependent person stops using the drug." But William McAuliffe and Robert Gordon (1974) presented data to show that, contrary to Lindesmith's belief, addicts do continue to experience *euphoria* following each injection of heroin. McAuliffe and Gordon argued that if it were not for the promise of euphoria, addicts would not persistently take the trouble to steal and hustle to get money for the next fix, and that if they only wanted to avoid withdrawal distress, they would quickly seek help at some drug treatment center. But this is not the case.

Both interpretations may well miss the mark. They above all reflect the researchers' own perceptions of what the experience of the drug effect means to them rather than to the addicts, who were not asked how they themselves actually felt. According to an ethnographic study, which encouraged addicts to express their feelings, most heroin addicts seek *something between* withdrawal avoidance and euphoria—more than the desperate avoidance of withdrawal distress but less than the intense euphoria they initially experienced. What they seek is "a temporary calm and serenity, feelings of normalcy, relaxation, and capability to provide them with a respite from the bleak harshness of their lives. It is the pursuit of normalcy rather than of euphoria that propels these heroin users to continue to use the substance." The pursuit of normalcy, however, does not involve the frantic, pathetic search for relief from the pain of withdrawal symptoms. Instead, heroin addicts see themselves in control rather than as "down-and-out dope fiends." They have a sense of pride in being able to achieve normalcy in a society that has relegated them to a lowly status (Hanson et al., 1985).

Although heroin is addictive, most users do not become addicts. A major reason is that heroin users typically get less and less pleasure from the drug after their early experiences of euphoria. As a former user says, "Luckily, it was no longer feeling good enough to make it worth getting busted for . . . Heroin had lost its immense power over me. It simply wasn't worth it. The magic ceased to happen long ago. There's only the memory . . . Right now I'd rather go out for a good dinner than shoot a bag of heroin" (Goode, 1981). There is also no truth to the old saw that "once a junkie, always a junkie." One study shows that, among the returning Vietnam veterans in 1971 who had been addicted to heroin while overseas, over 90 percent were no longer addicted about eight months after their return home (Maddux and Desmond, 1980; Robins et al, 1973). Even if permanently addicted to heroin, people do not necessarily suffer severe damage to their health. The drug may be harmless when compared with other psychoactive drugs. Unlike cigarette smoking and alcohol drinking, prolonged use of heroin does not necessarily damage the organs, tissues, or cells of the human body. As long as heroin addicts do not neglect other aspects of their lives, they can remain as healthy as the nonuser. As Jerome Jaffe (1965), the physician who later served as President Nixon's adviser on drug problems, observed,

> The addict who is able to obtain an adequate supply of the drug through legitimate channels and has adequate funds, usually dresses properly, maintains his nutrition, and is able to discharge his social and occupational obligations with reasonable efficiency. He usually remains in good health, suffers little inconvenience, and is, in general, difficult to distinguish from other persons.

A good example is the physician addict. Although they use a much greater quantity of narcotics than "street junkies," physician addicts generally manage to maintain their health and practice their profession. They are only less efficient in their work when compared with their addiction-free colleagues (Cooms, 1997).

On the other hand, street junkies are far more likely to suffer the consequences of narcotics laws. Because of these laws, heroin's black market prices are usually so high that the addicts, who are mostly poor, have to spend a great deal of their time frantically searching for money to buy the next fix. The frantic search for money tends to involve the user in committing burglaries, shoplifting, gambling, prostitution, and other acquisitive crimes, which creates a great deal of stress and strain. By the time they get enough money to buy a packet of "junk," they are likely to be both physically drained and emotionally stressed out. In addition, there is no way for them to know how pure or potent the packet is—its heroin content may range from zero to 99 percent. If they are used to no more than 5 percent heroin and happen to buy a packet of 50 percent, they may die of an overdose (Smolowe, 1993).

Cocaine and Crack

Also known as "coke," "snow," and "toot," cocaine is derived from the leaves of coca plants. At least 90 percent of the coca plants in the world are grown on the mountains of Peru and Bolivia, whose governments sometimes treasure the crop as one of their major exports. The coca leaves, however, are processed into cocaine in Colombia, and from where the final product is smuggled into the United States (Wren, 1997).

Before it became illegal at the turn of this century, cocaine was commonly used as a local anesthetic, for offsetting fatigue and depression, and for curing morphine addiction and stomach disorder. It was even chosen as the official remedy of the Hay Fever Association. Sigmund Freud, the founder of psychoanalysis, not only prescribed cocaine for his patients to treat those ills, but also used the drug himself to stay alert and ward off melancholy. Cocaine was also a major ingredient in numerous patent medicines and in many soft drinks, such as Coca-Cola. In 1885, a well-known pharmaceutical company promoted cocaine as a wonder drug, claiming that it could "supply the place of food, make the coward brave, the silent eloquent, free the victims of alcohol and opium habit from their bondage, and, as an anesthetic, render the sufferer insensitive to pain." One of the best, most popular wines in the late nineteenth century, marketed under the name of Vin Mariani, contained some cocaine. It won endorsement from Pope Leo XIII, Pope Pius X, President McKinley, the kings of four countries (Spain, Greece, Norway, and Sweden), and many famous writers and artists. The French sculptor who designed the Statue of Liberty swore that if he had only drunk Vin Mariani earlier, he would have been able to build that lady hundreds of meters higher (Musto, 1986; Goode, 1981).

By the turn of the twentieth century, when laws were passed to make cocaine illegal, it had become widely used as a pleasure drug. At that time most of the users were the powerless, such as African Americans, lower-class whites, and criminals. But since the 1960s cocaine has become a symbol of wealth or status, mostly used by affluent whites. It is the most expensive drug, sometimes called "the champagne of drugs" or "caviar among drugs." Usually snorted, the drug is in the form of white powder—hence also called "powder cocaine." One can seek a greater high by resorting to "freebasing," which involves purifying the drug with ether and then smoking it. Since 1986, however, an increasing number of youths, especially those from poor and working-class families, have used crack cocaine—or simply, "crack." It is a less pure form of cocaine but can still produce an intense high because users typically smoke it rather than snort it.

Crack is much cheaper than pure cocaine, which may explain its popular use among the poor and the young.

As a stimulant, cocaine increases the heartbeat and raises blood pressure and body temperature. A snort in each nostril can produce a euphoric lift that lasts for half an hour or so. The cocaine high may be described objectively as an intensely vivid, sensation-sharpening experience. In the view of users themselves, the drug (1) provides exhilaration—a sense of elation, well-being, or a voluptuous, joyous feeling; (2) enhances self-confidence, supplying a sense of mastery and competence in what the user does; and (3) increases energy and suppresses fatigue, enabling the user to continue physical and mental activity more intensely and longer—such as by working for two or three days and nights straight without any sleep. Some users claim that cocaine is an aphrodisiac, but most deny it and there is increasing evidence that sustained use of cocaine can cause sexual dysfunction and impotence (Goode, 1981).

Cocaine is physically addictive; it produces such withdrawal symptoms as exhaustion and stomach cramps after its use is discontinued. Cocaine is particularly noteworthy for being extremely psychologically addictive, due largely to the high quality of pleasure the user can derive from it. Coming down from a high usually causes such a deep gloom that the only remedy is more cocaine. Bigger doses follow, and soon the urge becomes a total obsession, with all its devastating consequences. As one cocaine user said, "I even hocked my wife's wedding ring. That's not me. Whoever said cocaine isn't addicting should be shot" (Rosenfeld, 1985). The powerful psychological addiction to cocaine has been demonstrated in laboratory experiments with animals. Once hooked on cocaine, rats and monkeys will prefer the drug to food, even though they have not eaten all day. They will keep on pressing the bar (which they have been trained to do) for a cocaine reward until they drop from exhaustion. Crack is even more addictive than plain cocaine. The rush comes and goes so much more quickly and intensely that the crack user can get hooked much faster. According to the National Institute on Drug Abuse, crack addiction develops after only six to ten weeks, while it takes three to four years for users to get hooked on regular cocaine. When snorted, the coke reaches the brain in about eight minutes to produce a much milder high than that from crack. But crack hits the brain within only seconds in an intensified, concentrated form (Lamar, 1986).

Most people who use cocaine find their experience positive. But the drug can also be extremely dangerous if taken in large doses or used frequently for an extended time. It can cause insomnia, impotence, extreme irritability, paranoia and other symptoms of psychosis, and the sensation of bugs crawling under the skin. A single overdose can also produce an effect like "lighting a fire in the brain," triggering severe headaches, nausea, and convulsions with the possibility of total respiratory and cardiovascular collapse. Crack puts its users even at higher risks. Since it swiftly and dramatically increases blood pressure and heart rate, crack can more easily lead to heart attacks and deaths. Most users of cocaine, however, do not experience these effects, primarily because they use cocaine moderately and infrequently.

Newly Popular Drugs: Meth and Roofies

Meth (methamphetamine), an injectable stimulant known on the street as "speed," "crank," or "crystal," has, since 1995, risen dramatically in popularity among drug users throughout the western United States. The drug itself is not new. During the Second World War, soldiers on both sides used it to reduce fatigue and enhance performance. Hitler was widely believed to be a meth addict. Later, in the 1960s, President John Kennedy also used the drug, and soon it caught on among so-called speed freaks. But because it was extremely expensive as well as difficult to obtain, meth was never close to being as widely used as cocaine. Today, however, largely because Mexican drug traffickers have made meth easily available in the West, its use has increased sharply in that region, especially in such cities as San Diego, San Francisco, Los Angeles, and Phoenix, where meth is about to supplant cocaine as the drug of choice. A growing number of users are white, 18-to-34-year-old working-class men and women, who like the fact that the high from meth lasts four or five times longer than that from cocaine. When used initially, meth is known to suppress appetite, create euphoria, boost self-confidence, and provide a burst of energy. But after users develop a tolerance for the drug, depression is likely to set in, followed by intense paranoia (Kirn, 1998; Witkin, 1995).

Unlike meth, which is a stimulant, another recently popular drug is a depressant. In tablet form, the drug is known on the street as "roofies," "rope," "the forget pill," and "roach." It is related to the sedative Valium but is ten times stronger. Roofies is actually Rohypnol, a prescription drug for severe insomnia. Rohypnol is sold over the counter in some 60 countries, and much of the drug used on the street in the United States is smuggled from Mexico and Colombia. The drug is particularly popular with teenagers in the South and Southwest, who like to combine the drug with alcohol for a quick high. This practice is apparently dangerous—it is what sent the grunge–rock star Kurt Cobain into a coma a month before he committed suicide. Like strong liquor, roofies make some users aggressive and fearless, but they often cause blackouts, with a total loss of memory. Consequently, some men use roofies to knock women out and then rape them, and it is from this use that the drug is also known as "the date-rape drug." The drug has also caused a great deal of concern about its potential for addiction and lethal overdosing (Cannon, 1999; Seligmann and King, 1996).

Social Dimensions of Drug Use

Drug use is not an individual behavior, engaged in simply by one person and affecting one person alone. It is social behavior, involving many drug users and affecting not only the drug user but also many other people—in fact, the entire society. Here we focus on four social dimensions of drug use: the extent of drug use in the United States, how U.S. society reacts to drug use, the impact of drug use on the spread of AIDS, and the influence of drug use on crime.

The Extent of Drug Use

The use of illegal drugs is quite common in the United States. About 12 percent of the U.S. population age 12 or older use illicit drugs every year, and half of them at least once a month. Of various age groups, young adults (ages 18 to 25) have the highest rate of drug use and teenagers (ages 12 to 17) the second highest. The United States as a whole has the highest rate of drug use among the industrial countries of the world, and U.S. high school seniors also have the highest rate among their peers in the industrial world (Sallett, Goode, and Pooler, 1999; Currie, 1993).

All this, however, should not be blown out of proportion. It is true that the United States leads the industrial nations in drug use. It is not true that drug use is so pervasive that it invades every nook and cranny, enslaving all classes of Americans to the same extent. Most drug problems, especially the most serious ones, such as drug addiction, death from drug overdose, or drug-related homicide, are for the most part confined to the lower classes, particularly to socially and economically oppressed minorities. Drug use and overdose among the non-poor, middle class, or affluent is generally far less common (Massing, 1997; Currie, 1993).

In fact, for Americans as a whole, the rate of drug use steadily declined from 1980 to 1992, and since 1992 the rate has remained about the same. But for teenagers, the rate has been rising, driven mostly by white youngsters smoking pot, as Figure 11.1 indicates. The sharpest increase in drug use has occurred

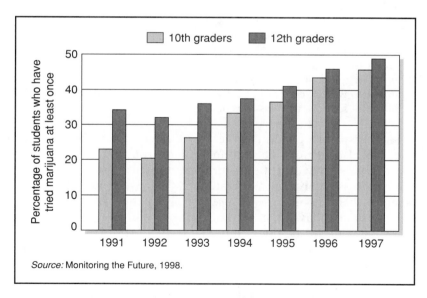

Source: Monitoring the Future, 1998.

FIGURE 11.1   Growing Drug Use Among Teenagers.

Source: Monitoring the Future, 1998.

among young teens, around age 13 (Sallett, Goode, and Pooler, 1999). Another noteworthy finding: African-American students in secondary school are now less likely than their white peers to use drugs because they are more likely to have observed at close hand how drugs wreck lives in black communities (Wren, 1996a; Bogert, 1994).

Moral Panic: Societal Reaction to Drug Use

Because drug use is widely condemned as deviant and dangerous, society tends to respond with a moral panic regardless of what the facts about the problem are (Goode and Ben-Yehuda, 1994). Thus the general public often seems to be seized with the terrible vision of huge masses of Americans shooting heroin, snorting cocaine, smoking pot, or using meth, roofies, or some other illicit drug. Even in the midst of a declining drug use in the last decade, *Newsweek* (1986) declared:

> An epidemic is abroad in America, as pervasive and as dangerous in its way as the plagues of medieval times. . . . It has taken lives, wrecked careers, broken homes, invaded schools, incited crimes, tainted businesses, toppled heroes, corrupted policemen and politicians, bled billions from the economy and in some measure infected every corner of our public and private lives.

In the year when the rate of drug use hit bottom, Mathea Falco (1992), former assistant secretary of state for international narcotics matters and drug-abuse adviser to Bill Clinton during the presidential campaign, also proclaimed:

> The horrors of drug abuse have become depressingly familiar: crack-addicted mothers abandoning their babies; young children dealing drugs instead of going to school; innocent citizens killed in gang shoot-outs; and sports stars dying from overdoses. . . . Drug abuse is at the heart of what many people think has gone wrong with America. It appears as either the cause or the effect of a wide range of problems which seem out of control: urban blight, the destruction of families, the failure of schools, the loss of economic productivity.

Such displays of moral panic about drug use are difficult to justify. Of course, illegal drugs can be extremely dangerous—if used improperly, incessantly, or excessively. But the majority of users use drugs responsibly—experimentally, occasionally, or moderately. If this were not the case, the huge numbers of baby boomers who used drugs in the 1960s, including President Clinton, would today have become hopeless junkies and the whole nation would have gone to the dogs. Should we, then, shut our eyes to our society's drug problem? Absolutely not. But instead of succumbing to moral panic, the family, school, and media can be more effective by calmly doing such things as providing youngsters with valid rather than "scare" information about drugs or encouraging them to avoid drugs (as has been successfully done with smoking) or to use drugs responsibly to avoid harming themselves or others (as has been successfully done with drinking and driving).

Drugs and AIDS

Intravenous (IV) injection of an illegal drug can spread HIV, the virus that causes AIDS, from one user to another. Most drug users with AIDS are addicted to heroin, and they have caught the deadly disease from sharing needles with other addicts. The connection between drugs and AIDS is remarkably strong in the United States. IV drug users with AIDS make up only about 7 percent of all AIDS cases in Holland, 3 percent in Sweden, and 2.9 percent in Canada. By sharp contrast, this figure is nearly 25 percent in the United States. The proportion is considerably higher in some U.S. cities: 40 percent in New York City and 65 percent in Newark. In fact, the spread of the AIDS virus has virtually stopped among gays, but continues among IV drug users (Currie, 1993). Why?

A major factor behind the sharp drop in the new incidence of AIDS among gays is the practice of safe sex. But many IV drug users refuse to practice safe needle use, continuing to share needles and rejecting clean needles even if easily available (Decker and Rosenfeld, 1992; Sibthorpe et al., 1991). Why do they take the terrible risk of HIV infection? One reason is that they are drug addicts rather than occasional drug users. Their craving for drugs is so overwhelming that they must shoot up right away and cannot be bothered with taking precautions (Sibthorpe et al., 1991). Another reason is that the essence of the addict's lifestyle is risk taking: "Their habit alone is daily dalliance with mortality. Given a life filled with risks—overdoses, hepatitis, jail—the threat of dying from AIDS seems, to many, merely redundant" (Goode, 1999). A third reason has to do with the difference in social background between the gays who practice safe sex and the IV drug addicts who spurn safe needle use. Most of the gays are relatively well-off white men, but the majority of the addicts are poor African Americans and Hispanics. Deprived of the opportunities for material success in a society that discriminates against them, the addicts are compelled to seek social status through bravado and daring. This includes taking on a dangerous drug, especially one that is widely known to be capable of killing the user. In other words, it is overwhelming poverty that makes life so bleak and empty that the risk-taking involved in unsafe drug use appears challenging and thrilling (Currie, 1993).

Drugs and Crime

Research in the United States and other countries has clearly shown a strong link between drug use and crime: People who use illegal drugs generally commit more crime than those who do not. It has been found that close to half of the crime suspects arrested in the United States had used illegal drugs in the prior three days while 55 percent of their counterparts in England had done the same. It is also a well-known fact that in the United States as drug use has declined since the 1980s so has the crime rate (Wren, 1999b; Walchak, 1996; Grapendaal, 1992; Harrison, 1992b). Does all this mean that drug use causes crime? The answer is yes, according to *drug enslavement theory*. The answer is no, according to *general deviance syndrome theory*.

According to drug enslavement theory, drug users are forced into a life of crime because they cannot afford to pay for their prohibitively expensive drug habits unless they rob or steal to get the money for their next fix. This may be true of "deficit users," who live in poverty, have inadequate education, lack job skills, face racial discrimination, and suffer other social disadvantages because they are relatively poor, uneducated, and economically unskilled. But the theory cannot be applied to "leisure users," who are well-off enough to find it unnecessary to commit crime for the purpose of raising funds for drug purchases (Harrison, 1992a).

According to general deviance syndrome theory, the high correlation between drug use and crime does not mean that drug use causes crime because most drug users with a criminal record have committed crime *before* using drugs. Becoming a drug user and continuing to commit crime as a drug user are cut from the same cloth—that is, from a general tendency toward deviance. Those with a general deviance syndrome are likely to get involved not only in one form of deviant activities (such as crime) but also in other forms of deviance (such as drug use and drug-related criminality). This syndrome was found in about 77 percent of the drug users in a study conducted at a Denver drug abuse center, while the syndrome was absent in the remaining 23 percent—who committed offenses only after becoming drug users (Swan, 1993). It seems clear that drug use does not by itself cause crime for most users, but drug use does *intensify* criminal tendency or *increase* the frequency of criminal activity. This may explain the "astronomical" number of offenses committed by drug users (Goode, 1999).

A Social Profile of Drug Users

As we have observed, the poor, particularly poor minorities, are considerably more likely than the nonpoor, the middle class, or the affluent to use illegal drugs. But the poor are *not* more likely to use *all* kinds of drugs. Research has shown that socioeconomic groups often differ from each other in the *type* of drugs they are likely to use. Moreover, *within each group,* not all members use drugs. Which members, then, are more likely than others to use drugs? Research has uncovered certain social and social-psychological characteristics that distinguish drug users from others. Let us therefore discuss (1) the connection between socioeconomic status and drug types, and (2) drug users' social and social-psychological characteristics.

Socioeconomic Status and Drug Types

Socioeconomic status—measured in terms of education, occupation, and income—is significantly related to the type of illicit drug being used. People of higher status tend to use certain drugs, whereas people of lower status tend to use other drugs (Goode, 1999).

There is a strong connection between higher status and marijuana: The higher the status, the more likely the use of marijuana. The drug is particularly popular among college and high school students; marijuana is by far their number one drug of choice.

Heroin is far and away the most popular among lower-status people, particularly those who live in poor, inner-city neighborhoods. The affluent, including their children of high school or college age, typically stay away from heroin. This has long been so, and even in the 1960s, when massive numbers of college and high school students experimented with all kinds of drugs, heroin remained at the very bottom of their drug choice. But since the mid-1990s more affluent whites have turned on to heroin, primarily because the drug is now pure enough to snort or smoke, with no risk of getting AIDS from sharing contaminated needles (Wren, 1999a; Leland, 1996).

Cocaine has long been associated with affluent people because of its high cost. Today, the drug is still more popular among the affluent than among the poor. But since the drug is much less expensive today, less affluent people have increasingly used it. The cheapest form of cocaine, crack, is particularly popular with the poor. In fact, crack has been called "the poor person's drug."

As for the newly popular drugs, meth and roofies, they seem to have a special allure among working-class and young people. As has been suggested, some working-class persons use meth to seek euphoria, an enhanced self-confidence, and a burst of energy, and some working-class women use the drug to lose weight because it can suppress appetite. Roofies is popular with young people who apparently like to drink, because as a depressant the drug has the same effect as alcohol, except of course, that it is far more potent. Information on the socioeconomic background of roofies users is not yet available.

While we have discussed users of different drugs separately, we should nonetheless note that the use of a particular drug does not necessarily mean that the individual uses or will continue to use only that drug. Most people who use drugs tend to use more than one type. In addition, under peer influence, they tend to graduate from using relatively soft drugs, such as cigarettes, liquor, or marijuana, to using "harder" drugs, such as heroin and cocaine. Still, most drug users favor a certain drug over others.

Social and Social-Psychological Characteristics

Drug users, in general, are distinguishable from nonusers for having certain social and social-psychological characteristics.

First, drug use varies with gender and age. Males are more likely than females to use drugs. This reflects the greater general tendency on the part of males to engage in deviant activities. Thus, the more deviant the drug use, the greater the gender difference. While men are only *slightly* more likely to use drugs at all, they are *considerably* more likely to use drugs regularly, and *extremely* more likely to use drugs heavily so as to become drug addicts (Goode, 1999). Young people are more likely to use drugs. The age group with the highest rate of drug use is 18 to 25 years old. Within this group, more drug users are older teenagers (ages 18 or 19) than are young adults (ages 24 or 25). The higher rate of drug use among younger persons can be attributed to freedom from parental supervision and, more important, freedom from adult responsibilities such as employment, marriage, and raising children. Research has long established that the unemployed, unmarried, and childless are more likely than those with jobs, spouses, and children to use drugs (Goode, 1999).

Second, drug use is related to parental and peer influences. Users are likely to have parents who use legal drugs such as tobacco cigarettes, alcoholic beverages, and prescription drugs for relieving tension and combating insomnia. From parents, then, drug users first learn to use legal drugs—before turning to illegal ones. Users are also more likely than nonusers to have poor relationships with their fathers (Molotsky, 1999; Hsu, 1993; Adler and Kandel, 1981). When used for the first time, the drugs are usually given by friends. It is little wonder that drug users have at least a few friends who also use the same drugs. Whether they will continue to use the drugs for an extended period also depends significantly on their friends' drug use (Osgood et al., 1996; Lacy, 1981).

Third, among high school students, the drug users, when compared with their nonusing peers, cut classes or skip whole days of school more frequently, are more likely to drop out of school, have weaker commitment to religion, and go out evenings for fun and recreation more often. In other words, young drug users are not as strongly tied to three major social institutions—the school, the church, and the home—as the nonusers (Bachman, Johnston, and O'Malley, 1981; Jessor, Chase, and Donovan, 1980).

Fourth, among those who have gone to college, drug users are more likely to have majored in the social sciences, fine arts, and humanities than in the natural sciences. They are also more likely to favor liberal politics, to be estranged from religion, and to have a generally permissive and anticonventional outlook. In short, compared with their peers who do not use drugs, drug users are more likely to be nonconformist, subscribing to what has been called the "hang-loose ethic."

> One of the fundamental characteristics of the hang-loose ethic is that it is *irreverent.* It repudiates, or at least questions, such cornerstones of conventional society as Christianity, "my country right or wrong," the sanctity of marriage and premarital chastity, civil obedience, the accumulation of wealth, the right and even competence of parents, the schools, and the government to head and make decisions for everyone—in sum, the Establishment. (Simmons and Winograd, 1967)

Not surprisingly, most of the young people who smoke pot today are children of the baby boomers who took to marijuana as their "drug of defiance" against conventional society (Morrow, 1996).

Becoming a Drug User

In their classic study of heroin use, Isidor Chein and his associates (1964) distinguished four stages in the process of becoming involved with the drug. These stages are *experimentation, occasional use* (once a week or less), *regular use* (once a day or more), and *futile efforts to break the habit.* Chein and his associates further note that a user may go through all these stages or may stop at any stage. One person may experiment but not repeat the experiment. Another may use heroin occasionally but never regularly. A third person may become a regular user but manage to break the habit. And a fourth person may go through all the stages to become hooked on heroin, despite strenuous efforts to kick the habit.

Among the users of various drugs, heroin users seem most likely to escalate into the last, fourth stage (addiction), with users of marijuana, cocaine, and other illicit drugs remaining in the earlier stages (experimental, occasional, and regular use).

Heroin is most addictive not only because of its chemical properties but, perhaps more important, because the majority of its users are relatively poor and use the drug to cope with the stresses of their life problems, such as low-paying jobs, unemployment, and racism. Since the relief brought by the drug is transitory and the stresses always recur, extended use of heroin is likely to occur; and since the drug is extremely addictive, its users have the greatest chance of getting hooked. On the other hand, users of marijuana, cocaine, and other drugs may be less likely to get addicted to the drugs because, unlike heroin users, they are mostly young people who use drugs for about the same reason they go to the movies, to a party, or out on a date—that is, drugs are a part of their social lives or recreational activities. As a nationwide study of high school seniors found, the reasons most often cited by users of marijuana and cocaine are "to have a good time with friends," "to feel good or get high," and "to see what it's like." Very few of the students mentioned "to get away from my problems," "to deal with anger and frustration," or "to get through the day" (Johnston et al., 1986). Therefore, without the compulsion to use drugs for dealing with difficult, intractable problems, they are more likely to remain occasional users.

Whatever stage drug users may end up in, how do they get involved in drugs in the first place? They usually have been offered the drug by their friends in a simple, casual way. This can be illustrated by the following accounts of how two young men had their first experiences with heroin (Chein et al., 1964):

> It was raining, and I was tired. I was standing in a doorway when this friend of mine came by. He said, "Want a pick-up [injection]?" I said "Sure," so we popped [took a shot].

> I was at a party. Everybody was having a good time. I wanted to be one of the crowd. I thought, if it didn't hurt them it wouldn't hurt me. That started the ball rolling. They were sniffing it that time. Two or three pulled out a few caps [heroin capsules] and said, "Here, if you want to, try." I accepted. They weren't trying to addict me; they just gave it to me.

Contrary to popular belief, it is not the strange drug peddler, the "merchant of death," who pushes drugs on the innocent young. Instead, it is their friends who introduce them to drug use (Osgood et al., 1996).

Once having tried the drug, would-be users may go through a learning process—with explicit or implicit instruction from their drug-introducing friends. Howard Becker (1963) has identified three steps in the process of learning to become a marijuana user.

The first step is learning the *technique* to get high. Since beginners tend to smoke marijuana like an ordinary cigarette, they may fail to induce the desired drug effects. Thus they may watch their experienced friends smoke or they may receive direct coaching from them on the proper way of smoking grass, such as inhaling deeply and then holding the smoke in the lungs long enough for the bloodstream to absorb the psychoactive substance of marijuana.

Becker's second step is learning to *recognize* the drug effects. After learning the proper technique of smoking marijuana, new users may still not get high. So they have to learn from friends that having cold feet, rubbery legs, intense hunger, and unawareness of the passage of time are some of the signs of a marijuana high.

The third step is learning to *enjoy* the drug effects. While being high, novices may have such feelings as dizziness, thirst, and tingling of the scalp; they may misjudge time and distance or feel themselves to be simultaneously at two places; they may hear or otherwise sense things in strange ways. These feelings may be unpleasant or even frightening to beginning drug users. They must learn to redefine these sensations as pleasurable; otherwise they will not use the drug again. New marijuana users usually learn to enjoy these experiences because of the encouragement and reassurances of experienced friends. These friends may tell them such things as, "You sure are lucky; I'd give anything to get that high myself. I haven't been that high in years."

With the use of cocaine, heroin, or other illegal drugs, the beginner may also have to learn the first step—the technique of using the drug. But the second and third steps—learning to recognize and enjoy the drug effects—may not be necessary, because the effects are usually more clear-cut and predictable than the effects of marijuana. In virtually all cases of initial cocaine use, for example, the user feels its effect as extremely pleasurable. Hence, there is no need for users of cocaine and other drugs to learn to recognize and enjoy the drug effects.

What Causes Illegal Drug Use?

There are over forty theories about some aspect of drug use. Some of these theories are designed to explain why some individuals are more likely than others to use or abuse drugs. These explanatory theories can be divided into three major types: biological, psychological, and sociological. According to biological theories, the causes of drug addiction inhere in biological factors, such as an inborn high tolerance for drugs or a metabolic disorder that creates a craving for an illicit drug in about the same way that diabetes creates a craving for insulin. According to psychological theories, the causes of drug use are specific personality traits, such as low self-esteem or unconventionality. And according to sociological theories, drug use stems from social forces, such as the drug subculture or peer influence (Goode, 1999). The first type of theory is the least credible, because scientific research has largely failed to support it. Also, the so-called biological causes could well be the effects of drug abuse. There are ample data to support the other two types of theory, and here we will discuss three specific examples.

Economic Deprivation Theory

After reviewing various studies conducted on drug use since the early 1950s, Elliott Currie (1993) concludes that "the link between drug abuse and deprivation is one of the strongest in 40 years of careful research." More specifically, he writes:

> Forty years of accumulated research, then, confirms that endemic drug abuse is intimately related to conditions of mass social deprivation, economic marginality, and cultural and community breakdown—in Europe as in the United States, in the eighties and nineties as in the sixties, among poor whites and Hispanics as well as inner-city blacks.

Currie further explains *why* poor people turn to drugs in response to poverty-related social conditions. An important first reason is that drugs can fulfill the need for *status*. In the larger, conventional society, the poor are denied legitimate avenues of attaining esteem, a sense of respect, or even a sense of community. As a consequence, there has developed in the poor neighborhood a drug culture that serves as an alternative source of esteem and respect. As one researcher found, "being in the drug culture is just like being a movie star. So many people depend on you, want to stop you in the street. The police is always on you. . . . You are a very important person." A second reason is that drugs can help the user *cope* with the harsh, oppressive realities of poverty. As Currie writes, "Drugs become a way of getting away from daily problems, medicating emotional anguish, relieving stress, escaping pain." A third reason is that drugs can provide a sense of *structure* or *purpose* to shattered lives. In the absence of steady work or stable family life, the poor cannot find the sense of structure that the nonpoor have. As a substitute, drug use helps relieve monotony and purposelessness among the poor. A fourth, unavoidable reason is that the poor communities are *saturated* with illicit drugs. Given the pervasiveness and easy availability of drugs along with the ubiquity of drug users, it is easy to drift passively into drug use without considering its consequences (Currie, 1993).

In short, grinding poverty can force people to use drugs as a way of meeting normal human needs that have been systematically thwarted by society. It is obvious that this kind of theory is useful for explaining drug use among the poor, but it is equally obvious that it cannot explain drug use among the affluent.

Cognitive Association Theory

While economic deprivation theory is intended to explain both drug use and abuse, cognitive association theory is designed to explain drug addiction alone. As Alfred Lindesmith (1968) explains,

> The power of the [drug] habit is derived basically from effects which follow when the drug is removed rather than from any positive effects which its presence in the body produces. Addiction occurs only when [drugs] are used to alleviate withdrawal distress, after this distress had been properly understood. . . . If the

individual fails to conceive of his distress as withdrawal distress brought about by the absence of [the drugs], he does not become addicted, but, if he does, addiction is quickly and permanently established through further use of the drug.

Lindesmith has collected convincing data to support the theory. He found that, among patients who had been given morphine to kill their postsurgery pain, some later became addicted to the drug but others did not. The difference had to do with whether the patients *knew* that their nausea and other symptoms of withdrawal sickness were caused by their suddenly discontinuing the use of morphine. Those who did—in other words, "cognitively associated" the withdrawal distress with their prior use of morphine—ended up addicted to the drug, because they demanded that they be given more morphine. By contrast, patients who experienced the same withdrawal sickness *without* knowing the cause of it did not become addicted. Why not? Because they were assured by their doctor that the discomfort was normal for a patient recovering from surgery and that it would eventually stop by itself. These patients then "toughed it out"—rather than demanding more morphine.

In sum, the cause of addiction is the drug user's *cognitive association* between withdrawal distress and prior drug use. To bolster the theory, Lindesmith further observes that the mentally ill, the mentally challenged, young children, and animals usually are immune to addiction because they cannot understand the meaning of withdrawal symptoms even if it is explained to them. The theory can also explain why people with average intelligence can easily get hooked on drugs once they experience withdrawal distress. However, a deeper reason for addiction, we may argue, is that most people in a modern, hedonistic society want to eliminate distress instantly rather than stoically endure it until it passes.

Social-Psychological Theory

From various studies we can derive a number of sociological and psychological factors that lead people from virtually all walks of life into drug use.

Among the sociological factors, some exert their influence from the higher societal or cultural level, while others more directly affect individuals in their immediate milieu consisting of family, friends, schoolmates, neighbors, coworkers, and others they meet often.

A prime example of societal factors is the legal drug culture of our society. Such psychoactive drugs as alcoholic beverages, tobacco cigarettes, and various sedatives and tranquilizers are pushed on the general public either directly or indirectly. Each year, the alcohol and tobacco industries spend millions of dollars on advertising—coaxing and seducing people to use their drugs. The pharmaceutical industry sends its sales representatives into doctors' offices with free samples of legal uppers and downers, and these "reps" talk the physicians into pushing the drugs on their patients. On the other hand, the general public demands these drugs to help ease their physical aches and pains, their psychological stresses and strains, a sense of social incompetence and awkwardness, or existential emptiness and boredom. Given

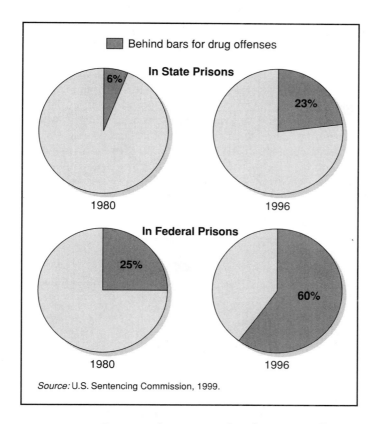

FIGURE 11.2   Increased Incarceration for Drug Offenses

this drug culture, many people become accustomed to using legal drugs, which makes it easy to try illegal ones. This is why many people use illegal drugs only after they have drunk or smoked, and many teenagers use illicit drugs only after they have long seen their parents drink or smoke. If a youngster says, "My parents drink—why can't I smoke grass?" it is difficult for adults to talk down that argument.

The social factors that more immediately sway individuals toward drug use can be drawn from various deviance theories, such as social control, differential association, social learning, structured strain, deviant opportunity, and deviant subculture theories. Their significance has been demonstrated by current research. Since these general theories have been discussed in some detail in Chapters 2 and 3, we will mention here only the variables that have been found most useful for explaining drug use. They are (1) lack of attachment to conventional persons or institutions, such as parents, teachers, clergy, and employers, or family, school, religion, and work, (2) having friends who use drugs, (3) being a member of a drug-using subculture, and (4) easy access to drugs (Kaplan et al., 1986; Marcos, Bahr, and Johnson, 1986; Elliott et al., 1985; Kandel, 1984).

As for the psychological reasons behind drug use, research has found the following factors significant: poor self-concept, low self-esteem, self-rejection; feelings of distress, powerlessness, or hopelessness; being unconventional or rebellious; receptivity to uncertainty, risk taking, or new experience; and expecting drugs to enhance status or mitigate life's problems (Kaplan et al., 1986; Jurich and Polson, 1984). Clinical evidence further suggests that people with a certain type of personal problem tend to prefer one particular drug after experimenting with various substances. They tend to use that preferred drug regularly because it helps relieve their specific problem. For example, those who are restless, aggressive, or given to violent eruptions tend to use heroin regularly because they find that it helps them "feel normal, calm, mellow, soothed, and relaxed." Those who often feel depressed, fatigued, bored, or shy are inclined to choose cocaine because they feel that it helps make them energetic, self-assured, and sociable (Khantzian, 1985).

The War on Drugs

The war on drugs consists of two basic strategies. One is *punitive:* using law enforcement to stop the supply of drugs and punish drug sellers and users. The other is *supportive:* using drug prevention (or education) and treatment to reduce the demand for drugs and help drug addicts. The U.S. government devotes most of its antidrug budget to law enforcement. One result is a sharp increase in the incarceration of drug offenders (see Figure 11.2). Can this emphasis on law enforcement over drug prevention and treatment solve the drug problem? Let us first analyze the punitive strategy by looking at how it has been applied in the past and how it is applied today. Then we will see how reaction to the punitive strategy has sparked a debate over legalizing drugs. Finally, we will examine the application of the supportive strategy to solving drug problems.

Historical Pattern

Historically, the war on drugs has turned out to be a war on powerless groups, particularly minorities.

The first attempt to battle drug use appeared in the form of a city ordinance against opium dens in San Francisco in 1875. The custom of opium smoking had earlier been introduced to this country by Chinese coolies, unskilled laborers who were imported to work on railroad construction crews. At first, their opium dens were tolerated. But soon the Chinese labor pool was seen to present a threat to the white labor market because they were hired and worked long hours for low wages. The white laborers started a campaign against the Chinese and their opium dens. The campaign, effectively led by the president of the American Federation of Labor, conjured "a terrible picture of how the Chinese entice little white boys and girls into becoming 'opium fiends,' [who were] condemned to spend their days in the back of laundry rooms" (Hill, 1973).

Consequently, a number of cities followed San Francisco in passing ordinances against opium dens. The antiopium laws were, in practice, anti-Chinese laws, because they provided "a legal basis for unrestrained and arbitrary police raids and searches of Chinese premises" (Helmer, 1975). In 1909 Congress enacted a law prohibiting the importation of opium for smoking. Then, in 1914, Congress passed the Harrison Narcotic Act outlawing the sale or possession of opium and its derivatives. By this time a socially undesirable class, including prostitutes, thieves, and hoodlums, had been known to use the forbidden drugs and therefore became "dope fiends" in the wake of the new law. In contrast, opiate users of higher social status were largely unaffected by the law since they were able legally to obtain the drugs from their physicians—the Harrison Act did not prohibit opiate use for "legitimate medical purposes."

Around 1900, many state laws and municipal ordinances were also enacted against the use of another drug—cocaine. These anticocaine laws were, in reality, antiblack laws. In those days, cocaine was widely used by blacks, but whites fearfully believed that a cocaine high could spur blacks to violence against whites, stimulate sexual assaults by black men on white women, improve blacks' pistol marksmanship, make blacks invulnerable to bullets, give blacks superhuman strength, and make them cunning and efficient. The anticocaine laws, then, were useful for controlling blacks and keeping them in "their place."

In 1937 Congress passed the Marihuana Tax Act. This antimarijuana law was, in effect, an anti-Hispanic law. The Mexican migrant workers in the West and Southwest had been known to smoke marijuana, and Anglo Americans, holding a strong prejudice against them, had spread rumors that "weed" often led the Mexicans to commit murder, rape, and other horrible crimes. In 1936, for example, a Colorado newspaper editor wrote to the Bureau of Narcotics: "I wish I could show you what a small marijuana cigarette can do to one of our degenerate Spanish-speaking residents. That's why our problem is so great: the greatest percentage of our population is composed of Spanish-speaking persons, most of whom are low mentally, because of social and racial conditions" (Himmelstein, 1983; Musto, 1973).

In the 1950s the social problem of heroin use was blamed on the communists. They were believed to push heroin as part of their conspiracy against the United States. The Narcotic Drug Control Act, enacted in 1956, was indeed very tough on heroin peddlers: It provided the death penalty for the sale of heroin to a person under 18 by one over 18 (Szasz, 1974).

In the 1960s horror stories about the effects of marijuana and other illicit drugs were widely publicized. One such story came in 1968 from Pennsylvania's governor, who subsequently became chairman of President Nixon's Marijuana and Drug Abuse Commission. The governor told the press that six college students stared at the sun while under the influence of LSD and were consequently blinded. Although the story was later exposed as a hoax, the general public had already erupted with fear about LSD and other illicit drugs. Then, many new federal and state laws were enacted to increase the severity of punishment for illicit drug use. All these harsh laws served to punish the youth who dared reject conventional values, scorn the establishment, and protest U.S. involvement in the Vietnam War.

Since the late 1960s, however, large numbers of conventional, middle-class whites have used drugs, particularly marijuana. Professional athletes, movie stars, rock stars, business executives, and other successful, respectable people have turned cocaine into a status drug. Drug use has stopped being associated exclusively with powerless minorities, antiestablishment youths, and social undesirables. Consequently, affluent, respectable drug users, instead of being treated like dangerous criminals, are today more likely to go free or receive light sentences. Nevertheless, racial minorities, particularly African Americans, continue to suffer the brunt of antidrug law enforcement.

Punitive Strategy: Law Enforcement

Compared with their affluent and white counterparts, the poor and minority drug users are more often arrested or imprisoned. In 1989, for example, African Americans constituted only 12 percent of the U.S. population, but they made up 40 percent of all arrests for various drug offenses. In the state of New York in 1988, over 90 percent of the prisoners serving time for drug felonies were African Americans and Hispanics (Currie, 1993). In 1995, 90 percent of those convicted of crack cocaine offenses in federal court were African Americans, who received much longer sentences than well-off white offenders convicted of selling powder cocaine (Isikoff, 1995). All this suggests how today's law enforcement against drugs continues the historical pattern of drug laws against minorities. Today's law enforcement does more than discriminate against African Americans and Hispanics; it worsens their drug problems by siphoning off government funds that could have been used for drug education and treatment programs. Thus, poor black and Hispanic communities continue to have the highest rates of drug addiction and other severe drug problems in U.S. society (Friedman, 1998).

Law enforcement is also aimed at poor foreign countries that produce most of the illicit drugs consumed in the United States. Our government has gone to great lengths in urging these countries to eradicate their narcotic plants. Millions of U.S. dollars have been offered in return for the destruction of the plants, and threats to cut off U.S. aid or oppose international lending have often been made to countries that fail to reduce drug production. Even U.S. soldiers and advisers have been dispatched to Latin American countries to destroy cocaine-producing plants and pursue drug lords. The U.S. Customs Service has also caught many people for trying to smuggle illicit drugs into the United States. In addition, the DEA (Federal Drug Enforcement Agency) and other law-enforcement agencies have often made headline news seizing tons of illicit drugs throughout the country.

Nevertheless, drugs are still easily available on the street, for the most part because as long as the demand for them is great, there are always some countries and many smugglers to supply them (Wren, 1996b).

Debate over Legalizing Drugs

The apparent failure of the law-enforcement approach has led to calls for legalization of drugs. Advocates of legalization contend that, like Prohibition (of alcohol) in the 1920s, current drug laws do more harm than good. They are said to generate many crimes, including homicides. As Milton Friedman (1989) argues, "Addicts are driven to associate with criminals to get the drugs [and] become criminals themselves to finance the habit." The drug laws are also said to encourage official corruption because huge profits from drug sales enable the criminals to bribe police to "look the other way." By legalizing drugs, the proponents argue, the government can take away obscene profits from drug traffickers, end police corruption, and reduce crime drastically. Finally, legalizers believe that with legalization the huge amount of money currently spent on law enforcement can be used for drug treatment and education, which will dramatically reduce drug use and addiction (Friedman, 1998; Carter, 1989).

But most Americans oppose legalization. They fear that, if drugs are legalized, drug use and addiction will skyrocket (Forbes, 1996). As William Bennett (1989), a former national drug policy director, says, "After the repeal of Prohibition, consumption of alcohol soared by 350%." A soaring rate of drug use and addiction, according to another opponent, will hurt the poor and minorities that already suffer the most even more (Rosenthal, 1995). Sociologist Elliott Currie (1993) also argues that legalization cannot solve the problem of widespread drug abuse and crime because the root cause of the problem is poverty, racism, or inequality. Thus, Currie proposes that the government eradicate the cause of the problem by providing employment to all, increasing the minimum wage, expanding the Job Corps, increasing health care for the poor, offering paid family leave, providing affordable housing, and reducing social inequality.

In late 1996 California and Arizona legalized the smoking of marijuana by cancer, AIDS, and other seriously ill patients, but it is doubtful that illicit drugs will soon be legalized for use by the general population. It is not just that the great majority of Americans viscerally oppose legalization (Rosenthal, 1995). They apparently know and appreciate one great achievement of the punitive strategy of antidrug law enforcement: ensuring that heroin, cocaine, and other hard drugs are not as easily available as tobacco cigarettes, alcoholic beverages, and other legal drugs.

Supportive Strategy: Prevention and Treatment

While the U.S. government pays more attention to the punitive strategy, the supportive strategy of preventing drug use via education and treatment for addicts and their drug addiction nonetheless exists. To prevent drug use, school programs, television commercials, and other educational efforts are focused on increasing public awareness of the harmfulness of drugs. Treatment involves hospitals, public-health agencies, and drug-treatment centers in programs for people with drug problems. Let us take a closer look at each of these two types of supportive strategy in the war on drugs.

Drug Prevention.   The most popular program of drug prevention is the Project D.A.R.E. (Drug Abuse Resistance Education). Adopted by more than 60 percent of the U.S. school districts, DARE involves a police officer teaching a drug education class at a local school. The aim of the program is to prevent drug use by teaching students about the perils of drug use and then showing them how to develop social skills, raise self-esteem, resist peer pressure to use drugs, and seek drug-free alternatives, such as tutoring younger children or developing a hobby. According to its administrators and supporters, DARE has, since its establishment in 1982, proven successful in achieving its goal (DeJong, 1986). But researchers have found otherwise: DARE does not significantly prevent drug use, although it does enhance children's self-esteem, polish their social skills, and improve their attitudes toward police (Elliott, 1995).

Nonetheless, parents of most children who have participated in the DARE curriculum seem to agree with its administrators that the program works. They can see that their own children do not use drugs. But they do not realize that, as researchers have generally discovered, DARE works only for children who, like their own, are unlikely to use drugs in the first place. More precisely, then, DARE does prevent drug use by *reinforcing* the existing antidrug attitude that most children have learned from parents. The fact remains that DARE—and other similar programs—does not work for children who are already at risk of using drugs. Who are these children? They are children with the following experiences:

- Family history of alcoholism
- Family history of criminality
- Poor parental child-rearing practices, such as lax supervision and constant criticism
- Parental drug use or permissive attitudes toward drugs
- Early antisocial behavior in school, especially aggressiveness
- Alienation and low commitment to getting an education
- Academic failure in middle to late elementary school education
- Socializing with friends who take drugs (Levine, 1986)

Apparently, drug education alone cannot work for children with these problems unless the family, school, community, and the larger society also work together to deal with the impact of these problems on the children.

Drug Treatment.   Three kinds of treatment exist for drug addicts. The first, *chemical treatment,* may include detoxification and maintenance therapy. *Detoxification* involves the use of a nonnarcotic chemical or a required rest to bring the patient into a drug-free state. Detoxification by itself cannot cure addiction because the craving for drugs remains, but it makes the patient more amenable to psychotherapy or other treatment programs designed to cure addiction.

Maintenance therapy involves a treatment center giving the patient a drug that has almost the same chemical makeup as that of the illicit drug. The substitute drug, such as methadone for heroin addicts, is able to prevent withdrawal distress and can be used regularly as a safe alternative to the street drug or as a supplement to a treatment designed to cure addiction (Massing, 1998).

A second type of drug treatment is *psychological therapy*, including aversion therapy, personal therapy, and group therapy. *Aversion therapy* involves making patients associate their drug of choice with some unpleasant experience. Thus, if drug addicts undergo a program where they are administered an electric shock every time they use their drug of choice, they are likely to stop using the drug. *Personal therapy* involves a psychotherapist helping patients discover and then seek to eliminate the psychological causes of their drug abuse, such as low self-esteem or inability to form sound relationships with others. *Group therapy* involves a group of drug addicts discussing and sharing with each other their lives and personal experiences with drug abuse.

A third type of drug treatment is *therapeutic community*. This involves drug addicts living together like members of a family. Cut off from outside contacts, including family and friends, these addicts support each other, helping each other live a drug-free life. The better-known therapeutic communities are Synanon, Odyssey House, and Phoenix House, but they can even be found in many prisons (Early, 1996).

It is difficult, if not impossible, to determine which of these treatments works better than others because patients in different programs vary in such significant factors as age, ethnicity, employment status, length of drug use, and degree of addiction. Thus, for example, a program that treats with great success patients who are only mildly addicted to drugs *cannot* be said to be more successful than another program that treats with little success patients who are heavily addicted. But many studies suggest that any treatment method can work better if the patients are employed and can earn a good income, receive adequate support from others such as family and friends, or are free from a drug-abuse subculture (Abadinsky, 1993).

Cigarette Smoking

As suggested before, compared with illegal drugs, legal drugs are far more prevalent and, over time, much more dangerous. The use of alcohol is the subject of the next chapter. Here we take a look at the smoking of tobacco cigarettes.

Since 1964, when the U.S. Surgeon General first announced the conclusion of a scientific study that smoking is causally related to lung cancer, there have been many reports about the serious health hazards of smoking. Consequently, laws have required warning labels for cigarettes, restriction of tobacco advertising and promotion, and smoke-free workplaces and public areas. In recent years the government has even forced the tobacco industry to pay more than $500 billion over 25 years ($20 billion annually) for health-care costs, an enormous sum in view of the fact that the tobacco business takes in around $30 billion a year. All these efforts have reduced smoking by about 40 percent over the last 30 years, and now the percentage of smokers in the United States is among the lowest in the world (Cooper, 1998; Sullum, 1998; Pollack, 1997).

Still, too many Americans continue to smoke regularly, making up at least 26 percent of the U.S. population. Worse, since 1990, smoking among teenagers has gone up sharply (see Figure 11.3). Now, for any given month, more than one-third of high school students smoke. Most of these young smokers are very likely to continue smoking in their adult lives, because research has shown that 75 percent of adult smokers started before age 18.

As teenagers, whites are much more likely than blacks to smoke (see Figure 11.3 again). Among adults, however, African Americans are more likely to smoke. Of various racial or ethnic groups, Native Americans have the highest percentage of smokers and Asian Americans the lowest. These racial differences in smoking may have something to do with education. Generally, as many studies have shown, the prevalence of smoking is three times higher among people with less than 12 years of education compared to those with more than 16 years of education (AHA, 1998). Ethnic groups with less education are thus more likely than other groups to smoke. There is also a gender factor in smoking: Within most ethnic groups, there are many more male smokers than female smokers, the exception being that, among white teenagers, females are more likely to smoke (see Figure 11.3).

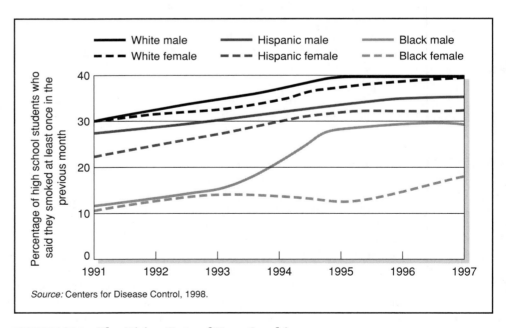

Source: Centers for Disease Control, 1998.

FIGURE 11.3   The Rising Rate of Teen Smoking

Given the terrible health hazards of smoking, why do smokers continue to smoke rather than quit? Are they irrational, or do they fail to appreciate the hazards of smoking? Many smokers have become addicted, so that they cannot quit. But others continue to smoke even if they could quit, because to them the benefits of smoking outweigh the costs. The benefits include releasing tension, feeling relaxed, and enjoying quiet companionship or lively conversation. It is, however, more than these benefits that cause smokers to continue smoking. Smokers are simply much less risk averse than nonsmokers. Contrary to popular belief, smokers are acutely aware of the hazards of smoking. In fact, they tend to greatly overrate the risks of smoking. In one study, for example, smokers placed the risk of lung cancer at 38 percent, while a more realistic risk is lower than 10 percent (Viscusi, 1992).

Whatever benefits smokers claim to enjoy from tobacco use, nonsmokers can still assert their right to be protected from harmful secondhand smoke. But smokers can claim their right to risk their own health by smoking. Faced with this conflict between smokers and nonsmokers, the government has so far tried to bring about a smoke-free society but one in which only smoking in public places is prohibited, not smoking per se.

Summary

1. How can illegal drug use be put in proper perspective? We should recognize that illegal drugs are not as widely used and dangerous as some legal drugs. Societal reaction to drugs varies with time and place. Moreover, illegal drugs are for the most part used moderately rather than uncontrollably.

2. What are the effects of various illegal drugs? As a stimulant, marijuana can produce euphoria, heighten sensitivity, improve perception, and increase appetite. It has even proven beneficial to the very ill. But if used to the point of intoxication, marijuana can impair judgment and memory. It is also addictive, and its users are more likely than nonusers to use hard drugs as well. As a depressant, heroin can soothe pain, anxiety, and tension—as well as produce what the user considers to be euphoria. It is highly addictive. Heroin addicts do not necessarily have their health or careers ruined by the drug, but they may suffer both effects if they are not socially privileged and financially successful. As a stimulant, cocaine sharpens the senses, provides exhilaration, enhances self-confidence, and boosts energy. It is also extremely addictive. Crack, the cheaper and smokable form of cocaine, is even more powerful and addictive. Meth and roofies are newly popular drugs, the former a stimulant and the latter a depressant.

3. What is the extent of drug use in the United States? The United States has the highest rate of drug use in the industrial world, but most of the drug problems are confined to the lower classes. Drug use in U.S. society steadily declined from 1980 until 1992, when it began to rise, largely fueled by young whites smoking pot. **How does U.S. society react to drug use by Americans?**

It usually reacts with moral panic, imagining drug use as a much more serious problem than it is.

4. Why are intravenous drug users very likely to get AIDS? IV drug users are reluctant to take precautions by avoiding the sharing of needles. The reasons for such reluctance include an overwhelming need for immediate drug experience, the user's risk-taking lifestyle, and the bleakness and emptiness of life resulting from grinding poverty. **Does drug use cause crime?** The answer is yes according to drug enslavement theory, but no according to general deviance syndrome theory.

5. What are drug users like? Users of marijuana and powder cocaine are more likely to be relatively affluent, while users of heroin and crack cocaine are more likely to be poor. Users of meth and roofies seem largely working-class and young. **What social and social-psychological characteristics distinguish drug users from nonusers?** Drug users are male and young, have drug-using parents and friends, lack strong ties to social institutions, have majored in non-sciences while in college, and are liberal or unconventional.

6. How does a person become a drug user? There are four stages in the process of becoming an illegal drug user: experimentation, occasional use, regular use, and addiction. A user may go through all these stages until becoming an addict, or may stop at the first, second, or third stage. In Becker's classic study of pot smokers, the smoker characteristically learns three things in a sequential manner: how to get high on the drug, how to recognize the nature of the high, and how to enjoy the high.

7. What causes drug use and addiction? According to Currie's economic deprivation theory, severe poverty causes the victims to use drugs to fulfill their need for status, to cope with the oppressive realities of poverty, and to gain a sense of purpose in their shattered lives, with the easy availability of drugs in their community. Lindesmith's cognitive association theory says that we can become addicted to heroin if we associate our withdrawal distress with our previous use of the drug. Finally, according to social-psychological theory, both sociological and psychological factors are involved in drug use—the former exemplified by the legal drug culture and lack of social control, and the latter by poor self-concept and low self-esteem.

8. What is the nature of the war on drugs? The war on drugs consists of two basic strategies. One is punitive, involving the use of law enforcement to stop the supply of drugs and punish drug sellers and users. Another strategy is supportive, involving the use of drug prevention or education to reduce the demand for drugs and the use of treatment to help drug addicts.

9. What is the nature of smoking? Although smoking can cause serious illnesses, more than one-fourth of Americans smoke regularly, primarily because they believe that the benefits of smoking outweigh the costs.

SUGGESTED READINGS

Coombs, Robert Holman. 1997. *Drug-Impaired Professionals*. Cambridge, Mass.: Harvard University Press. An interview-based analysis of the nature and causes of drug addiction among doctors, lawyers, and other professionals.

Currie, Elliott. 1993. *Reckoning: Drugs, the Cities, and the American Future*. New York: Hill and Wang. An analysis of the worsening drug problems in largely poor minority neighborhoods of large cities across the United States.

Decker, Scott, and Richard Rosenfeld. 1992. "Intravenous drug use and the AIDS epidemic: Findings from a 20-city sample of arrestees." *Crime & Delinquency, 36,* 492–509. Shows how AIDS counseling alone—without drug treatment—largely fails to reduce high-risk drug use.

Early, Kevin E. (Ed.). 1996. *Drug Treatment Behind Bars: Prison-Based Strategies for Change*. Westport, Conn.: Praeger. A collection of articles on the therapeutic communities in U.S. prisons.

Elliott, Delbert S., David Huizinga, and Suzanne S. Ageton. 1985. *Explaining Delinquency and Drug Use*. Beverly Hills, Calif.: Sage. Testing ideas from structured strain, social control, and social learning theories but finding peer influence to have the greatest impact on youth's drug use.

Erickson, Patricia G., and Yuet W. Cheung. 1992. "Drug crime and legal control: Lessons from the Canadian experience." *Contemporary Drug Problems, 19,* 247–277. A study of past prohibitions on alcohol, heroin, cannabis, and cocaine in Canada, which shows the ineffectiveness of excessive reliance on the criminal law for curbing drug use.

Falco, Mathea. 1992. *The Making of a Drug-Free America: Programs That Work*. New York: Times Books. Showcasing effective programs on drug prevention, treatment, and law enforcement.

Goode, Erich. 1993. *Drugs in American Society*. 4th ed. New York: McGraw-Hill. A comprehensive text on the subject, covering drug use in general, many specific drugs such as alcohol, marijuana, and cocaine, and theories of drug use.

Hanson, Bill, George Beschner, James M. Walters, and Elliott Bovelle (Eds.). 1985. *Life with Heroin: Voices from the Inner City*. Lexington, Mass.: Lexington Books. A sensitive probe into the subjective world of poor African-American users of heroin.

Harrison, Lana D. 1992. "International perspectives on the interface of drug use and criminal behavior." *Contemporary Drug Problems, 19,* 181–201. A cross-national analysis of how the drugs–crime connection exists mostly among the lower classes but is weaker in countries with stronger welfare systems.

Harrison, Lana, and Joseph Gfroerer. 1992. "The intersection of drug use and criminal behavior: Results from the national household survey on drug abuse." *Crime & Delinquency, 38,* 422–443. Suggests a strong link between drugs and crime in the United States, though young age, poverty, and minority status are also strongly related to crime.

Massing, Michael. 1998. *The Fix*. New York: Simon & Schuster. An analysis of the U.S. drug problem with practical recommendations for treatment as opposed to law enforcement.

Venturelli, Peter J. 1994. *Drug Use in America: Social, Cultural, and Political Perspectives*. Boston: Jones and Bartlett. An anthology of articles on drug use among the youth, women, and minorities as well as on drug prevention and decriminalization.

CHAPTER

12 Drinking and Alcoholism

On a typical American campus, serious weekend partying begins on Friday. Asked after midnight, "Why do you drink so much?" most students give a succinct answer. "Stress!" says a business major outside a bar. Watched by a bored bouncer, he staggers away. . . . "Stress," whispers a female student as she leans on a wall to avoid falling. Nearby are two bull-necked young men, one wearing a T-shirt with the slogan "Take Me Drunk, I'm Home" and the other's stating, "From Zero to Horny in 2.5 Beers." They lift up the disoriented and giggling young woman by the ankles over a beer keg. Hanging upside down, she seizes its plastic hose and begins to gulp. . . . "Outrageous, awesome, major stress," says a third student outside a club, helping her too-drunk-to-walk friend get into a car. The friend, hair soaked with beer, promptly hangs out the window, hiccuping for a few seconds and then vomiting (Matthews, 1993).

Binge drinking, which is often defined by researchers as consuming five or more drinks at one sitting, is relatively common on U.S. campuses. According to a national survey, about 44 percent of the students binge at least once within a two-week period (Wechsler et al., 1995). Stress is a contributing factor as most binge-drinking students believe, but other factors are also involved (Wechsler et al., 1995; Linsky, Colby, and Straus, 1991). In this chapter we will discuss those factors along with other facets of drinking and alcoholism.

The Extent of Drinking and Alcoholism

Despite the prevalence of binge drinking on the campuses, most Americans do not become alcoholics, who by definition have lost control over drinking and consequently have problems with health, work, or personal relationships. Only about 7 percent of U.S. adults are alcoholics. Fully 60 percent are moderate drinkers, among whom the men consume no more than two drinks a day and the women no more than one drink. And a large minority, one-third of the adult population, are teetotalers, who completely abstain from drinking (Chase, 1996, 1995; Rowe, 1995). Globally, Americans also appear to be moderate drinkers, ranking neither among the heavy-drinking nations nor among the practically dry ones, as Table 12.1 suggests. This pattern of moderate drinking has become more popular since the early 1980s. Since that time, moreover, abstinence has

TABLE 12.1   Alcohol Consumption: A Global View

	Rank in Per Person Consumption		
	Liquor	*Beer*	*Wine*
Russia	1	10	7
France	2	8	1
Japan	3	6	9
U.S.A.	4	4	6
Switzerland	5	5	3
Britain	6	3	5
Australia	7	2	4
Czech Republic	8	1	8
Italy	9	9	2
Mexico	10	7	10

Source: World Drink Trends, 1994; *Newsweek,* January 22, 1996, p. 54.

increased and heavy drinking has declined, chiefly because of rising health consciousness and caution about the hazards of drinking and driving (Chase, 1996).

Still, alcohol is far more widely used than all illegal drugs, and its abuse is the most widespread of all drug abuses. Alcoholism is also one of our nation's biggest health problems, surpassed only by heart disease and cancer, and drunk driving is the number one cause of death among young people (ages 16 to 24). The economic cost of alcohol problems is enormous, as much as $90 billion a year in reduced industrial production, illness, and traffic accidents (Brake, 1994; Heien and Pittman, 1993).

Myths about Alcohol Abuse

Though prevalent and serious, alcohol problems do not seem to shock the general public. If we, as hosts or hostesses, continually invite our guests to have another drink, we are not considered dope pushers at all. Every year beer manufacturers are allowed to encourage drinking at many college campuses. For student functions, these beer pushers, as a university president observed, "contact student groups, offering to provide bands, bandstands, and even hats for the occasion—all with the logo of the particular brand. Their stated effort is to promote brand loyalty among students, but a result also can be to encourage drinking" (Hey, 1986). Most important, the beer and liquor commercials vie with one another in pushing the drug on a massive audience. It is little wonder that only a small minority of Americans see alcohol use and abuse as a serious problem; most would rather consider the use of other drugs—marijuana, cocaine, and heroin—a serious problem. From this lack of public concern about drinking, there have emerged a number of misconceptions about alcohol and its abuse. Although some of the popular beliefs (e.g., "Drinking on an empty stomach can get you drunk fast") are indeed correct, many are false.

One commonly held notion is the myth that most alcoholics, who have long been disparaged as "skid-row bums," are homeless. The fact is that homeless alcoholics constitute only a very small minority—0.4 to 5 percent—of the entire alcoholic population in the United States (Welte and Barnes, 1992). The overwhelming majority of alcoholics are ordinary people who live with their families.

A second, widely believed idea is that mixing different kinds of alcoholic drinks can make a person drunk faster. Actually, it is not the mixture of different drinks, but the total amount of alcohol consumed and the length of time taken to consume it that determine the speed of intoxication.

A third belief held by many people is that drinking black coffee or dousing one's head with cold water can sober one up. In fact, there is no effective method for getting over intoxication other than waiting for the alcohol to leave the body—with the length of the waiting period depending on the percentage of alcohol in the bloodstream.

A fourth popular misconception is that drinking only beer is unlikely to make one an alcoholic. The truth is that beer drinkers are more likely to become alcoholics when compared with drinkers of gin, Scotch, or any other kind of alcoholic beverage. Perhaps because beer is less potent than the other drinks, people tend to drink it for hours on end, and extended, heavy drinking is very likely to lead to alcoholism.

According to a fifth—and seductive—myth, sex becomes more exciting after several drinks. However, since alcohol is a depressant rather than a stimulant of the central nervous system, a drinker may find it more difficult to perform sexually even if he or she feels less inhibited. As Shakespeare writes in *Macbeth*, drinking "provokes the desire, but it takes away the performance." A common problem with heavy drinking for men is loss of erections, particularly among the middle-aged. Also, a drunk man trying to arouse his partner sensitively is like a gorilla trying to play a violin (Hammond and Jorgensen, 1981).

What Alcohol Does to Its Users

Ever since Stone Age people became intoxicated from drinking the liquid oozing from fruit left too long in a warm place, alcohol has been bringing both joy and grief to humankind. Today, for example, most Americans who drink do get a great deal of enjoyment from it, but some end up getting misery from it by becoming alcoholics. Alcohol plays a significant role in holy ceremonies, making people feel religious, but it also has a hand in most cases of murder and aggravated assault. These conflicting effects of alcohol have spawned conflicting ideas in the folk wisdom about alcohol. For example, one Chinese proverb says that "Three glasses of wine can set everything right," yet another states that "Medicine may heal imaginary sickness but wine can never dispel real sorrow." In the Bible we are told that "Wine maketh glad the heart of man," but we are also warned that "Wine is a mocker, strong drink is raging" (Fort, 1973). What exactly does alcohol do to or for its users? Let us take a closer look.

Mental and Physical Impact

Alcohol is a drug since it affects our mental and physical activity. Although it is not a stimulant, alcohol is popularly thought of as one. A stimulant increases the functional activity of the body and mind. But alcohol is a depressant; it belongs to the same class of drugs as anesthetics, sedatives, and narcotics. As a depressant, alcohol reduces our mental and bodily functioning.

> At the sensorimotor level . . . alcohol is an incompetence producer. Its effects on the drinker's equilibrium, for instance, may result in his stumbling, bumping into things, knocking them over, falling down. . . . In addition, things may be dropped or otherwise broken, judgments of time and distance may be thrown askew, tasks may be poorly executed. . . . What is more, we all know that when a person is drunk, these sorts of alcohol-produced failings are both unintentional and beyond the drinker's power to overcome by sheer volition. (MacAndrew and Edgerton, 1969)

Alcohol, then, greatly reduces the drinker's sensorimotor skill—that is, mental and physical functional activity. By itself, however, alcohol does not diminish the drinker's moral competence (Graham et al., 1979; MacAndrew and Edgerton, 1969). It does not, for example, cause people to insult their friends or to make an unwelcome pass at a member of the opposite sex. But the general public believes that alcohol produces moral failings. This popular belief, in the manner of a self-fulfilling prophecy, is so strong that many people in our society do indeed show moral failings after a few drinks. When sober again, they insist that alcohol has made them behave badly, thereby exculpating themselves, with the support of the general public.

Knowing that they will not be condemned for their immoral behavior while drunk, many men in our society often try to get themselves and their women friends drunk. But not all achieve their goal. Some are able to get drunk enough to feel uninhibited; others may get too sick or too drowsy to do or feel anything. This is because one group is more, or less, intoxicated than the other. What is it that determines the different degrees of intoxication? A number of factors:

1. A small-sized person may become intoxicated after drinking only one beer, but a large-sized person may stay sober after three or four. Because alcohol is diluted in the bloodstream, a 100-pound woman cannot tolerate as much liquor as a 200-pound man.

2. The higher the percentage of alcohol in a beverage, the quicker the intoxicating effect. Thus a 90-proof whiskey (containing 45 percent alcohol) is more powerful than a 6-proof beer (containing 3 percent alcohol). Obviously, the greater the amount of alcohol consumed, the more potent the intoxicating effect.

3. Alcohol is not digested as food; it goes through the walls of the stomach and small intestine and is absorbed directly into the bloodstream. So food in the stomach can retard absorption of alcohol and weaken its intoxicating impact; on the other hand, drinking on an empty stomach will result in quick absorption and quicker intoxication.

4. An individual with a higher level of tolerance for alcohol—through more frequent, heavier drinking—will become less intoxicated than one with lower tolerance if both consume the same amount of alcohol.

Health Effects

A small intake of alcohol can be socially, psychologically, and even physically beneficial. Studies have shown, for example, that occasional or moderate drinking helps rural whites alleviate the tension and pressure of their harsh lives. The aged residents of nursing homes who drink alcoholic beverages moderately also enjoy improved sleep, heightened morale, and general well-being. Moreover, moderate drinkers are generally healthier, live longer, or have lower death rates than abstainers. Moderate drinkers are also much less likely than teetotalers to suffer from heart disease (Burros, 1996; Shapiro, 1996; Neff and Husaini, 1985;

Rosenberg et al., 1981). But the fact that a little bit is good does not mean that a lot would be better. The key, encouraging word here is *moderate*, which, as we have mentioned, means having two drinks a day for men and one drink a day for women. If men and women consume more, they are likely to harm their health in various ways.

The most common damage done to the body by immoderate, heavy drinking involves the liver. The constant intake of alcohol, coupled with malnutrition common among problem drinkers, can destroy liver cells and thereby cause fat to accumulate in the liver. The resulting scarred and fatty liver—a condition called *cirrhosis* of the liver—is a major cause of serious illness and premature death in heavy drinkers. Cirrhosis can also lead to sexual impotence. Although at least 60 percent of all cirrhotics who have stopped drinking recover from the disease within five years, their sexual impotence persists (Andreasen and Black, 1991).

Heavy drinking is also likely to cause heart disease and strokes. For one thing, heavy drinkers tend to have clogged blood vessels in the heart and thus suffer from *coronary heart attacks* more often than moderate drinkers. In addition, they are likely to suffer from *cardiomyopathy,* which involves the weakening of the heart muscle, or *hemorrhagic strokes,* which occur when a blood vessel in the brain leaks or ruptures (NIAAA, 1993).

When combined with heavy smoking, heavy drinking further increases the risk of developing cancer of the mouth, throat, and other areas of the body that are frequently assaulted by alcohol. The causal impact of alcohol abuse on these cancers seems more indirect than direct: (1) Alcohol acts as an irritant to the tissues of mouth, throat, and other related organs, thereby making them more vulnerable to *carcinogens* (cancer-causing agents) that invade them. (2) Some alcoholic beverages carry their own carcinogens. (3) Poor diet in the heavy drinker facilitates the work of these carcinogens. And (4) the heavy use of alcohol enhances the cancer-causing impact of smoking (NIAAA, 1993).

Finally, heavy use of alcohol can cause a whole array of other health problems, such as:

■ Alcoholic myopathy, a muscle disease with such symptoms as swelling and severe muscle cramps

■ Impaired memory and ability to learn

■ Premature aging, with neuropsychological performance more characteristic of much older persons

■ Fetal alcohol syndrome, characterized by damage to the fetus's central nervous system, small infant weight and size, and various birth defects (Stark, 1987; Miller, 1986; Bolter and Hannon, 1980; Eckardt, Ryback, and Paulter, 1980)

Social Consequences

Moderate drinking can bring social benefits, such as sociability and hospitality or relaxation and recreation with others (Heath, 1995), but excessive use of alcohol helps bring about a number of negative social consequences. One is a relatively high rate of *automobile accidents,* the leading cause of death among young people in the United States. Over half of each year's automobile deaths and injuries can be traced to excessive drinking. As the National Institute on Alcohol Abuse and Alcoholism has found, "Most people killed in traffic accidents after drinking . . . have very high blood alcohol concentration, averaging twice the level of alcohol considered legally impairing" (NIAAA, 1993). A certain group of young people are especially likely to get involved in auto accidents and deaths. Compared with their peers, they are not just more likely to drink excessively but to use illicit drugs, violate various traffic laws, enjoy taking risks, and exhibit aggressiveness or hostility toward others (Donovan, 1993).

Another consequence is a high rate of *criminal offenses.* Offenses directly related to drinking include public drunkenness, driving while intoxicated, disorderly conduct, vagrancy, and violation of liquor laws. Such offenses result in so many arrests that they put a severe strain on the operation of the criminal justice system. Since 1970 many treatment programs for problem drinkers have helped reduce the number of arrests for alcohol-related offenses, but such offenses still constitute the largest arrest category today (U.S. Census Bureau, 1999). The majority (over 90 percent) of the crimes committed by students on college campuses are also alcohol-related. The perpetrators usually commit multiple crimes, including vandalism, fighting, theft, and alcohol violations. They are more likely than other students to have low grade-point averages, to be athletes, and to drink heavily (Engs and Hanson, 1994; Towson State, 1993).

Heavy drinking further plays a significant part, albeit indirectly, in the commission of more serious, violent crimes, such as homicide, aggravated assault, and forcible rape. As Figure 12.1 indicates, alcohol is implicated in 42 percent of all violent crimes in the United States. Those who commit these crimes seem to use

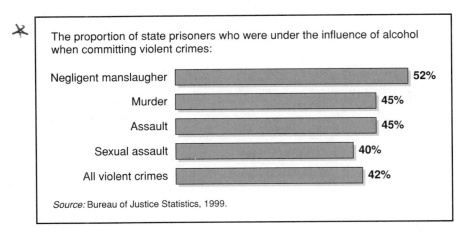

The proportion of state prisoners who were under the influence of alcohol when committing violent crimes:

Negligent manslaugher	52%
Murder	45%
Assault	45%
Sexual assault	40%
All violent crimes	42%

Source: Bureau of Justice Statistics, 1999.

FIGURE 12.1   Alcohol and Violent Crimes

alcohol as an excuse for expressing their aggression. Alcohol can thus become dynamite in the hands of an aggressive person. In one experimental study, subjects with a history of arguments and other aggressive acts were more likely to get involved in interpersonal aggression after they had done some heavy drinking (Boyatzis, 1975).

A Social Profile of Drinkers

Some Americans are more likely than others to use or abuse alcohol. The difference lies in a number of sociocultural factors, such as gender and age, racial and ethnic background, religious affiliation, socioeconomic status, and regional location.

Gender and Age

Drinking is a characteristically male activity. Compared with women, men are not only more likely to drink but also more likely to consume more when they drink and far more likely to get into trouble with drinking. It has been estimated that men are at least four times more likely than women to become alcoholic. But this gender difference has been narrowing over the years, as women have been achieving more equality in various aspects of life. According to many studies, over the last 30 years a significant increase in drinking as well as drinking problems has occurred among college women. The researchers attribute this finding to the women's greater career pressures, their stronger desire for achieving gender equality by behaving like "one of the boys," and declining social stigma about women getting drunk. Nevertheless, men still drink more and have more alcohol problems than women (Rowe, 1995; Gross, 1993; Hanson and Engs, 1992; Perkins, 1992; Engs and Hanson, 1985).

One reason for the gender difference is that drinking and drunkenness are more socially acceptable for males than for females. Another reason is that, as a result of gender-role socialization men are more concerned with their masculinity, such as their need for dominance and emotional control, which is further reinforced by the peer pressure to "drink like a man" (Carey, 1993). Research has indeed shown a strong link between masculine concerns and alcohol use or abuse (Huselid and Cooper, 1992).

Apparently more concerned with their masculinity than older men, young men are more likely to drink and to do so heavily. But the age difference in alcohol consumption among women is not as great as that among men, because women are generally uninterested in being masculine. Younger women, though, are still significantly prone to drink more than older women. This suggests that the age factor can have its own, independent influence on drinking, without being affected by the gender factor (Hanson, 1995; Hunter, Hannon, and Marchi, 1982).

Racial and Ethnic Background

Americans of different races and ethnicities tend to have different rates of alcohol use and abuse. Apparently, the culture of the countries from which their ancestors came continues to influence the drinking pattern of today's Americans.

African Americans.   Compared with whites as a broad group, African Americans are somewhat less likely to drink but significantly more likely to become alcoholics. Moreover, as they get older, African American heavy drinkers are more likely than their white peers to continue drinking heavily (Nielsen, 1999). Thus, as a group, African Americans suffer from a higher rate of alcohol-related diseases, such as alcohol fatty liver, hepatitis, liver cirrhosis, and esophageal cancer (Herd, 1991). This is largely because African Americans have a much higher rate of *poverty*—and many studies have indeed indicated a strong link between poverty and drinking problems. The alcoholism among poor African Americans can be said to reflect a futile attempt to use alcohol "as a mechanism to escape the stresses of poverty, discrimination, and deprivation" (Neff and Husaini, 1985). Poor blacks, some research suggests, are more likely to abuse alcohol because poverty has caused them to have low self-esteem and little racial pride (Harper and Saifnoorian, 1991). By contrast, middle- and upper-class blacks have higher self-esteem and greater racial pride, which enables them to benefit from traditional Afrocentric values of kinship and spirituality that discourage alcohol abuse. Not surprisingly, many studies have found black college students to be much less likely to use and abuse alcohol than even their white peers, let alone poor blacks (Hanson, 1995; Herd, 1991).

Hispanic Americans.   Like African Americans, Hispanic Americans are also more likely than Anglos to drink heavily. This has long been attributed to the Hispanic value of machismo, which emphasizes the importance of masculinity in the form of male dominance, toughness, and honor. But, according to more recent research, machismo does *not* affect heavy drinking among Hispanics: Hispanics who drink heavily show no greater interest in machismo when compared with those who drink in moderation. Ironically, though, machismo affects heavy drinking among Anglos (Neff et al., 1991). Apparently, in Hispanic culture, men are not expected to prove their machismo through heavy drinking but rather through some other means, such as exhibiting physical courage or sexual prowess. The social expectation for men to prove their manhood through heavy drinking appears instead to be a part of the Anglo culture. A more credible explanation for the higher rate of drinking problems among Hispanics is their higher rate of poverty. Generally, more successful Hispanic groups, such as Cubans and Dominicans, are less likely than others, such as Puerto Ricans and Guatemalans, to abuse alcohol (Hanson, 1995).

Native Americans.   Compared with African and Hispanic Americans, Native Americans have more serious problems with alcohol. They suffer from higher rates of such problems as alcoholic cirrhosis, arrests for public drunkenness, and alcohol-related accidental deaths. These problems have been attributed to socio-cultural factors, particularly the fact that the life of Native Americans as a poor minority is filled with stress, while the traditional culture that provides them with a sense of pride and dignity has been diminished or destroyed through long years of colonization by Europeans and other immigrants (Schaefer, 1981). However, it is doubtful that the same alcohol problems plague all of the Native American tribes, who, after all, number over 300. While Native Americans as a group have more drinking problems than other Americans, some tribes do have few problems and others have many. Generally, tribes with "an individualistic hunting-gathering tradition" have a higher incidence of alcohol abuse than tribes with "an agricultural tradition stressing communal values and ceremonies" (Hanson, 1995).

Irish Americans.   Irish Americans have one of the highest rates of alcoholism in U.S. society. A major reason can be traced to the traditional Irish culture, which accepts heavy drinking as normal and treats the drunk as a lovable person:

> [In Ireland] drunkenness . . . is laughable, pleasurable, somewhat exciting, a punctuation of dull routine to be watched and applauded, and drunken men are handled with care and affection. The drunkard is handled with maternal affection, often referred to as "the poor boy," with a special connotation of sympathy, love, pity, and sorrow. If married, the drunkard is compassionately classed by his wife with "the min, God help us!" The man who is drunk is sometimes regarded with envy by the man who is sober (Bales, 1962).

Italian and Chinese Americans.   Americans of Italian or Chinese ancestry have one of the lowest rates of alcoholism, although they often drink. This is largely because Italian Americans usually drink with meals, do not encourage solitary drinking as a means of drowning sorrows, and have strong sanctions against drunkenness. Similarly, Chinese Americans drink a lot but are relatively free from alcoholism. Like the Italians, the Chinese usually drink with meals, particularly on such special occasions as family ceremonies (births, weddings, rites for the dead) and national and religious celebrations. The Chinese do not think of drunken behavior as funny or comical. They look at it with contempt because they believe that drunkenness can seriously disrupt interpersonal relationships and that only moderate, controlled drinking is a social lubricant (Hanson, 1995).

Religious Affiliation

American Jews start drinking at a very young age, but they have one of the lowest rates of alcohol problems. This has been the case for many years and is still true today. The reason has long been assumed to be the culture of Orthodox Judaism—more specifically, the fact that Jews use wine only for religious rituals and consider it sacrilegious to use the alcohol to get drunk. But sociologist Barry

Glassner (1991) finds that Orthodox Judaism cannot fully explain the persistent low rate of drinking problems among Jews. Many Jews today are no longer very religious; instead, they are nominal, nonpracticing, or inactive Jews, who do not go to the synagogue or keep kosher. Instead, there are four factors that reinforce each other in protecting Jews against alcoholism.

One is the widespread belief among Jews that excessive drinking is a non-Jewish characteristic, while *moderate drinking* is a *Jewish trait.* Jews often use the Yiddish expression *shikker vie a goy* (drunk as a Gentile) and feel that it is not Jewish to get drunk. A second factor that protects Jews against alcoholism is the practice of *moderate drinking since childhood.* They have as children had many opportunities to learn to associate drinking with special positive events, such as religious services, weddings, or dinners. On such occasions, controlled drinking is expected, and excessive drinking is condemned. A third factor is the support for moderate drinking and disapproval of excessive drinking that Jews receive from *their peers.* This kind of peer support and pressure is effective in insulating Jews from alcohol abuse because most of their friends are Jewish. A fourth factor is the Jews' *conscious attempts to avoid excessive drinking* even under social pressures—from non-Jews—to do otherwise. If they are encouraged by non-Jews to drink more than they wish, Jews will often simply say no or will take a few sips rather than gulp down the whole drink (Glassner, 1991).

Conservative Protestants such as Pentecostals and Southern Baptists prohibit the use of alcohol by the faithful. Thus, they have the largest proportion of nondrinkers and the lowest proportion of heavy drinkers when compared with Catholics and liberal Protestants. But if they drink, conservative Protestants are more likely to end up being problem drinkers. One explanation is that conservative Protestants, having been brought up in a religion that preaches total abstinence from liquor, have not learned how to drink in moderation. Another explanation is that the drinking problem of conservative Protestants who drink is merely a part of their overall pattern of deviation from their religious training. Thus, whatever causes their larger pattern of deviance, such as broken homes or joblessness, also causes their alcohol abuse (Orcutt, 1991).

Socioeconomic Status

Proportionately more people of the higher socioeconomic levels drink when compared with those of the lower levels. Yet there are more problem drinkers and alcoholics from the lower classes. There may be two explanations for this paradoxical finding. One is that drinkers of different classes use alcohol for different purposes. Drinkers of higher social classes seem more likely to use alcohol as a facilitator of social interaction, but lower-class drinkers tend more to drink as a way of trying to solve personal problems. This may explain why, when drinking, lower-class persons drink significantly more and faster than higher-class persons (Hunter, Hannon, and Marchi, 1982). It is apparent that a large consumption of alcohol can make the lower-class drinkers lose self-control, which in turn makes it harder to solve problems. They may in consequence keep drinking to attempt to achieve a goal that gets progressively harder to achieve the more they drink. Another explanation is that there may in fact be no real difference in alcoholism between the higher and lower classes. Lower-class people may only *appear* more prone to alcoholism because they are not as successful as the higher classes in hiding problem drinking.

The first explanation appears more convincing because the lower classes do have a greater number of distressful life experiences that are associated with drinking problems. Such experiences include family breakdown (marital violence, separation, or divorce) and job loss. Research has consistently found that people with these kinds of experiences suffer from higher rates of alcoholism than those without (Catalano et al., 1993).

Regional Location

Alcohol consumption is highest in the Northeast and West, lowest in the South, and intermediate in the Midwest (see the first column in Table 12.2). The states that have higher rates of alcohol use are generally more urbanized, which suggests that cities and suburbs have proportionately more drinkers than rural areas and small towns. One explanation for the greater consumption of alcohol in more urbanized regions attributes it to the greater stresses and strains of their urban life. Another explanation is that regions with higher rates of alcohol use probably have more favorable attitudes toward alcohol, less legal restrictions, and weaker traditions of temperance or prohibition against alcohol.

While the South has the lowest level of alcohol consumption, it has the highest rate of drunkenness, as indicated by the second column in Table 12.2. In fact, compared with other regions, the South has higher rates of alcoholism and alcohol-related fights, accidents, and problems with work, the police, spouses, and friends (Hilton, 1991). In other words, Southerners are less likely than others to drink, but if they do drink, they are more likely to become problem drinkers.

TABLE 12.2 Region and Drinking

Region	Current Users*	Drunk Every Week**
Northeast	54.1%	3.9%
West	54.2%	6.9%
Midwest	48.6%	3.8%
South	44.9%	8.7%

*Who have used alcohol at least once in the past month.

**Male drinkers who are drunk every week.

Source: Statistical Abstract of the United States, 1995, p. 143; Walter B. Clark and Michael E. Hilton (Eds.), *Alcohol in America* (Albany, N.Y.: State University of New York Press, 1991), p. 267

This apparent contradiction between less alcohol consumption and more problem drinking in the South should not be surprising. It is analogous to what we have observed in regard to the religiously conservative and the lower class, who are less likely than others to drink but, if drinking, are more likely to abuse alcohol. The reasons given earlier are (1) the failure to learn moderate drinking in the case of the religiously conservative and (2) the use of alcohol as a futile attempt to solve personal problems in the case of the lower class. What about the reason for the higher rate of drinking problems in the South? The reason is having a higher proportion of religiously conservative and lower-class people than other regions.

What Is Alcoholism?

There is no universally accepted definition of alcoholism. The most popular definition was offered by the World Health Organization in 1952: "Alcoholics are those excessive drinkers whose dependence upon alcohol has attained such a degree that it shows . . . an interference with their bodily and mental health, their interpersonal relations, and their smooth social and economic functioning (Cahalan, 1970). This elaborate definition can be boiled down to a shorter sentence like the one offered more recently by psychiatrist Donald Goodwin (1991): "Alcoholism involves a compulsion to drink, causing damage to self and others." Thus alcoholics can be identified on the basis of certain problems that they have as a result of drinking. But those just given in the two definitions are too broad, not specific enough. In a 1991 report from the National Institute on Alcohol Abuse and Alcoholism (NIAAA), specific problems are presented in the form of 33 statements, of which ten are presented here:

1. I have often taken a drink the first thing when I get up in the morning.

2. I deliberately tried to cut down or quit drinking but was unable to do so.

3. Once I started drinking it was difficult for me to stop before I became completely intoxicated.

4. I have had a quick drink when no one was looking.

5. I have skipped a number of regular meals while drinking.

6. I have awakened the next day not being able to remember some of the things I had done while drinking.

7. I have lost a job, or nearly lost one, because of my drinking.

8. My drinking contributed to getting hurt in an accident (in a car or elsewhere).

9. A physician suggested I cut down on drinking.

10. I have stayed away from work or gone to work late because of a hangover.

According to NIAAA, if a person says yes to at least one of those statements, that person may be identified as an alcoholic. But there is no certainty that a person having any one of these problems is necessarily an alcoholic. Consider the implication of statement 10. Many college students have occasionally stayed away from class because of a hangover from having drunk too much at a party the night before, but they are not necessarily alcoholics, because such experience has occurred only once or twice rather than repeatedly. It is safe to say, however, that the more of the listed problems people have, the more likely they are alcoholics. The problems can be classified into four types (Schuckit, 1984):

1. *Excessive drinking* over an extended period.

2. *Psychological addiction,* an irresistible craving for alcohol.

3. *Physical addiction,* experiencing physical discomfort when drinking stops.

4. *Alcohol-related problems,* such as divorce, car accident, or inability to work because of uncontrolled drinking.

Once a person is identified as an alcoholic, social scientists may still disagree on how to label the alcoholic's problem. Some label it *alcoholism* because they consider it a disease, but others call it *problem drinking* because they see it as a behavior. Still others simply regard alcoholism as chronic drinking, more serious than problem drinking. For our purposes, we use interchangeably various labels, including not only alcoholism and problem drinking but also abusive drinking, uncontrolled drinking, and alcohol abuse. But no matter what label we use, it is intended to mean having those four problems.

Becoming an Alcoholic

When people take a drink for the first time in their lives, they do not immediately, nor inevitably, become alcoholics (Hasin, Grant, and Endicott, 1990). They usually go through a sequence of events that may culminate in being totally dependent on alcohol. That sequence, according to E. M. Jellinek (1952) the influential pioneer in the study of alcoholism, consists of four stages.

Social Drinker

In the first, prealcoholic stage, prospective alcoholics *begin as social drinkers.* Through drinking, they discover their ability to experience some relief from tensions (Orcutt, 1993). But the more they drink, the less their tolerance for tensions; the less their tolerance for tensions, the more they want to drink to seek relief. This results in a vicious circle of more and more episodes of drunkenness and hangover. At the same time, the more individuals drink, the greater their tolerance for alcohol, so that they have to consume more and more alcohol to get drunk. These experiences increase the psychological and physiological impact of alcohol on the drinker. But people in this stage can still control their drinking so that they can continue to function normally in their occupational and social world.

Psychologically Addicted

In this second stage, social drinkers begin to show signs of abusing alcohol if they start to experience blackouts. A *blackout* is an attack of amnesia or memory loss, but it is quite different from passing out. When people drink beyond their alcohol-tolerance level, they may pass out on the spot, totally incapable of interacting with others. On the other hand, individuals experiencing blackouts may be the life of the party, or at least talk with others and move about freely; but the next day they cannot remember what they did.

By now they have become *psychologically addicted* to alcohol, having a strong craving for the drug. The craving is so great that they will drink a lot, drink alone, and drink in the morning. Such excessive drinking begins to hurt their relations with relatives, friends, and fellow workers, and they may feel guilty about drinking too much. Still, they feel they could not help having the strong attraction to alcohol. But they still can stop abusing alcohol if they are determined to do so.

Physically Addicted

In this third stage, the drinkers become *physically addicted* in the sense of having chills, shakes, and other withdrawal distresses when not drinking. By now they could not stop drinking even if they wanted to, because they have lost control over drinking. Therefore, once they start drinking, they tend to keep doing so until the supply is gone or they are too drunk to continue. Although they cannot control their drinking, they typically insist that they can stop if they really want to. To prove that they can, they will go on the wagon for a while or change their drinking patterns—switching types of liquor, trying different ways of mixing it, and altering speeds of consuming it.

But the more these drinkers think they can control their drinking—and the more they try to control it—the more they lose control. Consequently, they begin to invent excuses and rationalizations for drinking. They may, for example, blame their spouses or bosses for causing so much tension that they need to drink for relief. The drinking can break up their relations to bosses, friends, and family. This makes them become even more attached to liquor, and, as a result, they often skip meals in favor of liquor. They are nonetheless still capable of being gregarious and sociable (Morey, Skinner, and Blashfield, 1984).

Hitting Bottom

In this last stage, the alcoholic becomes isolated and withdrawn from others. They now *hit bottom* with total dependence on alcohol, exhibiting spectacular, bizarre behavior. A typical example is drinking and being intoxicated continuously for several days without doing anything else. They are haunted by the tremendous fear that alcohol may be taken away from them. They must have a drink just to be able to get up in the morning. They may be so far gone that to get liquor into their mouths becomes an almost impossible task to perform. But they usually work very hard at it—spending hours stumbling, crawling, vomiting, trembling, and failing to achieve the goal three or four times before finally succeeding in keeping a drink down. Since they rarely eat, they often suffer from malnutrition. They also suffer from delirium tremens, which can produce terrifying hallucinations—such as seeing millions of little flies chasing, suffocating, or eating them.

Unique Drinking Problems

Female alcoholism and college binge drinking appear unique in different ways. The medical profession routinely diagnoses men with alcoholism if they show symptoms of the problem but tends to dismiss women with the same symptoms as merely having a problem with their "nerves." Binge drinking in college is also unusual: Since 1981 this problem has continued to be prevalent while the number of *nondrinking* college students has increased significantly (Celis, 1995).

Female Alcoholism

Perhaps because they are generally expected not to drink as heavily as men do, women tend not to be diagnosed as alcoholics, even when they are known to drink like a fish. "I used to carry a big purse full of beer into my psychiatrist's office and drink right through the sessions," recalled a woman about her past alcoholism. "He never said a word to me about it. As I look back, I think I was probably challenging him to say something, to help me. But he never dealt with it." Unable or unwilling to see alcoholism as the source of their female patients' distraught states, doctors often diagnose the problem as merely "nerves," anxiety, depression, or some other emotional ailment, and proceed to prescribe tranquilizers, antidepressants, and other psychoactive drugs, which they are far less likely to do for male patients. It is little wonder that women alcoholics are twice as likely as their male counterparts to be addicted to other drugs besides alcohol (Sandmeier, 1992, 1980).

The medical profession probably should not be faulted for their lack of knowledge about female alcoholics because most researchers in the field have long studied only male alcoholics. Nevertheless, the few studies that have been done on female alcoholics show them to be different in some ways from their male counterparts. First, women are more likely to have a family history of alcoholism. Second, women have their first drink and first intoxication at an older age. Third, women are more likely to experience a stressful event, such as physical or sexual abuse, traumatic loss of loved ones, or loneliness, that precipitates alcoholic drinking. Fourth, women often drink abusively after their husband or boyfriend has become a heavy drinker, but men rarely join their wives or girlfriends in becoming abusive drinkers. And fifth, women drink more at home, while men drink more in bars or some other public places (Lisansky, 1991).

College Binge Drinking

In 1981 about 25 percent of college students reported abstaining even from an occasional beer within a one-year period, but today the figure has nearly doubled to 47 percent (Celis, 1995). But the proportion of students engaging in binge drinking remains about the same as it was in 1981. Apparently, the nationwide effort to raise the legal drinking age to 21 in the late 1980s has not discouraged binge drinking among many students under that age. Today, about 44 percent of the students (50 percent of the men and 39 percent of the women) binge at least once within a two-week period. In addition, there seems to be a relentless quality to the pursuit of intoxication, as suggested by many students seeking to binge and get drunk rather than simply drinking in moderation (see Figure 12.2). College students are also much more likely than nonstudents to engage in binge drinking and to drink with the intention to get drunk (Celis, 1994).

What lies behind this binge drinking? The stress from having to work hard for good grades is one contributing factor (Linsky, Colby, and Straus, 1991). But the social pressure to get drunk so as to fit in and not to be seen by others as "uptight" or antisocial is an even more important factor. This may explain why residents of a fraternity or sorority and students who regard parties as a very important part of college life are considerably more likely than others to engage in binge drinking. Along with these three characteristics (the feeling of stress, residing in a fraternity or sorority, and adoption of a party-centered lifestyle), the

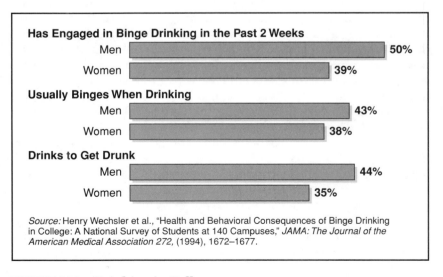

Source: Henry Wechsler et al., "Health and Behavioral Consequences of Binge Drinking in College: A National Survey of Students at 140 Campuses," *JAMA: The Journal of the American Medical Association 272*, (1994), 1672–1677.

FIGURE 12.2 Drinking in College

following have been found to be associated with binge drinking (Goldberg, 1998; Wechsler et al., 1995):

- Being male
- Being white
- Having parents with a college degree
- Majoring in business
- Engaging in risky behaviors, such as smoking pot or cigarettes
- Being involved in athletics
- Having indulged in binge drinking as high school seniors

What Causes Alcoholism?

Researchers from various academic disciplines have offered different theories about the development of alcoholism. Medical scientists and psychiatrists believe that some people are genetically vulnerable to alcoholism. Psychologists attribute alcoholism to certain personality traits collectively called the alcoholic personality. And sociologists ascribe alcoholism to a unique set of environmental factors. Let us take a close look at each theory.

A Biological Predisposition

Some medical scientists have long assumed that alcoholism originates from various physical problems such as nutritional deficiencies, glandular disorders, and malfunctions of the central nervous system. Each of these physical factors is thought to cause a strong craving for alcohol, which then leads to alcoholism. But the medical scientists have been criticized for confusing effect with cause. The physical problems that the medical scientists assume are the causes of alcoholism may well be the effects of alcoholism. In other words, the prolonged, frequent, and heavy consumption of alcoholic beverages is very likely to damage the alcoholic's health, bringing on those physical problems.

Medical and psychiatric researchers have also argued that alcoholism is genetically determined. To support this argument, they point to studies showing, for example, that identical twins have higher concordance rates for alcoholism than fraternal twins. (That is, if an identical twin is alcoholic, the chances of the other identical twin becoming alcoholic are relatively high, but if a fraternal twin is alcoholic, the chances of the other fraternal twin becoming alcoholic are significantly lower.) Since identical twins are more genetically alike than fraternal twins, it is assumed that the cause of alcoholism is genetic.

In the early 1990s, some medical researchers purportedly discovered the so-called *A1 gene*, which is supposed to make people vulnerable to alcoholism. The A1 gene was found to deprive its carrier of the feeling of pleasure. Therefore, according to the researchers, people born with this defective gene are driven to constantly use alcohol—or some other drug—as a means of seeking the pleasure that genetically normal people can enjoy without excessive drinking. In analyzing the blood of 159 people, the researchers found the A1 gene in 50 percent of the alcoholics they studied, compared with only 21 percent of nonalcoholics (Noble et al., 1991; Parsian et al., 1991).

Another kind of evidence is also used to support the genetic theory of alcoholism. According to many studies, a majority (two-thirds to three-fourths) of Chinese and Japanese have a "flushing response" to alcohol. After they drink a small amount of alcohol (fewer than one or two beers), their faces and upper body parts will blush, to be accompanied by a sensation of warmth, nausea, and general discomfort. Because of this physiological reaction, apparently genetic in origin, many Asians cannot tolerate heavy drinking and therefore are unlikely to become alcoholics. By contrast, Caucasians, particularly white males, do not have this response. As a consequence, they are more able to literally hold their liquor—capable of guzzling a large quantity of alcohol without getting drunk. Given their greater tolerance for alcohol, they are more likely to become alcoholics (Nakawatase et al., 1993; Goodwin, 1991).

All this suggests that the biological factor may contribute to the development of alcoholism. But there is no direct evidence that the biological factor causes alcoholism. The biological factor can, at best, only serve as a predisposition to drink excessively, but whether people with that predisposition will actually become alcoholics depends on social and psychological factors (Bower, 1992).

The Alcoholic Personality

Many psychologists attribute alcoholism to one or more negative personality traits. These traits include being antisocial, rebellious, egocentric, gregarious, hyperactive, passive-dependent, depressed, anxious, and hostile. Alcoholics are also assumed to have weak ego, poor self-concept, low frustration tolerance, and neurotic guilt. Such personality deficits have supposedly been found in alcoholics (Donovan, 1986). There is no consensus among the personality researchers as to how many of those traits make up what they call the *alcoholic personality*. To some, only one trait—especially being *antisocial*—reflects the alcoholic personality; to others, many more constitute the alcoholic personality. Another problem with the personality theories is that the traits are often contradictory, such as being hyperactive versus depressed or being hostile versus gregarious. A third problem is that most of the personality researchers focus on adults who have become alcoholics rather than using the prospective, longitudinal method of examining children and then reexamining them when they become adults. As a result, the effects of alcoholism are often confused with the causes. There is evidence that chronic drinking causes rather than results from impulsivity, low self-esteem, anxiety, or depression (Vaillant, 1995; Vaillant and Milofsky, 1982).

Other psychologists consider the need for *dependency* to be the key factor in the development of alcoholism. According to William McCord and Joan McCord (1960), for example, the alcoholic's need for dependency stems largely from a stressful and erratic home environment where the mother often comforts the child with loving indulgence but also often terrifies the child with outright rejection. These conflicting childhood experiences are said to intensify the individual's need for love—the need for dependence on others. But this heightened need is not easy to satisfy, so that the individual becomes overwhelmed with *anxiety,* which in turn leads the person to use alcohol in order to get rid of the anxiety. But David McClelland and his colleagues (1972) contend that the need for *power,* rather than the need for dependency, is the driving force behind alcoholism. As McClelland says, "Societies and individuals with accentuated needs for personalized power are more likely to drink more heavily in order to get the feeling of strength they need so much more than others."

While McClelland regards the concern for power as the cause of alcoholism, the McCords do not necessarily disagree. This is because the McCords acknowledge the power desire as the other, *conscious* aspect of the same alcoholic personality that is characterized by the *unconscious* need for dependency. In these psychoanalytic terms, heavy drinking can be said to provide an appearance of toughness to make the alcoholic feel consciously like a powerful person, which in turn suppresses (i.e., keeps unconscious) the alcoholic's anxiety as a dependent person. In effect, heavy drinking simultaneously fulfills both the conscious need for power and the unconscious need for dependency. It is difficult, however, to demonstrate empirically the concept of the unconscious.

Social and Cultural Forces

In sociology there are two major explanations for alcoholism. One is a strictly sociological theory, useful for explaining why some *groups* have higher alcoholism rates than others. The other theory is social-psychological, explaining why some *individuals* become alcoholics but others do not.

Explaining Individual Differences.   According to a classic social-psychological theory in sociology, the unique factor that turns individuals into alcoholics is the fit between vulnerable personality traits on the one hand, and certain drinking-group values and activities on the other (Trice, 1966). This fit will come about under the following four conditions:

1. People must have the qualifications to be a candidate for alcoholism, namely, the vulnerable personality features. These personality features are the same as some of those identified by psychologists as the traits of the alcoholic personality. As Harrison Trice (1966) says, "A potential alcoholic has intense dependency needs and sharp feelings of worthlessness, self-hate, and inadequacy, which produce an unusual need to be looked upon by others and by himself as a 'man.'" Such dependent individuals have deep anxiety about their own adequacy, which makes them highly susceptible to the influence of drinking groups.

2. Once they join drinking groups, they find that they fit right in. Members of drinking groups characteristically believe that drinking is a sign of masculine prowess. They are fond of encouraging a new member to "drink like a man," and praising him for being able to "hold his liquor." This is what the prospective male alcoholic badly needs because of his "unusual need to be looked upon by others and by himself as a 'man.'"

3. After drinking and enjoying his status as "a man" for some time, the individual finds it necessary to consume more and more liquor to prove his manhood. He reaches the point where he becomes an excessive drinker who has lost self-control. It is at this point that his drinking groups stop rewarding him for his alcohol consumption and start rejecting him as a loser. This is because the same social value that encourages a person to drink like a man also emphasizes the importance of self-control—presumably another aspect of the same masculine character.

4. After being ostracized by the drinking groups that initially encouraged the use of alcohol, the abusive, uncontrolled drinkers seek out more tolerant drinking companions, namely, other abusive, uncontrolled drinkers. In such company, the abusive drinkers encourage each other to drink more and more, until finally they are securely locked into alcoholism.

In short, psychologically vulnerable individuals and their drinking peers come together to generate a force that gradually causes the individuals to become alcoholics.

Explaining Group Differences.   According to another classic sociological theory, three factors work together to create a high rate of alcoholism: (1) the production of acute inner tensions in people by their culture, (2) a culturally induced attitude toward drinking as a means of relieving those inner tensions, and (3) the failure of the culture to provide suitable substitute means for resolving the inner tensions (Bales, 1946).

To take the first factor, *culturally produced inner tensions* include feelings of anxiety, guilt, conflict, suppressed hostility, and sexual frustration. To show the way in which a culture can bring about these inner tensions in its members, Bales presented the case of Irish peasants, noted for their drunkenness during the past several centuries. Irish parents instilled fear, insecurity, and anxiety in their children by disciplining them with the threat of "bogey men," "spooks," and "fairies," and by smothering them with affection at one moment and beating them in a fit of anger at the next. The boys often had to stay on the farm, continuing to work for their father until he retired or died. "So long as they stayed on the farm," Bales observed, "they had to work for him as 'boys' and were treated as boys, even though they might be 45 or 50 years old." This created a huge reservoir of suppressed hostility against the father. Kept under the father's thumb as "boys," these physically mature men could neither marry nor dally in premarital sexual escapades. Such a situation generated powerful sexual tensions.

Acute inner tensions can become a powerful motivating force for compulsive drinking if *the culture has induced in people the attitude that liquor is excellent for relieving the tensions and many other problems,* the second factor. The Irish farmers are said to have such a culture. When going to fairs to buy or sell livestock, they treat each other with a few drinks in order to "soften the other guy up," so that they typically come home in a heavy state of intoxication. But their wives usually treat them with care and affection; their mothers lovingly call them "my poor boy"; and their friends, acquaintances, and others regard their intoxication with envy instead of pity. The Irish also consider alcohol an effective folk remedy for "keeping the cold out of the stomach," curing stomachache, combating insomnia, increasing the feeling of physical and sexual strength, and even getting rid of hangovers. With this attitude, the Irish find it natural to resort to drinking as a means of drowning their personal problems as well. The result is their relatively high rate of alcoholism.

In coping with a culturally induced stress, people will turn to alcohol if they *cannot find another method of resolving the stress,* the third factor. For Jews and Italians, eating seems to be the method of dealing with tension. Many Muslims are said to turn to hashish as well as strong tea and coffee. The Brahmins in India and Japanese are believed to rely on opium. As a result of their having culturally approved alternatives to the use of alcohol for resolving tension, these groups have low rates of alcoholism. But the Irish, being without an alternative to drinking, have a higher rate of alcoholism.

Of the three types of theories, the sociological theories appear the most satisfactory. As psychologists McCord and McCord (1960) wrote, "Sociologists have produced impressive evidence demonstrating that rates of alcoholism are significantly related to the social factors." But we should not overgeneralize. People who are psychologically vulnerable and exposed by peers to heavy drinking do not necessarily become alcoholics, nor do the majority of the Irish indulge in excessive drinking. What the sociological theories suggest is that people with those social and cultural experiences are more likely than others to become alcoholics.

Controlling Alcohol Use and Abuse

Like illegal drug use, alcohol use or abuse has been subjected to various attempts to control it, but has proven to be a persistent aspect of American life.

Legal Measures

One way to control alcohol use involves the coercive power of the law. Let us see how this has been carried out in the past and present.

The Past. In colonial days, the Puritans enjoyed drinking beer and rum in moderation. They condemned only excessive drinking. Then, in the early nineteenth century, there arose a crusade for total abstinence. This crusade, often called the temperance movement, eventually culminated in the enactment of the Eighteenth Amendment (popularly known as "Prohibition") in 1919. During the next 14 years, drunkenness did not disappear from the face of America. On the contrary, Prohibition turned out to be such a disastrous failure that it was repealed by the Twenty-first Amendment in 1933 (Gusfield, 1991; Wilkinson, 1970).

In some ways similar to the efforts past and present at outlawing psychoactive drugs discussed in the preceding chapter, Prohibition originated chiefly from an attempt to control the powerless segments of society. In postcolonial America, the temperance movement first emerged as an attempt on the part of the aristocracy of wealth to control the new upsurge of democracy among the masses, who happened to engage in some drinking. Later the emergent, dominant middle classes (independent farmers, small-business owners, and self-employed professionals) used the temperance movement to stir up prejudice and discrimination against Irish and German immigrants, Catholics and Jews, and the urban lower classes. The middle classes felt that their puritanical values of hard work were threatened by the "ne'er-do-well, unambitious, and irreligious" immigrants and poor Americans who traditionally drank. But by the time Prohibition came into effect, a new, more powerful group (salaried professionals, white-collar workers, and managerial employees) had begun to emerge from within the middle class. Unlike the old middle class, who advocated total abstinence from drinking, the new one supported moderate use of alcohol, which contributed to the demise of Prohibition. Since then, moderate drinking, as opposed to total abstinence, has continued to be the norm of not just the middle class but of most Americans as well (Gusfield, 1991).

The Present. The Clinton administration wanted to discourage alcohol abuse by imposing a "sin tax" on hard liquor, though not on beer or wine. The increased tax on liquor is designed to help pay some of the enormous, multibillion-dollar expenses for treating diseases caused by heavy drinking. This seems to be a sensible measure against alcohol abuse, a far cry from the total prohibition of alcohol in the past. But the liquor lobby was so powerful that Clinton changed his mind (Cohn and Hager, 1993).

However, a crusade against teenage drinking and drunk driving has been quite successful. Since 1982 many organizations such as MADD (Mothers Against Drunk Driving) and SADD (Students Against Drunk Driving) have effectively aroused public outrage at drunk driving for causing many traffic deaths. They have succeeded in pressuring legislators to be tougher in dealing with drunk drivers. But their biggest achievement has come from lobbying the federal and state governments to raise the minimum drinking age to 21, and by the late 1980s virtually all the states had. Crusaders against drunk driving have often argued that the higher drinking age can save many lives. Indeed, most research has proven the crusaders correct: The number of alcohol-related car crashes, along with teenage drinking per se, has declined significantly since the early 1980s (O'Malley and Wagenaar, 1991). There is a limit to what the law can accomplish, though.

For example, the incidence of alcohol-related deaths on the roads rose in 1995, and this rise has been attributed to a decline in media coverage of drunk driving (Wald, 1996). The drinking age law has also helped create a phenomenon called *frontloading,* in which underage young people drink alcoholic beverages in private before attending a social event where proof of legal age is required for drinking (Gorman, 1994; Hughes and Dodder, 1992).

Therapeutic Approaches

While the law against drunk driving or underage drinking treats alcohol users and abusers as offenders, the therapeutic way of dealing with drinking problems is based on the assumption that abusive drinkers are patients who need help.

Detox and Treatment Centers. In the early 1970s the popular belief in alcoholism as a disease led to the enactment of laws in over 20 states that treat alcohol abusers as patients rather than criminals. In those states today violators of the public drunkenness law are no longer thrown into jail. They are instead taken to public detoxification centers for treatment and then, if necessary, sent to halfway houses or aftercare facilities where they are helped to stay "on the wagon." Unfortunately, many who have come out of detox centers or halfway houses will go back in again. In fact, research has shown that "detox doors revolve much faster than jail doors." The major reason is that many patients refuse to see themselves as alcoholics and to follow the center's rules for making a recovery (such as attending meetings or talking about drinking problems), two major conditions that have been proven essential for recovering from alcoholism (Rubington, 1991).

For other alcoholics, who do not violate the public drunkenness law, there are numerous community-based alcohol treatment centers throughout the country. These centers provide mostly outpatient services, offering hospitalization only as a last resort. Services include primarily psychological counseling and therapy because the centers are most often operated under the guidance of psychiatrists and psychologists. Much of the psychological treatment involves the use of aversion therapy or a combination of this with group therapy. Group therapy brings together a number of alcoholics (and, in many cases, their spouses and children) and tries to guide them back to sobriety through a series of sessions that include lectures, educational films, and discussions about drinking problems. Aversion therapy calls for the use of electric shock or nausea-inducing drugs designed to condition the alcoholic to feel sick at the very odor of liquor. Generally, this aversion therapy is effective only for a short time—the urge to drink returns within 6 to 12 months. The combination of this therapy with group treatment is more effective. However, most centers are underutilized, so that the enormity of alcohol abuse in the society as a whole remains largely untouched (Roman and Blum, 1991). A more popular—and effective—method does not involve any professional therapist, but simply alcoholics and ex-alcoholics themselves. It is the AA (Alcoholics Anonymous) method.

Alcoholics Anonymous.   Founded in 1935, AA is today the largest and most successful organization for helping alcoholics (Weisner, 1995). The only requirement for joining AA is the desire to stop drinking. Once having joined the organization, new members may choose another AA member as a sponsor. Sponsors are recovering alcoholics ready to come to a new member's aid whenever needed. The treatment involves attending a series of meetings where any number of alcoholics share their drinking histories. These meetings may be held in offices, schools, churches, lodges, or private homes, and they are open to alcoholics and nonalcoholics alike. At a typical meeting, a volunteer "leader" will begin by saying something like "Hello, I'm John, and I'm an alcoholic." He or she may then introduce some AA members who will discuss their experiences with alcohol as well as their recovery from the drinking problem. Afterward, others may follow suit, relating their own experiences. A crucial part of these sessions is that one admit to oneself and other AA members that one is an alcoholic and is powerless over alcohol.

This program is widely considered the most successful method ever devised for coping with alcoholism. Not surprisingly, it has spawned similar organizations such as Al-Anon (for spouses and other close relatives and friends of alcoholics) and Alateen (for alcoholics' teenage children). Their aim is to help members understand alcoholism and themselves, as well as learn how to live with and help their alcoholic relatives. Apparently, the effectiveness of the AA method is due in great measure to the *group support* provided to alcoholics by people who have deep, personal understanding of drinking problems. Group support is particularly important for alcoholics because they are typically "escape drinkers" (who drink alone in a futile attempt to solve personal problems) rather than social drinkers (who participate in drinking with other people for dietary, religious, or social reasons as the Italians, Jews, Chinese, or higher-status people characteristically do). Research has suggested that AA offers what those alcoholics have always sought before they started to drink heavily, namely, social acceptance, a more positive identity, and feelings of normalcy and confidence, the benefits of group support (Hurlburt, Gade, and Fuqua, 1984). AA can provide those benefits because it has effectively become its members' family. As a member said at an AA meeting,

> I lost everything. Family, home, wives, kids, job, everything. Even my parents turned against me. . . . I finally found you people. Now you're my family. Wherever I go, you're there. . . . You give me everything I ever wanted and ever looked for. I feel like I'm needed again. (Denzin, 1991)

Can Alcoholics Learn to Drink Moderately?   AA assumes that alcoholism is an incurable disease. This is why AA often pronounces "once an alcoholic, always an alcoholic." Since they are not expected to fully recover, even members who have remained sober for years are always considered to be, and are called, recovering— *not* recovered—alcoholics. To continue staying sober, AA insists, recovering alcoholics must completely stay on the wagon. Even taking a small sip of wine, AA believes, will cause recovering alcoholics to relapse into uncontrolled drinking because they still have the disease. Therefore, to AA, alcoholics can never learn to drink moderately, and to talk about moderate drinking can only give alcoholics an excuse to keep on drinking.

But an increasing number of researchers argue that alcoholism is not a disease over which the problem drinker has no control. It is, instead, an unhealthy behavior pattern that can be changed by learning to engage in controlled, moderate drinking. According to moderation theorists, studies in the United States have shown that many alcoholics can learn to drink moderately without suffering a relapse, and studies in many European countries have also demonstrated the ability of alcoholics to learn to drink in moderation without relapsing into uncontrolled drinking (Rotgers, 1996; Sobell and Sobell, 1993; Institute of Medicine, 1990). We should note, however, that most of these alcoholics may well be merely "problem drinkers" who have not developed a severe addiction to alcohol. But for "hard-core alcoholics," who have long been severely addicted to the drug, AA's insistence on abstinence may still be the safer way of dealing with the addiction (Marriott, 1995).

Summary

1. **What is the extent of drinking and alcoholism in the United States?** Most Americans drink, but only moderately, while a large minority (one-third) abstain from drinking and a small minority (7 percent) suffer from alcoholism.

2. **What are some popular myths about alcohol use?** They are as follows: alcoholics are mostly homeless; mixing different kinds of drinks accelerates intoxication; drinking black coffee or pouring cold water on the head can get rid of drunkenness; drinking only beer cannot make one an alcoholic; and sex becomes more exciting after several drinks.

3. **What are the effects of alcohol?** Alcohol is a depressant drug, and as such, it reduces the drinker's mental and physical ability but not moral competence. How much the mental and physical ability declines depends on the level of intoxication—the percentage of alcohol in the bloodstream. The latter, in turn, depends on such factors as the body size and weight of the drinker, the type and amount of alcoholic beverages consumed, the quantity of food in the stomach, and the drinker's level of tolerance for alcohol. Taken in moderate amounts, alcohol can provide some health and social benefits. But heavy drinking is likely to damage the liver, bring about sexual impotence, and cause heart disease, strokes, cancer, and other health problems. Alcohol abuse further contributes to a number of social problems such as automobile injuries and deaths and criminal offenses.

4. **Who is more likely than others to use or abuse alcohol?** Those who are more likely to drink are males, young adults, liberal Protestants and Catholics, higher-status persons, and residents of the Northeast and West. But those who

are more likely to end up as alcoholics are lower-status persons, and African, Hispanic, Irish and Native Americans.

5. What is alcoholism? It involves drinking excessively, being psychologically and physically addicted, and experiencing alcohol-related problems. **How does a person become an alcoholic?** The person first begins as a social drinker, then becomes psychologically and physically addicted, and finally hits bottom with total dependence on alcohol. **In what ways are female alcoholism and college binge drinking unique?** The medical profession tends to brush aside female alcoholism as a minor problem even though it is as serious as male alcoholism, and college binge drinking continues to be as prevalent as before even while abstinence has increased on the campus.

6. What causes alcoholism? According to the biological theory, alcoholism is brought on by some problem inside the body such as a nutritional deficiency, a defective gene, or a lack of flushing response. Psychologists attribute alcoholism to the alcoholic personality, which includes being antisocial, the need for being dependent on others, and the need for power. According to one classic sociological theory, alcoholism develops from a social situation in which psychologically vulnerable individuals are pressured by drinking companions to drink heavily. According to another sociological theory, a culture causes alcoholism by producing acute inner tensions in people, encouraging people to view drinking as useful for relieving tensions, and failing to provide suitable substitutes for alcohol in reducing stress.

7. How has U.S. society tried to control alcohol abuse? By legal and therapeutic methods. The law prohibiting the sale of alcohol in the 1920s and early 1930s failed to eradicate drunkenness, and the prohibition reflected an attempt to control the powerless segments of society. The Clinton administration has planned to discourage alcohol abuse but to no avail. Still, the crusade against teenage drinking and drunk driving since the early 1980s has produced positive results. Therapeutic approaches have also been used to control alcohol abuse. They include treating public drunkenness as a disease rather than a crime, providing treatment at community centers, and offering social support through groups organized by alcoholics themselves, of which the largest and most successful is Alcoholics Anonymous. AA insists that alcoholics must completely abstain from drinking, but a growing number of researchers find that alcoholics (more precisely, problem drinkers) can learn to drink in moderation.

SUGGESTED READINGS

Catalano, Ralph et al. 1993. "Job loss and alcohol abuse: A test using data from the epidemiologic catchment area project." *Journal of Health and Social Behavior, 34* (September), 215–225. Alcohol abuse is found to be more common among those who have been laid off than among those who have not.

Clark, Walter B, and Michael E. Hilton (Eds.). 1991. *Alcohol: Drinking Practices and Problems.* Albany, N.Y.: State University of New York Press. A collection of articles presenting the results of several survey studies on alcohol use and abuse in the United States.

Denzin, Norman K. 1993. *The Alcoholic Society: Addiction and Recovery of the Self.* New Brunswick, N.J.: Transaction Publishers. Analyzing the various scholarly views on alcoholism and the experiences of drinking as well as recovering from alcoholism.

Heath, Dwight B. (Ed.). 1995. *International Handbook on Alcohol and Culture.* Westport, Conn.: Greenwood. A collection of articles on the drinking norms and practices of 27 countries.

Martin, Jack K., Paul M. Roman, and Terry C. Blum. 1996. "Job stress, drinking networks, and social support at work: A comprehensive model of employees' problem drinking behaviors." *Sociological Quarterly, 37,* 579–599. A study of how stressful working conditions, drinking networks, and social support at work influence problem drinking among employees.

Orcutt, James D. 1993. "Happy hour and social lubrication: Evidence on mood-setting rituals of drinking time." *Journal of Drug Issues, 23,* 389–407. This study indicates a reduction in stress among college students when they engage in social drinking during weekday evenings.

Perkins, H. Wesley. 1992. "Gender patterns in consequences of collegiate alcohol abuse: A 10-year study of trends in an undergraduate population." *Journal of Studies on Alcohol, 53,* 458–462. The data show that college men continue to have many more alcohol abuse and alcohol-related problems than college women.

Pittman, David J., and Helene Raskin White (Eds.). 1991. *Society, Culture, and Drinking Patterns Reexamined.* New Brunswick, N.J.: Rutgers Center of Alcohol Studies. A large collection of articles presenting the social scientific views on various aspects of alcohol use and abuse.

Roman, Paul M. (Ed.). 1991. *Alcohol: The Development of Sociological Perspectives on Use and Abuse.* New Brunswick, N.J.: Rutgers Center of Alcohol Studies. A set of essays on the contributions made by sociologists to the understanding of drinking and alcoholism.

Sayette, Michael A., et al. 1993. "Alcohol and aggression: A social information processing analysis." *Journal of Studies on Alcohol, 54,* 399–407. Alcohol use is found to be associated with aggressive responses to provocation.

13 White-Collar and Governmental Deviance

On a sunny day in November 1991, Walter Krug, age 37, was cruising along in his 1988 Chevy pickup truck on a highway near Stanton, Texas. Suddenly another pickup blew a tire, went out of control, veered into Krug's lane and hit him from the side. The violent impact ruptured the gas tank of Krug's vehicle, shooting out fuel that exploded in a huge fireball. Unable to extricate himself, Krug was burned to death. "He would have survived the crash," Krug's family lawyer said, "if not for the fire. But there shouldn't have been a fire." Threatened with a lawsuit, the pickup's manufacturer, General Motors, settled out of court. Krug was one of more than 300 people killed since 1973 in collisions involving exploding gas tanks in similar pickups manufactured by GM. According to GM documents released in November 1992, the automaker had known since 1983 that the fuel tanks could be made much less vulnerable to side-impact collision. But the company's executives had never tried to do anything about it. By 1992, they even refused to recall some 5 million dangerous GM pickups after more than 300 motorists had been killed. This was worse than the havoc wreaked by the Ford Pinto, the 1970-era compact car with a similarly flawed gas-tank design that led 27 drivers to their fiery deaths (Margolick, 1993; McCarroll, 1992).

The auto company has, through its executives, perpetrated *white-collar crime* (or, more broadly, *white-collar deviance*), an offense committed by a white-collar person. Most white-collar deviance can be divided into *corporate deviance*, committed by an organization like GM through its executives or managers, and *occupational deviance,* carried out by an individual as part of an occupation. In this chapter we will take a closer look at the definition of white-collar deviance, the characteristics of corporate and occupational deviance, and the uniqueness of white-collar deviance. We will also analyze various facets of *governmental deviance,* which is white-collar deviance committed in government or politics. Finally, we will try to explain why some people get involved in white-collar and governmental deviance.

What Is White-Collar Deviance?

When sociologist Edwin Sutherland first introduced the concept of white-collar crime in 1939, he defined it as an offense committed by "the upper, white-collar class, which is composed of respectable, or at least respected, business and professional men." Ten years later Sutherland (1949) tried to flesh out the concept:

> White-collar crime may be defined approximately as a crime committed by a person of respectability and high social status in the course of his occupation. Consequently, it excludes many crimes of the upper class, such as most of their cases of murder, adultery, and intoxication, since these are not customarily a part of their occupational procedures.

In this classic definition, two things characterize white-collar crime: (1) It is *occupationally* related, carried out during the course of the offender's occupation, and the occupation involved is *white-collar* as opposed to blue-collar. (2) The economic deviant is a relatively *respectable, high-status* person. By "high-status persons," Sutherland referred to people ranging from business managers and executives to "wage-earning class, which wears good clothes at work, such as clerks in stores" (Sutherland, 1983).

What distinguishes the commission of white-collar crime from the commission of blue-collar or street crime is more than the act itself. It also involves *how* the act is executed. Thus, white collars are more likely to commit an offense with skill, with sophistication, or, most important, with the resources of power, influence, or respectability for avoiding detection, prosecution, or conviction. If blue collars try to commit the same act, they usually do not—and, perhaps, cannot—

do it in the same way as white collars. This is why blue collars are far more likely to be arrested, prosecuted, or convicted if they commit the same crimes as white collars (Shapiro, 1990).

While talking about high-status people engaging in economic deviance, Sutherland also had in mind *corporations* participating in similar deviant activities. The concept of corporate deviance was crucial for understanding the sociological nature of white-collar deviance in general. See how Sutherland used the examples of corporate deviants to show what he thought was the absurdity of explaining deviance in psychological terms:

> We have no reason to think that General Motors has an inferiority complex or that the Aluminum Company of America has a frustration-aggression complex or that U.S. Steel has an Oedipus complex, or that the Armour Company has a death wish or that the DuPonts desire to return to the womb. (Sutherland, 1956)

Therefore, for our purposes, white-collar deviance includes both occupational and corporate deviance. It may be noteworthy that we broaden the concept of white-collar *crime* by replacing it with "white-collar *deviance.*" This is because what sociologists have traditionally called white-collar crime includes not just criminal offenses but civil and other noncriminal offenses. (A civil offense is legally not a crime because it involves violating a civil rather than a criminal law.) We use the term *white-collar deviance* to refer to both criminal and noncriminal forms of economic deviance carried out by high-status people as part of their occupation for personal gain (hence *occupational deviance*) or on behalf of their corporation (hence *corporate deviance*).

Corporate Deviance

Corporate deviance can be divided into four major types: deviance against employees, deviance against customers, deviance against the government, and deviance against the environment.

Deviance against Employees

For many years corporations have been expected to ensure that their employees remain free from known hazards in the work environment. This expectation was finally turned into a law in 1970, and a federal agency, known as OSHA (Occupational Safety and Health Administration), was established to enforce the law. But many workers today are still exposed to various kinds of pollutants in the work environment, for example, coal dust, cotton dust, and radiation. Although these substances have been found to cause cancer, leukemia, and other serious illnesses, corporations tend to ignore or deny the problem rather than take corrective action, such as eliminating the exposures to make their plants safer (Frank, 1993).

Sociologists David Ermann and Richard Lundman (1996, 1982) have suggested three reasons for corporations' tendency to be negligent about their employees' health and safety. The most obvious and important reason is corporate concern with *profit maximization.* Corporate executives are inclined to ignore health hazards in their plants because elimination of these hazards will eat into their companies' profits.

A second reason for the negligence about workers' safety is the nature of *corporate structure.* One of the major characteristics of corporations is that executives are rewarded for seeking short-term success only. Thus, in determining whether to ignore or eliminate health hazards, corporate executives tend to focus on how great a profit they will derive from a certain decision in a few months or years rather than in 10 or 20 years. It is no wonder that they usually decide against spending what appears, at the moment, to be a large amount of money to improve their employees' working conditions. They simply fail to consider the long-term consequences of such a decision, such as facing the high cost of numerous lawsuits filed against them by their many disabled employees. Another important characteristic of corporate structure is that it motivates executives to judge employees' worth impersonally, focusing only on their contribution to production. As a result, employees tend to be treated as if they were machines—and as machines, they are easily replaceable. If some workers become disabled or die, others can be found easily and quickly to take their place. Such a callous attitude toward employees can understandably lead corporate executives to disregard employee health and safety.

A third reason for corporate deviance against employees is *the government's reluctance to take action against offending corporations.* OSHA often avoids using threats or penalties to deter offenses; instead, negotiation and persuasion are routinely employed to obtain compliance. In cases where citations and fines are used as a last resort, the companies are allowed to have their penalties reduced if they correct their "deficiencies." In addition to this weak enforcement policy, the government has cut back on OSHA enforcement personnel. Moreover, many states prohibit injured employees from suing their employers unless they are able to prove that the injury was intentional. In other words, employers cannot be sued for negligence (Frank, 1993).

Deviance against Customers

There are many different forms of corporate deviance against customers. The most common ones involve dangerous foods, unsafe products, frauds, deceptive advertising, and antitrust violations.

Dangerous Foods. The food industry has been known to seek greater profits by selling adulterated or contaminated foods. Meat-packing companies often sell their products without being certain that the meat is safe for human consumption. That's why health experts advise consumers to make sure that their hamburgers are cooked fully. Many people took this advice to heart in 1993 when nearly 400 people were stricken with *E. coli,* a dangerous colon bacterium, after eating hamburgers at Jack in the Box restaurants. Four children later died from the bacterial infection. According to U.S. Agriculture Department and state health officials, the bacteria could have been killed if Jack in the Box had cooked the hamburgers to a higher temperature (155 degrees instead of 140). But the problem originated in the slaughterhouse where the meat had been contaminated with feces (McDowell, 1996).

Foods can also be adulterated. Hormel Company, for example, has once taken stale meat returned by its retail-store customers and then "reconditioned," repackaged, and resold it for a higher profit to other stores—without the legally required reinspection by the U.S. Department of Agriculture officer in charge. As a researcher found, "Spareribs returned for sliminess, discoloration, and stickiness were rejuvenated through curing and smoking, renamed Windsor Loins, and sold in ghetto stores for more than fresh pork chops" (Wellford, 1972).

In fact, it is customary for the food industry to use all kinds of chemical additives in its products, many of which have been suspected by government scientists to cause cancer and other diseases. The apparent purpose is not only to keep the foods from spoiling, but to make them look fresh and appealing as well as to give them the right taste and aroma. Sodium nitrites and nitrates, for example, are added to keep meat products looking blood-red. However, the real purpose behind all this is the pursuit of the big buck. As one food marketer says, "The profit margin on food additives is fantastically good, much better than the profit margins on basic, traditional foods" (Simon, 1996).

Unsafe Products.   The profit motive also underlies the manufacturing and selling of unsafe products by car, drug, tobacco, and other industries. Tobacco companies, for example, have long known that smoking causes cancer and is addictive, but they continue to make and sell cigarettes (Noah, 1997). Dealing in unsafe products also appears frequently in the pharmaceutical industry. Drug companies are often found committing such product-safety offenses as the sale of impure, overstrength, out-of-date, or nonsterile products. The far more serious offense of fraudulent safety-testing of drugs has also been uncovered many times. Experimental rats and monkeys that had developed terrible symptoms like tumors and blindness in drug trials were replaced by healthy animals. Dead animals were "resurrected" in lab reports—rats that had died from using a new drug reappeared later in the data as alive (Braithwaite, 1993). Falsification of clinical data such as these has set drug companies afoul of the law. In 1990, for example, Bolar's high-blood-pressure drug, Generic Dyazide, was recalled because it was found defective and the company was fined $10 million for having forged documents in seeking FDA approval (Gorman, 1992). (FDA is the federal government's Food and Drug Administration.)

More prevalent than presenting grossly phony data to the FDA is the profit-driven tendency to withhold data from the FDA about a drug's negative side effects. Consequently, many potentially dangerous drugs get FDA approval, and the consumers are, in effect, used as guinea pigs. After using the drugs at their own expense, sometimes for a lengthy period of time, consumers will know whether the medical products are dangerous. Of course, by the time they discover the danger, it is too late. They have already suffered and sometimes died. When this happens, the general public is bound to be greatly scandalized. One of the drug scandals of the 1990s involves Dow Corning's silicone-gel breast implants. In 1992 some customers complained that the implants leaked, ruptured, or caused autoimmune disorders. The FDA was forced to investigate, and found from the company's internal documents that the manufacturer of the breast implants knew about the problems way back in the mid-1970s (Pontell and Calavita, 1993).

Frauds. Fraudulent practices can be found in various industries such as banking, insurance, real estate, and securities. They are all extremely lucrative, largely made possible by inadequate government control. Let us take a closer look at the nature of bank and insurance frauds.

One of the greatest bank frauds in recent U.S. history involves a number of savings and loan (S&L or thrift) institutions in the 1980s, which cost taxpayers an astounding $1.4 trillion. In a span of only five years, from 1987 through 1992, a staggering 95,045 criminal charges were filed against S&L officials. The suspected frauds can be divided into three types: (1) illegal nonbanking activities—violating banking laws by engaging in unsafe practices, such as concentrating investment in one high-risk area, say, construction loans, without having conducted any marketability study; (2) collective embezzlement—using ownership of an S&L to steal depositors' money, which has prompted a California state official to say, "The best way to rob a bank is to own one"; and (3) covering up—falsifying records to make the institutions look normal or financially healthy. A major cause of all these frauds was the dismantling of "most of the regulatory infrastructure that had kept the thrift industry together for decades" (Pontell and Calavita, 1993; also see Truell and Gurwin, 1992).

Fraud is also a big problem in the insurance industry. Insolvencies among insurance companies have more than tripled in the last ten years, and at least 30 percent—and perhaps as much as 50 percent—of these failures were the result of insiders' fraudulent activities. Government regulation is even more inadequate in the insurance industry. There are federal agencies policing banks, savings and loans, securities, and commodities, but there is none for the insurance industry. There are state agencies for regulating insurance, but they are mostly inefficient. They are typically underfunded and understaffed; New Mexico, for example, has only five staff regulators to monitor 1600 insurance companies. The most common insurance frauds include phony assets and small-business scams. In the phony assets scheme, an insurance company lies about its assets to show that it has the sufficient amount required by law. In small-business scams, a firm administers an MEWA ("Multiple Employer Welfare Arrangement," whereby several small employers combine their money to insure health coverage for their workers) and simply steals the money until it cannot pay any claims (Headden and Witkin, 1993).

Deceptive Advertising. Closely similar to fraud is deceptive advertising. Most advertising is mere puffery, an exaggerated claim for a product. Examples follow (Simon, 1996):

> "Nestle makes the very best chocolate"
>
> "GM—always a step ahead"
>
> "Wheaties, Breakfast of Champions"
>
> "Every kid in America loves Jell-O brand gelatin"
>
> "Seagram's, America's Number One Gin"

Although these claims are false, they are legal.

But another form of false advertising is illegal because it involves products with more serious consequences for the consumer, as the following case illustrates (Simon, 1996):

> The Federal Trade Commission ruled that Anacin had falsely advertised its product by claiming that it: (1) relieved nervousness, tension, stress, fatigue, and depression; (2) was stronger than aspirin; (3) brought relief within twenty-two seconds; (4) was highly recommended over aspirin by doctors; and (5) was more effective for relieving pain than any other analgesic available without prescription.

For such an illegal act, however, the company is not subject to punishment as a common criminal. The offender is merely required to sign a document stating an agreement to stop the illegal activity. Obviously, the intent of the law here is not to punish the offender, but to stop the illegal action and prevent further damage (Coleman, 1994).

Antitrust Violations. Antitrust laws prohibit companies from conspiring to reduce or eliminate competition. If there is little or no competition, prices will go up and consumers will have no choice but to pay them. To violate the antitrust laws, companies selling the same kind of products usually get together to fix prices that are abnormally high. Sometimes corporations prevent new competition from entering the market, as can be illustrated by the two largest credit-card companies, Visa and MasterCard, barring banks from issuing American Express and Discover cards (Frank and Wilke, 1997). Antitrust violations consequently can produce enormous profits. Although profit is an obvious prod to antitrust violations, at least three subtle forces may be at work also: (1) a history of cooperation among corporations; (2) an oligopolistic market, dominated by only a few companies, which makes cooperation easy; and (3) lack of public awareness of antitrust violations (Ermann and Lundman, 1996, 1982).

These three elements of antitrust violations can be found in the baby-food industry. Virtually every U.S. family with an infant has bought baby formula, a commercial concoction of milk and vitamins. A few parents may complain about the high price of baby formula, but most do not know that the high price stems largely from antitrust violations. These violations involve three formula companies that, with a long-standing cozy relationship, have dominated the formula industry. Their antitrust violations started in 1980 when the largest of the three companies, Abbott Laboratories, conspired with the other two to prevent a new competitor, Nestle, from entering the formula market in the United States. More specifically, Abbott persuaded its two rivals to agree to a formula-industry code of business practice that prohibits, among other things, consumer advertising. This has hampered Nestle's ability to sell its formula because it relied heavily on advertising. Abbott and the other two giant companies did not have to advertise because they depended on hospitals and doctors to market their products. Since they have dominated the market, they have been able to keep the price of their formulas very high (Jamieson, 1994; Burton, 1993b).

Deviance against the Government

Most corporate deviance against the government involves tax evasion. But tax evasion by corporations is not always illegal. Because of their pervasive and powerful political influence, large corporations can legally evade taxes through tax breaks provided by legislation and through tax loopholes made possible by the complexity of tax laws. This is why, according to a Congressional study, the top 148 corporations paid less than half of the official tax rate on profits and 10 percent of these corporations paid no taxes at all (Sloan, 1997; Coleman, 1994).

But taking advantage of the loopholes may go too far and become illegal. Consider, for example, the law that exempts from taxation the profit made by U.S. companies located abroad. To take advantage of this loophole, many giant American companies make themselves multinational corporations by setting up subsidiaries in foreign countries that have very low corporate tax rates and then make it appear that most of their profits are earned abroad. Suppose an item is produced in the United States at a cost of $100 and is sold to an Irish subsidiary for $100. Because there is no profit from this transaction, no U.S. tax is paid. But then the subsidiary resells the item for $200, earning a $100 profit. The company pays only a 4 percent tax ($4) in Ireland, thereby evading the 48 percent tax in the United States. With the Irish subsidiary, then, the American company evades a lot of taxes by making it appear that most of its profits come from the foreign subsidiary (Martz, 1991).

In committing deviance against the government, corporations do not evade payment of taxes alone. They also give huge sums of campaign donations to both political parties to influence legislation toward favoring their business interests (Sabato and Simpson, 1996; Hunt, 1995). Moreover, in today's global economy, giant U.S. corporations may even bribe foreign governments or engage in some other activities abroad that are forbidden by U.S. law. An example is Baxter International Inc., the world's largest hospital-supply company, which in 1993 pleaded guilty to a felony charge of violating the U.S. law that prohibits cooperating with the Arab boycott of Israel. Since 1985 Baxter had tried to enter the vast, lucrative market of the Arab world. Arab boycott authorities would not cooperate unless Baxter first ceased its business in Israel, which Baxter finally did (Burton, 1993a). Most of the illegal activities engaged in by U.S. companies involve giving bribes worth millions of dollars to foreign officials. Still, compared with their European and Asian counterparts, U.S. corporations are much less likely to use payoffs to do business abroad, an extremely common practice in global economy (Milbank and Brauchli, 1995).

Deviance against the Environment

Most corporations in one way or another dump their wastes onto the land and into the air and water, primarily because they find it too costly to develop ecologically safer alternatives or antipollution devices. They are also unwilling to clean up the mess or to assume liability for the health of citizens affected by it, because to do so would cut into their profits. According to the U.S. Congress, corporations in the petrochemical, metals, electrical, and transportation industries are the more severe polluters of the environment (Barnett, 1993).

Environmental pollution affects practically all of us in some way. As Ralph Nader (1970) said, "The efflux from motor vehicles, plants, and incineration of sulfur oxides, hydrocarbons, carbon monoxide, oxides of nitrogen, particulates, and many more contaminants amounts to compulsory consumption of violence by most Americans. There is no full escape from such violent ingestions, for breathing is required." According to one EPA (Environmental Protection Agency) study, residents in poor or minority neighborhoods suffer significantly more than others. This is because landfills, garbage incinerators, toxic dump sites, and environmentally hazardous plants tend to be located near the homes of the poor and minorities (Suro, 1993).

The federal government has, since the early 1970s, tried to combat environmental pollution but with little success throughout the decade. Then, in 1980, Congress passed a law called the Comprehensive Environmental Response Compensation and Liability Act, popularly referred to as the Superfund program, intended to clean up some of the worst uncontrolled hazardous waste sites in the nation. In the early 1980s the Superfund program got off to a shaky start because the EPA was "soft" on environmental offenses. Many corporations that polluted the environment were left alone, and the few guilty ones were given every opportunity to negotiate cleanup settlements with the EPA. However, toward the late 1980s, the EPA aggressively began to enforce the Superfund law against guilty corporations. Today, these corporations are under a great deal of EPA pressure to pay for the cleanup. The industry and its insurance companies, though, have been advocating that all the cleanup costs be paid for through taxation. They argue that the general public should help pay for the cleanup because it has enjoyed many products of the industry, having in effect benefited from the production that created hazardous wastes (Barnett, 1993). Given today's widespread opposition to higher taxes, it is doubtful that the general public would like the idea of shelling out more money. Besides, many hold the corporations rather than themselves responsible for industrial waste.

Occupational Deviance

Compared with the offenses committed by corporations, those perpetrated by individual white-collar employees for their own gain are usually less costly to the victims. But they still cost considerably more than the common crimes committed by the lower classes. There are many different forms of deviant activities in white-collar occupations, but we will analyze only the most common and costly ones.

Employee Theft

Theft by employees from the companies where they work is extremely common and costly. In the 1990s, it accounts for at least 2 percent of sales, costing an estimated $120 billion a year (Buss, 1993). Both businesses and consumers suffer. Because of employee theft, more than a thousand businesses go under every year, and the remaining, nonetheless successful businesses pass the cost of employee theft to consumers by raising prices. According to various expert estimates, about 30 percent of U.S. employees plan to steal from their employer, another 30 percent are basically good employees but may occasionally succumb to the temptation, and 40 percent are basically honest (Buss, 1993). As one sociological study concluded, employee theft "is undoubtedly the most pervasive and costly form of property deviance of any kind in the United States" (Douglas and Waksler, 1982).

Most employee thieves are middle class. They are "predominantly solid, respectable citizens who pay taxes, root for major league stars, believe in the 'American way of life' and the virtues of hard work and honesty, and are quickly angered by the thought of welfare chiselers, street hoodlums, and the permissiveness and immorality which they believe is upsetting an established social order" (Altheide et al., 1978). Why, then, do these straight arrows steal? Various researchers have provided at least four explanations (Hollinger and Clark, 1983; Altheide et al., 1978; Conklin, 1977):

1. Employee theft has much to do with *large and impersonal* corporations. Employees tend to feel little or no loyalty to such corporations, regarding them as abstract entities rather than real people. To the employee thief, stealing from a large and impersonal company is like stealing from nobody. The general public may feel the same way. As Jack Douglas and Frances Waksler (1982) say, "If someone steals your $20 calculator, you may well expect sympathy from others; if an employee of IBM steals one, people are less likely to say 'Poor IBM.'"

2. A society with a tradition of *union–management conflict,* such as the United States, tends to have a high incidence of employee theft, because workers feel exploited by and resentful toward the company. Employee theft is thus an expression of the workers' desire to get back at the company. That's why employee theft is more common in cases where workers feel underpaid or abused by their employers, or frustrated by lack of promotions or salary

raises. Such workers regard their stealing not as real theft but as an informal compensation, which they feel they fully deserve (Greenberg, 1996).

3. Workers may steal if they *find their jobs too boring*. Stealing on the job, then, becomes interesting and challenging. One study of employee thieves in a midwestern clothing store found that those who stole for the satisfaction of getting away with it outnumbered those who stole for money alone or on impulse. When not stealing, employees unhappy with their jobs tend to engage in various counterproductive activities, such as doing sloppy work, coming to work late or leaving early, taking extra-long lunch hours or coffee breaks, using a sick leave without being sick, and drinking or using drugs on the job.

4. Employee thieves do not see themselves as criminals. This *noncriminal self-image* receives ample reinforcement from the popular stereotype of real criminals as those who commit street crime. Moreover, for fear of bad publicity, many companies are reluctant to have their crooked employees prosecuted. They merely fire the culprits, who later can get hired by other companies because their former employer does not want to publicize the theft. Some of the victimized firms play along with their thieving employees, pretending not to know what is going on. Since they pay the workers low wages, they expect them to supplement their meager income by taking home some merchandise.

Embezzlement

Embezzlement is a form of employee theft, but "embezzlement" is often used to refer to the stealing of money, while "employee theft" usually denotes stealing merchandise. Though less costly than employee theft, embezzlement costs $27.2 billion in one year, and commercial banks lose about five times as much money to embezzlers as they do to armed robbers (Thompson et al., 1992; Conklin, 1977).

Embezzlers range from relatively low-level employees to top executives. Many low-level employees who embezzle are middle-class bank tellers who occasionally steal several hundred dollars to solve some financial problems such as overdue bills or medical expenses. Top-level employees, of course, would make away with much more. In 1991, for example, Donald Houde, a trusted 9-year employee who was the systems director of Denver's Mile Hi Cablevision, was discovered to have embezzled $30,000 every month from the cable television company until he got caught. By then his loot had accumulated to nearly $2 million (Thompson et al., 1992).

Like Houde, most embezzlers are in management positions. Typically, they are white males in their thirties, well-paid, married with one or two children, and living in a respectable neighborhood. Embezzlers are basically hardworking, honest people; some are even pillars of their communities. Why do they steal? According to a classic explanation by sociologist Donald Cressey (1971), prospective embezzlers usually go through a social-psychological process that consists of three phases.

In the first phase, they encounter what they perceive to be an *unshareable* financial problem. They are too embarrassed to share this problem with their spouses, friends, or other people who are ordinarily available for help in financial matters. The reasons include being heavily in debt from gambling, or having a mistress, or simply feeling too much pride to ask others for help.

In the second phase, the individuals become aware of an *opportunity* for secretly solving the financial problem. The opportunity is typically embedded in the very position of trust that they hold by virtue of their respectable occupation.

And in the final, third phase, which is the most crucial, they *rationalize* away the criminal nature of embezzlement, defining the act as merely getting a temporary loan rather than as committing a theft. They expect to return the money later. As one embezzler put it, "I figured that if you could use something and help yourself and replace it and not hurt anybody, it was all right" (Coleman, 1994). This rationalization clinches the decision to carry out the embezzlement. However, compared with those in higher positions in a company, people in lower positions are less likely to rationalize—they tend more to admit that their embezzlement is a crime (Benson, 1985; Zeits, 1981).

Financial Frauds

The most common form of financial frauds involves the failure to pay income taxes. Over half of all taxpayers have been found to evade taxes to some extent. Middle- and upper-income people, especially businesspeople and lawyers, are the most common culprits. Why is tax evasion so prevalent? A major reason is the complexity of income tax laws. There are numerous ambiguous legal definitions of what constitutes income, deductions, depreciation, exemptions, and credits. These items can therefore be computed and manipulated in different ways, with the result that people with the same income end up paying different amounts of taxes. In effect, how much people pay depends on how well they play the "tax game." Generally, because of being able to hire smart tax accountants or lawyers, higher-income persons can play the game better than others (Coleman, 1994). The richest ones can thus boast that they pay little or no taxes; as Leona Helmsley, one of the wealthiest real estate entrepreneurs in the United States, once said, "Only little people pay taxes."

Less common than tax evasion is violation of securities law. But since most violators are professional stockbrokers and stock traders, the cost per violation is much higher. A popular form of violation by stockbrokers is defrauding customers through sales of worthless securities. Suppose a male stockbroker personally owns a lot of stock in a company that is on the verge of bankruptcy. He gets his friends on Wall Street to put out phony news releases and market analyses that make the stock look like a sure winner. After providing this fraudulent information to his clients, the stockbroker sells them all his stock. The clients, of course, lose a bundle when the company goes under and the stock hits bottom (Coleman, 1994). Increasingly more prevalent than this securities fraud are sweepstakes schemes, phony Internet stocks, and identity theft, such as using someone's Social Security number or other personal data to get credit cards or loans (Eaton, 1999).

Another form of securities violation is insider trading. It involves an insider of a company, such as its owner or one of its executives, buying or selling its stock on confidential information, not available to the general public, such as advance knowledge about a new product or unanticipated company profits or losses. Insiders can make a killing if they buy a lot of stock in their company before the public knows about the new product or unanticipated profit, because the price of the stock will rise significantly after the release of the information. Such insider trading puts the general public at a distinct disadvantage, undermining the fair and honest operation of our securities markets (Szockyj, 1993).

Deviance in the Professions

There are as many forms of professional deviance as there are professions. Here we focus on just three: medical misconduct, lawyerly lawlessness, and accounting abuse.

Medical Misconduct.   Many forms of criminal conduct take place in the medical profession. We will discuss just a few.

One is *fee splitting*, which involves a doctor receiving kickbacks from another for referring patients. The doctor who receives the kickbacks is usually a general practitioner referring his patients to a surgeon or specialist. Fee splitting not only hits the patients in their pocketbooks; it can also maim or kill them. The reason is that doctors who seek kickbacks typically send their patients to the surgeon who splits the largest fee rather than the surgeon who does the best surgery. Unfortunately, the surgeon who splits the largest fee tends to be the worst, most dangerous surgeon, who, because of incompetence, must offer maximum kickbacks to get business (Green, 1990).

A second form of medical misconduct is *unnecessary surgery*. In one study in which 1356 patients recommended for surgery were examined, researchers at Cornell Medical School found that 25 percent of the operations were not needed. The figures were even higher for certain parts of the body: 50 percent of pacemaker implants, 36 percent of eye surgeries, 31 percent of gall-bladder removals, 29 percent of prostate surgeries, 43 percent of hemorrhoid operations, and 32 percent of knee surgeries (Green, 1990). The basic cause of these unnecessary operations is apparently the desire for maximum profits rather than honest misdiagnosis. As research has shown, surgeons who are highly paid by insurance companies on a fee-for-service basis perform considerably more operations than surgeons who are paid much less by HMOs (health maintenance organizations) on a flat salary (Coleman, 1994).

A third form of medical misconduct is *fraudulently claiming payment* for services. This usually involves billing insurance companies and the state and federal Medicaid and Medicare programs for services never rendered, double-billing them for services rendered, or billing them for expensive physician services when, in fact, the services have been performed by nurses or other nonphysicians. Such fraudulent practices seem particularly common among doctors who lack competency and success in their profession and work in poor neighborhoods (Coleman, 1994).

Lawyerly Lawlessness.　　Legal lawlessness is widespread, marked mostly by the practice of overcharging clients. According to an auditor who works full-time investigating lawyers' bills, overcharging appears in about 90 percent of the cases he is hired to examine. In one survey, more than 60 percent of lawyers themselves said that they had personal knowledge of bill padding (Budiansky et al., 1995).

The opportunities for profiteering have much to do with the intangible nature of legal work. Unlike plumbers, who render a tangible, visible service by unclogging a stuffed drain or fixing a leaky faucet, lawyers often provide such intangible services as giving a few words of advice, making a telephone call, filling out and filing a form, writing a letter, preparing a document, talking to another attorney or a government agent, negotiating with somebody, or some other similar action that the client is rarely able to observe. Therefore, although any of these actions may take only a few minutes, an attorney can charge an hour's or even several hours' fee for them. It is difficult for the clients to dispute the high fee, because they cannot see what the lawyer does behind closed doors (Stevens, 1995; Green, 1990).

Even when the clients can see the lawyer in action, especially at court appearances, there are still ample opportunities for fraudulent charging of fees. For one thing, a lawyer can intentionally delay the resolution of a case so as to have more court appearances and charge the client accordingly. Lawyers are tempted to engage in this confidence game if the client is rich. But a confidence game can also be played on poor clients, though by the reverse of delay. This tactic involves shortening the duration of a case in order to maximize the number of clients and hence the profit the lawyer can have. The lawyer can pretend to work hard on the client's behalf while persuading the client to plead guilty so that the case can be brought to a quick conclusion (Coleman, 1994).

Regardless of how they inflate their hours of service, this tendency in lawyers has inspired jokes such as this one: "A lawyer appeared at the gates of heaven and began loudly protesting that he was only 42—much too young to die. 'That's funny,' St. Peter replied. 'According to the hours you've billed, we thought you were 93.'" (Budiansky et al., 1995).

Accounting Abuse.　　In preparing tax returns for companies and individuals, accountants may assist their clients in falsifying their income or deductions in order to pay less taxes. But this is not a profitable area for accounting abuses, because tax preparation provides only a small portion (no more than 23 percent in 1993) of the accounting profession's revenues. Most of the profession's $46 billion annual revenues comes from examining corporations' financial statements. Thus, most of the abuse involves fraud or negligence in the course of doing audits (Wells, 1993).

The job of auditing a corporation's books to make certain that their accounting is accurate is extremely important in ensuring the stability and health of the nation's economy. If a company is truly as well run as the accountant says it is, then the bank that lends it money and the public that invests in it by buying its stock and becoming its shareholders have a good chance of earning a profit later. But if the accountant says the company is financially sound and strong while, in fact, it is about to go bankrupt, the bank and investors will likely lose their money. But the bank itself can also collude with crooked companies in defrauding their shareholders and investors, with assistance from the lender's own accountants in covering up the seedy deals. Today, accountants face more than 4000 liability suits—double the total of seven years ago—and as much as $15 billion in damages. Most of these suits charge the accountants with failure to uncover fraud (Wells, 1993).

The major cause of this accounting abuse is obviously the conflict of interest that is built into the accountant's position as an auditor paid by the company to audit itself. Accountants find it hard to resist the proverbial temptation of not biting the hand that feeds them. They may insist that they can be totally independent of the company so as to be able to examine its books objectively, but the fact remains that they are financially dependent on that company. If they overzealously investigate the company, they will lose the job the next time around. In short, the conflict of interest prevents accountants from doing what they are supposed to do—detect fraud in the company they audit (Wells, 1993).

What Makes White-Collar Deviance Unique?

White-collar deviance is distinguishable from common crime in a number of ways. The most distinctive aspect of white-collar deviance is the rational execution of the offense to maximize profit, along with the use of power, influence, or respectability to minimize detection. Equally distinctive but less obvious are: (1) the deviant's respectable self-image, (2) the victim's unwitting cooperation, and (3) society's relative indifference toward the offense.

The Deviant's Respectable Self-Image

White-collar deviants typically see themselves as respectable individuals rather than as common criminals. This self-image plays an important part in the perpetration of various white-collar deviances.

White-collar deviants usually express their respectable self-image through certain rationalizations. Corporate executives convicted of price fixing have been found to argue that their unlawful price-fixing schemes are far from being criminal. Instead, they view themselves as having really served a worthwhile purpose for the nation's economy by "stabilizing prices," and they congratulate themselves for having effectively helped their companies by "recovering costs." There is no such thing as price fixing in their book. Embezzlers, as we have observed, tend to define their stealing as only "borrowing," insisting that they will pay the money back soon. Perpetrators of the more common employee theft feel that they actually do not steal anything from their companies, because the companies are believed to make up the losses by using them as tax deductions and charging customers higher prices. Tax offenders tend to see themselves as victims rather than offenders. They would argue that they are just unlucky enough to get caught for doing something that practically everyone else does. As a convicted tax offender said, "Everybody cheats on their income tax, 95 percent of the people. Even if it's for $10 it's the same principle. I didn't cheat. I just didn't know how to report it" (Benson, 1985).

What all these different types of white-collar offenders have in common is their denial of criminal intent. They admit that they have committed the act that landed them in prison, but regard their actions as mistakes only, not acts motivated by a guilty, criminal mind. In short, they find it hard to see themselves as real criminals. As one businessman, who is in prison for price fixing, said about himself: "Having been in business for 33 years, you don't just automatically become a criminal overnight" (Benson, 1985). Even Charles Keating, who was in prison for conviction on numerous counts of bank fraud and racketeering in 1989, never admitted guilt for his actions (Zagorin, 1997).

The Victim's Unwitting Cooperation

In contrast to such common crimes as murder, robbery, rape, and assault, white-collar deviance requires an unwitting cooperation from its victims. This cooperation is unwitting because it is based on the victim's carelessness or ignorance. In a home improvement scheme, for example, the victims do not bother to check the work history of the fraudulent company that solicits them, and they sign a contract without examining its contents for such matters as the true price and the credit terms. Some victims purchase goods through the mail without checking the reputation of the firm. Doctors may prescribe untested drugs after having relied on only the drug company's salespeople and advertising. Lest we blame the victims, we should realize the difficulty for them to know they are being victimized, even if they want to find out the true nature of their victimization. Grocery shoppers, for example, are hard put to detect such dangerous substances as residues of hormones, antibiotics, pesticides, and nitrites in the meat they buy.

Society's Relative Indifference

While ignorance or carelessness leads the victim to cooperate unknowingly with white-collar deviants, society's indifference to their offense is a blessing knowingly bestowed on them. Generally, little effort is made to catch white-collar deviants, and if, on rare occasions, they are caught, they seldom go to jail. Even if they are sent to prison, they are not likely to be placed in a harsh institution or to stay there for long.

Since the early 1980s, however, there have been some signs that our society has become more concerned about white-collar deviance. Many large corporations have been prosecuted for illegal activities. In 1985 a Chicago judge gave the most severe sentence ever (25 years) to three company executives for an employee's death resulting from their failure to correct unsafe plant conditions. The day after the sentencing, the *Detroit Free Press* asked its readers if murder is "too harsh a charge for negligent employers." An overwhelming 80 percent of those calling in said no (Cahan et al., 1985). Sociologists have also found that respondents in their studies rated white-collar offenses as serious as street crimes (Geis, 1984).

Does all this mean that justice can now be expected to be *collar*-blind? Hardly. Most obviously, not a single white-collar offender has been sentenced to death, let alone actually executed, for causing the deaths of many workers or customers, although many lower-class criminals have been executed for killing one person. Moreover, most white-collar criminals, especially the big-time ones that steal tens or hundreds of millions, continue to be punished less severely than street criminals. From 1987 through 1992, federal agents charged a staggering 95,045 white-collar individuals and corporate executives with various bank and S&L frauds, but more than 75 percent of these charges were dropped from prosecution. The few that were convicted of bank fraud received an average of only 2.4 years in prison, compared with 7.8 years for traditional bank robbery (Pizzo and Muolo, 1993).

It is doubtful that the government can wage an all-out war on white-collar crime because many such criminals are just too powerful, influential, or respectable. After a jury convicted a wealthy businessman of defrauding an S&L out of $55 million, the judge reduced his sentence to only six months in a halfway house—not a real prison—and a mere $2 million in restitution, letting him keep the remaining $53 million profit from the crime. When the prosecutor objected, the judge explained: "This man has a unique ability, and I think it can be carried out honestly as well as dishonestly. People who are able to accomplish what he has . . . are also stimulating the economy of this country and helping those of us who are professionals to exist" (Pizzo and Muolo, 1993). Moreover, the general public does not seem to feel as threatened by white-collar offenders as by violent street criminals. Average Americans may say that they consider white-collar offenses just as serious as street crimes, but they are not likely to put this into action if they serve on a jury in a corporate crime case. As one prosecutor says, "Look, I can wave a pair of bloody underwear in front of a jury and have their undivided attention. But I can wave $100 million in phony loan statements in front of the same jury and just watch their eyes glaze over" (Pizzo and Muolo, 1993).

Causes of White-Collar Deviance

From analyzing the literature on white-collar crime, we can find three basic reasons why, among corporations and white-collar personnel, some are more likely than others to engage in deviant activities. These three reasons are related to the general concepts of the power theory presented in Chapter 3 to explain why and how power can cause deviance.

Deviant Motivation: Fear of Loss and Greed for Gain

Some evidence suggests that fear and greed have much to do with deviant activities in the white-collar world. It is well-known to Wall Street observers that fear and greed are the two most powerful human emotions driving the stock market. The fear of loss causes investors to sell stocks, which brings down their prices. If the fear is great and widely shared, it will cause a market crash. On the other hand, the greed for gain causes investors to buy more stocks, which raises their prices. If the greed is great and widely shared, it will cause a market boom. All this means in economic terms that when the supply of a stock rises—as a result of many investors wanting to sell their shares of the stock—its price falls, and when the demand for a stock rises—as a result of many investors wanting to buy more shares of the stock—its price rises.

Just as fear and greed drive the stock market, these motives seem to propel white-collar deviance. The fear of loss, such as the fear of losing one's house from mortgage foreclosure or the fear of a company going bankrupt, has been found to be associated with white-collar deviance. The deviance is characteristically the type that produces a relatively low profit or high risk of arrest, such as bank embezzlement and credit fraud. This usually involves low-level white-collar workers and small, new, or unsuccessful companies (Wheeler, 1992; Weisburd et al., 1991). The greed for gain—in order to prove to oneself how successful one can be or to turn an already large and successful corporation into an empire—is also likely to cause white-collar deviance. But the deviance is characteristically one that produces huge profit, such as buying political influence with huge donations or violating an antitrust law. It usually involves big-time executives and large, well-established, successful corporations. The greed is a by-product of success. As one researcher on white-collar crime says, "Greed is distinguished as a want that can never be satisfied: Success is ever-receding; having more leads to wanting more again" (Braithwaite, 1992).

The greed is not a psychological abnormality, though. It derives from the culture of competition, which celebrates greed as the engine of capitalism that drives people to get rich. This cultural encouragement of greed came through loud and clear when Ivan Boesky, before he was prosecuted and convicted of insider trading in the 1980s, was the honored commencement speaker at the School of Business Administration of the University of California at Berkeley. He told the graduates: "Greed is all right. . . . I want you to know that. I think greed is healthy. You can be greedy and still feel good about yourself." The audience roared with appreciative laughter and applause (Martz, 1986). The business graduates could identify with Boesky probably because greed is basically the same as excessive, boundless ambition, a product of the U.S. culture of success, which greatly emphasizes the importance of achieving material success in our lives.

In short, the greater the fear of loss or the greed for gain, the stronger the motivation for engaging in white-collar deviance.

Deviant Opportunity: The Benefit of High Position and Power

By itself the deviant motivation in the form of fear or greed is not enough to compel a person or corporation to engage in economic deviance. The deviance is more likely to occur if opportunities exist for carrying it out. Generally, the higher the individual's position is in a company, the more likely the "deviantly" motivated individual is to carry out a profitable deviant act, basically because of easier access to the company's resources. Thus managers, officers, or owners can be expected to be more likely than lower-level personnel to steal from the company. Relatively high status and prestige in society also make it easier to defraud unsuspecting victims because status and prestige lend the appearance of legitimacy and trustworthiness and reduce the target's guard against being victimized (Weisburd et al., 1991). A combination of high position, status, and prestige can thus provide the greatest opportunity for deviant activities, which in turn is likely to turn a deviant motivation into a deviant action.

For the same reason, the more power corporations have, the more likely they are to commit corporate crime. There is evidence to support this statement. In one study, for example, large corporations constituted only 42 percent of all companies investigated, but accounted for 70 percent of all violations—compared with 20 percent for medium-sized companies and 10 percent for small firms (Clinard and Yeager, 1980).

Weak Social Control: Lax Law Enforcement

It is widely known that law enforcers do not exercise as much control over white-collar deviance as over street crime. As we have indicated, for example, the penalty for bank fraud committed by a bank's executive or owner averages only 2.4 years in prison, compared with 7.8 years for bank robbery perpetrated by a lower-income person. As a result, white-collar crime by the rich and powerful can be expected to be more prevalent than street crime by the poor and powerless. Sometimes the government even directly encourages the rich to engage in deviance with its deregulation policies, as we can see from the proliferation of banking frauds in the 1980s after the government deregulated the banking industry (Glasberg and Skidmore, 1998).

Some studies, however, claim to have found that the overwhelming majority of white-collar criminals are far from rich and powerful but instead are pitiful middle-class people such as the bank teller who, saddled with overdue bills, embezzles only a few hundred dollars (Weisburd et al., 1991). The sample of such studies is usually a biased one, representing mostly the losers among white-collar criminals, namely, those who are prosecuted or convicted for their crimes. But the plain fact is that most white-collar criminals, particularly those who are rich and powerful, are not caught, which is, in fact, a powerful testimony to the relative lack of law enforcement against them.

Law enforcers are not entirely to blame for the weaker control experienced by more powerful deviants. The huge power commanded by such deviants plays a role too. In the pharmaceutical industry, for example, the government's regulatory agencies may try to confiscate drugs that have not been properly tested. But powerful drug companies can use their considerable resources to stop the confiscation. They may bribe the regulatory agents or pay unethical medical researchers to produce fraudulent evidence that the drugs are safe. To ensure against prosecution for bribery, some pharmaceutical companies even have employees who are, as part of their job description, responsible for going to jail. If a head has to "go on the chopping block," it would be the heads of these employees (Braithwaite, 1993, 1992).

In brief, more powerful corporations and individuals are more likely than others to engage in deviant activities because of weaker social control.

Governmental Deviance

Most of us seem to be ambivalent about our government officials. On the one hand, we expect them to break the law every now and then and we may, when seeing one of them get caught, remark, "There goes another crook." Mark Twain expressed this popular sentiment well when he said way back in 1894: "It could probably be shown with facts and figures that there is no distinctly American criminal class except Congress." On the other hand, we respect and admire them for being our leaders, often so much so that we would scramble in a crowd to get their autographs or shake their hands with a sense of pride and honor. Given these conflicting feelings of revulsion and respect, we nonetheless try to be objective in analyzing governmental deviance. This type of deviance essentially involves the abuse of power by government officials or politicians running for elected office. Here we focus on three types of governmental deviance: political corruption, election improprieties, and official violence.

Political Corruption

Political corruption is usually associated with graft or bribery—the abuse of power for personal gain. It may take the form of an outright bribe, in which case the public official accepts the money offered by a briber who expects a favor in return. Outright bribe routinely takes place in poor countries because it has become a part of their culture (Omestad, 1997). Outright bribe is far less common in the United States. The types of political corruption that occur more often in this country include kickbacks, management of public funds for personal gain, and illegal use of mail privileges.

Receiving Kickbacks from Businesses. The federal government spends an enormous sum of taxpayer money on goods and services supplied by various businesses. The officials in charge of purchasing these goods and services may find it hard to resist kickbacks from the companies they are dealing with. To receive kickbacks, though, the officials will allow businesses to send the government outrageous bills. Thus, repair contractors and suppliers have been known to bill the government for work that was never done and for materials that were never delivered. Officials in the U.S. Defense Department are also known to have paid hundreds of dollars for a hammer and hundreds more for a toilet seat.

Abusive Management of Public Funds. The management of public funds is a potential source of political corruption. City or state treasurers can be tempted to misuse the millions of dollars for personal gain, especially because there are many subtle, unprosecutable ways to do it. In deciding which bank to deposit an enormous sum of public money into, government officials may base their decision on whether it will profit themselves financially and politically. Thus, they may choose a bank of which they are shareholders; or a bank that will give their family members or business associates loans at low interest rates; or a bank that has promised to contribute substantially to their political campaigns.

Abusing the Frank. The most common form of official corruption is probably the abuse of the frank—the privilege of sending mail free of charge. Our Founding Fathers intended the frank to be for official use only, namely, for answering letters from constituents. However, members of Congress routinely abuse the frank for personal purposes by sending out campaign information to ensure reelection. They, in effect, turn the franking system into a "taxpayer-funded propaganda machine" (Sabato and Simpson, 1996). As a Congressman explained to his new press aide, "We are going to mail, mail, mail and then mail some more. You're going to mail until you run out of ideas. Then you're going to talk to the rest of the staff and mail until they run out of ideas. After that you're going to come to me and mail until *I* run out of ideas. And when that happens, we're going to staple my picture to pages of the goddamn Yellow Book and mail them out, too, and lemme tell you, you can't *ever* run out of them sons of bitches" (Jackley, 1992).

Election Improprieties

Our representative democracy requires that we, the masses, have the right to choose our leaders. This right, however, often has little meaning to those who want to be our leaders. Therefore, various devious means are often used to win elections.

Denial of Voting Right. The masses of citizenry are encouraged to participate in the presidential election. But in reality it is the electoral college—consisting of political leaders, not the populace—that selects the president. This should largely be blamed on the writers of the Constitution rather than on current political leaders, but it is important to realize that the "voters" are in a way bypassed to let political leaders decide who should be president (Simon, 1996).

Political Dirty Tricks. Dirty tricks are often employed to ensure victory in an election. They include spreading rumors about the opponent's strange character, kinky sex life, or association with drug kingpins; having individuals in the audience at the opponent's rally heckle or ask embarrassing questions; defacing the opponent's billboards; and stealing the opponent's campaign mail. A more sophisticated form of dirty trick is the "telephone sleaze" in which campaign workers call voters, say they are conducting a nonpartisan survey, then ask loaded questions such as, "Did you know Senator Jones wants to vote against the banning of child pornography?" (Sabato and Simpson, 1996).

Campaign Finance Abuses. Candidates for elected office often solicit and receive huge campaign contributions from monied interests (large corporations and wealthy individuals) and the donors expect the politicians to return the favor if elected. Incumbent legislators running *unopposed* also receive large contributions from the rich with the same expectation. As a result, the rich can gain access to the White House and Congress that ordinary citizens cannot. All this, in effect, involves the buying and selling of political influence or access to elected officials. Recently, for example, prominent bankers who had contributed heavily to Clinton's reelection campaign were invited to the White House to discuss banking regulations with the President and the nation's senior banking regulator, while executives of the giant tobacco company Philip Morris, a huge contributor to the Republicans, were able to discuss their concerns with Republican Congressional leaders (van Natta and Fritsch, 1997; Wertheimer, 1996).

Official Violence

There is a long history of governmental violence against various groups of citizens in the United States. The government, for example, drove Native Americans out of their lands and killed many of them in the early period of U.S. history. Today, most official violence involves police brutality against citizens, especially African and Hispanic Americans in large cities. When complaints of police brutality are brought against some officers, they are often dismissed as being without merit. If some complaints are admitted as legitimate, they are blamed on "only a few bad apples" in the police department. But these bad apples are usually kept on the force to rot rather than thrown out. Consequently, in nearly every large city's police department, there's a small group of officers committing most of the police brutality. Some police forces have begun to use a civilian review board to prevent police brutality, but most refuse to subject themselves to outside control, believing that they can police themselves (Kappeler, Sluder, and Alpert, 1998; Gleick, 1995; Herbert, 1995).

As a democracy, however, the United States commits *democide* (the killing of people by their government) to a much smaller extent than many other nations. For the 20th century, democratic states account for only about 1 percent of all government-sponsored murders throughout the world. The vast majority of such killings have been carried out by Communist and authoritarian governments. The most notorious have been the Soviet Union, China, and the Khmer Rouge, which liquidated about one-third of the Cambodian population. Moreover, the governments of poorer nations commit democide on a larger scale than do richer nations. Apparently, the authorities in poor countries view life as cheap. But as the economy of these nations improves, the incidence of democide tends to decline, because "even ruthless dictators need tax revenue, and you can't collect taxes from dead people" (Scully, 1997).

Official Ways of Neutralizing Deviance

Government officials take great care to cover up their deviant acts. Even after such acts have been uncovered, the officials rarely admit their guilt. Instead, they automatically attempt to neutralize their deviance—to make it appear as if they had done nothing wrong. Such an attempt has been called "the ritual of wiggle." There are different ways for government officials to wiggle out of their deviant activities. Let us take a look at their most common techniques of neutralization (Lieberman, 1973).

Denying the Obvious

Public officials tend to deny that any wrongdoing has occurred, no matter how strong the suspicion or how clear the reality. The denial is as frequently and honestly repeated as possible. Even a popular president like Ronald Reagan found it hard to tell the truth. In late 1986, when the arms deal with Iran shocked the nation, he insisted that he did not know of the diversion of funds to the Nicaraguan rebels, although it was clear to many Americans that he did. In a nationwide poll, 47 percent of the respondents said that he was "lying" (the exact word used in the question) while only 37 percent said that he was telling the truth (Church, 1986). More recently, President Clinton denied that there was anything wrong with him having coffees or lunches in the White House with his wealthy contributors. He said, for example, "I think it is an appropriate thing and can be a good thing for the President and for the Secretary of the Treasury to meet with a group of bankers and listen to them and listen to their concerns" (Mitchell, 1997).

Ignoring the Deviance

If an illegal act is a private one committed by individual officials, they ignore it by disconnecting their phones, going into hiding or on a trip away from the press, or simply saying "no comment." If the government is supposed to take action against its officials for some lawbreaking, it resorts to evasive responses by insisting that the facts do not conclusively and absolutely warrant governmental intervention. The government, for example, has failed to address itself adequately to the issue of the legality of the United States' involvement in the Vietnam War. Even if they have been found guilty, officials still tend to act as if their deviance is not really deviant. In 1997, for example, after House Speaker Newt Gingrich was reprimanded and fined $300,000 for years of unethical conduct, he dismissed his misdeeds as only comparable to jaywalking (Weisman, 1997).

Accusing the Accuser

In the case of private offense, the individual official may threaten or actually file a libel suit against the journalist who publicized the offense. Although it is almost impossible to prove libel, the official hopes that the suit will divert public attention from the official's own wrongdoing. The government hopes for the same thing when it accuses its accuser. This is why the Nixon administration often attacked the news media for distorting facts when its illegal activities were publicized. Also, when CBS-TV News broadcast its critical documentary *The Selling of the Pentagon,* a House committee launched an investigation into CBS-TV News rather than into the Defense Department. In 1992, when Senator Brock Adams of Washington State was accused by a woman for sexually molesting her, he claimed she was mentally ill, though eight other women had independently alleged similar sexual harassment by him (Trost and Thomas, 1993).

Promising to Take Action

When high government officials are under intense pressure to do something about a certain incident, they will publicly promise to take action to deal with it. Yet, behind the scenes, the promised action is not seriously carried out. In the 1970s, when the Watergate scandal broke, the Attorney General promised to make the Justice Department's investigation of the scandal "the most extensive, thorough and comprehensive investigation since the assassination of President Kennedy." But it was only a promise; nothing came of it. In the 1980s, when confronted with the scandal of selling arms to Iran and diverting funds to the Nicaraguan rebels, President Reagan kept repeating that he wanted all the facts to come out. Yet he did not try very hard to get the facts out. He did not even demand from his aides, who were the key figures in the scandal, an accounting of what they did (Church, 1986). More recently, President Clinton repeatedly announced his intent to help clean up the system that effectively encourages politicians to sell access or influence for large campaign contributions. But he continued to raise funds for his political party by soliciting huge donations from big corporations and wealthy individuals (Mitchell, 1997).

Justifying the Deviance

This method of neutralization is rationalization par excellence. Although they have implicitly admitted their wrongdoing with their promise to deal with it, the guilty officials rationalize that it was necessary for them to commit the deviant act. This should not be surprising, because it has the support of the popular belief that the end sometimes justifies the means. Thus, many officials justify unlawful wiretapping on the grounds that the danger of not using it against suspected criminals or terrorists is too great. In the early 1970s, President Nixon, the CIA, and the FBI even justified domestic surveillance of U.S. citizens in the interest of national security. In the 1950s and 1960s, top U.S. military and intelligence officials insisted that it was necessary to use unsuspecting Americans as guinea pigs for mind-control experiments by sneaking powerful mind-altering drugs into their drinks because there had been reports of Soviet success at mind control (Budiansky et al., 1994). In 1997 President Clinton defended his solicitation of big political donations, saying, "I do not believe you will ever get the politics out of politics. And that's not bad" (Mitchell, 1997).

Causes of Governmental Deviance

A review of various studies on governmental deviance suggests at least three important causes of the problem: the superabundance of ambiguous laws, governmental complexity, and power.

Superabundance of Ambiguous Laws

Government officials operate under a *superabundance of ambiguous laws*—lack of clearcut laws for controlling official action. This enormous collection of ambiguous laws has been described by a legal scholar "as a wall of lattice-work: the thin strips of wood represent all of our legal rules, but the pervasive holes are very prominent; indeed, but for the holes there would be no design at all" (Lieberman, 1973). The "holes" referred to in the quote are popularly known as *loopholes*, meaning the ambiguity of laws through which the intent of the laws can be evaded. Therefore, the superabundance of ambiguous laws inevitably creates a "discretionary wilderness" where government officials are relatively free to rely on their own judgment and self-interest to interpret the law. The kind of interpretation opens up a great deal of opportunity for officials to engage in deviant activities, whenever they so desire, with impunity.

In fact, as is well known among historians studying the U.S. presidency, many laws are purposely ambiguous, designed to give presidents a lot of room to do their job. "The Reagan Administration," for example, "has followed the lead of its predecessors in emphasizing semantic interpretations to exempt its actions from various laws. As the Truman Administration called the Korean war a 'police action' to circumvent the necessity for a declaration of war, so the Reagan Administration has said that its assistance to the Nicaraguan rebels was part of a strategy of 'interdicting' supply lines to El Salvador's communist insurgents rather than of undermining the Sandinista Government of Nicaragua" (Tolchin, 1986). Earlier, Presidents Lyndon Johnson and Richard Nixon had also skirted the law when they sent troops into combat in Vietnam without the benefit of a congressional declaration of war. More recently, President Bill Clinton went around the law to raise money for his reelection campaign. Once, for example, after President Clinton received word that a rich man wanted to donate $5 million to his campaign fund, he instructed his White House deputy chief of staff to handle the matter, although it is against the law for a government official to raise campaign funds (Isikoff, 1997).

Governmental Complexity and Power

Given the intricate, complex nature of the government as a huge organization, it is inevitable that its members cannot have complete information and responsibility regarding what and how they should do their jobs in the organization. Due to this lack of information and responsibility, then, officials tend to get involved in deviant activities (Ermann and Lundman, 1996).

This explanation, however, implies that officials are not to blame for committing deviance because, given the lack of information and responsibility, they do not knowingly or intentionally get involved in deviance. Thus, the concept of governmental complexity can best be used to explain *unintentional* deviance among government officials. As for their *intentional* deviance, which essentially involves an abuse of power, it may be better explained by the power theory that we have developed in Chapter 3 and applied to white-collar deviance earlier in this chapter. According to the power theory, there are three reasons why government officials tend to purposely abuse their power: stronger deviant motivation, greater deviant opportunity, and weaker social control. Due to their relatively high position in society, governmental officials tend to be too ambitious, thereby more likely to experience relative deprivation, which would motivate them to employ deviant means to achieve their high goals. They are further encouraged to abuse their power because they enjoy abundant opportunities for doing so and are not subject to stringent social control, thanks again to their lofty position in society.

Summary

1. What is white-collar deviance? Traditionally called white-collar crime, white-collar deviance includes both criminal and noncriminal forms of economic deviance carried out by high-status people as part of an occupation for their personal gain (hence occupational deviance) or on behalf of their corporation (hence corporate deviance).

2. What is the nature of corporate deviance? It can be divided into four types on the basis of who or what their victims are. Deviance against employees involves a corporation ignoring its employees' health and safety; deviance against customers involves a corporation dealing in dangerous foods or unsafe products, engaging in commercial frauds or deceptive advertising, and violating antitrust laws; deviance against the government includes evading payment of taxes, using campaign donations to buy influence, and bribing foreign governments or committing other illegal acts abroad; and deviance against the environment involves polluting the environment.

3. What is the nature of occupational deviance? Carried out for the employees' own gain rather than on behalf of their company, occupational deviance includes employee theft, embezzlement, tax and securities violations, and deviance in such professions as medicine, law, and accounting.

4. How does white-collar deviance differ from common, street crime? White-collar deviance is distinguishable for its rational execution of the offense as well as the offender's respectable self-image, the victim's unwitting cooperation, and society's relative indifference toward the offense.

5. What causes white-collar deviance? Generally, the causes of white-collar deviance are stronger deviant motivation, greater deviant opportunity, and weaker social control. The motivation involves the fear of loss and greed for gain. The opportunity inheres in a higher position in a company or in the more powerful corporation. And weaker control comes from less stringent law enforcement against white-collar deviance.

6. What is the nature of governmental deviance? Government deviance involves the abuse of power by government officials or candidates for elected office. Such deviance appears in different forms, including political corruption, election improprieties, and official violence. Political corruption includes receiving kickbacks from businesses, abusing the management of public funds, and abusing the frank. Election improprieties include denial of the right to really elect the president, playing dirty tricks on the election opponent, and the buying and selling of political influence that favors the rich over ordinary citizens. Official violence involves mostly police brutality against crime suspects and innocent citizens, especially African and Hispanic Americans.

7. What would government officials do if their illegal activities were revealed to the public? They would try to neutralize their deviance. This neutralization takes the form of denying the obvious, ignoring the deviance, accusing the accuser, promising to take action, and justifying the deviance.

8. What causes governmental deviance? The causes of governmental deviance include the superabundance of ambiguous laws, governmental complexity, and power that creates deviant motivation, deviant opportunity, and weak control.

SUGGESTED READINGS

Coleman, James William. 1994. *The Criminal Elite: The Sociology of White Collar Crime.* 3d ed. New York: St. Martin's. A comprehensive review of the literature on white-collar crime, dealing with the types, characteristics, origins, and legal control of the crime.

Dabney, Dean A., and Richard C. Hollinger. 1999. "Illicit prescription drug use among pharmacists—Evidence of a paradox of familiarity." *Work and Occupations, 26* (February), 77–106. A study of how expert knowledge of prescription drugs coupled with the opportunity to obtain them leads pharmacists to drug abuse.

Ermann, M. David, and Richard J. Lundman (Eds.). 1996. *Corporate and Governmental Deviance.* 5th ed. New York: Oxford University Press. A collection of articles dealing with the characteristics of elite deviance, its impact on people, and societal reactions to it.

Friedrichs, David O. 1996. *Trusted Criminals: White Collar Crime in Contemporary Society.* Belmont, Calif.: Wadsworth. A comprehensive text covering various types and characteristics of white-collar deviance.

Green, Gary S. 1990. *Occupational Crime.* Chicago: Nelson-Hall. Deals with various kinds of crime committed in the course of one's occupation, as well as the concept, measurements, explanations, and control of occupational crime.

Poveda, Tony G. 1994. *Rethinking White-Collar Crime.* Westport, Conn.: Praeger. An analysis of the theoretical issues about the definition, explanation, and social control of white-collar crime.

Sabato, Larry J., and Glenn R. Simpson. 1996. *Dirty Little Secrets: The Persistence of Corruption in American Politics.* New York: Times Book. Discusses how corruption flourishes in the current political system that serves big-money interests more than the ordinary citizenry.

Schlegel, Kip, and David Weisburd (Eds.). 1992. *White-Collar Crime Reconsidered.* Boston: Northeastern University Press. A collection of articles by various sociological researchers on the definitions, theories, victimization, and control of white-collar crime.

Simon, David R. 1999. *Elite Deviance.* 6th ed. Boston: Allyn and Bacon. A survey of various forms of elite deviance, including corporate deviance, international deviance, and political deviance.

Simon, David R., and Frank E. Hagan. 1999. *White Collar Deviance.* Boston: Allyn & Bacon. Presents various aspects of white-collar deviance.

Sutherland, Edwin H. 1983. *White Collar Crime: The Uncut Version.* New Haven: Yale University Press. A classic on white-collar crime, with introductory remarks by contemporary sociologists Gilbert Geis and Colin Goff.

Weisburd, David, Stanton Wheeler, Elin Waring, and Nancy Bode. 1991. *Crimes of the Middle Classes: White-Collar Offenders in the Federal Courts.* New York: Yale University Press. An empirical study of middle-class white-collar offenders who get caught for their crimes.

14 Disreputable Economic Deviance

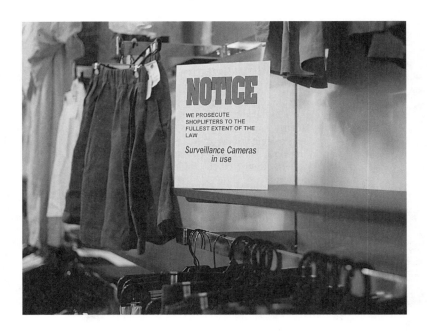

On a warm September morning in a peaceful town near Washington, D.C., a 34-year-old research chemist was driving her 22-month-old daughter to preschool. At a stop sign two strangers approached her gold BMW, forced her from the car, and sped off. But, with her left arm caught in the harness strap of her seat belt, she was dragged face down across the rough pavement for nearly two miles. Before the carjackers stopped to dump her mutilated body in the road, they threw out her toddler daughter. The child, still strapped in her car seat, miraculously survived. An hour later the two carjackers crashed the car in a corn field and were arrested (Turque, 1992).

Carjacking, as the horrible crime just described is called, is an example of disreputable economic deviance, disreputable because it is an economic deviance far more widely and strongly condemned than white-collar deviance. In this chapter we will discuss various forms of disreputable economic deviance, including robbery, auto theft and carjacking, burglary, shoplifting, and organized crime.

Robbery

Robbery is simultaneously both a property and violent crime. It is a property crime because it involves illegally taking the victim's property; it is a violent crime for the use of violence or threat of violence against the victim in its commission. We will first examine these two connected facets of robbery, and then look at the patterns of robbery, such as where or when robbery usually occurs, what robbers are like, and why they commit robbery.

Robbery as a Property Crime

As a property crime, robbery is a relatively rational, calculated act, and as such, it involves making rational decisions. The decision making consists of a sequence of three elements: (1) deciding to rob mostly for financial gain, (2) deciding what target to rob, and (3) deciding how to carry out the robbery (Conklin, 1972).

Deciding to Rob for Money.   For most robbers the decision to rob is based on their desire for money. But psychiatrists tend to assume that armed robbers are basically abnormal, suffering from a sense of inadequacy and failure and therefore committing robbery with a firearm as a way of seeking self-adequacy and power. One armed robber is quoted as saying, "When I have a gun in my hands nothing can stop me. It makes me feel important and strong. With a revolver you're somebody" (Gabor et al., 1987). This may be true of some robbers, but *most* bank robbers are *primarily* interested in money, just like the notorious Willie Sutton. When asked why he robbed banks, Sutton replied, "Because that's where the money is." The pursuit of power in robbery, if it exists, is only a *secondary* motive (Haran and Martin, 1984).

Deciding Which Target to Rob.   Once they have decided to rob, would-be robbers have to select a certain target. Target selection is generally based on two factors: (1) Robbers usually consider *lucrative* establishments—such as banks, grocery stores, and other places where large sums of cash are available—as potential targets. (2) They usually select from among these targets one with a *lower risk of arrest*. Thus, most robbers choose, for example, to hold up a branch bank in an outlying commercial area with few people that is close to a highway, rather than the main bank in the busy central business district.

Deciding How to Rob.   This last decision involves varying degrees of planning. At one extreme, some robbers, particularly professional ones who are after a big score, plan their crimes with great care and minute detail. At the other extreme, some robbers, especially amateur ones who suddenly feel the need for a small sum of cash, commit robbery on the spur of the moment, with hardly any planning. The majority of robberies are more carefully planned than not, as evidenced by the relatively low rate of arrest for such a crime—usually only about one out of four robberies ends in arrest (FBI, 1996).

Robbery as a Violent Crime

There are two facets to robbery as a violent crime: One involves actual violence, the other potential violence. Because they do not carry a weapon, *unarmed robbers* usually have to resort to *actual violence* to subdue the victim; hence the crime is also called *strong-arm robbery*. But *armed robbers* tend more to rely only on *potential violence*—the threat of force—made to appear real and frightening to the victim by the sight of a weapon.

Unarmed Robbery and Actual Violence.   Unarmed or strong-arm robberies are often viewed by the public as less dangerous than armed robberies. But, in reality, the opposite is true: Unarmed robberies are far more likely to result in injury to the victims. According to one study, 66 percent of unarmed-robbery victims, compared to only 17 percent of armed-robbery victims, were injured (Feeney and Weir, 1975). Of course, armed robberies are more likely to result in the victim's death. But the likelihood of fatality is extremely small: Victims die in fewer than one percent of all robberies carried out with a gun (Wright, Rossi, and Daly, 1983; Feeney and Weir, 1975).

Unarmed robberies are more dangerous because offenders believe that victims are more likely to resist when there is no weapon involved than when there is a weapon. As one unarmed robber says, "In strongarms, you have to put [the victim] out of commission for a few minutes. When you haven't got a gun or knife, he won't do anything. He'll tell you to go to hell or turn on you. So all you can do is knock him out" (Luckenbill, 1981).

Armed Robbery and Potential Violence.   As a threat of force, potential violence in armed robbery rarely turns into real violence because the use of a weapon, particularly a firearm, often ensures the successful execution of the crime. There are four ways in which a weapon can help robbers accomplish their goal efficiently (Conklin, 1972).

First, the weapon creates a *buffer zone* between offender and victim. Many robbers believe that the firearm is the most effective weapon because it frightens the victim the most. With the firearm holding the victim at a distance, the robber can cover a large area and can also control many victims at the same time. Second, the weapon *intimidates* the victim, making it unnecessary for the robber to resort to violence. If the show of a weapon fails to intimidate the victims enough to give up their money, the offender often tries to increase the level of intimidation by cocking the pistol or holding it to the victim's head. If this attempt also fails, the robber may be compelled to use the weapon for the third purpose— to *make good the threat*. A few robbers stab or shoot the victim, but most simply strike—without seriously hurting—the victim on the side of the head or in the stomach to show that they "mean business." If this still does not work and the victim resists strongly, most robbers would not hesitate to kill the victim. According to an analysis of over 815 robberies reported to Chicago police, only a few (7 percent) of the victims did resist actively and most of them were killed (Meer, 1985). Fourth, the weapon *ensures escape* after the completion of the crime, as robbers use the weapon to prevent the victims, witnesses, and even police officers from interfering with their escape.

Patterns of Robbery

Robbery is basically a *big-city* crime. The robbery rate in large cities is many times higher than in rural areas. Relatedly, the more urbanized a region, the higher its rate of robbery. This is because, unlike homicide, which typically occurs between acquaintances as offender and victim, robbery involves mostly strangers—and opportunities abound for encountering strangers in large cities. Thus, as the northeastern states are more urbanized than the southern states, so the northeastern states have a higher robbery rate (U.S. Census Bureau, 1999).

Robbery occurs most frequently in the *cold winter* months, reaching its peak in volume during the holiday season in December, when stores are making more money and people are carrying more cash with them on the streets. There are additional reasons for the higher frequency of robbery in the winter than in other seasons. The cold weather keeps most people off the streets, thereby making it easier for robbers to victimize lonely individuals without having any discouraging witnesses around. The cold weather also makes it look natural for robbers to wear a heavy coat, which is ideal for hiding a shotgun or other weapon. The increase in hours of darkness in the winter further enhances the opportunity for robbing without getting caught. All these factors involve the opportunity for committing robbery. Other factors have to do with the increased motivation for committing the crime. One such factor is a higher rate of unemployment in the winter, which largely comes from the loss of seasonal jobs such as construction, tourism, and other outdoor work. Another motivational factor is the economic pressure from the rising cost of living in the winter, because there is greater need for money to be spent on such goods as clothing, shelter, and heating (Landau and Fridman, 1993).

Most robberies (about six out of ten) take place *outdoors,* on the streets and highways. Of those that occur indoors, the general public assumes that a significant number take place in banks. But *bank robbery is relatively rare,* accounting for only about 6 percent of indoor robberies (see Figure 14.1). Since the early 1990s, though, bank robberies have increased significantly. This is largely because it is much more convenient to rob banks today. There are now far more banks providing long hours, in addition to the proliferation of sleepless automatic-teller machines, whose patrons can be easily robbed. Unlike the banks built 100 years ago like fortresses, many banks today make themselves vulnerable to robbery by having potted plants, subdued lighting, and open teller stations. The road system further makes it easy for robbers, since it takes less than a minute after the heist

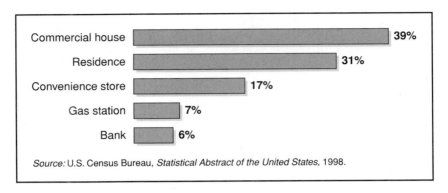

Source: U.S. Census Bureau, *Statistical Abstract of the United States*, 1998.

FIGURE 14.1   Locations of Indoor Robberies

to zoom away on the freeway. This may explain why California, which has the nation's most extensive network of freeways, has many more bank robberies than any other state (Johnston, 1997; Kaplan, 1991).

Most of the robberies today are *armed.* Over the years, armed robberies have increased faster than unarmed ones. Most of these robberies involve the use of firearms rather than knives and other cutting instruments, and are more likely to be committed by adults than youngsters. In contrast, unarmed robberies, which include purse snatching, mugging, and other violent confrontations, involve youngsters more often than adults. Compared with armed robberies, unarmed robberies also take place closer to the offender's home. This is largely due to the spontaneity and predominance of foot travel in unarmed robbery—as opposed to the planned nature of armed robbery and the common use of a vehicle in its commission (FBI, 1996; Capone and Nichols, 1976).

In contrast with violent crimes such as homicide and rape, which are predominantly intraracial in nature, robbery is more likely to be *interracial*—involving blacks robbing whites (Wilbanks, 1985). This is probably because robbery is more premeditated and impersonal than homicide and rape. "More premeditated" suggests that the robber, being more rational and calculative, would rather victimize people with more money than those with less, and "impersonal" implies that the robber would rather rob strangers than relatives, friends, or acquaintances. This victim profile—having more money and being strangers—is more likely to fit whites than blacks. Therefore, black offenders tend more to rob whites than other blacks.

Amateur and Professional Robbers

There are two kinds of robbers: amateurs and professionals. Compared with professionals, amateurs generally commit robbery for smaller sums of money with less planning and skill and higher risks of arrest. Adults are more likely than youngsters to be professionals, and youngsters tend more to be amateurs.

Amateur Robbers. Amateur robbers can further be divided into three types: (1) opportunist robbers, (2) addict robbers, and (3) alcoholic robbers (Haran and Martin, 1984; Conklin, 1972).

The majority of amateur robbers are *opportunist robbers.* Usually committing such forms of theft as larceny and shoplifting, opportunists infrequently rob. When they do rob, they tend to target individual persons rather than commercial establishments. Typical targets are older women with purses, drunks, cab drivers, and people who walk alone on dark or empty streets. The criteria for choosing such targets are the victim's easy accessibility and vulnerability rather than large sums of cash. Perhaps because such targets are easy to rob, opportunists rarely carry firearms and often have no weapon of any kind. Yet they are likely to form a gang, three or four young opportunists working together to overpower the victim in a strong-arm robbery. So the group itself operates as a weapon of sorts, comparable in threatening power to a knife.

Since the early 1980s, however, opportunist robbers have caused a surge in bank robberies, which are traditionally associated with professional robbers. This new breed of bank robber is mostly young and unsophisticated. There is little planning to their heists. Confederates are casually chosen and form loose groups thrown together "for the job." The robberies are so amateurishly conceived that the amount of loot is often the result of pure chance. The average take is about $3,000, but it does not seem much because it has to be split two, three, or four ways (Kaplan, 1991; Haran and Martin, 1984).

Addict robbers commit robbery to buy their next "fix." Like opportunists, addicts rarely go after lucrative targets and thus often commit robberies that yield small sums of money. But due to the high cost of their drug habit, the robbers desperately carry out more acts of property crime than the opportunist. Moreover, addicts are more reluctant to resort to physical force and thus more likely to use a firearm.

Among amateurs, *alcoholic robbers* are least likely to engage in robbery, and most likely to be caught when they rob. They usually do not plan their crime; neither do they try to make their crime easier by seeking a vulnerable victim. Instead, they often get involved in a situation that unexpectedly leads to a robbery. They may get into fistfights, or drunkenly assault people, and then take away their victims' money as an afterthought. The random nature of the alcoholic's crime may be illustrated by one alcoholic who walked into a liquor store to buy a bottle of whiskey. After he had given the clerk the money to pay for it, the clerk asked whether he wanted anything else. At that instant, the alcoholic decided that he did, telling the clerk to hand over all the money in the register. Surprised and angered, the clerk refused. During the ensuing fight, the alcoholic managed to take some money and then fled.

Professional Robbers. Professionals carefully plan their robberies, execute them with one or more accomplices and with skill, and make away with large sums of money. There are two types of professional robbers, one more specialized in robbery than the other. The more specialized ones commit robbery almost exclusively; the less specialized, being also committed to other forms of crimes, commit robbery only occasionally but nonetheless with professional skill. The first type of professional robber was more common in the past, while the second type is more common today.

Professional robbers as a whole have a strong commitment to robbery as a way of earning a living, and seek a series of big scores to support an expensive, hedonistic lifestyle. After executing a robbery, professionals often leave the city for a few weeks, perhaps taking a trip to a resort area. Once there, they spend the money like millionaires, to satisfy luxurious whims and pleasures. When the supply of money is depleted, they will start developing specific plans for more robberies. At other times they just keep their eyes open, watching for possible scores. Since they are mostly interested in big scores, they will typically rob commercial establishments that contain large sums of money. Because these targets generally take greater precaution against theft than individuals do, professional robbers usually have developed considerably more skill and do more careful planning than amateur offenders, who usually rob individuals of smaller sums of money.

Professional robbers tend to see their crime as an honest enterprise. Unlike burglary and other thefts, which involve furtiveness or deception, robbery calls for an open, direct, face-to-face confrontation with the victim. It is this quality of candor that, in the eye of the professional robber, transforms the crime into an honest activity. Professional robbers even consider their crime more honest than the business activity of the companies they victimize. As one of them explains, "To me this is perfectly honest, because these companies are cheating people anyway. When you go and just take it from them, you are actually more honest than they are. Most of the time, anyway, they are insured and make more money from the caper than you do" (Irwin, 1970).

Causes of Robbery

Two sociological theories seem useful for explaining robbery. One focuses on the *motivation* to commit robbery and the other on the *opportunity* for committing robbery as the causes of the crime. According to the first theory, the motivation is socially created *relative deprivation,* the feeling of frustration from failing to realize a heightened expectation in the lower classes, and to the second theory, the opportunity is provided by the *economic abundance* in the larger society.

Relative Deprivation.   John Conklin (1972) has used the concept of relative deprivation to explain the surge in robbery rates in major U.S. cities during the 1960s. Conklin noticed that from 1960 to 1969 the social and economic condition of poor African Americans improved significantly as a result of the federal government's many antipoverty and civil rights programs. But at the same time the rates of robbery among poor African Americans also went up significantly. Conklin attributed this ironical increase in robbery rates to relative deprivation among the poor blacks: The absolute improvement in their life induced them to hold higher expectations of enjoying as many opportunities as whites, but when they failed to realize these expectations, they felt frustrated and, as a consequence, tended to commit robbery.

Economic Abundance. Leroy Gould (1969) has used not only the concept of relative deprivation but also economic abundance to explain why the rate of property crime that had remained relatively low during the 1930–1943 period of economic scarcity rose sharply during the period of abundance from 1944 to 1965. As Gould says, "Increases in the amount of property would serve to increase the relative deprivation of those who were still not sharing in the ownership of the property, while at the same time *making it easier for these people to steal the property for their own use.*"

According to Gould, people with money problems feel particularly frustrated when they know that many others are doing very well because of the general affluence around them. At the same time, the society's economic abundance creates a lot of opportunities for committing robbery. Many banks, especially branch banks, are located close to highways and shopping centers—a convenience obviously designed for customers but tempting to robbers as well (Johnston, 1997; Duffala, 1976; Gould, 1969). The opportunities for robbery are also available in many other business establishments and private residences, where the robber can find a great deal of money, jewelry, and other precious objects. Since people have more money, they are also likely to carry more cash with them on the streets. In brief, economic abundance enhances what some sociologists have called "target suitability" for robbery (Cohen, Cantor, and Kluegel, 1981).

Auto Theft and Carjacking

Auto theft is the most significant property crime. As Table 14.1 shows, from 1986 to 1996, car theft continued to increase, while other property crimes, especially burglary, declined.

TABLE 14.1 Property Crimes, 1986–1996

Crime	Rate per 100,000 population		
	1986	*1996*	*Change from 1986 to 1996*
Auto theft	507.8	525.9	+3.6%
Larceny/theft	3,010.3	2,975.9	–1.1%
Robbery	225.1	202.4	–10.1%
Burglary	1,344.6	943.0	–29.9%

Source: U.S. Census Bureau, *Statistical Abstract of the United States*, 1998.

Characteristics and Trends

Many people seem to associate auto theft with teenagers stealing a car for purposes of "joy riding"—driving the car for a while and then abandoning it. Indeed, joy riding was quite common in the 1960s and 1970s. But since the early 1980s, it has become increasingly rare. Now, in the 1990s, most auto thieves steal cars in order to sell them for a quick and handsome profit. In fact, auto theft has become big business. Every year, about 1.5 million cars are stolen, costing at least $7 billion, which accounts for nearly half of all the property lost to crime (FBI, 1996; Nikkel, 1995).

The overwhelming majority of auto thefts do not involve any violence against the victim because the offender typically steals the car when the owner is not around. However, since 1990, there has been a trend toward the use of violence to force drivers to give up their cars. Cars have been hijacked at highway rest stops, gas stations, fast-food outlets, car washes, red lights, and shopping-mall parking lots. In a typical carjacking, a single robber puts a pistol to the head of a startled driver. Some carjackers would do a "bump and run" by staging a minor rear-end accident. When the unsuspecting motorist gets out to investigate the damage, one robber holds up the victim while the other drives off with the victim's car. A few of these carjackings, like the one described in the beginning of this chapter, are extremely violent, resulting in the victim's being severely beaten or brutally killed (Hyatt, 1993; Witkin, 1992).

According to the U.S. Justice Department, every year in the 1990s there were about 49,000 attempted carjackings and in half of these cases the offender got away with the car. Most of the carjackers are African Americans, but so are most of their victims. The most vulnerable to carjacking are people who are most likely to become victims of violent crime in general. They include men more than women, blacks more than whites, Hispanics more than non-Hispanics, the divorced more than the married, and urban residents more than rural or suburban dwellers (Klaus, 1999).

What Causes the Upsurge?

Why has auto theft increased much more than other property crimes? The *motivation* for committing auto theft appears to be about the same as for other property crimes. Like other property criminals, car thieves have a strong motivation for monetary gain. Their criminal motivation derives largely from the poor, lower-class environment where they have suffered deprivation resulting from income inequality, racial discrimination, or society's failure to fulfill aspirations for decent jobs. But auto thieves are unique in being offered abundant *opportunities* for stealing cars.

First, *inadequate law-enforcement* makes it easy to steal cars without getting caught. Overwhelmed by violent crime, the police have too little time left for dealing with auto theft. Of the nation's 500,000 police officers, fewer than 3000 (less than one percent) investigate auto theft. Moreover, prisons are so overcrowded with violent offenders that most car thieves do not serve any time—they are simply set free on probation. A second reason for the rise in auto theft is the *increased profitability* of stolen cars and car parts, the demand for which has gone up sharply. Some of this new demand comes from foreign countries, to which some 200,000 "hot" cars are shipped a year, compared with just a few thousands a decade ago, because a stolen American car can now double or triple in value there. Auto-repair shops also like to buy the parts removed from stolen cars because the illegal items are sold cheaper and delivered faster than legal ones from the manufacturer. A third reason for the growth in auto theft is *increased insurance fraud.* To collect insurance money, a car owner can contract with a thief to steal the car, abandon the automobile on a city street for any thief to steal, or simply run the vehicle into a river (Christian, 1995; Witkin, 1992).

What about the upsurge in carjacking? The three factors that have just been observed to be associated with auto theft can also explain the sharp increase in carjacking. But there is an additional, ironical reason: *the increased sophistication of the car's security devices,* such as the alarm systems, steering-wheel locks, and ignition-control systems. These antitheft devices are likely to encourage car thieves, particularly young amateurs, to hijack a car, because it is considerably easier to rob a motorist at gunpoint than to steal a car parked somewhere with its engine turned off (Bradsher, 1999; Witkin, 1992).

Burglary

Compared with other property crimes, burglary has declined significantly (see Table 14.1). Nevertheless, the number of break-ins is still great enough to cause concern among many Americans. According to an ABC News/*Washington Post* poll in the early 1990s, nearly a third of adults surveyed said that they "worry a great deal" about burglary (Sussman, 1992).

Modus Operandi

Burglars are characteristically rational and calculating in executing their crime. Thus, most burglaries are committed during the day when the homes are empty because the occupants are at work, at school, or out shopping. The most popular time for burglars to do their thing is between 9 and 11 a.m. and from 1 to 3 p.m. These are the hours when people are most likely to go out. Contrary to popular belief, burglaries are *not* crimes of the night, because breaking into a house at night may cause a confrontation with its occupants. There are exceptions, though. A few cat burglars may break into a home without waking up its occupants. This is especially easy to do in houses with loud window air conditioners. As a burglar says, "If you can't hear the air conditioner when you're asleep, you can't hear me when I break into your home." A few other burglars would work at night only if the family is away on vacation (Sussman, 1992; Cromwell, Olson, and Avary, 1991).

To ensure that the house they want to break into is empty, most burglars have a bag of tricks at their disposal. One common trick is to pass themselves off as a door-to-door salesperson. They knock on a door or ring a doorbell, ready to deliver a sales pitch. A similar stratagem is to knock on the door, ready to ask for a nonexistent person ("Is Mr. Smith home?") or directions to a nearby address. If nobody answers the door, they may quickly break into the house. But the more cautious burglars would leave a card in the door. If the card is still there the next day, it is a sure sign that the family is away. Another common trick is to get the prospective victim's name from the mailbox, look up the telephone number, and repeatedly make the call. If nobody answers, the house is assumed to be unoccupied (Cromwell, Olson, and Avary, 1991).

After making sure that nobody is in the house, most burglars still want to find out whether there is a burglar alarm. If there is, the burglars will go away. They will even pass over a house with a mere sign or window sticker that says the house is protected by an alarm system. They do not want to take chances with anyone who takes some precaution against burglary. As one burglar says, "Why take a chance? There's lots of places without alarms. Maybe they're bluffing, maybe they ain't." Dogs are another effective deterrent. Most burglars will stay away from a house if they know there is a dog in it. Even small dogs deter burglary, because, as one burglar explains, "Little dogs yap too much. The neighbors look to see what they are so excited about. I don't like little yapping dogs" (Cromwell, Olson, and Avary, 1991).

Causes of Burglary

Like other property crimes, burglary can be explained by deviant motivation and opportunity. But the specific nature of motivation and opportunity for burglary is not the same as that for other economic deviances.

In the case of burglaries, the primary motivation is the desire to obtain money to *meet expressive needs*, specifically the needs to maintain a "fast life," to party, and to use drugs and alcohol. Burglars have developed these needs from their street culture that emphasizes partying as the most important purpose of life (Wright and Decker, 1994).

The opportunity for committing burglary largely comes from the frequent *absence of capable guardians*. Capable guardians are people whose presence deters others from committing crime. Members of a family can become capable guardians against burglary simply by being present in their home. But there is no guardianship against burglary in many homes when husbands and wives go to work and children go to school. Moreover, the lack of community integration, as indicated by the absence of many neighbors watching each other's homes, reduces the neighbors' capability as antiburglary guardians (Lynch and Cantor, 1992).

Shoplifting

Shoplifting has become a scary word, conjuring up an image of thieves mingling with customers. Who wants to shop at a store known to be crawling with thieves? Understandably, store owners, to avoid frightening away customers, euphemistically refer to shoplifting as "shrinkage." Whatever it is called, shoplifting has become a serious problem in the United States. It costs U.S. shops up to $13.5 billion a year. This is roughly equivalent to 2 percent of their total merchandise, compared with 1.5 percent for shops in Canada and less than 1 percent in Japan (Klemke, 1992; *The Economist*, 1991). Ultimately, however, it is the honest customers who are forced to pay for the cost of shoplifting because prices of goods are routinely raised to reduce the loss from shrinkage.

A Social Profile of Shoplifters

Only a few shoplifters are *boosters,* professional criminals who shoplift for profit. Most shoplifters are *snitches,* amateurs who steal articles of small value for personal use. Most studies do not distinguish between boosters and snitches, and the following profile of shoplifters presumably applies to both.

Shoplifting is predominantly a juvenile offense. Individuals under age 21 are most likely to shoplift and, among these youngsters, those between ages 11 and 15 have the highest rate of shoplifting. The rate is lowest for people above age 50. Still, older shoplifters are more often featured in newspapers and magazines than their numbers warrant, because they can offer heartrending stories like, "I'm tired of eating dog food and I felt like eating a decent piece of meat" (Klemke, 1992).

The general public seems to believe that shoplifting is mostly a female crime. Some criminologists have also assumed the same thing. But this assumption was based on old studies that dealt with *apprehended* shoplifters only. Apprehended shoplifters do not represent the population of shoplifters, most of whom are not caught by the police. In more recent studies, when random samples of ordinary people were asked whether they had shoplifted, men turned out to be more likely than women to commit the crime (Klemke, 1992).

The lower class, the unemployed, the homeless, and drug addicts also have clearly higher rates of shoplifting. But the impact of race is less clear. Blacks are more likely than whites to shoplift in cases where the items taken are relatively expensive, while whites are more likely to take things of little value (Klemke, 1992).

Causes of Shoplifting

Like other property crimes, shoplifting can be explained by criminal motivation and opportunity. But a unique configuration of motivations and opportunities differentiates shoplifting from other crimes.

There are both economic and social-psychological motivations for shoplifting. As for economic motivations, *poverty* is a factor, as suggested by the evidence that poor people are more likely than others to shoplift and that shoplifting becomes more common when unemployment is high. But severe economic hardship alone cannot explain all cases of shoplifting. In fact, many shoplifters are merely *frugal customers*, who can afford to buy the things they need but are driven to steal them by a desire to stretch their budget through bargain hunting as encouraged by the consumption-driven society. Also, many young shoplifters commit the offense because they do not have the money to buy designer jeans, fancy shoes, and other fashionable items that enhance peer acceptance (Klemke, 1992).

Of the social-psychological motivations for shoplifters, the most common is the *sense of thrill, excitement,* or *fun* that shoplifters expect to experience when committing the crime. Another important motivation is the *desire for social acceptance,* which makes youngsters in particular highly vulnerable to peer pressure. When asked why they shoplift, many would say "because my friends are doing it." A third motivation is a cluster of *rationalizations* that the shoplifter can use to justify the crime before committing it. Thus many shoplifters deny responsibility (saying, for example, "My friends make me do it" or "I'm high or drunk"); deny injury to the victim ("It's only a cheap bottle of perfume" or "It's such a big store they won't miss it"); or argue that the victim deserves it ("It serves them right because they rip us off every time we buy something from them"). Armed with these rationalizations, shoplifters are able to decriminalize their offense, thereby continuing to see themselves as respectable, law-abiding citizens rather than as criminals (Klemke, 1992).

Those economic and social-psychological motivations seem by themselves powerful enough to cause people to shoplift, because the opportunities for shoplifting are so available to everybody. Anyone can, without any difficulty, walk into a store as a prospective shoplifter in the guise of a customer. And the risk of being apprehended for shoplifting is minimal, thanks to the laxness of law-enforcement against such offense.

Organized Crime

The entertainment media, such as the movie *The Godfather,* first shown more than 20 years ago and recently rereleased, often romanticize mobsters as men of honor, courage, and toughness but also sensationalize them as ruthless killers. Actually, the participants in organized crime, like the average Americans, try to achieve the American Dream, except by more socially disreputable, deviant means. Let us take a closer look at organized crime.

Organizational Structure

There are many different organized crime groups in the United States, each consisting of members of the same race or ethnicity. The best known and most powerful is *the Mafia,* also called *la Cosa Nostra, the mob,* or *the syndicate.* Composed mostly of Italian Americans, the Mafia is a relatively loose, informal confederation of diverse groups of professional criminals operating independently in large cities around the country. Each group is known to law enforcers as a crime family identified by the name of its founder, such as Genovese, Gambino, or

Bonanno. Each family consists of a *hierarchical structure* of positions, ranging from the highest to the lowest as follows: "don" or boss, underboss, lieutenants, counselor, and "soldiers" or button men (so-called because they do the bidding of the higher-ranking members when the latter "push the button"). The boss of each family directs the criminal activities of the members of his family.

Members are governed by *a code of conduct*. The most important rules in the code concern *loyalty* ("Be loyal to the family") and secrecy ("Don't squeal on fellow members). If these rules are violated, the individual will be murdered. That's why the U.S. government has to spend an enormous sum of money on the witness-protection program, providing informers with new identities, houses in different locations, and new jobs.

Those two basic characteristics of organization—a well-defined hierarchy of positions and a code of conduct—also exist, with some variation, in many other ethnic crime groups, such as those dominated by African Americans, Hispanic Americans, and Asian Americans. But these ethnic gangs not only differ among themselves but also from the Italian-American Mafia in regard to the nature of their deviant activities.

Organized Crime Activities

The largest criminal organization is the 6000-strong Herrera family founded by immigrants from Mexico, operating mostly in Southern California. They are notorious for smuggling heroin into the United States. Then there are some 200 Colombian crime families in Florida who engage in cocaine smuggling. Chinese, Vietnamese, Korean, and Japanese gangs have been found on the East and West Coasts, active in smuggling drugs and extorting money from businesses in their communities. Scores of other groups can be found in various cities: Israelis dominating insurance fraud in Los Angeles, Cubans running illegal gambling operations in Miami, Canadians engaging in gun-smuggling and money-laundering in Miami, Russians carrying out extortion and contract murders in New York, and so on (Kleinknecht, 1996; President's Commission, 1986). Despite their differences, all these groups have one thing in common: They specialize in one or two forms of economic deviance while confining their operation to a limited area, usually an ethnic community. In contrast, Italian-American crime groups operate *all over the country*, engaging in a *variety* of deviant activities such as those disclosed below.

Selling Illegal Goods and Services. The illegal goods and services sold by the Mafia include illicit gambling, loan sharking, and narcotics. *Illicit gambling* includes betting on horse races, lotteries, and sporting events. But it has become less profitable today because of the increasing legalization of lotteries and off-track betting. Illicit gambling now brings in only about $2 billion a year, which is small potatoes in view of the Mafia's annual income of at least $60 billion (Angelo, 1992; President's Commission, 1986).

Far more profitable is *loan sharking*, the lending of money at exorbitantly high rates, typically more than 100 percent a year. In fact, when the economy is in a depression or recession, hordes of businesspeople and bill-payers are forced to borrow money from loan sharks at up to between 200 and 300 percent annual interest. Since customers can put up only their bodies as security for the loan (if they had valuable property, they would have gone to a legitimate loan company), it seems logical that the loan sharks may resort to violence or the threat of violence to ensure repayment. But the loan sharks hardly need to threaten violence, let alone actually use it, because they already have a bad *reputation* for being violent, which is enough to scare the borrowers (Block, 1991).

In the field of *illicit drugs,* the Italian-American Mafia operates for maximum profit at minimum risk of interference from law enforcers. They restrict their activities to importing and wholesale distribution, letting independent drug pushers take over the risky business of selling narcotics on the street. The narcotics trade is the most lucrative source of revenues for organized crime. Not surprisingly, the "new Mafias"—consisting of African Americans, Asians, or Hispanics—rely on drug trafficking as their *primary* source of income.

Engaging in Large-Scale Thefts and Racketeering.   The Mafia steals in a big way. Small-scale thefts such as holdups and burglaries are left to independent criminals. The mob turns to wholesale operations instead: They steal huge quantities of negotiable stocks and bonds as well as credit cards and airline tickets, whole carloads of merchandise (sometimes with the car itself) from docks, railway stations, and international airports, and millions of dollars' worth of automobiles, which they furnish with proper engine identification numbers and registration papers necessary for selling them. To sell these "hot" items, they have fences who work like big-time merchandising operators.

Another form of organized crime activity is known as racketeering. It may take the simple form of a "protection racket," which involves the extortion of money from legitimate businesspeople. They are given the proverbial offer they cannot refuse: the sale of the mob's "insurance policy" against such "accidents" as the burning of their stores and the breaking of their store windows or their heads—to be carried out by the mobsters if the businesspeople refuse to buy the "insurance." The more elaborate and more common form is *labor racketeering.* This involves the manipulation of workers' employers and unions. Racketeers may forcibly offer businesspeople a "sweetheart contract," whereby the employers pay them a fee for having their employees join the racketeers' nonexistent union; extort money from employers by threatening them with labor strife; or demand that the employing company put their relatives on the company's payroll.

Corrupting Public Officials.   To help ensure success in all the above patterns of activities, it may be necessary to corrupt the appropriate public officials. The mob usually targets three kinds of officials: law enforcers, politicians, and officials in licensing, supervisory, or regulatory agencies (Block, 1991). The manner of corruption is outright bribery or, in the case of politicians, contribution to a political campaign. The goal is to have their "political front person" pass laws favoring their interests and prevent the passage of laws damaging to their illegal activities, to have the police and other law enforcers ignore their criminal activities, or to get regulatory agencies to turn a blind eye to their illegal way of operating legitimate businesses—such as threatening competitors with violence.

Infiltrating Legitimate Businesses.   This activity is the most profitable and yet the safest for the mobsters to engage in. The types of businesses that they have infiltrated include Las Vegas casinos, nightclubs and restaurants, hotels and motels, trucking companies, wholesale food distributors, as well as the industries of banking and investment, insurance, real estate, electronics, health services, stock brokerage, and prepaid telephone cards. The Mafia's penetration into these legitimate businesses is so deep that many law-abiding citizens routinely deal with it. Even the FBI, always busy fighting organized crime, once unknowingly hired a mob's moving company (Raab, 1997; President's Commission, 1986). By acquiring any one of those legitimate businesses, the mobsters aim to achieve certain objectives: to gain respectability, to establish a legitimate source of income for paying taxes and thus avoid income tax prosecution, to invest "bad" money (from racketeering and other illegal activities) in a legitimate business for legitimate profit, and to use the legitimate business as a front for carrying out illegitimate schemes.

The most common objective of entering a legitimate business is the last one, because it produces the most profit. An illegitimate scheme may involve insurance fraud: taking over businesses and then hiring professional arsonists to burn buildings and their contents in order to then collect on the fire insurance. Increasingly, to avoid detection by law enforcers, the Mafia has resorted to the more sophisticated methods of fraud typically used by white-collar and corporate criminals like those we discussed in the preceding chapter.

Ethnicity and Organized Crime

The roots of organized crime reach deep into the American past. During the eighteenth century, there were pirates at many U.S. ports and rivers, as well as robbers, gamblers, and slave-snatchers operating mostly in the rural, frontier settings. The frontier lawlessness continued to reign throughout the nineteenth century. It spawned such legendary train- and bank-robbery gangs as the Reno brothers and the Jesse James gang.

Toward the end of the last century, many criminal gangs began to emerge in the cities. The major ones were Irish, Jewish, and Italian, but these three groups were not equally powerful at the same time. The Irish dominated the organized crime scene in the first two decades of this century, controlling large cities' political machinery and such industries as construction, trucking, public utilities, and the waterfront. Then, in the 1920s, the Jews took over the dominant position in organized crime, controlling gambling and labor racketeering. In the same decade Prohibition (the law against the manufacture and sale of liquor) began to prepare the Italians to succeed the Jews. By the end of Prohibition in the early 1930s, the Italians were firmly in control of organized crime. In fact, Italian dominance has continued to this day, largely because of Prohibition.

Prohibition ushered in a new era of organized crime. Before Prohibition, criminal groups were mostly local in the scope and extent of their activities, confined to single ethnic neighborhoods. During and after Prohibition, however, the Italian gangs went beyond the local setting to control criminal activities of more extensive territories—covering the entire country. Prohibition brought this about by making bootlegging a complex, large-scale operation. The illicit alcohol had to be manufactured, transported, and distributed to thousands of retail outlets across the country. Successful bootlegging required complex operations involving huge breweries and distillers, giant warehouses, fleets of tank cars and trucks, and protection from hijackers. It also required the bribery and cooperation of the Coast Guard, customs officials, politicians, and police. Since the liquor came from Europe or Canada, it further required international as well as interstate connections (Hills, 1980; Homer, 1974).

All this explains why the Mafia is the only crime group that exists in all the major U.S. cities today. But, since the early 1980s, the Mafia has lost some of its dominance over the underworld. The country's most celebrated Mafia boss in recent years, John Gotti, has finally been convicted and sentenced to prison. Most of the other Mafia bosses have also been put away. Every single one of the nation's 24 Mafia families has some members now doing time. The Mafia has also suffered severe internal problems. Threatened with long imprisonment unless they talk, many mafiosi are willing to violate the organization's sacred code of "omerta" (silence or secrecy) by testifying in court against fellow members. The Mafia membership is also shrinking because the crime families' children and grandchildren prefer to pursue conventional careers as lawyers, doctors, or businesspeople. Given all these problems plaguing the Mafia, criminal gangs of other ethnicities that have emerged over the last three decades are tempted to move in on the lucrative crime markets that the Italians have monopolized for the last 60 years (Kleinknecht, 1996; Reuter, 1995).

But it will take some time for some of the new ethnic gangs to wrest the underworld leadership from the Italians. The history of ethnic succession in organized crime—the leadership first held by the Irish, then by the Jews, and finally by the Italians—suggests that an ethnic gang has to go through at least four stages before it can attain supremacy in the U.S. underworld. In the first stage, common street criminals get together to *form gangs in their own ethnic neighborhood* where they extort or otherwise victimize its residents. In the second stage, confined to the same area, different gangs are compelled to *compete with one another* in dominating the local crime scene. Frequent violent conflict occurs, including murders. In the third stage, the gangs *resolve their conflict* by forming a larger crime organization that allocates turfs to gangs and settles intergang disputes by peaceful means. The organization, stronger than each individual gang, is powerful enough to move its crime operations beyond the ethnic neighborhood and into the larger society. In the fourth stage, various ethnic crime organizations fight with one another, resulting in the emergence of *one ethnic organization as the victor,* which then dominates the underworld across the country. This is what the Italians have been doing since they became victorious over the Jews and Irish in the 1930s (O'Kane, 1992).

Today, African-, Hispanic-, Asian-American, and other gangs are stuck in the second stage, as shown by the constant conflicts among ethnic gangs in their own ethnic neighborhoods. Most of the conflicts are drug-related, because the new ethnic gangs typically rely on drug trafficking as the primary source of their income. This is reminiscent of the 1930s when the Italians were also in the second stage, finding themselves locked in a liquor war comparable to the drug war of today. In fact, the new ethnic gangs seem to have taken over drug trafficking and other traditional street crime activities but only in their own ethnic communities, as the Italians did in the 1930s. But none of these new ethnic gangs—or the nonethnic motorcycle gangs—has managed to have the Mafia's success in developing a diversified portfolio that includes not just drug trafficking but many other crime activities throughout the country (Kleinknecht, 1996; Nordland, 1992). In short, the Mafia has been losing its power, but no other ethnic crime organization has emerged to replace it as the dominant force in organized crime.

Organized Crime in Global Perspective

We have so far seen what organized crime is like in the United States. To learn more about organized crime, we may need to know what it is like in other societies. Let us, then, take a tour of the underworld in Italy, Japan, Hong Kong, and Russia.

The Mafia in Italy. The Italian Mafia engages in about the same activities as its U.S. counterpart does: illegal gambling, racketeering or extortion, and drug trafficking as well as bribing government officials and infiltrating legitimate businesses. But the Italian Mafia has long enjoyed greater social and political influence. They are particularly influential in the areas where they operate, even moreso than the government itself. Victims of robbery, for example, have a much greater chance of getting their property back if they seek help from the Mafia than if they go to the police. In the case of an abduction, a mafioso can mediate between the kidnapper and the victim's family—the kidnapper gets only a portion of the ransom demanded and the victim is freed unharmed—whereas police intervention may endanger the victim's life. In fact, common criminals are so scared of the Mafia that they rarely do their thing. In Corleone, Sicily, where Italy's most powerful and bloodiest crime family lives, there is hardly any theft or robbery. "Here," observes an Italian journalist, "the Mafia offers, at no cost and without need for violence, services more efficient than the government's" (Nicastro, 1992).

The Mafia is also very influential in politics. It has its own political machine, capable of delivering votes to win elections for some members and others. Most of the elected officials are not mafiosi but many have turned to the syndicate for help during election. It is therefore easy for the mob to get lucrative contracts for public works or government projects, from which enormous profits can be made legally as well as illegally—such as through faked repairs and padded expenses. Not surprisingly, public funds have become the biggest source of the Mafia's income (Moody, 1993; *The Economist,* 1992).

Since 1992, however, the Mafia has been under siege. The problem started with its assassination of two widely admired judges who had made Mafia-busting their life's work. The ensuing public outrage forced the government to crack down on organized crime. Sweeping antiracketeering laws were soon passed, giving law enforcers unprecedented power in nailing the mafiosi, such as the power to use phone taps widely, to search or confiscate properties, and to guarantee protection for state's witnesses. The witness protection program has proven the most effective in fighting organized crime. It has persuaded more than 300 mafiosi to collaborate with the authorities. As a result, many high-ranking mafiosi, like their peers in the United States, have been arrested, prosecuted, or imprisoned (Moody, 1993; *The Economist,* 1992).

But it is doubtful that the Italian mob will be crushed completely. Similar anti-Mafia campaigns were carried out in the 1960s and early 1980s, yet the mob later reemerged as powerful as ever. A major reason is that there is a great deal of unemployment and poverty in the areas where organized crime flourishes. Another important reason is that the mob provides jobs and security in the areas under its control (Walston, 1986).

The Yakuza in Japan. The *Yakuza,* which literally means "good-for-nothing," consists of about ten crime "families," each comparable to a huge corporation. The largest Yakuza family comprises over 750 gangs, with each gang—which average 25 to 30 members—having its own subgangs, and each subgang having its own subordinate gangs. Such a huge, complex organizational structure makes for loose control. Thus a typical Yakuza organization is far less centralized than the U.S. Mafia family. Each of the numerous subgangs within the Yakuza family is given considerable flexibility and autonomy, the freedom to engage in any business, legal or illegal, as long as it pays a monthly fee and fulfills other obligations to the organization as a whole (Delfs, 1991a).

The Yakuza's recruits typically come from backgrounds similar to those of their U.S. peers. Most are lower-class youths who have been rejected by Corporate Japan, such as school dropouts, drug users, or members of motorcycle gangs. Before being initiated into the Yakuza, these social rejects must undergo an apprenticeship that usually lasts five years. They learn the values and customs of the syndicate, such as taking responsibility for one's failure by cutting off the little pinkie or, most important, being absolutely loyal to the boss, who is considered more important than one's wife and children, or life itself. At the end of the apprenticeship the recruits join the Yakuza and earn four times as much as the average salaried person. They see themselves as modern-day samurai (noble, heroic warriors), feeling tough, brave, and smart. These former social rejects also look down on ordinary people, considering them to be fools for working much harder for far lower pay (Delfs, 1991a).

Aside from its traditional operations in prostitution, gambling, and narcotics, the Yakuza has, since the 1980s, moved deeply into many legitimate businesses largely because of increased demands for its criminal talent. By the end of the 1980s, many banks had accumulated a lot of nonperforming loans, that is, loans which their customers—both businesses and consumers—cannot pay. The banks were forced to sell the Yakuza the bad debts cheaply, which was better than getting nothing at all. The Yakuza was glad to buy the debts because it could effectively collect payment from the borrowers—naturally, through threats of violence or worse. This has enabled the Yakuza to entrench itself in the banking business today (Kaplan, 1998; WuDunn, 1996; Delfs, 1991b).

The Yakuza is heavily involved not only in banking and other legitimate business but also in politics. The mob contributes huge sums of money to leaders of various political parties. This is not only because the Yakuza wants to influence government policy, but also because the politicians need the money to win elections. Thus, there exists "a symbiotic relationship of mutual benefit and need between the underworld and open society, one in which businesspeople and politicians actively seek out Yakuza as clients and also as providers of various unique and essential services" (Delfs, 1991b).

Unlike the crime organizations in most other countries, the Yakuza gangs are legal in Japan. This is why the Yakuza display their names on the front of their headquarters and members proudly wear their gang's lapel pin in public. But, like their counterparts in the United States and Italy, in recent years the Yakuza has been under considerable pressure from the government. The Japanese government has passed an anti-Yakuza law that defines as illegal any organization in which more than 12 percent of the members are convicted criminals. Many Yakuza gangs faced the prospect of having to dissolve and discontinue their criminal operations.

However, the law has stirred protests from the Yakuza and its supporters, who argued that gangsters have the same right as everybody else to earn a living. In addition, Yakuza sympathizers have argued that the law will turn heretofore open organized crime into an underground organization, which will become less controllable by law enforcers, as it is in the United States. Other supporters have also contended that the Yakuza's decline will cause a rise in street crime committed by freelance criminals, as the Yakuza has traditionally been more effective than the police in deterring street crime. At any rate, since the law was put into effect in 1992, many Yakuza gangs have started to circumvent it by formally expelling some members in order to reduce the proportion of members with criminal records. This means that most Yakuza gangs can still continue their business as usual (Sterngold, 1992; Delfs, 1991c).

The Triads in Hong Kong. A former British colony that was returned to China in 1997, Hong Kong is an extremely prosperous city. Under the banner of international capitalism, the frenzied pursuit of money has transformed the city into the world's third-largest financial center, close behind New York and London. The frenzied pursuit of money has also turned the city into probably the world's largest haven of organized crime. According to Hong Kong police, at least 50 crime organizations thrive in the city. The organizations are called the Triads. A Triad is symbolized by an equilateral triangle whose three sides represent the basic Chinese concepts of heaven, earth, and man, suggesting the great unity and power of the organization. Altogether there are over 300,000 Triad members, which clearly dwarfs the Yakuza membership (80,000) in Japan and particularly the Mafia membership (2000) in the United States (Kaplan, 1998; Posner, 1988).

A multibillion-dollar underworld empire, the Triads annually acquire an income estimated to exceed the former colony's gross domestic product (the total value of all the goods and services produced in Hong Kong). Part of this income derives from traditional crime activities, such as illegal gambling, prostitution, extortion, as well as infiltration of numerous legitimate businesses. These activities are highly lucrative, but most of the Triad money comes from the astronomically more profitable heroin business. Unlike their traditional crime activities, which are limited to the local market, the Triads' heroin business is global, with huge quantities of their illicit drug sold in Europe, the United States, and other prosperous countries (Godson and Olson, 1995; Posner, 1988).

The enormous wealth makes the Triads a popular source of employment for poor ambitious teenagers. These Hong Kong youngsters have lived since birth in tiny apartments in a ramshackle building packed with thousands of families. They believe that they can become rich by joining a Triad, but they must first prove themselves to be tough, ruthless, and smart in their neighborhood's delinquent gangs. When being initiated into a Triad, they must swear absolute loyalty to the organization 36 times, each time with the reminder from a Triad leader that death comes to all traitors. The initiation rite also includes taking some blood from the recruits, mixing it with wine, and having the new members drink it. They are expected to always remember that there are only two choices for Triad members—loyalty or death (Posner, 1988).

These new members start out doing most of the dirty work as the organization's foot soldiers. Their jobs range "from vandalizing cars at garages in order to force money from the owners to throwing live snakes and rats into crowded restaurants that refuse to pay promptly" (Posner, 1988). They also learn to extort money from numerous businesses by "asking" them for loans or "persuading" them to hire some extra employees who do not show up for work. Later, with considerable experience of this type in hand, smarter, ambitious Triad members infiltrate legitimate businesses to commit such white-collar crimes as credit-card and business fraud, counterfeiting, and embezzlement. Starting out mostly with toughness, and then with brains, a Triad member can eventually rise to the top of the syndicate as a very wealthy crime boss (Posner, 1988).

As in the United States, Italy, and Japan, the Hong Kong government has, since the early 1990s, tried to crack down on the Triads. New laws were passed requiring testimony from victims against Triad members and allowing confiscation of crime proceeds. Various businesses, particularly banks and accountants, are mandated to report any suspicious activities, because the authorities hope to find and confiscate the Triads' drug-trafficking profits. Ordinary citizens are also obliged to testify or otherwise provide information about dangerous criminals. Refusal to testify may result in a 12-month prison term or $13,000 fine. These anti-Triad battles are unlikely to win the war on organized crime for three reasons: (1) The public has so far found police protection frighteningly inadequate for testifying against powerful Triads. (2) The Triads can easily transfer their drug and other dirty money out of Hong Kong, as some have done before. (3) The Triads have penetrated legitimate businesses so deeply that most of their illegal acts cannot be detected (Mosher, 1992).

The Mafiya in Russia. Organized crime *already* existed in the former Soviet Union when the country was still under tight control by the Communist regime (Handelman, 1995; Vaksberg, 1991). But the replacement of communism by *capitalism* has enabled the "Mafiya" to greatly expand their traditional operations as well as move into new areas of criminal activities.

For decades the prohibition of private enterprise under the Soviet command economy created severe shortages of merchandise at state stores. As a consequence, considerable opportunities opened up for black marketeers to sell merchandise in the illicit private marketplace. Most of these black marketeers were ordinary citizens who legally obtained an extra supply of, say, sugar from their relatives in another city and then sold it to neighbors or friends. But some black marketeers were outright criminals, who as part of a criminal network received shipments of goods, such as quality fur hats, from their colleagues, the "suppliers," working in state factories (Handelman, 1995).

Today, these organized criminals have greatly expanded their criminal enterprises. They now obtain from government bureaucrats and industrial managers through bribery all kinds of commodities—from gold to petroleum—in order to smuggle them abroad for sale at below the world price. They are also involved in theft and sale abroad of missiles and nuclear-bomb-making materials, such as enriched uranium. They have declared open season on the Russian military, stealing such weapons as tanks, rocket launchers, and assault rifles. Aside from these unique criminal activities, Russian mobsters operate the same kinds of rackets that are run in other countries, such as extortion, prostitution, drug trafficking, money laundering, and contract killing, except that they are far more ruthless. Many businesspeople have been gunned down for refusing to pay protection or extortion money (Duffy and Trible, 1994).

Most of the Russian crime groups lack the hierarchical structure of the American Mafia, the Japanese Yakuza, or the Hong Kong Triads. They are unpredictable and volatile enough to be called *disorganized* crime (Mitchell, 1992). Collectively, however, they have become more powerful than their foreign peers. According to a 1994 report prepared for the Russian president, a large majority (70 to 80 percent) of commercial banks and private enterprises in major cities are forced to pay a tribute of 10 to 20 percent of their profits to organized crime. The Russian Mafiyas, the report concludes, have the country by the throat, squeezing the life out of the private sector and even holding the government hostage. The Russian crime gangs have looted so much money that they are now operating in more than 50 countries from Britain to Malaysia. In North America alone there are already over 30 Russian crime syndicates trafficking in everything from narcotics to prostitution in more than 17 cities (Friedman, 1999; Bohlen, 1994).

Cross-Cultural Conclusions.   At this juncture, after analyzing organized crime in various societies, we may reach several conclusions about the subject.

The first point to be made is that organized crime is basically the same in most societies for being an hierarchal organization that engages in crime activities. Organized crime differs from one society to another only in intraorganizational unity and criminal activities. Members' loyalty to the organization seems stronger in Japan and Hong Kong than in the United States and Italy today. The Hong Kong Triads engage in drug trafficking much more extensively than their counterparts in other countries. The Triads, along with their peers in Japan, Italy, and Russia, seem to have penetrated legitimate business and politics more deeply than have the crime organizations in the United States.

The second conclusion is that there is no validity to Daniel Bell's (1962) theory that organized crime is a uniquely American way for ambitious poor people to become rich. Organized crime, as we have observed, serves the same function in Japan and Hong Kong.

A third conclusion to be drawn is that organized crime is more pervasive, influential, or powerful in the four societies we examined than it is in the United States. The reason may be partly cultural in that organized crime in Italy, Japan, and Hong Kong is more socially acceptable and integrated into the legitimate world of business and politics. The reason may also be partly economic: The less mature the capitalism of a country is, the less controllable and hence the more prevalent its organized crime. This point shows most clearly in the contrast between the United States and Russia.

The fourth conclusion from this analysis must be that it is extremely difficult, if not impossible, to get rid of organized crime, as shown by the failure of antisyndicate measures in various countries. This is particularly true in Japan and Hong Kong because of the underworld's deeper penetration into the conventional upperworld. By comparison, however, U.S. authorities are more successful in prosecuting mobsters, especially in recent years. Does this mean that we can eradicate organized crime in the United States? Let us take a closer look at this issue.

The War on Organized Crime in the United States

In the 1980s the federal government began in earnest to crack down on organized crime. Special strike forces were set up in 26 cities to arrest and prosecute numerous mobsters and seize their assets. This was done by pulling together the resources of the Justice Department's lawyers, the FBI, the Drug Enforcement Administration, the Department of Labor, the Internal Revenue Service, the Customs and Postal Services, and the Bureau of Alcohol, Tobacco, and Firearms in order to ensure that the mobsters did not slip through the law-enforcement cracks. These federal agents also had the cooperation of local police, a far cry from the situation in the past when they distrusted each other and often collided in their organized-crime investigations. President Ronald Reagan also helped out by removing the limits on court-ordered wiretaps. With these electronic weapons, federal agents were able to listen in on countless conversations among mobsters in their cars, social clubs, and other places where they met. The federal agents were even successful in using the threat of heavy sentences to pressure many mafiosi to violate their crime family's centuries-old tradition of silence by testifying against their former partners. These turncoats were mostly the new generation, who found a long prison sentence too stiff a price to pay for family loyalty.

Because of the combination of all these factors, the war on organized crime showed impressive results. In only four years, from 1981 to 1985, 2554 mafiosi were prosecuted and 809 convicted. Toward the end of 1986, three crime bosses and five other mafiosi were convicted of running the Mafia as members of its commission and of committing such crimes as murder, extortion, and racketeering (Magnuson, 1986). The campaign against organized crime has been even more successful in the 1990s, as none of the nation's 24 Mafia families has escaped successful prosecution (Nordland, 1992).

All this has undoubtedly dealt a serious blow to the Mafia. But it does not signal the death of organized crime. Those who have escaped the dragnet are now much more careful in concealing their activities and identities. They have begun to shift increasingly to more sophisticated, less detectable white-collar crimes (Raab, 1997, 1994). They have also stopped attracting public attention by shedding their former flamboyant lifestyles. It is doubtful that they would again behave like the mobster who turned himself into "a one-man parade" everywhere he went and impressed others by tipping a bartender $100 just for keeping the ice cubes cold (Pileggi, 1986).

Perhaps most important to the future, it seems impossible to stamp out organized crime because the two basic social causes of such deviance remain: (1) a strong demand for illicit drugs and other vices or a great opportunity for illicit gain in the white-collar and corporate world, and (2) a contingent of the ambitious poor or immigrants who cannot achieve the American Dream the conventional way.

Summary

1. What are the characteristics of robbery? Robbery has the characteristics of both a property and violent crime. As a property crime, robbery is a rational act, which involves making rational decisions about the execution of a robbery. As a violent crime, robbery is carried out with actual or potential violence against the victim; unarmed or strong-arm robbery involves actual violence, while armed robbery involves potential violence.

2. What are the patterns of robbery? Most robberies are committed in large cities, during the cold winter months, and most occur outdoors. While bank robbery is relatively rare, it has increased significantly. Most robberies are armed, and robberies are more interracial than such violent crimes as homicide and rape.

3. How do amateur robbers differ from professional robbers? The amateurs are generally younger, and tend to commit robbery for smaller sums of money with less planning and skill and a higher risk of arrest. In addition, professional robbers have a stronger commitment to robbery as a way of earning a living and see their crime as an honest enterprise. **What causes robbery?**

According to sociological theories, the causes of robbery are relative deprivation in the lower classes and economic abundance in the larger society.

4. What are the characteristics of auto theft and carjacking? Most auto thieves steal cars for the purpose of selling them for a quick and handsome profit. While a great majority of auto thieves quietly steal cars left alone by their owners, a few thieves resort to violence by hijacking cars. **What causes the recent great increase in auto theft and carjacking?** The causes include inadequate law enforcement against car theft, increased profitability of stolen cars and auto parts, and increased insurance fraud. The increased sophistication of the car's security devices is an additional factor behind the upsurge in carjacking.

5. How do burglars go about breaking and entering? They try to avoid confrontations with victims by breaking into empty houses, which explains why most burglaries occur during the day when people go out to work rather than during the night. **What causes burglary?** The causes include the offender's expressive needs for maintaining a fast life, partying, and using drugs and alcohol, and the deviant opportunity provided by the frequent absence of capable guardians against burglary.

6. Who shoplifts? Shoplifters are mostly young persons under age 21. They are more likely to be men and to be lower class, unemployed, homeless, or addicted to drugs. **What causes shoplifting?** Causes of shoplifting include economic motivations such as being poor and trying to be frugal, and social-psychological motivations such as the desires for thrill, social acceptance, and rationalizations.

7. What is the nature of organized crime as an organization? It has a well-defined hierarchy of positions and a code of conduct governing the behavior of members. **What crime activities do organized criminals participate in?** While most ethnic crime groups specialize in drug trafficking or only a few crimes, the Italian-American Mafia gets involved in many diverse deviances that include selling illegal goods and services, engaging in large-scale thefts and racketeering, corrupting public officials, and infiltrating legitimate businesses.

8. How is ethnicity associated with organized crime? Toward the end of the last century, the most powerful crime groups were Irish, Jewish, and Italian. Organized crime was first dominated by the Irish, then by the Jews, and finally, beginning in the 1930s, by the Italians. Prohibition—the period in which alcohol was made illegal—helped the Italians develop a nationwide dominance of organized crime, which continues to this day. Since the early 1980s, pressure from law enforcement has chipped away the Italian dominance, and other ethnic groups, particularly African, Hispanic, and Asian Americans, have emerged. But the Italian Mafia still retains its nationwide leadership in the underworld.

9. How does organized crime in other countries resemble or differ from that in the United States? Organized crime is basically the same in various societies with regard to organizational structure and crime activities, which vary only in degree and extent. Organized crime is also cross-societally the same, as a means for the ambitious poor to achieve success. But organized crime is more pervasive and powerful in other countries than it is in the United States. And government attempts to crack down on organized crime are less successful in other countries than in the United States.

10. How has the U.S. government dealt with organized crime? Since the early 1980s, the federal government has consolidated its various law-enforcement efforts—with impressive results—toward putting organized crime out of business. Numerous mobsters, and their bosses, have been successfully prosecuted and put away. But the demise of organized crime is doubtful because the criminals tend to become more careful in concealing their activities and identities— and, perhaps most important, the basic social causes of organized crime continue to exist.

SUGGESTED READINGS

Block, Alan A. (Ed.). 1991. *The Business of Crime: A Documentary Study of Organized Crime in the American Economy.* Boulder, Colo.: Westview. A collection of government reports on organized crime's infiltration and control of garment, air freight, waste disposal, and other industries.

Cromwell, Paul E., James N. Olson, and D'Aunn Wester Avary. 1991. *Breaking and Entering: An Ethnographic Analysis of Burglary.* Newbury Park, Calif.: Sage. A thoroughgoing look into the world of burglary.

Gabor, Thomas. 1987. *Armed Robbery: Cops, Robbers, and Victims.* Springfield, Ill.: Charles C. Thomas. An empirical study of robbery in Canada, with relevance to the same crime in the United States.

Handelman, Stephen. 1995. *Comrade Criminal: Russia's New Mafiya.* New Haven, Conn.: Yale University Press. Offers a guide to the frontierlike, ruthless, and chaotic world of organized crime in Russia.

Kenney, Dennis J., and James O. Finckenauer. 1995. *Organized Crime in America.* Belmont, Calif.: Wadsworth. A textbook on organized crime, covering its history, crime activities, and association with various groups of Americans, as well as the attempts to deal with organized crime.

Kleinknecht, William. 1996. *The New Ethnic Mobs: The Changing Face of Organized Crime in America.* New York: Free Press. A detailed presentation of organized crime among various ethnic minorities in the United States.

Klemke, Lloyd W. 1992. *The Sociology of Shoplifting: Boosters and Snitches Today.* Westport, Conn.: Praeger. A comprehensive theoretical and empirical analysis of various aspects of shoplifting.

O'Kane, James M. 1992. *The Crooked Ladder: Gangsters, Ethnicity, and the American Dream.* New Brunswick, N.J.: Transaction. An analysis of how a succession of ethnic minorities has been using organized crime to climb the ladder of success in the United States.

Tunnell, Kenneth D. 1992. *Choosing Crime: The Criminal Calculus of Property Offenders.* Chicago: Nelson-Hall. An empirical study of robbers, burglars, auto thieves, and other property offenders with focus on how they have come out with their motivation and decision to commit the crime.

Wright, Richard T., and Scott H. Decker. 1994. *Burglars on the Job: Streetlife and Residential Break-ins.* Boston, Mass.: Northeastern University Press. A close-up analysis of how burglars do their crime and live their lives.

REFERENCES

Abadinsky, Howard. 1993. *Drug Abuse.* 2d ed. Chicago: Nelson-Hall.

Abu-Sharif, Bassam. 1996. "The face of terrorism, then and now." *New Perspectives Quarterly, 13* (Fall), 59–61.

Adler, Israel, and Denise B. Kandel. 1981. "Cross-cultural perspectives on developmental stages in adolescent drug use." *Journal of Studies on Alcohol, 42,* 701–715.

Adler, Jerry. 1996. "Adultery: A new furor over an old sin." *Newsweek,* September 30, 54–60.

Agnew, Robert. 1995. "Strain and subcultural theories of criminality." In Joseph F. Sheley (Ed.), *Criminology: A Contemporary Handbook.* 2d ed. Belmont, Calif.: Wadsworth.

AHA (American Heart Association). 1998. "Tobacco smoke biostatistical fact sheet." http://www.amhrt.org.

Akers, Ronald L. 1968. "Problems in the sociology of deviance: Social definition and behavior." *Social Forces, 46,* 463–464.

Akers, Ronald L. 1985. *Deviant Behavior: A Social Learning Approach.* 3d ed. Belmont, Calif.: Wadsworth.

Akers, Ronald L. 1998. *Social Learning and Social Structure: A General Theory of Crime and Deviance.* Boston: Northeastern University Press.

Alder, Christine. 1984. "The convicted rapist: A sexual or a violent offender?" *Criminal Justice and Behavior, 11,* 157–177.

Alder, Christine. 1985. "An exploration of self-reported sexually aggressive behavior." *Crime & Delinquency, 31,* 306–331.

Alessio, Vittoria. 1996. "Born to be gay?" *New Scientist, 151,* September 28, 32–35.

Altheide, David L. 1981. "Airplane accidents, murder, and the mass media: Comment on Phillips." *Social Forces, 60,* 593–596.

Altheide, David L., et al. 1978. "The social meanings of employee theft." In John M. Johnson and Jack D. Douglas (Eds.), *Crime at the Top.* Philadelphia: Lippincott.

Altman, Lawrence K. 1999. "New York study finds gay men using safer sex." *New York Times,* June 28, pp. A1, A17.

Amir, Menachem. 1971. *Patterns in Forcible Rape.* Chicago: University of Chicago Press.

Anderson, C. A. 1989. "Temperature and aggression: Ubiquitous effects of heat on occurrence of human violence." *Psychological Bulletin, 106,* 74–96.

Anderson, George M. 1977. "Prostitution: Old problem, new conflicts." *America,* April 16, 350–354.

Anderson, K. E., Hugh Lytton, and David M. Romney. 1986. "Mothers' interactions with normal and conduct-disordered boys: Who affects whom?" *Developmental Psychology, 22,* 604–609.

Andreasen, Nancy C., and Donald W. Black. 1995. *Introductory Textbook of Psychiatry.* Washington, D.C.: American Psychiatric Press.

Angelo, Bonnie. 1992. "Wanted: A new godfather." *Time,* April 13, p. 30.

Anslinger, Harry J., and W. S. Thompkins. 1953. *The Traffic in Narcotics.* New York: Funk and Wagnalls.

APA (American Psychiatric Association). 1994. *Diagnostic and Statistical Manual of Mental Disorders,* 4th ed. Washington, D.C.: APA.

Archer, Dane, and Rosemary Gartner. 1984. *Violence and Crime in Cross-National Perspective.* New Haven, Conn.: Yale University Press.

Armstrong, Louise. 1993. *And They Call It Help: The Psychiatric Policing of America's Children.* Reading, Mass.: Addison-Wesley.

Arrigo, Bruce A., and Thomas J. Bernard. 1997. "Postmodern criminology in relation to radical and conflict criminology." *Critical Criminology, 8,* 39–60.

Athens, Lonnie. 1985. "Character contests and violent criminal conduct: A critique." *Sociological Quarterly, 26,* 419–431.

Avio, Kenneth L. 1979. "Capital punishment in Canada: A time-series analysis of the deterrence hypothesis." *Canadian Economic Review, 12,* 647–676.

Bachman, Jerald G., Lloyd D. Johnston, and Patrick M. O'Malley. 1981. "Smoking, drinking, and drug use among American high school students: Correlates and trends, 1975–1979." *American Journal of Public Health, 71,* 59–69.

Bachman, R., and Karl A. Pillemer. 1991. "Retirement: Does it affect marital conflict and violence?" *Journal of Elder Abuse and Neglect, 3,* 75–88.

Bailey, William C. 1980. "Deterrence and the celerity of the death penalty: A neglected question in deterrence research." *Social Forces, 58,* 1311.

Bailey, William C. 1984. "Poverty, inequality and city homicide rates: Some not so unexpected findings." *Criminology, 22,* 531–550.

Bailey, William C. 1998. "Deterrence, brutalization, and the death penalty: Another examination of Oklahoma's return to capital punishment." *Criminology, 36,* 711–733.

Bailey, William C., J. David Martin, and Louis Gray. 1974. "Crime and deterrence: A correlational analysis." *Journal of Research in Crime and Delinquency, 11,* 124–143.

Baker, Jean A. 1998. "Are we missing the forest for the trees? Considering the social context of school violence." *Journal of School Psychology, 36,* 29–44.

Bales, Robert F. 1962. "Attitudes toward drinking in the Irish culture." In David J. Pittman and Charles R. Snyder (Eds.), *Society, Culture, and Drinking Patterns.* New York: Wiley.

Bales, Robert Freed. 1946. "Cultural differences in rates of alcoholism." *Quarterly Journal of Studies on Alcohol, 6,* 480–499.

Ball-Rokeach, Sandra J. 1973. "Values and violence: A test of the subculture of violence thesis." *American Sociological Review, 38,* 739–743.

Barnako, Frank. 1998. "Sex sites: $1 billion and growing fast." *CBS MarketWatch,* October 8.

Barnett, Harold C. 1993. "Crimes against the environment: Superfund enforcement at last." *The Annals of the American Academy of Political and Social Science, 525* (January), 119–133.

Barnett, Ola W., and Alyce D. LaViolette. 1993. *It Could Happen to Anyone: Why Battered Women Stay.* Newbury Park, Calif.: Sage.

Barnett, Ola W., Cindy L. Miller-Perrin, and Robin D. Perrin. 1997. *Family Violence Across the Lifespan: An Introduction.* Thousand Oaks, Calif.: Sage.

Baron, James N., and Peter C. Reiss. 1985. "Same time, next year: Aggregate analyses of the mass media and violent behavior." *American Sociological Review, 50,* 347–363.

Barry, Kathleen. 1995. *The Prostitution of Sexuality.* New York: New York University Press.

Bart, Pauline B., and Patricia H. O'Brien. 1984. "Stopping rape: Effective avoidance strategies." *Signs, 10,* 83–101.

Bart, Pauline B., and Patricia H. O'Brien. 1985. *Stopping Rape: Successful Survival Strategies.* New York: Pergamon.

Baum, Alice S., and Donald W. Burnes. 1993. *A Nation in Denial: The Truth About Homelessness.* Boulder, Colo.: Westview Press.

Bawer, Bruce. 1993. *A Place at the Table: The Gay Individual in American Society.* New York: Poseidon Press.

Bayer, Ronald. 1985. "AIDS and the gay community: Between the specter and the promise of medicine." *Social Research, 52,* 588–589.

Bayer, Ronald. 1987. *Homosexuality and American Psychiatry: The Politics of Diagnosis.* Princeton, N.J.: Princeton University Press.

Bechhofer, Laurie, and Andrea Parrot. 1991. "What is acquaintance rape?" In Andrea Parrot and Laurie Bechhofer (Eds.), *Acquaintance Rape: The Hidden Crime.* New York: John Wiley & Sons.

Beck, Melinda. 1990. "Trading places." *Newsweek,* July 16, pp. 48–54.

Becker, Howard S. 1963. *Outsiders: Studies in the Sociology of Deviance.* New York: Free Press.

Becker, Howard S. 1974. "Labelling theory reconsidered." In Paul Rock and Mary McIntosh (Eds.), *Deviance and Social Control.* London: Tavistock.

Beckerman, Nancy L. 1995. "Suicide in relation to AIDS." *Death Studies, 19,* 223–234.

Begley, Sharon. 1996. "Born happy?" *Newsweek,* October 14, pp. 78–80.

Begley, Sharon. 1999. "Why the young kill." *Newsweek,* May 3, pp. 32–35.

Bell, Daniel. 1962. *The End of Ideology.* New York: Free Press.

Belluck, Pam. 1998. "Black youths' rate of suicide rising sharply." *New York Times,* March 20, pp. A1, A18.

Belluck, Pam. 1998. "In little city safe from violence, rash of suicides leaves scars." *New York Times,* April 5, pp. 1, 21.

Benedict, Jeffrey R. 1998. *Athletes and Acquaintance Rape.* Thousand Oaks, Calif.: Sage.

Benjamin, Harry, and R. E. L. Masters. 1964. *Prostitution and Morality.* New York: Julian.

Bennett, Amanda. 1992. "Back from hell: Lori Schiller emerges from the torments of schizophrenia." *Wall Street Journal,* October 14, pp. A1, A8.

Bennett, William J. 1989. "A response to Milton Friedman." *Wall Street Journal,* September 19, p. A32.

Benson, Michael L. 1985. "Denying the guilty mind: Accounting for involvement in white-collar crime." *Criminology, 23,* 585–607.

Berendzen, Richard, and Laura Palmer, 1993. *Come Here: A Man Overcomes the Tragic Aftermath of Childhood Sexual Abuse.* New York: Villard Books. 90.

Bergen, Raquel Kennedy. 1996. *Wife Rape: Understanding the Response of Survivors and Service Providers.* Thousand Oaks, Calif.: Sage.

Berger, Joseph. 1994. "The psychotherapeutic treatment of male homosexuality." *American Journal of Psychotherapy, 48,* 251–261.

Berk, Richard A., and Phyllis J. Newton. 1985. "Does arrest really deter wife battery? An effort to replicate the findings of the Minneapolis spouse abuse experiment." *American Sociological Review, 50,* 253–262.

Berke, Richard L. 1998. "Chasing the polls on gay rights." *New York Times,* August 2, Section 4, p. 3.

Berkowitz, Leonard. 1969. "The frustration-aggression hypothesis revisited." In Leonard Berkowitz (Ed.), *Roots of Aggression.* New York: Atherton.

Bernard, Thomas J. 1984. "Control criticisms of strain theories: An assessment of theoretical and empirical adequacy." *Journal of Research in Crime and Delinquency, 21,* 353–372.

Berrill, Kevin T. 1992. "Anti-gay violence and victimization in the United States: An overview." In Gregory M. Herek and Kevin T. Berrill (Eds.), *Hate Crime.* Newbury Park, Calif.: Sage.

Berthelsen, Christian. 1999. "Women are speaking out to heal trauma of rape." *New York Times,* April 4, p. 17.

Bettridge, Brenda J., and Olga Eizner Favreau. 1995. "Suicidal behavior among adolescent females: The cry for connection." In Silvia Sara Canetto and David Lester (Eds.), *Women and Suicidal Behavior.* New York: Springer.

Bissland, James H., and Richard Munger. 1985. "Implications of changing attitudes toward mental illness." *Journal of Social Psychology, 125,* 515–517.

Blakely, Mary Kay. 1983. "The New Bedford gang rape." *Ms.*, July, p. 53.

Blank, Jonah, Jason Vest, and Suzie Parker. 1998. "The children of Jonesboro." U.S. News & World Report, April 6, pp. 16–22.

Blau, Judith R., and Peter M. Blau. 1982. "The cost of inequality: Metropolitan structure and violent crime." *American Sociological Review, 47,* 114–129.

Block, Alan A. 1991. *The Business of Crime.* Boulder, Colo.: Westview.

Blumenfeld, Warren J. (Ed.). 1992. *Homophobia: How We All Pay the Price.* Boston: Beacon.

Blumenfeld, Warren J., and Diane Raymond. 1993. *Looking at Gay and Lesbian Life.* Boston: Beacon.

Blumstein, Alfred. 1995. "Violence by young people: Why the deadly nexus?" *National Institute of Justice Journal,* August, pp. 2–9.

Blumstein, Philip, and Pepper Schwartz. 1990. "Intimate relationships and the creation of sexuality." In David P. McWhirter, et al. (Eds.), *Homosexuality/Heterosexuality.* New York: Oxford University Press.

Bode, Ken. 1978. "New life for the oldest profession." *New Republic,* July 8, pp. 21–25.

Boeringer, Scot B. 1996. "Influences of fraternity membership, athletics, and male living arrangements on sexual aggression." *Violence Against Women, 2,* 134–147.

Boffey, Philip M. 1986. "Schizophrenia: Insights fail to halt rising toll." *New York Times,* March 16, p. 1.

Bogert, Carroll. 1994. "Good news on drugs from the inner city." *Newsweek,* February 14, pp. 28–29.

Bohlen, Celestine. 1994. "Graft and gangsterism in Russia blight the entrepreneurial spirit." *New York Times,* January 30, p. 1.

Bolter, John F., and Roseann Hannon. 1980. "Cerebral damage associated with alcoholism: A reexamination." *Psychological Record, 30,* 165–179.

Boor, Myron. 1981. "Methods of suicide and implications for suicide prevention." *Journal of Clinical Psychology, 37,* 70–75.

Bower, Bruce. 1992. "Alcoholism: Nurture may often outdo nature." *Science News, 141,* February 1, p. 69.

Bower, Bruce. 1994. "Mental disorders strike about half of U.S." *Science News,* January 22, p. 55.

Bowers, William J., and Glenn L. Pierce. 1980. "Deterrence or brutalization: What is the effect of execution?" *Crime and Delinquency, 26,* 453–484.

Boyatzis, Richard E. 1975. "The predisposition toward alcohol-related interpersonal aggression in men." *Journal of Studies on Alcohol, 36,* 1196–1207.

Bradsher, Keith. 1999. "For car thieves, a technological arms race." *New York Times*, March 28, Section 4, p. 3.

Brady, James. 1983. "Arson, urban economy, and organized crime: The case of Boston." *Social Problems, 31,* 1–27.

Braithwaite, John. 1985. "White collar crime." *Annual Review of Sociology, 11,* 1–21.

Braithwaite, John. 1989. *Crime, Shame and Reintegration.* New York: Cambridge University Press.

Braithwaite, John. 1992. "Poverty, power, and white-collar crime." In Kip Schlegel and David Weisburd (Eds.), *White-Collar Crime Reconsidered.* Boston: Northeastern University Press.

Braithwaite, John. 1993. "Transnational regulation of the pharmaceutical industry." *The Annals of the American Academy of Political and Social Science, 525,* January, 13–14.

Brake, Mike. 1994. "Needed: A license to drink." *Newsweek,* March 14, p. 11.

Breault, K. D. 1986. "Suicide in America: A test of Durkheim's theory of religious and family integration, 1933–1980." *American Journal of Sociology, 92,* 628–656.

Breault, K. D. and Karen Barkey. 1982. "A comparative analysis of Durkheim's theory of egoistic suicide." *Sociological Quarterly, 24,* 321–331.

Brecher, Edward M. (and the Editors of *Consumer Reports*). 1975. "Marijuana: The health questions." *Consumer Reports, 40,* 143–145.

Breggin, Peter. 1997. *Empathy and the Creation of a Healing Presence.* New York: Springer.

Brinson, Susan L. 1992. "The use and opposition of rape myths in prime-time television dramas." *Sex Roles, 27,* 359–375.

Brody, Jane E. 1997. "Quirks, oddities may be illnesses." *New York Times,* February 4, pp. B9, B11.

Brooke, James. 1996. "To be young, gay and going to a high school in Utah." *New York Times,* February 26, pp. A1, B8.

Brown, Judith K. 1992. "Introduction." In D. A. Counts, J. K. Brown, and J. C. Campbell (Eds.), *Sanctions and Sanctuary: Cultural Perspectives on the Beating of Wives.* Boulder, Colo: Westview.

Brown, Marjorie E. 1979. "Teenage prostitution." *Adolescence, 14,* 665–680.

Browne, Angela. 1987. *Why Battered Women Kill.* New York: Free Press.

Browne, Angela. 1993. "Violence against women by male partners: Prevalence, outcomes, and policy implications." *American Psychologist, 48,* 1077–1097.

Brownmiller, Susan. 1975. *Against Our Will: Men, Women and Rape.* New York: Simon & Schuster.

Brownmiller, Susan. 1993. "Making female bodies the battlefield." *Newsweek,* January 4, p. 37.

Brozan, Nadine. 1986. "Gang rape: A rising campus concern." *New York Times,* February 17, p. 18.

Bruni, Frank. 1997. "In an age of consent, defining abuse by adults." *New York Times,* Section 4, p. 3.

Bruyn, Severyn T. 1966. *The Human Perspective in Sociology.* Englewood Cliffs, N.J.: Prentice Hall.

Bryan, James H. 1966. "Occupational ideologies and individual attitudes of call girls." *Social Problems, 13,* 441–450.

Bryant, Marshall A. 1977. "Prostitution and the criminal justice system." *Journal of Police Science and Administration, 5,* 384.

Budiansky, Stephen, et al. 1994. "The cold war experiments." *U.S. News & World Report,* January 24, pp. 32–38.

Budiansky, Stephen, et al. 1995. "How lawyers abuse the law." *U.S. News & World Report,* January 30, pp. 50–56.

Bullough, Bonnie. 1993. "The causes of homosexuality: A scientific update." *Free Inquiry, 13* (Fall), 40–47.

Bumiller, Elisabeth. 1999. "Deny rape or be hated: Kosovo victims' choice." *New York Times,* June 22, pp. A1, A13.

Burgess, Ann Wolbert. 1995. "Rape trauma syndrome." In Patricia Searles and Ronald J. Berger (Eds.), *Rape and Society.* Boulder, Colo.: Westview.

Burgess, Robert L., and Ronald L. Akers. 1966a. "A differential association-reinforcement theory of criminal behavior." *Social Problems, 14,* 128–147.

Burgess, Robert L., and Ronald L. Akers. 1966b. "Are operant principles tautological?" *The Psychological Record, 16,* 310.

Burr, Chandler. 1996. *A Separate Creation: The Search for the Biological Origins of Sexual Orientation.* New York: Hyperion.

Burros, Marian. 1996. "In an about-face, U.S. says alcohol has health benefits." *New York Times,* January 3, pp. A1, B6.

Burt, Martha R. 1991. "Rape myths and acquaintance rape." In Andrea Parrot and Laurie Bechhofer (Eds.), *Acquaintance Rape.* New York: Wiley.

Burton, Thomas M. 1993a. "Caught in the act." *Wall Street Journal,* March 26, pp. A1, A5.

Burton, Thomas M. 1993b. "Spilled milk." *Wall Street Journal,* May 25, pp. A1, A6.

Buss, Dale. 1993. "Ways to curtail employee theft." *Nation's Business,* April, p. 36.

Butterfield, Fox. 1992. "Seeds of murder epidemic: Teen-age boys with guns." *New York Times,* October 19, p. A8.

Butterfield, Fox. 1995. "Many cities in U.S. show sharp drop in homicide rate." *New York Times,* August 13, pp. 1, 10.

Butterfield, Fox. 1996. "Gun violence may be subsiding, studies find." *New York Times,* October 14, p. A6.

Butterfield, Fox. 1999. "Prisons brim with mentally ill, study finds." *New York Times,* July 12, p. A10.

Byrne, C. A., et al. 1999. "The socioeconomic impact of interpersonal violence on women." *Journal of Consulting and Clinical Psychology, 67,* 362–366.

Cahalan, Don. 1970. *Problem Drinkers.* San Francisco: Jossey-Bass.

Cahan, Vicky, et al. 1985. "A murder verdict jolts business." *Business Week,* July 1, p. 24.

Cahill, Tom. 1985. "Rape behind bars," *The Progressive,* November, p. 32.

Cain, Albert C., and Irene Fast. 1966. "Children's disturbed reactions to parent suicide." *American Journal of Orthopsychiatry, 36,* 873–880.

Calhoun, Lawrence G., James W. Selby, and C. B. Abernathy. 1984. "Suicide death: Social reactions to bereaved survivors." *Journal of Psychology, 16,* 255–261.

Calhoun, Lawrence G., James W. Selby, and Michael E. Faulstich. 1980. "Reactions to the parents of the child suicide: A study of social impressions." *Journal of Consulting and Clinical Psychology, 48,* 535–536.

Calhoun, Lawrence G., James W. Selby, and Peggy B. Walton. 1985–86. "Suicidal death of a spouse: The social perception of the survivor." *Omega, 16,* 283–288.

Califia, Pat. 1994. *Public Sex: The Culture of Radical Sex.* Pittsburgh, Penn.: Cleis Press.

Campbell, Jacquelyn C. 1989. "Women's responses to sexual abuse in intimate relationships." *Health Care for Women International, 8,* 335–347.

Canetto, Silvia Sara, and David Lester (Eds.). 1995. *Women and Suicidal Behavior.* New York: Springer.

Cannon, Angie. 1999. "Sex, drugs, and sudden death." *U.S. News & World Reports,* May 24, p. 73.

Caplan, Gerald M. 1984. "The facts of life about teenage prostitution." *Crime & Delinquency, 30,* 69–74.

Capone, Donald L., and Woodrow W. Nichols, Jr. 1976. "Urban structure and criminal mobility." *American Behavioral Scientist, 20,* 199–213.

Carey, Kate B. 1993. "Situational determinants of heavy drinking among college students." *Journal of Counseling Psychology, 40,* 217–220.

Carlson, Margaret. 1995. "The sex-crime capital." *Time,* November 13, pp. 89–90.

Carrithers, David W. 1985. "The insanity defense and presidential peril." *Society, 22* (July/August), 22–27.

Carse, Alisa L. 1995. "Pornography: An uncivil liberty?" *Hypatia, 10,* 155–182.

Carter, Bonnie Frank, and Allan Brooks. 1991. "Child and adolescent survivors of suicide." In Antoon A. Leenaars (Ed.), *Life Span Perspectives of Suicide: Time-lines in the Suicide Process.* New York: Plenum.

Carter, Hodding. 1989. "We're losing the drug war because prohibition never works." *Wall Street Journal,* July 13, p. A15.

Cashdan, Sheldon. 1972. *Abnormal Psychology.* Englewood Cliffs, N.J.: Prentice Hall.

Castro, Janice. 1993. "What price mental health." *Time*, May 31, pp. 59–60.

Catalano, Ralph, et al. 1993. "Job loss and alcohol abuse: A test using data from the epidemiologic catchment area project." *Journal of Health and Social Behavior, 34*, 215–225.

Cazenave, N. A., and Murray A. Straus. 1990. "Race, class, network embeddedness, and family violence: A search for potent support systems." In M. A. Straus and R. J. Gelles (Eds.), *Physical Violence in American Families*. New Brunswick, N.J.: Transaction.

Celis, William 3rd. 1994. "More college women drinking to get drunk." *New York Times*, June 8, p. B8.

Celis, William 3rd. 1995. "Tradition on the wane: College drinking." *New York Times*, February 5, pp. 1, 16.

Chambliss, William J. 1969. *Crime and the Legal Process*. New York: McGraw-Hill.

Chambliss, William, and Robert Seidman. 1971. *Law, Order, and Power*. Reading, Mass.: Addison-Wesley.

Chappell, Duncan, Gilbert Geis, Stephen Schafer, and Larry Siegel, 1971. "Forcible rape: A comparative study of offenses known to the police in Boston and Los Angeles." In James M. Henslin (Ed.), *Studies in the Sociology of Sex*. New York: Appleton-Century-Crofts.

Chase, Marilyn. 1995. "Beneficial drinking: After abstinence, before trying one on." *Wall Street Journal*, July 3, p. B1.

Chase, Marilyn. 1996a. "Health journal." *Wall Street Journal*, August 26, p. B1.

Chase, Marilyn. 1996b. "Americans seem to drink a lot or hardly at all." *Wall Street Journal*, December 30, p. B1.

Chein, Isidor, Donald L. Gerard, Robert S. Lee, and Eva Rosenfeld. 1964. *The Road to H.* New York: Basic Books.

Cherry, Rona, and Laurence Cherry. 1973. "Depression: The common cold of mental ailments." *New York Times Magazine*, November 25, p. 38.

Chesnais, Jean-Claude. 1992. "The history of violence: Homicide and suicide through the ages." *International Social Science Journal, 44*, 217–234.

Chesney-Lind, Meda. 1997. *The Female Offender: Girls, Women, and Crime*. Thousand Oaks, Calif.: Sage.

Christensen, Russ, and Peter W. Dowrick. 1983. "Myths of mid-winter depression." *Community Mental Health Journal, 19*, 177–186.

Christian, Nichole. 1995. "New generation of car thieves restructures the business." *Wall Street Journal*, July 19, p. B1.

Church, George J. 1986. "What he needs to know." *Time*, December 22, pp. 17–18.

Clausen, John A., and Carol L. Huffine. 1975. "Sociocultural and social-psychological factors affecting social responses to mental disorder." *Journal of Health and Social Behavior, 16*, 405–420.

Clifton, A. Kay, and Dorothy E. Lee. 1995. "Gender socialization and women's suicidal behaviors." In Silvia Sara Canetto and David Lester (Eds.), *Women and Suicidal Behavior*. New York: Springer.

Clinard, Marshall, and Daniel J. Abbot. 1973. *Crime in Developing Countries*. New York: Wiley.

Clinard, Marshall B., and Peter C. Yeager. 1980. *Corporate Crime*. New York: Free Press.

Cloud, John. 1998. "For better or worse." *Time*, October 26, pp. 43–44.

Cloward, Richard, and Lloyd E. Ohlin. 1960. *Delinquency and Opportunity: A Theory of Juvenile Gangs*. New York: Free Press.

Cochrane, Raymond. 1983. *The Social Creation of Mental Illness*. London: Longman.

Cohen, Albert K. 1955. *Delinquent Boys: The Culture of the Gang*. New York: Free Press.

Cohen, Albert K. 1966. *Deviance and Control.* Englewood Cliffs, N.J.: Prentice Hall.

Cohen, D., M. Llorente, and C. Eisdorfer. 1998. "Homicide-suicide in older persons." *American Journal of Psychiatry, 155,* 390–396.

Cohen, Lawrence E., David Cantor, and James R. Kluegel. 1981. "Robbery victimization in the U.S.: An analysis of a nonrandom event." *Social Science Quarterly, 62,* 645–657.

Cohen, Murray, Ralph Garofalo, Richard Boucher, and Theoharis Seghorn. 1971. "The psychology of rapists." *Seminar in Psychiatry, 3,* 310.

Cohn, Bob, and Mary Hager. 1993. "The power of sin." *Newsweek,* October 4, p. 51.

Coleman, James William. 1994. *The Criminal Elite: The Sociology of White Collar Crime.* 3d ed. New York: St. Martin's.

Collier, Theresa J. 1993. "The stigma of mental illness." *Newsweek,* April 26, p. 16.

Colvin, Mark, and John Pauly. 1983. "A critique of criminology: Toward an integrated structural-Marxist theory of delinquency production." *American Journal of Sociology, 89,* 513–551.

Committee on Cultural Psychiatry. 1989. *Suicide and Ethnicity in the United States.* New York: Brunner/Mazel.

Conant, Marcus. 1997. "This is smart medicine." *Newsweek,* February 3, p. 26.

Conklin, John E. 1972. *Robbery and the Criminal Justice System.* Philadelphia: Lippincott.

Conklin, John E. 1977. *"Illegal but Not Criminal": Business Crime in America.* Englewood Cliffs, N.J.: Prentice Hall.

Cookson, Peter W., Jr., and Caroline Hodges Persell. 1985. *Preparing for Power: America's Elite Boarding Schools.* New York: Basic Books.

Cooper, Matthew. 1998. "Turning up the heat." *Newsweek,* April 13, pp. 50–51

Cowley, Geoffrey. 1997. "Can marijuana be medicine?" *Newsweek,* February 3, pp. 22–27.

Coyne, James C., and Geraldine Downey. 1991. "Social factors and psychopathology: Stress, social support, and coping processes." *Annual Review of Psychology, 42,* 401–425.

Cressey, Donald R. 1971. *Other People's Money: A Study in the Social Psychology of Embezzlement.* Belmont, Calif.: Wadsworth.

Cromwell, Paul F., James N. Olson, and D'Aunn Wester Avary. 1991. *Breaking and Entering: An Ethnographic Analysis of Burglary.* Newbury Park, Calif.: Sage.

Crossen, Cynthia. 1996. "Losing it." *Wall Street Journal,* December 3, pp. A1, A10.

Crosset, Todd W., J. Ptacek, M. A. Mcdonald, and J. R. Benedict. 1996. "Male student-athletes and violence against women: A survey of campus judicial affairs offices." *Violence Against Women, 2,* 163–179.

Crossette, Barbara. 1995. "A global gauge of greased palms." *New York Times,* August 20, p. E3.

Cross-National Collaborative Group. 1992. "The changing rate of major depression: Cross-national comparisons." *JAMA (Journal of American Medical Association), 268,* 3098–3105.

Cullen, Francis T. 1984. *Rethinking Crime and Deviance Theory.* Totowa, N.J.: Rowman & Allanheld.

Currie, Elliott. 1993. *Reckoning: Drugs, the Cities, and the American Future.* New York: Hill and Wang.

Daly, Kathleen, and Meda Chesney-Lind. 1988. "Feminism and criminology." *Justice Quarterly, 5,* 101–143.

Danigelis, Nick, and Whitney Pope. 1979. "Durkheim's theory of suicide as applied to the family: An empirical test." *Social Forces, 57,* 1081–1106.

Dank, Barry M. 1971. "Coming out in the gay world." *Psychiatry, 34,* 180–197.

Davis, Alan J. 1982. "Sexual assaults in the Philadelphia prison system and sheriff's vans." In Anthony M. Scacco, Jr. (Ed.), *Male Rape.* New York: AMS Press.

Davis, Bernard D. 1990. "Right to die: Living wills are inadequate." *Wall Street Journal,* July 31, p. A12.

Davis, Kingsley. 1971. "Sexual behavior." In Robert Merton and Robert Nisbet (Eds.), *Contemporary Social Problems.* 3d ed. New York: Harcourt Brace Jovanovich.

Davis, Nanette J. (Ed.). 1993. *Prostitution: An International Handbook on Trends, Problems, and Policies.* Westport, Conn.: Greenwood.

Davis, Nanette J., and Clarice Stasz. 1990. *Social Control: The Production of Deviance in the Modern State.* New York: McGraw-Hill.

Davison, Gerald C., and John M. Neale. 1996. *Abnormal Psychology.* 6th ed. New York: Wiley.

"Deadwood's defunct houses." *Time,* July 28, p. 77.

Decker, Scott, and Richard Rosenfeld. 1992. "Intravenous drug use and the AIDS epidemic: Findings from a 20-city sample of arrestees." *Crime & Delinquency, 38,* 492–509.

Deitz, Sheila R., et al. 1984. "Attributions of responsibility for rape: The influence of observer empathy, victim resistance, and victim attractiveness." *Sex Roles, 10,* 261–280.

DeJong, William. 1986. "Project DARE: Teaching kids to say no to drugs and alcohol." *NIJ Reports,* no. 196, pp. 2–5.

DeKeseredy, Walter S., and Martin D. Schwartz. 1996. *Contemporary Criminology.* Belmont, Calif.: Wadsworth.

Delfs, Robert. 1991a. "Clash of loyalties." *Far Eastern Economic Review, 155,* November 21, pp. 30, 34.

Delfs, Robert. 1991b. "Feeding on the system." *Far Eastern Economic Review, 155,* November 21, pp. 28–30.

Delfs, Robert. 1991c. "Legal conduct." *Far Eastern Economic Review, 155,* November 21, pp. 34–35.

Denham, Susanne A., Susan M. Renwick, and Robert W. Holt. 1991. "Working and playing together: Prediction of preschool social-emotional competence from mother-child interaction." *Child Development, 62,* 242–249.

DenHouter, Kathryn V. 1981. "To silence one's self: A brief analysis of the literature on adolescent suicide." *Child Welfare, 60,* 3.

Denzin, Norman K. 1991. "The AA group." In David J. Pittman and Helene Raskin White (Eds.), *Society, Culture, and Drinking Patterns Reexamined.* New Brunswick, N.J.: Rutgers Center of Alcohol Studies.

Dickermann, Mildred. 1995. "Wilson's panchreston: The inclusive fitness hypothesis of sociobiology re-examined." *Journal of Homosexuality, 28,* 147–183.

Diller, Lawrence H. 1998. *Running on Ritalin.* New York: Bantam Books.

Dobash, Russell P., R. Emerson Dobash, Margo Wilson, and Martin Daly. 1992. "The myth of sexual symmetry in marital violence." *Social Problems, 39,* 71–91.

Doblin, Rich, and Mark A. R. Kleiman. 1993. "Marijuana as medicine." *Wall Street Journal,* February 19, p. A13.

Dobrzynski, Judith H. 1996. "For more and more job seekers, an aging parent is a big factor." *New York Times,* January 1, pp. 1, 24.

Dodge, David L. 1985. "The over-negativized conceptualization of deviance: A programmatic exploration." *Deviant Behavior, 6,* 17–37.

Dohrenwend, Bruce D., and Barbara Snell Dohrenwend. 1974. "Psychiatric disorders in urban settings." In S. Arietti and G. Caplan (Eds.), *American Handbook of Psychiatry.* New York: Basic Books.

Dohrenwend, Bruce P. 1975. "Sociocultural and social-psychological factors in the genesis of mental disorders." *Journal of Health and Social Behavior, 16,* 365–392.

Dohrenwend, Bruce P., and Barbara Snell Dohrenwend. 1976. "Sex differences and psychiatric disorders." *American Journal of Sociology, 81,* 1447–1454.

Dollard, John, Neal E. Miller, Leonard W. Doob, O. H. Mowrer, and Robert R. Sears. 1939. *Frustration and Aggression.* New Haven: Yale University Press.

Donnerstein, Edward, et al. 1987. *The Question of Pornography: Research Findings and Policy Implications.* New York: Free Press.

Donovan, James M. 1986. "An etiologic model of alcoholism." *American Journal of Psychiatry, 143,* 5–6.

Donovan, John E., 1993. "Young adult drinking-driving: Behavioral and psychosocial correlates." *Journal of Studies on Alcohol, 54,* 600–613.

Dorpat, T. L. 1967. "Suicide in Murderers." In Marvin Wolfgang (Ed.), *Studies in Homicide.* New York: Harper & Row.

Douglas, Jack D. 1967. *The Social Meanings of Suicide.* Princeton, N.J.: Princeton University Press.

Douglas, Jack D. (Ed.). 1970. *Deviance and Respectability.* New York: Basic Books.

Douglas, Jack D., and Frances C. Waksler. 1982. *The Sociology of Deviance.* Boston: Little, Brown.

Dowd, Maureen. 1983. "Rape: The sexual weapon." *Time,* September 5, pp. 27–29.

Drummond, Tammerlin. 1995. "Not in Kansas anymore." *Time,* September 25, pp. 54–55.

Dubin, Louis I., and Bessie Bunzel. 1933. *To Be or Not To Be.* New York: Harrison Smith and Robert Haas.

Duffala, Dennis C. 1976. "Convenience stores, armed robbery, and physical environmental features." *American Behavioral Scientist, 20,* 227–246.

Duffy, Brian, and Jeff Trimble. 1994. "The wise guys of Russia." *U.S. News & World Report,* March 7, p. 45.

Dugger, Celia W. 1999. "Calcutta's prostitutes preach about condoms." *New York Times,* January 4, pp. A1, A8.

Dunkle, John H., and Patricia L. Francis. 1990. "The role of facial masculinity/femininity in the attribution of homosexuality." *Sex Roles, 23,* 157–167.

Dunlap, David W. 1995. "Two steps forward for homosexuals." *New York Times,* October 18, p. A12.

Durkheim, Émile. 1897/1966. *Suicide.* New York: Free Press.

Dutton, Donald G. 1986. "Wife assaulters' explanations for assault: The neutralization of self-punishment." *Canadian Journal of Behavioral Sciences, 18,* 381–390.

Dutton, Donald G. 1994. "Patriarchy and wife assault: An ecological fallacy." *Violence and Victims, 9,* 167–182.

Dworkin, Andrea. 1982. "Pornography and grief." In Laura Lederer (Ed.), *Take Back the Night: Women in Pornography.* New York: Bantam Books.

Early, Kevin E. 1992. *Religion and Suicide in the African-American Community.* Westport, Conn.: Greenwood.

Early, Kevin E. 1996. *Drug Treatment Behind Bars: Prison-Based Strategies for Change.* Westport, Conn.: Praeger.

Early, Kevin E., and Ronald L. Akers. 1995. "'It's a white thing': An exploration of beliefs about suicide in the African-American community." In Alex Thio and Thomas Calhoun (Eds.), *Readings in Deviant Behavior.* New York: HarperCollins.

Eaton, Leslie. 1999. "Assault with a fiscal weapon." *New York Times,* May 25, pp. C1, C25.

Eckardt, Michael J., Ralph S. Rybak, and Charles P. Pautler. 1980. "Neuropsychological deficits in alcoholic men in their mid-thirties." *American Journal of Psychiatry, 137,* 932–936.

Edmundson, Mark. 1999. "Save Sigmund Freud." *New York Times Magazine*, July 13, pp. 34–35.

Edwards, Hodee. 1993. "Rape defines sex." *Off Our Backs, 23* (August), 16–17.

Ehrlich, Isaac. 1975. "The deterrent effect of capital punishment: A question of life and death." *American Economic Review, 65,* 397–417.

Eigen, Joel Peter. 1981. "Punishing Youth Homicide Offenders in Philadelphia," *Journal of Criminal Law and Criminology, 72,* 1075.

Einstadter, Werner, and Stuart Henry. 1995. *Criminological Theory: An Analysis of Its Underlying Assumptions.* Fort Worth, Texas: Harcourt Brace.

Elliott, Jeff. 1995. "Drug prevention placebo." *Reason, 26* (March), 14–21.

Elliott, Robert E., et al. 1985. *Explaining Delinquency and Drug Use.* Beverly Hills, Calif.: Sage.

Ellis, Elizabeth M., Beverly M. Atkeson, and Karen S. Calhoun. 1981. "An assessment of long-term reaction to rape." *Journal of Abnormal Psychology, 90,* 263–266.

Elmer-Dewitt, Philip. 1995. "On a screen near you: Cyberporn." *Time,* July 3, pp. 38–45.

Emanuel, Ezekiel J. 1996. "Euthanasia and physician-assisted suicide." *Lancet, 29,* 1805–1810.

Emanuel, Ezekiel J. 1997. "The painful truth about euthanasia." *Wall Street Journal,* January 7, p. A18.

Engs, Ruth C., and David J. Hanson. 1985. "The drinking patterns and problems of college students: 1983." *Journal of Alcohol and Drug Education, 31,* 65–83.

Engs, Ruth C., and David J. Hanson. 1994. "Boozing and brawling on campus: A national study of violent problems associated with drinking over the past decade." *Journal of Criminal Justice, 22,* 171–180.

Erikson, Kai T. 1962. "Notes on the sociology of deviance." *Social Problems, 9,* 307–314.

Erlanger, Howard S. 1974. "The empirical status of the subculture of violence thesis." *Social Problems, 22,* 280–292.

Erlanger, Steven. 1991. "A plague awaits." *New York Times Magazine,* July 14, p. 26.

Ermann, David, and Richard J. Lundman. 1982. *Corporate Deviance.* New York: Holt, Rinehart and Winston.

Ermann, M. David, and Richard J. Lundman (Eds.). 1996. *Corporate and Governmental Deviance: Problems of Organizational Behavior in Contemporary Society.* 5th ed. New York: Oxford University Press.

Essex, Marilyn, et al. 1980. "On Weinstein's 'Patient attitudes toward mental hospitalization: A review of quantitative research.'" *Journal of Health and Social Behavior, 21,* 393–396.

Falco, Mathea. 1992. *The Making of a Drug-Free America: Programs That Work.* New York: Times Books.

Farberow, Norman L. 1970. "Ten years of suicide prevention–Past and future." *Bulletin of Suicidology,* No. 6, p. 9.

Farberow, Norman L. 1991. "Adult survivors after suicide: Research problems and needs." In Antoon A. Leenaars (Ed.), *Life Span Perspectives of Suicide: Time-lines in the Suicide Process.* New York: Plenum.

Faris, Robert E. L., and H. Warren Dunham. 1939. *Mental Disorders in Urban Areas.* Chicago: University of Chicago Press.

Farley, Melissa. 1994. "Prostitution: The oldest use and abuse of women." *Off Our Backs, 24,* 14–15.

Farrington, David P. 1977. "The effects of public labelling." *British Journal of Criminology, 17,* 112–125.

Farrington, David P., S. G. Osborn, and D. J. West. 1978. "The persistence of labelling effects." *British Journal of Criminology, 18,* 277–284.

FBI (Federal Bureau of Investigation). 1996. *Uniform Crime Reports.* Washington, D.C.: Government Printing Office.

Feeney, Floyd, and Adrianne Weir. 1975. "The prevention and control of robbery." *Criminology, 13,* 104.

Feldman, Douglas A. 1985. "AIDS and social change." *Human Organization, 44,* 343–348.

Felson, Richard B., and Henry J. Steadman. 1983. "Situational factors in disputes leading to criminal violence." *Criminology, 21,* 39–74.

Ferguson, Frances. 1995. "Pornography: The theory." *Critical Inquiry, 21,* 670–695.

Fields, Suzanne. 1993. "Rape as sport: The culture is at the root." *Insight on the News, 9* (May 3), 19–20.

Fillion, Kate. 1991. "Rape on campus." *Chatelaine, 64* (August), 33–35.

Fineman, Howard. 1993. "Marching to the mainstream." *Newsweek,* May 3, pp. 42–44.

Fineman, Howard, and Bob Cohn. 1993. "The mystery of the White House suicide." *Newsweek,* August 2, p. 16.

Finkelhor, David. 1984. *Child Sexual Abuse: New Theory and Research.* New York: Free Press.

Finkelhor, David, and Kersti Yllö. 1987. *License to Rape: Sexual Abuse of Wives.* New York: Free Press.

Finkelhor, David, et al. 1989. "Sexual abuse and its relationship to later sexual satisfaction, marital status, religion, and attitudes." *Journal of Interpersonal Violence, 4,* 379–399.

Firth, Raymond. 1961. "Suicide and risk-taking in Tikopia society." *Psychiatry, 24,* 4.

Fisher, Helen E. 1992. *Anatomy of Love: The Natural History of Monogamy, Adultery, and Divorce.* New York: Norton.

Fishman, Scott M., and David V. Sheehan. 1985. "Anxiety and panic: Their cause and treatment." *Psychology Today,* April, p. 26.

Fleishman, Ellen Gerschitz. 1983. "Sex-role acquisition, parental behavior, and sexual orientation: Some tentative hypotheses." *Sex Roles, 9,* 1051–1059.

Foderaro, Lisa W. 1995. "Mentally ill gaining new rights, with the ill as their own lobby." *New York Times,* October 14, pp. 1, 8.

Folse, Kimberly A., and Dennis L. Peck. 1995. "A phenomenological analysis of suicide." In Alex Thio and Thomas Calhoun (Eds.), *Readings in Deviant Behavior.* New York: HarperCollins.

Forbes, Malcolm S. Jr. 1996. "Wrong approach," *Forbes,* March 11, pp. 25–26.

Ford, Amasa B., et al. 1979. "Violent death in a metropolitan county: Changing patterns in suicides (1959–1974)." *American Journal of Public Health, 69,* 459–464.

Fort, Joel. 1973. *Alcohol: Our Biggest Drug Problem.* New York: McGraw-Hill.

Fox, James Alan. 1994. "American killers are getting younger." *USA Today: The Magazine of the American Scene,* January, pp. 24–26.

Fox, James Alan. 1996. "Trends in Juvenile Offending." *National Institute of Justice Journal,* August, pp. 15–23.

Fox, James A., and Jack Levin. 1998. "Multiple homicide: Patterns of serial and mass murder." *Crime and Justice: A Review of Research, 23,* 407–455.

Fox, James Alan, and Marianne W. Zawitz. 1999. "Homicide trends in the United States." U.S. Department of Justice, Bureau of Justice Statistics.

Fox, Richard G. 1971. "The XYY offender: A modern myth?" *Journal of Criminal Law, Criminology, and Police Science, 62,* 59–73.

Frank, Nancy. 1993. "Maiming and killing: Occupational health crimes." *The Annals of the American Academy of Political and Social Science, 525,* 107–118.

Frank, Stephen E., and John R. Wilke. 1997. "Visa, MasterCard may face antitrust suit." *Wall Street Journal,* February 7, p. A3.

Fredriksen, K. I. 1989. "Adult protective services: A caseload analysis." *Journal of Interpersonal Violence, 4,* 245–250.

Freud, Sigmund. 1961. *Civilization and Its Discontents,* trans. and ed. James Strachey. New York: Norton.

Freund, Matthew, et al. 1991. "Sexual behavior of clients with street prostitutes in Camden, N.J." *Journal of Sex Research, 28,* 579–591.

Friedman, Milton. 1989. "An open letter to Bill Bennett." *Wall Street Journal,* September 7, p. A18.

Friedman, Milton. 1998. "There's no justice in the war on drugs." *New York Times,* January 11, p. 19.

Friedman, Robert I. 1999. "White collar and dangerous." *New York Times,* August 27, p. A25.

Fuller, Richard C., and Richard R. Myers. 1941. "Some aspects of a theory of social problems." *American Sociological Review, 6,* 27–32.

Gabor, Thomas, et al. 1987. *Armed Robbery: Cops, Robbers, and Victims.* Springfield, Ill.: Charles C. Thomas.

Gagnon, John H., Martin Levine, and Peter Nardi (eds.). 1997. *Encounters with AIDS: The Impact of the HIV/AIDS Epidemic and the Gay and Lesbian Communities.* Chicago: University of Chicago Press.

Gallagher, Bernard J. 1980. *The Sociology of Mental Illness.* Englewood Cliffs, N.J.: Prentice Hall.

Gallup, George. 1985. "Loss of support for death penalty." *San Francisco Chronicle,* February 4, p. 11.

Gamwell, Lynn, and Nancy Tomes. 1995. *Madness in America: Cultural and Medical Perceptions of Mental Illness before 1914.* Ithaca, N.Y.: Cornell University Press.

Garfinkel, Harold. 1967. *Studies in Ethnomethodology.* Englewood Cliffs, N.J.: Prentice Hall.

Garland, David. 1993. *Punishment and Modern Society: A Study in Social Theory.* Chicago: University of Chicago Press.

Geerken, Michael R., and Walter R. Gove. 1977. "Deterrence, overload, and incapacitation: An empirical evaluation." *Social Forces, 56,* 424–447.

Geis, Gilbert. 1984. "White-collar and corporate crime." In Robert F. Meier (Ed.), *Major Forms of Crime.* Beverly Hills, Calif.: Sage.

Geis, Gilbert. 1992. "White-collar crime: What is it?" In Kip Schlegel and David Weisburd (Eds.), *White-Collar Crime Reconsidered.* Boston: Northeastern University Press.

Geis, Gilbert, and Robley Geis. 1979. "Rape in Stockholm: Is permissiveness relevant?" *Criminology, 17,* 315.

Gelles, Richard J. 1985. "Family violence." *Annual Review of Sociology, 11,* 347–367.

Gelles, Richard J. 1993. "Constraints against family violence." *American Behavioral Scientists, 36,* 575–586.

Gelles, Richard J. 1995. *Contemporary Families: A Sociological View.* Thousand Oaks, Calif.: Sage.

Gelles, Richard J., and Murray A. Straus. 1987. "The cost of family violence." *Public Health Reports, 102,* 638–641.

Gelles, Richard J., and Murray Straus. 1988. *Family Violence.* Beverly Hills, Calif.: Sage.

Gelman, David. 1993. "Tune in, come out." *Newsweek,* November 8, pp. 70–71.

Gelman, David, et al. 1994. "The rapist: An overview." In Karin L. Swisher , Carol Wekesser, and William Barbour (Eds.), *Violence Against Women.* San Diego, Calif.: Greenhaven.

George, Robert, Fred Wulczyn, and David Funshel. 1994. "A foster care research agenda for the 90s." *Child Welfare, 73,* 525–549.

Gianelli, Diane M. 1999. "Oregon suicide report contains some surprises." *American Medical News,* 42, March 8, pp. 9, 11.

Gibbs, Jack P. 1966. "Conceptions of deviant behavior: The old and the new." *Pacific Sociological Review, 9,* 9–14.

Gibbs, Jack P. 1971. "Suicide." In Robert Merton and Robert Nisbet (Eds.), *Contemporary Social Problems.* New York: Harcourt Brace Jovanovich.

Gibbs, Jack P. 1975. *Crime, Punishment and Deterrence.* New York: Elsevier.

Gibbs, Nancy. 1993a. "R for Death." *Time,* May 31, p. 37.

Gibbs, Nancy. 1993b. "'Til death do us part." *Time,* January 18, p. 41.

Gibbs, Nancy. 1995. "Love and let die." In Robert Emmet Long (Ed.), *Suicide.* New York: Wilson.

Gidycz, Christine A., and Mary P. Koss. 1991. "The effects of acquaintance rape on the female victim." In Andrea Parrot and Laurie Bechhofer (Eds.), *Acquaintance Rape.* New York: Wiley.

Gilbert, Neil. 1995. "Realities and mythologies of rape." In Alex Thio and Thomas C. Calhoun (Eds.), *Readings in Deviant Behavior.* New York: HarperCollins.

Gillespie, Michael, Valerie Hearn, and Robert A. Silverman. 1998. "Suicide following homicide in Canada." *Homicide Studies, 2,* 46–63.

Gillespie, Terry. 1996. "Rape crisis centers and 'male rape': a face of the backlash." In Marianne Hester et al. (Eds.), *Women, Violence and Male Power.* Philadelphia: Open University Press.

Giordano, Peggy C. 1983. "Sanctioning the high-status deviant: An attributional analysis." *Social Psychology Quarterly, 46,* 329–342.

Girard, Chris. 1993. "Age, gender, and suicide: A cross-national analysis." *American Sociological Review, 58,* 553–574.

Glasberg, D. S., and D. Skidmore. 1998. "The dialectics of white-collar crime: The anatomy of the savings and loan crisis and the case of Silverado Banking, Savings and Loan Association." *American Journal of Economics and Sociology, 57,* 423–449.

Glaser, Daniel. 1956. "Criminality theories and behavioral images." *American Journal of Sociology, 61,* 433–444.

Glass, Shirley P., and Thomas L. Wright. 1992. "Justifications for extramarital relationships: The association between attitudes, behaviors, and gender." *Journal of Sex Research, 29,* 361–387.

Glassner, Barry. 1991. "Jewish sobriety." In David J. Pittman and Helene Raskin White (Eds.), *Society, Culture, and Drinking Patterns Reexamined.* New Brunswick, N.J.: Rutgers Center of Alcohol Studies.

Gleick, Elizabeth. 1995. "The crooked blue line." *Time,* September 11, pp. 39–42.

Gleick, Elizabeth. 1996. "Putting the jail in jailbait." *Time,* January 29, pp. 33–34.

Glick, Daniel, et al. 1999. "Anatomy of a massacre." *Newsweek,* May 3, pp. 25–31.

Godson, Roy, and William J. Olson. 1995. "International organized crime." *Society,* January/February, pp. 18–29.

Goe, W. Richard, Ted L. Napier, and Douglas C. Bachtel. 1985. "Use of marijuana among rural high school students: A test of a facilitative-constraint model." *Rural Sociology, 50,* 409–426.

Goetting, Ann. 1989. "Patterns of marital homicide: A comparison of husbands and wives." *Journal of Comparative Family Studies, 22,* pp. 341–354.

Goetting, Ann. 1995. *Homicide in Families and Other Social Populations.* New York: Springer.

Goffman, Erving. 1961. *Asylums.* Garden City, N.Y.: Anchor.

Gold, Martin. 1958. "Suicide, homicide, and the socialization of aggression." *American Journal of Sociology, 43,* 651–661.

Goldberg, Carey. 1997. "Way out west and under the influence." *New York Times,* March 16, p. E16.

Goldberg, Carey. 1998. "Little drop in college binge drinking." *New York Times,* September 11, p. A12.

Goldner, Norman S. 1972. "Rape as a heinous but understudied offense." *Journal of Criminal Law, Criminology and Police Science, 63,* 402–407.

Goleman, Daniel. 1986. "Aid in day-to-day life seen as hope for schizophrenics." *New York Times,* March 19, pp. 1, 12.

Goleman, Daniel. 1992. "A rising cost of modernity: Depression." *New York Times,* December 8, p. B6.

Goode, Erica. 1999. "Study on child sex abuse provokes furor on findings." *New York Times,* June 13, p. Y25.

Goode, Erich. 1981. "Drugs and crime." In Abraham S. Blumberg (Ed.), *Current Perspective on Criminal Behavior.* New York: Knopf.

Goode, Erich. 1990. "Crime can be fun: The deviant experience. *Contemporary Sociology, 19,* 5–12.

Goode, Erich. 1991. "Positive deviance: A viable concept?" *Deviant Behavior, 12,* 289–309.

Goode, Erich. 1994. "Round up the usual suspects: Crime, deviance, and the limits of constructionism." *The American Sociologist,* Winter, pp. 90–104.

Goode, Erich. 1997. *Deviant Behavior.* 5th ed. Upper Saddle River, N.J.: Prentice Hall.

Goode, Erich. 1999. *Drugs in American Society.* 5th ed. New York: McGraw-Hill.

Goode, Erich, and Nachman Ben-Yehuda. 1994. *Moral Panics: The Social Construction of Deviance.* London: Blackwell.

Goodwin, Donald W. 1991. "The etiology of alcoholism." In David J. Pittman and Helene Raskin White (Eds.), *Society, Culture, and Drinking Patterns Reexamined.* New Brunswick, N.J.: Rutgers Center of Alcohol Studies.

Gordon, Margaret T., and Stephanie Riger. 1989. *The Female Fear.* New York: Free Press.

Gorman, Christine. 1992. "Can drug firms be trusted?" *Time,* February 10, p. 43.

Gorman, Christine. 1994. "Higher education: Crocked on campus." *Time,* December 19, pp. 66–67.

Gottesman, Irving I. 1995. "Genetic factors contribute to schizophrenia." In David Bender and Bruno Leone (Eds.), *Mental Illness: Opposing Viewpoints.* San Diego, Calif.: Greenhaven.

Gottfredson, Michael R., and Travis Hirschi. 1990. *A General Theory of Crime.* Newbury Park, Calif.: Sage.

Gould, Leroy C. 1969. "The changing structure of property crime in an affluent society." *Social Forces, 48,* 51.

Gouldner, Alvin W. 1968. "The sociologist as partisan: Sociology and the welfare state." *The American Sociologist, 3,* 103–116.

Gove, Walter R. 1970. "Societal reaction as an explanation of mental illness: An evaluation." *American Sociological Review, 35,* 882.

Gove, Walter R. (Ed.). 1980. *The Labelling of Deviance: Evaluating a Perspective.* 2d ed. Beverly Hills, Calif.: Sage.

Gove, Walter R. 1982. "Labelling theory's explanation of mental illness: An update of recent evidence." *Deviant Behavior, 3,* 307–327.

Gove, Walter R. 1984. "Gender differences in mental and physical illness: The effects of fixed roles and nurturant roles." *Social Science and Medicine, 19,* 77–84.

Gove, Walter R., and Michael Hughes. 1980. "Reexamining the ecological fallacy: A study in which aggregate data are critical in investigating the pathological effects of living alone." *Social Forces, 58,* 1157–1177.

Gove, Walter R., Maurigia Tovo, and Michael Hughes. 1985. "Involuntary psychiatric hospitalization: A review of the statutes regulating the social control of the mentally ill." *Deviant Behavior, 6,* 287–318.

Graham, Dee L. R., with Edna I. Rawlings and Roberta K. Rigsby. 1994. *Loving to Survive: Sexual Terror, Men's Violence, and Women's Lives.* New York: New York University Press.

Graham, Kathryn, William Turnbull, and Linda LaRocque. 1979. "Effects of alcohol on moral judgment." *Journal of Abnormal Psychology, 88,* 442–445.

Grapendaal, Martin. 1992. "Drugs and crime in an accommodating social context: The situation in Amsterdam." *Contemporary Drug Problems, 19,* 303–326.

Graves, William F. 1964. "The deterrent effect of capital punishment in California." In Hugo Adam Bedau (Ed.), *The Death Penalty in America.* Garden City, N.Y.: Doubleday.

Gray, Susan H. 1982. "Exposure to pornography and aggression toward women: The case of the angry male." *Social Problems, 29,* 387–398.

Green, Edward, and Russell P. Wakefield. 1979. "Patterns of middle and upper class homicide." *Journal of Criminal Law and Criminology, 70,* 172–181.

Green, Gary S. 1990. *Occupational Crime.* Chicago: Nelson-Hall.

Greenberg, David F. (Ed.). 1981. *Crime and Capitalism: Readings in Marxist Criminology.* Palo Alto, Calif.: Mayfield.

Greenberg, Michael, and Dona Schneider. 1994. "Violence in American cities: Young black males is the answer, but what was the question?" *Social Science and Medicine, 39,* 179–187.

Greenberg, Scott. 1996. "Why do workers bite the hands that feed them? Employee theft as a social exchange process." *Research in Organizational Behavior, 18,* 111–156.

Greenhouse, Cheryl M. 1992. "Household survey shows few changes in Americans' illicit drug use." *NIDA Notes, 7* (March/April), 5–6.

Greenhouse, Linda. 1999. "Sex harassment in class is ruled schools' liability." *New York Times,* May 15, pp. A1, A24.

Greenwald, Harold. 1970. *The Elegant Prostitute.* New York: Walker.

Greer, Frank I., and Rhona Strasberg Weinstein. 1979. "Suicide prevention outreach: Callers and noncallers compared." *Psychological Reports, 44,* 387–393.

Griffin, Susan. 1971. "Rape: The all-American crime." *Ramparts,* September, pp. 4–5.

Gross, William C. 1993. "Gender and age differences in college students' alcohol consumption." *Psychological Reports, 72,* 211–216.

Grossman, Dave. 1995. *On Killing: The Psychological Cost of Learning to Kill in War and Society.* Boston: Little, Brown.

Groth, A. Nicholas, and H. Jean Birnbaum. 1979. *Men Who Rape.* New York: Plenum.

Groth, A. Nicholas. 1983. "Rape: Behavioral aspects." In S. H. Kadish (Ed.), *Encyclopedia of Crime and Justice.* New York: Free Press.

Gunnell, David, Helen Wehner, and Stephen Frankel. 1999. "Sex differences in suicide trends in England and Wales." *The Lancet, 353,* 556–557.

Gusfield, Joseph R. 1991. "Status conflicts and the changing ideologies of the American temperance movement." In David J. Pittman and Charles R. Snyder (Eds.), *Society, Culture, and Drinking Patterns,* pp. 101–120.

Hammer, Joshua, and Brook Larmer. 1997. "We're in no rush." *Newsweek,* January 13, pp. 47–48.

Hammond, D. Corydon, and Gary Q. Jorgensen. 1981. "Alcohol and sex: A volatile cocktail." *USA Today: The Magazine of the American Scene,* July, pp. 44–46.

Handel, Warren. 1982. *Ethnomethodology: How People Make Sense.* Englewood Cliffs, N.J.: Prentice Hall.

Handelman, Stephen. 1995. *Comrade Criminal: Russia's New Mafiya.* New Haven, Conn.: Yale University Press.

Hanson, Bill, George Beschner, James M. Walters, and Elliott Bovelle. 1985. *Life with Heroin: Voices from the Inner City.* Lexington, Mass.: Health.

Hanson, David J. 1995. "The United States of America." In Dwight B. Heath (Ed.), *International Handbook on Alcohol and Culture.* Westport, Conn.: Greenwood.

Hanson, David J., and Ruth C. Engs. 1992. "College students' drinking problems: A national study, 1982–1991." *Psychological Reports, 71,* 39–42.

Haran, James F., and John M. Martin. 1984. "The armed urban bank robber: A profile." *Federal Probation, 48* (December), 51.

Harman, Lesley, D. 1985. "Acceptable deviance as social control: The case of fashion and slang." *Deviant Behavior, 6,* 1–15.

Harper, Frederick D., and Elaheh Saifnoorian. 1991. "Drinking patterns among black Americans." In David J. Pittman and Helene Raskin White (Eds.), *Society, Culture, and Drinking Patterns Reexamined.* New Brunswick, N.J.: Rutgers Center of Alcohol Studies.

Harries, Keith D. 1990. *Serious Violence: Patterns of Homicide and Assault in America.* Springfield, Ill.: Charles Thomas.

Harrison, Lana D. 1992a. "The drug-crime nexus in the USA." *Contemporary Drug Problems, 19,* 257–258.

Harrison, Lana D. 1992b. "The intersection of drug use and criminal behavior: Results from the National Household Survey on Drug Abuse." *Crime & Delinquency, 38,* 422–443.

Harry, Joseph. 1983. "Parasuicide, gender, and gender deviance." *Journal of Health and Social Behavior, 24,* 350–361.

Harry, Joseph, and Mary C. Sengstock. 1978. "Attribution, goals, and deviance." *American Sociological Review, 43,* 278–280.

Hasin, Deborah S., Bridget Grant, and Jean Endicott. 1990. "The natural history of alcohol abuse: Implications for definitions of alcohol use disorders." *American Journal of Psychiatry, 147,* 1537–1541.

Hasin, Deborah S., et al. 1990. "Multiple alcohol-related problems in the United States: On the rise?" *Journal of Studies on Alcohol, 51,* 485–493.

Hayes, Lindsay M. 1995. *Prison Suicide: An Overview and Guide to Prevention.* Washington, D.C.: U.S. Department of Justice.

Headden, Susan, and Gordon Witkin. 1993. "Preying on the helpless." *U.S. News & World Report,* May 24, pp. 48–52.

Heath, Dwight B. 1995. "Some generalizations about alcohol and culture." In Dwight Heath (Ed.), *International Handbook on Alcohol and Culture.* Westport, Conn.: Greenwood.

Heidensohn, Frances. 1995. *Women and Crime.* 2d ed. New York: New York University Press.

Heien, Dale M., and David J. Pittman. 1993. "The external costs of alcohol abuse." *Journal of Studies on Alcohol, 54,* 302–307.

Helmer, John. 1975. *Drugs and Minority Oppression.* New York: Seabury.

Hendin, Herbert. 1979. "A saner policy on suicide." *Psychology Today,* May, p. 115.

Hendin, Herbert. 1995. *Suicide in America.* New York: Norton.

Hendin, Herbert. 1997. *Seduced by Death: Doctors, Patients, and the Dutch Cure.* New York: Norton.

Henneberger, Melinda, and Michel Marriott. 1993. "For some, youthful courting has become a game of abuse." *New York Times,* July 11, pp. 1, 14.

Henry, Andrew, and James Short. 1954. *Suicide and Homicide.* New York: Free Press.

Henry, William A. III. 1993. "Gay parents: Under fire and on the rise." *Time,* September 20, pp. 68–71.

Henry, William A. III. 1994. "Pride and prejudice." *Time,* June 27, pp. 54–59.

Henslin, James M. 1970. "Guilt and guilt neutralization: Response and adjustment to suicide." In Jack D. Douglas (Ed.), *Deviance and Respectability.* New York: Basic Books.

Henslin, James M. 1988. "Structuralism and individualism in deviance theory." *Deviant Behavior, 9,* 211–223.

Hepburn, John R. 1977. "Social control and the legal order: Legitimated repression in a capitalist state." *Contemporary Crises, 1,* 84.

Herbert, Bob. 1995. "Killer cops." *New York Times,* September 15, p. A15.

Herd, Denise. 1991. "Drinking patterns in the black population." In Walter B. Clark and Michael E. Hilton (Eds.), *Alcohol in America.* Albany, N.Y.: State University of New York Press.

Herdt, Gilbert. 1990. "Developmental discontinuities and sexual orientation across cultures." In David P. McWhirter, et al., *Homosexuality/Heterosexuality.* New York: Oxford University Press.

Herman, Ellen, and Martin B. Duberman. 1995. *Psychiatry, Psychology, and Homosexuality.* New York: Chelsea House.

Herman, Judith Lewis. 1995. "Considering sex offenders: A model of addiction." In Patricia Searles and Ronald J. Berger (Eds.), *Rape and Society.* Boulder, Colo.: Westview.

Hess, John H., and Herbert E. Thomas. 1963. "Incompetency to stand trial: Procedures, results, and problems." *American Journal of Psychiatry, 119,* 713–720.

Hey, Robert P. 1986. "This fall's biggest campus problems." *Christian Science Monitor,* August 29, p. 6.

Heyl, Barbara Sherman. 1977. "The madam as teacher: The training of house prostitutes." *Social Problems, 24,* 545–555.

Hickey, Eric W. 1991. *Serial Murderers and Their Victims.* Pacific Grove, Calif.: Brooks/Cole.

Hill, Herbert. 1973. "Anti-oriental agitation and the rise of working-class racism." *Society, 10,* January/February, p. 52.

Hills, Stuart L. 1980. *Demystifying Social Deviance.* New York: McGraw-Hill.

Hilton, Michael E. 1991. "Regional diversity in U.S. drinking practices." In Walter B. Clark and Michael E. Hilton (Eds.), *Alcohol in America: Drinking Practices and Problems.* Albany, N.Y.: State University of New York Press.

Hilts, Philip J. 1987. "AIDS infection found in 11% of U.S. prostitutes." *Washington Post,* March 27, pp. A1, A10.

Himmelstein, Jerome L. 1983. *The Strange Career of Marijuana: Politics and Ideology of Drug Control in America.* Westport, Conn.: Greenwood.

Hinrichsen, Gregory A., Nancy A. Hernandez, and Simcha Pollack. 1992. "Difficulties and rewards in family care of depressed older adults." *Gerontologist, 32,* 486–492.

Hirschi, Travis. 1962. "The professional prostitute." *Berkeley Journal of Sociology, 7,* 44–45.

Hirschi, Travis. 1969. *Causes of Delinquency.* Berkeley and Los Angeles: University of California Press, 1969.

Hirschi, Travis. 1973. "Procedural rules and the study of deviant behavior." *Social Problems, 21,* 166–171.

Hirschi, Travis, and Michael R. Gottfredson (Eds.). 1994. *The Generality of Deviance.* New Brunswick, N.J.: Transaction.

Hoffman, Bruce. 1998. *Inside Terrorism.* New York: Columbia University Press.

Holden, Constance. 1985. "Genes, personality, and alcoholism." *Psychology Today,* January, pp. 38–44.

Hollinger, Richard C., and John P. Clark. 1983. *Theft by Employees.* Lexington, Mass.: Lexington Books.

Hollingshead, August B., and Frederick C. Redlich. 1958. *Social Class and Mental Illness.* New York: Wiley.

Holmes, Ronald M., and James E. DeBurger. 1985. "Profiles in terror: The serial murderer." *Federal Probation, 49,* 29–34.

Holmes, Ronald M., and Stephen T. Holmes. 1992. "Understanding mass murder: A starting point," *Federal Probation, 56,* 53–61.

Holmstrom, Lynda Lytle, and Ann Wolbert Burgess. 1983. *The Victim of Rape.* New Brunswick, N.J.: Transaction Books.

Holzman, Harold R., and Sharon Pines. 1982. "Buying sex: The phenomenology of being a john." *Deviant Behavior, 4,* 105.

Homer, Frederic D. 1973. *Guns and Garlic: Myths and Realities of Organized Crime.* West Lafayette, Ind.: Purdue University Press.

Hornblower, Margot. 1993. "The skin trade." *Time,* June 21, p. 45.

Horwitz, Allan V., Susan C. Reinhard, and Sandra Howell-White. 1996. "Caregiving as reciprocal exchange in families with seriously mentally ill members." *Journal of Health and Social Behavior, 37,* 149–162.

Hsu, Lee-Nah. 1993. "Drug use and the family." *World Health, 46* (November), 31–33.

Huff-Corzine, Lin, Jay Corzine, and David C. Moore. 1986. "Southern exposure: Deciphering the South's influence in homicide rates." *Social Forces, 64,* 906–924.

Hughes, Stella P., and Richard A. Dodder. 1992. "Changing the legal minimum drinking age: Results of a longitudinal study." *Journal of Studies on Alcohol, 53,* 568–575.

Human Rights Watch. 1995. *Rape for Profit: Trafficking of Nepali Girls and Women to India's Brothels.* New York: Human Rights Watch.

Humphreys, Laud. 1970. "Tearoom trade: Impersonal sex in public places." *Transaction, 7,* 17–18.

Humphreys, Laud. 1972. *Out of the Closets.* Englewood Cliffs, N.J.: Prentice Hall.

Hunt, Albert R. 1995. "The best Congress money can buy." *Wall Street Journal,* September 7, p. A15.

Hunter, Patricia A., Roseann Hannon, and David Marchi. 1982. "Alcohol consumption in natural settings as a function of sex, age, and income level." *Journal of Studies on Alcohol, 43,* 387–392.

Hurlburt, Graham, Eldon Gade, and Dale Fuqua. 1984. "Personality differences between Alcoholics Anonymous members and nonmembers." *Journal of Studies on Alcohol, 45,* 170–171.

Huselid, Rebecca Farmer, and M. Lynne Cooper. 1992. "Gender roles as mediators of sex differences in adolescent alcohol use and abuse." *Journal of Health and Social Behavior, 33,* 348–362.

Hyatt, Ralph. 1993. "Carjacking: A sign of the times." *USA Today: The Magazine of the American Scene, 22,* September, pp. 40–41.

Ibrahim, Farah A. 1995. "Suicidal behavior in Asian-American women." In Silvia Sara Canetto and David Lester (Eds.), *Women and Suicidal Behavior.* New York: Springer.

Institute of Medicine. 1990. *Broadening the Base of Treatment for Alcohol Problems.* Washington, D.C.: Academy Press.

Irwin, John. 1970. *The Felon.* Englewood Cliffs, N.J.: Prentice Hall.

Isikoff, Michael. 1995. "Crack, coke and race." *Newsweek,* November 6, p. 77.

Isikoff, Michael. 1997. "The White House shell game." *Newsweek,* February 10, pp. 34–35.

Itzin, Catherine (Ed.). 1993. *Pornography: Women, Violence, and Civil Liberties: A Radical View.* New York: Oxford University Press.

Jackley, John L. 1992. *Hill Rat: Blowing the Lid Off Congress.* Washington, D.C.: Regnery Gateway.

Jackson, James O. 1996. "The lost children." *Time,* March 25, pp. 44–45.

Jackson, Lois, et al. 1992. "Varied potential risks of HIV infection among prostitutes." *Social Science and Medicine, 35,* 281–286.

Jackson, Thomas L. 1996. *Acquaintance Rape: Assessment, Treatment, and Prevention.* Sarasota, Florida: Professional Resource Press.

Jacobs, Jerry. 1967. "A phenomenological study of suicide notes." *Social Problems, 15,* 60–72.

Jaffe, Jerome H. 1965. "Drug addiction and drug abuse." In Louis S. Goodman and Alfred Gilman (Eds.), *The Pharmacological Basis of Therapeutics.* New York: Macmillan.

Jamieson, Katherine M. 1994. *The Organization of Corporate Crime: Dynamics of Antitrust Violation.* Thousand Oaks, Calif.: Sage.

Janus, Samuel S., and Cynthia L. Janus. 1993. *The Janus Report on Sexual Behavior.* New York: Wiley.

Jasper, Jann. 1992. "Rape: Are you at risk?" *New Woman, 22,* 80–86.

Jellinek, E. M. 1952. "Phases of alcohol addiction." *Quarterly Journal of Studies on Alcohol, 13,* 673–684.

Jenness, Valerie. 1990. "From sex as sin to sex as work: COYOTE and the reorganization of prostitution as a social problem." *Social Problems, 37,* 403–420.

Jessor, Richard, James A. Chase, and John E. Donovan. 1980. "Psychosocial correlates of marijuana use and problem drinking in a national sample of adolescents." *American Journal of Public Health, 70,* 604–613.

Johnson, Dirk. 1993. "Gay-rights debate prompts new wave of 'coming out'." *New York Times,* June 30, p. A1.

Johnston, David. 1997. "The mystery of the violent bank jobs." *New York Times,* March 30, p. E4.

Johnston, Lloyd D., et al. 1986. *Drug Use Among American High School Students, College Students, and Other Young Adults.* Rockville, Md.: National Institute on Drug Abuse.

Jones, Ann. 1994. *Next Time, She'll Be Dead: Battering & How to Stop It.* Boston: Beacon.

Jones, Franklin D., and Ronald J. Koshes. 1995. "Homosexuality and the military." *American Journal of Psychiatry, 152,* 16–21.

Jones, Peter, et al. 1993. "Premorbid social underachievement in schizophrenia: Results from the Camberwell Collaborative Psychosis Study." *British Journal of Psychiatry, 162,* 65–71.

Jurich, Anthony P., and Cheryl J. Polson. 1984. "Reasons for drug use: Comparison of drug users and abusers." *Psychological Reports, 55,* 371–378.

Kahan, Dan M. 1997. "It's a shame we have none." *Wall Street Journal,* January 15, p. A14.

Kamisar, Yale. 1998. "Details doom assisted-suicide measures." *New York Times,* November 4, p. A27.

Kandel, Denise B. 1984. 'Marijuana users in young adulthood." *Archives of General Psychiatry, 41,* 200–209.

Kanin, Eugene J. 1984. "Date rape: Unofficial criminals and victims." *Victimology: An International Journal, 9,* 95–108.

Kanin, Eugene J. 1985. "Date rapists: Differential sexual socialization and relative deprivation." *Archives of Sexual Behavior, 14,* 219–231.

Kanin, Eugene J., and Stanley R. Parcell. 1981. "Sexual aggression: A second look at the offended female." In Lee H. Bowker (Ed.), *Women and Crime in America*. New York: Macmillan.

Kantor, Glenda, and Murray A. Straus. 1990. "The 'drunken bum' theory of wife beating." In M. A. Straus and R. J. Gelles (Eds.), *Physical Violence in American Families*. New Brunswick, N.J.: Transaction.

Kantrowitz, Barbara. 1991. "Striking a nerve." *Newsweek,* October 21, pp. 38, 40.

Kantrowitz, Barbara. 1996. "Gay families come out." *Newsweek,* November 4, pp. 50–57.

Kaplan, David A. 1991. "The bank robbery boom." *Newsweek,* December 9, p. 63.

Kaplan, David A., and Daniel Klaidman. 1996. "A battle, not the war." *Newsweek,* June 3, pp. 24–30.

Kaplan, David E. 1998. "Yakuza Inc." *U.S. News & World Report,* April 13, pp. 40–47.

Kaplan, Howard B. 1972. *The Sociology of Mental Illness*. New Haven, Conn.: College and University Press.

Kaplan, Howard B., et al. 1986. "Escalation of marijuana use: Application of a general theory of deviant behavior." *Journal of Health and Social Behavior, 27,* 44–61.

Kappeler, Victor E., Mark Blumberg, and Gary W. Potter. 1993. *The Mythology of Crime and Criminal Justice*. Prospect Heights, Ill.: Waveland.

Kappeler, Victor E., Richard D. Sluder, and Geoffrey P. Alpert. 1998. *Forces of Deviance: Understanding the Dark Side of Policing*. 2nd ed. Prospect Heights, Ill.: Waveland.

Kart, Gary S. 1990. *The Realities of Aging*. 3d ed. Boston: Allyn and Bacon.

Katchadourian, Herant. 1985. *Fundamentals of Human Sexuality*. 4th ed. New York: Holt, Rinehart and Winston.

Katz, Bonnie L. 1991. "The psychological impact of stranger versus nonstranger rape on victims' recovery." In Andrea Parrot and Laurie Bechhofer (Eds.), *Acquaintance Rape*. New York: Wiley.

Katz, Jack. 1988. *Deductions of Crime: Moral and Sensual Attractions in Doing Evil*. New York: Basic Books.

Kaufman, Arthur, et al. 1980. "Male rape victims: Noninstitutionalized assault." *American Journal of Psychiatry, 137,* 221–223.

Kaufman, Joan, and Edward Zigler. 1987. "Do abused children become abusive parents?" *American Journal of Orthopsychiatry, 57,* 186–192.

Kaufman, Joan, and Edward Zigler. 1993. "The intergenerational transmission of abuse is overstated." In Richard J. Gelles and Donileen R. Loseke (Eds.), *Current Controversies on Family Violence*. Newbury Park, Calif.: Sage.

Kaysen, Susanna. 1993. *Girl, Interrupted*. New York: Turtle Bay Books/Random House.

Kempf, Kimberly L. 1993. "The empirical status of Hirschi's control theory." In Freda Adler and William S. Laufer (Eds.), *New Directions in Criminological Theory*. New Brunswick, N.J.: Transaction.

Kendall-Tackett, Kathleen A., Linda Meyer Williams, and David Finkelhor. 1993. "Impact of sexual abuse on children: A review and synthesis of recent empirical studies." *Psychological Bulletin, 113,* 164–180.

Kendler, Kenneth S. 1983. "Overview: A current perspective on twin studies of schizophrenia." *American Journal of Psychiatry, 140,* 1413–1425.

Kendler, Kenneth S., et al. 1993. "The prediction of major depression in women: Toward an integrated etiologic model." *American Journal of Psychiatry, 150,* 1139–1148.

Kessler, Ronald C., and Harold W. Neighbors. 1986. "A new perspective on the relationships among race, social class, and psychological distress." *Journal of Health and Social Behavior, 27,* 107–115.

Kessler, Ronald C., and James A. McRae, Jr. 1983. "Trends in the relationship between sex and attempted suicide." *Journal of Health and Social Behavior, 24,* 98–110.

Kessler, Ronald C., et al. 1985. "Social factors in psychopathology: Stress, social support, and coping processes." *Annual Review of Psychology, 36,* 560–561.

Kessler, Ronald, et al. 1994. "Lifetime and 12-month prevalence of DSM-III-psychiatric disorders in the United States." *Archives of General Psychiatry, 51,* 8–19.

Kety, Seymour S. 1974. "From rationalization to reason." *American Journal of Psychiatry, 131,* 957–963.

Khantzian, Edward J. 1985. "The self-medication hypothesis of addictive disorders: Focus on heroin and cocaine dependence." *American Journal of Psychiatry, 142,* 1259–1264.

King, David R. 1978. "The brutalization effect: Execution publicity and the incidence of homicide in South Carolina." *Social Forces, 57,* 683–687.

Kinsey, Alfred C., et al. 1948. *Sexual Behavior in the Human Male.* Philadelphia: Saunders.

Kinsey, Alfred C., et al. 1953. *Sexual Behavior in the Human Female.* Philadelphia: Saunders.

Kirk, Stuart A., and Herb Kutchins. 1992. *The Selling of DSM: The Rhetoric of Science in Psychiatry.* New York: Aldine de Gruyter.

Kirk, Stuart A., and Herb Kutchins. 1994. "Is bad writing a mental disorder?" *New York Times,* June 20, p. A11.

Kirkpatrick, Clifford, and Eugene Kanin. 1957. "Male sex aggression on a university campus." *American Sociological Review, 22,* 52–58.

Kirn, Walter. 1998. "Crank." *Time,* June 22, pp. 26–32.

Kite, Mary E., and Bernard E. Whitley, Jr. 1996. "Sex differences in attitudes toward homosexual persons, behaviors, and civil rights: A meta-analysis." *Personality and Social Psychology Bulletin, 22,* 336–353.

Kitsuse, John I. 1962. "Societal reaction to deviant behavior: Problems of theory and method." *Social Problems, 9,* 247–256.

Klaus, Patsy. 1999. "Carjackings in the United States, 1992-96." *Bureau of Justice Statistics Special Report,* March, U.S. Department of Justice.

Kleck, Gary. 1979. "Capital punishment, gun ownership, and homicide." *American Journal of Sociology, 84,* 882–910.

Kleck, Gary. 1990. "Rape and resistance." *Social Problems, 37,* 149–162.

Kleck, Gary, and M. Hogan. 1999. "National case-control study of homicide offending and gun ownership." *Social Problems, 46,* 275–293.

Klein, Richard. 1996. "Secure, and Dangerous." *New York Times,* August 2, p. A15.

Kleinfield, N.R., and Kit R. Roane. 1999. "Subway killing puts harsh light on the suspect's mental torment." *New York Times,* January 11, pp. A1, A18.

Kleinknecht, William. 1996. *The New Ethnic Mobs: The Changing Face of Organized Crime in America.* New York: Free Press.

Klemke, Lloyd W. 1992. *The Sociology of Shoplifting: Boosters and Snitches Today.* Westport, Conn.: Praeger.

Knight, Raymond A., et al. 1985. "Classification of sex offenders: Perspectives, methods, and validation." In Ann Wolbert Burgess (Ed.), *Rape and Sexual Assault: A Research Handbook.* New York: Garland.

Knutson, Jeanne N. 1996. "The terrorists' dilemmas: Some implicit rules of the game." In Conor Gearty (Ed.), *Terrorism.* Aldershot, England: Dartmouth.

Kolata, Gina. 1992. "The burdens of being overweight: Mistreatment and misconceptions." *New York Times,* November 22, pp. 1, 18.

Kolb, Lawrence C., and H. Keith H. Brodie. 1982. *Modern Clinical Psychiatry.* 10th ed. Philadelphia: Saunders.

Kopelowicz, Alex, and T. George Bidder. 1992. "Outcome of schizophrenia." *American Journal of Psychiatry, 149,* 426.

Koss, Mary P. 1995. "Hidden rape: Sexual aggression and victimization in a national sample of students in higher education." In Patricia Searles and Ronald J. Berger (Eds.), *Rape and Society.* Boulder, Colo: Westview.

Koss, Mary P., and J. A. Gaines. 1993. "The prediction of sexual aggression by alcohol use, athletic participation, and fraternity affiliation." *Journal of Interpersonal Violence, 8,* 94–108.

Koss, Mary P., et al. 1987. "The scope of rape: Incidence and prevalence of sexual aggression and victimization in a national sample of higher education students." *Journal of Consulting and Clinical Psychology, 55,* 162–170.

Kristof, Nicholas D. 1996a. "Asian childhoods sacrificed to prosperity's lust." *Time,* April 14, pp. 1, 6.

Kristof, Nicholas D. 1996b. "Guns: one nation bars, the other requires." *New York Times,* March 10, p. E3.

Krohn, Marvin D. 1995. "Control and deterrence theories of criminality." In Joseph F. Sheley (Ed.), *Criminology: A Contemporary Handbook.* 2d ed. Belmont, Calif.: Wadsworth.

Krohn, Marvin D., William F. Skinner, James L. Massey, and Ronald L. Akers. 1985. "Social learning theory and adolescent cigarette smoking: A longitudinal study." *Social Problems, 32,* 454–471.

Kuo, Wen H. 1984. "Prevalence of depression among Asian-Americans." *Journal of Nervous and Mental Disease, 172,* 449–457.

Kuo, Wen H., and Yung-Mei Tsai. 1986. "Social networking, hardiness and immigrant's mental health." *Journal of Health and Social Behavior, 27,* 133–149.

Kushner, Howard I. 1985. "Women and suicide in historical perspective." *Signs, 10,* 543.

Kushner, Howard I. 1995. "Women and suicidal behavior: Epidemiology, gender and lethality in historical perspective." In Silvia Sara Canetto and David Lester (Eds.), *Women and Suicidal Behavior.* New York: Springer.

Kutchins, Herb, and Stuart A. Kirk. 1997. *Making Us Crazy.* New York: The Free Press.

Kutner, L. 1962. "The illusion of due process in commitment proceedings." *Northwestern University Law Review, 57,* 383–399.

Labaton, Stephen. 1995. "As pornography arrests grow, so do plans for computer stings." *New York Times,* September 16, pp. 1, 8.

Labovitz, Sanford. 1968. "Variation in suicide rates." In Jack P. Gibbs (Ed.), *Suicide.* New York: Harper & Row.

Lacayo, Richard. 1995. "How safe is safe?" *Time,* May 1, pp. 68–72.

Lacayo, Richard. 1998. "The new gay struggle." *Time,* October 26, pp. 32–36.

Lacy, William B. 1981. "The influence of attitudes and current friends on drug use intentions." *Journal of Social Psychology, 113,* 65–76.

LaFree, Gary D. 1982. "Male power and female victimization." *American Journal of Sociology, 88,* 312–313.

LaFree, Gary D., Barbara F. Reskin, and Christy A. Visher. 1985. "Jurors' responses to victims' behavior and legal issues in sexual assault trials." *Social Problems, 32,* 389–406.

LaGrange, Randy L., and Helene Raskin White. 1985. "Age differences in delinquency: A test of theory." *Criminology, 23,* 19–45.

Laing, R. D. 1965. *The Divided Self.* Baltimore, Md.: Penguin Books.

Laing, R. D. 1967. *The Politics of Experience.* New York: Ballantine.

Laing, R. D. 1985. *Wisdom, Madness and Folly.* New York: McGraw-Hill.

Lamar, Jacob V. 1986. "Crack," *Time*, June 2, p. 17.

Lamb, Michael. 1998. "Cybersex: Research notes on the characteristics of the visitors to online chat rooms." *Deviant Behavior, 19,* 121–135.

Lamberti, Joseph W., Nathan Blackman, and James M. A. Weiss. 1967. "The sudden murderer." In Marvin Wolfgang (Ed.), *Studies in Homicide.* New York: Harper & Row.

Landau, Simha F., and Daniel Fridman. 1993. "The seasonality of violent crime: The case of robbery and homicide in Israel." *Journal of Research in Crime and Delinquency, 30,* 163–191.

Landau, Sybil. 1974. "Rape: The victim as defendant." *Trial, 10* (July/August), 19–22.

Lanning, Kenneth V. 1992. *Child Molesters: A Behavioral Analysis.* Arlington, Va.: National Center for Missing and Exploited Children.

Lapham, Lewis H. 1985. "Supply-side ethics." *Harper's,* May, pp. 10–11.

Lauderdale, Pat, Jerry Parker, Phil Smith-Cunnien, and James Inverarity. 1984. "External threat and the definition of deviance. *Journal of Personality and Social Psychology, 46,* 1058–1068.

Laumann, Edward O., et al. 1994. *The Social Organization of Sexuality: Sexual Practices in the United States.* Chicago: University of Chicago Press.

Lavelle, Marianne. 1998. "The new rules of sexual harassment." *U.S. News & World Report,* July 6, pp. 30–31.

Lawson, Annette. 1988. *Adultery: An Analysis of Love and Betrayal.* New York: Basic Books.

Lear, Martha Weinman. 1972a. "Q. If you rape a woman and steal her TV, what can they get you for in New York? A. stealing her TV." *New York Times Magazine,* January 30, pp. 62–63.

Lear, Martha Weinman. 1972b. "What can you say about laws that tell a man: If you rob a woman, you might as well rape her too—The rape is free." *Redbook,* September, p. 83.

Lecomte, D., and P. Fornes. 1998. "Homicide followed by suicide: Paris and its suburbs, 1991-1996." *Journal of Forensic Sciences, 43,* 760–764.

Lederer, Laura (Ed.). 1982. *Take Back the Night: Women on Pornography.* New York: Bantam Books.

Lee, Matthew R., and William B. Bankston. 1999. "Political structure, economic inequality, and homicide: A cross-national analysis." *Deviant Behavior, 20,* 27-55.

LeGrand, Camille E. 1973. "Rape and rape laws: Sexism in society and law." *California Law Review, 61,* 929–930.

Leland, John. 1995. "Bisexuality." *Newsweek,* July 17, pp. 44–50.

Leland, John. 1996. "The fear of heroin is shooting up." *Newsweek,* August 26, pp. 55–56.

Lemert, Edwin M. 1951. *Social Pathology.* New York: McGraw-Hill.

Lemert, Edwin M. 1972. *Human Deviance, Social Problems, and Social Control.* 2d ed. Englewood Cliffs, N.J.: Prentice Hall.

Lemonick, Michael D. 1996. "Defining the right to die." *Time,* April 15, p. 82.

Leonard, Eileen B. 1982. *Women, Crime, and Society: A Critique of Criminology Theory.* New York: Longman.

Lester, David. 1983. *Why People Kill Themselves.* Springfield, Ill.: Charles C. Thomas.

Lester, David. 1985. "Accidental deaths as disguised suicides." *Psychological Reports, 56,* 626.

Lester, David. 1988. "Toward a theory of parasuicide." *Corrective and Social Psychiatry, 34,* 24–26.

Lester, David. 1989. *Questions and Answers About Suicide.* Philadelphia: Charles Press.

Lester, David. 1990. "Suicide, homicide and the quality of life in various countries." *Acta Psychiatrica Scandinavica, 81,* 332–334.

Lester, David. 1991. "Childlessness, suicide and homicide." *Psychological Reports, 69,* 990.

Lester, David, and Bruce L. Danto. 1993. *Suicide Behind Bars: Prediction and Prevention.* Philadelphia: Charles Press.

Lester, David, and Mary E. Murrell. 1980. "The influence of gun control laws on suicidal behavior." *American Journal of Psychiatry, 137,* 121–122.

LeVay, Simon. 1996. *Queer Science: The Use and Abuse of Research into Homosexuality.* Cambridge, Mass.: MIT Press.

LeVay, Simon, and Elisabeth Nonas. 1995. *City of Friends: A Portrait of the Gay and Lesbian Community in America.* Cambridge, Mass.: MIT Press.

Levi, Ken. 1981. "Becoming a hit man: Neutralization in a very deviant career." *Urban Life, 10,* 47–63.

Levin, Jack, and James Alan Fox. 1985. *Mass Murder: America's Growing Menace.* New York: Plenum.

Levine, Art. 1986. "Drug education gets an F." *U.S. News & World Report,* October 13, pp. 63–64.

Levinson, David. 1988. "Family violence in a cross-cultural perspective." In V. B. Van Hasselt et al. (Eds.), *Handbook of Family Violence.* New York: Plenum.

Levy, Steven. 1995. "No place for kids?" *Newsweek,* July 3, pp. 47–50.

Lewin, Tamar. 1993a. "Colorado ban on gay rights laws is ruled unconstitutional." *New York Times,* December 14, p. A11.

Lewin, Tamar. 1993b. "Rape and the accuser: A debate still rages on citing sexual past." *New York Times,* February 12, p. B12.

Lewin, Tamar. 1995. "Parents poll finds child abuse to be more common." *New York Times,* December 7, p. A17.

Lewis, Helen Block. 1985. "Depression vs. paranoia: Why are there sex differences in mental illness?" *Journal of Personality, 53,* 150–178.

Lewis, Neil A. 1995. "Clinton plan would let FBI infiltrate menacing groups." *New York Times,* April 25, p. A9.

Lieberman, Jethro K. 1973. *How the Government Breaks the Law.* Baltimore, Md.: Penguin.

Liebling, Alison. 1992. *Suicides in Prison.* London: Routledge.

Lindesmith, Alfred R. 1968. *Addiction and Opiates.* Chicago: Aldine.

Link, Bruce G. 1982. "Mental patient status, work, and income: An examination of the effects of a psychiatric label." *American Sociological Review, 47,* 202–215.

Link, Bruce G., Bruce P. Dohrenwend, and Andrew E. Skodol. 1986. "Socio-economic status and schizophrenia: Noisome occupational characteristics as a risk factor." *American Sociological Review, 51,* 242–258.

Link, Bruce G., Jerrold Mirotznik, and Francis T. Cullen. 1991. "The effectiveness of stigma coping orientations: Can negative consequences of mental illness labeling be avoided?" *Journal of Health and Social Behavior, 32,* 302–320.

Link, Bruce G., Mary Clare Lennon, and Bruce P. Dohrenwend. 1993. "Socioeconomic status and depression: The role of occupations involving direction, control, and planning." *American Journal of Sociology, 98,* 1351–1387.

Linsky, Arnold S., John P. Colby, Jr., and Murray A. Straus. 1991. "Stress, drinking culture, and alcohol problems: A partial test of Bales' theory." In David J. Pittman and Helene Raskin White (Eds.), *Society, Culture, and Drinking Patterns Reexamined.* New Brunswick, N.J.: Rutgers Center of Alcohol Studies.

Linz, Daniel, and Neil Malamuth. 1993. *Pornography.* Newbury Park, Calif.: Sage.

Linz, Daniel, Edward Donnerstein, and Steven Penrod. 1984. "The effects of multiple exposures to filmed violence against women." *Journal of Communication, 34,* 130–147.

Lisanky, Edith S. 1991. "Women and alcohol: Psychosocial aspects." In David J. Pittman and Helene Raskin White (Eds.), *Society, Culture, and Drinking Patterns Reexamined*. New Brunswick, N.J.: Rutgers Center of Alcohol Studies.

Liska, Allen E., and Mark D. Reed. 1985. "Ties to conventional institutions and delinquency: Estimating reciprocal effects." *American Sociological Review, 50,* 547–560.

Lockwood, Daniel. 1985. "Issues in prison sexual violence." In Michael Braswell et al., *Prison Violence in America*. Cincinnati, Ohio: Anderson.

Loff, Bebe, and Stephen Cordner. 1998. "Australian doctor reveals details of assisted suicides." *The Lancet, 352,* 1838.

Loftin, Colin, and Robert Nash Parker. 1985. "An error-in-variable model of the effect of poverty on urban homicide rates." *Criminology, 23,* 269–285.

Lonsway, Kimberly A., and Louise F. Fitzgerald. 1994. "Rape myths are attitudes and generally false beliefs about rape." *Psychology of Women Quarterly, 18,* 133–164.

Lorenz, Konrad. 1966. *On Aggression*. New York: Harcourt, Brace and World.

Luckenbill, David F. 1977. "Criminal homicide as a situated transaction." *Social Problems, 25,* 176–186.

Luckenbill, David F. 1981. "Generating compliance: The case of robbery." *Urban Life, 10,* 25–46.

Luckenbill, David F. 1985. "Entering male prostitution." *Urban Life, 14,* 131–153.

Luckenbill, David F. 1986. "Deviant career mobility: The case of male prostitutes." *Social Problems, 33,* 283–296.

Lunde, Donald T. 1975. "Our murder boom." *Psychology Today,* July, pp. 40–42.

Lyman, Stanford M. 1995. "Without morals or mores: Deviance in postmodern social theory." *International Journal of Politics, Culture and Society, 9,* 197–235.

Lynch, James P., and David Cantor. 1992. "Ecological and behavioral influences on property victimization at home: Implications for opportunity theory." *Journal of Research in Crime and Delinquency, 29,* 335–362.

Lynn, Barry W. 1986. *Polluting the Censorship Debate: A Summary and Critique of the Final Report of the Attorney General's Commission on Pornography*. Washington, D.C.: American Civil Liberties Union.

MacAndrew, Craig, and Robert B. Edgerton. 1969. *Drunken Comportment*. London: Nelson.

Macdonald, John M. 1971. *Rape*. Springfield, Ill.: Charles C. Thomas.

Macdonald, John M. 1995. *Rape: Controversial Issues*. Springfield, Ill.: Charles C. Thomas.

MacKinnon, Catherine A. 1993. *Only Words*. Cambridge, Mass.: Harvard University Press.

Maddux, J. F., and D. P. Desmond. 1980. "New light on the maturing out hypothesis in opioid dependence." *Bulletin on Narcotics, 32,* 15–25.

Madge, Nicola, and John G. Harvey. 1999. "Suicide among the young—The size of the problem." *Journal of Adolescence, 22,* 145–155.

Madigan, Lee, and Nancy C. Gamble. 1991. *The Second Rape: Society's Continued Betrayal of the Victim*. New York: Lexington Books.

Magnuson, Ed. 1986. "Headhunters," *Time,* December 1, p. 32.

Maguire, Kathleen, and Ann L. Pastore (Eds.). 1996. *Sourcebook of Criminal Justice Statistics— 1995*. Washington, D.C.: Government Printing Office.

Mancoske, Ronald J., et al. 1995. "Suicide risk among people living with AIDS." *Social Work, 40,* 783–787.

Mandoki, Catalina A., and Barry R. Burkhart. 1991. "Women as victims: Antecedents and consequences of acquaintance rape." In Andrea Parrot and Laurie Bechhofer (Eds.), *Acquaintance Rape*. New York: Wiley.

Mann, Coramae Richey. 1996. *When Women Kill.* Albany, N.Y.: State University of New York Press.

Mann, Judy. 1985. "Campus gang-rape report." *Washington Post,* December 20, p. B3.

Mao, Tse-tung. 1967. *Selected Works of Mao Tse-tung, Vol. 1.* Peking: Foreign Languages Press.

Marcos, Anastasios C., Stephen J. Bahr, and Richard E. Johnson. 1986. "Test of a bonding/association theory of adolescent drug use." *Social Forces, 65,* 135–169.

Marcus, Eric. 1992. *Making History: The Struggle for Gay and Lesbian Equal Rights.* New York: HarperCollins.

Marcus, Eric. 1993. *Is It a Choice?* New York: HarperSanFrancisco.

Margolick, David. 1993. "Verdict against G.M. fuels debate on huge punitive jury awards." *New York Times,* February 6, p. 6.

Margolin, Leslie. 1992a. "Beyond maternal blame: Physical child abuse as a phenomenon of gender." *Journal of Family Issues, 13,* 410–423.

Margolin, Leslie. 1992b. "Deviance on record: Techniques for labeling child abusers in official documents." *Social Problems, 39,* 58–70.

Markoff, John. 1992. "Though illegal, copied software is now common." *New York Times,* July 27, pp. A1, C4.

Marks, Alan. 1980. "Socioeconomic status and suicide in the state of Washington: 1950–1971." *Psychological Reports, 46,* 924–926.

Marks, Alan, and C. Shannon Stokes. 1976. "Socialization, firearms, and suicide." *Social Problems, 23,* 622–629.

Marriott, Michel. 1995. "Half steps vs. 12 steps." *Newsweek,* March 27, p. 62.

Martin, Patricia Yancey, and Robert A. Hummer. 1995. "Fraternities and rape on campus." In Alex Thio and Thomas C. Calhoun (Eds.), *Readings in Deviant Behavior.* New York: HarperCollins.

Martin, William T. 1984. "Religiosity and United States suicide rates, 1972–1978." *Journal of Clinical Psychology, 40,* 1166–1169.

Martinez, Ramiro, Jr. 1996. "Latinos and lethal violence: The impact of poverty and inequality." *Social Problems, 43,* 131–146.

Martz, Larry. 1986. "True greed." *Newsweek,* December 1, p. 48.

Martz, Larry. 1991. "The corporate shell game." *Newsweek,* April 15, pp. 48–49.

Marx, Gary T. 1981. "Ironies of social control: Authorities as contributors to deviance through escalation, nonenforcement, and covert facilitation." *Social Problems, 28,* 221–246.

Massing, Michael. 1998. *The Fix.* New York: Simon & Schuster.

Massing, Walter, and Matthias C. Angermeyer. 1985. "The monthly and weekly distribution of suicide." *Social Science and Medicine, 21,* 433–441.

Masters, William H., and Virginia E. Johnson. 1979. *Homosexuality in Perspective.* Boston: Little, Brown.

Mathias, Robert. 1992. "Drug use among high school seniors continues 16-year decline." *NIDA Notes, 7* (May/June), 12–13.

Mathis, James L. 1972. *Clear Thinking About Sexual Deviations.* Chicago: Nelson-Hall.

Matthews, Anne. 1993. "The campus crime wave." *New York Times Magazine,* March 7, p. 41.

Matthews, Victor M. 1968. "Differential identification: An empirical note." *Social Problems, 14,* 376–383.

Matza, David. 1969. *Becoming Deviant.* Englewood Cliffs, N.J.: Prentice Hall.

Mauro, Robert. 1996. "Suicide—not the answer." *Accent on Living, 41* (Winter), 68–69.

May, William F. 1991. "The molested." *Hastings Center Report, 21,* 9–17.

McAuliffe, William E., and Robert A. Gordon. 1974. "A test of Lindesmith's theory of addiction: The frequency of euphoria among long-term addicts." *American Journal of Sociology, 79,* 795–840.

McCaghy, Charles H. 1968. "Drinking and deviance disavowal: The case of child molesters." *Social Problems, 16,* 43–49.

McCaghy, Charles H., and James K. Skipper, Jr. 1969. "Lesbian behavior as an adaptation to the occupation of stripping." *Social Problems, 17,* 262–270.

McCaldon, R. J. 1967. "Rape." *Canadian Journal of Corrections, 9,* 45.

McCarroll, Thomas. 1992. "Was GM reckless?" *Time,* November 30, p. 61.

McClearn, Gerald E. 1969. "Biological bases of social behavior with specific reference to violent behavior." In Donald J. Mulvihill, Melvin Tumin with Lynn Curtis (Eds.), *Crimes of Violence,* Vol. 13. Washington, D.C.: Government Printing Office.

McClelland, David C., et al. 1972. *The Drinking Man.* New York: Free Press.

McCord, William. 1995. "Death with dignity." In Robert Emmet Long (Ed.), *Suicide.* New York: Wilson.

McCord, William, and Joan McCord. 1960. *Origins of Alcoholism.* Stanford, Calif.: Stanford University Press.

McDowell, Bill. 1996. "Jack in the Box battles back with some help from a clown." *Advertising Age, 67,* November 25, p. 11.

McIntosh, John L. 1991. "Epidemiology of suicide in the United States." In Antoon A. Leenaars (Ed.), *Life Span Perspectives of Suicide: Time-lines in the Suicide Process.* New York: Plenum.

McKegney, F. Patrick, and Mary Alice O'Dowd. 1992. "Suicidality and HIV status." *American Journal of Psychiatry, 149,* 396–398.

McLanahan, Sara S., and Jennifer L. Glass. 1985. "A note on the trend in sex differences in psychological distress." *Journal of Health and Social Behavior, 26,* 328–336.

McMullen, Richie J. 1990. *Male Rape: Breaking the Silence on the Last Taboo.* London: GMP Publishers.

McNeil, Donald G. 1998. "Mugabe attacks, and gay Zimbabweans fight back." *New York Times,* July 14, p. A4.

McNeil, Donald G., Jr. 1995. "For gay Zimbabweans, a difficult political climate." *New York Times,* September 10, p. 3.

McNeil, Donald G., Jr. 1999. "Condoms for women gain approval among Africans." *New York Times,* July 24, pp. A1, A6.

McWhirter, David P., and Andrew M. Mattison. 1984. *The Male Couple: How Relationships Develop.* Englewood Cliffs, N.J.: Prentice Hall.

Medea, Andra, and Kathleen Thompson. 1974. *Against Rape.* New York: Farrar, Straus and Giroux.

Meer, Jeff. 1984. "Profile of a victim." *Psychology Today,* May, p. 76.

Meer, Jeff. 1985. "Living through robbery." *Psychology Today,* May, p. 20.

Meier, Robert F., Steven R. Burkett, and Carol A. Hickman. 1984. "Sanctions, peers, and deviance: Preliminary models of a social control process." *The Sociological Quarterly, 25,* 67–82.

Meiselman, Karin C. 1990. *Resolving the Trauma of Incest: Reintegration Therapy with Survivors.* San Francisco: Jossey-Bass.

Menard, Scott. 1995. "A developmental test of Mertonian anomie theory." *Journal of Research in Crime and Delinquency, 31,* 136–174.

Merry, Engle. 1980. "Manipulating: Streetwalkers' strategies for safety in the city." *Ethnos, 45,* 157–175.

Merton, Robert K. 1938. "Social structure and anomie." *American Sociological Review, 3,* 672–682.

Merton, Robert K. 1957. *Social Theory and Social Structure,* rev. ed. New York: Free Press.

Merton, Robert K. 1971. "Social problems and sociological theory." In R. K. Merton and Robert Nisbet (Eds.), *Contemporary Social Problems.* 3d ed. New York: Harcourt Brace Jovanovich.

Merton, Thomas. 1973. *The Asian Journal of Thomas Merton.* New York: New Directions.

"A message from Sicily." 1992. *The Economist.* July 25, pp. 47–48.

Messerschmidt, James W. 1986. *Capitalism, Patriarchy, and Crime: Toward a Socialist Feminist Criminology.* Totowa, N.J.: Rowman & Littlefield.

Messner, Steven F. 1982. "Poverty, inequality, and the urban homicide rate." *Criminology, 20,* 102–114.

Messner, Steven F. 1983. "Regional and racial effects on the urban homicide rate: The subculture of violence revisited." *American Journal of Sociology, 88,* 997–1007.

Messner, Steven F. 1986. "Modernization, structural characteristics, and societal rates of crime: An application of Blau's macrosociological theory." *Sociological Quarterly, 27,* 27–41.

Messner, Steven F., and Kenneth Tardiff. 1985. "The social ecology of urban homicide: An application of the routine activities' approach." *Criminology, 23,* 241–267.

Messner, Steven F., and Reid M. Golden. 1992. "Racial inequality and racially disaggregated homicide rates: An assessment of alternative theoretical explanations." *Criminology, 30,* 421–445.

Michael, Richard P., and Doris Zumpe. 1983. "Sexual violence in the United States and the role of season." *American Journal of Psychiatry, 140,* 883–886.

Michael, Robert T., et al. 1994. *Sex in America: A Definitive Survey.* Boston: Little, Brown.

Milbank, Dana, and Marcus W. Brauchli. 1995. "Greasing wheels." *Wall Street Journal,* September 29, pp. A1, A14.

Miller, Howard L., et al. 1984. "An analysis of the effects of suicide prevention facilities on suicide rates in the United States." *American Journal of Public Health, 74,* 340–343.

Miller, JoAnn L. 1991. "Prostitution in contemporary American society." In Elizabeth Grauerholz and Mary A. Koralewski (Eds.), *Sexual Coercion.* Lexington, Mass.: Lexington Books.

Miller, Laurence. 1986. "Pickled brains age faster." *Psychology Today,* January, p. 16.

Miller, M., and D. Hemenway. 1999. "The relationship between firearms and suicide: A review of the literature." *Aggression and Violent Behavior, 4,* 59–75.

Millett, Kate. 1973. *The Prostitution Papers.* New York: Avon.

Milner, Christina, and Richard Milner. 1972. *Black Players.* Boston: Little, Brown.

Minor, W. William. 1984. "Neutralization as a hardening process: Considerations in the modeling of change." *Social Forces, 62,* 995–1019.

Mishara, Eric. 1983. "R. D. Laing's new home." *Omni,* August, p. 35.

Mitchell, Alison. 1992. "Russian émigrés importing thugs to commit contract crimes in U.S." *New York Times,* April 11, pp. 1, 18.

Mitchell, Alison. 1997. "President regrets top U.S. regulator met with bankers." *New York Times,* January 29, pp. A1, A12.

Mitchell, Richard G. Jr. 1984. "Alienation and deviance: Strain theory reconsidered." *Sociological Inquiry, 54,* 330–345.

Mitchell, Roger E., and Rudolf H. Moos. 1984. "Deficiencies in social support among depressed patients: Antecedents or consequences of stress?" *Journal of Health and Social Behavior, 25,* 438–452.

Mithers, Carol Lynn. 1980. "Date rape: When "nice guys' won't take NO for an answer." *Mademoiselle,* November 8, pp. 210–211.

Mixson, Paula M. 1995. "An adult protective services perspective." *Journal of Elder Abuse and Neglect, 7,* no. 2–3, 69–87.

Modan, Baruch, et al. 1992. "Prevalence of HIV antibodies in transsexual and female prostitutes." *American Journal of Public Health, 82,* 590–591.

Moen, Phyllis, Julie Robison, and Donna Dempster-McClain. 1995. "Caregiving and women's well-being: A life course approach." *Journal of Health and Social Behavior, 36,* 259–273.

Molotsky, Irvin. 1999. "Study links teen-age substance abuse and paternal ties." *New York Times,* August 31, p. A14.

Monahan, John. 1992. "Mental disorder and violent behavior." *American Psychologist,* April, pp. 511–521.

Montagu, Ashley. 1968. "Chromosomes and crime." *Psychology Today,* October, pp. 42–49.

Moody, John. 1993. "Gotcha, Godfather!" *Time,* January 25, p. 47.

"The moon and murder." *Sky and Telescope, 70,* 28.

Moreau, Ron. 1992. "Sex and death in Thailand." *Newsweek,* July 20, p. 50.

Morey, Leslie C., Harvey A. Skinner, and Roger K. Blashfield. 1984. "A typology of alcohol abusers: Correlates and implications." *Journal of Abnormal Psychology, 93,* 408–417.

Morganthau, Tom. 1997. "The war over weed." *Newsweek,* February 3, pp. 20–22.

Morin, Stephen F., et al. 1984. "The psychological impact of AIDS on gay men." *American Psychologist, 39,* 1288–1293.

Morris, Allison. 1987. *Women, Crime, and Criminal Justice.* New York: Basil Blackwell.

Morris, Jeanette, and Lisa A. Cubbins. 1992. "Dating, drinking, and rape." *Psychology of Women, 16,* 179–191.

Morris, Monica B. 1977. *An Excursion into Creative Sociology.* New York: Columbia University Press.

Morrow, Lance. 1996. "Kids & pot." *Time,* December 9, pp. 26–30.

Mosher, Stacy. 1992. "Trouble with Triads," *Far Eastern Economic Review, 155,* July 23, p. 19.

Muecke, Marjorie A. 1992. "Mother sold food, daughter sells her body: The cultural continuity of prostitution." *Social Science and Medicine, 35,* 891–901.

Mulvihill, Donald J., and Melvin M. Tumin with Lynn A. Curtis. 1969. *Crimes of Violence,* Vol. 11. Washington, D.C.: Government Printing Office.

Murray, John B. 1986. "Marijuana's effects on human cognitive functions, psychomotor functions, and personality." *Journal of General Psychology, 113,* 25–40.

Musto, David F. 1973. *The American Disease: Origins of Narcotic Control.* New Haven, Conn.: Yale University Press.

Musto, David F. 1986. "Lessons of the first cocaine epidemic." *Wall Street Journal,* June 11, p. 30.

Mydans, Seth. 1997. "Australia, edgy, faces reality of assisted suicide." *New York Times,* February 2, p. 3.

Myers, Mary Beth, Donald Templer, and Ric Brown. 1984. "Coping ability of women who become victims of rape." *Journal of Consulting and Clinical Psychology, 52,* 73–78.

Myerscough, Rodney, and Stuart Taylor. 1985. "The effects of marijuana on human physical aggression." *Journal of Personality and Social Psychology, 49,* 1541–1546.

Nader, Ralph. 1970. "Foreword" to John C. Esposito, *Vanishing Air.* New York: Grossman, p. viii.

Nakawatase, Tomoko V., et al. 1993. "The association between fast-flushing response and alcohol use among Japanese Americans." *Journal of Studies on Alcohol, 54,* 48–53.

Nathan, Debbie. 1995. "Justice in Wenatchee." *New York Times,* December 19, p. A19.

National Institute on Alcohol Abuse and Alcoholism (NIAAA). 1983. *Alcohol and Health.* Rockville, Maryland: NIAAA.

Neff, James Alan, and Baqar A. Husaini. 1985. "Stress-buffer properties of alcohol consumption: The role of urbanicity and religious identification." *Journal of Health and Social Behavior, 26,* 207–222.

Neff, James Alan, et al. 1991. "Machismo, self-esteem, education and high maximum drinking among Anglo, black and Mexican-American male drinkers." *Journal of Studies on Alcohol, 52,* 458–463.

Nelson, Mariah Burton. 1994. *The Stronger Women Get, the More Men Love Football: Sexism and the American Culture of Sports.* New York: Harcourt Brace.

Nettler, Gwynn. 1970. *Explanations.* New York: McGraw-Hill.

Nettler, Gwynn. 1974. "On telling who's crazy." *American Sociological Review, 39,* 893–894.

Nettler, Gwynn. 1984. *Explaining Crime.* 3d ed. New York: McGraw-Hill.

Newmann, Joy P. 1986. "Gender, life strains, and depression." *Journal of Health and Social Behavior, 27,* 161–178.

Nicastro, Franco. 1992. "All is quiet in Corleone." *World Press Review,* December, p. 13.

Nichols, Margaret. 1990. "Lesbian relationships: Implications for the study of sexuality and gender." In David P. McWhirter, et al. (Eds.), *Homosexuality/Heterosexuality.* New York: Oxford University Press.

Nicholson, M.E., et al. 1998. "Trends in alcohol-related campus violence: Implications for prevention." *Journal of Alcohol and Drug Education, 43,* 34–52.

Niebuhr, Gustav. 1998. "Laws aside, some in clergy quietly bless gay 'marriage'." *New York Times,* April 17, pp. A1, A20.

Nielsen, Amie L. 1999. "Testing Sampson and Laub's life course theory: age, race/ethnicity, and drunkenness." *Deviant Behavior, 20,* 129–151.

Nieradzik, Krystyna, and Raymond Cochrane. 1985. "Public attitudes towards mental illness—The effects of behavior, roles, and psychiatric labels." *International Journal of Social Psychiatry, 31,* 23–33.

Nikkel, Cathy. 1995. "Car theft $7.5 billion a year international business." *Motor Trend, 47,* November, pp. 26–27.

Noah, Timothy. 1997. "OK, OK, cigarettes do kill." *U.S. News & World Report,* March 31, pp. 29–30.

Noble, Ernest P., et al. 1991. "Allelic association of the D_2 dopamine receptor gene with receptor-binding characteristics in alcoholism." *Archives of General Psychiatry, 48,* 648–654.

Nordland, Ron. 1992. "The 'Velcro Don': Wiseguys finish last." *Newsweek,* April 13, p. 35.

Norman, Michael. 1998. "Getting serious about adultery." *New York Times,* July 4, pp. A13, A15.

Norris, Joel. 1989. *Serial Killers.* New York: Anchor Books.

Nunnally, Jim C., Jr. 1961. *Popular Conceptions of Mental Health.* New York: Holt, Rinehart and Winston.

O'Boyle, Michael, and Elisif A. A. Brandon. 1998. "Suicide attempts, substance abuse, and personality." *Journal of Substance Abuse Treatment, 15,* 353–356.

O'Hanlan, Katherine A. 1996. "Homophobia is a health hazard." *USA Today: The Magazine of the American Scene, 125,* November, pp. 26–29.

O'Kane, James M. 1992. *The Crooked Ladder: Gangsters, Ethnicity, and the American Dream.* New Brunswick, N.J.: Transaction.

O'Malley, Patrick M., and Alexander C. Wagenaar. 1991. "Effects of minimum drinking age laws on alcohol use, related behaviors and traffic crash involvement among American youth: 1976–1987." *Journal of Studies on Alcohol, 52*, 478–491.

Omestad, Thomas. 1997. "Bye-bye to bribes." *U.S. News & World Report,* December 22, pp. 39-44.

Onstad, Katrina. 1996. "The cyberporn flap: An update." *Canadian Business, 69,* Fall, p. 58.

Orcutt, James D. 1991. "Beyond the 'exotic and the pathologic': Alcohol problems, norm qualities, and sociological theories of deviance." In Paul M. Roman (Ed.), *Alcohol: The Development of Sociological Perspectives on Use and Abuse.* New Brunswick, N.J.: Rutgers Center of Alcohol Studies.

Orcutt, James D. 1993. "Happy hour and social lubrication: Evidence on mood-setting rituals of drinking time." *Journal of Drug Issues, 23,* 389–407.

Osgood, D. Wayne, et al. 1996. "Routine activities and individual deviant behavior." *American Sociological Review, 61,* 635–655.

O'Sullivan, Chris S. 1991. "Acquaintance gang rape on campus." In Andrea Parrot and Laurie Bechhofer (Eds.), *Acquaintance Rape.* New York: Wiley.

Overall, Christine. 1992. "What's wrong with prostitution? Evaluating sex work." *Signs, 17,* 705–724.

Palmer, Stuart. 1960. *A Study of Murder.* New York: Crowell.

Parker, Robert Nash. 1989. "Poverty, subculture of violence, and type of homicide." *Social Forces, 67,* 983–1007.

Parker, Robert Nash. 1994. "Violent crime." In Joseph F. Sheley (Ed.), *Criminology: A Contemporary Handbook.* Belmont, Calif.: Wadsworth.

Parker, Robert Nash, and M. Dwayne Smith. 1979. "Deterrence, poverty, and type of homicide." *American Journal of Sociology, 85,* 614–624.

Parker, Robert Nash, with Linda-Anne Rebhun. 1995. *Alcohol and Homicide: A Deadly Combination of Two American Traditions.* Albany, N.Y.: State University of New York Press.

Parsian, Abbas, et al. 1991. "Alcoholism and alleles of the human D2 dopamine receptor locus: Studies of association and linkage." *Archives of General Psychiatry, 48,* 655–663.

Parsons, Talcott. 1951. *The Social System.* New York: Free Press.

Paternoster, Raymond, and Leeann Iovanni. 1986. "The deterrent effect of perceived severity: A reexamination." *Social Forces, 64,* 751–777.

Patsiokas, Anne T., George A. Clum, and Richard L. Luscomb. 1979. "Cognitive characteristics of suicide attempters." *Journal of Consulting and Clinical Psychology, 47,* 478–484.

Paveza, Gregory J., et al. 1992. "Severe family violence and Alzheimer's disease: Prevalence and risk factors." *Gerontologist, 32,* 493–497.

Pear, Robert. 1999. "House backs ban on using medicine to aid in suicide." *New York Times,* October 28, pp. A1, A20.

Peck, Dennis L. 1984. "Lethality of method of suicide among a youthful sample of committers: An examination of the intent hypothesis." *Psychological Reports, 55,* 861–862.

Peck, Dennis L. 1985–1986. "Completed suicides: Correlates of choice of method." *Omega, 16,* 309–323.

Peck, M., and A. Schrut. 1971. "Suicidal behavior among college students." *HSMHA Health Report, 86,* 149–156.

Pedersen, Daniel. 1996. "Death in Dunblane." *Newsweek,* March 25, pp. 25–29.

Pelka, Fred. 1995. "Raped: A male survivor breaks his silence." In Patricia Searles and Ronald J. Berger (Eds.), *Rape and Society.* Boulder, Colo.: Westview.

Pennebaker, James W., and Robin C. O'Heeron. 1984. "Confiding in others and illness rates among spouses of suicide and accidental-death victims." *Journal of Abnormal Psychology, 93,* 473–476.

Peplau, Letitia Anne. 1981. "What homosexuals want." *Psychology Today,* March, pp. 28–38.

Peplau, Letitia Anne, and Susan D. Cochran. 1990. "A relationship perspective on homosexuality." In David P. McWhirter, et al. (Eds.), *Homosexuality/Heterosexuality.* New York: Oxford University Press.

Perkins, H. Wesley. 1992. "Gender patterns in consequences of collegiate alcohol abuse: A 10-year study of trends in an undergraduate population." *Journal of Studies on Alcohol, 53,* 458–462.

Perkins, Roberta. 1991. *Working Girls: Prostitutes, Their Life and Social Control.* Canberra: Australian Institute of Criminology.

Pescosolido, Bernice A., and Robert Mendelsohn. 1986. "Social causation or social construction of suicide? An investigation into the social organization of official rates." *American Sociological Review, 51,* 80–101.

Peterson, M. A., et al. 1980. *Doing Crime.* Santa Monica, Calif.: Rand.

Peterson, Ruth D. 1992. "Rape and dimensions of gender socioeconomic inequality in U.S. metropolitan areas." *Journal of Research in Crime & Delinquency, 29,* 162–177.

Petrovich, Michael, and Donald I. Templer. 1984. "Heterosexual molestation of children who later became rapists." *Psychological Records, 54,* 810.

Pfuhl, Erdwin, and Stuart Henry. 1993. *The Deviance Process.* 3d ed. New York: Aldine.

Phillips, David P. 1974. "The influences of suggestion on suicide." *American Sociological Review, 39,* 340–354.

Phillips, David P. 1979. "Suicide, motor vehicle fatalities, and the mass media: Evidence toward a theory of suggestion." *American Journal of Sociology, 84,* 1150–1174.

Phillips, David P. 1980a. "Airplane accidents, murder, and the mass media: Towards a theory of imitation and suggestion." *Social Forces, 58,* 1001–1024.

Phillips, David P. 1980b. "The deterrent effect of capital punishment: New evidence on an old controversy." *American Journal of Sociology, 86,* 139–148.

Phillips, David P. 1981. "The complementary virtues of qualitative and quantitative research: Reply to Altheide." *Social Forces, 60,* 597–599.

Phillips, David P. 1982. "Reply to Zeisel." *American Journal of Sociology, 86,* 171–172.

Phillips, David P. 1983. "The impact of mass media violence on U.S. homicides." *American Sociological Review, 48,* 560–568.

Phillips, David P. 1993. "Adequacy of official suicide statistics for scientific research." *Suicide & Life-Threatening Behavior, 23,* 307–319.

Phillips, David P., and Kenneth A. Bollen. 1985. "Same time, last year: Selective data dredging for negative findings." *American Sociological Review, 50,* 364–371.

Pieper, R. 1979. "Identity management in adolescent male prostitution in West Germany." *International Review of Modern Sociology, 9,* 239–259.

Pileggi, Nicholas. 1986. *Wiseguy: Life in a Mafia Family.* New York: Simon & Schuster.

Piliavin, Irving, Rosemary Gartner, Craig Thornton, and Ross L. Matsueda, 1986. "Crime, deterrence, and rational choice." *American Sociological Review, 51,* 101–119.

Pillemer, Karl A., and David Finkelhor. 1988. "The prevalence of elder abuse: A random sample survey." *The Gerontologist, 28,* 51–57.

Pittman, Frank III. 1993. "Beyond betrayal: Life after infidelity." *Psychology Today,* May/June, p. 36.

Pizzo, Stephen P., and Paul Muolo. 1993. "Take the money and run." *New York Times Magazine,* May 9, p. 26.

"The plague among us." 1986. *Newsweek.* Editorial. June 16.

Platt, Steven. 1984. "Unemployment and suicidal behavior." *Social Science and Medicine, 19,* 93–115.

Pollack, Andrew. 1997. "Overseas, smoking is one of life's small pleasures." *New York Time,* August 17, p. E5.

Ponse, Barbara. 1984. "The problematic meanings of 'lesbian.'" In Jack D. Douglas (Ed.), *The Sociology of Deviance.* Boston: Allyn and Bacon.

Pontell, Henry N., and Kitty Calavita. 1993. "White-collar crime in the savings and loan scandal." *The Annals of the American Academy of Political and Social Science, 525* (January), 31–45.

Porter, Roy. 1996. "Born that way?" *New York Times Book Review,* August 11, p. 8.

Posner, Gerald L. 1988. *Warlords of Crime.* New York: McGraw-Hill.

Post, Shelley. 1982. "Adolescent parricide in abusive families." *Child Welfare, 61,* 445–455.

Post, Tom. 1993. "A pattern of rape." *Newsweek,* January 4, pp. 32–36.

Potterat, John J., et al. 1990. "Estimating the prevalence and career longevity of prostitute women." *Journal of Sex Research, 27,* 233–243.

President's Commission on Organized Crime. 1986. *The Impact: Organized Crime Today.* Washington, D.C.: Government Printing Office.

"The pride of Olean." 1975. *Newsweek,* January 13.

Quindlen, Anna. 1994. "Sex for sale." *New York Times,* November 26, p. 15.

Quinney, Richard. 1965. "Suicide, homicide, and economic development." *Social Forces, 43,* 401–406.

Quinney, Richard. 1974. *Critique of Legal Order: Crime Control in Capitalist Society.* Boston: Little, Brown.

Quinney, Richard. 1975. *Criminology.* Boston: Little, Brown.

Quinsey, Vernon L., Anne Maguire, and George W. Varney. 1983. "Assertion and over-controlled hostility among mentally disordered murderers." *Journal of Consulting and Clinical Psychology, 5,* 550–556.

Raab, Selwyn. 1994. "Mob tightens secretive style in retreat from prosecutors." *New York Times,* May 29, pp. 1, 13.

Raab, Selwyn. 1997. "Officials say mob is shifting crimes to new industries." *New York Times,* February 10, pp. A1, A10.

Rakatansky, Herbert. 1996. "Suicide acceptable on operatic stage, not in real life." *American Medical News, 39* (November 4), 21–22.

Rapaport, Karen R., and C. Dale Posey. 1991. "Sexually coercive college males." In Andrea Parrot and Laurie Bechhofer (Eds.), *Acquaintance Rape.* New York: Wiley.

Rapaport, Karen, and Barry R. Burkhart. 1984. "Personality and attitudinal characteristics of sexually coercive college males." *Journal of Abnormal Psychology, 93,* 216–221.

Ratey, John J., and Catherine Johnson. 1997. *Shadow Syndromes.* New York: Pantheon Books.

Reese, Michael. 1986. "One family's struggle." *Newsweek,* January 13, p. 56.

Reibstein, Larry. 1997. "Whose right is it?" *Newsweek,* January 20, p. 36.

Reinisch, June M. 1990. *The Kinsey Institute New Report on Sex: What You Must Know to Be Sexually Literate.* New York: St. Martin's.

Reiss, Albert J., Jr. 1961. "The social integration of queers and peers." *Social Problems, 9,* 102–120.

Resenfeld, Sam A. 1985. "The lady is addictive." *Psychology Today* (January), p. 20.

Reuter, Peter. 1995. "The decline of the American Mafia." *Public Interest,* Summer, 89–99.

Riccio, R. 1992. "Street crime strategies: The changing schemata of streetwalkers." *Environment and Behavior, 24,* 555–570.

Richards, Bill. 1992. "Burden of proof." *Wall Street Journal,* December 8, pp. A1, A8.

Richardson, Deborah R., and Georgina S. Hammock. 1991. "Alcohol and acquaintance rape." In Andrea Parrot and Laurie Bechhofer (Eds.), *Acquaintance Rape,* pp. 83–95. New York: Wiley.

Rickgarn, Ralph L. V. 1994. *Perspectives on College Student Suicide.* Amityville, N.Y.: Baywood.

Ridley, Mark. 1996. "The gay brain." *Natural History, 105* (August), 10–11.

Rimer, Sara. 1993. "Campus lesbians step into unfamiliar light." *New York Times,* June 5, p. 6.

Rimm, Marty. 1995. "Marketing pornography on the information superhighway." *Georgetown Law Journal, 83,* 1849–1934.

Robins, Lee N. 1973. *The Vietnam Drug User Returns.* Washington, D.C.: Government Printing Office.

Robins, Lee N., et al. 1984. "Lifetime prevalence of specific psychiatric disorders in three sites." *Archives of General Psychiatry, 41,* 949–958.

Rodgers, Bryan, and Susan L. Mann. 1993. "Re-thinking the analysis of intergenerational social mobility: A comment on John W. Fox's 'Social class, mental illness, and social mobility.'" *Journal of Health and Social Behavior, 34,* 165–172.

Rodino, Peter W. 1986. "Will handgun foes be over a barrel?" *New York Times,* March 28, p. 27.

Roman, Paul M., and Terry C. Blum. 1991. "The medicalized conception of alcohol-related problems: Some social sources and some social consequences of murkiness and confusion." In David J. Pittman and Helene Raskin White (Eds.), *Society, Culture, and Drinking Patterns Reexamined.* New Brunswick, N.J.: Rutgers Center of Alcohol Studies.

Rose, Harold M., and Paula D. McClain. 1990. *Race, Place, and Risk: Black Homicide in Urban America.* Albany, N.Y.: State University of New York Press.

Rosenau, Pauline M. 1992. *Postmodernism and the Social Sciences.* Princeton, N.J.: Princeton University Press.

Rosenberg, Lynn, et al. 1981. "Alcoholic beverages and myocardial infarction in young women." *American Journal of Public Health, 71,* 82–85.

Rosenblum, Karen E. 1975. "Female deviance and the female sex role: A preliminary investigation." *British Journal of Sociology, 26,* 169–185.

Rosenfeld, Sam A. 1985. "The lady is addictive." *Psychology Today,* January, p. 20.

Rosenhan, D. L. 1973. "On being sane in insane places." *Science,* January 19, p. 256.

Rosenthal, A. M. 1995. "The cruelest hoax." *New York Times,* January 3, p. A11.

Rosenthal, Elisabeth. 1999. "Suicide gains ground on women in rural China." *New York Times,* January 24, pp. 1, 8.

Ross, Michael W., and Willem A. Arrindell. 1988. "Perceived parental rearing patterns of homosexual and heterosexual men." *Journal of Sex Research, 24,* 275–281.

Rotgers, Frederick, et al. 1996. *Treating Substance Abuse: Theory and Practice.* New York: Guilford.

Rowe, Paul M. 1995. "Alcoholism in USA." *Lancet, 345,* April 1, 860.

Rubington, Earl. 1991. "The chronic drunkenness offender: Before and after decriminalization." In David J. Pittman and Helene Raskin White, (Eds.), *Society, Culture, and Drinking Patterns Reexamined.* New Brunswick, N.J.: Rutgers Center of Alcohol Studies.

Ruch, Libby O., Susan Meyers Chandler, and Richard A. Harter. 1980. "Life change and rape impact." *Journal of Health and Social Behavior, 21,* 248–260.

Rudestam, Kjell Erik. 1977. "Physical and psychological responses to suicide in the family." *Journal of Consulting and Clinical Psychology, 45,* 162–170.

Ruiz, Dorothy S. 1982. "Epidemiology of schizophrenia: Some diagnostic and sociocultural considerations." *Phylon, 43,* 315–326.

Russell, Diane E. H. 1984. *Sexual Exploitation.* Beverly Hills, Calif.: Sage.

Russell, Diane E. H. 1986. *The Secret Trauma: Incest in the Lives of Girls and Women.* New York: Basic Books.

Russell, Diane E. H. 1990. *Rape in Marriage.* Bloomington: Indiana University Press.

Rust, Paula C. 1995. *Bisexuality and the Challenge to Lesbian Politics: Sex, Loyalty, and Revolution.* New York: New York University Press.

Sabato, Larry J., and Glenn R. Simpson. 1996. *Dirty Little Secrets.* New York: Times Books.

Sachs, Andrea. 1993. "9-Zip! I love it!" *Time,* November 22, pp. 44–45.

Sagarin, Edward. 1969. *Odd Man In.* Chicago: Quadrangle.

Sagarin, Edward. 1975. *Deviants and Deviance.* New York: Praeger.

Sagarin, Edward. 1985. "Positive deviance: An oxymoron." *Deviant Behavior, 6,* 169–181.

Saghir, Marcel T., and Eli Robins. 1980. "Clinical aspects of female homosexuality." In Judd Marmor (Ed.), *Homosexual Behavior: A Modern Reappraisal.* New York: Basic Books.

Sallett, Alphonse, Erich Goode, and William Pooler. 1999. "The death of a paradigm? The onset and dynamics of an adolescent drug epidemic, 1991–1998." Unpublished paper.

Sanborn, Donald E., and Charlotte J. Sanborn. 1978. "Sex, season and suicide." *Psychological Reports, 42,* 1332.

Sanday, Peggy Reeves. 1981. "The socio-cultural context of rape: A cross-cultural study." *Journal of Social Issues, 37,* 5–27.

Sanday, Peggy Reeves. 1990. *Fraternity Gang Rape: Sex, Brotherhood, and Privilege on Campus.* New York: New York University Press.

Sanday, Peggy Reeves. 1996a. *A Woman Scorned: Acquaintance Rape on Trial.* New York: Doubleday.

Sanday, Peggy Reeves. 1996b. "Rape-prone versus rape-free campus cultures." *Violence Against Women, 2,* 191–208.

Sandmaier, Marian. 1980. "Alcoholics invisible: The ordeal of the female alcoholics." *Social Policy, 10* (January/February), 25–30.

Sandmaier, Marian. 1992. *The Invisible Alcoholics: Women and Alcohol.* 2d ed. Bradenton, Fla.: Blue Ridge Summit.

Sapp, M., et al. 1999. "Attitudes toward rape among African American male and female college students." *Journal of Counseling and Development, 77,* 204–208.

Sarrel, Philip M., and William H. Masters. 1981. "Sexual molestation of men by women." *Archives of Sexual Behavior, 11,* 117–131.

Sarrel, Philip, and Lorna Sarrel. 1982. "Can a man be raped by a woman?" *Redbook,* May, p. 94.

Satel, Sally. 1996. "The madness of deinstitutionalization." *Wall Street Journal,* February 20, p. A22.

Scarce, Michael. 1997. *Male on Male Rape: The Hidden Toll of Stigma and Shame.* New York: Insight books.

Schaefer, James M. 1981. "Firewater myths revisited: Review of findings and some new directions." *Journal of Studies on Alcohol,* Supplement No. 9 (January), 108–109.

Scheff, Thomas J. 1964. "Social condition for rationality: How urban and rural courts deal with the mentally ill." *American Behavioral Scientist, 7,* 21–27.

Scheff, Thomas J. 1966. *Being Mentally Ill.* Chicago: Aldine.

Scheff, Thomas J. 1974. "The labeling theory of mental illness." *American Sociological Review, 39,* 448–449.

Schemo, Diana Jean. 1996. "Indians in Brazil, estranged from their land, suffer an epidemic of suicide." *New York Times,* August 25, p. 7.

Schiffren, Lisa. 1996. "Gay marriage, an oxymoron." *New York Times,* March 23, p. 37.

Schlosser, Eric. 1997. "The business of pornography." *U.S. News & World Report,* February 10, pp. 42–50.

Schmitt, Richard B. 1996. "Defenses down." *Wall Street Journal,* February 29, pp. A1, A6.

Schuckit, Marc A. 1984. "Overview: Epidemiology of alcoholism." In Marc A. Schuckit (Ed.), *Alcohol Patterns and Problems.* New Brunswick, N.J.: Rutgers University Press.

Schur, Edwin M. 1984. *Labeling Women Deviant.* New York: Random House.

Schutz, Alfred. 1962. *Collected Papers I: The Problem of Social Reality.* ed. Maurice Natanson. The Hague: Martinus Nijhoff.

Schutz, Alfred. 1964. *Collected Papers II: Studies in Social Theory,* ed. Arvid Brodersen. The Hague: Martinus Nijhoff.

Schwartz, Martin D. 1987. "Gender and injury in spousal assault." *Sociological Focus, 20,* 61–75.

Schwartz, Martin D. 1988. "Ain't got no class: Universal risk theories of battering." *Contemporary Crisis, 12,* 373–392.

Schwartz, Martin D. 1995. "Date rape on college campuses." In Alex Thio and Thomas Calhoun (Eds.), *Readings in Deviant Behavior.* New York: HarperCollins.

Schwartz, Martin D., and Carol A. Nogrady. 1996. "Fraternity membership, rape myths, and sexual aggression on a college campus." *Violence Against Women, 2,* 148–162.

Schwartz, Martin D., and Walter S. DeKeseredy. 1997. *Sexual Assault on the College Campus: The Role of Male Peer Support.* Thousand Oaks, Calif.: Sage.

Schwartz, Sharon. 1991. "Women and depression: A Durkheimian perspective." *Social Science and Medicine, 32,* 127.

Schwendinger, Julia R., and Herman Schwendinger. 1983. *Rape and Inequality.* Beverly Hills, Calif.: Sage.

Scott, Joseph E., and Steven J. Cuvelier. 1987. "Sexual violence in Playboy magazine: A longitudinal content analysis." *The Journal of Sex Research, 25,* 534–539.

Scull, Andrew. 1988. "Deviance and social control." In Neil J. Smelser (Ed.), *Handbook of Sociology.* Newbury Park, Calif.: Sage.

Scully, Diana. 1990. *Understanding Sexual Violence: A Study of Convicted Rapists.* Boston: Unwin Hyman.

Scully, Diana, and Joseph Marolla. 1984. "Convicted rapists' vocabulary of motive: Excuses and justifications." *Social Problems, 31,* 530–544.

Scully, Diana, and Joseph Marolla. 1985. "Riding the bull at Gilley's: Convicted rapists describe the rewards of rape." *Social Problems, 32,* 251–263.

Scully, Gerald W. 1997. "Murder by the state." Paper published by the National Center for Policy Analysis at the University of Texas, Dallas.

Sedlak, Andrea J. 1991. *National Incidence and Prevalence of Child Abuse and Neglect: 1988. Revised Report.* Rockville, Md.: Westat.

Segal, Lynne. 1993. "Does pornography cause violence?: The search for evidence." In Pamela Church Gibson and Roma Gibson (Eds.), *Dirty Looks: Women, Pornography, Power.* London: BFI Publishing.

Seidman, Steve. 1994. "Queer theory/sociology: A dialogue." *Sociological Theory, 12,* 166–177.

Seligmann, Jean, and Patricia King. 1996. "'Roofies': The date-rape drug." *Newsweek,* February 26, p. 54.

Selkin, James. 1975. "Rape." *Psychology Today,* January, p. 74.

Sellin, Thorsten. 1938. *Culture Conflict and Crime*. New York: Social Science Research Council.

Serrill, Michael S. 1993. "Defiling the children." *Time,* June 21, pp. 53–55.

"Sexual therapists." 1979. *The Economist*. December 2, p. 26.

Shapiro, Joseph P. 1995. "Death on trial." In Robert Emmet Long (Ed.), *Suicide*. New York: Wilson.

Shapiro, Joseph P. 1996. "The elderly's vulnerability to abuse is exaggerated." In A. E. Sadler (Ed.), *Family Violence*. San Diego, Calif.: Greenhaven.

Shapiro, Laura. 1996. "To your health?" *Newsweek,* January 22, pp. 52–54.

Shapiro, Susan P. 1990. "Collaring the crime, not the criminal: Reconsidering the concept of white-collar crime." *American Sociological Review, 55,* 346–365.

Sharpe, Anita. 1997. "Psyched up." *Wall Street Journal,* January 24, pp. A1, A11.

Sheehy, Gail. 1971a. *Hustling*. New York: Delacorte.

Sheehy, Gail. 1971b. "Nice girls don't get into trouble." *New York,* February 15, p. 30.

Sheila Balkan, Ronald J. Berger, and Janet Schmidt. 1980. *Crime and Deviance in America: A Critical Approach*. Belmont, Calif.: Wadsworth.

Shenon, Philip. 1996. "AIDS epidemic, late to arrive, now explodes in populous Asia." *New York Times,* January 21, pp. 1, 8.

Shenon, Philip. 1997. "New study faults Pentagon's gay policy." *New York Times,* February 26, p. A8.

Shenon, Philip. 1999. "Pentagon moving to end abuses of 'don't ask, don't tell' policy." *New York Times,* August 13, pp. A1, A12.

Sherman, Lawrence W., and Richard A. Berk. 1984. "The specific deterrent effects of arrest for domestic assault." *American Sociological Review, 49,* 261–272.

Shihadeh, Edward S. 1994. "Economic inequality, family disruption, and urban black violence: Cities as units of stratification and social control." *Social Forces, 73,* 729–751.

Shihadeh, Edward S., and James Flynn. 1996. "Segregation and crime: The effect of black social isolation on the rates of black urban violence." *Social Forces, 74,* 1325–1352.

Shilts, Randy. 1993. *Conduct Unbecoming: Gays and Lesbians in the U.S. Military*. New York: St. Martin's.

Shneidman, Edwin S. 1975. "Classification of suicidal phenomena." In Simon Dinitz, Russell R. Dynes, and Alfred C. Clarke (Eds.), *Deviance*. New York: Oxford University Press.

"Shoplifting in America."1991. *The Economist*. January 19, p. 65.

Short, James F. Jr. 1960. "Differential association as a hypothesis: problems of empirical testing." *Social Problems, 8,* 14–25.

Shotland, R. Lance, and Lynne Goodstein. 1983. "Just because she doesn't want to doesn't mean it's rape: An experimentally based causal model of the perception of rape in a dating situation." *Social Psychology Quarterly, 46,* 220–232.

Shrout, Patrick E., et al. 1992. "Mental health status among Puerto Ricans, Mexican Americans, and Non-Hispanic whites." *American Journal of Community Psychology, 20,* 729–749.

Shute, Nancy. 1997. "The drinking dilemma." *U.S. News & World Report,* September 8, pp. 55–65.

Sibthorpe, Beverly, et al. 1991. "Needle use and sexual practices: Differences in perception of personal risk of HIV among intravenous drug users." *Journal of Drug Issues, 21,* 699–712.

Siegal, Lewis J., and Jacob H. Friedman. 1955. "The threat of suicide." *Diseases of the Nervous System, 16,* 45.

Silbert, Mimi H., and Ayala M. Pines. 1981. "Occupational hazards of street prostitutes." *Criminal Justice and Behavior, 8,* 397–398.

Simmons, J. L. 1965. "Public stereotypes of deviants." *Social Problems, 13,* 223–224.

Simmons, Jerry L., and Barry Winograd. 1967. *It's Happening.* Santa Barbara, Calif.: McNally and Loftin.

Simon, David R. 1996. *Elite Deviance.* 5th ed. Boston: Allyn and Bacon.

Simon, William, and John H. Gagnon. 1974. "The lesbians: A preliminary overview." In Gagnon and Simon (Eds.), *Sexual Deviance.* New York: Harper & Row.

Simons, Marlise. 1993. "The sex market: Scourge on the world's children." *New York Times,* April 9, p. A3.

Simons, Marlise. 1995. "Dutch doctors to tighten rules on mercy killings." *New York Times,* September 11, p. A3.

Sloan, Allan. 1997. "A sexy new loophole." *Newsweek,* February 3, pp. 37–38.

Smart, Reginald G. 1991. "AIDS and drug abuse in Canada: Current status and information needs." *Journal of Drug Issues, 21,* 73–82.

Smith, Michael D. 1990. "Patriarchal ideology and wife beating: A test of a feminist hypothesis." *Violence and Victims, 5,* 257–273.

Smith, Wesley J. 1993. "The whispers of strangers." *Newsweek,* June 28, p. 8.

Smolowe, Jill. 1993. "Choose your poison." *Time,* July 26, p. 57.

Smolowe, Jill. 1996. "The unmarrying kind." *Time,* April 29, pp. 68–69.

Smyth, Angela, and Chris Thompson. 1990. *SAD: Seasonal Affective Disorder.* New York: Unwin.

Sobell, Mark B., and Linda C. Sobell. 1993. *Problem Drinkers: Guided Self-Change Treatment.* New York: Guilford.

Socall, Daniel W., and Thomas Holtgraves. 1992. "Attitudes toward the mentally ill." *The Sociological Quarterly, 33,* 435–445.

Socarides, Charles, et al. 1997. "Don't forsake homosexuals who want help." *Wall Street Journal,* January 9, p. A10.

Specter, Michael. 1995. "Gay Russians are 'free' now but still stay in fearful closet." *New York Times,* July 8, pp. 1, 4.

Specter, Michael. 1998. "Traffickers' new cargo: Naïve Slavic Women." *New York Times,* January 11, pp. 1, 6.

Spitzer, Steven. 1975. "Toward a Marxian theory of deviance." *Social Problems, 22,* 638–651.

Spohn, Cassia, and Julie Horney. 1992. *Rape Law Reform: A Grassroots Revolution and Its Impact.* New York: Plenum.

Srole, Leo, et al. 1962. *Mental Health in the Metropolis.* New York: McGraw-Hill.

Stack, Steven. 1979. "Durkheim's theory of fatalistic suicide: A cross-national approach." *Journal of Social Psychology, 107,* 161–168.

Stack, Steven. 1982. "Suicide: A decade review of the sociological literature." *Deviant Behavior, 4,* 49–51.

Stack, Steven. 1983. "The effect of religious commitment on suicide: A cross-national analysis." *Journal of Health and Social Behavior, 24,* 362–374.

Stack, Steven. 1986. "A leveling off in young suicide." *Wall Street Journal,* May 28, p. 30.

Stack, Steven. 1987. "Celebrities and suicide: A taxonomy and analysis, 1948–1983." *American Sociological Review, 52,* 401–412.

Stack, Steven. 1991. "Social correlates of suicide by age: Media impacts." In Antoon A. Leenaars (Ed.), *Life Span Perspectives of Suicide: Time-lines in the Suicide Process.* New York: Plenum.

Stack, Steven, and Jim Gundlach. 1992. "The effect of country music on suicide." *Social Forces, 71,* 211–218.

Stark, Elizabeth. 1987. "Forgotten victims: Children of alcoholics." *Psychology Today,* January, pp. 58–62.

Steffensmeier, Darrell. 1996. "Gender and crime: Toward a gendered theory of female offending." *Annual Review of Sociology, 22,* 459–487.

Steffensmeier, Renee Hoffman. 1984. "Suicide and the contemporary woman: Are male and female suicide rates converging?" *Sex Roles, 10,* 613–631.

Steinberg, Jacques. 1999. "The coming crime wave is washed up." *New York Times,* January 3, Section 4, p. 4.

Stengel, Erwin. 1969. *Suicide and Attempted Suicide.* Baltimore, Md.: Pelican.

Stephens, Joyce. 1995. "The pseudocidal female: A cautionary tale." In Silvia Sara Canetto and David Lester (Eds.), *Women and Suicidal Behavior.* New York: Springer.

Sterngold, James. 1992. "Japan takes on the mob, and the mob fights back." *New York Times,* June 15, pp. A1, A6.

Stevens, Amy. 1995. "Ten ways (some) lawyers (sometimes) fudge bills." *Wall Street Journal,* January 13, pp. B1, B10.

Stolberg, Sheryl Gay. 1998. "Assisted suicides are rare, survey of doctors finds." *New York Times,* April 23, pp. A1, A15.

Stolberg, Sheryl Gay. 1999. "Science looks at Littleton, and shrugs." *New York Times,* May 9, pp. 1, 4.

Stone, Elizabeth. 1992. "Off the couch." *New York Times Magazine,* December 6, pp. 50–53, 78–89.

Straus, Murray A. 1991. "Discipline and deviance: Physical punishment of children and violence and other crime in adulthood." *Social Problems, 38,* 133–154.

Straus, Murray A., Richard J. Gelles, and Suzanne K. Steinmetz. 1980. *Behind Closed Doors.* Garden City, N.Y.: Anchor Books.

Struckman-Johnson, Cindy. 1991. "Male Victims of Acquaintance Rape." In Andrea Parrot and Laurie Bechhofer (Eds.), *Acquaintance Rape.* New York: Wiley.

Sturdevant, Saundra Pollock, and Brenda Stoltzfus. 1992. *Let the Good Times Roll: Prostitution and the U.S. Military in Asia.* New York: New Press.

Suitor, Jill J., Karl Pillemer, and Murray A. Straus. 1990. "Marital violence in a life course perspective." In Murray A. Straus and Richard J. Gelles (Eds.), *Physical Violence in American Families: Risk Factors and Adaptations to Violence in 8,145 Families.* New Brunswick, N.J.: Transaction.

Sullum, Jacob. 1998. *For Your Own Good: The Anti-Smoking Crusade and the Tyranny of Public Health.* New York: Free Press.

Suro, Roberto. 1993. "Pollution-weary minorities try civil rights tack." *New York Times,* January 11, pp. A1, A12.

Sussman, Vic. 1992. "To stop a thief." *U.S. News & World Report,* March 30, pp. 55–58.

Sutherland, Edwin H. 1939. *Principles of Criminology.* 3d ed. Philadelphia: Lippincott.

Sutherland, Edwin H. 1949. *White-Collar Crime.* New York: Holt, Rinehart and Winston.

Sutherland, Edwin H. 1956. "Crimes of corporations." In Albert K. Cohen, Alfred Lindesmith, and Karl Schuessler (Eds.), *The Sutherland Papers.* Bloomington: Indiana University Press.

Sutherland, Edwin H., and Donald R. Cressey. 1978. *Criminology.* 10th ed. Philadelphia: Lippincott.

Swan, Neil. 1993. "Researcher's problem, which comes first: Drug abuse or antisocial behavior?" *NIDA (National Institute on Drug Abuse) Notes, 8* (May/June), 6–7.

Sweet, Ellen. 1985. "Date rape: The story of an epidemic and those who deny it." *Ms.*, October, p. 58.

Swiss, Shana, and Joan E. Giller. 1993. "Rape as a crime of war." *JAMA: The Journal of the American Medical Association, 270,* 612–615.

Symanski, Richard. 1974. "Prostitution in Nevada." *Annals of the Association of American Geographers, 64,* 361–375.

Szasz, Thomas. 1974a. *Ceremonial Chemistry.* Garden City, N.Y.: Anchor.

Szasz, Thomas. 1974b. *The Myth of Mental Illness,* rev. ed. New York: Harper & Row.

Szasz, Thomas. 1994. "Mental illness is still a myth." *Society,* May/June, pp. 34–39.

Szockyj, Elizabeth. 1993. "Insider trading: The SEC meets Carl Karcher." *The Annals of the American Academy of Political and Social Science, 525* (January), 46–58.

Szwarcwald, C.L. et al. 1999. "Income inequality and homicide rates in Rio de Janeiro, Brazil." *American Journal of Public Health, 89,* 845–850.

Tannenbaum, Frank. 1938. *Crime and the Community.* New York: Columbia University Press.

Tedeschi, James T., and Richard B. Felson. 1994. *Violence, Aggression, & Coercive Actions.* Washington, D.C.: American Psychological Association.

Teplin, Linda A. 1985. "The criminality of the mentally ill: A dangerous misconception." *American Journal of Psychiatry, 142,* 593–598.

Thio, Alex. 1973. "Class bias in the sociology of deviance." *The American Sociologist, 8,* 1–12.

Thio, Alex. 1974. "The phenomenological perspective of deviance: Another case of class bias." *The American Sociologist, 9,* 147–148.

Thio, Alex. 1975. "A critical look at Merton's anomie theory." *Pacific Sociological Review, 18,* 139–158.

Thompson, Terri, et al. 1992. "Crime and the bottom line." *U.S. News & World Report,* April 13, p. 57.

Thornton, Bill, and Richard M. Ryckman. 1983. "The influence of a rape victim's physical attractiveness on observers' attributions of responsibility." *Human Relations, 36,* 549–562.

Tittle, Charles R. 1969. "Crime rates and legal sanctions." *Social Problems 16,* 408–423.

Tittle, Charles R. 1980. "Labelling and crime: An empirical evaluation." In Walter R. Gove (Ed.), *The Labelling of Deviance: Evaluating a Perspective.* 2d ed. Beverly Hills: Sage.

Tolchin, Martin. 1986. "On breaking, or bending, or ignoring the law." *New York Times,* November 28, p. 12.

Torrey, E. Fuller. 1974. *The Death of Psychiatry.* Radnor, Pa.: Chilton.

Torrey, E. Fuller. 1997. *Out of the Shadows: Confronting America's Mental Illness Crisis.* New York: Wiley.

Totman, Jane. 1978. *The Murderers: A Psychosocial Study of Criminal Homicide.* San Francisco: R and E Research Associates.

Toufexis, Anastasia. 1992a. "Bisexuality: What is it?" *Time,* August 17, p. 49.

Toufexis, Anastasia. 1992b. "Do mad acts a madman make?" *Time,* February 3, p. 17.

Towson State. 1993. "A study on campus crime by Towson State University's Center for the Study and Prevention of Campus Violence," reported in *New York Times Magazine,* March 7, p. 40.

Trad, Paul V. 1991. "The ultimate stigma of mental illness." *American Journal of Psychotherapy, 45,* 463–466.

Traver, Nancy. 1992. "Children without pity." *Time,* October 26, p. 46.

Trice, Harrison M. 1966. *Alcoholism in America.* New York: McGraw-Hill.

Troiden, Richard R. 1979. "Becoming homosexual: A model of gay identity acquisition." *Psychiatry, 42,* 362–373.

Trost, Cathy, and Paulette Thomas. 1993. "Sexual politics." *Wall Street Journal,* March 10, p. A6.

Troyer, Ronald J., and Gerald E. Markle. 1982. "Creating deviance rules: A macroscopic model." *Sociological Quarterly, 23,* 157–169.

Truell, Peter, and Larry Gurwin. 1992. *False Profits: The Inside Story of BCCI, the World's Most Corrupt Financial Empire.* Boston: Houghton Mifflin.

Turque, Bill. 1992. "A new terror on the road." *Newsweek,* November 23, p. 31.

U.S. Census Bureau. 1996. *Statistical Abstract of the United States.* Washington, D.C.: Government Printing Office.

U.S. Congress, Office of Technology Assessment. 1990. *Indian Adolescent Mental Health* (OTA-H-446). Washington, D.C.: Government Printing Office.

Unnithan, N. Prabha, Lin Huff-Corzine, Jay Corzine, and Hugh P. Whitt. 1994. *The Currents of Lethal Violence: An Integrated Model of Suicide and Homicide.* Albany, N.Y.: State University of New York Press.

Vachss, Alice S. 1994. *Sex Crimes: Ten Years on the Front Lines Prosecuting Rapists and Confronting Their Collaborators.* New York: Holt.

Vaid, Urvashi. 1995. *Virtual Equality: The Mainstreaming of Gay and Lesbian Liberation.* New York: Anchor Books.

Vaillant, George E. 1995. *The Natural History of Alcoholism Revisited.* Cambridge, Mass.: Harvard University Press.

Vaillant, George E., and Eva S. Milofsky. 1982. "The etiology of alcoholism: A prospective viewpoint." *American Psychologist, 37,* 494–503.

Vaksberg, Arkady. 1991. *The Soviet Mafia.* New York: St. Martin's.

Valente, Sharon M. 1993. "Suicide and elderly people: Assessment and intervention." *Omega: Journal of Death & Dying, 28,* 317–331.

van Biema, David. 1997. "Fatal doses." *Time,* February 17, p. 72.

van Gelder, Paul J., and Charles D. Kaplan. 1992. "The finishing moment: Temporal and spatial features of sexual interactions between streetwalkers and car clients." *Human Organization, 51,* 253–263.

van Natta, Don Jr., and Jane Fritsch. 1997. "$250,000 buys donors' best access to Congress." *New York Times,* January 27, A1, A10.

van Poppel, Frans, and Lincoln H. Day. 1996. "A test of Durkheim's theory of suicide—Without committing the 'ecological fallacy'." *American Sociological Review, 61,* 500–507.

Vaughan, Diane. 1983. *Controlling Unlawful Organizational Behavior: Social Structure and Corporate Misconduct.* Chicago: University of Chicago Press.

Viscusi, W. Kip. 1992. *Smoking: Making the Risky Decision.* New York: Oxford University Press.

Voeller, Bruce. 1990. "Some uses and abuses of the Kinsey scale." In David P. McWhirter, Stephanie A. Sanders, and June Machover Reinisch (Eds.), *Homosexuality/Heterosexuality.* New York: Oxford University Press.

Walchak, David G. 1996. "Drugs and violent crime." *Police Chief, 63,* March, p. 6.

Wald, Matthew L. 1996. "A fading drumbeat against drunken driving." *New York Times,* December 15, p. E5.

Walker, Lenore F. 1979. *The Battered Woman.* New York: Harper & Row.

Walker, Lenore F. 1990. *Terrifying Love: Why Battered Women Kill and How Society Responds.* New York: Harper Perennial.

Wallace, Harvey. 1996. *Family Violence: Legal, Medical, and Social Perspectives.* Boston, Mass.: Allyn and Bacon.

Waller, Willard. 1936. "Social problems and the mores." *American Sociological Review, 1,* 922–933.

Walston, James. 1986. "See Naples and die: Organized crime in Campania." In Robert Kelly (Ed.), *Organized Crime: A Global Perspective.* Totowa, N.J.: Rowman & Littlefield.

Warshaw, Robin, and Andrea Parrot. 1991. "The contribution of sex-role socialization to acquaintance rape." In Andrea Parrot and Laurie Bechhofer (Eds.), *Acquaintance Rape.* New York: Wiley.

Wartik, Nancy. 1995. "Jerry's choice: Why are our children killing themselves?" In Robert Emmet Long (Ed.), *Suicide.* New York: Wilson.

Wasserman, Ira. 1984. "Imitation and suicide: A reexamination of the Werther effect." *American Sociological Review, 49,* 427–436.

Watts, Alan. 1966. *The Book: On the Taboo Against Knowing Who You Are.* New York: Collier Books.

Weber, Thomas E. 1987. "The X files." *Wall Street Journal,* May 20, pp. A1, A8.

Wechsler, Henry, et al. 1995. "Correlates of college student binge drinking." *American Journal of Public Health, 85,* 921–926.

Weicker, Lowell P., Jr. 1985. "Dangerous routine." *Psychology Today,* November, pp. 60–62.

Weiner, Tim. 1998. "Military discharges of homosexuals soar." *New York Times,* April 7, A21.

Weinstein, Raymond M. 1981. "Mental patients' attitudes toward hospital staff." *Archives of General Psychiatry, 38,* 487.

Weinstein, Raymond M. 1983. "Labeling theory and the attitudes of mental patients: A review." *Journal of Health and Social Behavior, 24,* 70–84.

Weis, Kurt, and Sandra S. Borges. 1973. "Victimology and rape: The case of the legitimate victim." *Issues in Criminology, 8,* 81–85.

Weisberg, Kelly. 1985. *Children of the Night: A Study of Adolescent Prostitution.* Lexington: Lexington Books.

Weisburd, David, et al. 1991. *Crimes in the Middle Classes.* New Haven: Yale University Press.

Weisheit, Ralph. 1992. "Patterns of female crime." In Robert G. Culbertson and Ralph Weisheit (Eds.), *Order Under Law.* Prospect Heights, Ill.: Waveland.

Weisman, Steven R. 1997. "Spin nation." *New York Times,* January 26, p. 12.

Weisner, Constance, et al. 1995. "Trends in the treatment of alcohol problems in the U.S. general population, 1979 through 1990." *American Journal of Public Health, 85,* 55–60.

Weitzer, Ronald. 1991. "Prostitutes' rights in the United States: The failure of a movement." *Sociological Quarterly, 32,* 23–41.

Wellford, Harrison. 1972. *Sowing the Wind: A Report from Ralph Nader's Center for Study of Responsive Law on Food Safety and the Chemical Harvest.* New York: Grossman.

Wells, Joseph T. 1993. "Accountancy and white-collar crime." *The Annals of the American Academy of Political and Social Science, 525* (January), 86–87.

Welte, John W., and Grace M. Barnes. 1992. "Drinking among homeless and marginally housed adults in New York state." *Journal of Studies on Alcohol, 53,* 303–315.

Wenz, Friedrich V. 1978. "Breadth of perspective and suicide threats." *Psychological Reports, 43,* 649–650.

Wertheimer, Fred. 1996. "Stop soft money now." *New York Times Magazine,* December 22, pp. 38–39.

Wheeler, Stanton, David Weisburd, and Nancy Bode. 1982. "Sentencing the white-collar offender: Rhetoric and reality." *American Sociological Review, 47,* 641–659.

Wheeler, Stanton. 1991. "The problem of white-collar crime motivation." In Kip Schlegel and David Weisburd (Eds.), *White-Collar Crime Reconsidered.* Boston: Northeastern University Press.

White, Jacquelyn W., and John A. Humphrey. 1991. "Young people's attitudes toward acquaintance rape." In Andrea Parrot and Laurie Bechhofer (Eds.), *Acquaintance Rape.* New York: Wiley.

"White Slavery." 1972. *Time,* June 5, p. 24.

Wiatrowski, Michael D., David B. Griswold, and Mary K. Roberts. 1981. "Social control theory and delinquency." *American Sociological Review, 46,* 525–541.

Wickelgren, Ingrid. 1999. "Discovery of 'gay gene' questioned." *Science,* April 23, p. 571.

Widom, Cathy Spatz. 1989. "The intergenerational transmission of violence." In Neil Alan Weiner and Marvin E. Wolfgang (Eds.), *Pathways to Criminal Violence.* Newbury Park, Calif.: Sage.

Wilbanks, William. 1984. *Murder in Miami: An Analysis of Homicide Patterns and Trends in Dade County (Miami) Florida, 1917–1983.* Lanham, Md.: University Press of America.

Wilbanks, William. 1985. "Is violent crime intraracial?" *Crime & Delinquency, 31,* 117–128.

Wilentz, Amy. 1985. "When brother kills brother." *Time,* September 16, p. 33.

Wilkerson, Isabel. 1993. "Foes of pornography and bigotry join forces. *New York Times,* March 12, p. A12.

Wilkins, James. 1967. "Suicidal Behavior." *American Sociological Review, 32* (1967), 286–287.

Wilkinson, Kenneth P. 1984. "A research note on homicide and rurality." *Social Forces, 63,* 445–452.

Wilkinson, Rupert. 1970. *The Prevention of Drinking Problems.* New York: Oxford University Press.

Williams, Kirk R. 1984. "Economic source of homicide: Reestimating the effects of poverty and inequality." *American Sociological Review, 49,* 283–289.

Williams, Kirk R., and Susan Drake. 1980. "Social structure, crime and criminalization: An empirical examination of the conflict perspective." *The Sociological Quarterly, 21,* 563–575.

Willwerth, James. 1993. "It hurts like crazy." *Time,* February 15, p. 53.

Wilson, Margo I., and Martin Daly. 1992. "Who kills whom in spouse killings? On the exceptional sex ratio of spousal homicides in the United States." *Criminology, 30,* 189–215.

Wilson, Mitchell. 1993. "DSM-III and the transformation of American psychiatry: A history." *American Journal of Psychiatry, 150,* 399–410.

Winerip, Michael. 1999. "Bedlam on the streets." *New York Times Magazine,* May 23, pp. 42–49, 56, 65, 68–70.

Winick, Charles, and Paul M. Kinsie. 1971. *The Lively Commerce.* Chicago: Quadrangle.

Witkin, Gordon. 1992. "Willing to kill for a car." *U.S. News & World Report,* September 21, pp. 40–43.

Witkin, Gordon. 1995. "A new drug gallops through the West." *U.S. News & World Report,* November 13, pp. 50–51.

Wittig, Monique. 1990. "The straight mind." In Russell Ferguson et al. (Eds.), *Out There: Marginalization and Contemporary Culture.* Cambridge, Mass.: MIT Press.

Wold, Carl I. 1970. "Characteristics of 26,000 suicide prevention center patients." *Bulletin of Suicidology,* no. 6, pp. 24–28.

Wolfe, Alan. 1998. "The homosexual exception." *New York Times Magazine,* February 8, pp. 46-47.

Wolfgang, Marvin E. 1958. *Patterns in Criminal Homicide.* Philadelphia: University of Pennsylvania Press, 1958.

Wolfgang, Marvin E. 1967. "A sociological analysis of criminal homicide." In Marvin E. Wolfgang (Ed.), *Studies in Homicide.* New York: Harper & Row.

Wolfgang, Marvin E., and Franco Ferracuti. 1967. *The Subculture of Violence: Towards an Integrated Theory in Criminology.* London: Tavistock.

Wren, Christopher S. 1996a. "Adolescent drug use rose in latest survey from 1995." *New York Times,* December 20, p. A8.

Wren, Christopher S. 1996b. "Why seizing drugs barely dents supply." *New York Times,* December 15, p. E4.

Wren, Christopher S. 1997. "Keeping cocaine resilient: Low cost and high profit." *New York Times,* March 4, pp. A1, A10.

Wren, Christopher S. 1999a. "A purer, more potent heroin lures new users to a long, hard fall." *New York Times,* May 9, p. 27.

Wren, Christopher S. 1999b. "Study compares U.S. and English drug crimes." *New York Times,* May 14, p. A10.

Wright, James D. 1995. "Ten essential observations on guns in America." *Society,* March/April, pp. 62–68.

Wright, James D., Joseph F. Sheley, and M. Dwayne Smith. 1992. "Kids, guns, and killing fields." *Society,* November/December, pp. 84–89.

Wright, James D., Peter H. Rossi, and Kathleen Daly. 1983. *Under the Gun: Weapons, Crime, and Violence in America.* New York: Aldine.

Wright, Richard T., and Scott H. Decker. 1994. *Burglars on the Job: Streetlife and Residential Break-ins.* Boston: Northeastern University Press.

"Wrist-cutting—A road to life, not death." 1976. *Psychology Today.* April, p. 20.

WuDunn, Sheryl. 1996. "Uproar over a debt crisis." *New York Times,* February 14, pp. C1, C4.

Wysocki, Diane Kholos. 1998. "Let your fingers do the talking: Sex on an adult chat-line." *Sexualities,* Vol. 1, pp. 425-352.

Yamamoto, J., et al. 1983. "Symptom checklist of normal subjects from Asian-Pacific islander population." *Pacific/Asian American Mental Health Research Center Research Review, 2,* 6–8.

Yesavage, Jerome A., et al. 1985. "Carry-over effects of marijuana intoxication on aircraft pilot performance: A preliminary report." *American Journal of Psychiatry, 142,* 1325–1329.

Yonkers, Kimberly A., and George Gurguis. 1995. "Gender differences in the prevalence and expression of anxiety disorders." In Mary V. Seeman (Ed.), *Gender and Psychopathology.* Washington, D.C.: American Psychiatric Press.

Young, T. J. 1991. "Suicide and homicide among Native Americans: Anomie or social learning?" *Psychological Reports, 68,* 1137–1138.

Zagorin, Adam. 1997. "Charlie's an angel?" *Time,* February 3, pp. 36–38.

Zeisel, Hans. 1982. "A comment on 'The deterrent effect of capital punishment' by Phillips." *American Journal of Sociology, 88,* 167–169.

Zeiss, Carol A. 1984. "Hypothesis on sexual violence 'not convincing'." *American Journal of Psychiatry, 141,* 1133.

Zeits, Dorothy. 1981. *Women Who Embezzle or Defraud.* New York: Praeger.

Zekeri, Andrew A. 1995. "Suicide and rurality in Alabama communities." *Social Indicators Research, 36,* 177–190.

Zillmann, Dolf, and Jennings Bryant. 1982. "Pornography, sexual callousness, and the trivialization of rape." *Journal of Communication, 32,* 10–21.

Zorza, Joan, and Laurie Woods. 1994. *Mandatory Arrest: Problems and Possibilities.* New York: National Center for Women and Family Law.

NAME INDEX

SUBJECT INDEX